THE POISONOUS CLOUD

Chemical Warfare in the First World War

L. F. HABER

CLARENDON PRESS · OXFORD

*This book has been printed digitally and produced in a standard specification
in order to ensure its continuing availability*

OXFORD
UNIVERSITY PRESS

Great Clarendon Street, Oxford OX2 6DP

Oxford University Press is a department of the University of Oxford.
It furthers the University's objective of excellence in research, scholarship,
and education by publishing worldwide in

Oxford New York

Auckland Bangkok Buenos Aires Cape Town Chennai
Dar es Salaam Delhi Hong Kong Istanbul Karachi Kolkata
Kuala Lumpur Madrid Melbourne Mexico City Mumbai Nairobi
São Paulo Shanghai Singapore Taipei Tokyo Toronto

with an associated company in Berlin

Oxford is a registered trade mark of Oxford University Press
in the UK and in certain other countries

Published in the United States
by Oxford University Press Inc., New York

© L. F. Haber 1986

ISBN 0-19-858142-4

Jacket illustration: men of the 2nd Btn.
Argyll and Sutherland Highlanders wearing mouthpads, 1915.
Imperial War Museum.

ACKNOWLEDGEMENTS

T H E book draws heavily on reports, memoranda, and letters in public archives. The material is bulky and is filed in boxes which line miles of shelving in the Public Record Office, the National Archives in Washington, and elsewhere. A small staff is employed to process enquiries and move the boxes from store to users. Although red tape is not unknown in these places, I have good cause to be grateful to these men and women who kept me supplied with the raw materials for my history. Thus, at the outset, I gladly acknowledge the help of the many unknown Civil Servants, particularly those in the old PRO in Chancery Lane, London, which was not designed to handle boxes quickly. Archivists and Librarians, of whom I got to know a good many, were ever helpful and patient with me. If I single out Rose Coombs, David Lance, and G. M. Bayliss from the Imperial War Museum, Archivdirektor C. F. Stahl from the BMA, and Oberregierungsarchivrat Dr Heyl from the BHSA, the reason is that I must on occasions have strained their endurance and their memories, both considerable, and belatedly I offer them my sincere thanks for the information they provided. A special word of thanks is also due to the staff at the Library of the University of Surrey, who dealt quickly and efficiently with my frequent requests for books and pamphlets from other libraries at home and abroad.

I have adopted the practice of referring to the help given to me by colleagues, research students, and friends at those points in the story where their intervention was particularly valuable. Here I want to remember those who have been involved with the project as a whole, who sent me their reminiscences or commented on outlines or drafts. Harold Hartley deserves pride of place, for it was he who launched me on this enterprise. Without his encouragement and his papers, I would not have got started. John Coates backed his reminiscences with correspondence notes and interviews on chemical warfare which he obtained during the 1930s when he prepared his lecture for the Chemical Society. He put all the documents at my disposal and so cleared up many questions concerning Haber's role between 1915 and 1918. Leslie Barley and J. Davidson Pratt talked to me and wrote at length, and I have used much of the material they provided. These eye-witnesses of chemical warfare in the First World War are dead. I remember them with affection and gratitude.

Two other helpers call for special mention. When one is researching and writing over a period of many years continuity suffers and repetition may become intolerable. My friend Peter Morgan volunteered to go through the typescript with the sharpness of mind and the critical judgement that have made his opinions so valuable to me for many years. I was particularly fortunate because he remembered his chemistry sufficiently to correct me on many details and his exposure to military life in Hitler's War enabled him to spot errors in my account of the Kaiser's War. Without his meticulous intervention at the final stage the book would be longer, frequently tedious and contain many mistakes. The University Press have their own rules and chemical warfare has to conform to them: I can only marvel at the work that goes into the publication of a difficult book and I want to take this opportunity of thanking Rupert Christiansen for editing the typescript and in the process correcting the style and improving the general appearance.

The man who could have been of the greatest help, my father, died fifty years ago. He could have plugged many holes and, as Hartley wrote later, 'put the record straight'. There is still no comprehensive biography of Fritz Haber nor for that matter an official German, British, or French history of chemical warfare in the First World War. Hartley urged me to look at the evidence that had recently become available and in so doing describe my father's many-sided activities in those years: I have done that in this book which I dedicate to them.

London, L. F. H.
September 1984

CONTENTS

LIST OF ILLUSTRATIONS

LIST OF MAPS

LIST OF TABLES AND DIAGRAMS

DIAGRAMS

ABBREVIATIONS AND GLOSSARY

The following abbreviations and technical terms have been used throughout the text of the book and in the index.

ADGS	Assistant Director Gas Services
AEF	American Expeditionary Force
BA	Bundesarchiv, Koblenz (Germany)
BASF *or* Badische	Badische Anilin- & Soda-Fabrik, Ludwigshafen (Germany)
BEF	British Expeditionary Force
BHSA	Bayerisches Hauptstaatsarchiv, Abt. IV, Kriegsarchiv, Munich
BIR	Bayerisches Infanterie Regiment
Blue Cross	German shell-marking to indicate it was filled with arsenical compounds. Used here as a collective noun for these materials
BMA	Bundesarchiv-Militärarchiv, Freiburg i.B. (Germany)
BRIR	Bayerisches Reserve Infanterie Regiment
cc	cubic centimetre
CCS	Casualty Clearing Station
CS-C	Chemical Sub-Committee of the Scientific Advisory Group of the Trench Warfare Department (later the Trench Warfare Research Department) of the Ministry of Munitions
CWC	Chemical Warfare Committee, London
CWD	Chemical Warfare Department of the Ministry of Munitions
CWS	Chemical Warfare Service, a branch of the USA armed forces
DA	Diphenylchloroarsine, code-named 'Clark' 1 by the Germans
DGS	Director of Gas Services, France
DM	Diphenylaminechloroarsine, also known as 'Adamsite' in Britain and USA
DMCG	Direction du Matériel Chimique de Guerre of the Ministère de l'Armement
FMA	French Military Archives, Château de Vincennes, nr. Paris
GQC	Grand Quartier Général, the GHQ of the French forces
gr	gram
HE	High explosive
IEEC	Inspection des Études et Expériences Chimiques, the French research and development organization for chemical warfare

IWM	Imperial War Museum, London
kg	Kilo or kilogram
KWI	Kaiser-Wilhelm-Institut für Physikalische Chemie und Elektrochemie in Berlin-Dahlem. Since 1953, Fritz-Haber-Institut der Max-Planck-Gesellschaft
m	metre
mg/m³	milligram(s) per cubic metre
MoM	Ministry of Munitions
MoM History	History of the Ministry of Munitions, XI, part 2, 'Chemical Warfare Supplies', n.d. [1921?], unpubl.
NA	United States National Archives, Washington, DC
OHL	Oberste Heeres-Leitung, the German supreme command
ppm	parts per million
PRO	Public Record Office, Kew, nr. London
RA	Royal Artillery
RAMC	Royal Army Medical Corps
RE	Royal Engineers
Rgt	regiment
SBR	small box respirator, the standard-issue British respirator 1916–18
Stogas	Stabs-Offizier, Gas, the equivalent of the Chemical Adviser in the BEF
t	metric tonne. Quantities are expressed in t throughout the book except where the capacity or other details of the British or American chemical warfare effort need to be given with great precision, when the number will be followed by *ton, tons,* or *long tons*. (Note: American short tons have been converted to t or long tons as appropriate.)
TNT	trinitrotoluene, one of the principal HE shell fillings in the First World War
TWD	Trench Warfare Department of the Ministry of Munitions
tr.	translated by the author
UAC	United Alkali Co. Ltd.
Yellow Cross	German shell-marking to indicate that contents were dichlorodiethyl sulphide and solvent. Used here as synonym for mustard gas or Yperite

1

PERSONAL INTRODUCTION

ANOTHER book on chemical warfare when the literature on the subject is already considerable calls for an explanation. In this particular case personal interests and new material are so closely knit that it is necessary to describe how I came to be committed to the task and what I am hoping to achieve.

In 1968 at the formal ceremony to commemorate the centenary of the birth of my father, Fritz Haber, there was an incident in the lecture theatre of the University of Karlsruhe where he had taught from 1894 to 1911. Two young men appeared on the rostrum and unfurled a banner with the following legend:

Feier für einen Mörder
Haber = Vater des Gaskriegs

There was a brief, complete silence, then the Chairman said something apposite and soothing, the youths disappeared as suddenly as they had come, and the speaker resumed. Some thought the incident was a muted expression of that student militancy which swept through Western Europe in 1968. Others were indignant that a scientific occasion should be so inconsiderately disturbed. I was taken aback and my first reaction was that the slogans were lies or at least grossly exaggerated. On further reflection it seemed to me truly astonishing that after half a century, chemical warfare could still generate so much emotion. What were the facts, and was all the fuss really justified? There the matter might have rested, but for another personal and this time determining intervention.

Harold Hartley was an unusual man. This is not the place to sketch his biography, but to note his connection with chemical warfare which, in his prime, marked the turning-point for him. In civilian life he taught physical chemistry at Oxford, but after the outbreak of war he joined up and in June 1915 he became Chemical Adviser to the 3rd Army, but he did not play a prominent role until he was promoted to Assistant Director Gas Service, in short, ADGS (Defence) two years later. Hartley attained the top post in November 1918 when he was appointed Controller, Chemical Warfare Department (CWD). His personality was more significant than his official function and rank. He possessed a lively intellect, the ability to ask the right questions, and a genuine interest in other people's work. These attributes, combined with a good Balliol background opened many doors to him and he was better informed than many of his seniors on the Staffs or in Whitehall. That came to be recognized and while winding down the CWD in 1919 he led the British section of an inter-allied team which visited the occupied areas of Germany in February of that year. He was struck by the close relationship between German chemical manufacture and the supply of munitions, the ingenious development of substitutes for materials in short supply and, specifically, by the existing facilities for war gas production. Hartley's views on the British chemical warfare effort were now carrying weight, his recommendations were listened to, and the German experience had taught him the significance of the industrial aspects of chemical warfare. As a result he played an indispensable part in the inter-war deliberations of the Chemical Warfare Committee. As part of Hartley's public, but not publicized, service he was asked to go to Berlin in 1921. In retrospect it seems odd that the British should have waited almost three years before 'debriefing' German scientists. But such had been the dilatoriness of the Reichswehr Ministry that repeated enquiries went unanswered or were left deliberately incomplete. A more subtle approach might yield better results. So, being a passable German speaker, a good physical chemist, an expert on chemical warfare and, not least, an honorary Brigadier-General and CBE he went to Berlin to speak, as he put it, to the 'great' Haber.

For Haber the war had been first the apex and then the nadir of his middle life. Appointed director of the newly created and privately endowed Kaiser-Wilhelm-Institut for Physical Chemistry (KWI) in 1911 he had moved from Karlsruhe to the Reich capital. The move from province to the centre underlined his growing fame as the man who had solved the problem of nitrogen fixation which had eluded other greater scientists. He was the embodiment of the romantic, quasi-heroic aspect of German chemistry in which national pride commingled with the advancement of pure science and the utilitarian progress of technology. Haber's patriotism was unusual even in an age when jingoism, into which it so frequently spills over, was condoned. He was a Prussian, with an uncritical acceptance of the State's wisdom, as interpreted by bureaucrats, many of them intellectually his inferiors. He was also ambitious, determined to succeed, and well aware that his Jewish origin was both obstacle and spur. At the outbreak of war he was in sole charge of a purpose-built centre for cross-disciplinary research into physics and chemistry. He immediately placed the facilities of the KWI at the disposal of the Government. In addition he became a voluntary consultant—behind the scenes—on what would now be called industrial mobilization. His involvement in chemical warfare began in December 1914 and was marked for the duration by strong purpose, great energy, a practical turn of mind, and outstanding administrative ability. Haber's greatest successes came in 1915—the year of the first gas attacks and the organization of gas-mask production—but his most important role was played in the last two years of the war when he tendered advice at the highest level and was officially in charge of German gas supplies and gas protection. His wide and burdensome responsibilities did not extend to the use of chemical warfare agents. Thus, powerful and yet powerless, he was early aware of the turning tide and the implications of defeat. His chemical weapon had failed, misused in other hands, but failed all the same.

The end of 1918 marked the end of Haber's active connection with chemical warfare, though he was never allowed to forget what he had done. I shall leave his post-war activites to the last chapter and confine myself here to this talks with Hartley because they have a bearing on the genesis of this book. They met in June 1921: each was curious about the other. Haber about the man who had done less for his country's war effort, but had been more highly rewarded—forgetting the cultural differences and the advantage of being on the winning side. Hartley wanted 'to fathom what was in Haber's mind when we knew that he was directing the German use of gas'. These talks were more than an intelligence interrogation. They extended beyond the organization of chemical warfare, the primary objective, to the state of German science and the progress of physical chemistry, and, as Hartley wrote later, 'I like to think we parted as friends. It was a great experience to have enjoyed his intimate confidence.'[1]

The immediate and direct outcome of the meeting was a long report which was never published and remains, owing to the lack of German material, the most comprehensive document on the development of that country's chemical warfare, its organization and purpose.

Many years later Hartley proposed to incorporate the report in his account of chemical warfare. The plan had to be postponed because the pressure of business prevented him from devoting time to literary projects. However, Hartley's interest in the subject never ceased, indeed it was revived at intervals owing to his place at the centre of the British chemical warfare scene in the 1920s and 1930s and his links with Haber which continued to influence him for half a century. Surely an exceptionally long period for the germination of an idea! The details merit recording.

Upon Haber's death in 1934, the Chemical Society asked J. E. Coates, a former pupil, to give the memorial lecture. Coates was careful and conscientious. Through interviews and correspondence he gathered a mass of personal impressions so that he was able to appreciate Haber's commitment to chemical warfare which, however awkward, had to be presented to a large audience of British chemists.[2] Hartley was repeatedly consulted over this delicate task and his comments were invaluable because he knew at first hand almost everyone connected with chemical warfare from 1915 onwards. Later he drafted a note, based on his report, which was factual and fair, though often critical on technical matters. Later still he went through Coates's drafts and suggested further changes.

Then there was a long gap. Hartley seems to have toyed from time to time with the project of a history and may have intended to combine it with an autobiography. In 1958 he was writing to C. G. Douglas 'some day I hope I shall live long enough to go through the final [volume of the official] history and with my own records try and give a true picture for the sake of posterity.' Douglas encouraged him—'I wish you would write a history of the gas services . . . I don't think they ever had adequate recognition and there ought to be a trustworthy record'—but Hartley thought it was premature: 'I have a slight feeling of reluctance to publish anything while Foulkes is alive as I don't want to upset him.'[3]

Coates, Douglas, and Foulkes will reappear later; they are introduced here to show that Hartley kept in touch with the participants. Soon afterwards there was another period of active interest. In 1960–1 he wrote at my request a chapter for Dr J. Jaenicke's biography of Fritz Haber which is still incomplete and remains unpublished. It was straightforward and factual, but often and deliberately anecdotal: Hartley thought that would add spice to the story, and so it did, but it also perpetuated myths. His correspondence at the time shows that he was anxious to put his story on record so as to correct what he considered to be the unfavourable bias of the Official History.[4] The deaths of collaborators and friends in the 1960s, among them Livens, Douglas, Auld, and Foulkes, reminded him that time was pressing. There were brief notes on gas warfare written in 1966, 1968, and 1969, but by then he was in his eighties and his energy was failing. He became very ill at the beginning of 1970 and I made it a habit to visit him regularly at his nursing home: our talks ranged widely and his interest in chemical warfare soon revived. He had ideas on the subject, a fantastic memory, and a mass of papers of which I will presently have more to say. According to Hartley, there was no definitive history of chemical warfare, and one was badly needed. I was unconvinced, at least until I had immersed myself in his papers. But there was another aspect: except for Coates's excellent memorial lecture[5] and Jaenicke's rather shorter eulogy of 1968, there is still no biography of my father. Novelists and others have indeed made him their subject, but—to put it charitably—their treatment of the war years has remained inadequate.

Hartley's powers of persuasion were notorious. Considering that I was insufficiently occupied he proceeded to 'hartle' me. The verb is active: 'I think', 'you do', 'it is successfully accomplished'.[6] He had charm, the ability to command loyalty, and a genuine interest in the activities of younger people. I set to work, read, interviewed him dozens of times, talked and corresponded with his surviving war-time colleagues, and eventually prepared a synopsis which, in its first version, embodied many of his ideas and some of mine. But towards the summer of 1972 his attention flagged—he was always tired, often in great discomfort, and too old and sick to find the strength to be committed to the project. He died in September of that year and I continued alone. The end result differs considerably from what we envisaged many years ago. That must be so, for one's ideas change as research and reflection open up new horizons. But I am grateful to Harold Hartley for having pointed me firmly in the general direction and for giving me this opportunity to do justice to one period of my father's life which he preferred to keep obscure and which no one has yet properly examined.

So far I have described the personal background to the book. Some would say that this is sufficient reason for writing it. But if one goes over previously cultivated ground it is necessary to demonstrate one's claim to have uncovered and used new material. Hence the following review of the novelty and value of the information which came into my hands after Hartley enlisted me.

For some years after the First World War, German authors had something of a corner in chemical warfare literature. There are some advantages even to defeat: as you have been beaten you might as well make a clean breast of it, since the victor knows what you have been up to. But does he? Hartley's trip to Berlin (and he was not the first investigator) shows that the Allies were ignorant of many aspects. Of course Hartley could not disclose the extent of his knowledge, in the first place because the Official Secrets Act prevented him from doing so; secondly he was reluctant to discard his trumps at the beginning of the game. The Germans obviously took a different view: they were good at military technology, and after 1919 their revelations consisted of interesting technical details, known to the Allies even before the Armistice, but not divulged by them. The first in the field was General Schwarte. He was the editor of an oft-quoted book which was hastily prepared and while boosting German achievements ignored those of the Allies. Chapter XI of his book is divided into three sections on chemical warfare, by Captain H. Geyer of the General Staff and by F. P. Kerschbaum and H. Pick of the KWI, respectively in charge of its offensive and defensive sections; they had nothing to say about their enemies![7] Schwarte was followed by Hanslian, a former pharmacist with the XXII Corps. The first edition of his *Der chemische Krieg* appeared in 1925; this was a slim book of 200 pages, essentially an enlargement of what Schwarte had put together. The second edition appeared in 1927. It was more substantial and relied extensively on foreign sources, notably American reports and the papers given by British and French specialists on different aspects of chemical warfare. Hanslian, like others, was recycling information, and his book—though elaborately documented—was incomplete in many respects, lacked numeracy, ignored organization, research, and development, and failed to evaluate the effort put into this form of warfare and the gains achieved. The third edition was in two parts, but only the first—the military part—was published. It is vast, badly written, and repetitive.[8] The section on Ypres 1915 was shortened (because Hanslian had written a booklet on the attack in 1934) and that on post-war developments expanded to 500 pages. He had access to German material, but relied in the main on the United States Chemical Warfare Service (CWS) whose experience of the war was necessarily limited, and on Soviet publications which were propagandist rather than informative.

All inter-war writers on the subject relied on Schwarte and Hanslian, repeated their 'facts' and left the interesting questions unanswered. The official histories did not fill the gaps, nor were they designed as technical studies. In any case their publication was slow. The German volumes fell victim to political change, to another war, and were not resumed until the 1950s. The British did not reach 1918 until 1947!

The 'classics', official and others, are not of much use if one is looking for a fresh approach. Hence the importance of the new material. It will be convenient to start with the Hartley papers and proceed from there to the national and specialist archives.

Hartley's collection on chemical warfare, which he kept in his room, comprised about twenty-five files, in no apparent order, containing the most diverse material.[9] I could not get him to explain either the sequence or the obvious gaps. Broadly speaking these files complement the material now at the Public Record Office. Four sets of papers are particularly important. First, the reports connected with the German cloud-gas attack at Ypres on 19 December 1915: this was the first occasion the Germans used large quantities of phosgene in the West and great care was taken by the Chemical Adviser and medical officers to record in minute detail the technical particulars of the discharge and the protective value of the British gas helmets. Secondly, there is a complete collection of *Gas Warfare*, a monthly bulletin which Hartley launched and edited after he became ADGS (Defence) in mid-1917. This was published by GHQ for circulation among gas officers, staff, and chemical warfare specialists in Whitehall. The interest and value of *Gas Warfare* lies in the dated reports on the use of gas by the British and German forces and in the statements of German prisoners to British intelligence officers which can be compared with the entries in German regimental diaries. Remarkable discrepancies between such statements and reports made elsewhere have thus come to light. Thirdly, there are the statistics on German gas bombardments and British casualties resulting therefrom between July and November 1918. Despite their considerable limitations the numbers permit at least a rough evaluation of the effectiveness of gas shells.[10]

Finally, there is the report on German Chemical Warfare Organization and Policy, a long undated document which, for the sake of brevity, I shall refer to as the Hartley Report. From internal evidence it would appear that the report was written in 1921–2, revised later, and duplicated for circulation in 1925. Owing to the significance of the document, its genesis and scope merit closer attention. The Treaty of Versailles required the Germans to supply technical information. As far as chemical warfare was concerned, the Allies were principally interested in manufacturing operations, the design of gas shell-filling equipment, the central chemical warfare depot at Breloh, the preparation of activated charcoal and the progress made with various organic arsenical compounds which were discharged as a particulate cloud.[11] The military branch of the Inter-Allied Control Commission had an Armaments Sub-Commission which endeavoured through questionnaires sent out in 1920 and 1921 to get information on these and other points. In this way Gen. E. Vinet, the French head of the Sub-Commission, his assistant Col. H. Muraour, and Dr H. E. Watts, an English chemist with chemical warfare experience, obtained many production statistics from the Germans. In July 1920 Vinet talked to Haber and drove with him to the chemical warfare establishments near Berlin. Vinet and his team concluded their investigations with typed reports, which in some respects went over the same ground as Hartley's report. The first in two parts respectively dated June and December 1920, contained sections on the field ammunition depots and on the organization of German chemical warfare. Some of the material was incorporated in a later document dated 22 March 1921 entitled 'Report on the Present Condition of the Installations set up for the Manufacture of Asphyxiating Gases in the German Chemical Factories'. This dealt specifically with the progress of dismantling.[12]

The British were not satisfied with this information and Hartley was carefully briefed regarding what to look for when visiting Germany in June 1921. He was asked to discover 'as far as possible' the extent of the dismantling of gas production facilities, the lines on which the Germans were working at the time of the Armistice, especially particulate clouds, and 'some information regarding the German war organisation for chemical warfare. This is a subject on which we have very little accurate data.'[13] Such was the background to Hartley's enquiries which, as his notebook[14] and the report show, were extremely thorough. He visited Berlin, Breloh, Munich, and Stuttgart, talked to Haber for altogether seventeen hours and had meetings with Haber's collaborators at the KWI, among them Epstein, Freundlich, Hahn, Kerschbaum, Regener, Willstätter; he also talked to Duisberg and Nernst. He met with great co-operation, except from one man, not named, but probably Regener at Stuttgart, an acknowledged authority on particulate clouds. Hartley checked the answers against other information available to him and Watts subsequently dealt with some supplementary questions. 'There seems to be no reason to think that the information given was inaccurate or that the experts were holding back anything so far as their work in the war was concerned. In some respects their frankness was surprising,' Hartley wrote later.[15] Gaps do remain, especially on particulate clouds and events on the Eastern Front, but any reassessment of the industrial and organizational aspects of German chemical warfare would be seriously incomplete without the Hartley Report.

London has, so far as I have been able to judge, the largest extant collection outside Russia of chemical warfare documents from 1914 to the 1930s. The Imperial War Museum obtained a mass of papers of value to the military aspects of gas, offence as well as defence: they consist of instructions, circulars, leaflets, reminiscences, and a large collection of photographs which are invaluable if one wishes to follow the minutiae of chemical warfare. The documents at the PRO are different and consist of three main collections. The first are the records of the Ministry of Munitions, specifically its Trench Warfare Supply Department and the Chemical Warfare Department. The second are the records of the War Office which comprise the Gas Directorate (DGS) in France, the research centre at Porton and Allied information, chiefly French, which Lefebure, a most energetic liaison officer, secured in Paris and forwarded. The War Office papers also include the inter-war series, among them—under the reference WO 33/1072—the Hartley Report, unobtainable for almost half a century. Finally, the United States CWS sent duplicates of its records to London, but for reasons which will emerge later I have only consulted a few of them. The British material at the PRO is daunting in its size. The Ministry of Munitions records comprise forty-one boxes, the Porton papers 387 boxes, and the DGS documents 154 boxes (about 700 files). A line had to be drawn somewhere: I examined the entire contents of all the Ministry and DGS boxes, but the Porton material was highly technical and I therefore confined myself to a search of forty-five boxes, taken at random.

The PRO papers became accessible after a change in legislation. The material just described was released from the late 1960s onwards and takes the story up to the 1930s. The unwary might think the collection is complete, but they would be mistaken. The more recent documents, say from the mid 1930s onwards, probably contain files which were not closed until after the Second World War, and therefore were not available to me when researching for this book. The earlier documents, from 1915 up to 1930 or 1935 are certainly not complete. The most charitable explanation is that in the rapid demobilization of the CWD in 1918–19 the clerks and their superiors were often careless and needlessly destructive. The gaps were widened by other causes: even Registries are not infallible and files sent out are not returned despite reminders. Thus documents get mislaid and disappear from circulation. They may also, of course, have been expressly secreted and may, at this time of writing, be collecting dust on some shelf, inadequately labelled and long forgotten. All the belligerents were obsessed by security in chemical warfare matters. The British and French codenames delighted their inventors, but probably confused the users more than they did the enemy. Whatever the reason, the incompleteness is apparent.[16] This can, in part, be made good by recourse to the Hartley papers, occasionally, interpolation (or, more crudely, guessing) will be justified and foreign documents sometimes provide valuable clues.

Last, but by no means least, there is the history of the Ministry of Munitions. Some people, under instruction from higher authority, meticulously preserved records of historical interest. These formed the raw material of a comprehensive history which was completed in small instalments, but was never published, and indeed did not become accessible to the public until the 1960s. The documents for the History of Chemical Warfare Supplies fill many folders and pride of length unquestionably goes to the 360 foolscap-page typescript by Major H. Moreland who had been in the Trench Warfare Supply Department in charge of 'Gas and Cylinders' from the outset and was promoted head of the Chemicals Section in 1916. Moreland gave his side of the story, and J. Davidson Pratt, who we shall meet later, wrote on the activities of the Chemical Warfare Committee. The drafts survive, largely confirm each other and enable us to see how chemical warfare was organized in the UK. Together with the Hartley Report, they illuminate the industrial – scientific – military relationship which previous writers perforce neglected.

It remains to note how far other archival material supplements the Hartley—PRO documents. Little has survived in Germany. Hartley used to tell of his first meeting with Haber who greeted him in Berlin with 'Why have you been so long in coming? I was looking forward to discussing all our records with you, but there has been a most unfortunate fire and they are all destroyed. Look at that hole in the roof.'[17] Alas, the story is apocryphal. There was no fire and the papers had been removed to the Reichswehr Ministry in 1919. It is likely that the records were extensive as each section at the KWI had compiled an account of the work done. These large tomes were treated as top secret and except for one appear not to have survived.[18] Together with the papers of the German War Ministry they formed part of the military archives at Potsdam which were largely destroyed in an air raid on 14 April 1945.[19] The surviving documents were combined with others from the naval and air force archives and eventually formed the core of the Bundesarchiv-Militärarchiv collection at Freiburg. The material on chemical warfare is scanty, though some valuable inter-war documents and personal notebooks and diaries are available, have been indexed, and can be used to check data from other sources. The files and routine reports of Section A10 (Chemical Supplies) of the War Ministry have not survived, with the exception of a few fragments and curiously a single, complete report (dated 21 December 1917) which was captured, translated after the war, and found its way into the Hartley papers.[20]

Fortunately, the archives of the German states suffered little damage. For my purposes by far the most important has been the Bavarian. Chance played a considerable role: the staff papers of the Bavarian Army Corps and of Prince Rupprecht's Army Group—which faced the British in Flanders for most of the war—were sent to Potsdam in 1919; they remained there until March or April 1945. A Bavarian officer, working in the archives, decided to save what he could lay his hands on, got them into a lorry and out of Prussia.[21] The rest were destroyed. What the unknown archivist salvaged was necessarily incomplete, but nevertheless contains invaluable material (since it is nowhere else available) on some critical episodes of German chemical warfare which have not hitherto appeared in published accounts by either side. The regimental records and diaries never left Bavaria: they are complete and are the only means of checking the claims made in *Gas Warfare* and elsewhere of the success of British gas attacks. In its proper place I will compare the claims with the records and draw attention to the significance of this evidence.

In terms of content the French archives occupy a position mid-way between the German and the PRO. A recent change in policy allows the public access to First World War material. The Archives Militaires at Vincennes have about 70 boxes—containing thousands of individual pieces as well as complete files—which bear directly on chemical warfare. But the material has not been properly collated: excepting the boxes of Direction du Matériel Chimique de Guerre (DMCG) papers, the records are scattered among the miscellaneous documents of the war. Such dispersal, accompanied by careless muddle in sorting and filing, greatly diminishes the value of what there is. There are many breaks in the sequence of the documents and absence of order, and no attempt was made, so far as I know, to prepare historical or general surveys as in Britain. One example will illustrate the general situation: the documents on cloud-gas discharges by the Germans and the French end with a report dated 21 October 1916,[22] but at the PRO there are official French reports on German gas attacks in January-February 1917. What has happened to the French papers at Vincennes? Similar remarks apply to the Archives Nationales in Paris where the parcels (!) of the Sous-Sécretaire d'État au Ministère de l'Armement (that is, the section corresponding to the Trench Warfare Supply Department of the Ministry of Munitions) are manifestly incomplete. They are deficient in material bearing on research, supply, and use, but most informative on gas masks and the state of the French chemical industry.

Personal circumstances caused me to take up the subject in the first place. The additional material, as it unfolded, then pointed my research into those areas where previous study enabled me to understand the problems involved and formulate questions which, even now, call for an answer. We can illustrate their nature by two quotations: 'Throughout the war the [German] enemy maintained an unbroken and unenviable priority in adopting and developing . . . offensive toxic substances'[23] Why? Secondly, in connection with the issue of British gas helmets which began on 10 May 1915: 'Henceforward, so far as concerned matters of defence, the initiative rested with the Allies'.[23] Again, why?

Previous writers have taken fundamental issues of offence and defence in chemical warfare for granted, and have launched themselves into tactical, moral, or personal aspects of poison gas. I do not intend to follow them, because these are outside my knowledge and experience. Moreover recent investigations have cleared up practically all remaining contentious issues in these areas.

So what particular contribution can be made towards a better understanding of chemical warfare by an economic historian, such as I am, with a special interest in the development of the chemical industry? It is, I think, to set out the new facts and comment upon them so that we can better appreciate the cause-and-effect relationship of a very sudden and extremely complex technological change with unique features in its application.

Technological change is profoundly influenced by the intensity and direction of research and development, and by diverse economic and social factors which form the background to chemical innovation and, in turn, are affected by it. In war the market economy becomes less important: supply is controlled, demand checked, and choice restricted. But development and application continue, indeed are pushed to the absolute limit of innovatory ability, because substitutes or passable alternatives, become essential. In recent years the mechanics of the process have become better known. We are, however, less familiar with the obstacles that the large-scale adoption of new techniques and processes encounter: 'where there is a will, there's a way', but the way will be obstructed if the basic technological environment is backward and if the methods of dealing with innovation are imperfect. Historians have become increasingly interested in the technical and socio-economic constraints to industrial change in the twentieth century, but few have investigated them in the context of military technology and none with regard to chemical warfare. This is odd, for von Bloch, who considered himself an economist and was the first to apply economic statistics to military matters, had seized the point eighty years ago: modern technology, he argued, improved weapons and also the ability to defend oneself against them. Hence a future war would be longer and ultimate victory would depend on political, economic, and social conditions; to appreciate the import of these conditions required the tools of political economy and of statistics.[24] Both were ignored by writers on military affairs in Bloch's day and indeed until very recently. A. M. Prentiss, whose book appeared in 1937, was the first to extend the study of chemical warfare to the industrial potential and even attempted a cost-benefit analysis of this mode of warfare.[25]

Economic investigations are obviously strengthened by a quantitative approach. The impression given by the supply of war gases in 1914–18 is generally one of improvisation and muddle. A systematic approach to organizational problems and other management aides, notably operational research, barely existed and certainly were not applied to chemical warfare materials. Yet even then there were people who thought numerately. Lanchester's N^2 law governing the strengths of opposing forces was, as he himself recognized, inapplicable to land warfare owing to the multiplicity of targets.[26] But that did not invalidate the basic principles which were that the assessment of relative strengths must be numerical and entail the measurement of strength. In retrospect it is surprising how few attempts have been made by previous writers, with the exception of Prentiss, to deal with this side of the subject.

The book would be incomplete if it concerned itself solely with impersonal facts and ignored those who made them. Personal war reminiscences abound, but I am deliberately restricting myself to two particular aspects: firstly, the relationship between two groups of professionals, chemists and soldiers; secondly, the impact on combatants of a wholly novel weapon against which the only defence was absolute confidence in an entirely new protective device, the respirator.

The relations between chemists and soldiers were by no means harmonious and, looking back, the alternation between mutual understanding and incomprehension correspondingly contributed to the effectiveness and failure of chemical weapons. I write 'alternation' advisedly, for there is much evidence of what would now be called communications failures. The friction between the two cultures existed even then and was not lessened by the passage of time. The uneasy relations were not confined to the front; they extended well to the rear, into the bureaucratic complexes which eventually 'managed' the war. Science and war were indeed interacting and after 1914 the subject attracted sustained attention. Sir William Pope made it the theme of his Presidential

Address to the Chemical Society. He noted that the necessity for applying science had come to be accepted during the war, but he was afraid that in peacetime science could be treated parsimoniously. He warned that it was 'again leaving the hands of the scientific man and being resumed by the lay administrator.'[27] This has been a common complaint ever since, though the scale of operations has vastly increased, and science policy has so far failed to solve the problem. But gas warfare 1915–18 can serve as a case study, *in vivo* as it were, of professional relations, suddenly, briefly and even dramatically involved in the practical applications of chemistry.

That brings me to another 'human angle' familiar to many through Sargent's painting of the gassed men on their way to the Casualty Clearing Station on the Amiens Road.[28] Defence against gas was a most unusual mixture of discipline, morale, and applied physiology. At the level of moral judgement the beastliness of chemical warfare (as distinct from other forms of warfare) has attracted immense attention, but what was it really like? Artists, poets, and novelists have given one version. I put it to the test, under admittedly ideal conditions, with chlorine and mouthpads made of dry, as well as urine-soaked, socks—the recommended protection of May 1915. The experiment did not turn me into an expert, but caused me to look for another version. Hence interviews with those who had experienced cloud gas and gas shell between 1915 and 1918. These old men had unexpected reactions which led me to the conclusion that the effectiveness of chemical weapons cannot be measured in purely statistical terms and requires some consideration of the post-war attitudes to gas and their effect on defence policies.

Between the wars, and even later, old battles were fought over with the same ammunition by those who had taken part, and their prejudices affected their perspective. By contrast I have the advantage of that detachment which comes from lack of involvement—the generation gap has its uses. That does not mean that I shall be invariably unbiased: I have already declared my personal interest and reviewed the fresh material which determined my approach. If new light can be shed on past events it is the historian's duty not merely to produce the evidence, but also to evaluate its significance relative to what was previously known; in brief to reassess the validity of historical judgements. That objective governs the scope of the book and also the manner of dealing with the subject-matter. It will be convenient to discuss both under five headings.

First, the time-span: chemical warfare began officially in 1915 and ended in 1918. These four years will be my chief concern. Though gas has been used sporadically since then, I have not studied these instances, but have relied in the main on specialist publications and the work of the Stockholm International Peace Research Institute.

Second, the range of the material and its limitations: the story deals with gas; other quasi-chemical activities such as smoke-generation or flame-throwers have been excluded. The emphasis is principally on the Western Front and on the activities of British, French, and German gas specialists and troops, the development of special research and development organizations by these three belligerents, and the resulting production of poison gas[29] and of gas masks. I am aware that on some occasions gas played a significant role on the Italian front and also in Poland, but the documentation was not accessible to me. Although there is some new material not available to historians writing before the late 1960s, it is not sufficient, except in rare instances, to alter received opinions. I would therefore have to go over previously trodden ground, and so have deliberately kept the discussion short. The review of the American chemical warfare effort is similarly limited, but for an entirely different reason: there is an abundance of information, but also a different timetable of events. US chemical warfare came very late: unimportant throughout 1917 and relying almost entirely on British experience and equipment, it only began to play a significant role at the very end of the war. Had the struggle continued into 1919 the American CWS would have occupied the principal position. However, during 1918 US soldiers exposed to German gas shelling suffered heavy casualties. Thus American experience in respect of offensive warfare is largely irrelevant and need not be stressed; but in respect of defence against gas it is interesting and meaningful and so given more emphasis.

Third, the chronology: it has been impracticable and often undesirable to keep to a strict date order. I am concerned with the manufacture and use of new weapons and the elaboration of defensive measures. This entails several studies in depth which are, in fact, essential digressions, deliberately inserted in the narrative at the point when their explanatory value is greatest, regardless of the chronological sequence. That explains why occasionally I have to back-track, and sometimes to run ahead.

Fourth, the purpose: I intend to investigate the circumstances that led the Germans to be the pacemakers in offence (though not defence) and the obstacles which prevented the Allies from responding speedily and effectively. Chemical backwardness was one factor, organization another, the initial lack of special skills a third. To the extent that the difficulties were overcome, most quickly and impressively in anti-gas protection, the Allied position improved. Various factors, notably raw material shortages, were later to hamper the Germans and in some respects they were less competent than the Allies had anticipated. Each side tended to overrate the other. To understand why, it is necessary to consider the people and the organizational structures available to do the job, and in particular to describe the enforced collaboration of chemists and soldiers.

Fifth, the conclusion: gas was one of the very few genuine new weapons of the First World War and unique in that it was not used in the next. Why was a weapon unrestrainedly used between 1915 and 1918 unused in 1939–45? That question has been carefully examined by Brown in the context of power politics.[30] But it also raises another question: was gas not used because the belligerents had in the earlier war been moving towards a chemical and operational stalemate, inasmuch as gas attacks could no longer overwhelm the defences against them? There were certainly signs of that in 1918. That, in turn, leads to another consideration: could it be that gas was a less effective weapon than its originators had expected and than its supporters later proclaimed it to be? The matter needs to be properly investigated: the resources devoted to gas production can be identified, and the industrial – military input side of the cost-efficiency model can even be quantified. The output side, that is the effect in terms of enemy casualties, ground gained, and extra strain on the opponent's resources is much more complex and the statistics are incomplete. In particular the data on casualties and the treatment of the gassed, which will be examined in a separate chapter, are unsatisfactory.[31] But the point that matters is whether the reliability of the numbers is sufficient to support the conclusions drawn from them. I think it is and will produce the evidence. The reader must then decide for himself. But it is not enough to write the conclusion as if it were an essay in descriptive statistics. Value judgements are surely relevant and have their proper place; suffice it to note here that the impact of chemical warfare on contemporaries was profound and cannot be ignored. Events and the personal reactions to them appear at first to be inextricably connected. In retrospect the facts and the impressions are often in conflict. Where does the truth lie? This is dangerous ground for an historian. But it is worth exploring, if only briefly in the last two chapters, in order to give a rounded picture of the effect of this extraordinary weapon.

2

FORERUNNERS IN FACT AND FICTION

THE gas cloud, first used in April 1915, had no precursors: it sprang, as it were, in its final form, on an unprepared enemy. This was certainly an unusual event in the history of military technology. With most other weapons the development can be traced over decades if not centuries. But gas, deadly or merely irritant, was different. As a weapon it existed principally in the imagination of writers. At rare intervals some ingenious and original mind would move from fantasy to reality, but the experiments were never conclusive. For had they been demonstrably successful they would have, we may be sure, encouraged other people to improve on the original. All the descriptions until 1915 are of unrelated incidents without antecedents and without sequel.

Thus there are a few reports of smoke from damp straw or other organic matter having been used occasionally in antiquity. Two millennia later Leonardo da Vinci described a shell containing very fine sulphur and arsenic dust which was to be thrown against enemy ships and galleys: details of this forerunner of irritants and so of tear gas are lacking. Then there is another gap, and the first evidence of a more sophisticated approach. Lord Dundonald's 'secret weapons' received a lot of attention because he was persistent, extremely long-lived and, according to his biographer, had 'achieved great results by small means'.[1] He proposed in 1811, 1845, and again in 1855 the use of smoke from burning coal tar and carbon disulphide.[2] For different reasons the French and later the Russians were spared these novel weapons. Similarly Stenhouse's combined stink and fire bomb of 1854 contained a liquid of which the active constituent was probably dimethylarsenious oxide, was not acceptable to the military.[3]

The above summary is not exhaustive, but digressions on technological curiosities do not alter the general picture that chemical weapons formed no part of military preparations. That conclusion is based not merely on the absence of mention in military treatises, but, more to the point, on supply constraints. The industrial-scale technology for making the gases and the means for delivering them did not exist until the very end of the nineteenth century. Consider the first war gases: chlorine and phosgene. Chlorine had been discovered towards the end of the eighteenth century and in aqueous solution had thereafter been used for many years as bleach. The bleaching liquor was replaced about the middle of the nineteenth century by bleaching powder (containing up to 35 per cent Cl_2) prepared from chlorine derived from hydrochloric acid (which, in turn, was a by-product of the Leblanc soda process and slaked lime).[4] While bleaching powder soon became an important industrial chemical, chlorine was not an article of commerce and armies did not have movable plants to generate the gas. Liquid chlorine in cylinders, which gained such a notoriety in 1915, was first offered to German bleachers by Badische Anilin- & Soda-Fabrik in the late 1880s, and unsuccessfully put on sale by the company's American representatives in 1892. Chlorine made electrolytically from brine began to replace Weldon-Deacon chlorine from the turn of the century onwards, but in the USA as well as Britain it tended to be converted into bleaching powder, and liquid chlorine in cylinders did not generally become available in the USA until about 1909 and even later in Britain.[5] The commercial history of phosgene is more recent. It was discovered in 1812 by Davy who prepared it by reacting carbon monoxide and chlorine in daylight. The compound was not used until the 1880s when Alfred Kern mentioned it in his patent for the manufacture of crystal violet (1883). There were patent complications, but once they had been removed, this triphenylmethane dye became, and long remained, extremely important. Thus a sustained demand was created for the intermediate, known as Michler's ketone, made by passing phosgene into dimethylaniline. Initially phosgene was manufactured only in Germany and was sold in steel bottles.[6] By the eve of the war there was equipment for making the compound in Germany, France, and Britain.

The condition of the chemical industry and its product mix, combined with ignorance among the potential users were the determining factors in the failure to contemplate the use of gas before the war. However, such an explanation would have no relevance to the development of gas masks. Their evolution is elaborately documented because protection against dangerous substances, be it mercuric sulphide (vermilion) manufacture in the first century or bleaching powder packing in the nineteenth, was a matter of continuing concern, as distinct from the occasional use of smoke in war.[7] Rescue services in coal mines and fire-fighting in densely packed urban housing or factories created a need for dependable breathing sets. Mouthpads first described by Pliny were used to protect the Victorians, albeit imperfectly, against 'noxious' atmospheres. An alternative solution was a long flexible breathing-tube with a charcoal filter: though recommended for firemen, it cannot have been of much value, since that kind of filter will not adsorb the particulate matter of smoke. Hence the development of regenerative sets based on the principle that the wearer carries his own supply of respirable air. Appliances comprising a supply of oxygen, a carbon dioxide absorber, and an impermeable bag, together with valves, gauges, and tubes had been envisaged in the eighteenth century but could not be constructed at the time. The first practicable set was designed by Dr T. Schwann in 1852–3 and within the next twenty or twenty-five years several different types were introduced. By the beginning of the twentieth century firms such as Siebe, Gorman and Co. in Britain or Drägerwerke in Germany supplied dependable though bulky precision-built regenerative sets to collieries, fire-brigades, sewage works, many industrial users, and submarine crews. The flexible corrugated rubber tube and the non-return expiratory valve, which were important components in the British respirator from 1916 onwards, had been introduced by Siebe, Gorman in the 1880s.[8]

We therefore have an interesting contrast in 1914: dangerous gases had been prepared, indeed chlorine and carbon disulphide were becoming industrial commodities, but militarily they were an unknown element. On the other hand protection against gases had reached an advanced stage. The equipment was available, and the manufacturers were improving it in the light of operating experience gained under the most diverse conditions. In principle then, defence was much stronger than attack, but given the state of knowledge among staff officers, the military significance of this fact was of no interest.

With hindsight it is easy enough to identify technological gaps, much more difficult to show the extent to which contemporaries appreciated the problem and consciously sought a solution. Military novels, and particularly science fiction, serve a useful role in this connection, if only as indicators of intellectual awareness. During the latter part of the nineteenth century writers often endowed their fictional belligerents with the most advanced technology. However, these literary fantasies wished away the obstacles, and not surprisingly, the defence was not allowed to develop sufficiently to cope with the attacks. Such reasoning remains incomprehensible, for it was based on the assumption that one side (the heroes) could learn, while the other (the villains) could not. Inconsistency may not matter among novelists who need not strive after logic, but the point is that in the 1890s and 1900s the facts were different: gas as a weapon was underdeveloped by comparison with the defences against it. Failure to remember this and continued wishful thinking on gas, based on the fallacies of science fiction, were shortly to lead to serious military blunders.

Alfred Robida, a well-known French engraver and caricaturist, first serialized and later (1887) issued in book form *La Guerre au vingtième siècle*, which was remarkably prescient: the enemy has chemists who prepare gas bombs and mines filled with *miasmes concentrées* and also with viruses; his specialist troops wear masks like helmets and oxygen cylinders. In short the pictures recall Dundonald's and Stenhouse's stink bombs, and the breathing sets then in use. The story next describes a French counter-attack with gas shells, the enemy retaliates with paralysing and asphyxiating chemicals and with itching powder. The French eventually discover a 'corrosive dew'—*du vitriol dans l'atmosphère*—which destroys the hostile batteries.[9] Although none of this was taken seriously at the time, Robida's fantasies became realities on the Western Front. H. G. Wells pitched *The War of the Worlds* (1898) in an altogether different key. He too had gas, 'Black Smoke', discharged from a portable rocket-launcher, which killed by inhalation and by touch; it was heavy, settled on the ground, and became innocuous in contact with water. The Martians cleared it with steam-jets, but they did not wear masks![10] Here again parallels may be drawn with mustard gas and the Livens projector with its phosgene projectile. Serving officers themselves occasionally took a hand. A group which included the professor of military art and history at the Staff College and a rear admiral, published *The Great War of 189—: A Forecast* in 1893. They anticipated a conventional war, say vintage 1890, and the only concession to contemporary technology was the appearance of a rigid airship which dropped a large bomb filled with blasting gelatine and liquid oxygen. The explosion was formidable and partly destroyed the town of Varna.[11] Another professional was Capitaine Danrit, the pseudonym of E. A. G. Driant, a regular soldier and later Député: he was an outright anti-German and in his numerous novels French equipment was always superior to German.[12]

Clarke has made a study of 'military science fiction' and has shown that it was an expression of international rivalries. He lists no less than 221 imaginary war books between 1890 and 1914, three-fifths of them in the eight years before the outbreak of war.[13] The bulk was mere literary xenophobia and scientifically nonsensical but the influence of these novels was cumulative and, judging by Wells's fame, far-reaching. Science fiction at its best heightened awareness of the destructive power of novel weapons and it is not fanciful to suggest that it appealed to some chemists and engineers by drawing their attention to the potential of gas. When war did break out, literature supplied as it were a link between scientific vision and the needs of the moment. Hence a flood of suggestions which combined Robida's inventiveness with first-year undergraduate chemistry, a sort of Heath Robinson approach to chemical warfare, preposterous, impractical, ignoring technological obstacles and defence. Nevertheless, enough of these extraordinary proposals survived the scrutiny of General Staffs and were later tried out. They gave the early chemical warfare efforts an unusually imaginative and do-it-yourself character. In these original, indeed fantastic, and distinctly unconventional military aspects, gas can trace a direct descent from science fiction.

Attempts to define the rights and obligations of belligerents and formalize the rules of war were given a fresh impetus by Tsar Nicholas II who convened the first Hague Peace Conference in 1899. He had been advised that technical progress was bound to affect warfare. Hence the objective of Hague I was not merely to mitigate the hardships of a future war, but specifically to prohibit new, that is hitherto unused, weapons.[14] Jack (later Lord) Fisher represented Britain, Capt. Mahan the USA, and Col. von Schwarzhoff Germany. They were career officers, experts in their profession and, as has been perceptively observed, 'such men could not be expected to bargain away the basis of their careers and prestige, and they were quite adept at discovering and articulating technical and tactical reasons for rejecting the Tsar's proposals.'[15] Gas was on the agenda. The delegates had no chemical advisers and, more importantly, there was no point of reference, no recorded experience, except in science fiction. How to prohibit a non-existent weapon? The delegates dealt with the problem as follows: 'The Contracting Powers agree to abstain from the use of all projectiles the sole object of which is the diffusion of asphyxiating or deleterious gases.'[16] The clause caused much discussion, but all the delegations (save that of the USA) eventually agreed to the resolution, thereby gaining goodwill without foregoing any existing defence interest. The USA, however, stood apart, on the ground that the clause was unrealistic and Mahan said that he could not see any logical difference between blowing up people in a ship whence they could scarcely escape or choking them by gas on land.[17] The arguments with their moral overtones need not detain us at this stage. Hague I was a comforting, but loosely worded document: or more precisely a declaration of intent for the Convention was toothless, there being no provision for inspection, nor for control—in short, each signatory was in honour bound to do his own policing.

Gas turned up again at the second Hague Conference convened by President Theodore Roosevelt in 1907. Hague II reaffirmed the earlier abstention clause and another on the avoidance of projectiles, weapons, and materials which might cause unnecessary suffering. It widened the restraints by prohibiting the use of 'poison or poisoned weapons' (Article XXIIIa). Implementation, however, remained unchanged from Hague I, so that enforcement continued to be unilateral. By 1914 this later Convention had been ratified by all the European belligerents in the forthcoming war except Italy; the USA and Turkey adhered later.

The spirit of the Conventions was surely clear enough: to stop new and potentially more awful weapons. But the letter was obscure and open to widely differing interpretations. Thus Hague I and II were a moral force to be reckoned with and at the same time ineffectual. The resulting long-term practical consequences assumed great significance after 1915 and continued to operate throughout the post-war years. When the Germans used gas at Ypres, they were held to be in breach of the Conventions on several counts. Public opinion was aroused and the Germans had to justify themselves, always a difficult task for a pioneer in warfare and doubly so in this instance. They argued at the time, and later, that (i) the Conventions did not cover gas blown from cylinders, (ii) the Allies had used gas first, (iii) gases were not poisons, and (iv) after the war, gas shells were implicitly excluded because they were not causing needless suffering.[18] The arguments continued endlessly between the belligerents and, long after peace had been signed, remained inconclusive. In trying to exculpate themselves the Germans sought to draw attention to uses of gas before April 1915 and their tactic henceforward was to cast doubt on the Allied assertion of surprised innocence. That raises the question: did the Germans have precursors and if so who innovated what and when? The answers, as so often, are unclear, but it is worthwhile examining the evidence if only for the light it throws on the state of pre-war preparedness.

Many writers on chemical warfare have asserted that the French police either 'considered' or actually employed tear gas to capture a gang of violent criminals in April 1912.[19] The facts are as follows: Jules Bonnot, the leader of the gang, and an associate were tracked down to a shed in the Paris suburb of Choisy-le-

Roi. The associate was killed by revolver shots, but Bonnot held out. The police thereupon dynamited part of the building, a fire broke out, and the dying gangster was finally overwhelmed. The entire action lasted about four hours. It was reported in minute detail by the press; not one of the papers suggested or even hinted at the proposed use of tear gas or its possible employment.[20]

Evidence of the use of tear gas, especially on a well-publicized occasion such as the capture of the notorious Bonnot would have been invaluable for propaganda purposes on a later occasion. The sequel, however, was prosaic. Messrs. Kling and Florentin, two chemists at the municipal laboratory of the City of Paris, became interested in riot control, investigated the use of lachrymatory agents, and recommended them to the police. The materials employed (which were not described) were to be filled into cartridges or hand grenades. It does not seem that the French police adopted tear gas, but supplies were prepared for the French corps of engineers and, as will be seen in the next chapter, were issued to the troops soon after the outbreak of war.[21] During the war, Commandant Nicolardot, then head of the chemical laboratory of the Section Technique de l'Artillerie, told Professor Crossley that he had warned his superiors as early as 1900 that the Germans would use chlorine and bromine, and he had even designed a simple mask. In 1905–6 he had recommended chloropicrin as shell filling and made a study of those gases which he thought were permissible under the Hague Convention.[22] None of this came to anything. Nicolardot may well have inflated his own role: but in any case intentions are not acts and except for the unspecified tear gas I have not found any material on French gas research or production before the war. I do not claim that this is conclusive, merely that if anything was done, it was handled with extreme discretion.

From Germany there are reports of some activity. A chemist at the Hoechst company worked on smoke generators for the navy.[23] More to the point, a long memorandum written by Col. Bauer, who played an important role in chemical warfare and who will make his appearance in due course, mentions that the army conducted experiments with gas, type not specified, before August 1914. The outcome, he wrote, had been 'negative' and actually delayed later work because the experts believed that the pre-war trials had been inconclusive.[24] Bauer's report is to some extent confirmed by a letter which Haber wrote years later to a war-time colleague in which he stated that when the Germans began their first wartime gas tests at the Wahn artillery range, the chemists were told by some airmen stationed there that 'trials had taken place with aeroplane bombs containing phosgene before or after [sic] the declaration of war', but had been abandoned as impracticable.[25] The story is imprecise and while it represents the first mention of phosgene in a military context, it gives no date. All one can say with confidence is that work had gone beyond the mere desk study of possible uses of poison gas.

One turns, with relief, to the more informative and probably more dependable British reports. They show that some people in the War Office were sufficiently interested in gas to put a carefully worded enquiry to the Foreign Office whether it was 'permissible' under Hague II to employ 'preparations giving rise to disagreeable fumes without causing permanent harm' and to introduce gas in high explosive shell. The Foreign Office ruled that both were admissible 'in view of indications that the subject was being considered in other countries'.[26] Accordingly 'stink pots' (possibly based on Dundonald's recipe) were investigated, but abandoned, and during 1913–14 the use of chloroacetone and benzyl chloride, both lachrymatory substances, in 'small' shell was studied. The Superintendent of Research reported unfavourably on the research on 29 August 1914 and the War Office stopped further work a month later.[27] The British efforts, despite the circumstantial reports, do not amount to much, though they indicate contemporary attitudes to the Hague Conventions. Indeed there was only one place where some working experience of gas was being obtained, and that unexpectedly was in Australia where arsenious chloride was being employed to destroy prickly pear. This interesting information, though no secret, did not reach the proper quarters until August 1915.[28]

The most one can say about gas and smoke is that by the eve of the war military awareness of chemicals had increased to the extent that some soldiers were willing to consider them and a very few, with a more innovating turn of mind, were even experimenting with various compounds. The substances used with the exception of phosgene, were not toxic. There were no military stocks of gases, nor of gas shell, save for very limited supplies of tear-gas grenades and cartridges in French hands. The forerunners were scientific curiosities and the belligerents of August 1914 had no conception of the practicalities of chemical warfare.

3

THE CHLORINE CLOUD

THE German advance of August 1914 into Belgium and France produced a rich crop of horror stories. Mutual antagonisms soon reached such a pitch that any allegation about the enemy's use of secret weapons (among them chemicals) was readily believed. Geyer wrote later that his colleagues at OHL when told of the use of gas by the French, dismissed the reports. Major Bauer, an important personage in our story and Geyer's chief, said the Germans had never concerned themselves with chemical warfare.[1] The claims and their validity will presently be examined in greater detail, meanwhile it is worth noting that the Germans were in a good position to check the accuracy of the allegations, for their troops came across abandoned French supply dumps, but they never found any French gas ammunition.[2] There was in fact a simple scientific explanation: the explosion of a shell or mine generates some carbon monoxide which in a trench or other hollow can build up to a dangerous concentration. Picric acid (trinitrophenol), widely employed by the Allies as a high explosive, when incompletely detonated has a peculiar odour, causes sneezing, and its bright yellow colour attracts attention. The German infantry were unfamiliar with it and therefore suspicious.

Nevertheless, within a few weeks of the outbreak of war several proposals were made in different countries to introduce unconventional weapons. These projects were vigorously promoted by individuals who badgered and bullied the professionals until the new materials were tested. The autumn of 1914 was, in this respect, the period of the scientific amateur and of science fiction. No more would have been heard of these fantastic plans but for the prestige of the initiators and the credulity of the officials they dealt with. In Britain, all these ideas were sifted by the Royal Society's War Committee, specifically by the Chemical Sub-Committee, and in this way cranks and specialists gained, as it were, some respectability. The proposals to use chemical weapons in some form or other need to be summarized, if only to show that the Western powers were interested in them, and indeed differed not in intent, but merely in the choice of materials and willingness to try them out.

We may conveniently begin where the last chapter ended—in Britain. Towards the end of September 1914 the War Office and the Admiralty prohibited the use of tear gas in shell, and on 16 October the former, when approached with the suggestion to drop bombs filled with aqueous hydrocyanic acid from planes, pointed out that this violated Hague II. Nevertheless the scientists busied themselves. Sir William Ramsay recommended acrolein to the members of the Royal Society sub-committee. It was known to have the properties of a tear gas, and also to be toxic in large doses, but was rejected not on those grounds, but because it oxidized to acrylic acid—now more familiar as a paint base.[3] J. F. Thorpe and H. B. Baker at Imperial College then began to study the tear gases, and Thorpe, who had worked on o-xylylene bromide, proposed it as a lachrymator. Again, this was found to be unsuitable, and during the latter part of November and throughout December they investiaged 'stink-bomb' ingredients among which certain benzyl compounds were most promising, but had to be rejected on account of the toluene shortage. After dozens of other substances had been examined the choice fell on ethyl iodoacetate which required no materials then scarce. Tests were made in a trench at Imperial College. Col. (later Gen. Sir Louis) Jackson[4] came from the War Office to attend them. He was more resistant to tear gas than the academics (or maybe he just shut his eyes tightly), but eventually he too succumbed. Further confirmation of the efficacy of the compound was provided by a lad who happened to be passing by. So the substance was adopted: to commemorate South Kensington it was code-named SK.[5] Having thus, after several weeks of research, identified a practical tear gas in January 1915, nothing more was done. At about the same time, Maurice Hankey, then secretary to the Committee of Imperial Defence, was sending the projects of some cranks, which had somehow found their way to his office, to the War Office: one inventor wanted to set fire to the atmosphere, another to spray the Germans with amyl nitrate, an inflammable liquid. Neither was practical, but they caused Hankey to recommend the study of chemical warfare to the War Office, so as to be ready to retaliate if the Germans should start it. Such awareness of chemical warfare at that high level was significant, and it was sustained by the increasing number of intelligence reports on the subject. As a result, official adherence to Hague II weakened, and in March 1915 Earl Dundonald's advice on chemical smoke-screens was belatedly accepted: the material was tested on 9 April 1915 and a Committee set up to examine its use.[6]

The French, by contrast, made more progress. They had in August 1914 small stocks of tear-gas cartridges and possibly also of hand grenades of which the active ingredient was ethyl bromoacetate. But at first the army did not call for them. Later, when it did and the cartridges were fired from a specially adapted and inaccurate rifle, the tiny amount of tear gas (say 19 cc per cartridge) went undetected.[7] The stocks of *cartouches suffocantes* were apparently used up during the autumn and a fresh order was placed in November. Bromine, then readily obtainable only from Germany and the USA, was scarce, so the active ingredient was changed to chloroacetone.[8]

The interesting question is this: what caused the French to order more tear gas? The obvious answer is the onset of trench warfare. But it is incomplete, for the cartridges were useless, whereas hand grenades would only be effective in large quantities and in close combat. The most likely explanation is that tear gas (regardless of the Hague Conventions) was going to be employed in the forthcoming spring offensive. The Germans captured a French circular, dated 21 February 1915, which described the chloroacetone cartridges and grenades, explained their use and while pointing out that in small quantities the chemical was not 'deleterious', recommended that goggles be worn for protection. Such written evidence of the proposed use of tear gas was of great value to the Germans and they later made the most of it. I have not been able to trace the genesis of this circular, so carelessly allowed to fall into enemy hands, but it is possible that it was premature and that it was distributed before the new weapon was available for field use. One document at Vincennes, dated 30 March 1915, refers to a large number of *engins suffocants* (i.e. hand grenades) having been ordered as well as 90,000 goggles—the latter to protect the French against German tear gas which had allegedly been introduced recently. Delivery was expected about 15 May.[9] There is evidence that these hand grenades were being manufactured during March–April 1915.[10] According to Trumpener, they were, by order of GQG No. 781 of 3 April 1915 placed at the disposal of the armies.[11]

The Germans claimed that the French had used tear gas in March 1915 in the Argonne,[12] but there is no confirmation and I am inclined to think that if such gas was used on that occasion, it was only on a small scale. Nevertheless the available information points to a clear French intent to introduce tear gas in Spring 1915. Their attitude reflected the growing belief that chemical substances, in addition to high explosive were needed to drive the enemy from casemates, dug-outs, and trenches and so weaken his defences.

The Germans reached the same conclusion by a different route, but instead of restricting themselves to tear gas they extended the concept to chlorine and so transformed the nature of chemical warfare. There are different versions of how it all began. The most plausible is that Gen. Falkenhayn, at the time Chief of the General Staff, instructed Bauer to call a meeting at the Wahn range (south east of Cologne, later the site of the airport) early in October 1914 to discuss methods for generating smoke or fire and also materials having lachrymatory and other irritating effects which would cause the enemy to break cover. Nernst and Duisberg attended. The former, an eminent physical chemist, was well known at OHL as a volunteer driver and a man of original ideas.[13] The latter, the leading figure in the German chemical industry, also knew Bauer and his office was not far away at the Bayer company in Leverkusen. Someone (it may have been Duisberg) suggested dianisidine chlorosulphonate, which causes violent sneezing, but is otherwise inoffensive. It was readily obtainable from Leverkusen, being derived from an important azo dye intermediate. Several hundred kilos were ordered, filled into shells and used at the capture of Neuve Chapelle on 27 October.[14] The Germans quickly and ingeniously modified the

105 mm howitzer shell so that the shrapnel, instead of being embedded in black powder, was surrounded by the chemical. It was expected that the explosion would grind and disperse the material. But in their hurry they failed to make tests, so that they did not discover until too late that the dispersal was small and the irritant action short.[15] This non-event was the more galling because the enemy were unaware of the first use of chemical shell! Production was stopped.

OHL had no chemist, but Col. Gerhard Tappen, the chief of the operations branch, had a brother, then working in the Heavy Artillery Department of the War Ministry. Hans Tappen was a chemist and had written a dissertation on benzyl bromides; he thus knew something of tear gas and recommended it to his brother. The moment was right, the connection influential, and Hans was assigned in November 1914 to Spandau where the ordnance works supplied him with shell cases lined with lead to resist the corrosive action of xylyl bromide. Bauer did not think much of the idea, but Gerhard Tappen pulled rank and insisted on trials which showed that a liquid shell-filling was practicable. Further tests, near Berlin in December 1914 and at Wahn on 9 January 1915 (the latter attended by Falkenhayn himself) showed that T-*Stoff*, the code name for both xylyl- and benzyl bromide, was a satisfactory filling. Orders were given for production to be increased and permission obtained to fill T-*Stoff* into 150 mm howitzer shell for field use.[16] Hans Tappen had meanwhile gone to Leverkusen where he developed other lachrymatory substances. The production of the different active agents which were given code names presented no particular technical problems, and as the scale of shell filling was initially small, the suppliers were instructed to deal with this too. Table 3.1 shows that by Spring 1915 three firms were involved.[17]

The Germans having adopted tear gas now faced an unexpected difficulty. Range tests indicated that the 150 mm howitzer shell was the best mode of delivery, but at the turn of the year there were not enough howitzers of this calibre.[18] That restricted the use of tear gas, and the first T-shell firing was delayed until 31 January 1915 when it took place against the Russians at Bolimów. As the ambient temperature was extremely low the liquid failed to vaporize, and so, once again, the Germans made a false start. To prevent this, bromacetone (B-*Stoff*) was added and the French were shelled with a mixture of T and B at Nieuport in March.[19] Though these beginnings were hardly impressive, the Allies were aware of something unusual going on, but uncertain how to react.[20] The howitzer problem had eased and during spring and early summer, the Germans used T-shells on about half a dozen occasions, in particular on 22 April in association with the chlorine cloud. Various attempts were made between February and April 1915 to add toxicity to the tear gas by mixing it with phosgene, but the modified filling was not apparently used in the field. The Germans (probably at Nernst's suggestion) also experimented with trench mortar bombs filled with phosgene or with a mixture of phosgene and chlorine. Haber gave a demonstration of these bombs at Wahn on 25 March

Table 3.1. *German Tear-Gas Materials, Manufacturers,*
and Start of Operations

Chemical compound	Code*	Manufacturer and Location	Production started	Shell-filling began
Xylyl bromide and benzyl bromide	T	Kahlbaum, Berlin	Dec. 1914	Jan. 1915
		Bayer, Leverkusen	Jan. 1915	Jan. 1915
		Hoechst, Höchst	Apr. 1915	Apr. 1915
Bromacetone	B	Bayer, Leverkusen	Dec. 1914	Jan. 1915
Bromomethyl-ethyl-ketone	BN	Hoechst, Höchst	Apr. 1915	n.a.
Methyl chlorosulphonate	—	Bayer, Leverkusen	Jan. (?) 1915	n.a.
Dichloromethyl chloroformate	K†	Bayer, Leverkusen	Jan. 1915	Jan. 1915

* Suffix -*Stoff* (= substance) omitted.
† When filled into trench mortar bombs the code letter was C.

1915. Once again Duisberg was present, and had cause to remember the occasion for he inhaled some of the gas and was lucky to get away with a slight case of pneumonia and a few days in bed.[21] An even earlier instance of a toxic material in shells occurred in December 1914 at Haber's institute: the object was to find a poisonous tear gas that could be carried and dispersed by cast iron shell, which despite its poor fragmentation was being pressed into service. Dr. O. Sackur, possibly inspired by Stenhouse's work sixty years before, was studying the action of dichloromethylamine on cacodyl chloride, a very unstable compound. There was an explosion, Sackur was killed instantly, and all work on the compound ceased.[22]

The story so far is nothing more than a listing of incidents. Each of them was small and, taken separately, unimportant, but as a whole they illustrate the piecemeal approach to chemical warfare and important differences between the belligerents. The British confined themselves to experiments. The French relied on their pre-war work on tear gases, extended it, and had every intention of using these materials in the first half of 1915. The Germans spasmodically investigated various proposals and such was the potential of their chemical industry, that whatever was suggested could be implemented at short notice. The scientific and technological ability of the German manufacturers was unquestioned. But the users, the artillery, remained half-hearted. There was considerable reluctance to integrate the novel chemical fillings in artillery procedures. How else to explain the intermittent use of tear gas in summer 1915 and the gap between filling shell with K-*Stoff* in January and issuing it in August? Vinet's statement[23] that during 1914–15, Bayer, Hoechst, and Kahlbaum filled 'about 1 mln projectiles' with various chemical warfare materials is unsupported by statistics and, in my opinion, grossly exaggerated. Given the reports of individual actions, a more likely figure would be a fifth to a quarter of Vinet's total.

But the main reason for the lack of interest and the absence of any urgency among the belligerents was the shortage of shell cases, propellants, and explosives; the Germans also temporarily lacked heavy howitzers. In conditions of scarcity the military opted for the familiar: they argued that this was not time for experiments even if the novel materials were worthwhile substitutes, and furthermore they had sufficient evidence to show that large quantities had to be used in order to be effective. Nevertheless if the stalemate of trench warfare was to be broken in 1915, a novel solution was required. It was found by Haber, and to the extent that he originated and developed the concept of the gas cloud, the Karlsruhe militants were right to call him the father of chemical warfare.

How did he become involved and make his contribution? He had been chiefly concerned with nitrogen supplies, though the institute was, as we have seen, carrying out some military scientific investigations. The trigger apparently was the testing of T-shell in mid December 1914: Haber was present and came away convinced that tear gas was useless on a small scale. He made his views known and suggested firing xylyl bromide bombs from trench mortars arranged in groups. He was thus anticipating Livens's projectors of 1916–17. Haber was told his idea was impracticable because the equipment could not be quickly supplied. We may digress here to note that in Britain Livens got a similar answer from the War Office, but went ahead regardless. Haber did not, instead—with his practical turn of mind—he suggested the next best thing, the discharge of gas from cylinders.[24] This time OHL was receptive, not least because the cylinders existed (or it was believed that they did) and chlorine was available. Haber declared that the gas would form a cloud which would drive the enemy out of the trenches into the open. The idea appealed. Before the year was out he was put in charge and, at the age of forty-six, to everyone's surprise, was raised from NCO in the Reserve to Captain. The promotion was as unconventional as the weapon.[25]

Was he a good choice? In Haber the OHL found a brilliant mind and an extremely energetic organizer, determined, and possibly also unscrupulous. Was chlorine a good choice? It was certainly Haber's choice, and given his prestige and position it was accepted. He was aware of its limitations and, personally brave, paid little attention to the risks. In a hurry to get chlorine to the front he underrated the drawbacks and gambled that the German infantry could do without protection. This was a miscalculation and it was aggravated by an even more serious mistake in the selection of the material. Phosgene, though not so readily available in the same quantity, would have achieved the hoped-for results much more effectively. But its use would have imposed some delay while masks and supplies were got ready. Hindsight helps of course: we have seen how the German interest in chemical warfare was becoming increasingly diversified, and as they were prepared to ignore the moral issue posed by the Hague Conventions they would have done better to damn the consequences and rely for their initial surprise on the more powerful weapon.

The German preparations took about two and a half months. The first hurdle was the formal acceptance, and Falkenhayn had to take the decision. OHL while considering gas 'unchivalrous' nevertheless hoped it would lead to a decisive solution in the West. The experts assured Falkenhayn that chlorine from cylinders was not a breach of Hague II and that there was no risk of early retaliation. Haber was not consulted by Falkenhayn about the legal aspect and subsequently wrote: 'Although he never asked for my opinion on the state of the law, he left me in no doubt that he accepted the limitations of international law which he intended fully to adhere to.'[26] The inconsistency between the attitude ascribed to the leadership and the actual policy suggests confusion and an attempt by Haber to cover up. He was invariably consulted on technical aspects, and is reported to have urged that gas should only be employed if the generals were sure of victory. Thus the unfolding of events allowed military optimism to overrule scientific common sense. In retrospect one can consider this an early instance of having an expert 'on tap, but not on top'. It was also the first of many instances of mutual incomprehension between chemists and regular officers. In the end Falkenhayn gave the go-ahead around the middle of January.[27]

Next, the site had to be chosen. The Army commanders were asked and with the exception of Duke Albrecht of Württemberg, commanding the 4th Army, all refused. His men faced Ypres. The refusals and the single acceptance were odd, because Ypres was not the best location. There were better sites in Artois north of Lens, and in Champagne east of Reims. More time and trouble at this stage would have saved disappointments later. But the chief of staff of the 4th Army, Ilse, together with Gen. Deimling, a middle-aged Württemberger who commanded the XV Corps in position between Hoge and Hill 60 were summoned to OHL on 25 January and told by Falkenhayn that gas would be used in the south-eastern sector.[28] They were optimistic at OHL and had convinced themselves that the capture of Ypres would be a major success; staff officers even justified trying out the new weapon against the British, on the ground that they were the most resolute and dangerous opponents.[29]

It is time to take a closer look at Ypres where in February 1915 the gas troops began their work. The town, though often shelled, still had its recognizable landmarks in the winter of 1914–15. The civilian population had remained and even in April 1915 farmers were working their fields.[30] The fighting of the previous November had halted the Germans north and east of the Yser canal at Bikschote and Langemark, say 8 km from the centre of the town. The line curved in a big semi-circle; the configuration was like a giant saucer of which

Ypres formed the centre and the front constituted the rim. To the north that rim was broken and the ground flat. To the east a ridge formed and continued south and south west where it terminated in mounds named Mt. Kemmel, Mt Noir, Mt des Cats, etc. The Germans held the higher ground (though not the hillocks). The arc of the salient from the canal in the north to St Eloois due south of the town was about 30 km: the line was not smooth, but had incisions and bulges. The term high ground is misleading, for the elevations above sea level can be counted in a few metres: Langemark 13, Poelkapelle 27, Hoge 43, St Eloois 40, Wijtschate 82, Ypres itself 18. In such country the 'heights' dominate the land, and the views from them are astonishing.

The salient was by no means ideal gas cloud country. In the first place the terrain is not even. Seen from a distance the landscape, like the Hampshire downs, appears smooth but upon approaching, little undulations, tiny valleys, and minuscule rivulets can be observed. Differences of 5 or 10 m on the ground, the height of a house or barn, are significant: they could and did favour or impede the advancing chlorine cloud. They certainly would make its progress less predictable. The Germans soon realized this and their eyes confirmed the contour lines of their maps. But they thought that the gas, if not pushed by the wind, would, owing to its density, 'run' downhill. Given the configuration of the terrain, that was debatable. Hence the importance of the wind.

The wind was among the most curious factors of the entire episode. Meteorology, as will be repeatedly noticed in later pages, dominated the gas cloud, indeed much of chemical warfare generally, and forecasting was an art rather than a science. Falkenhayn having picked on Ypres, had also chosen the place where weather conditions were least predictable. The town is about 30 km from the Belgian coast, just over 40 km from Dunkirk: thus westerly on-shore winds are likely to predominate. The Germans knew this. They could have readily enlarged their knowledge. The Channel ports necessarily kept weather records and inland there were observatories in Belgium and France, among which those of Douai and Laon (both in German hands) kept detailed records of relative humidity, rainfall, and wind direction, and sometimes also speed.[31] The information, had the Germans studied it, would have given them pause to think. Within a month of the first German gas discharge, Lt.-Col. J. Annesley an amateur meteorologist, assembled the statistics from Dunkirk, Laventie, Douai, Arras, and Amiens to show wind direction and speed in the previous twenty years. He found that on average the wind blew from the German quarter, that is the east, north-east, and south-east, on 116 days a year (32 per cent) and from the Allied quarter, that is the west, north-west, and south-west, on 162 days (44 per cent). For 87 days (24 per cent) it blew from north or south, which suited neither side. Annesley also investigated wind speeds in northern France and Belgium and took as his upper limit point 8 m/sec (18 mph), twice the maximum later adopted by the belligerents. He found that from June to September inclusive wind speeds below that limit were, on average, encountered one day in two. In other months the conditions were less favourable.[32] But the German gamble was even greater, because in Deimling's sector the right winds were extremely rare, and around Bikschote, though the position was better, they were 'capricious'.[33]

At first, however, the Germans were concerned with organization and training. A regular officer, Otto Peterson, in his mid fifties and lately in command of the engineers of Königsberg, was promoted colonel and put in charge of the operation. Originally he had 500 men, drawn from the reserve, known collectively as Pionierkommando or Disinfektionstruppe Peterson. They began their training at Wahn towards the end of January. No one knew how to set about this, for there was no precedent to draw upon. Carrying and entrenching the heavy cylinders obviously required practice, and that was relatively simple. Communications were more difficult, but signals could be taught and remembered. What was totally lacking was experience and what could not be drilled was how to mesh with the infantry at the front. Even as late as April training was still minimal.[34]

The force gradually increased to 1,600 and on 27 April the Kommando was formally constituted as Pionier Rgt. 35, commanded by Major von Zingler who had come from the Cavalry.[35] Headquarters were at Geluwe a village on the Ypres–Menin road. There the 'observers' also foregathered in February and March, recruited on the old boy net by Haber and animated by his fierce desire to succeed. They were a remarkable group. Haber himself, an academic in uniform, paunchy, rarely without a cigar, pockets bulging, surrounded by young acolytes who managed to look respectful, busy, and unconventional in dress and bearing.[36] Otto Hahn, who commmanded a machine-gun section, was prevailed upon by Haber to become an 'observer'. So were James Franck, Gustav Hertz, and others who were later to become distinguished scientists.[37] But for the present they could be seen at Wahn and in the Ypres Salient, helping with training, visiting the front to determine the emplacement of cylinders, and taking meteorological observations.

All this bustling activity could not compensate for the lack of gas trials. The first experimental discharges had taken place in January at Wahn, which was then flat heathland interspersed with scrub and very different terrain from the cultivated fields, ditches, and ridges of Flanders. After the decision had been taken to adopt chlorine, security became extremely tight. Large-scale tests were prohibited, but occasional experiments with dug-in cylinders were allowed. The object of these exercises was to see how Peterson's specialists, provided with oxygen breathing-sets for the occasion would cope when required to open several cylinders in a given time.[38] There was apparently only one full-scale rehearsal. It took place on 2 April at Beverloo, the Belgian army training-ground near the Dutch frontier. Haber and Bauer accidentally rode into the gas cloud and were lucky to get out before they were seriously gassed.[39]

For part of January and most of February there were discussions over the disposition of the cylinders. Initially OHL had requisitioned 6,000 large commercial cylinders each holding 40 kg of chlorine, a total of 240 t of gas. In addition 24,000 half-size and more manageable cylinders each containing 20 kg were ordered, and all were delivered during April. All told, about 700 t of chlorine were ordered. At this point the gap between expectation and achievement became wide, and was indeed never closed. Had the original intention been fulfilled, the quantity would have sufficed for about 23 km of front at the rate of 30 t/km, equivalent to 1½ small cylinders = 30 kg of chlorine) per metre of front.[40] Various circumstances led to some changes which bewildered later commentators. We can, however, safely ignore the minutiae of the alternations and also the details of the time-consuming, complicated preparations and concentrate on the chief points. First, the cylinders. A central filling point would have been desirable, but there was no time to build one, and the improvised filling stations at railheads were wasteful and unnecessarily conspicuous.[41] Secondly, transport. This created endless trouble. The commercial cylinders were 1.20 to 1.50 m tall, heavy (say 85 kg) and as unwieldy as a corpse. Extra carrying parties had to be organized over a period of several weeks. Thirdly, digging in: work began in Deimling's sector in February and was completed on 10 March. The proximity of the opposing front lines, often less than 50 m apart, created immense difficulties. The work had to be done at night, some noise was inevitable, the Allies were alert, and shell-fire came down on the Germans. According to Deimling there were two such incidents at the beginning of March, in both of which the Germans had casualties: in the second they lost three killed and fifty injured by gas. These were the first gas casualties on the Western Front.[42]

We may be sure that Haber and Peterson had many anxious moments. They now realized that the southern ridges were badly placed as regards wind. Moreover, the lines zigzagged so that some blow-back was probable and German chlorine would harm unprotected Germans. So, late in March, it was decided to install the cylinders to the north and north-east of Ypres opposite a sector then held by the French. Work began on 5 April and was completed on 11 April, when 1,600 large and 4,130 small cylinders, containing say 150 t of chlorine, were dug in along 7 km of front, running approximately from Bikschote in the north to Poelkapelle in the north-east. The density had been cut by a third from 30 t/km to 21 t/km, but this was compensated for by clustering the cylinders in batteries of ten each, connected by a manifold to a single discharge pipe. One Pionier tended each battery.[43] Later in April and during May more cylinders were dug in along the line Frezenberg-Hoge. Particulars of the total numbers of cylinders emplaced and of gas discharged in the second battle of Ypres—the two are not identical because some filled cylinders were later dug out—have frequently been published. But the figures do not tally and the German records are incomplete. According to Prentiss, a thorough student of the subject, 498 t (about 70 per cent of the total ordered) were discharged.[44] Higher figures are certainly wrong since they take no account of the lower density adopted by the Germans in April. My own view is that 330–50 t, half the original order, was the upper limit.

The dangerous nature of chlorine was well known, but initially it was considered unnecessary to issue the infantry with the mouthpads then employed to protect workers in chemical factories. These pads consisted of cotton waste, periodically moistened by steeping in sodium thiosulphate, and kept in a small satchel. Peterson's men, however, were thought to be specially at risk and Haber ordered Draeger's oxygen breathing sets on 30 January. They were of the standard mine rescue type, bulky but effective. By 24 March (that is, after the installation of the cylinders south-east of Ypres had been completed), 1,000 had reached the Salient. Another 2,000 were delivered during the following four weeks. That was roughly sufficient for the Pionier regiments then in the process of being formed. Haber's urgent request, dated 25 March, for a further 3,000 suggests a last-minute change of mind and the extension of protection to machine gunners and possibly some infantry. But time was running out and he later told Hartley that the troops were left unprotected because 'it was impossible to convince the military authorities beforehand of the necessity for providing special equipment.'[45] At the very last moment, probably as a result of the gas casualties in Deimling's sector and Haber's own accident, pads were issued. The first lot had to be held over the mouth and nose—how were the men to fight?—but after 15 April some of the troops were issued with pads that had tapes.[46] These hasty, final improvisations showed remarkable lack of foresight and, incidentally, served to alert Belgian intelligence.

The German commanders meanwhile were becoming impatient. Fourth Army HQ decided on 8 April to attack from the north towards the Pilkem 'ridge', 4 km from the German lines and roughly 10-15m above them. The first gas alert order was given on 14 April at 2230 and cancelled at 0145 on 15 April. The second alert was on 19 April at 1500, but was countermanded. By then OHL had become cautious and owing to the Russian threat on the Austro-Hungarian front became reluctant to commit reserves earmarked for the east to something as uncertain as the follow up to a gas attack. The third alert was given on 21 April at 1700, postponed first to 0400 on 22 April, then to 0900 and then to the afternoon.[47]

The rising tension at XXVI Reserve Corps headquarters and especially among the assault divisions under von Hügel can be imagined. The troops, the Pionierkommando, and the specialists had had very little rest and were on edge. They were sure the Allies had been alerted. They had indeed. Three weeks earlier the French, then still in the south of the Salient, were told by prisoners of the installation of cylinders, and there was visual evidence of gas cylinder explosions in March. But the French ignored these warnings and later ones in April from a deserter as well as from Belgian sources which provided more details of the situation in the north. With few exceptions the French did not bother, and Foch—then commanding the French troops in Belgium—was at fault in neglecting all precautions.[48]

The British and the Canadians who were taking over the southern and north-eastern portions of the Salient from the French treated the reports more seriously.

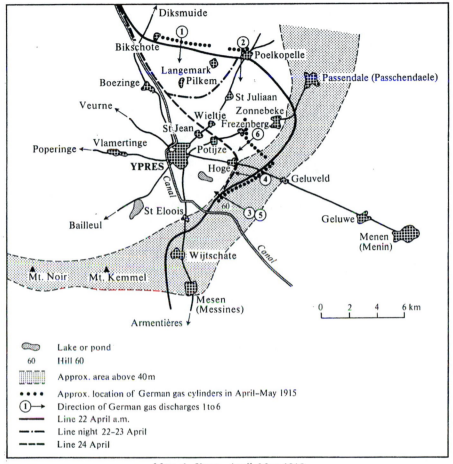

Map. 1. Ypres, April–May 1915

In the first half of April, Col. Jackson at the War Office warned of a chemical attack—he surmised arsenic—and on 14 April he wrote to the DMO that 'it is advisable to prepare against such an attack'. The memorandum went from the DMO to the Army Medical Services and thence to Professor Ramsay's sub-committee of the Royal Society.[49] At the highest level, Hankey was told at GHQ BEF 'that the Germans were notoriously preparing something of this kind, but it was believed to be intended for use in trenches captured by us and not for offensive purposes.'[50] There was a good deal of foreknowledge, and among the British it helped speed things up *after* the event. It is also interesting to note that the significance of the reports was more appreciated in the rear than at the front. In the Salient there was the most knowledge but also the least understanding of the implications. In truth how were these men, totally ignorant of science, going to deal with something that was entirely outside their frame of reference? And so, on Wednesday 21 April, Col. Mordacq, commanding the 90th French Brigade, went to Pilkem to ensure that the relief scheduled for the night of Wednesday to Thursday would proceed smoothly. All went well, though the Germans were nervous and firing intermittently. The 45th Algerian Division (which included Mordacq's men) had barely settled in their wretchedly built shallow trenches when the Germans began shelling them intensively with high explosive and T-*Stoff*. The afternoon was warm and a light breeze was blowing from the north-east towards the 87th Territorial Division and the neighbouring Algerians.[51] It was just after 1700 on Thursday, 22 April.

The simultaneous opening of almost 6,000 cylinders which released 150 t of chlorine along 7000m within about ten minutes was spectacular. The front lines were often very close, at one point only 50 m apart.[52] The cloud advanced slowly, moving at about 0.5 m/sec (just over 1 mph). It was white at first, owing to the condensation of the moisture in the surrounding air and, as the volume increased, it turned yellow-green. The chlorine rose quickly to a height of 10−30 m because of the ground temperature, and while diffusion weakened the effectiveness by thinning out the gas it enhanced the physical and psychological shock. Within minutes the Franco-Algerian soldiers in the front and support lines were engulfed and choking. Those who were not suffocating from spasms broke and ran, but the gas followed. The front collapsed.[53]

The Germans advanced cautiously. They too were taken by surprise and followed the cloud, delayed not by resistance, but by patches of gas in low ground and ruins. Within an hour or so they had captured Langemark and Pilkem, and by dusk at 1930 were approaching the canal on their right. They had taken about 2,000 prisoners and fifty-one guns. Now they stopped, having reached their first objectives. German hesitations and darkness saved the French by giving them time to regroup on the west bank. Together with the Canadians they attacked the German positions during the night but could not shift them. The Germans, for their part were also troubled and their elation at the initial success soon turned to disappointment when on 23 April their Divisions, upon being ordered to advance, met with increasingly stiff resistance.[54]

Such was the confusion in the first twenty-four hours that no one, friend or foe, thought clearly: people reacted to rapid changes in the position. Reflection came later and with it recriminations. Hartley asked Nernst and Haber in 1921 for their views on the event. Both agreed that it had been an experiment (they used the word *Versuch*), and that it had been badly handled—insufficient gas had been released and the soldiers had lacked imagination.[55] These were the natural reactions of disappointed innovators. In fairness to them it needs to be said that on the level of military technology, the 22 April had been an event of the first importance. The professionals looked at it rather differently. Some declared it had been a big muddle, others sought to exculpate themselves by laying the blame on rival shoulders.[56]

The British had great difficulty obtaining reliable information from the Salient where the second battle of Ypres was now raging. Gen. French's dispatch to the War Office at 1750 on 23 April displayed uncertainty about the gas, and called for protection and also retaliation.[57] Forty-eight hours after the cloud they were still waiting for full reports in London. But Hankey, writing to Asquith presciently noted, 'the normally prevailing wind in France is westerly, so that if this form of warfare is to be introduced we, in the long run, shall have an enormous advantage.'[58]

For the present, however, the Germans retained their chemical initiative. On 24 April at 0200 they released about fifteen t of chlorine against the left flank of the 2nd Canadian Brigade which the flight of the Algerian troops had left uncovered. The lines were further apart at that point and some of the Canadians managed to protect themselves against gas. This time the ground was cool and the cloud did not rise, but drifted compactly at a height of 2 m, pushed by a 'fair' wind of 3.7 m/sec (8 mph) towards the Canadians. They held their ground at first (and some stood on the parapet thereby avoiding the worst of the swiftly moving chlorine) but later gave way and abandoned St Juliaan at 1500.[59] The battle then mounted in violence as the Germans gradually edged closer to Ypres and in so doing forced the Canadian Division and the 27th and 28th British Divisions into a smaller Salient.

During the latter stages of Second Ypres, the Germans used gas on at least four other occasions. The first three did not entail fresh preparations, since the cylinders had been dug in almost two months before. The discharges took place on the higher ground of the ridge where the lines were close and indented. There was thus considerable danger to the Germans whilst simultaneously the British troops were gaining experience and were on some occasions protected by primitive mouthpads. The general objective was to weaken British resistance just before an attack and to delay the movement of supplies and reinforcements from Ypres to the front. No statistics of the quantity involved have survived. Assuming that the entire stock in Deimling's sector installed at the original rate of 30 t/km was used up, attacks Nos. 3 to 5 taken together would have entailed a maximum of a hundred t. The final attack, No. 6, was on a slightly narrower front with small cylinders and the quantity, at the less dense rate of installation is likely to have been of the order of 70−80 t of chlorine.

The third release of gas took place in the late afternoon of 1 May, near Hill 60, against the 1st Dorsets. A mere sixty cylinders were emptied, but the wind changed suddenly and both sides suffered casualties. On the next occasion, the night of 5 to 6 May, a large number of cylinders were opened on a 1400 m front south of Hoge. Although the British had been issued with mouth-and-nose pads, they had considerable casualties, and had to yield ground. The fifth attack, on 10 May, was again in the area of Hill 60 and probably used up the remaining cylinders. British casualties were small. The last gas discharge took place at 0245 on 24 May and came from newly installed cylinders, south-east of Frezenberg. The lines were close, and the wind favourable throughout the operation which was deliberately spread over forty to forty-five minutes, so as to replenish the cloud continuously. Despite the issue of mouthpads the British−Canadian forces suffered considerably from gas. This last chlorine cloud preceded a major German assault which yielded them some ground north and east of Hoge. That local victory and the evident exhaustion of both sides marked the end of Second Ypres: the front in the Salient remained unchanged for the next two years.[60]

Gas had been used six times during the battle. The Allies were bent on revenge, but overlooked the problems. The Germans, by contrast, began to realize that the tactical value of their new weapon was limited. Having first made, and then been disappointed by, their big technical effort, they now saw that the whole matter had to be approached more systematically. The right location had to be found, both as to terrain and as to meteorological conditions. Having found it, the optimum width had to be decided upon—too wide would merely repeat Ypres, too narrow would lead to a counter-attack by the enemy on both flanks and trap the Germans in a noose. Most important of all, the experience gained in April–May indicated the difficulties encountered in combining a gas discharge with an infantry attack.[61] Chlorine therefore remained on trial and the Germans decided to continue their experiments on the Eastern Front where they hoped conditions would be more favourable to chemical warfare.

Russian documents have not been available to me and with one exception the following account is based entirely on German sources. They occasionally conflict, so that it has not been possible to establish the truth on many details; but there is, fortunately, general agreement on the salient points. In April 1915, someone at OHL proposed to Gen. von Mackensen, commanding on the Carpathian Front, that the gas troops might help with his forthcoming offensive at Gorlice. The new intake of men—soon to be constituted as Pionier Regiment 36 could thus obtain practical experience. Haber, von Goslich (the OC designate), and several observers went to the Carpathians at the end of the month or early in May. Some of Peterson's troops followed but when they arrived on 2 or 3 May they found Mackensen about to move and the terrain totally unsuitable;[62] it was then decided to transport all of them direct to the 9th Army front 50–60 km west of Warsaw. The Germans had been entrenched there since the end of 1914 and had fired the first T shells at Bolimów in January. Their left flank rested on the Vistula, and the line followed the Bzura river and its confluent, the Rawka which they had crossed. Rail communications to the west through the junction of Łowicz were good. The Germans occupied the attractive and undamaged village of Nieborów, but Sochaczew, a large village to the north-east, was in no man's land. The local population had remained and the German observers and gas troops found the rustic scene a complete change from Flanders. Some of the forests had been shelled, but there was plenty of cover. The fields were in crop, the trees in leaf, and it was hot. The Russians were disposed in an irregular line, bulging towards the Germans in the marshes of the Bzura. The ground behind them was flat and slightly above the German positions. The lines were much further apart than in the West. Both sides had trouble digging trenches, for below the shallow layer of top soil was sand.

In this country, entirely different from the Salient, the Germans carried out three large gas discharges.[63] Their specific objective was to support the infantry in local attacks by incapacitating the Russians and generally to distract the attention of the defenders from the main thrusts of the German advance.[64] The operations also had two subsidiary purposes—first to practise the integration of the gas troops with the infantry and secondly to try out phosgene. It is not possible from the surviving documents to tell whether the Germans used phosgene in the first of their three gas clouds, nor whether the proportion was 5 or 20 per cent.[65] We can only speculate on their reasons. If they were hoping for some synergistic effect, they were (although this cannot be demonstrated) probably disappointed. Alternatively they may have thought a gas mixture would be better suited to the climatic conditions of Eastern Europe. I think it most likely that they were following up the tests at Wahn mentioned earlier, but found themselves short of phosgene and so, perforce, had to dilute it in chlorine. The piecemeal introduction of phosgene was certainly in keeping with their entire approach so far to chemical warfare. But even this could be turned to advantage: operations in the east attracted less publicity among the Allies and neutrals so that large-scale tests of novel weapons might escape attention. Moreover the Russians were entirely unprotected, unlikely to retaliate, and perhaps would not even notice the experimental addition of phosgene.

The Germans began to install cylinders around the middle of May. They used small cylinders, probably filled in Germany, grouped in batteries as at Ypres. The first discharge of 220 t was made on 31 May on a width of 12 km, the main impact being south of the Bzura and east of the Rawka towards the hamlets of Sucha and Humin. The winds were westerly and the cylinders were opened at intervals between 0300 and 0500. In a few sectors where the Germans feared blow-back, gaps were left. The cloud passed over crowded Russian trenches where a relief was taking place and they suffered heavily. However the German infantry had no experience of this kind of warfare and were surprised when their reconnaissance in force was checked by pockets of resistance. There were unexpected losses. The day ended unsatisfactorily for the Germans: they counted 374 of their own dead and wounded and a further 56 were gassed because they had no protection.[66]

Gas was released a second time on a front of 6 km on 12 June at 0330, along the Bzura towards the Pisia. The sector overlapped that of the first discharge, but conditions were sufficiently tranquil on this front to enable the Germans to remove the cylinders, refill them from rail tank cars and dig them in again. The effort entailed can be imagined. Hahn was present on that day and witnessed the panic as the wind changed direction and the cloud blew back into the German lines. The men, even then, were insufficiently protected and trained. He rallied them, the wind changed again, and they advanced 6 km. The Russians and the Germans both had losses. The latter counted 1,100 dead and wounded, including 350 injured by gas.[67]

The third attack took place at dawn on 6 July between Humin and Borzymów and at the other end of the line, east and west of Sochaczew. Nine thousand

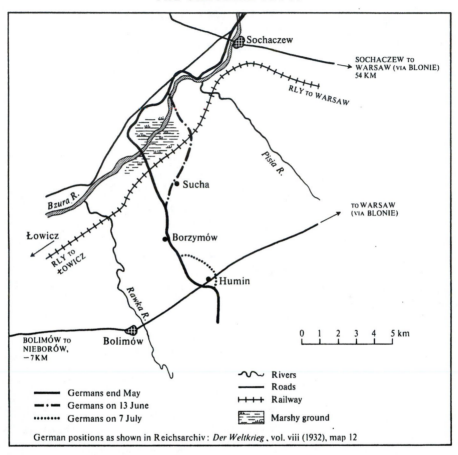

Map 2. The Western Approaches to Warsaw, May–July 1915

cylinders (say 180 t) were available, but it appears that not all were discharged. The Russians anticipated the attack, held their positions lightly, and consequently suffered little. Once again the cloud changed direction and drifted along the German lines; as a result 1,450 Germans were gassed of whom 138 later died.[68]

The harassing attacks continued intermittently, and it is difficult to make any sense out of them, except that the specialists were given their head. For example Nernst's trench mortar-bombs, filled with B- and C- *Stoff* were tried out again on 30 July and 1 August on the northern front. He busied himself investigating the effects among the prisoners, but little of military value emerged and he and his bombs faded from the chemical warfare scene.[69] Another experiment was designed to test extremely dense clouds against a large fixed obstacle, the Russians fortress of Osowiece north-east of Warsaw. Conditions on 6 August were ideal: a quiet sector, flat ground, a cool night, wind speed 1½ m/sec (3.4 mph). The Germans had massed 12,300 cylinders tightly along a 4 km front and released 220 t (55 t/km) at 0400. But the Russians had taken precautions and as soon as the cloud was spotted, enormous fires were ignited and their strong upward draught deflected the gas. They held the fortress for another fortnight. They also spoilt another planned discharge by evacuating the town of Lomza.[70]

Between 22 April and 6 August 1915 the Germans released approximately 1,200 t, of gas, over two-thirds of it in the east. It yielded them an immediate and large benefit on the first occasion at Ypres. The sequel, particularly in the east, turned out to be less satisfactory, and it may be doubted whether the large gas clouds along the Bzura and the Rawka had any connection with the fall of Warsaw which the Russians evacuated in August. The chief gain from all this laborious activity, Langemark and Pilkem excepted, was experience, which pointed unmistakably to one firm military–technical conclusion from which several important consequences flowed: the gas cloud was totally dependent on the direction and strength of the wind. Given the state of the meteorological art, neither could be predicted with confidence. It followed that gas could not be used to precede an infantry attack. The synchronization of discharge times with the advance of large bodies of men on a front of several kilometres was impossible. Hence the question: what other profitable employment could be found for the two Pionier regiments and the observers? The obvious answer, disbandment, did not occur to anyone since manpower shortages were not acute. The other answer, which was not yet perceived in those terms, though it became the accepted solution, was to abandon the gas cloud as a tactical weapon and use it as a novel addition to psychological warfare. Gas would not merely inflict casualties, but also distress and generally demoralize the enemy. The experience in the east showed that against untrained and unprotected troops gas could be a potent weapon in weakening resistance.[71]

The new purpose of chemical warfare, modest after the initial high hopes of late winter and early spring, left two difficulties unsolved. First, it was necessary to distinguish gas from other casualties in order to measure the results of a discharge. At this stage, in spring and early summer 1915, the belligerents barely knew their own, let alone the enemy's losses, but for external consumption manipulated what numbers there were. The Germans were concerned in their foreign propaganda to minimize the results so as to deflect the opprobrium of their first use of poison gas. They claimed that on 22 April their hospitals dealt with a mere 200 gas victims, of whom twelve died later. The Allies, on the contrary, had every interest to inflate the figures, and asserted that the total wounded and killed were 15,000 and 5,000 respectively.[72] Neither claim is believable nor will the facts ever be established. But the impact of gas casualties was becoming significant, and during the second half of the year the Germans as well as the Allies took steps to systematize and extend their medical records. In the short run there was a rather more important problem. For internal purposes the higher the enemy casualties (actual or imagined) the greater the *raison d'être* of the gas troops and the chemists. But the German losses from their own gas were visibly mounting and opposition to cloud gas was growing among infantry officers. The supporters of chemical warfare in its modified form had therefore to alter their approach. Henceforth the first priorities were the protection and anti-gas training of the German soldier.

The execution of these defensive objectives therefore became the principal scientific and administrative challenge faced by the Germans in the latter part of 1915. For the time being they deliberately played down the offensive value of gas and the interest shifts from the front to the rear. But among the Allies the order was reversed. Their reflex reaction to the events of April had been to improvise protection. That done, they turned to retaliation. The Anglo-French developments which we must now describe, reflect, as in a mirror, the German initiative.

4

THE ALLIED REACTION

Urge that immediate steps be taken to supply similar means of most effective kind for use by our troops. Also essential that our troops should be immediately provided with means of counter-acting effect of enemy gases which should be suitable for use when on the move.

Sir John French, Dispatch No. 140 to War Office,
23 April 1915

Retaliation and defence were bracketed together, though the latter was considered more important and accorded higher priority throughout 1915. A comparison with the steel helmet springs to mind. Head wounds were long considered among the occupational risks of soldiering which may explain why it took until Spring 1916 before British and German troops were issued with steel helmets. But protection against gas was linked with morale, chemical warfare was an unanticipated danger, and the novelty of gas necessarily caused apprehension if not fear. The troops' confidence must not be undermined by gas. If the men thought they were defenceless they might panic and retreat. That had to be prevented, hence protection was essential, and even improvisations were better than nothing, provided always that they quickly got into the trenches. Everywhere there was the same urgency during 1915, but before describing the different solutions to the problem of gas defence, it is necessary to consider briefly the nature of poison gas, because the chemical and physical characteristics of the material determined the effect it would have.

That is a simple proposition, but it has been obscured by the tendency of post-war writers to go into unnecessarily complicated detail and to overtook the fact that practical obstacles eliminated the use of most poisons. In short the aggressor's choice was severely limited, while—by contrast—the defender's response was complicated by the necessity to achieve universal protection. The discussion of gas warfare can be simplified without loss of accuracy by listing in Table 4.1[1] the properties of five substances which, with the exception of tear gas, comprised the armoury of chemical warfare from April 1915 to mid-1917.

All the chemical warfare materials listed in Table 4.1 are—as we shall soon see − dangerous poisons, but that does not make them equally suitable. It is possible to think of many criteria for selecting them, but the most relevant are density and boiling-point. Obviously the heavier the substance relative to air, the better. That, one might have thought, would have ruled out hydrogen cyanide, the more so as it is innocuous at the concentrations that can be produced

Table 4.1. *Chemical Warfare Materials used in 1915–1917*

Chemical	Formula	Molecular weight	Density at 20°C gm/ml	Boiling- point (°C)	Vapour density relative to Air=1	Vapour pressure mmHg at 20°C
Chlorine	Cl_2	71	1.40	−35.0	2.5	4993
Phosgene	$COCl_2$	99	1.38	7.5	3.5	1173
Chloropicrin	CCl_3NO_2	164	1.66	112.0	5.7	19
Trichloromethylchloroformate (commonly called Diphosgene)	$Cl.CO.O-$ CCl_3	198	1.65	128.0	6.9	10
Hydrogen Cyanide	HCN	27	0.69	26.5	0.9	603

and sustained in the field. Nevertheless the irrational element in chemical warfare led to its adoption, and—contrary to commonsense and to scientific realism—it was retained for several years. Chloropicrin and diphosgene are relatively heavy liquids and their low vapour pressure means that they can only be dispersed by the detonation of a shell or the propellant action of a light gas. That left the chemists with chlorine and phosgene. The former has the lowest boiling-point of the five substances and hence the highest vapour pressure; the resulting extremely high rate of diffusion obviously diminished the military value of the gas. Phosgene emerges, by elimination, as the most suitable material for chemical warfare, except that in cold weather it will not vaporize, and that defect was easily overcome by adding a little chlorine.

In 1915 and for much of 1916 the shell shortage left the chemists with no choice and perforce they had to concentrate on the practical problems of generating gas clouds. The objective was clear—to maintain a high concentration over the target area. The difficulty lay in predicting the likelihood of achieving the desired effect. As the gas leaves the cylinder it diffuses and gradually rises. The shape of the cloud approximates in theory that of a wedge or a cone cut along its length—the pointed end being the battery of cylinders with the broad end nearest the enemy lines. The concentration over the target is thus a function of the initial volume, the rate of discharge, and the distance travelled; it will not be uniform and will be lower at the edges. Time plays a complex role. The duration of the discharge can be controlled, but wind speed, which cannot be forecast accurately, will have a variable effect on the time taken by the cloud to travel over a given distance. Finally, the ambient temperature is important: it is measurable before the discharge, but at and near the point of emission the emerging gas will cool the atmosphere, increase its density, and so add another variable to the equation.

The physical constants set theoretical parameters, but what really mattered in 1915 in the absence of a theory was working experience with large volumes of gas. Obviously that was not available at first and later in the war there were neither enough time nor resources to formulate cloud-gas theories, investigate them empirically and test them by actual observation.[2] In other words, the belligerents had no scientific backing for what they were doing. All that could be achieved was to follow some elementary rules as closely as possible and hope that luck would lead to success. Wind speed—ideally 2 to 4 m/sec.—and direction were, of course, critical, and so was ambient temperature – preferably cold or at least cool. These conditions fixed the best time for a gas discharge as the hours before dawn when the wind (if any) is generally steady and rising air currents are at their daily low point. Because periods of stable conditions were so rare the reliability of weather forecasts was particularly important. But meteorology was still at an early stage. Rain could, even then, be accurately forecast, but that was less valuable than the likely wind direction, on which the experts were often of a different mind. The least reliable forecasts were of wind speed and this was precisely the statistic to which the greatest significance was attached. The force of the wind was commonly measured 10 m above ground, but that height was irrelevant for gas clouds. Meteorologists had absolutely no experience of forecasting wind-speeds at a height of 2 m; so they guessed and were more often wrong than right. Although anemometers were soon sprouting along the parados of reserve and support trenches and the information was systematically collated by field observatories, this particular branch of meteorology remained the weak point of cylinder operations.[3]

Gas attacks lacked precision, but gas defence was even more uncertain. The attacker had to answer the question, how effective is my weapon; the defender, how dangerous is it? Both turned to the literature on industrial toxicology, but the description of the occupational hazards of bleaching-powder packing provided no guide to protection against chemical warfare. So the answers had to be worked out experimentally, using animals and occasionally man. From the outset there was much confusion, and though the techniques were gradually improved and the routine tests standardized, misleading information continued to circulate unchallenged between the wars, and even recently toxicity figures have been published which omit to note the defects of the data. Since the scientific characteristics of gas warfare and its usefulness form an important theme of this book, a digression on the measurement of its dangerous nature is warranted. We may conveniently begin by considering the figures shown in Table 4.2. The differences between the numbers are so striking that one is bound to view them with extreme scepticism. The first column is based on British tests in the latter part of the war. Incapacity in man is a subjective criterion, and in this context means no more than that after 'a few seconds' the soldier was no longer able to fight. The second column is perhaps better known as 'Haber's Constant', the product of concentration (in ppm) and time (in minutes) to cause death; in theory, though not in practice, a short exposure to a high concentration is therefore equivalent to a longer exposure at a low concentration. The Germans used cats and grossed up the results to correspond to the body weight of man. The lower the figure, the greater the toxicity. The Americans experimented on many different species and obtained widely differing results. It is certain that

Table 4.2. *Estimated Toxicity of Chemical Warfare Materials used in 1915–1917*[4]

Chemical	~ Incapacity in 'a few seconds' (First World War) (mg/m³)	Concentration required to cause death (mg/m³)		
		First World War	USA 1930s*	USA 1950s*
Chlorine	240	7,500	5,600	1,900
Phosgene	41	450	500	320
Chloropicrin	134	1,000	2,000	n.a.
Trichloromethylchloroformate (Diphosgene)	40	500	500	320
Hydrogen Cyanide †	552	1,000	200	200

* 10 minutes' exposure.   † Instantaneously fatal at levels shown.

the research done in Washington was not known to the Germans and did not influence the composition of their filters in the last months of the war.[5] The figures in the third column are derived from experiments on dogs and mice. They may be compared with those in column 2 by adjusting the German data to ten minutes which reduces the concentration to one-tenth of that shown. For example, ten minutes exposure to chlorine at 750 mg/m³ would be fatal according to Haber's Constant, while the same outcome would result from 5,600 mg/m³ according to the Americans. The numbers in the final column are based on more advanced statistical treatment but like the others have been grossed up from animals to adult male body weight. The discovery of the sigmoidal shape of the curve relating cumulative mortality to dosage, and its logarithmic transformation into a straight-line plot dates from the 1920s.[6] The technique does not appear to have been applied to poison-gas investigations until the 1930s or even later. The significance of this approach is that it allows the determination within narrow confidence limits of the dosage (expressed as LD_{50}) required to kill half the animals in the sample. Hence the data in column 4 should be the most accurate and it is valuable in drawing attention to the large discrepancies with the earlier tests.

The technical discussion cannot be pursued further because the details of sample size and of experimental conditions are not available.[7] But some general comments, though based on hypotheses, are relevant. The Germans attached no particular military importance to Haber's Constant during the war. They used it chiefly for ranking substances, a 'sieve' which ensured that compounds with a high number were rejected. The Allies lacked such a rough and ready device until the end of the war so that they spent much time in useless development work. These practical details of military toxicology have some wider implications. If we accept the American LD_{50} numbers in column 4 as reliable, then we have the explanation for the relatively small number of deaths from gas because the concentration achieved in the field was usually below the levels indicated. A further conclusion to be drawn from the American data is that the threat posed by gas was exaggerated during and after the war. The exaggeration stemmed from ignorance and its effect on defence was to weaken the scientific approach and to enhance the psychological element in the reaction to a novel danger. The various mask designs towards the end of 1915 can be attributed to a large extent to the different views held in the principal countries on the toxic nature of gas. The chemists and physiologists could not be rigorously objective: subjective responses to gas accordingly played the more important role at the time and had far-reaching results. The British, and in their wake the Americans, overrated toxicity, and adopted masks which over-protected. The French, Russians, Italians, and even the Germans (the low Haber Constant for phosgene notwithstanding) took the opposite view and their designs, according to the British, gave insufficient protection. The casualty statistics which appeared years later give no clear verdict: the figures do not show that the penalty for under-protection was a higher casualty rate, nor do they indicate that the reward of over-protection was that fewer were killed by gas.

In April 1915 the prime danger was chlorine. (Tear gas never assumed the importance of the more toxic gas, and protection was a matter of issuing tight-fitting goggles.) The simplest defence against an acid gas is neutralization, and the choice fell on sodium thiosulphate, a soluble alkali, widely used in photography. The few German troops that had been issued with mouthpads, were also supplied with thiosulphate crystals, and were instructed in the preparation of a solution and how to dampen the pads with it. The general distribution of the equipment began in northern France in May and was completed further south during July.[8]

The Allied reaction to the events of 22 April was a mixture of panic and determination. The *Daily Mail* was quickly off the mark and appealed to the women of England to protect their menfolk by making pads out of cotton wool and to put them into sachets fashioned out of butter muslin or flannelette. On 28 April, the War Office, publicly appealed for this type of protection. The next day women crowded the Army Clothing Depot in Pimlico, and in their thousands the pads were sent off at once to Flanders. They reached the troops within 72 hours. Haldane and other physiologists were indignant: 'This respirator is useless when dry and allows no air to pass when wetted', and there were casualties in the Hill 60 sector during May, because some men failed to heed the warning.[9] Haldane had a right to be angry for his vigorous intervention yielded more valuable results. On 23 April he had been to see the Secretary of State for War, on 25 April the chief chemist of the Doncaster Coal Owners' Association, which had a gas chamber, told him that woven fabrics were better absorbents than cotton pads, and on 26 April he was in France. Within a week, Haldane had seen enough to recommend elementary safety measures such as breathing through moistened earth packed lightly in a bottle which had had its bottom knocked out. Alternatively the men were advised to breathe through socks steeped in urine. Immediately after Haldane's return to Oxford, on 1 May, he, H. B. Baker, and A. Mavrogordato, carried out further tests, and decided to elaborate the German pad: they adopted cotton waste held in place by black cotton netting as used for ladies' veils—a material of which supplies were then readily available. Properly impregnated with thiosulphate, the 'Black Veil Respirator' as it came to be known, was said to protect against a 0.1 per cent concentration of chlorine (1,000 ppm), for up to five minutes. This was not safety as defined in the second column of Table 4.2, but it was better than nothing. At any rate, cotton waste and cotton netting were ordered by the ton and shipped to France. Later this pad was manufactured in Britain, and by 20 May nearly everyone in the BEF had been issued with one.[10]

The French were just as quick. Emergency instructions were circulated on 23 April and two days later the Ministère de la Guerre received an urgent order for 100,000 small water-proof pouches each holding a muslin bag containing cotton waste. So prompt was the response that the first batch, including sacks of thiosulphate, left Paris for the north on 27 April. Within the next fortnight 200,000 pads were sent to the troops in Flanders and Artois, and later in May a further 300,000 were distributed to the armies on the Somme and further east. Soon there were complaints: the mouthpads, copied from the Germans, were considered unsafe and on 4 June, the Ministère ordered two million of the 'English type'—local versions of the Black Veil. But there were delays, and not until August was Albert Thomas, the Minister responsible, able to assure GQG that all was in order. By the middle of that month 1.16 million pads and 1.34 million pouches had been produced. Attention next concentrated on goggles—the French were always worrying about tear gas—when it was discovered that 650,000 ordered in late Spring were useless because the celluloid was not firmly fixed in the frame. Even the President of the Republic asked Thomas for reassurance and was told on 26 August that larger quantities of better-quality goggles had been sent to the troops.[11]

The Germans and the British considered the mouthpads a temporary solution. The Germans gambled that the Allies would be unable to retaliate for a long time, and decided to retain the pads until they had a good respirator; some snout-like pads, complete with nose-clips and metal frame, were captured, but there is no evidence that Haber's collaborators seriously considered their large-scale manufacture.[12] The British, however, spent much time devising and improving impregnated wool helmets which they considered gave better protection and were more comfortable than pads. The first designs are ascribed to Cluny-McPherson, and to Watson at GHQ: the hoods were tested at the Royal Army Medical College, London, on 10 May and found valuable. They were made initially of 'Viyella' fabric, which had been dipped into a solution of thiosulphate (hence 'Hypo'), bicarbonate of soda, and glycerine—the last to keep the alkalis moist and prevent them from irritating the skin. A mica window, later replaced by celluloid or cellulose acetate, allowed the wearer to see, but not to shoot straight. The hood was meant to be tucked into the top of the shirt and held tight by the tunic or the shirt button. Breathing in was easy enough, but a lot of carbon dioxide (which did not react with the soda compounds) accumulated in the hollows around the cheeks and under the chin. The physiologists disapproved, the men disliked the hot, stuffy, and very uncomfortable hoods, as well as the complicated drill of putting on, taking

Fig. 1. Early protection: British soldiers wearing various types of pads and masks, vintage 1915. L. to r.: a French pad (possibly Tambuté's model); black veil; mouthpad (German?); 'Hypo' helmet; 'Tube' or phenate-hexamine helmet. (Imperial War Museum)

off, and folding without damaging the brittle plastic window. Nevertheless it was decided to produce the 'Hypo' helmet at once: manufacture began in the second week of May and all the troops had been supplied with one by 6 July. Considering that impregnation, drying, cutting out the cloth, and stitching in the windows required machinery and factory organization, it was a remarkable effort to make and dispatch several hundred thousand in a matter of six to seven weeks.[13]

Mouthpads, helmets, and goggles were necessary improvisations, but without instruction, practice, and discipline insufficient against gas. This was recognized, but the systematic organization which is vital to what came to be called 'active defence' was lacking until 1916. In the first confused days of April and May 1915, a few individuals took the initiative, were encouraged from on high, and like L. J. Barley found themselves itinerant lecturers reiterating the same message of keeping calm. A useful contribution was also made by chemists and chemistry students who had enlisted in the Special Companies of the Royal Engineers, but were hurriedly sent to France and, after brief training, dispersed among the BEF to work as Anti-Gas Instructors. In July, when the emergency was over, they returned to Woolwich, to prepare for retaliation.[14] At GHQ meanwhile, the Director-General of Medical Services took charge, appointed Chemical Officers—later renamed

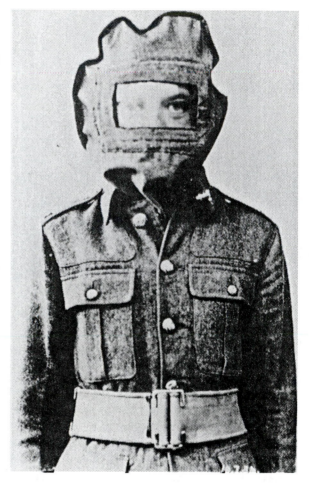

Fig. 2. Early protection: the 'Hypo' helmet with mica window, June 1915. (Porton)

Chemical Advisers—to each army and assumed responsibility for the early defences against gas and the issue of instructions. The latter combined practical advice with statements of the obvious such as to change pads 'when the respirator no longer stops the entrance of the gas.' The Adjutant General was also active and his orders emphasized that 'all ranks must be constantly drilled in the use of respirators.'[15] French instructions concerning gas were extremely detailed, but those issued by the 2nd Army on 1 November 1915 made no mention of training and practice.[16] The Germans handed over gas defence and training to the medical services, and the military pharmacists were ordered to take charge of the issue and maintenance of pads and, later, of masks. They were also instructed to examine unexploded shells and enemy masks; in 1916 Haber's people became responsible for these duties. From the outset German circulars stressed the confidence

Fig. 3. Men of the 2nd Btn. Argyll and Sutherland Highlanders wearing mouthpads. Photograph taken in May or June 1915 at Bois Grenier. The bottles contain (or are supposed to contain) sodium thiosulphate solution, then commonly called 'hypo'. (Imperial War Museum)

factor—the pad offered good protection, practice in wearing it and regular drill enhanced its value. In any event, German artillery and rifle fire would break up the chlorine cloud, so that the soldier had nothing to fear![17] And so it turned out in 1915.

Protection and training combined to give confidence and steadfastness when the cloud advanced. A report on the events of 24 May, the last occasion the Germans used gas against the British at Second Ypres, shows what could happen in a crisis. In the area of the Menin Road – Sanctuary Wood the British were on slightly lower ground and extremely close to the German positions when the gas was released. The soldiers, sometimes only 10 m and never more than 250 m from the enemy, heard the discharge, saw the gas, but stood their ground and at first used the pads correctly, redipping them in thiosulphate solution when the chlorine came through. But as the cloud kept moving on 'the men became excited and could not be prevented from putting their respirators to their mouths without squeezing them dry'. As a result they could not inhale through them, became panicky, and, fearing they 'were being suffocated . . . dipped them at shorter intervals, breathing hard between dips instead of holding their breaths.' There were many bad gas casualties, and the officers who moved about to show their men how to adjust the pads

Fig. 4. French 'Tampon P2', three separate gauze layers, covered by muslin or similar fabric. Impregnated before issue to troops. Issued from August to October 1915. (Imperial War Museum)

were also gassed or wounded as they failed to take cover from the intense shell-fire.[18]

When the Germans moved their specialists east and the chlorine cloud vanished temporarily from the Western Front, gas discipline relaxed. The new drafts which reached France during the summer had no experience of chemical warfare and their apprehension diminished as the weeks went by. The French had encountered chlorine only once, and though occasionally troubled by tear gas, did not bother with anti-gas training so that the effectiveness of their mouthpads was not tested. Barbusse, an eye-witness of the battles in Artois, and a careful observer, noted that the men used the waterproof pouches to store tobacco.[19] When gas warfare was resumed in the autumn a heavy penalty was paid for unpreparedness and indifference.

From the outset there were significant differences between the British and the French in the tempo and timing of retaliation. Kitchener moved fast. Col. Jackson, soon to be promoted and put in charge of the Trench Warfare Department at the new Ministry of Munitions, was entrusted with the preparations. About the end of May he was ready with a plan for deploying chlorine cylinders along a front of 5 km, to surprise the Germans with a gas cloud. This was not very original thinking. However, he had no choice but to follow German precedent, for the alternative of gas shell was outside his scope because they were the responsibility of the Director of Artillery. Jackson did not lack for volunteers, because the old boy net operated smoothly in the small circle of professional chemists. Alexander Keogh, the Rector of Imperial College, got together a group of twenty-one staff and former students, and the Institute of Chemistry also circularized its members. But their training in offensive warfare was postponed until the emergency had passed: the young chemists were hurriedly sent to France and became temporary instructors; for part of May and all of June they lectured on pads and protection.[20]

In London meanwhile the experts were seriously examining the most unusual substances and the weirdest contrivances in the hope of finding something that would hurt the Germans and satisfy revenge. Ethyl iodoacetate (SK) investigated earlier in the year, was now hastily and expensively produced in various laboratories and by 21 May about 120 kg were available. That and some other irritants, collectively described as 'annoyers', were quickly filled into hand grenades and shipped to France. In this way small quantities of sulphur dioxide, carbon disulphide, sulphur chloride with bromine, calcium arsenide, and even capsicine (a pepper extract), got to Flanders, and sometimes were actually thrown at the Germans. Within a month or so the occasional chemical 'hates' had been recognized as useless and were stopped.[21] Although they went unnoticed by the enemy, they served at least one useful purpose by demonstrating that this was no way to organize retaliation. In the first place it was essential to weed out impracticable ideas and compounds; secondly links with manufacturers had to be strengthened; and, finally some co-ordinating body of makers and users with a leavening of academic chemists was urgently required to develop the entire chemical warfare effort.

Such a threefold approach took months to run smoothly, but some progress was made during the late spring and summer of 1915. The Cassel Cyanide Co. began to manufacture SK on a pilot plant scale and was soon making 250 kg a day — sufficient for about 750 hand grenades. Jackson even got the Ordnance people to carry out static tests with 4.5" howitzer shell filled with SK. But the burster charge, 112–40 gr of TNT, was so powerful that it dispersed the SK too widely, thereby rendering it ineffective.[22] It was evident that high explosive and chemical effect could not easily be combined, that chemical shell design needed to be thoroughly investigated, and that the burster charge together with priming tube had to be different. The shell crisis was then at its height, no one had time for gas shell and the matter was postponed.

The shell episode was a minor diversion from the main job—the preparation of a cloud-gas attack. The first trials with chlorine cylinders were made at the Castner–Kellner works, Runcorn, on 4 June. Jackson and Major (later General) C. H. Foulkes, RE, commanding the special gas troops which were being formed, attended. They were impressed, and a fortnight later, a meeting at Boulogne entrusted the firm with the entire supply of chlorine. Castner–Kellner was the only British works with a chlorine liquefaction plant—its capacity being 5 long tons a week. It was told to raise it to 150 long tons a week, and to procure the cylinders, valves, and syphon tubes. The commercial type cylinder was made from solid drawn steel, had a diameter of 20 cm (8"), was about 1.65 m high and weighed, filled, 54–9 kg, the chlorine content being about 27 kg. It is not known how many were ordered in June, but by the end of September six thousand or thereabouts had been requisitioned or newly produced. They held altogether 160–70 long tons of chlorine.[23]

During July, the preparations for the British counter-stroke began in earnest. The chemist–instructors were sent back to Woolwich, promoted at once to full corporals (a procedure that caused much comment) and ordered to train the volunteers which made up Special Companies Nos. 186 to 189 of the Royal Engineers. Foulkes, who had seen service in the Boer War and been decorated for bravery at First Ypres, was a conscientious commander and in seven weeks he was able to instil his men with enthusiasm and even some knowledge of trench warfare practice. The first batch of cylinders reached France in mid-month and training was intensified. The cylinders were provided with carrying handles through which rope slings passed which were then attached to a pole. Three men had to carry, man-handle, push, and pull the unwieldy load at night along crowded trenches. The discharge pipes, two for each cylinder, were over 3 m long and when fitted together formed an inverted U over the parapet. The pipes were cumbersome and the preferred method was to carry them upright. On arrival at the trench, the cylinders were placed against the parapet and the connection made between pipe and cylinders; the work entailed removing the cap and the blind nut. All this had been practised thoroughly day and night at the base, but when the 'carry-in' began in September, the real thing was very different from the dummy runs.[24]

The Germans were aware that something was afoot. They anticipated retaliation, expected chlorine, but lacked details. The security cover for the Special Companies was military hygiene. (Even in this respect the British followed the enemy.) It held at first, but during July the Germans began to be worried. Prince Rupprecht of Bavaria who commanded the northern group of German armies issued a warning that gas attacks could be expected and anti-gas instructions were widely circulated. The transport of thousands of cylinders through the densely populated mining districts could not be hidden and by mid September the Germans must have known the scale of British preparations.[25]

On the subject of retaliation, the French GQG was all energy and valorous sentiments, but lower down very little was happening. One difficulty was the lack of chlorine. On enquiry it was found that phosgene was produced on a very small scale at Calais. So the French chose that gas, but they still needed chlorine to make it. The British were approached, but could not spare any until after the forthcoming battle. During September Jackson negotiated a contract with the French to fill chlorine cylinders for them at Runcorn at the rate of 50 t a week and dispatch a further 2 t a week direct to Calais. The first deliveries were made in October.[26] The technical obstacles do not explain all the delays, and right from the start French chemical warfare had a half-hearted air which it never lost. Thus, Gen. Curmer, who was in charge of engineering at GQG, asked army commanders in July to suggest possible sites for cloud-gas attacks, but several weeks passed before the Ministère de la Guerre was even approached about providing the men to operate the cylinders. Eventually two 'Compagnies Z' were formed from men invalided out of the army or exempt. By mid November this motley collection of 800 men was ready, but their technical competence was small, their physique poor, and senior officers were reluctant to use them for any operation. Someone recommended a reorganization, a third company was formed, the unfit were weeded out, and Commandant Soulié appointed to lead the special troops. But he was stationed at Versailles and told to look after training—hardly a prescription for aggressive gas warfare, and by comparison with what Foulkes had been and continued to be doing (and telling the French about it), it amounted to indifference.[27]

In one respect, however, the French were innovators. They decided in July that they would use chemical shell as soon as practicable, and the next month they began filling 75 mm shells with perchloromethyl mercaptan. This is a tear gas of no military value, but Joffre gave it his blessing, and hoped that 50,000–80,000 shells filled with the liquid would be available for the autumn offensive. The lower of the two figures was attained and the shells, which do not appear to have incommoded the Germans, were wasted.[28]

In the latter part of 1915, Allied retaliation was entirely unco-ordinated. The British were about to launch their first gas attack, the French were intending to organize themselves, and the Russians talked grandly of creating clouds with chlorine, phosgene, and even less credibly, with chloropicrin. They were not taken

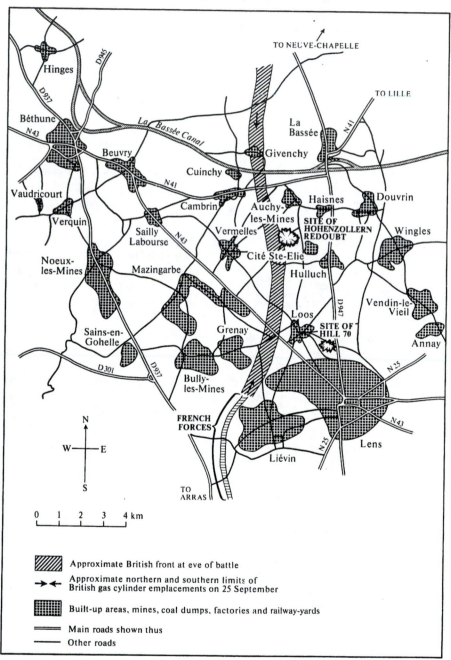

Map 3. Loos, September 1915

very seriously in London, for it was known that their chemical supply problems surpassed those of the western allies.[29] And so the first large-scale cloud gas discharge was left to the British at Loos.

The British took less than three months to prepare for retaliation, but the battle of Loos did not achieve anything and the chlorine cloud, which had so greatly impressed Haig at a demonstration a few weeks before was a failure. Nevertheless it was the start of their cylinder attacks: they made that mode of chemical warfare peculiarly their own and retained it long after the other belligerents had abandoned it. Foulkes, who had played the leading role, emerged from the non-event with his reputation intact and was able to turn failure into a spring-board for the later growth of the Special Companies. Loos and the autumn campaign of the French have been fully described elsewhere, and for the general background I have relied on Liddell Hart and Isorni.[30]

The terrain over which the battle was fought is good gas country: flat fields without hedges and ditches, no special topographical features, except, in the distance, the slag-heaps, winding-gear, and smoke-stacks of the pits, brick-works, and factories of Lens. A map of the district confirms the judgement of the eye— the contour lines are far apart. Time has not wrought many changes and this corner of Artois remains rural except around Lens. The mining villages of Auchy, Hulluch, Vermelles, and Loos have been rebuilt and grown a little. The Hohenzollern Redoubt stood where is now the Cité Madagascar. Only Puits 14, Hill 70, and some other landmarks have gone, bulldozed away for the northern by-pass of Lens. The British attack was in an easterly direction towards the Lens–La Bassée road (now the D 947) and beyond it. It was expected that the chlorine would flow smoothly over the flat ground and would encounter no obstacle until it reached the slag-heaps, several kilometres from the starting-point, and the low ridge, 5 km north-east of Lens, where there is now an aerodrome.

Three gas companies were available. The 1,400 men were told to finish training on 4 September. For the next three weeks they supervised the unloading of the cylinders, pipes, and other equipment, arranged carrying parties and placed the cylinders, in groups of twelve, in bays at about 400 points between Grenay (at the junction with the French) in the south to just north of Givenchy. In this manner, along a 10 km front, 5,100 cylinders, holding about 140 tons of chlorine, were 'emplaced', though not—as was the German way—dug in under the firestep. Another 400 cylinders (11 t) were installed further north near Neuve-Chapelle. The cylinders were not packed as closely as at Second Ypres in Spring, chiefly because the line curved and the front north of the La Bassée Canal was at risk from discharges further south. But the staff expected that 14–15 t/km would produce a thick enough cloud for the initial thrust, and, in order to heighten the effect, smoke candles were to be lit concurrently with the discharge. For the rest, all hoped that the Germans would be surprised and disorganized by chlorine carried on a gentle wind in the right direction. The most ludicrous security precautions were taken, down to labelling gas 'accessory', although the cylinders on their way to the front were easily recognized by civilians and troops. But foreknowledge was a less important factor in determining the success or failure of the entire operation than the speed and direction of the wind.

On 15 September, the original date for the attack, the atmospheric conditions were ideal. Ten days later when the battle began they were unfavourable. Gold, the chief meteorologist, was at Hinges, Haig's HQ, where reports came in from observers at the front, weather stations east and south of Béthune, and further afield from the French. On 24 September this last source inexplicably failed. Tension rose at Hinges. During the late afternoon and throughout the night of 24–5 September, the recordings were phoned through, logged, and interpreted. Gold predicted that the wind would moderate and change direction slightly. Between midnight and 0200 its speed fell from 1.3–1.8 m/sec to less than 1 m/sec, and in places there was dead calm. The direction, initially steady from the south-west, veered one or two points towards south. All this was according to forecast, but the timing was wrong: the changes took place much earlier than expected and as zero hour, 0550, approached the prognosis got worse.[31] The entire battle-plan was now in jeopardy. The gas, instead of being pushed diagonally towards the Germans, would move sluggishly, if at all, between the lines which were rarely more than 400 m apart, and around the Hohenzollern Redoubt and near the Canal were even closer. Haig wanted to cancel the gas discharge, was told it was too late and gave the order to proceed.

Henry Williamson was at Loos and his readers will recall that Phillip Maddison with his section of three Sergeants and thirty Corporals were near the Vermelles – Hulluch road. Williamson-Maddison was in charge of 14 emplacements and his men had to deal with 168 cylinders. The strain was frightful—the last-minute excitement over wrong-sized spanners was only solved by scrounging the right size from others. At 0550 the cylinders were opened and the barrage began. There was much confusion among the men of the Special Companies, this being their first experience of a gas discharge. Less excusable was the belated discovery of faulty materials: a few copper pipes split, flexible pipes leaked, some spanners were too soft to turn stiff valve-spindles, sometimes the spindles themselves broke, parapet pipes burst, and in general it was difficult to connect pipes to fresh cylinders for there was no branch-pipe system. Hence there was, as later reports put it, 'a certain amount of gas leakage' in the British trenches and after the event one group of critics noted that 'the mechanical arrangements were ill adapted for their requirements.'[32] Still, the cylinders were opened, the cloud emerged, hissing, mixed with the smoke from the candles and, seen from a distance, the effect was spectacular. At the front itself, matters looked different. In the sector between Vermelles and the Canal, the gas drifted slowly at first, then stopped. The infantry assault began at 0630 and in the centre the soldiers, wearing their gas helmets, were forced to advance through the dense chlorine towards the German barbed wire which the artillery had failed to demolish. The enemy gave ground, for some of their first lines were under gas and owing to smoke, visibility was poor. Further south, where less gas had been released, the British took Loos and for a time the

Germans considered the position 'extremely serious.'[33] But the German withdrawal could not be exploited. It was then decided to open the remaining cylinders near Neuve Chapelle to support a diversionary bombing raid. This was done on 27 September at 1700 when the wind blew from the right quarter and at the right speed of 1.8 m/sec. The little operation was a success. The main battle continued but by 29 September the Germans had driven the British back to their starting line.

Gas had failed at Loos. The first aim, retaliation, had been replaced by the more ambitious one—to save manpower and shells by forcing the enemy line with gas. On looking back, it is obvious that this was expecting too much of the chlorine cloud. The disappointment was all the greater because of excessive optimism before the battle. However the enthusiasts, among them Foulkes, were well satisfied; nor did he alter his first opinion. In 1921 he summed up the work of the Special Companies at Loos with the words—'Altogether . . . it was no mean performance' and years later he asserted in his book that gas 'influenced the battle to a marked extent whether the effect was material or moral.'[34] This is a travesty of the facts. The Germans reported 21,000 killed and wounded at Loos up to 29 September, the British casualties up to 13 October, when the last engagement ended, were 60,000. The Germans did not count their gas casualties separately, but the VII Corps (which held the line from Givenchy southwards) reported that 106 men had been gassed and evacuated for treatment; none died from the effects of chlorine. The German medical staff noted a good deal of vomiting, and Haber later wrote to the Kaiser that the men in one Division gave way when the cloud approached. This is confirmed by Pollitt who was at the Hohenzollern Redoubt and saw the Germans retreat in front of the gas. He noted that it 'never caught up with them' which explains why they had such small gas casualties.[35]

The Germans were not inconvenienced for long; the British, on the other hand, suffered considerably from their own chlorine. Graves who was just south of the Canal observed British gas casualties, and near the Hohenzollern chlorine hung about in shell holes and trenches, and caught the British who were sheltering from German shells.[36] The total British gas casualties between 25 and 27 September were 2,632, of whom seven died. The 2nd Division astride the Canal and the 15th Division just opposite Loos suffered most, 1,052 and 464 respectively.[37] The gas casualty rate was 4.4 per cent of all killed and wounded at Loos, a relatively high proportion by comparison with later gas attacks. The belligerents drew several lessons. The British needed better respirators and more practice. The development of the former was henceforward pursued with even greater intensity, whilst the latter was achieved by carrying out several small gas discharges. The first took place on 13 October to support an attack on the Hohenzollern Redoubt. It accomplished nothing, except that the Germans retaliated with tear gas. Only the British suffered gas casualties on that occasion. Thereupon the Special Companies were withdrawn for training; they went into action again on either side of the canal on the night of 21–2 December: 940 cylinders (almost 30 t) were opened. In February 1916 they carried out small operations near Laventie and further north at Le Touquet, near Armentières, with 330 and 400 cylinders respectively. The Germans suffered some casualties,[38] and Foulkes obtained the reinforcements which he needed to carry out his ambitious plans for 1916.

The Germans also learnt something from Loos. They too looked to their gas defences and now began to think of gas not as an alternative to artillery, but as a weapon to cause confusion and damage morale. The battles in Champagne gave them their opportunity. The circumstances were as follows: the second thrust of the Allied autumn offensive was a French attack along a front of 30 km in northern Champagne, from the valley of the Suippe to the Argonne forest. Timed to coincide with Loos, the assault faltered on the first day owing to a break in the weather. But the French persisted until 30 September and resumed between 6 and 14 October. They made a few dents in the German position. The Germans intended to use gas and sent Pionier Regiment 36, followed by 35, to Vouziers on the upper Aisne with instructions to install cylinders. But the terrain is hilly, the lower ground marshy, and access difficult—in short, bad gas country, so the Germans scrapped the plan. The French thought differently, and Pétain who was in command in that sector, was ordered at the beginning of November to recapture a position with the help of gas. The weather broke again, the ground became impassable, and Soulié's men only managed to install two-thirds of the cylinders before they collapsed exhausted. The discharge was planned for 3 or 4 December, but had to be postponed several times and was finally cancelled in mid-December. Some of the equipment had become so coated with mud that it was no longer usable.[39] That ended French retaliation with gas for 1915; it had been a futile effort, characterized by amateurishness and irresponsibility.

To relieve pressure on the Germans between the Suippe and the Aisne, OHL ordered a diversion around Reims in the hope that the French would withdraw troops from the main battle. The Germans occupied the higher ground east of Reims, which offered them good observation and vantage-points for cloud-gas discharges. Their lines circled the town at a distance of about 5 km and at the Pompelle Fort turned east. Pompelle remained in French hands throughout the war and guards the junction of the N44 with the N31. The fort looks down on the Aisne canal, and in turn is under observation from the slopes of Mt. de Berru occupied by the Germans from 1914 to 1918. The N31, an old Roman road, runs due east from Pompelle to a point near Aubérive, then turns south. During the war it marked for 20 km the position of the French. The Germans were dug in to the north, the hillocks of the Massif de Moronvillers behind them. The road rises from 107 to 126 m, Mt. Cornillet, Mt. Haut, Mont sans Nom, are 200–50 m high. Between the plain and the hills are ridges which provide cover on the reverse slopes and the possibility of digging caves and sheltered approach paths through the chalk. The Germans dominated the scene and used the railway along the Suippe to bring up supplies. They probably had one or two mobile filling-stations in the valley where the gas was transferred from rail tank cars to cylinders. This job used to worry the Germans a great deal and they employed a special detachment of Gaspioniere, supervised by chemists, for this work and for nothing else. Haber established himself at Warmeriville and the gas troops were billetted nearby. The

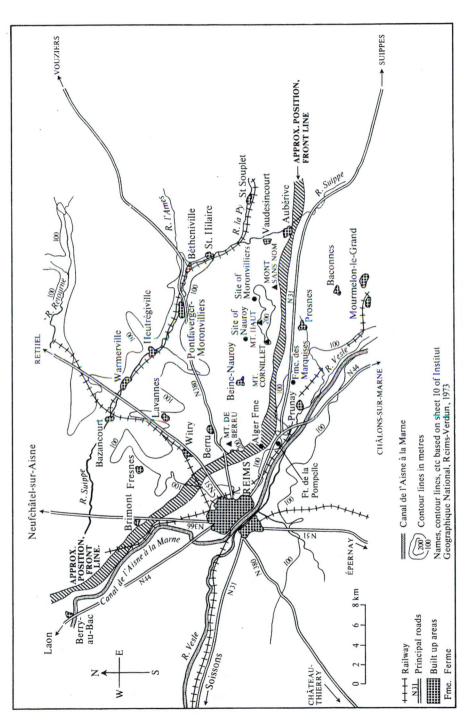

Map 4. Champagne Front, 1915–1917

cylinders were dug in methodically and undetected. It was decided to launch a major operation as soon as the new respirators had been issued.[40]

The German records of the chlorine clouds in Champagne have been destroyed, and one has to rely on Heber who wrote more than twenty years after the event: he is often unreliable and uninformative just when precise details are necessary.[41] Heber says that the Germans discharged altogether 34,500 cylinders, but I think he is double-counting, and 24,200 is a more likely figure. The cylinders were all of the new small size, holding 20 kg of gas, so that a little under 500 t were involved. The Germans used, for the first time on the Western Front, phosgene in the ratio of one to four of chlorine.

The first cloud attack began at 0815 German time on 19 October: the morning was cool and dry, the wind steady from NNW at a speed of 1.6–2 m/sec. The width of the front was 12 km, and about 14,000 cylinders were used, say 23 t/km—so that the initial concentration was rather less dense than at Ypres half a year earlier. The Germans, wearing their new masks, attacked the Alger farm, on the other side of the road from Pompelle, and Marquises, another fortified building 6 km east. They captured both. At Pompelle the cloud was thick, but the French who had been alerted by a heavy bombardment, kept calm, put on their mouthpads, and counter-attacked. By nightfall the Germans had retreated from both strong points. They tried again the following afternoon between Pompelle and Prunay, emptying about 4,400 cylinders along 3 km (29 t/km). They refilled the cylinders and tried for a third time, on 27 October, on a front of 5 km with 5,000 cylinders (24 t/km) between Marquises and Prosnes. Once more they did not seize and hold the French trenches. But in one important respect they had achieved at least one of their objectives: the three gas attacks caused the French over 5,700 casualties, including 500 killed.[42] That done, the pioneers packed up and some were sent north of Verdun where, on 26 November, they opened their cylinders in the area of Malancourt–Forges Bethincourt. The French had had advance warning from prisoners, but still lost 387 men, including 57 who died from gas.[43]

Bad gas protection and poor discipline were responsible for these heavy losses. The Germans were unaware of the effect they had achieved and instead of continuing against a weak enemy transferred their attentions to the more alert and careful one. The gas cloud at Ypres on 19 December has received far more attention than the autumn attacks. Several of those present wrote about the event afterwards, their stories tally in all essential details, and the incident will serve to show the state of attack and of defence in chemical warfare at the end of the year.

Towards the end of October Pionier Rgt. 36 was sent from Champagne to the Ypres Salient to install cylinders around Hoge (see map in Chapter 3). The wind was unfavourable, so the cylinders were moved to the area between the Ypres Canal and Wieltje, north of the town, and dug in late in November and at the beginning of December. The British were aware of these activities and very concerned about them, for their gas helmets offered insufficient protection against phosgene which, it was widely believed, would be used by the Germans. While the Germans were waiting impatiently for a favourable north-easterly wind, the British were raiding the enemy lines to capture prisoners for interrogation. They got their man on 16 or 17 December, grilled him, discovered the location of the cylinders, and were dismayed to learn that they contained pure phosgene. Gas precautions were tightened up and the men placed on extreme alert, so that when the Germans opened the cylinders at 0515 on the 19th, the British were ready for them. Heber, who was there, wrote that 9,300 cylinders were opened, say 180 t of gas, in the now usual 80:20 chlorine–phosgene ratio. So the German prisoner had been wrong, which was just as well, for the concentration in that small sector of 4–5 km averaged at least 36 t/km and the brisk north-easterly, variously recorded at 3.1 to 3.6 m/sec, pushed the gas quickly into the British lines. The land was flat, the volume high, and the gas spread far behind the front—it was noticeable at Vlamertinge, 8.5 km from the point of discharge. Only calmness and excellent discipline prevented a disaster, and the helmets were just about good enough for the occasion. Roughly 25,000 troops were in the area at the time, of whom 1,069 were gassed; 116 died from the consequences of the attack.[44] The Germans claimed later that they had merely intended to disturb and harass, and that they had made no preparations for an infantry attack. Be that as it may, vigilance and care had blunted the German objective. The British had cause to congratulate themselves, and their reaction to the event was to introduce systematic anti-gas training throughout the BEF.

In the winter of 1915–16 gas warfare consisted essentially of chlorine clouds (including up to 20 per cent of phosgene) and two or three kinds of tear-gas shell. How can one reconcile such a small range of toxic or irritating compounds with so much scientific effort? A year after its introduction gas was still at such an early stage of development that the civilians at home had little understanding of what was needed at the front. Conversely people at GHQ or Army HQ men were often wondering what the 'boffins'—the term had not yet been coined—were going to offer them next. Research and development in Britain and France, though not in Germany, was carried on in small groups, usually in university laboratories, under conditions of extreme secrecy, unplanned and unco-ordinated. A chemist, working on a new idea might be unaware of others working in the same area. The committees that were being formed to prevent this sort of thing, were still unsure of their role, unfamiliar with the ways of bureaucrats and unable to communicate with the military. Instead of sifting proposals and speeding development, they added to the confusion. The scientists were often bewildered by the requirements of the soldiers. What did they want? Tear gas to incapacitate, smoke to hide, poison gas to injure or kill? And in what form were the substances—assuming they could be made and delivered within the required time-span—to be used: as shell, trench mortar-bomb, or (physical conditions permitting) as clouds? Were they to be employed on their own or in combination with traditional weapons? These important questions called for urgent answers which needed to straddle military and physical sciences, but which could not be given for lack of experience and mutual understanding. Meanwhile the field was left open to improvisation, muddle, and cranks, and the armies became increasingly cautious about the use of gas, until more progress had been made towards closing the gap between offence and defence.

The theoretical diversity of chemical weaponry was immense, but in practical terms most could be dismissed. Some examples will show how absurd and unscientific was the thinking on gas warfare in its first year or two. It will also be seen why potentially valuable substances were passed over while useless compounds continued to be produced. Ingenuity began at the top. Gen. Charteris, the head of Intelligence at GHQ, was full of ideas: machine-gun bullets filled with gas, infecting the German potato crop, dropping gas bombs from planes, manufacturing lightweight gas cylinders. Not all his schemes were crazy, and lesser mortals than Charteris had even stranger proposals which they vigorously promoted. A drawing survives in the French archives showing a carbon monoxide generator installed in the front line connected to a vessel holding sulphur chloride whence a pump delivered the mixture by pipe line to the German trenches! Such flights of fancy need not be taken any more seriously than a British idea to disperse coal dust over the Germans, ignite it, and smother them under an apocalyptic fire cloud. Others thought of hydrogen chloride or of mixtures of chlorine with various other poisonous substances in the hope of achieving a synergistic effect. As to delivery methods, spring guns and catapults were built and tested to see how far they could throw gas-filled containers.[45]

Gradually less time was spent on science-fiction stuff, but even in the autumn and winter of 1915–16 much energy continued to be devoted to the development of useless substances because eminent men had become identified with them and were able to devote large resources to their pet projects. The French, for example, experimented with various tear gases. I have already mentioned that perchloromethyl mercaptan was useless, but it had one merit—it could be easily prepared by the action of gaseous chlorine on carbon disulphide. There were other lachrymators which, whatever their effectiveness, required to be filled into specially lined shell cases, a disadvantage which limited their appeal to the ordnance departments. The French spent much time on acrolein, rejected by the British in 1914, and after Moureu had found a stabilizer, began to fill it from 1916 onwards into hand grenades. Another fashionable substance was arsine, not so dangerous as phosgene, but at the time more difficult to protect against. This poison was to be produced by breaking two vessels, thereby allowing calcium arsenide to combine with hydrochloric acid; the design of a foolproof device and a projectile to carry it were still engaging British chemists in February 1916.[46]

Hydrogen cyanide, though also useless, was not irrelevant and warrants a digression. No death from it was ever reported, but the fatal nature of the poison was a continuing theme for most of the war. Afterwards British chemists used to ridicule the French for their obsession with hydrogen cyanide, conveniently forgetting that there were some important people in London who caused it to be given far more attention than it deserved; the Germans also took the non-existent danger seriously. It was well known that above a given threshold level, cyanide acts indirectly on the central nervous system and causes almost instant death. If one ignored, as most people did, the difficulty of producing the necessary concentration in the field, one could consider it an extremely promising weapon. Indeed there were many stories that the Germans were making cyanide bombs, or, alternatively, were proposing to flood abandoned trenches with the poison, so that the advancing Allies would die like rats. The greatest attraction of the poison to its promoters lay in its appeal to the emotions and connotations of death. There was also a practical consideration: the manufacture of hydrogen cyanide requires no chlorine, and the Allies adopted the former because they initially lacked adequate supplies of the latter. The French went ahead, made hydrogen cyanide, and charged it into shells as early as July 1915. The material is so light (see Table 4.1) that it has to be weighed down and the French employed various chlorides—including titanium tetrachloride to generate smoke—for that purpose; consequently they were obliged to double the number of shell for a given concentration. They gave the gas the code name 'Vincennite' but delayed its introduction until July 1916, when it was first employed on the Somme.[47]

The British initiative came from the Admiralty where Churchill's imagination was fired by hydrogen cyanide. F. A. Brock, of the fireworks business, then serving in the RN Air Service, discovered that Thomas Tyrer prepared it in aqueous solution for medical purposes. In order to weigh down the substance Brock added chloroform and thickened the mixture with cellulose acetate dope to make a syrup which he called 'Jellite'. He found an adventurous pilot to take several carboys of Jellite on his plane and drop them over the marshes of the Thames Estuary. Some broke. This harmless test was considered sufficiently encouraging to warrant the construction of a large plant at Stratford. It produced the first batch of Jellite on 13 September 1915 and within ten days, 120 glass jars, each containing 15 kg of the stuff were at Boulogne docks. Somebody in France thought that Jellite was too dangerous on-shore and the Navy was obliged to return the consignment to Stratford. The incident did not put an end to the nonsense: the works continued to make Jellite for stock, and in July 1916 Whitehall authorized its use for shell filling. By then 50 t of hydrogen cyanide were stored at Stratford, then a built-up area. The Admiralty began mixing it with chlorides, just as the French did, and to fill shells which were never fired. After many delays the War Office officially abandoned hydrogen cyanide in December 1917: the shells were dumped, production stopped, and 300 t of sodium cyanide sold to the French who persisted with that particular chemical side-show.[48]

The chemical improvisations and experiments had been extended from the very beginning to chemical shell, and as evidence of the unreliability of the gas cloud mounted, so support for artillery grew. Shells, unlike clouds, were not affected by the weather. Their delivery over the range of a field gun, say 6½–7 km (heavier artillery reached up to 10 km), was not only more precise, but also well beyond the limits within which cylinder operations were normally effective. Besides, the armies were thoroughly familiar with artillery and it was hoped that gas could be readily added to the gunners' activities. Why, given these favourable circumstances, did it take so long for gas shell to become an accepted mode of warfare? The chief objection in 1915–16 was that a lot of metal was needed to carry a little gas. In the high explosive shell, the low power-to-weight ratio was not such a great disadvantage, for the explosive energy of TNT was enhanced by the fragmentation of the steel casing. By contrast fragmentation was undesirable with gas: only a small bursting charge was needed to open the shell—the liquid or gas would disperse through momentum and evaporation.

Initially shell cases designed to take HE were filled with tear or poison gas. Their efficiency was low: for a field gun shell the proportion of chemical to total weight (filled and fused) was 6–7 per cent, except for the French 75 mm which, because of its special construction, had a ratio of 9–10 per cent. Specially designed shell cases for chemicals, with longer and thinner walls were introduced in 1917, and doubled the carrying capacity.[49] At first the Germans and the French used whatever was at hand, even cast iron. But that, like steel, was attacked by bromine compounds, so that the case had to be lined with lead. As this was very time-consuming, work began on ceramic liners and later on glass-lined shell cases.[50]

The special problems encountered with tear-gas fillings were aggravated by others of a more general nature which were not so readily solved. A minor difficulty was caused by ranging. The French practice of adding smoke-producing substances to gas shell helped their observers and alerted the enemy whose suspicions would be confirmed by the characteristic 'plop' sound of the detonation. The Germans, even with gas, ranged with special mortar shell containing HE and smoke. A major difficulty was the need for rapid fire to put down a gas concentration sufficiently dense to make an impact on the enemy. Firing rates vary inversely with calibre. Field guns such as the British 18 pdr or the French 75 mm could be fired at 15–20 rounds a minute, but for a heavier gun, say the British 4.5″ (11.4 cm) howitzer, 4 rounds a minute represented rapid fire. Thus to equal the contents of a single British cylinder, about 60 rounds of phosgene shell had to be fired from an 18 pdr or 27 from the howitzer. Fuses were unsatisfactory, and instant impact fuses were only introduced in the second half of 1916. Even so some gas, unlike HE, was wasted because the shell embedded itself in the fraction of a second before detonating. Finally, there was the pattern of firing. This technicality could only be answered by trial and error. Until then, the different views held on tangential and overlapping shell bursts necessarily entailed a great waste of shell.[51] All these obstacles imposed a threshold on the use of gas shells: below that limit (100 shells is the number sometimes quoted in British artillery instructions) a gas bombardment was totally useless. It is interesting to observe that it took until 1917 to realize this.

The objections to gas shell meant that it had to overcome considerable resistance before it became acceptable to the artillery. In addition there was another factor which dominated everything else—the supply of shell cases generally. For the British, who were chronically short throughout 1915–16, that was the key issue. The incremental benefit from more HE shell was so great, that few were prepared to experiment with novel designs, let alone release conventional shell cases for filling with gas. The French were better placed, and the production of 75 mm cases was sufficiently large to permit the diversion of a significant number to chemical warfare. (The slightly higher gas content ratio may also have played a part.) They began filling in the second half of 1915. The Germans filled tear gas throughout 1915, but unwisely added TNT, and so largely wasted both. They did not begin the systematic study of gas shell design until late winter or early spring of 1916, probably in response to the examination of French blinds filled with gas. Then they acted with great speed: they abandoned fragmentation immediately, adopted drawn or forged steel, and introduced impact fuses of high sensitivity.[52] It is likely that the Germans caught up with the French in the latter half of 1916.

Filling or 'charging' gas shell caused difficulties throughout the war, which will be considered at greater length in their proper place: here we may note that some of the problems can be ascribed to the obstinacy of ordnance experts reluctant to change their ways. A more serious matter was that the introduction of gas disturbed the basic principles of filling: long runs on mass production lines and the avoidance of all complications. The chemists upset the entire approach—'We should aim at simplicity both from the point of view of manufacture and use in the field', said Hartley after the war.[53] But from the start uniformity never had a chance, and variety increased irresistibly, so that the contrast between HE and chemical warfare materials remained wide. TNT was the chief explosive: it is stable, melts at 80°C, has a specific gravity 1.60 times that of water, and may be safely poured. Gases and the various liquids under consideration have different physical properties— though diphosgene and chloropicrin have densities similar to TNT which is one of the reasons why the Germans adopted them. While the filling technique varies with each material, the objective remains unchanged—to get the weight right: this was easy for TNT which could be readily filled to the 'dead firing weight' required by the inspectors to within the ±0.5 per cent (equivalent to ±40 gr for a British field-gun shell of around 8 kg). But with liquids of different densities that method was impracticable and the shell was filled to a constant percentage volume, with an allowance of 10–12 per cent for gas expansion. The British, who filled from the side of the shell, required accurate gauges to measure small differences in level on a relatively large surface. The French, on the other hand, filled through the nose to a constant level: their task was easier, because the surface area is small, so that small differences in the level have no significant effect on weight. Hence all they needed was a simple valve controlled by a mercury filled U-tube. Their system was quick and safe. The Germans filled to a constant volume through the nose. The final, proof weight, was adjusted by lead shot. The French perversely threw away the advantage of simplicity in their method, by filling 'heavy', i.e. overweight shell, with hydrogen cyanide, and 'light' or underweight shell with phosgene. The practice entailed a lot of unnecessary handling of shell cases, and appears to have been abandoned during 1917.[54]

The Germans, who had been first with chemical shell, got the chemical manufacturers to do the filling, but Hoechst and Bayer refused to enlarge their plants, and the war ministry was obliged to build special factories. The French organization was simple and practical: in July 1915 they installed lines for filling poison gas at Aubervilliers, and tear gas at Vincennes. A year later, Aubervilliers was a plant with a capacity of 31,000 shells per 9 hour day (about three times the size of the largest British installation), and the French claimed they could increase it by forcing the pace and introducing double shifts. The first British filling lines at Watford and Walthamstow began work in February 1916, but as gas shell played a minor role throughout 1916, inefficient practices were tolerated and became firmly embedded, so that far-reaching changes were necessary at a later stage of the war.

German gas-shell production in or about December 1915 was 24,000 a month, the French made less than that. The British were still giving batch orders, the largest being for 10,000 4.5" SK shell ordered late in October 1915, but not completed until the following April.[55] In all three countries, the output of gas shells was a fraction of the HE production.

Technical obstacles and organizational failures delayed the introduction of gas shell. The Hague Conventions, though directed against their use, were ineffective. Nevertheless enquiries were made by French and British officials before toxic shells were formally authorized in the first half of 1916. The Germans, though they had made up their minds rather earlier, gave 'practically no importance . . . to gas shell in spite of a special artillery staff attached to Army HQ, to develop its use', until well into the battle of Verdun.[56]

The French are usually considered the pioneers of the poison gas shell, and their use of phosgene shells in the Verdun sector in Spring 1916 is an important landmark in the history of chemical warfare. But we would be wrong to ascribe to them (or for that matter to the other belligerents) a systematic approach to the subject. Joffre had called for phosgene filling in October 1915, and stressed the need for trial shoots. When, at last, they were held on 29 December, he was disappointed by the results—only 20 per cent of the animals were killed. A month later GQG and Albert Thomas were still arguing over the effectiveness of gas shell. Other types of gas shell were being prepared and by August 1916, the French had 9 different chemical fillings of which only two could be considered deadly.[57] Ideas, projects, and confusion were not the preserve of the French. Much was done empirically, a great deal miscarried, and so increased the hostility of many senior officers to gas. Although the scale of this activity was modest by comparison with conventional warfare, it nevertheless created stirrings which were picked up and amplified by unscientific spies and intelligence officers. The belligerents were alerting each other with reports of novel poisons and delivery methods, however useless the former and inadequate the latter. The significance of these signals for 1916 lay not so much in the increased sophistication of gas attack, but in the progress made with gas defence to which high priority had been given since April 1915.

The improvised gas defences which I described at the beginning of the chapter satisfied no one. The summer and autumn were anxious months for the Allies; they worried chiefly about phosgene. From July onwards they were able to offer a little protection against the gas, but what if the Germans were to release phosgene undiluted with chlorine? The Anglo-French experts tended to overrate the inventiveness and nastiness of their opponent and in their endeavours to anticipate him introduced minor improvements on several occasions. These successive changes cast doubt on the value of the previously issued equipment, and so invited a cynical response to gas protection at a time when confidence needed to be maintained at all costs. The Germans, on the other hand, were sure the Allies would not catch up quickly, but they ran great risks and suffered losses from blow-back because their pads gave insufficient protection. As a precaution they issued oxygen breathing-sets to the gas troops, medical companies, machine gunners, and sometimes to artillery observers.[58]

Good organization, drive, and willingness to chance it gave the Germans the initiative. Haber was put in charge, and he was certainly the right man for the job. He was unfamiliar with the basic principles, but being extremely practical he realized that theoretical solutions alone were insufficient and that large-scale manufacture combined with raw material economy were equally necessary for successful gas defence. The first meeting on defence was held at the end of April, and Haber at once asked several firms to submit designs. During May and June, Bayer and Auergesellschaft were working on prototypes, while the Berlin institute installed equipment for testing the action of chemicals on gases. Towards the end of June or early in July various types of respirators, including one that resembled the British Small Box Respirator of 1916, were submitted for evaluation. The final choice, made at the end of July, fell on the model submitted by the Auergesellschaft. Haber immediately placed large orders for essential components. He also selected the teams of chemists who were put to work under extremely gifted section heads such as Herzog, Quasebart, Pick, and for a short time Willstätter. Their main tasks were to monitor production, establish and operate an inspection and quality control service, and further develop the basic design. It was an imaginative solution to a complex problem, and built on the German tradition of organized team-work. Haber carried a great responsibility, for the entire operation worked to a strict timetable which allowed for no failures: the product had to be right first time, or the troops would be issued with useless masks.[59]

The British approach was different. Individuals, rather than groups, worked independently of each other and at different tempos. Officially, the centre of defence research was the Royal Army Medical College, and E. F. Harrison was the moving spirit there. In France the Central Laboratory at GHQ played the chief role, and its head Professor (later Lt.-Col.) W. Watson and his assistant B. Mouat Jones, were invaluable as men of ideas and as links with the Chemical Advisers (who also generated constructive suggestions) and with the Director of Medical Services BEF. Haldane, then the greatest Allied authority on the physiology of respiration, was not formally consulted, because of his outspoken views on the incompetence displayed by senior officers in April. Nevertheless he contributed indirectly and unofficially by advising former students and friends notably C. G. Douglas ad B. Lambert who were working on gas defence at

Oxford.[60] All were urged on by Foulkes and his staff and subjected to other, sometimes conflicting pressures. Such a manner of proceeding led to confusion and delays, and also caused much avoidable personal friction and irritation. But it suited the temperament of the majority of its practitioners and had the great merit of ensuring a careful examination of the alternatives and a thorough study of the details.

The French documents tell a different story. Although they convey the same impression of purposeful activity, no names emerge, nor is there much evidence of anyone thinking through the entire problem. Rather it is a case of coping with unforeseen crises. There were several reorganizations in summer 1915 and the committee chairmen changed, but it is by no means clear what functions the eminent scientists on the various bodies fulfilled. No one considered gas defence from first principles, and systematic work on the French respirator did not begin until the winter of 1915–16 and then continued at a slow pace for the next eighteen months or so.[61]

The varied attitudes to the organization and implementation of gas defence in the second half of 1915 led to major differences in the anti-gas equipment supplied, and the differences continued throughout the war and indeed into the 1920s and 1930s. This is a curious outcome for there was no dispute over the objective. But the way of achieving this objective—defence against gas— was by no means the same and was often powerfully influenced by irrational considerations.

It was not difficult, even in 1915, to write the specification for a respirator: it had to give protection for several hours against all known gases likely to be employed, must be easy to put on, comfortable to wear, afford good visibility, allow speech, require little or no maintenance, and withstand rough conditions. So much for the military side. In addition the device must be simple to manufacture by unskilled hands from parts produced by the million to close tolerances from readily available materials. All these conditions have to be met in the *ideal* respirator of which it can be said that the whole is greater than the sum of the parts. That was (and remains) unattainable. One or two of the criteria can be jettisoned, and something practical will still emerge. Hence the question—what price safety? Complete protection could be achieved but the soldier would be completely useless. A compromise was therefore essential between the theoretical optimum respirator and makeshift improvisations. The compromise required answers to many questions, of which three were especially important.[62] (The reader may find it helpful at this stage to look at the photographs (Figs. 1–8) and judge for himself how closely the final products conformed to the criteria and provided solutions to the questions listed below.)

1. *Should the system be closed with its own oxygen supply or carbon dioxide convertors, or open, that is capable of removing the poison gas from the air?* On grounds of bulkiness, all the belligerents rejected the former.
2. *What should be the configuration of the face line?* If hood, snout,

or mask were an integral part of the anti-gas defence, they had to seal
off the face. Alternatively they need only protect eyes and skin, in which
case they could be loose fitting, but then the lungs needed to be protected
by a filter, and breathing in and out restricted to the mouth. The Germans
and the French chose the first, the British and Americans the second.

3. *Should the filter box be directly fitted to the mask, or connected by a tube
   to a box carried separately?* The one needed to be light and small, the other
   could be heavy and large. The Germans, and later the Russians and the
   French picked the former, the British and Americans, the latter.

The merits of the alternatives were endlessly debated, but no single conclusion
emerged. The details, often interesting, would take us too far afield. Two
examples must suffice to illustrate the differences. Damage to the British mask
did not impair its value (except against tear and mustard gas) for the reasons
set out in (2) above. However, a nose clip to prevent nasal inhalation inevitably
became an essential feature. Many believed that artificially blocking the nose
was 'unnatural': Cummins, an important figure in the British defence organization, was against the nose clip and even after the decision had been taken to
adopt it, he wrote that 'the German pattern is the best in this respect, and the
more slavishly we copy it, the better.' His French colleague, Flandin, agreed
with him.[63] Yet the nose clip was retained and proved its value. Some Germans
admired the British design, nose clip and all! Pick, also an authority on the
subject, praised its configuration and criticized the German mask on account
of its dead space around the cheek bone (the result of having folds to wipe away
moisture inside the lenses): carbon dioxide accumulated in that space and
affected breathing. The British avoided this by having a non-return valve at
the end of the mouthpiece which made expiration much easier and helped men
tolerate the greater breathing resistance caused by the tube which in effect
doubled the distance to the lungs.[64]

The second example will show the complexities involving the materials which
were to remove and render innocuous the toxic gases. At first the pads and hoods
were impregnated with an alkali to neutralize acid gases. Later, when phosgene
was feared, sodium phenate replaced thiosulphate as the impregnant. Then it
was discovered that carbon dioxide reacted with the phenate to form salts which
tended to rot the fabric of the anti-gas helmets. So the material was changed
from Viyella wool-cotton mixtures to flannelette, and—to make doubly sure—a
non-return valve, fitted to a tube like a pipe stem, was provided for breathing
out. That problem was specifically British, for the other belligerents did not
bother with hoods or helmets.[65] A general problem for all however, was the
limited neutralizing power of soluble alkalis, which were in any event useless
against tear gas. An oxidizing material, such as sodium permanganate, and an
adsorbent like charcoal were recognized as the best constituents of the filter
box since they would deal with tear as well as toxic gases. As early as July 1915.
Lambert and Sadd in Britain were working on soda-lime-permanganate granules

as oxidizers, while in Germany, Willstätter and two assistants devised and tested in three weeks during August, a single-layer drum filter. It consisted of pumice or diatomite granules, impregnated with potassium carbonate and dusted with charcoal. The filter gave protection against chlorine, but failed against chlorine–phosgene mixtures and tear gas. It was impracticable to withdraw the old filters, so Willstätter was recalled and set to work again in November. He designed a three-layer filter: the outer one remained unchanged and neutralized chlorine, the middle one contained charcoal granules, the inner one pumice granules treated with potash and hexamine to break down any of the phosgene that had not been adsorbed on the charcoal. The addition of hexamine had also been considered by the Russians and the French as an ingredient for impregnating solutions during July and August, but owing to poor liaison the British did not hear of it until later.[66] Although it is readily prepared from formaldehyde and ammonia, and was on sale before the war, there was great anxiety about supplies. Mouat Jones, upon hearing the names of British manufacturers, wrote that the information 'is really invaluable and will no doubt exercise an important function in saving the British Empire from premature collapse'.[67] The exaggeration reflects the tenseness of those concerned with defence. The outcome was yet another change in the formulation of the dipping fluid.

It is time to leave the details and turn to the broader narrative to show the tempo of improvements. British anti-gas protection went through many evolutionary changes. Even while the 'Hypo' helmet was being issued to troops in June its replacement was investigated. Better visibility and gas-proof windows or eyepieces were needed. That was simple, and glass goggles in flanged frames replaced transparent plastic sheet.[68] Phosgene was the greater worry. The wildest rumours circulated, and the Adjutant General was even moved to write to the Secretary of State for War—'I desire to call your attention to the very grave situation that may arise if the enemy succeeds in using this gas before we are provided with some means of neutralising it.'[69] But the new impregnating mixture containing sodium phenate was difficult to prepare, dipping and drying presented unexpected snags, and the hood had to be altered to take the mouthpiece. The new design, known as the 'P' or 'Tube' helmet, was agreed on in mid July and a trial batch of fifty reached France ten days later. Some further changes in the impregnating procedure were found necessary, but John Bell, Hills and Lucas were able to start manufacture towards the end of the month. The P helmet began to be issued about four weeks later: Haig's men wore the uncomfortable contraption at Loos, and it remained in general use, though unsafe against concentrated phosgene, until replaced by the PH helmet in 1916. The latter was dipped in a solution of sodium phenate-hexamine and the first batches were produced early in January 1916. Shortly afterwards a version with improved goggles, known as the 'PHG' helmet made its appearance.[70]

The intensive preoccupation with the P and PH helmets probably slowed down the development of the British respirator, which was later called 'Harrison's

Fig. 5. Sentry, wearing 'PH' helmet, ringing alarm. The photograph was taken near Fleurbaix (south of Armentières) in June 1916. (Imperial War Museum)

Tower' or Large Box Respirator and became the precursor of the 'Small Box Respirator' (SBR). Lambert's design shown to Hartley in mid-July 1915, was ingenious, but another month went by before he felt sufficiently confident to send a prototype to France for testing. The Chemical Advisers merely considered it promising and further changes had to be made. Cummins tested Lambert's improved version together with Sadd's and Pilgram's on 25 September, and found that Lambert's was the best. Now, at last, it was possible to get a decision from GHQ. On 1 November Cummins's judgement was formally endorsed and the staffs immediately called for large supplies. They were to be disappointed: the final design took time, as did the organization of manufacture, which began in February 1916. About 200,000 were issued to the Special Companies and to machine gunners. Production stopped in summer 1916—the 'Tower' was too bulky to be satisfactory. It consisted of a half-face mask of impregnated butter muslin. A mouthpiece and flexible tube (with non-return valve) connected to a large filter or box of about 1000 cc capacity carried in a haversack under the left shoulder. Padded goggles, worn separately, completed the outfit (see Fig. 6), which complied only in some respects with the criteria listed previously.[71]

The Germans made much faster progress with their mask because they were not distracted by interim solutions. Production began in September 1915 and, whenever possible, readily available machinery was used to press or cut out the

Fig. 6. Large Box Respirator ('Harrison's Tower'), final design. Note half face mask, padded goggles, and flexible tube leading to filter box. This model is being demonstrated by an Australian chaplain at Fleurbaix, June 1916. (Imperial War Museum)

components. For example the circular filter was connected to the face piece by a screw fitting: this was of the same dimensions as those used for Osram street-lamps and meant that the machines for making lamp bases and sockets could be turned at once to the mass production of these important components. The value of the interchangeable filter was demonstrated after Willstätter's improved filling had been tested: all that needed to be done was to change the filling routine and insert wire mesh between each layer. Everything else remained the same. Manufacture of the new filter unit began in January 1916.[72]

The French pads and muzzles succeeded each other rapidly, but minor changes only improved the quality marginally, and they remained unsatisfactory. Different alkalis were tried: thiosulphate, sodium ricinoleate, sodium sulphani-late, sodium phenate, and from late October onwards (possibly as a result of the experience gained in the Champagne battles) hexamine was added to the dipping solution. They retained the basic design of having numerous layers of muslin, up to thirty-two or so, which were dipped into different solutions and then formed into a thick pad covering mouth and nose. It was uncomfortable and visibility was extremely poor. Tambuté, an outfitter in civil life, designed in October a sort of muzzle or snout which extended over the chin, but it took a long time to put on and adjust. So Gravereaux, towards the end of 1915, devised a fabric mask, called the M2, which remained in use until the end of the war (see Fig. 7). The impregnants were unchanged and the muslin layers were retained. The novel features were the waterproof cover which extended to and surrounded the celluloid goggles and the better design of the shape. The M2 could be quickly put on, had a large surface area and imposed no constraint on respiration. The French always attached great importance to this last factor, but the price of comfort was safety. The mask was not gas tight, nor could it be further improved so that later in the war when new gases were introduced, it became useless; and lastly, unless it was frequently reimpregnated and kept dry it quickly deteriorated.[73]

To what extent were the aims of gas defence achieved? The question admits of a subjective as well as of an objective answer. Both merit attention because the answers were collated and provided the feedback which became the starting-point for many of the small improvements. Once the first fright was over, the troops took a great dislike to the mouthpads, and they were widely criticized. The British gas helmets were generally considered uncomfortable: most of the men I asked disliked them, but became resigned to wearing them. The French were so dissatisfied with their first anti-gas devices that they went so far as to compare them with the British 'Hypo' helmet; the latter was found to offer

Fig. 7. M2 mask worn by French colonial soldier, Somme, September 1916. (Imperial War Museum)

better protection (which was hardly surprising), but the soldiers thought it terribly uncomfortable and GQG did not pursue the matter.[74] Wearability played a big role in the French design: the M2 mask was intended to be comfortable, and the Americans later on aimed to make the wearing of their masks as natural as possible. I have read few complaints of the SBR and the German mask.

The scientific answer to the effectiveness of gas defences presupposes that comparisons be made on a uniform basis. That was rarely done, and the claims made by each belligerent on behalf of his mask are rarely dependable and sometimes border on the imaginary. Weight and volume are the only dependable facts, and must be assessed in conjunction with comfort and safety. The British Large Box Respirator weighed 2582 gr, the SBR 1475 gr, the German respirator 510 gr; in every case the weight of the canvas or metal holder is excluded. The volume of the filter mass in the SBR was 623 cc, that of the German container 239 cc, and of its French copy, the ARS model 1918, 202 cc. I have not been able to discover the weights of the various French pads and muzzles, but they are unlikely to have been heavier than the German mask.[75]

Safety means resistance to gas of a given concentration for a minimum amount of time. At this point, the lack of comprehensive statistics weakens the value of those that are available. For example, the first German filters when tested on man by the British, offered 'complete' protection against 400 ppm of chlorine and 200 ppm of phosgene, but we do not know how long it took the filter to 'break down'—after the wearer first detected gas. All one can do with the experimental data is to use it as an indicator of the progress made in the filter components. Thus the prototype Large Box Respirator broke down at 100 ppm of chlorine. Early in 1916 the resistance improved to 1000 ppm (about 1 gr/m^3). When the SBR was introduced, it broke down at 100 ppm of phosgene, but within months 1000 ppm was obtained and in 1917, 10,000 ppm was reached and held for 45–60 minutes.[76] The various numbers may be compared with those in column 1 of Table 4.2 above to show the improvement in safety. If one believes the French, the M2 mask performed even better for up to four or five hours. The continuing heavy French casualties whenever the Germans turned on their cylinders gave the lie to these claims, but the remarkable thing is that French officials clung to them for years.[77]

The greater safety provided by respirators was the outcome of an enormous amount of applied research, and the gradual raising of the quality of the materials used. The Germans devoted much attention to fabrics. Their first choice had been rubberized cotton, but shortages forced them to look for substitutes and eventually to adopt specially tanned leather. They were able, from the outset, to prepare a reactive charcoal from spruce and fir by the zinc chloride process. Bayer improved the technology further. By contrast the British had no supply problems with cotton and rubber solutions, but charcoal long presented difficulties. At first they relied on animal charcoal, then on wood, and finally on coconut shells as raw materials. Since the content of their filter was larger, the inferior quality of the charcoal was compensated by greater volume. The British (and to a lesser extent the Germans, the French, and the Americans) made a thorough study of the soda-lime-permanganate granules. Such compounds had been used for laboratory reactions for years, but now a hard, yet absorbent material was urgently needed as neutralizer and oxidizer. Lambert and Harrison took from August to December 1915 to produce a suitable granule from slaked lime, cement, and sodium permanganate. Further minor changed in the formulation which led to better quality were made after 1916.[78]

Some of the work was on the border line between systematic development and serendipity. The nose clip of the SBR, that small but essential component, went through several stages before returning to its original shape. The Germans added piperazine to the filter to neutralize such formaldehyde as was formed when hexamine reacted with phosgene, but the additive, intended to make things more comfortable for the wearer made little difference. All belligerents investigated anti-dimming compounds, without however discovering any that worked better than spittle, and that was of limited use! To finish with this catalogue of details, there were the French experiments on the reaction of a fatty substance with an acid: but what was effective in the toilet-article business, merely caused irritation to the wearer. The improvements were hardly worth the trouble, but the French persisted with the result and they changed their pads and muzzles five times between August 1915 and February 1916.[79]

Where the design was simple and the components interchangeable—the German replaceable screw-in filter is the best example— alterations could be easily accommodated. That was an important consideration to senior commanders who cared little for technical details and much for the best protection. This had interesting consequences. Ideally, defence should anticipate attack, in 1915–16 it followed—as soon as better mask designs became available they were rushed into production. Inevitably there were delays, but fortunately for the belligerents the gas cloud discharges were spasmodic, so that the weakness of the defences did not, except on 22 April, lead to disaster.

The German approach paid off in that they were the first to equip their armies with the final model. Issue to the troops began in mid or late September, probably in Flanders, and continued in Champagne during October. It was completed by December 1915 or January 1916 on the Western Front. The distribution of the new three-layer filter started at the end of January. Although the exchange of filters was simplicity itself and called for no extra training, the task took longer than expected, perhaps on account of the preparations for the battle of Verdun, and was only finished in April.[80]

The French faced problems of the same order of magnitude as the Germans, but their reaction was totally different: they did not hold with the Germans' methodical approach to distribution, and during 1915 they never completed an issue. As a result it was noted that in the long autumn battles, reinforcements occasionally carried masks different from those worn by the men they relieved. Only the infrequent use of gas clouds by the Germans saved the French from major casualities. In February 1916 the distribution of the M2 mask began and was completed by late spring.

For the British the task was simpler, there being fewer troops and the BEF was concentrated in a small area of northern France. The 'Hypo' helmets were issued in matter of four weeks and the job was completed on 6 July. The 'P' or 'Tube' helmet was introduced in September, but the distribution got caught up with the battle of Loos and was not finished until the first part of December.[81] It offered some protection against phosgene, but the 'PH' helmet, which was superior in this respect, only became available to the troops from February 1916 onwards, and the issue was not completed until about June of that year.

The facts and near-facts leave many questions unanswered. The most important is whether collaboration or mere copying would have speeded up the process of providing not merely some protection, but the best available protection. The British and the Germans thought along those lines: the former rejected the German mask because it was judged inadequate, the latter rejected the SBR for lack of rubber. These two were the best, why did the others not chose them? National dignity and foolish jingoism were the chief reasons. The French were kept informed of British research and were given specimens for trying out. They stubbornly clung to their designs and when they eventually, in 1918, introduced their own mask, the ARS, it was an improved copy of the German. At the very end of the war, when particulate clouds were tested for 1919, the ARS was found wanting and the French were once more offered the SBR with special filters. Weygand wrote back firmly that the French *Étoile Noire* filter gave complete protection against arsenical compounds.[82]

The French high command may well have been offended by the contempt with which the British and the Germans treated the M2, and thereby rendered more determined to promote French respirators among the less well-endowed Allies. The marketing drive ignored quality, but emphasized the beneficial effect on morale. The recipients, who lacked everything, were presumably pleased with second or third best. The Russians accepted what they were given or sold. Surplus 'Hypo' helmets and French snouts began to arrive during the winter of 1915–16. They were useless against weak concentrations of phosgene: the Russians knew this, but instead of adopting the 'PH' helmet when it became available, went ahead with their own designs. One, which was issued in April 1916 followed the French snout, but with fewer layers: the impregnating fluid contained hexamine and acetic acid—the latter presumably to break down hydrogen cyanide. Another design, ready several months later, used charcoal: the Koumant—Zelinski mask was a weird-looking device (see Fig. 8), but a fine specimen of rubber-moulding technology. It was not of much use owing to the brittleness of the charcoal, the rapid heat build-up, and resistance to breathing. By the time issue began in the second half of 1916, the western Allies were shipping hundreds of thousands of 'PH' helmets and M2 masks to the Russians, who were left to deal with all the difficulties caused by a multiplicity of types,

Fig. 8. Russian Koumant–Zelinski
mask: face piece of rubber.
The small box attached to
face piece holds charcoal.
Note stopper under box;
this was removed before use.
Issued from second half of
1916 onwards.
(exhibit, Imperial War Museum)

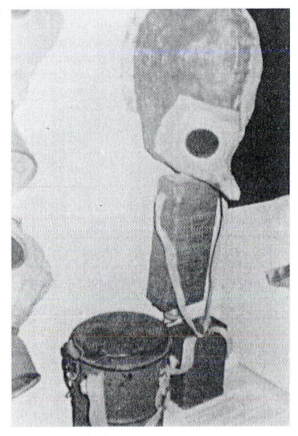

spares, and training instructions. Fortunately the gas war was virtually over
on the Eastern Front and the various anti-gas measures faded out during
1917.[83] That was the year the Italians discovered the failure of their respirator,
a copy of the M2 with twice the thickness of impregnated gauze, but without
hexamine in the dipping fluid. When the Austro-German forces used phosgene
at Caporetto in October, the Italians found that their mask left them
unprotected.[84] The shock of defeat helped to make the SBR acceptable. The
Americans, more practical than the Europeans, bought the SBR when their own
design failed under severe testing.

The story has run ahead of chronological order to show that false pride and
pig-headedness played a significant role in gas defence. By the end of 1915,
the basic design problems had been solved. But quality improvements and the
organization of production still had to be tackled, though even here considerable
practical experience was accumulating. Nevertheless, the second best, or even
worse, continued to be widely employed and caused avoidable casualties.

Throughout 1915 and for most of 1916, gas clouds dominated chemical warfare. The Germans sporadically employed tear-gas shell, which caused temporary inconvenience and, on at least one occasion, the capture of several thousand French prisoners who were led away, helplessly weeping.[85] But up to the end of 1915, chlorine was the chief weapon. At Ypres in April–May and on the Eastern Front, the Germans used about 1,200 t of gas. Their autumn operations on the western front consumed, in round numbers, a further 800 t, so that the year's total was of the order of 2,000 t. The British figure was around one-tenth of that, the French, nil.[86] The military–scientific effort which began on 22 April caused 20,000–30,000 casualties including killed, injured, and incapacitated soldiers taken prisoner. (The range is so wide because precise records were not kept.)

Some casualties could have been avoided by better masks, many more by better gas discipline and frequent practice. The British were aware of the role of training, but the stream of New Army men that poured into France in the summer and autumn overwhelmed the instructors. The facilities were ludicrously inadequate. For example Barley spent every day (except Mondays) from July onwards giving talks and demonstrations. He visited every unit of the 2nd Army, had practice trenches built, and installed his equipment. He must have been a familiar sight, sitting astride a chlorine cylinder, manipulating its valves, urging apprehensive soldiers to walk through the gas-filled trench and inhale whiffs of the stuff. Improvisation became routine, but was no substitute for systematic instruction which did not begin until January 1916 when Barley gave the first intensive course to three NCOs who then spread the message among the Divisions.[87]

The anxieties concerning phosgene resulted in the appointment of officers whose duties extended beyond training, to responsibility for anti-gas equipment and stores, to the issue of instructions or warnings and, not least, to chemical warfare intelligence generally. Three chemists, McCombie, Barley, and Hartley were promoted to the rank of captain and posted as Chemical Advisers to the 1st, 2nd, and 3rd Armies respectively in early summer. Hauptmann Braun carried out the same duties in the 6th German Army from October 1915 onwards.[88] I have searched the documents, but have not found particulars of officers who carried out similar work in the French armies.

Gas defence was more than the prompt distribution of pads, helmets, or respirators, the issue of circulars and of simple drill. It had to be seen to work, hence the care of gas casualties and the achievement of high recovery rates was not only common humanity, but a key factor in maintaining morale. Effective treatment demonstrated that the threat posed by the new weapon could be contained.

The symptoms of gas injury, were known and had been described in the literature of occupational diseases. But he dangers facing troops attacked with chlorine were of a different order of magnitude to those encountered by packers in a bleaching-powder factory. On the battlefield it was not possible to anticipate the duration of the cloud, nor to estimate its concentration, let alone to escape from it. These considerations, not the aetiology of the sickness, were the novel elements and determined its course. A few examples will illustrate the varied nature of the poisoning. Duisberg and Haber rode into the cloud and escaped, as we have seen, with slight inflammation of the lungs and a few days in bed. Lt. Kerpen, near the Hohenzollern Redoubt on 25 September, fell into a shell hole where the chlorine was especially dense, choked, and felt as if he had soap bubbles in his chest. They got him out, he spent weeks in hospital and convalescing, and was eventually invalided out of the army because he could not breathe deeply. The men in the photograph (Fig. 9) had been caught at 1930 on 1 May 1915 near Hill 60.[89] Of the 13 brought to the Casualty Clearing Station four died during the night and two in the morning, the others were *in extremis*. Later, with poetic licence, Wilfred Owen portrayed the sensation:

> Gas! Gas! Quick boys!—an ecstasy of fumbling
> Fitting the clumsy helmets just in time;
> But someone still was yelling out and stumbling
> And flound'ring like a man in fire or lime . . .
> As under a green sea, I saw him drowning. . . .
>
> And watch the white eyes writhing in his face,
> His hanging face, like a devil's sick of sin;
> If you could hear, at every jolt, the blood
> Come gargling from the froth corrupted lungs,
> Obscure as cancer, bitter as the cud . . . [90]

Fig. 9. British gas casualties: group of men severely gassed in Ypres sector on 1 May 1915—the photograph was taken the following morning. (Public Record Office)

The severity of the illness depended on the amount of the gas breathed in
and its concentration. Most people recovered quickly, but those badly gassed
went down within a few hours with severe inflammation of the lungs. The patient
coughed, retched, vomited, and these violent spasms aggravated the strain on
the heart which was being deprived of oxygen because of the inflammation of
the bronchi and air sacs. People seldom died as the clouds passed over, but
after three or four hours the sick reached a critical stage from which they
recovered after sleeping, or deteriorated further. In the latter event death within
twenty-four hours followed invariably and was due to heart failure caused by
pulmonary oedema, a drowning of the lungs in fluid released within them. The
inhalation of phosgene did not cause spasms and so was more insidious than
chlorine. Its inflammatory action was more localized and took a little longer
to develop; in all other respects it was more dangerous. The differences in the
initial stages of chlorine and phosgene poisoning were of considerable practical
importance and will be examined in their proper place in the next chapter.[91]

The circumstances of chemical warfare—the sporadic cloud-gas attacks
accompanied by hundreds of casualties—complicated the task of the medical
personnel. In the BEF sufficient clinical evidence was only becoming available
towards the end of 1915 and the pathology remained uncertain for another year.
The early handbooks were elementary—one learnt as one went along.[92] Rapid
evacuation, fresh air, and absolute calm were accepted as essential, but difficult
to implement because throughout 1915 the motor ambulance and the casualty
clearing system were still being developed. No attempt was made to separate
gas casualties from the other wounded, and the doctors, nurses, and auxiliaries
were at first unfamiliar with the details of treatment.[93] They hoped, somehow,
to give relief and allow the patient's body to recover from the inflammation
of the lungs. The Germans provided oxygen cylinders as early as April 1915,
and their VIIth Corps had issued small oxygen bottles to first-aid posts by
September, but the breathing appliances were still very crude and wasteful.
Venesection was practised by all the belligerents because it reduced the volume
of blood and so eased the work of the heart. The doctors experimented with
different drugs and argued with each other about the effects. Morphine was
widely employed in severe cases and at least alleviated the patient's suffering
in his final agony. Atropine to reduce spasm and the secretion of fluid from
the bronchial lining was in vogue during 1915–16. Sal ammoniac was often found
beneficial, but heart stimulants such as camphor and digitalin were not
considered particularly valuable. Since acid gases reduce the P_H of the blood,
attempts were made even in 1915 to raise alkalinity by administering sodium
lactate and other mild alkalis. These amateurish attempts were refined later,
but it is interesting to note that there was no therapeutic for inflammation caused
by gas (as distinct from bacteria or staphylococci) until the introduction of
cortisone in the 1950s. A recent article on phosgene poisoning, recommends
massive doses of cortisone and modern versions of First World War
medicines.[94] But for the gas victims of that conflict their best hope lay in

careful, intensive, and sympathetic nursing, and drugs were merely adjuncts of varying degrees of usefulness.

This chapter has been taken up with the Allied reaction to the events of 22 April. The variety of the response, from retaliation with gimmicks and with gas, to protection and treatment, sufficiently demonstrates the complex nature of the new weapon. At the opening of 1916, the cumulative experience showed that improvisation was no longer enough. On the technical level the scientists appeared to have learnt most – they were beginning to identify objectives and perceive the chemical means of implementing them. But on the military level, the approach remained pragmatic. Ideas emerged, were sometimes accepted and tried out, but there was no theory to underpin the tactical thinking of staffs. In short more questions were raised than answered: should gas clouds precede a major offensive or support a minor raid? Was the aim solely to harass and inflict maximum loss at minimum cost? Should the suitability of the terrain or the condition of the particular enemy formation govern the intensity and frequency of a gas-cylinder operation? To the cloud all targets were alike, it was therefore a general purpose weapon which inevitably entailed some wasteful application. The last consideration led to the question whether chemical shell, a specific weapon, should be taken seriously.

The Germans were most familiar with offensive chemical warfare, but had reached no consensus. At OHL, Bauer (supported by the experts) was for it, his chief, Falkenhayn, against it because of the danger of blow-back. That being so, why not develop gas shell? But the Germans were surprised when the French took the initiative with the 75 mm phosgene shell. What were they waiting for during the winter months, particularly as they were scathing about the low quality of the French anti-gas defences? Bauer and others blamed their seniors at OHL for missing many opportunities, but that was after the event and the collapse of 1918. They conveniently overlooked that they had not provided enough troops and cylinders to produce a cloud sufficiently large to open the front for a breakthrough and wide enough to minimize danger from the flanks. Falkenhayn's circular of 13 January 1916, probably drafted by Bauer or his assistant Geyer, listed the uses of clouds, hinted at some of the problems, but provided no guidance. Army and Corps staffs must have found the document confusing and its language commonplace. The statement that the enemy's respirators had been improved was bracketed with the recommendation to double the concentration to one large cylinder (i.e. 40 kg of gas) per metre of front.[95] In short, more of the mixture as before, no imagination, and no mention of gas shell.

The British attitude was different. The Cabinet endorsed retaliation and the War Office told the specialists to get on with it. After Loos the politicians lost interest, except Churchill: then, as later, he remained interested in chemical weapons and supported them. In October 1915 he urged the Dardanelles Committee to use gas at Gallipoli: he was humoured, a party was sent there, but the weather changed and the evacuation in December put an end to the plan.[96] At a less exalted level, Foulkes worked away improving the equipment and the training of his men. Little time was spent on tactical theories, but practical suggestions were quickly implemented. W. H. Livens, who was later to make a major contribution to gas warfare, adapted armoured flexible hose to novel purposes and designed four-way connections. The cumbersome parapet pipes were cut in half and the general housekeeping improved. Section officers were made responsible for discharge control which cut the risk of blow-back because the man on the spot was henceforth empowered to overrule commands from the rear. Finally anti-gas drill was formalized and schools for instructors, complete with staff and practice trenches, set up at the beginning of 1916.[97] These activities indicated a fierce determination to beat the Germans at their own game, but as we shall see, they came to fruition when the value of this particular mode of gas warfare began to be questioned.

Some of the French senior officers were eagerly pressing for action. Foch asked 'Les munitions nous les aurons. Les gaz les aurons nous?', but he didn't bother about the tedious details, notably protection against German gases. Although Joffre worried, his instructions of 26 December regarding the introduction of gas warnings did not extend to respirator drill. As to offence, the French at the end of the year were hoping to retaliate in February, though Soulié was overwhelmed with equipment shortages and the lack of properly trained troops.[98]

Among the belligerents there was an urgent need for fresh thinking on gas. Those who reflected on the progress made with respirators felt bound to conclude that chlorine was losing its military value.[99] What should take its place? Phosgene and chloropicrin were the obvious choices. In what form should they be delivered? The clouds were only one of several means, but at this stage of the war the potential of the gas shell was neither clearly nor widely appreciated. It would be wrong to speak of the winter months of 1915–16 as a turning-point in chemical warfare, it was only a pause in which defence was moving ahead. If this continued, there would soon be deadlock unless offence again progressed.

5

PHOSGENE

DURING 1916 the nature of chemical warfare changed gradually, but decisively—the gas shell came to replace the gas cloud. The complicated details form the theme of the following pages, but at the outset it may be useful to draw attention to the widening range of war gases which now came to include phosgene, trichloromethylchloroformate (called diphosgene by the Anglo-Americans), and chloropicrin. These substances were not newly discovered. Phosgene had been for many years a minor but valuable process chemical; diphosgene had first been described in 1840 and on half a dozen occasions subsequently, and its manufacture patented in Germany in 1900; chloropicrin had been prepared and frequently examined since 1840, the most recent occasion being 1914.[1] In short there was plenty of information in the public domain. The significance resided in their conspicuous use on the battlefield and the speed with which the belligerents were able to transform speciality products into tonnage chemicals. Thus, 1916 marked a distinct escalation in chemical warfare and produced evidence on the contemporary state of applied chemistry which governed the industry's ability to deliver chemical weapons.

The development of offensive materials reacted on defence and by increasing the strain heightened the psychological effect of gas which, in turn, had far reaching implications for systematic anti-gas training and on equipment design. Chlorine and tear gas are easy to identify and to guard against. Now there was greater variety but no foolproof means of detecting the danger. Instruments were crude and quickly damaged, animals had variable responses. Man's sense of smell was held to be the best safeguard, but the nose is fallible, its sensitivity is quickly blunted and powerfully influenced by imagination. Phosgene smells faintly of silage and, unlike chlorine, inhalation causes no spasm. It is therefore very difficult to distinguish between safe and lethal concentrations. But experience showed that smokers could identify traces of phosgene by its peculiar taste.[2] The penalty of ignorance was injury, so identification, response, precaution, and morale were links in a complex chain of discipline and safety measures to which all were made to conform.

The Germans never had any trouble making war gases, the French a good deal, the British (except for liquid chlorine) all the time. In this chapter, I intend to concentrate on the Allies, for manufacturing problems determined the course of their chemical warfare during 1916. Phosgene quickly became the centre of Anglo-French interest. Their gas experts were unfamiliar with it, but aware of its physical characteristics (see Chapter 4) determined on early practical tests which were held at Calais towards the end of June 1915 and demonstrated its potential for cylinder operations. Several weeks then passed while chemists, manufacturers, staff officers, and civil servants consulted and corresponded, but in August the decision was taken to order phosgene from the United Alkali Company (UAC) and de Laire. The former had made it to order before the war and now undertook to deliver a ton a day by the end of October; the latter owned a small plant at Calais and claimed he could supply at once, but haggled over the price. The optimists were in the ascendant and were confident that ample supplies would be available for 1916. When they did not materialize and UAC failed altogether to deliver the goods, there were complaints and recriminations.

The causes are of considerable interest. There were two ways of preparing phosgene. One, employed in laboratories and by occasional suppliers like UAC, consisted of reacting concentrated sulphuric acid with carbon tetrachloride. Since only half the chlorine contained in the carbon tetrachloride emerged as a constituent of phosgene, this route was obviously uneconomic. The other method was to pass approximately equal volumes of chlorine and carbon monoxide over charcoal which acts as catalyst. This was the process used by the Germans; its general outlines were known at the time, but the process details, which were all-important, were not accessible to the Allies. De Laire, however, asserted that he knew them, but that the terms of his licence did not allow him to disclose the information. It is probable that he had obtained it from the Germans via some intermediaries. At any rate the surviving documents, though extensive, shed no light on the legal background. Suffice it to say that he prepared almost pure carbon monoxide by burning special hydrogen-free coke in oxygen. His liquid chlorine was obtained from Castner-Kellner at Runcorn and the catalyst was animal charcoal. His plant was crude and labour-intensive. Nevertheless in the space of 23 months, ending in November, 1917, his average conversion efficiency, calculated on the chlorine intake, was 87 per cent. Poulenc Frères and Accumulateur Alcalin, who began making phosgene in 1916, had rather better designed plants, but a fractionally lower efficiency. UAC at Gateshead-on-Tyne and Widnes obtained carbon monoxide from producer gas, which yielded 30 per cent carbon monoxide, and used chlorine from their Weldon plants which yielded about 70 per cent Cl_2. Wood charcoal was the catalyst. The reaction of these impure materials produced phosgene which was so dilute that it could not be separated from the unreacted gases by refrigeration. Accordingly it had to be dissolved in tetrachloroethane and recovered by fractional distillation. The other British supplier, Electro-Bleach at Middlewich, obtained carbon monoxide by a different route, but without better overall results. Efficiencies varied considerably, the wartime average being 63 per cent, a figure which probably allowed for the chlorine content of the lost tetrachloroethane.[3]

The extraordinary thing about the story is not the initial failure, but that incompetent chemists and engineers were allowed to muddle on and indeed were encouraged instead of being sacked. Phosgene-making plant was ordered, arrived in bits and pieces after long delays, and was slowly installed at Gateshead, Widnes, and Middlewich. Production in the first half of 1916 was minuscule and during the second half at the rate of a few tons a week. By March 1917, the British companies' weekly capacity was 35 tons of phosgene, but in practice they averaged less than half that amount. The annual totals speak for themselves: 131 tons in 1916 and 561 tons the following year. De Laire also needed much prodding: he had promised to start deliveries to the British on 1 December 1915, but failed to do so. His excuse was that he did not have enough equipment and men to deliver phosgene to both allies. The British were upset, for their gas operations depended on phosgene, and they could not rely on Gateshead which started three months behind schedule and was often closed for repair. So the Ministry of Munitions hurriedly sent a chemist, A. T. de Mouilpied, to Calais to help organize the filling section. Some civilian workers followed him in January 1916, but he was unable to manage them and for several weeks they did no work and were frequently drunk. The situation was becoming intolerable. Foulkes stepped in, replaced de Mouilpied by a competent engineer, J. Kenner, and dispatched 200 of his Special Brigade men to Calais in March. The troubles at Gateshead and Calais strengthened de Laire's bargaining position and for many months he was ably supported by French officials who reasoned that if the British needed phosgene so badly, they would have to pay for it. The first negotiations took place in the closing months of 1915, but the evidence is too fragmentary to establish even the approximate price. Later agreements governed the price paid for de Laire's phosgene in 1916 and it is apparent that he had to concede a large reduction after mid 1916. The prices are compared in the following table with the payments made by the French Government to the two other suppliers. Both Governments undertook to supply liquid chlorine free at works and the 'rate of exchange' of chlorine to phosgene was therefore of some significance in the overall cost of phosgene.

The figures suggest that in the course of the year the French came to

Table 5.1. *Approximate Price paid per tonne for Phosgene by British and French Governments in 1916*[4]

Particulars	£/t	t of free Cl_2 supplied per t $COCl_2$ bought
British Govt./de Laire: Jan./Feb. 1916	47	2.0
British Govt./de Laire: June 1916	47	1.5
British Govt./de Laire: Sept. 1916	34	1.5
French Govt./Poulenc Frères: mid-1916	50	1.2
French Govt./Accumulateur Alcalin: end 1916	34	1.2

Note: On a molecular weight basis and ignoring all conversion losses, 0.7 t Cl_2 is required for 1 t $COCl_2$.

believe that the British were going to solve their production problems, and so they moderated their demands significantly. At the end of 1916 the Ministère de l'Armement paid as much as the Ministry of Munitions, but drove a harder bargain over the supply of free chlorine and so saved themselves some money. Nevertheless, the contracts were sufficiently profitable to cause de Laire and his competitors to install large phosgene-making capacity. By March 1917 the French companies were able to guarantee 50 t a week to the British Government alone. Later that year their output increased still further and their deliveries to the Ministry of Munitions rose from 1,389 t in 1916 to 2,773 in 1917.[5]

The chlorine—phosgene deals were by far the most important exchanges of their kind, indeed it is difficult to visualize Anglo-French chemical warfare operations without them. They illustrate the difficulties that can result from chemical engineering backwardness and management failures. Problems of a different nature also occurred on the other side. The Germans were not plagued by technological weaknesses, but they too failed to correct mistakes quickly, and in this instance the Allies were the beneficiaries.

Where the Allies used phosgene as shell filling, the Germans relied on diphosgene, code-named '*Grün Kreuz*' (green cross) or '*Perstoff*'. Their method of manufacture involved the triple chlorination of methyl chloroformate, an accelerator such as ultra-violet light, and apart from chlorine, methanol and phosgene.[6] The necessary process plant is substantial. At first sight diphosgene seems an unlikely poison 'gas' (see Table 4.1 for its characteristics), and its preparation is complicated. Hartley considered it to be the biggest mistake made by the German chemical warfare experts, but, in my opinion, he exaggerated.[7] It was not unreasonable for the Germans to adopt diphosgene when they decided on a filling for gas shell. They had plenty of electrolytic capacity for chlorine manufacture and the Bayer Co., which played a leading role in the first months of chemical warfare, had been supplying dichloromethyl chloroformate (K-*Stoff*) during 1915. In the following spring the Germans were in such a hurry that they did not carry out thorough shoots, and so failed to give due weight to the disadvantages of diphosgene in the field, in particular a lower toxicity than phosgene and slow evaporation. They were aware of these defects, but evidently deemed them of secondary importance compared to the ease and safety of filling shell, factors to which they attached prime, indeed excessive importance. With diphosgene there was no risk of vaporization in the shell which might disturb the ballistics, nor of leakage through the cement seal of the screwed shell head then used by the Germans. These considerations settled the matter: in April 1916, the factory at Leverkusen was instructed to start manufacture at once, and in September Hoechst also became a supplier.

It is nevertheless a remarkable fact that the Germans never changed their minds about diphosgene. The construction of refrigerated filling-plants, and the introduction of drawn shells virtually eliminated the danger of filling with phosgene. But the Germans retained diphosgene, indeed the capacity was enlarged and Leverkusen and Hoechst reached production peaks respectively in April and May 1918. Diphosgene was, next to mustard gas, their principal chemical shell-filling compound, and about 11,500 t were delivered during the war.[8] The episode remains inexplicable, for the Germans were relying on an inferior material which required three times as much chlorine as phosgene—a compound simpler to make and superior as a poison. They knew that their enemies, ever quick to copy them, did not, on this occasion, follow suit, a sure sign that they considered diphosgene second-best. Why did the Germans not test the one against the other and draw the consequence? Diphosgene was not the only instance of insufficient testing and of administrative inflexibility. The results were to impair the effectiveness of their chemical warfare and considerably diminish the Allied gas casualties.

Chloropicrin, the third of the new chemical warfare materials was adopted by all the belligerents, but only the British used it extensively for shell filling. Its preparation was simple: bleaching powder was dissolved in water and mixed with picric acid, also dissolved in water, in enamelled or lead-lined iron vessels. The reaction takes about two hours, steam is then blown into the vessel, chloropicrin forms and is separated from the water. The end-product is a liquid, not a gas (see Table 4.1) and is suitable as a filling for shell. Chloropicrin is a tear gas rather than a poison gas and attracted attention in Britain as early as June 1915 when Jackson was told about it. Then there were the usual delays before Lever Bros. were asked to investigate it in the autumn. Their research confirmed that chloropicrin was easy to make but that the liquid by-products—a mixture of phenol and bleach liquor—polluted streams and waterways. For this reason Lever Bros. declared themselves unable to produce it and their only remaining connection with the compound was its codename *PS*, for Port Sunlight. Gen. Butler, the Master Gunner of the 1st Army, wanted it for shell filling and Foulkes hoped to employ it for his cylinder operations.[9] But there were no supplies. The Russians, though, were able to make a little and surprised the Germans with it. They retaliated swiftly and by summer 1916, 'Klop' as they called it, was supplied by Bayer for shell filling. In Britain meanwhile, the Ministry of Munitions got a firm to put up a pilot plant, but not until April 1916 was the decision taken to build a works for making 40 tons a week at Cleckheaton. A second works, at Burslem, produced its first batch two months later. It had taken just a year from the initial proposal to the first delivery, though the supply of high-grade picric acid had still not been assured.[10] *PS* was, next to chlorine, the principal British contribution to chemical warfare. Altogether about 8,000 tons were manufactured: as a cylinder filling, with chlorine as propellant, it proved useless, but as a shell filling it began to reach the front in the latter part of 1916.

Volumes X and XI of *Der Weltkrieg* are silent on the use of gas and, in the absence of official German information, it is necessary to rely on other sources which are not only incomplete, but also sometimes inconsistent. Thus, owing to the lack of records, the exact number of German cylinder operations is not known but is unlikely to have exceeded twenty during 1916. The method and pattern differed from those of the previous year. The Germans began by using a 80:20 mixture of chlorine and phosgene, but changed the ratio to 50:50. In the summer the arrangement of the cylinders was altered by bunching them in batteries of up to twelve between traverses and increasing the volume by packing up to 250 small cylinders (each holding 20 kg Cl_2) along 100m of front: that yielded a maximum capacity of 50t/km, well above the level of 1915. The Germans also adopted the practice of fully opening the cylinders at short intervals. The effect of these measures was to create and maintain a dense cloud and the resultant high concentrations inflicted heavier casualties.[11]

The German cloud-gas attacks always took place in quiet sectors. Their new tactics called for immense preparations and the procedure never varied. The Gaspioniere and their bulky equipment were ordered to proceed to a particular area where they dug in the cylinders and waited for suitable weather. Their activities attracted attention and what the Allies did not observe themselves they got from prisoners and deserters. Thus they were always forewarned and on the alert when the Germans released gas. The Pioniere then had to remove their paraphernalia under retaliatory shelling, and eventually re-formed at base, awaiting fresh orders. If their operations are analysed, it is seen that the Germans took on each enemy in turn. The first gas cloud of the year was on 21 February and was directed against the French along a front of 7 km from Fouquescourt to Lihons south of the Somme. It was one of the largest operations on the Western Front and the three short waves propelled by a steady easterly wind of 5–6 m/sec caused many casualties.[12] The Germans then moved north and late in April the British suffered three attacks, two of them in the area between Hulluch and Loos. It was the turn of the French in May (two gas clouds) and of the British once more in June. Some Pioniere were next ordered to the Isonzo Front, to reinforce the Austrian specialists who were installing cylinders at San Michele di Carso. They released gas on 29 June, caused some Italian casualties, but suffered injury themselves when the cloud moved back over their lines. In the second half of the year the Germans were busy on the Eastern Front, where they carried out seven or eight cloud-gas attacks between July and October, east of Vilna, in northern Poland, and finally near Riga.[13] They did not have enough gas troops to keep up the pressure on both fronts, and there was only a single operation in the west, on August 8 at Wieltje near Ypres. It was to be the last cloud-gas discharge against the British, and like the first some fifteen months earlier in the same sector, caused considerable casualties.[14]

The events at Hulluch on 27 and 29 April are of particular interest for the German documents have survived and supplement the detailed British records, so that the complete story is available.[15] Earlier in the month the Germans had installed around 7,400 cylinders, along a front of 3 km from Cité St Elie southwards to Loos (see Map 3). The ground is flat, the terrain featureless, and the trenches which were close at this point had been left undisturbed since the previous October. The preparations were meticulous, and on the 27 at 0500 British time the first cloud was released from 3,800 cylinders near St Elie and at Loos, at a rate of about 50 t/km. The wind blew from the north-east at 1.4 to 2.2 m/sec depending on the location, and the gas soon reached the British trenches. A second cloud followed at 0700, and in its wake the Bavarians carried out their raid. The British casualties from gas totalled 486, of whom 135 died. The operation was repeated two days later, this time in the centre of the line west of Hulluch. The dawn was hazy and warm, and the wind at 0545 was gentle, but variable. About 3,600 cylinders were opened (say 48 t/km) and the cloud moved slowly at 1.0–1.2 m/sec towards the British lines. Five minutes later the wind dropped, then turned, and the chlorine – phosgene mixture flowed over the German front and support lines. There was much confusion and even panic when the valves were not or could not be closed quickly, so that perversely the gas became denser as it blew back over the Bavarians. Just a little north, at the Hohenzollern Redoubt, the Germans also released gas, but there the cloud travelled steadily at 2.0–2.4 m/sec and it was the British who suffered casualties—almost 800 men, of whom a quarter died.

Later, when the crisis was over, and the German chemical observers compared notes they agreed that thick ground mist between Loos and Hulluch had formed a dense cold layer which stopped the gas. This meteorological phenomenon was not the complete explanation and the 1,500 German casualties (some fatal, many serious) bore witness to serious failures of equipment and organization. The general staff ordered an enquiry. It was found that the men of the 1st Bavarian Division (which suffered most severely) had far too many masks in poor condition or damaged. Even when the masks were in perfect order, the concentration of the gas was, in many places, so high that the filter could not cope, broke down, and allowed the gas to penetrate the mask. The CO of Pionier Rgt. 36 was also at fault. A few days previously he and some of his men had taken part in a demonstration of a respirator with a redesigned face line. It had worked faultlessly in a dense cloud containing 75 per cent phosgene. On returning to Hulluch the new masks were issued to all the gas troops and in the hurry of the final preparations no one bothered to check the exact fit. To cap it all the specialists neglected to order the evacuation of the first line. Within about three weeks there was another incident in Champagne.[16]

These blow-backs and accidents were most serious and worse than being hit by one's own artillery—for the gunners could be stopped, but the cloud was beyond control. The findings of the official German enquiry caused great concern: the injury to the troops, the effect on morale, the casualties among the specialists, were less readily tolerated in 1916 than a year earlier in Poland. Infantry officers were openly voicing their dislike of cylinder operations and their opposition put a stop to the use of trench mortars firing gas bombs.[17] OHL was forced to take notice: the General Staff did not disband Peterson's command, but it lost interest in the Gaspioniere. Army commanders took the hint and, except in the east, henceforth rarely asked for gas troops. The tally in the west was indeed unimpressive. The eight operations had yielded no ground and, at considerable cost to the Germans, had injured or killed fewer than 5,000 British and French. In the terrible year of Verdun and the Somme such chemical diversions were clearly irrelevant. But while the Germans were rapidly becoming disenchanted with gas clouds, the British were developing a growing enthusiasm for this mode of warfare.

The Allies' intention to fight a vigorous and effective gas war were beset by so many obstacles, none of them caused by the enemy, that their plans were frustrated and their operations made little impact on the Germans. The supply of gas, as we saw, imposed unexpected delays. In Britain there was also initially a lack of cylinders, for the Admiralty proposed to use them for filling captive balloons, and at the beginning of 1916 commandeered all stocks at the makers. When that problem had been sorted out and deliveries resumed, the Ministry of Munitions discovered that 9,000 cylinders were stocked at Runcorn, but could not be filled until valves had been found. That particular difficulty was resolved in March and chlorine deliveries to France increased rapidly. By the end of June 17,000 cylinders, each holding about 30kg gas had been dispatched and within four to five weeks another 75,000 followed. Roughly half were sent empty for filling at Calais. An elaborate routine was established for transport to France and for the return of the empties to Hanley where a special cleaning- and filling-station was being established. As far back as the previous autumn (before the Germans had made up their minds) the decision was taken to use a 50:50 chlorine:phosgene mixture, code-named 'White Star'. It remained the chief cylinder filling throughout the war, but until March 1916 supplies were insufficient even for training purposes.[18]

Gas troops without gas were under-employed and invited ridicule, and their commanders were often at loggerheads with the Staff. In short, the beginning of 1916 was distinctly inauspicious, but Haig decided to raise the special companies to Brigade strength and received the necessary War Office authority on 25 January. Brigadier H. T. Thuillier, RE, was appointed Director of Gas Services (DGS) and given two assistants, Foulkes for offensive operations, and S. L. Cummins, RAMC, for anti-gas measures.[19] Thuillier, a quiet, reflective man, was well liked. He spent much of his time creating and supervising the development of gas defences and smoothing over the continual friction between GHQ, the Ministry of Munitions, and the War Office. He did not get on with Foulkes and, operationally, left him a free hand. Foulkes played a big role in British chemical warfare. His reminiscences *'Gas!'—The Story of the Special Brigade*, which appeared in 1934, were written in the style of the *Boys' Own Paper*, and were an odd mixture of historical confusion and technical precision; they showed no false modesty. He was brave, thorough, convinced of the usefulness of gas warfare, and absolutely determined to see the Special Brigade play a major role in the big summer offensive. Just the man for the job. He raged over the failure of White Star deliveries, and his intervention at Calais and treatment of de Mouilpied made him many enemies in London. But he did not care so long as his men got what they needed.[20]

In January, the four special companies were withdrawn for training to Helfaut. Drafts from home and volunteers from France joined the veterans of 1915 and by about May, the Special Brigade numbered around 5,500 officers and men. Most were destined for cylinder operations, but Major G. P. Pollitt was put in command of the gas-mortar companies and Lt. W. H. Livens was in charge of flame-throwers. A detachment of 200 men was working in de Laire's factory, filling and dispatching White Star cylinders.

The preparations for the Somme dominated British activities throughout spring. To Foulkes's chagrin, Haig and Rawlinson, who commanded the 4th Army, envisioned a minor part for gas, principally to distract the enemy during the run up to the battle and later to create diversions in quiet sectors. Foulkes, who had planned to release large clouds in the manner of the Germans the year before, had to scale down his operations. Having committed himself to the new tactics, he sought to justify them and henceforth claimed that they had been successful. Every favourable observation, every intelligence report, every POW statement, was used to magnify the work of the Special Brigade. But when the official history appeared, all its efforts rated only a few lines. GHQ did, for a time, in late summer, loyally support Foulkes and reminded the 1st, 2nd, and 3rd Armies (which were not involved in the battle) that 'there was no better means of causing casualties to German reserves' than by subjecting them to gas clouds from stocks which were now ample. However, few Corps and Divisional commanders, to whom the details were delegated, took the hint and acted vigorously.[21]

For most of May and June the men of the Special Brigade assisted by hundreds of infantry were busily 'carrying in'. The new tactics led to the installation of 24,000 cylinders at scores of points along the line from Maricourt near the Somme, then the junction with the French, to Ypres. The first British cloud gas operation since January took place on 24 June, north of Beaumont Hamel. It was quickly followed by many others, including a large one at Monchy-au-Bois, chiefly in the open, gently rolling downland between Arras and the Ancre river. During the last week of June about 13,000 cylinders, approximately 400 t of White Star, were discharged. The battle began on 1 July, and the diversionary gas attacks, often followed by raiding parties, were transferred elsewhere, to Arras, around Armentières, and to the sector between Loos and the canal at La Bassée. Between 11 July and 31 August, twenty separate operations were launched; then the frequency increased, but the scale diminished except for occasional major events; for example on 30 August at Monchy (37 t), and on 5 October at Hulluch and Nieuport which required 75 and 54 t respectively. To the end of November there were altogether 110 operations which called for 38,600 cylinders, equivalent to about 1,160 t of gas. Allowing for the three big clouds in August and October, that gives an average of 9 t of gas for each operation.[22] Table 5.2 shows the variable pattern of the attacks and indicates the peak reached just before the offensive.

Table 5.2. *British Gas Cylinder Operations, June to November 1916*[23]

Month	Cylinders	Weight of gas in t^*
June	13,260	398
July	4,890	147
August	4,950	149
September	3,240	97
October	8,520	256
November	3,720	112
Total for period	38,580	1,159
Total for year 1916	40,200	1,206

* Assuming 30 kg gas per cylinder.

The Germans, releasing large clouds on a front of several kilometres, caused a few thousand casualties. There was no reason to believe that the British attacks, each of them tiny compared with the German effort, would inflict serious losses on the enemy. But Foulkes did. The summer and autumn marked the high point of British cylinder operations, and even after the Somme battles were over they continued, and were resumed—though on a small scale—in February and March 1917. The dispersal and frequency of British operations along the entire front meant that few soldiers in the BEF were unacquainted with the work of the Special Brigade. Sassoon noticed the cylinders in June in his sector of the Somme, and a few months later Manning's anti-hero, Bourne, discovered that carrying cylinders between Mazingarbe and Vermelles was excessively hard work.[24] Considered purely as a public relations exercise, Foulkes had been successful. But battalion commanders whose men were injured by German artillery fire, which began as soon as the clouds were spotted, took a different view. The Brigade itself suffered heavily during July, 82 being killed by shell fire, 57 by gas, and 601 injured.[25]

Cost-effectiveness calculations were not made in those days, but there were critics, who thought it absurd that so many people should be employed, even in war, to such little purpose as carrying cylinders into the trenches, opening them, carrying them back to lorry pick-up points, and repeating the cycle. Livens was one of the critics and even before he went to France in August 1915 he had been toying with the idea of thin-walled gas-bombs projected from tubes. But he became involved with flame-throwers and had no time for experiments. In 1916 he altered his first concept and designed a device which could be manhandled in all weathers in a narrow trench. It would be dug in a short distance behind the first line. A salvo would be fired remotely and the projectiles would create a pool of gas in the enemy positions. There would be a substantial manpower saving compared with cylinders. Livens made his first tests in July on the Somme. He employed drums filled with oil and the results were spectacular, but unsatisfactory. He altered the drums to increase the ratio of contents to total weight and increased the range to 350 yards. His improved projectiles, containing chlorine, were used in the capture of Thiépval on 26 September—an important date in the technical history of warfare, for a few tanks also made their appearance. On the next occasion, at the capture of Beaumont Hamel on 13 November, Liven's 86 gas projectiles carried altogether one ton of chlorine.[26] Cloud gas would have been useless in the two battles. The British were left in possession and counted several hundred gas casualties, visible proof of the effectiveness of high concentrations and surprise on a well-trained and well-protected enemy. Livens's ingenuity had produced a novel chemical weapon which could be safely used by one side while seriously harassing the other.

Neither ambitiousness, nor perseverance, let alone personal initiative, characterized the French Compagnies Z under Soulié's command. GQG might advise, recommend, and encourage, but few senior officers at Army or Corps level took chemical warfare seriously. How did this come about? It is likely, but can only be confirmed in one instance, that some projected attacks were vetoed because of possible danger to French civilians in German-held territory. French farmers were still working their fields close to the front in quiet sectors such as the Somme or the Aisne in the first half of 1916.[27] But the prime cause, for which there is supporting evidence, was the lack of chlorine. The French were building electrolytic plants, but for most of the year they were dependent on British supplies. The situation was no better for phosgene. Joffre had asked Thomas on 18 December 1915 to fill 10 per cent of all cylinders with phosgene from that date onwards, but the directive could not be implemented for another ten months because the available supplies (principally from Calais) were earmarked for the British and the shell-filling programme.[28]

The scale of the French cylinder operations was small: the first one north of Reims, on 14 February, used up 1,300–1,400 cylinders and another, east of Reims, in June, fewer than 1,000. Even so, Soulié's men—of whom there were about 1,600 at mid-year—were stretched to the limit. The purpose of their work remains unclear, for no attempt was made by the infantry to follow up with raids let alone a major attack. The soldiers waited apprehensively for the German artillery fire which would follow the opening of the cylinders and hoped that retaliation would soon stop. There were also the usual blow-backs, a particularly bad one occurring early in July, south of the Somme: the French reported 204 gas casualties, six of them fatal. The Germans never even mentioned the incident.[29]

In the second half of the year there were fewer, but apparently larger, gas clouds. The supply situation was improving, but such had been the effect of Verdun on French morale that many Divisional commanders avoided provoking the German artillery unnecessarily. It is claimed that the French carried out twenty cloud-gas attacks, but I have only been able to trace half that number. Senator Cazeneuve and Deputé Laval, who took a spasmodic interest in chemical warfare, were told by Gen. Ozil that up to the end of January 1917, almost 3,000 t of gas had been discharged from 70,000 cylinders. But he offered no other quantitative details beyond mentioning that on 5 December, 1916, 220 t had been released: he failed to give the location, nor did the Germans report it.[30] We may be sure that if the Compagnies Z had achieved anything, the official historians would have reported it and the archives yielded the evidence. But there are no complete records and very few clues, except that the number of gas troops was not increased during the year—a sure sign of indifference at GQG.

The other belligerents had even less to show. The Italian front offered few suitable sites, and the prevailing winds were from the north or east. The Russians were reported to be using cloud gas on two occasions in October 1916, once in January 1917, and once again two months later. The details are not known to me, but supply constraints are likely to have handicapped the Russian gas troops.[31]

As 1916 waned, so did interest in cloud gas, except among the British, and even in that quarter there were growing doubts. But Foulkes's stubbornness was not grounded in stupidity: if you were committed to chemical warfare and you had no shells, you might as well continue with cylinders and seek to improve techniques. So 1917 was to witness British technical refinements, while the other belligerents developed gas shells which became the dominant chemical weapons in the last eighteen months of the war.

The introduction of lethal gas shells is rightly considered a turning-point in chemical warfare, because it added two new features: control instead of dependence on the vagaries of wind and weather, and choice of gases for particular targets instead of the indiscriminate cloud. The development has been credited to the French, but it did not take the Germans entirely unawares. Their reaction was so prompt that one suspects they too had been working along similar lines. Hanslian asserted that the French fired phosgene-filled shell at Verdun on 21 February 1916, at night; they also used HE and tear gas so that the Germans were not always aware of the exact nature of the gases employed. Although he gave no source, his story was accepted and repeated. But Vinet, a well-informed French gas specialist, had previously written that the first occasion was in March and the targets of the French artillery were the German positions in the Woëvre plain, east of Verdun. The Corps commander was Deimling (who had supervised the first cylinder installations around Ypres the year before), and, according to Vinet, he complained to Haber 'that in reply to the terrible French shell there was only available shell filled with Eau de Cologne.' Vinet and Hartley talked to Haber, who certainly knew the facts, in 1920 and 1921 respectively, two to three years before the publication of

Hanslian's book. Neither Vinet nor Haber ever went into details, and with good reason, for the first use of gas shell was a breach of the Hague Convention. To dmit responsibility for the introduction would have been difficult to justify in 1916 or to explain away in the 1920s. Hartley's claim that the French shells inflicted 'severe casualties' on the Germans cannot be confirmed, for the French records are unenlightening on this point, and *Der Weltkrieg* has nothing to say.[32]

I believe the circumstances were as follows: we have seen in the previous Chapter that the French carried out trial shoots with toxic shell at Satory in December 1915. They were unsatisfactory and the resulting arguments were going to be settled by further shoots on 19 and 21 February: on the first occasion no animal was killed, on the second about half of them died.[33] By then, small lots of phosgene shell had been issued, presumably for trying out on active service. The outbreak of violent fighting at Verdun quickly exhausted the stocks of conventional ammunition, and the experimental shells were fired—in February or March, the precise date does not matter—before formal authority had been given. The French used the 75 mm gun: its quick firing-action was theoretically an advantage, but in practice it was not the best weapon for gas because the shell has a high residual speed, a flat trajectory, and a negligible carrying capacity. The first meant the shell embedded itself before detonation, thus wasting gas, the second that reverse slopes were not accessible, the third that only 0.600–0.650 kg of phosgene was carried so that heavy shelling was essential to achieve a lethal effect.[34]

The Germans got Green Cross (which denoted diphosgene) shell so quickly to the front, that I think they had made their choice and carried out static tests before the French fired their shells. Large production orders were placed with Bayer in April and the decision taken to use 77 mm shell, which carried only a little more than the French 75, but was of monobloc construction, which made for easy filling, and was in stock.[35] Systematic test shoots did not take place at the time, for the Germans wanted to employ Green Cross at once on a massive scale. An ambitious plan has survived, undated but probably made in March or April, for firing 120,000 Green Cross shell from light howitzers together with 50,000 HE shell in the area Avocourt-Côte 304–Pont des Enfants on the left bank of the Meuse below Verdun. Bauer's hand and Haber's advice were at work, for the large use of gas (say 250 t) and the minor role assigned to HE presaged later saturation shoots designed to overwhelm enemy machine gunners and field artillery just before the infantry went in. But on this occasion the gas shells were not available and the capture of Avocourt (end of March) and of Côte 304 (beginning of May) was preceded by conventional artillery barrages.[36]

Initially the German gas shoots were on a limited scale and took place at long intervals. According to a French source and to Hanslian the first German use of toxic shell on the Western Front took place in the area of Douaumont on 9 March, the second in the night of 4–5 April, the third on 7 May near Tavannes (13,800 shells), the fourth in the night of 19–20 May at Chattancourt (13,000 shells). Hanslian mentions that 116,000 Green Cross shells were fired in the night of 22–3 June just before the assault on Thiaumont and Souville which marked the climax of the battle for Verdun. The concentration was too high for the French masks, they broke down, and the French artillery which had been the principal target fell silent. The Germans advanced, seized their first objectives, but were unable to exploit their success for lack of reserves. In the context of gas it was second Ypres again. They tried once more towards Souville, on 9–10 July, and this time expended 63,000 gas shells. But the French gunners had been issued with the M2 mask and were not incapacitated; they manned their guns and halted the last major German attack on Verdun.[37]

By then interest was shifting to the Somme where the French again took the initiative. Between 27 June and 6 July they fired an estimated 30,000 shells from 155 mm guns. They were, at this time, relying mainly on shell filled with hydrogen cyanide and additives to weigh down this light gas. The French were enthusiastic about it, and even Thuillier, usually level-headed, caught their optimism and declared that they were 'using Vincennite shells in quantity and with great effect . . . [and considered the gas] to be the most effective of chemical shell fillings.' But Hartley's notes show that the British discounted German prisoners' stories of gas casualties inflicted by Vincennite.[38] It is certain that the Germans were not seriously bothered by this gas.

They too fired toxic gas on the Somme, the British being the chief targets. There were at least a dozen bombardments during July, four occasions in August and five in September, and Green Cross caused altogether 2,800 casualties. Then the Germans slowed down and the British were issued with the new respirator. In the last three months of the year, thirteen gas shellings were recorded which resulted in 1,300 casualties.[39]

The increasing intensity of German gas bombardments, although the frequency remained low, reflected the gradual change in their tactics. Initially the Germans had much trouble with shell filling. Their first installation at Mancieulles, east of Verdun, though well located, was extremely crude. But they were adept at organizing and co-ordinating production, transport, filling, and dispatch to the front and from June onwards the supply position improved. In the second place they had only one toxic gas—diphosgene—which was not an all-round chemical weapon. Since the essence of artillery warfare was flexibility combined with specificity, the Germans were handicapped at this stage by lack of choice. The introduction of mustard gas and arsenical compounds in mid-1917 was therefore, for them, the ulimate development of chemical warfare. Finally, and most important, it was necessary to convince the artillery of the usefulness of gas shell. This was difficult and took longer than expected. Here was a technical innovation for which there was no precedent and which called for learning by experience and new procedures from people with a conventional and conservative attitude to warfare. The first known German gas-shell instructions are dated 6 August 1915. They applied to tear gases, recommended their use when there was little wind and high humidity, advised against ranging with gas and allowed a target width of 150 m per battery. Even then artillery staffs were told that results could only be achieved by the expenditure of a considerable number of shell. However the details show that the numbers were extremely modest: 'area targets', e.g. trenches and assembly points, required 2,660 shells/km^2 and 'specific targets', such as battery emplacements, 3,200 shells/km^2. In order to compare these figures with gas clouds and with later gas shoots it is necessary to assume that only heavy howitzers firing 150 mm shell carrying 6 kg of Green Cross would be used. On that basis, which is favourable to the shell, the numbers represent 16 and 19 t respectively, distributed evenly over 1 km^2. These concentrations were much too low to cause casualties. The Germans realized this after they had appointed special gas-shell advisers to Army artillery staffs. Their gunners, if they followed instructions, were generally wasting Green Cross shells, but the experts eventually made their influence felt, especially on the Somme, and the British losses testified to the effectiveness of higher concentrations. By the end of 1916 the Germans had learnt enough to change their tactics and new top-secret instructions were issued in mid February 1917.[40] They spelt out the most favourable atmospheric conditions (wind speed not above 1.5 m/sec), mentioned that lower concentrations were obtained with shell than with cloud and stressed the importance of 'nourishing' the target by slow fire over a period of several hours. Above all the instructions recognized the need for much greater expenditure of shell. Area shoots called for a mixture of 21,000 light, medium, and heavy shells per km^2, fired at varying tempos for six to eight hours. This was equivalent to 42 t of Green Cross distributed over 1 km^2—a lesser concentration than the dense clouds of 1916, but sufficient to force the enemy to wear masks for hours on end.

It is likely that the French gunners taught the Germans some valuable lessons, for they aimed at battery positions and shelled them methodically at a slow, but steady rate, so as to keep the enemy artillery 'neutralized' for many hours. They were, however, unable to apply these tactics for lack of gas shells until the autumn of 1916. The first gas bombardment of this kind occurred on the Somme at Pressoire in the night of 9–10 October when they fired 4,000 75 mm and 4,400 heavier shells on a few German batteries. Later that month, just before the reoccupation of Fort Douaumont, they carried out two bombardments— spread over 38 hours altogether—on its entrance which received 3,000 155 mm shell.[41] Slow fire on individual targets made good sense, but the French (unlike the Germans who copied them) threw away the advantage by filling shell with hydrogen cyanide which was innocuous at the concentrations they achieved.

The British hardly concerned themselves with gas shell for the Ministry of Munitions was unable to supply it. The Ministry could be excused, for the War Office did not formulate precise requirements until 5 February 1916 and another month passed before the Government formally authorized the construction of a filling plant. Then there was uncertainty over the filling: phosgene or rather White Star was preferred, but unobtainable at the time, whereas the Admiralty could quickly supply Jellite (see p. 63) for which it had no use and which was indeed useless. Not that it really mattered, for there were delays over the drawings and specifications of the chemical shell case, of which 35,000 a week were to be supplied, but were not available. GHQ was unable to make up its mind about quantities until mid May and only asked London for permission to retaliate with Jellite on 17 July. Permission was obtained ten days later and gas shells apparently filled with White Star were used for the first time at the battle of Flers between 13 and 15 September.[42] For the remainder of the year few gas shells were fired by the Royal Artillery. No trial shoots were organized and the artillery staffs were indifferent. Crossley concluded his report to Jackson: 'I could not help feeling that the artillery are not in reality interested in the subject of gas shells or their possible utility.'[43]

The introduction of toxic gas shells was a breach of the Hague Convention. Within a few months it had been accepted by all the belligerents. Supply constraints and ignorance, not moral scruples, delayed or prevented the use of shells. The organization of supply will occupy us in the next chapter; here it is only necessary to draw attention to the negligible role that gas shells played in the intensive fighting of 1916. According to Horne, the French and the Germans used altogether 37 million shells at Verdun between 21 February and 15 July.[44] Less than one per cent were filled with chemicals and, by comparison with conventional weapons, they caused negligible losses. In their preparations for the Somme between 27 June and 6 July, the French fired 1.7 million rounds of which 30,000 were filled with gas. The British used 410,000 HE and 9,000 gas shells to capture Flers.[45] The chemical war had indeed taken a new turn, but its significance would not become apparent for another year.

Poison gas was used more often in 1916 than in 1915 and the casualties were much higher despite the general issue of pads or masks. Nevertheless, the official line was that gas casualties occurred by mischance or alternatively were caused by failure to follow instructions and warnings—in short, the careless soldier put his life at risk. It was a good approach, for it strengthened gas discipline while rejecting any suggestion that the masks might be to blame. But the truth was that the masks were unsatisfactory and much research and development was devoted to their improvement.

The German respirator was given a new and supposedly better face line and a coiled wire frame pressed the fabric face-piece tightly against the cheeks and thus stopped gas from entering. The issue of the three-layer filter (which replaced the single-layer device distributed the previous autumn) was completed in April. At about the same time the Germans took several practical steps which showed that they were aware, months before Livens launched his projectiles, of the danger of a surprise gas attack. Accordingly the face-piece and filter unit were, henceforth, issued screwed together, ready for action. A canister, made of corrugated metal was provided and was so ingeniously designed that the mask was always carried at the ready, but did not chafe or become twisted in its special container. That did not exhaust German inventiveness and during June 1916 the composition of the filter was once again changed to permit easier breathing. The men were taught that the basic design was so good that it called for no change, and that the various improvements in no way altered the personal link between the soldier and his gas mask.[46]

The British respirator went through an entirely different evolutionary process of which I described the beginning in the previous Chapter. The year opened with the 'P' helmet in general use, but from late January 1916 onwards, the 'PH' helmet began to appear in France. For most British soldiers it remained the only protection until autumn. Its peculiar smell, bearable but uncomfortable, remained for many one of the indelible memories of the Somme. The rash and the untrained were frightened by it, thought gas was coming through, panicked, tore off their helmets, and became casualties. The disciplined majority, aware that the odour was innocuous (caused by the reaction of sodium phenate with chlorine), put up with it and came to no harm. Visibility was poor and the provision of special goggles—hence 'PHG' helmet—made things worse. In the heavy November rains the helmets became filthy, soggy, and, as one eye-witness pointed out, 'probably quite useless'.[47] It was known, though for obvious reasons not spread about, that the PH helmet would not stop chloropicrin; fortunately the Germans did not think much of Klop and so did not employ it widely in 1916.[48]

The distribution of the Large Box Respirator started during February and continued until June. The cumbersome and heavy appliance was both an experiment that failed and a digression which diverted energies from the Small Box Respirator (SBR).[49] It is interesting that none of the primary sources consulted by me explain why it took more than a year after the first military use of chlorine to devise, test, and approve the SBR. The responsibility for the delays must be shared by frequent minor design changes, bureaucratic incompetence, and excessive caution. At any rate the prototype was at last ready in May 1916 and at the end of the month a few pre-production models were sent to France for comparison with the German respirator. The SBR, designed and developed by Harrison and his assistants at the RAMC, Millbank and at the Boots factory in Nottingham, was a complex piece of equipment consisting of almost twenty components, some of which required complicated manufacturing operations with special materials. But it was, without doubt, the best respirator then available and the long gestation period was followed by immediate acceptance. The first order for 0.1 million was placed on 16 June, within a week it had been raised to 0.5 million, and the preparations had been so thorough that by July output was at the rate of 30,000 a day.[50] Hartley claimed later that the appearance of the SBR put an end to the German cloud-gas operations against the British. If true, this particular cause-and-effect relationship would demonstrate convincingly that attack and defence had reached stalemate. But the evidence does not support his assertion. The last German gas cloud was released at Wieltje on 8 August. The first issue of the SBR for training instructors began ten days later. The 2nd British Army at Ypres

Fig. 10. British 'PHG' helmet, final version, February or March 1916. Note the large goggles in their gas-tight mountings. (Porton)

Fig. 11. Inspecting the SBR. The photograph was taken on 1 January 1918 at Étricourt. (Imperial War Museum)

received theirs between the end of August and 19 September. A week later the issue to the 1st Army (holding the sector from Fromelles to Roclincourt north of Arras) was authorized and completed during the latter part of October. Thus the protection of troops stationed in the most suitable gas terrain remained incomplete for over two months after the last German cylinder attack, and British troops were not entirely safeguarded until the distribution had gradually worked its way through the 3rd Army (Arras) in November, the 5th Army (Albert) in December, and the 4th Army (Somme front from Le Sars to the junction with French 10th Army) in January–February 1917.[51]

The French went their own way and when offered the SBR, turned it down. The Tambuté snout-like pads impregnated with hexamine were useless, but the Government continued to order them from the Boussac company until the beginning of March at the rate of 10,000 a day. The improved face mask designed by Gravereaux, known as the M2, had its share of administrative delays and the first order for 0.6 million was not placed until 6 February 1916. Others followed in quick succession. Between May and November 1916 altogether 6.2 million masks were dispatched to the armies, and by the end of the year every

French soldier had also been issued with a metal box to hold his respirator. The M2 was not only inferior to the SBR, but what was worse, it was approved and distributed while it still had major defects. In particular the eye pieces were made of celluloid. Nothing illustrates better the failure of the French anti-gas services than this little detail: the opinion of the gas defence specialists serving with the forces was that the celluloid would mist up quickly, and also buckle and crack unless it was handled carefully. But the Ministère de l'Armement experts disagreed, the design was not changed, and when the Germans opened the phosgene cylinders the French suffered big losses.[52]

On the Eastern Front the Russians used British gas helmets (probably the PH type) of which several hundred thousand were sent out during the summer of 1916. That was a fraction of what was needed, but supplies of their own masks, in particular the Koumant–Zelinski were insufficient. The few German cylinder operations, caused heavy casualties because the Russian troops were ill-equipped and had not been taught how to defend themselves.[53]

After Verdun and the Somme every soldier in France had some knowledge of gas, though only a few at first hand. Anti-gas training was universally recognized as essential, but many (perhaps the majority) paid lip-service to the principles and neglected implementation. Lazy or careless officers left it to NCOs to give a brief talk and hand out the instructional leaflets. But as Auld observed: 'it can hardly be realised what alarm and distrust may exist in the raw recruit with regard to gas until he has been given some instruction.'[54] Baynes has recently drawn attention to the role of drill to enforce discipline and to co-ordinate movements so that even the stupid can master the routine effectively, and—in danger—will be able, as if by reflex action and without thinking, to protect themselves.[55] The principle had been recognized by good soldiers before the war, but gas created unusual practical difficulties because of the frequent changes of equipment and the introduction of new substances or of novel tactics. For example the Germans adopted denser concentrations and phosgene:chlorine mixtures at Ypres in December 1915, Hulluch and Wulverghem in April 1916, against which the 'P' and 'PH' helmets offered only limited protection. On all three occasions hundreds were killed or injured. How could the men be trained to safeguard themselves against the heightened danger, unless they were told about it, but once told would not their morale suffer? And what should be done about phosgene poisoning for which the best treatment was complete rest? Did that not offer every opportunity for shamming? Medical Officers were supposed to know, but did not or could not, and there were soldiers accused of malingering who had indeed respired gas and were to die within a few hours of the delayed action effect of phosgene.[56]

The answer to this complex problem was not to be found in drill alone, but in practical experience, supplemented by regular training and by self-discipline, and also by the constant vigilance and care of company and battalion commanders. Otto von Trotta, who commanded regiment No. 357 of the Guards Reserve Division, insisted on mustering his men with masks and giving them

Fig. 12. German troops putting on respirators. Note containers for holding mask. The photograph was taken in Spring 1917. (Imperial War Museum)

gas-chamber practice twice a month in the early part of 1916, during which he spotted defective respirators. But the careless Bavarians had overlooked this precaution and at Hulluch their infantry suffered severely. We may be sure that von Trotta's men disliked fussy inspections in rest quarters, but no doubt they were able to put on their masks in the regulation seven seconds and later in five seconds. We may also be sure that conscientious British officers got their men to take care of the SBR and fit it in six seconds.[57]

The British and the Germans took this aspect of defence against gas with increasing seriousness and dealt with it systematically. First the instructors were trained, then they taught the men, though my information suggests that instruction was sometimes perfunctory so that experience was bought expensively by the new drafts.[58] Besides, the infrequent cylinder attacks and the intermittent gas shellings, which characterized the year, caused discipline to relax after some time. Other influences were at work too. At Hulluch, the Irish had the most severe casualties among British troops and this was attributed to 'the Irish temperament' which does not submit 'to the irksome restraint imposed by . . . anti-gas measures'.[59] They may also, on that occasion, have been influenced by news of the Easter Rising a few days before. Temperament and attitudes could not be ignored. The French soldiers were apparently unable to learn the meticulous drill which the clumsy snouts called for if they were to fit properly. Their own gas troops were insufficiently trained and unlike the British were not volunteers, but combed out reservists. Not surprisingly when the Germans launched their big cloud at Fouquescourt and Lihons on 21

February 1916, some of the French infantry lost their heads and ran. A year later in Champagne anti-gas training and discipline were still not good enough. The M2, though easier to put on than the pads or snouts, had in many cases not been properly adjusted or was damaged: the men could not see properly and a few panicked; some of the officers were careless or negligent and so set a bad example. Even the Germans had problems: their Turkish and Bulgarian allies could never be sufficiently trained in gas defence to make them dependable in a crisis on the Western Front, and that, according to Geyer, was one of the chief reasons why they were not employed there.[60]

The introduction of phosgene changed the time and place of treatment. In 1915 most of the gas deaths had occurred at the front, but the following year the proportion of fatalities at Casualty Clearing Stations (CCS) increased sharply.[61] This was due not only to the better organization of evacuation to the CCS which benefited all the injured, but also and mainly to the delayed action of phosgene poisoning. For up to two or three hours, sometimes longer, the casualty suffered little or no discomfort. Thereafter, by which time the man was on his way to or already at the CCS, his condition would deteriorate very quickly with symptoms of general collapse and tendency to circulation failure from drowning of the lungs. If the patient survived the first 24 hours and was able to avoid pleurisy in the next 48 hours, he was sure to survive and within a few weeks would be capable of resuming light duties. Diagnosis and prognosis were now more accurate than in April and May 1915, but treatment had not progressed beyond rest, the use of a few drugs, venesection, and oxygen—the last, administered over a period of many hours, offering the best hope. But supplies often ran out when casualties mounted and selection became unavoidable. The hopeless cases were given massive morphine injections to ease their final agony and make it less distressing to the other injured in the ward who had a chance of surviving.[62]

Initially much effort was devoted to collective defence and many ingenious ideas were tried out which were of greater psychological than practical value. Gongs, klaxons, and sirens appeared, were found useful and became a permanent feature, but the practice of lighting fires as the cloud drew near was abandoned even before gas shells were introduced. Dug-outs were generally provided with impregnated blankets and they kept the gas out provided care was taken. The Germans installed extractor fans in the deep shelters driven into the chalk of Champagne, but these ventilating feats were exceptional. All kinds of sprays were tried out to break up gas concentrations in trench bottoms or battery positions.[63] There were also the Ayrton fans, promoted by the widow of the physicist who was herself a scientist. Her unceasing efforts overcame every obstacle and the big fly-swats eventually reached France, but were rarely allowed far forward. An instruction film at the Imperial War Museum, shows three men, moving like weird ballet dancers rhythmically raising, beating-down, and shovelling out foul air! A later generation might be forgiven for thinking it a sketch from Joan Littlewood's *Oh, What a Lovely War!*

Mrs Ayrton and her ridiculous fans will serve as end-point of one phase of gas warfare in which the amateur could still make a contribution, sometimes silly, occasionally inspired. But times were changing. The gas shell would transform the situation, open another chapter, and renew the contest between offence and defence. As 1916 ended, the former appeared to be marking time and the number of gas troops ceased to grow. Defence, on the other hand, was still growing fast: respirator supply and maintenance, alarm systems and instruction, were part of an expanding organization which affected everyone and no one was left who had not heard of gas, if only from the instructors. Thus an elaborate relationship developed: anti-gas training and drill were essential, in that they raised confidence and so maintained or even boosted morale. But they also caused widespread apprehension and set the imagination working. The real thing, when it came, often turned out to be less awful. The dread of chemical warfare, once aroused, was sustained and disseminated by the precautions taken against gas rather than by exposure to it.

6

CHEMISTS AT WAR

THIS and the following chapter form the core of the book. In them, I seek answers to two important questions: how does one introduce an entirely new weapon, and what are the obstacles preventing the achievement of that objective? There is a great deal of evidence and several ways in which it can be displayed. I decided to begin with the scientific community and then move on to the organization of research and development. The chapter ends by considering the users—the gas troops and those who were responsible for defence against gas. The other part of the story can be conveniently reviewed in the next chapter which will be concerned with the administrative and industrial aspects of chemical warfare and the extent to which they meshed with the activities of scientists and soldiers.

Chemists were unaccustomed to the novelty and tempo of the work for which they had volunteered, but generally they adapted themselves. What they found more difficult to adjust to was the direction of their work: the emphasis was on speed, on hurried testing, and on development to semi-works scale with the minimum delay. The traditional way of proceeding systematically, beginning with the establishment of theoretical foundations and of progress through the exchange of information, took too long or was prohibited on grounds of security. Thus there were bound to be mistakes and false trails were pursued at unnecessary length; there was also frustration at the apparently purposeless activity and sometimes boredom. Personal clashes surfaced frequently and under the unusual circumstances had a disproportionate bearing on the effectiveness of chemical research. All these factors were especially noticeable in offensive research and development and were only rarely encountered in the activities concerned with respirator design.

Before the war, research was followed by development and that in turn by production. Between 1915 and 1918 they were generally pursued in parallel and the time scale was so compressed that even when there was useful feedback it often remained ineffective. In peace, the market was the final arbiter, but in war the test and 'proofing' stages were the critical hurdles, and so field trials assumed an altogether disproportionate role.

By far the greatest problem, one that was never completely solved, was to find the right men. Academic chemists, used to working on their own were unaccustomed to collaboration with technologists. And industrial chemists, however good at product development, were unfamiliar with the different outlook of professional soldiers and the rigid procedures of military bureaucrats. A few figures will illustrate the scale. By the end of the war at least 5,500 people (including the lesser belligerents more than 6,000) were engaged in chemical research and development. Between a quarter and a third of them had a university degree, but the majority consisted of 'assistants' such as chemistry students, laboratory technicians, hospital dispensers, and other aides, as well as men from the medical, sanitary, engineering, or ordnance branches of the armed forces. The work was the exclusive preserve of men until 1918 when women became a significant minority. The approximate distribution is shown in Table 6.1.

Table 6.1. *Approximate Number of Scientists and Assistants in Chemical Warfare Research and Development, 1918*[1]

	With University First Degree or Higher	Unqualified or with Technical College Diploma	Total
Germany	150	1,850	2,000
USA	1,200	700	1,900
UK	120	1,340	1,460
France	110	n.a.	110 +
Total	1,580	3,890	5,470 +

Note: The British figures have been rounded and include those working at Porton.

There is no information to show growth towards the 1918 peak, nor can the figures be split between offence and defence. All that can be said with confidence is that during 1915 and 1916 the belligerents devoted the bulk of their research and development manpower to anti-gas measures, that the balance changed during 1917, and that in 1918 the emphasis shifted to weapon development. In terms of scientific effort, gas warfare absorbed less than 10 per cent of the practising chemists; the overwhelming majority worked in industry (especially in explosives factories), served in the forces, or retained their civilian occupations.

The above numbers, though relatively small in each country, were too large to be accommodated in a single university and would have swamped the laboratories of the chemical companies, with the possible exception of one of the big German enterprises. Yet it was desirable to concentrate research in one place, if only on grounds of security and to minimize duplication. Haber realized this at once and seizing the initiative placed his institute at Dahlem at the disposal of the German war office; he thereby saved time and quickly achieved results. The arrangement was formalized from the end of 1916 onwards when the entire staff lost their civilian status and came under military discipline. The US Bureau of Mines, which was responsible for chemical warfare research until June 1918, was aware of the German precedent and adopted a similar, though more ambitious policy. In mid-1917 it took over the American University in

Washington, converted and enlarged it, and gradually transferred all research and development from the branch laboratories, temporarily established in about thirty universities, to the new centre.[2] The British handled the matter differently. Those departmental heads who became connected with tear- and other gases were paid by the Ministry of Munitions for the use of their laboratories and assistants. The chemistry departments at Imperial College and at Birmingham University were the first 'centres' (the word inflates the scale of the work done). During 1917 Pope's laboratory at Cambridge, Irvine's at St Andrews, and Morgan's at Finsbury Technical College became involved. These five, expanded and re-equipped, became responsible for the bulk of offensive research. By contrast, defensive research long remained at the Royal Army Medical College at Millbank in London, though the physiology departments at Oxford and later University College, London, Bedford College, the Lister Institute, and the animal station at the School of Agriculture, Cambridge, also played important roles.[3] Unlike the other belligerents, the British had a Central Laboratory at GHQ, France, which became involved in chemical warfare from summer 1915 onwards. The French solved the laboratory problem by simply commandeering the necessary facilities in Paris. By 1918, the chemistry, pathology, and physiology departments of sixteen medical schools, institutes, or the University itself had been taken over in whole or in part. Analytical investigations were left to the Laboratoire Municipal where the police had extensive forensic laboratories and the necessary trained staff, under Professor A. Kling who proved to be an outstanding organizer and energetic director.[4] Not enough is known of the laboratories in other belligerent countries to draw any worthwhile conclusions.[5]

Everywhere the laboratories' facilities—except in the physiological departments—were not purpose-designed, so that most of the fittings and some of the equipment had to be improvised. This and the prevailing congestion enhanced the risks of handling toxic substances. Such unsatisfactory and dangerous working conditions added to the problems of chemical warfare research and the difficulties increased when, following the introduction of new gases in 1917, the scientific effort was stepped up. The buildings and sheds became inadequate, and various shortages prevented or delayed the installation of essential equipment. Scientific manpower was also becoming extremely scarce, for the armies would not release the specialists, so that civilians, notably teachers, had to be directed into laboratories.[6] The increasingly severe constraints, human no less than material, were a major obstacle to the early completion of projects and contributed to the inadequacy of the development work. When the war ended, many unfinished studies were in the pipeline.

What did all these people do? Their contemporaries were led to believe that their work was of the utmost national importance and highly secret. The facts were simpler: the chemists and their colleagues from other scientific disciplines were engaged in adaptive improvisation rather than in purposive research. Where offence was concerned, Heath Robinson, who flourished at the time, would have been more at home than the chemists who were preparing hundreds of molecular combinations with a skill which had been more fruitfully applied a few years earlier to dyestuffs or pharmaceuticals. But until 1917 and even into 1918 there was no logic behind their method, because the approach to chemical warfare was irrational and of the 'suck it and see' kind. Haber told Hartley that no systematic progress had been made in research during the war. The 'best' substances had been discovered and described before 1914. He spoke deprecatingly of the study of fifteen mustard-gas analogues and of the 'more than a hundred arsenic derivatives', examined at his institute up to November 1918. Willstätter, interviewed by Hartley a few days later, had been less involved and was more detached, but he confirmed that German research had not been very serious.[7] The same could be said *a fortiori* of the Allies.

The scientists generated an enormous mass of paper on the details of offensive warfare and achieved only minor improvements to defence in the last two years of the war when research was at its most intensive. A few examples will make the point. The French issued no fewer than seventeen reports on horse-masks and their work on medical research fills eleven boxes at the PRO.[8] And that is not the end of it, for their principal physiologist, Mayer, and his assistants wrote no less than 750 monographs on subjects connected with defence, and another 984 on various offensive materials. In Britain, the Chemical Advisory Committee generated 75 routine reports in the two years to 1917; its successor was more prolific and produced 35 in less than nine months. But these were only the tips of an iceberg. On mustard gas, Professor Irvine and his staff managed to issue 70 reports between August and December 1917, without noticeably advancing its manufacture. Even more impressive are the abstracts of the research and development work commissioned by the British committees: they were duly collated and thousands of entries fill eight volumes that have lain undisturbed these many years.[9] The German material was destroyed or simply disappeared. One study on chlorarsines had been found by Dr Jaenicke and its weighty bulk bears witness to much earnest study at Dahlem. The Americans, once they got into their stride, outdistanced everyone else; the fortnightly reports of the fourteen sections of the Research Division of their Chemical Warfare Service, though mere summaries, take up five boxes.[10] Generally speaking, and subject to some exceptions on defence research, scientists appeared to be working aimlessly and writing copiously. Scientific intelligence based on the systematic collection, collation, and interpretation of every sort of information remained haphazard until the latter part of the war. Haber had a few young men whom he sent off on special duty when it appeared necessary and the Central Laboratory, GHQ, took a sporadic interest in the matter. But it is worth noting that the British only launched a thorough-going literature survey in November 1917 and employed for that purpose one chemist and four part-time assistants: the idea was that their initial identifications would be passed on to teams of students who would prepare specimens. The first results began to appear in September 1918—just over two months later the little group was disbanded.[11]

For most of the time the research workers did not know what to look for. When they had a promising lead, they often failed to follow it up. They appeared to be spending as much time attending meetings or writing reports as working at their benches. In the absence of military guidance on end-uses, even German *Wissenschaftler* can be excused for overlooking the obvious. In the Allied camp cranky ideas retained the attention of serious people until ridicule caused them to be abandoned.[12] On the offensive, the objectives were so unclear and the method of application by shell or cloud so unreliable and crude, that much of the research was purposeless and men were wastefully employed recycling received knowledge. No wonder the results were so disappointing. On top of all that the work was always dangerous, particularly for those who handled defective cylinders or unexploded shells. Kling was asked by a British colleague how he dealt with the latter. He answered pithily, 'si nous ne réussissons pas, nous le saurons jamais, car l'explosion . . . ne nous épargnera pas',[13] and survived the war.

Defence research also caused much waste and endless paper work, but here, at least in the critical first few months, the scientists knew what was wanted and how to set about finding an answer. Later, the design of the respirator, its fitness for the purpose, the quality of its components, and the physiological effects of poison or tear gas were subjects of continuous and thorough study. Defence was an area where feedback led to improvements and bureaucratic delays were minimized. Even the French whose record on anti-gas work was otherwise undistinguished were, for once, innovators. Their Centres Médico-Légaux, travelling forensic laboratories, proved invaluable and were later adopted in a modified form by some of the Allies.[14]

The gas mask commanded attention throughout the war. Its key component was charcoal. The Germans, whose initiative has been described in a previous chapter, had chosen a small drum-type filter and were therefore obliged to pay particular attention to the quality of the charcoal. In this area, much valuable original work was done at Haber's institute on the structure of cellulosic matter and on the physical determinants of absorption power, and it has stood the test of time. The SBR's much larger filter capacity posed fewer problems. Even so the British and later the Americans, studied charcoal thoroughly so that here too quality improved and the growth of knowledge was soundly based.[15]

A great deal of defence research was concerned with the minutiae of respirator parts on which a man's life could depend. Few problems remained unsolved at the end of the war, but no answer was found to an important one—the misting up of the eye pieces. Development often overlapped research and produced unexpected difficulties, nowhere more so than in the interpretation of the observers' reactions to different concentrations of gas. Initially these test procedures were haphazard and the responses entirely qualitative.[16] By 1918 the methods had been tightened up. The physiologists and chemists were also becoming aware that repeated exposure to very dilute gas (e.g. one part of cyanoarsine per 100 mln) dulled the sense of smell. From there it was only a short step to the effects of imagination. Thus research moved into the general area of the psychology of perception and thence to the subject of masking the odour of gases. Some physiologists were studying the reflexes of dogs, mice, and birds in the hope of training animals to give early warning of gas. Meanwhile physicists and engineers were working on electro-mechanical gas detectors. All this activity snowballed, but was premature because the scientists were badly served by the instruments and the statistical techniques then available, and in any case they were instruments to work in inter-disciplinary teams. I do not know whether the Germans took the same interest in the more esoteric aspects of defence research, but late in 1916 Foulkes felt it was time to criticize the attention paid to detectors and to bring the specialists down to earth: 'there is the question of principle as to whether troops should depend for their safety . . . on an automatic device . . .'[17] The undertone of self-reliance, discipline, and morale will occupy us later. Meanwhile his observations did not stop all experiments, but they showed an awareness of the widening gulf between research and its value to the combatants in the field.

The above brief and critical survey of research and development is not intended to lead to a comparison of its quality as between the belligerents—I believe this to be impossible. Its purpose is to help answer the question whether a better or different organization and direction of scientific manpower would have prevented mistakes. However, before we come to that, it is necessary to introduce two other aspects of the scientific side of chemical warfare. The first is concerned with the timing and scale of major investigations and, in this connection, with unscientific attitudes to physical or chemical problems. The second is concerned with the method and thoroughness of the testing procedures.

The Germans surprised the Allies when, in July 1917, they fired shells filled with dichlorodiethyl sulphide, commonly called mustard gas or Yellow Cross (after the German shell markings), at targets in the Ypres sector. We will leave manufacturing problems and the military aspects to later chapters and concentrate here on the scientific steps taken to emulate the enemy. The British and the French quickly identified the unknown substance and as the literature references were accessible it was thought that the first and most important step would be to repeat in the laboratory what Guthrie, Meyer, and Clarke had already described.[18] Initially everything appeared to be entirely straightforward, and Professor Irvine, at St Andrews, was asked to investigate. His first report was considered by the Chemical Advisory Committee on 7 August, less than a month after the introduction of the substance. Irvine had followed Meyer's route; he had obtained low yields and doubted whether ethylene chlorohydrin, required for the intermediate material, would be readily available. He therefore proposed to adopt Guthrie's route, but by mid September it became obvious that he could not cope on his own with an increasingly complex investigation. Pope was now called in and from late October onwards he concentrated on Guthrie's method, starting with sulphur monochloride. Irvine meanwhile persevered with Meyer's process, but the weeks passed and little progress was made. Accordingly a third group under Lapworth at Manchester was set up to investigate sulphur dichloride. By the end of the year, the three-pronged approach involved ten to twelve qualified chemists as well as assistants and technicians. The reaction conditions and the quality of the ethylene had been identified as the chief problem areas, but the laboratory work remained inconclusive. The investigation was therefore widened again. The research department of Nobel's Explosives started to work on variants of Meyer's and Clarke's routes, Professor Kipping studied a process which involved bromine, while Morgan at Finsbury and Hill at Cambridge worked respectively on the butyl and propyl analogues of mustard gas. In January 1918 the laboratory investigations occupied twenty to twenty-five research chemists, and other groups at Porton and Millbank were studying persistency, the nature of the burns, and the treatment of the infection caused by the gas. By contrast fundamental work on the molecular structure of these sulphur chlorides began later under Francis at Bristol, but remained incomplete at the end of the war. Indeed a full understanding of the mechanism of sulphur–chlorine reactions was not attained until the 1940s.

The outcome of four to five months of intensive activity (equivalent to many man-years of research) was considerable confusion and growing frustration which spilled over into increasingly acrimonious personal relations. But a solution was near. On 17 January 1918, Pope, who had emerged as the leading personality on the academic side, wrote encouragingly to the Chemical Warfare Committee on sulphur dichloride. The Committee at once sent some chemists from Castner–Kellner to Manchester where Lapworth demonstrated the use of this material as starting-point. The Castner–Kellner people were able to repeat the experiment at Runcorn. All seemed set fair, when Pope reopened the issue eleven days later by recommending the adoption of sulphur monochloride and a reaction temperature of 50° to 70° C. He applied for a provisional patent and began to lobby vigorously for what he claimed was a 'novel' process giving high yields. Irvine was asked to verify, but when he compared the laboratory specimen of mustard gas with German material from unexploded shells, he found that it was 30 per cent weaker. This evidence notwithstanding the monochloride route now became front runner. Lapworth's group faded out because the quality of the mustard gas he got from sulphur dichloride was even worse, and the continuing difficulties over ethylene chlorohydrin presaged the forthcoming end of all work on Meyer's process.

A great deal of laboratory work was done by Pope's staff to prove the superiority of his process and in March or early April the firm of Chance and Hunt was called in and placed their entire research staff at the disposal of the Government: working at 55° to 65° C they got nowhere, and the scientific problems now became envenomed by personal strife. Pope appealed to Churchill (13 April) in a long memorandum. He explained that his process 'is, from the manufacturing point of view almost as perfect as an organic chemical process can be . . . . Progress was not, however, rapid: my descriptions of the process were examined by others who were unable to reproduce my results and my products were examined physiologically and pronounced comparatively innocuous.'[19] Pope was wrong, but with Churchill's support the monochloride process was backed at the highest level. Nevertheless, Chance and Hunt continued for the rest of April and in May to experiment with lower reaction temperatures and found, as the French had weeks earlier, that the highest yields were obtained at 30° to 35° C. But in Whitehall the results of the research team were ignored.[20]

The British side of the mustard-gas story has been described at length because it is fully documented. Elsewhere the approach differed only in scale and timing. American work began towards the end of September 1917 under J. B. Conant who had been called from Harvard to take charge of four chemists in the Organic Research Unit No. 1 at the American University. They spent the next four to five months struggling with Meyer's route and like their British colleagues had difficulties with the ethylene chlorohydrin supply. Conant was in touch with Pope and by mid January 1918 knew about the difficulties at Cambridge and Manchester. His unit had been enlarged and the next two months were spent studying the optimum conditions for the monochloride-ethylene reaction and designing a pilot plant. By mid-March, the Americans, using rather less manpower than the British, had reached about the same stage, although another two months were needed before the pilot plant produced satisfactory batches of mustard gas.[21]

The French had similar problems. They too failed over the supply of ethylene chlorohydrin, turned to Guthrie's description, and were kept posted by Pope. Like him they had first started with the dichloride, then switched to the monochloride, and about January 1918 had three teams going. Moureu and Job headed one, Bertrand another, and J. de Kap Herr, an organic chemist, the third. They made better progress than the Anglo-American groups because they were the first to realize that success depended on low operating temperatures, precise temperature control of the exothermic reaction, and—an important detail—on constant stirring of the reactants.[22] Their pragmatic approach paid off and the French were able to start the production of mustard gas three to four months ahead of Britain and the USA.

Despite all their efforts the Allies were unable to copy the route followed by Meyer and Clarke and successfully adopted by the Germans. It took them from August 1917 to the following spring to complete the research and development stage of the Guthrie process. The delays were not caused by lack of objective or absence of instructions: the remit had been clear—make mustard gas! The trouble was that in the first place the theoretical foundations were thin and there was insufficient time to strengthen them. Good laboratory work could not make up for that. Secondly the chemical engineering experience and process plant know-how which might have pointed to short-cuts was lacking a weakness that the considerable qualifications of the Allied chemists could not compensate for. By contrast, the Germans were extremely well provided in this respect and never had any difficulties over mustard gas. Indeed Badische Anilin had been preparing ethylene chlorohydrin on a substantial scale for the indigo synthesis before the war.[23]

One would be wrong to generalize about the scientific community from the particular case of mustard gas. The story of one group of arsenical compounds, the aromatic arsines, illustrates another facet. At the suggestion of Emil Fischer a variety of arsenicals began to be investigated at Haber's institute in 1916.[24] It was found that the materials were extremely irritating to nose and throat and could have side effects such as nausea and depression. Thus the substances might become wonder weapons—debilitating the enemy, penetrating his respirator so that he would be forced to cast it off and become exposed to toxic gases. Such science-fiction scenarios were not wishful thinking, for in great secrecy an intensive research and development effort was started at the KWI and later in France and in Britain directed at achieving precisely those results.

The Germans were first off the mark. Some work on aromatic arsines in the latter months of 1916 led them to believe that manufacture and military application were practicable and, as we shall see, they went ahead during 1917. But the preliminary studies were superficial and fundamental enquiries into the *modus operandi* of these solids was called for: diphenylchloroarsine and diphenylcyanoarsine (given the code names Clark 1 and Clark 2 or Zyanclark respectively) had to be dispersed. But the heat of a shell detonation dissipates so quickly that the materials fragment and do not form a cloud of particles. Discrete pieces of Clark 1 or 2, unless minute, are useless, and that suggested the alternative of sublimation into microscopic particles. Hence the first necessity was to develop special experimental techniques to study the formation of these aerosols, their characteristics in suspension, and their behaviour upon adsorption by a filter. The Germans were most secretive and Hartley was briefed in 1921 to obtain details. He learnt that Erich Regener, an X-ray specialist, had joined the KWI in September 1917 and a few months later was put in charge of Section K whose purpose was to study the physical nature of particulates, the best ways of generating these dispersions and the effectiveness of various types of filters. But Regener who held a chair at Stuttgart University where Hartley visited him, was uncommunicative. He did say that little fundamental work was done in the last two years of the war, that aliphatic as well as aromatic arsine compounds had been investigated and that a sublimating device, the *Gas Büchse*, had been designed. Most of this had been known, but he eventually admitted that the sublimator generated particles down to 10^{-6} mm (10μ) which behaved like a gas without becoming diluted. If this were true, the Germans had indeed devised a wonder weapon! But had the Germans regularly achieved these results and could they be measured? Regener would not answer these important questions for they would have disclosed the effectiveness of the *Gas Büchse* as well as the type of instrument used to count and determine the homogeneity of the particles in the test chamber. Regener, an expert on microscopic particles, only disclosed the absolute minimum of significant knowledge.[25] But even less comprehensible than the neglect of fundamental research was the attitude of the artillery specialists who had convinced themselves of the value of these substances. Haber was aware of the gaps in knowledge, but if he protested against the premature introduction of Clark 1 and 2 he was not successful, and Hartley hinted at personal differences to explain the amateurish approach taken at the KWI. There was, as the scientists must have been aware, a danger to the German troops because the phenyl arsines, if finely dispersed, could penetrate the German respirator, the filter unit of which was not large enough to allow the insertion of adsorbent paper, unless the charcoal content was reduced. But the artillery specialists considered that these arsines would be particularly effective against enemy gun positions and recommended immediate adoption as a shell filling. However, if they were right, the materials would assuredly handicap the German assault troops who were going to attack these positions.[26]

French, British, and American scientists were also engaged in research on substituted arsines. Vinet's account of French chemical warfare, revealing in other respects, quickly passes over the research carried out by Job, Moureu, and their collaborators in 1917–18. The documents on the subject in the French archives are missing—withheld or destroyed. British information on the subject is also incomplete. Work on 'aerial colloids', Donnan's expression for particulate clouds, was methodical and inconclusive. It began in August 1917 when C. T. R. Wilson, then the greatest authority on charged particles, was asked to lead the physical investigation. He failed to produce any results and by mid January following, the CWC appointed a special sub-committee to spur him on. Nothing happened and two months later he ceased to be connected with chemical warfare. Donnan now took charge and his laboratory at University College, London, set to work at once on the behaviour of particles. R. R. Whytlaw-Gray, a science master at Eton College, whose hobby was the measurement of minute objects was asked to investigate a reliable method of counting arsenical particles. But neither Donnan's team nor Whytlaw-Gray made worthwhile progress so that at the end of the war the British found themselves in a situation not unlike that of the Germans. But, as with the Germans, product development was ahead of fundamental work, although the German example of shell filling with arsenical compounds was not followed. It was decided in June 1918 to make diphenylchloroarsine (code-named DA) and disperse it with the British equivalent of the *Gas Büchse*. Later in the year the preparation of other compounds including 'Adamsite' (diphenylaminechloroarsine), developed by chemists at the American University, was begun.[27] (Summary particulars of four substances will be found in Table 6.2. The 'Blue Cross' materials, which will be repeatedly mentioned in later chapters, were used by the Germans in large quantities.)

Despite the lack of detail enough information is available to leave no doubt that the belligerents deployed a considerable scientific effort in the area of

CHEMISTS AT WAR

Table 6.2. *Particulars of four Arsenical Compounds
developed in the First World War**

Chemical Name	Diphenylchloro-arsine	Diphenylcyano-arsine	Ethyldichloro-arsine	Diphenylamine-chloroarsine
Common Name	Blaukreuz or Blue Cross	Blaukreuz or Blue Cross	Blaukreuz or Blue Cross	Adamsite
British Code	DA	DC	DL	DM
German Code	Clark 1	Clark 2 or Zyanclark	Dick	—
Molecular Weight	264	255	175	277
Specific Gravity (water = 1)	1.3	1.4	1.7	1.6
B. Pt. (C°)	333	377	156	410
Vapour Pressure (min at 20°C)	negl.	negl.	2.29 mmHg	negl.
Physical Property at Ordinary Temperature	Solid	Solid	Liquid	Solid
Melting-Point (C°)	39	35	−65	193
Main Chemicals used in Manufacture	Arsenic trichloride or sodium arsenite, benzene or aniline, sodium or hydrochloric acid	Potassium cyanide, diphenylchloro-arsine (after 1918 other materials were used)	Arsenious oxide, chlorine, ethyl alcohol and solvent	Arsenic chloride and benzene or aniline

* Sartori, M.: *The War Gases* (1939) and Prentiss, A. M.: *Chemicals in War* (1937).

arsenical compounds. All were handicapped by the lack of suitable instruments and the physical and physiological studies remained incomplete. The development of the products as shell fillings or as a cloud of particulates was also incomplete, and their military value was negligible because no effective means of delivery was found.

Muddle, obtuseness, and careless mistakes were frequent where offence research was concerned. Why was it that so many facts went unperceived, or were ignored, by so many? Chemists could plead ignorance and lack of time (though these same obstacles also arose in gas defence): the state of knowledge and the scientific instruments of 1915–18 could not be compared with the situation in the Second World War. All the same, some doubts as to the competence of the men or the institutional framework within which they operated remain. There was, for instance, the failure to follow up some unusual ideas and to look beyond the immediate objective. Among them were dimethyl sulphate, calcium arsenide, and arsine itself. The first two were proposed by British chemists in summer 1915, but were rejected. Ernest Starling demanded another investigation in February 1916, and dimethyl sulphate was rejected a second time. Arsine was suggested to the Ministry of Munitions late in 1916, but the idea was turned down. All three were dismissed because they were 'fairly harmless', an odd description applied to arsine! As for the other two, they should have been taken further because of their slow, cumulative action and their delayed toxic effect; dimethyl sulphate also injures the skin: these characteristics pointed to a different form of chemical warfare where the aim was not to kill quickly, but to incapacitate the enemy through injury and to deny him a tactically valuable area by poisoning it.[28] In the end these and other ideas might not have worked, but they were never tried. It is possible that the chemists were not prepared to explore further unconventional concepts. Their 'customers'—regular officers and officials—would expect quick and unambiguous results, so adding to their problems. But there were occasionally serious errors of judgement which went uncorrected for months if not years. Mustard gas affords a good illustration. The Germans spotted it quite early, simply because their literature research was so well organized. But in 1916 its toxicity was considered too low by comparison with phosgene, and Haber decided not to proceed with it. No one appears to have remembered that Meyer, thirty years earlier, had written of its blistering action. But at the beginning of 1917 the investigations were resumed. This time the persistence of the substance was what attracted attention and I take this as evidence that there was some new thinking on gas warfare generally. Once again blisters and conjunctivitis were ignored, so that when they introduced mustard gas the Germans were unaware of its vesicant action and did not know that it could cause temporary blindness.[29] There was the same ignorance on the Allied side. Professor Starling also 'discovered' mustard gas in 1916 and being a physiologist observed the blisters, but did not note the effect on the eyes, nor the persistence of the liquid, which the Germans had spotted. Starling told Thuillier what he knew and when asked what was the effective range of the damage, answered that it would not exceed a few yards—the diameter of an HE detonation. Whereupon Thuillier lost interest.[30] Independently of the British, the French had also considered mustard gas: at the beginning of 1916, Dr Chevalier had drawn attention to the literature references. Moureu had at once studied the chemistry and Mayer the physiological action. In March 1916 Mayer got some samples from Moureu, noted the blisters they caused, but reported that the substance was less toxic than phosgene or hydrogen cyanide. That closed the matter.[31]

What is one to make of these incidents?—except that men looking for one thing, rarely looked elsewhere. Why were there so few chemists willing to investigate further an unconventional idea or an unexpected result? Developing and testing outside the research laboratory emerge as weak areas. But that is not the complete explanation. Many chemists wore blinkers and far too often the lax organization of research and development was powerless against obstinate, though eminent, men. A good example is provided by the attitude of the French scientific establishment to hydrogen cyanide. The Germans rejected it twice, the British used it briefly, but the French retained it almost till the end. They added materials to prevent its rapid diffusion, but the fact that this entailed the greater expenditure of shells to obtain the same effect never troubled their chemists. After the war, Vinet admitted that the gas was militarily useless, but he maintained that his French colleagues 'have established the possibility of obtaining by this use overwhelming results'.[32] But his assertion was unsupported by evidence. The Germans also had their blind spots: they relied on diphosgene as their principal shell filling and, as Hartley put it later, 'probably saved us a large number of casualties.'[33] Comparative shoots would soon have established the greater killing-power of phosgene and would have demonstrated the need to achieve a high concentration quickly. Similar stupidities characterized the British use of 'Green Star'—a mixture of chloropicrin and hydrogen sulphide —which was injurious at close quarters to the men of the Special Brigade, but innocuous to the enemy just across no man's land. After more than a year of working with the substance, it was withdrawn.[34]

Where anti-gas was concerned fewer mistakes were made or tolerated and generally speaking, good sense prevailed. Only the French with their pads and snouts (to which I have already referred) and the Italians can be criticized for indifference and carelessness. Writing of Italian scientists in the last year of the war, Barley observed that they 'think . . . our standards of protection are most [*sic!*] unnecessarily high'.[35]

Beyond ignorance which could not be quickly remedied for there was not enough time, there was also lack of imagination, unpardonable obstinacy, folly, and idleness. The chemists and physicists whom I have named were not incompetent academics—many were among the luminaries of their profession. What had come over them? Were they unable to give of their best under pressure? Did differences of opinion turn into personal feuds in which government officials and soldiers became embroiled? Did national scientific pride obstruct the adoption of better enemy or allied materials? There can be no conclusive answers because I am dealing here with the endeavours of a small group of self-selected scientists whose individual actions were not predetermined by some overall scheme of things, but were pragmatic and indeed random. What I have been trying to show so far is that there were too many avoidable mistakes by too many members of the scientific community. We need to consider next whether they were corrected or compounded at the development and testing stage.

In war the place of individual customers is taken by a single buyer. The test of competition in the market is replaced by formal, official trials. If the product conforms to specification, then research, development, and production may be said to have meshed successfully. In reality it is not as simple as that, but the performance test marks the point where the scientists meet those who have been giving them their orders.[36] In 1915–18 both sides did not know the demarcation lines and were groping to find them. There were also added complications when a product, which had been satisfactory in the laboratory and passed muster at the field trials, failed on active service. (Occasionally the reverse was true.) This perplexed the scientists and may have caused them to belittle the value of animal tests and static trials under controlled conditions, on the grounds that they were artificial. Hartley and I think Haber, too, were of that opinion. But some useful data was obtained in this way; the precise results could be compared and there is evidence that the British were able to draw valuable lessons from trial shoots with hydrogen cyanide and chloropicrin which led them to redesign the burster for gas shells.[37] The French took much trouble over their trial shoots and maintained uniform conditions as to range and target arrangements; they also tended to use the same animal species. Nor did they mind the expenditure of shell. Between February 1916 and January 1918 they fired 5,179 shells in 30 separate trials for phosgene and hydrogen cyanide. It may be thought that it took them a long time to prove the worthlessness of the latter, but as regards the former they discovered an interesting fact: the effectiveness of a phosgene shoot was not in strict proportion to the payload of the shell, a smaller shell, fired more rapidly than the large, gave comparatively better results. Hence they continued to rely on the 75 mm gun.[38]

The German procedures for testing gas shells were entirely different. After trying out the substance in a large gas chamber on animals or on human volunteers, they experimented with small samples in a specially adapted 42 cm shell case to observe the behaviour of the gas upon detonation. If the tests showed promise static trials were held in the open: a 'barrage' was simulated by simultaneously exploding twenty to twenty-five shells of various calibres. The observers then left their dug-outs, some with, some without masks and walked towards the site of the explosion, and, as best as they could, noted down their impressions. (Field trials with gas clouds took place in Belgium or behind the Eastern Front.) These pseudo-scientific tests were manipulated to give a favourable impression to the people from the Artillerie Prüfungs Kommission and the representatives of OHL. As a result the gas filling often did not come up to expectations in the field. I have already mentioned diphosgene, and the story was repeated with Clark 1 and 2. In 1918, the Germans increased the HE content of their mustard gas shell. It therefore ceased to make the customary 'plop' sound of the small burster charge of the regular gas shell, and so confused the Allies. But, unknown to the Germans, the greater explosive power thinly scattered the toxic substance over a wider area, thereby diminishing its effectiveness.[39]

It was not only in the thoroughness of the trials, but also in the facilities provided for them that there were major differences between the Allies and the Germans. The British bought 1,200 hectares at Porton, near Salisbury, in January 1916. The site was carefully chosen: standing outside the main buildings and looking east one is struck by the similarity of the Hampshire Downs at this point to the gentle ridges east of Ypres. Much gas was to be used in both places in the next two-and-a-half years and when the war ended, Porton had expanded to around 2,600 hectares (say 10 square miles). The experimental section comprised laboratories, workshops, and animal houses and the entire complex remained the centre of British chemical warfare research and development for the next half century.[40] The Americans were assigned about 6,000 hectares by the French Government near Chaumont (Haute Marne), but before they could develop Hanlon Field in the image of Porton, the war ended. They went home and acquired an equally large site at Lakehurst, NJ. The French originally made do with the grounds at Satory near Versailles and with the artillery ranges at Fontainebleau, but later they adapted a site in the flat plain of the Rhône estuary at Entressen.[41] The Germans, by contrast, did very little. At first they used the ranges at Mummersdorf and Doeberitz, but the area was too populated, so that security and safety were unsatisfactory. In 1917 they decided to take over 1,000 hectares at Breloh, 90 km NE of Hanover and 5 km from Münsterlager on the main Berlin-Bremen line. Whatever its merits as a training area for German and later British soldiers, it was not a good site for large-scale experiments with gas. It was too small, the range narrow, the terrain flat and wooded, the soil sandy, conditions not resembling those encountered on the Western Front. The station was opened in April 1918 before all the equipment had been installed. However, the builders were slow, priorities remained unfulfilled, and by November of that year little more had been done. The late start and the incomplete facilities seriously handicapped the Germans. The fruits of their research were likely to remain unproven unless thoroughly tested. Haber and like-minded colleagues recognized that, but were unable to make the point with the Kriegsministerium and its chief von Wrisberg. The lack of rapport between chemists and military bureaucrats over this matter was detrimental to the entire German chemical warfare effort.[42]

Where the Germans were hasty and also over-confident of the lethal power of their chemicals, the Allies were apt to go to the other extreme and tended to be excessively thorough. Critics later accused the Porton staff of holding trials for the sake of the thing, regardless of their value to the artillery. The introduction of the Livens projector, the most cost-effective chemical device of the war, bears them out. Initially Porton was unwilling to test the projector because it was deemed too dangerous. The first trial—a mere forty projectiles— was held in March 1917. Meanwhile the Special Brigade had gone ahead: within four weeks of that Porton trial, the battle of Arras opened with the discharge of hundreds of phosgene projectiles which contributed to its initial success. GHQ was convinced and ordered projectors by the thousand, but at Porton they continued methodically to test from May to September.[43] The circumstances were exceptional in that Livens was the inventor as well as the developer, and his men the ultimate users. But the story illustrates the key role of linking applied science with military end uses. When the connection was weak, the results were unsatisfactory. But even a strong coupling did not ensure success. It sometimes happened that a product or appliance was refined unnecessarily when it would have been better to rethink the weapon *ab initio* along simpler lines. This approach was especially important for the Allies who needed to compensate for lower product quality by greater care and ingenuity in ensuring optimum end-use. In order to achieve that result—difficult, but not impossible—it was essential to organize and manage the entire research and development work in a purpose-oriented manner. And that created fresh problems.

The manner in which scientists organized themselves was as significant as their collective scientific ability. The committees that were created to direct and co-ordinate research and development therefore played or could have played important roles. Their members were usually chemists or physiologists (with a few representatives from other disciplines) and were primarily engaged in academic, as distinct from industrial, research. Scientists acting as administrators were rare in the first two years of chemical warfare. Thus there were no differences between those serving on committees and those who remained at universities: both were professional academics, accustomed to working singly or in small groups, unused to the taking of quick decisions.

The chief British characteristic was the separation, until October 1917, of research management into entirely distinct groups for offence and defence. This nonsensical division had venerable ancestry. The Royal Society set up on 12 November 1914 a sub-committee 'to consider chemistry in relation to the war'. Sir William Ramsay was in the chair; H. B. Baker, W. H. Perkin, Sir Edward Thorpe, and G. T. Beilby (a distinguished industrialist) were members; A. W. Crossley, Professor of Chemistry at King's College, London, became secretary. It did not concern itself with chemical warfare. In mid June 1915, Col. Louis Jackson was co-opted, but that did not signify any change in policy, and the new chairman, R. Meldola, was eminent but elderly. The Royal Society had also created the Physiology (War) Committee, and its members played an important part in organizing defence against gas. Sir Alfred Keogh, the Director-General Army Medical Services, recommended the members to the Society: Starling became the first chairman of the committee which included Barcroft, Bayliss, Boycott, Edkin, Fletcher, J. S. Haldane, F. G. Hopkins, and later also Leonard Hill and Meakins. C. G. Douglas of the RAMC represented 'the users' in the BEF. The secretary was Dr Morley Fletcher, who was also secretary of the Medical Research Committee, set up under the National Insurance Act. The Committee decided that it would concentrate on supervising toxicological research and the study of respiratory diseases. In particular, Barcroft at Cambridge and Haldane at Oxford were given more assistance and formed, as it were, the core of basic research which could build solidly on pre-war work.[44]

From the outset, there was a great difference in the attitudes taken towards offensive and defensive research. The development of protection against gas was accorded the highest priority. Keogh was fortunate in his choice of Col. (later Gen. Sir) William Horrocks whom he put in charge of the Anti-Gas Department at the War Office. He, in turn, appointed P. S. Lelean head of Research and Development and took over the Army Hygiene Laboratory at the RAMC College, Millbank. The work-load grew fast and before the year was out Starling had replaced Lelean and been given two assistants, E. F. Harrison and J. A. Sadd, to deal respectively with chemical research and respirator design. In 1916, all development work was transferred to Starling's department at University College, while Millbank devoted itself exclusively to fundamental research. By then the organization had adopted its final shape and was working smoothly. It was compact and maintained close liaison with the Royal Society's Committee and the BEF. A sense of purpose animated the senior staff and communicated itself to others. Horrocks dispensed with elaborate committee procedures, ran the Department along simple lines, and in Harrison picked an organizer of genius. He was a pharmacist in his late forties, who had worked for Boots and then as an independent consultant. He quickly made his mark at Millbank, took charge of the SBR development in 1916, then directed the Anti-Gas Department and still later was promoted to Deputy Controller, and then to Controller, Chemical Warfare Department. He died of the 'flu and overwork just before the Armistice.[45]

Meanwhile, and very differently, offensive research and development were getting under way. We have seen in an earlier chapter how Professors Baker and J. F. Thorpe (the nephew of Sir Edward), helped by Beilby and Jackson, had taken an interest in tear gas. On 23 June 1915 all four were moved from the War Office to the Trench Warfare Department of the newly formed Ministry of Munitions. A new Department of State normally creates turmoil, but on this occasion the confusion was immense. Its *raison d'être* was to do something about the supply of munitions, but our little group were told to concentrate on novel weapons for trench warfare, among them gas, which, it was thought, would be more readily available than shell cases and HE. This was a big job, and it could not be done because of three obstacles. The first was Jackson. Promoted to Brigadier and the new post of Director-General Trench Warfare Department (TWD), he was given a civilian financial adviser, Mr (later Sir) Alexander Roger, an accountant and director of an investment trust. Neither choice was happy. The two men were not on good terms and had no contacts with the War Office or the BEF. Secondly, there was another Director-General, Mr (later General) du Cane who was responsible for Munitions Design. When gas shell began to be seriously considered in 1916 he proceeded to encroach on territory hitherto considered the domain of the TWD. Finally there was the Inventions Branch (later the Munitions Inventions Department) which was meant to sift proposals and develop the less cranky ones. It was not long before its people overlapped the chemists.

At the end of June 1915 Jackson's scientists became the Scientific Advisory Group and Roger chaired their meetings. Dr R. Glazebrook of the National Physical Laboratory, W. B. Hardy, a physiologist, and Sir Boverton Redwood, an oil specialist, were added to provide diversity and bulk. Crossley left the Royal Society Committee, donned uniform, and acted as executive secretary. Jackson and his seven men would have been hard pressed if they had confined themselves to the development of poison gas, trench mortars, and similar specialist weapons. But they were also charged, albeit rather vaguely, with scientific intelligence, cost control, and relations with contractors. These jobs would have surpassed the abilities of giants, but they were ordinary men and, unlike their RAMC colleagues at Millbank, they were badly organized. Still, everyone began with a will, but after September they met only rarely. Roger remained chairman of the Advisory Group until December 1915 when he realized that it was ineffective and handed over to Jackson. Relations between the two deteriorated fast and in the ensuing power-struggle Roger emerged victorious and was promoted Director-General Trench Warfare Supply. Jackson ceased to be head of TWD and was moved sideways to Director-General Trench Warfare Research.

The Scientific Advisory Group was useless. It had a Chemical Sub-Committee (CS-C), consisting of Baker, Beilby, Boverton Redwood, and Thorpe. They met frequently between July 1915 and November 1917, but carried no more weight, though they were joined by John Cadman from Birmingham University (March 1916), Richard Threlfall (December 1916), and a representative from the War Office contracts branch. Crossley, as ever, was secretary. At first it met daily at Imperial College, but as the members had no clear instructions, they assumed that they were responsible for research, supply, and end-use of 'various gases, liquids and solids . . . for offensive purposes in trench warfare'. Respirators were excluded by definition, explosives and shells were the responsibility of other departments in the Ministry. The isolation of offensive research from other chemical warfare developments was a mistake, and resulted in duplication, vexation, and delay. The inclusion of gas supply showed unawareness of the limitations of academic scientists and ignored the growing power of Roger who considered himself rightly to be in sole charge of production and negotiations with manufacturers. To round off this sorry record of mis-organization and inter-departmental rivalries, it needs to be added that the War Office was determined to keep the Sub-Committee members out of France and would not let them communicate direct with GHQ. Crossley was assigned liaison duties within the Ministry and with the French, but not with the BEF.[46]

How did the sub-committee members pass their time when they were not attending meetings—401 all told? They dealt with many research problems, with weapon design, and with tests at Porton. Some concerned themselves with gas production and the failures of British phosgene plants, others surveyed German literature or tested the enemy's weapons, and all attended the rare information exchanges with Russian or French specialists. Mustard gas never appeared in the minutes until Yellow Cross shells exploded in Flanders. The pace, after the first frantic months, was leisurely and indecisive. Trouble-shooting was badly needed, but only Cadman was good at it. He knew what was wrong, tried his hand at progress-chasing, and had the temerity to order about the Contractors. This upset the administrators and they got rid of him: in July 1917 he was promoted and left chemical warfare. Crossley was everywhere, and probably of some use. But his colleagues disliked him and influential people became irritated with this pernickety chemist who had taken to soldiering with the zest of a martinet. He too was promoted, appointed head of Porton, and so had to give up his secretaryship in 1916. Dr A. Scott, FRS, a less troublesome man, succeeded him. Jackson, in charge of research, was held responsible for every failure and in particular (though unfairly) for the lack of poison gas. So his complaints about Roger and his often sensible plans for reform carried little weight with successive Ministers of Munitions. There were some trifling gestures: the sub-committee was renamed Chemical Advisory Committee and a link with the BEF via the War Office was created. But that did not amount to much and the crowning insult was demotion, hard to bear for a full Director-General, when Jackson and the Committee were taken over by du Cane and henceforth had to confine themselves to the general oversight of research at Porton and Imperial College, and rather more vaguely elsewhere.[47]

The Ministry was notorious for quarrels and intrigues, but in this particular instance the repercussions were important. The weakness of the research and development organization delayed the implementation of chemical warfare generally and the narrow outlook of the committee members prevented any fruitful collaboration with Horrocks's people. He actually made the first move, but between July 1916 and October 1917 there were only five meetings between the Anti-Gas Department and the Chemical Advisory Committee. They were of little use to either side.[48]

The German use of mustard gas created as much alarm as their introduction of chlorine. The initial reaction of the Chemical Advisory Committee was to urge the secondment of officers with active service experience to Porton, useful, but not likely to produce dichlorodiethyl sulphide. Its next move, in September 1917, was to appoint an 'Advisory Panel' of twelve scientists: Irvine was among them, but Pope at Cambridge and Frankland at Birmingham were not, though both were doing chemical war work. The Committee was manifestly incapable of handling the scientific side of the new weapon, nor could it answer the repeated demands for the means to retaliate. GHQ became increasingly concerned, the more so as the Germans were also firing off Blue Cross shells, the particles of which were thought to penetrate the SBR. Hartley, in charge of anti-gas measures in France, was sent over to investigate. Pope, soon to become the leading scientific personality in gas warfare, complained to Hartley: 'no chemist outside London is allowed any effective part in the work. The country is full of excellent chemists who are as capable as anyone in Germany of working out the question of what can be done in the production of unpleasant materials—Perkin, Kipping, Wynne, Lapworth, Henderson, Patterson, Orton, McKenzie, etc. have been available all along.' British chemical warfare research, he added 'is being run in the spirit of the little village publican doing his two barrels a week'.[49] This was hard, and allowing for some exaggeration, true.

At a much higher level, Churchill the new Minister of Munitions, was preparing to overhaul the entire Ministry. Specifically regarding chemical warfare—of which he was an active supporter—a complete reconstruction was put in hand. The Department of Chemical Warfare (CWD) was set up and Gen. H. L. Thuillier, at one time Director of Gas Services BEF, appointed Controller. He took charge at the end of October and became President of the Chemical Warfare Committee (CWC) which, at long last, co-ordinated the supervision of all aspects of offensive and defensive research, development, supply, and use. Militants, including Pope, were invited to join and specialists such as K. B. Quinan, the expert on chemical plant construction, became members. The Special Brigade was represented usually by its CO, Crossley and others came from Porton, the Army Chemical Advisers often attended, and there were some civil servants from the Supply Sections and the War Office. Finally, about twenty eminent scientists, the 'Associate Members', could be called upon if required— among them, as an afterthought, Jackson, now shunted into a siding.[50]

More than tact and diplomacy were needed to set such a motley group to work. Thuillier was a good chairman and when he returned to active command twelve months later, Harrison briefly succeeded him. But new faces, more money, and enthusiasm were not enough to energize research and link it solidly with development. A systematic approach and a smooth routine were also called for. At the first meeting on 27 October, Thuillier established the ground rules: Friday morning was reserved for offensive research, the afternoon for development and supply; Saturday morning was devoted to anti-gas work. The secretariat took charge of the agendas and of the chemical intelligence branch. There was not time enough for long discussions and Harrison, Irvine, Pope, and Crossley often took the lead and acted as rapporteurs. Proposals were submitted, accepted, or rejected. In this way 800–50 compounds, suitable for offensive purposes, were reviewed between October 1917 and February 1919. A few were approved and assigned to research teams who had to report periodically on their progress. When there was controversy, say a paper was challenged on scientific grounds, the Committee referred the matter to a third member to check and arbitrate. Particularly complex matters, such as mustard-gas production or decontamination, were reviewed at special conferences which everyone was expected to attend.[51] Considering the pressure of events (to which Jackson's group had succumbed), one is struck by the business-like approach to the management of research and development. But the intensive and purposeful activity and smooth organization of the last year of the war could not make up for lost time. Nor were they able to solve the continuing production difficulties which necessitated yet another purge and reshuffle in spring 1918.

The French organized chemical warfare research and development in a simple, logical manner. Immediately after the first German cloud-gas attack, the Director-General of Engineering at the Ministère de la Guerre invited Kling to take charge of the investigation into the effects of gas; at the same time Professor F. Heim became responsible for anti-gas research and Weiss, the head of the mines inspectorate, for the supply of breathing sets. This arrangement lasted until July 1915, when the Minister set up the Service du Matériel Chimique de Guerre, initially under Weiss who was replaced by Gen. Ozil a few weeks later.

The Service had broadly the same functions as the British CWD in 1918. One branch or department was responsible for all research and development, another for application and pilot plant operation, the third for purchases and dispatch. The first, Inspection des Études et Expériences Chimiques (IEEC) was a co-ordinating body under the chairmanship of Col. (later Gen.) Perret. He also chaired the two research committees, but left the scientific side to their respective vice-chairmen; Charles Moureu, an organic chemist and professor at the Collège de France, handled offensive studies and Charles Achard, professor of clinical medicine at the Sorbonne, dealt with defence. An important feature of the sub-committees was that they were small—they had about ten members each, that several members sat on both, and that they shared the same secretariat under Dr (later Professor) Terroine. Hartley who knew many of the IEEC people, considered Lebeau, a Professor at the École de Pharmacie, the 'most active', praised Moureu, but Grignard, the most eminent of the French chemists, 'cut no ice'.[52]

Whatever the scientific abilities of individuals, the French approach to research organization had considerable merit. The close links between offence and defence were extremely useful, and through Perret, Ozil knew at first hand what the IEEC was doing and could integrate the scientists' work with that of the other departments. Secondly the rather formal meetings which took place every two to three weeks represented a review of progress and served to set new objectives; on paper there was the closest co-ordination of research. Thirdly, all the laboratories were in Paris. The extreme centralization of French science, so nefarious on other occasions, proved to be a blessing in this instance. The academics could be readily contacted, their laboratories were at hand, they could—if they were so minded—meet easily, and they acted almost as delegates of their groups. The usual practice was for the chemical and pharmacological departments to distribute research assignments on offensive materials among themselves; the medical departments and the Val-de-Grâce hospital—the training college for the French medical corps—took charge of defence research and of the anti-gas training courses. Kling continued to run the Centres Médico-Légaux. He and Nebout, a gunner who was Perret's special adviser, were given additional duties: the former helped with the planning of gas attacks the latter lectured to artillery staffs on gas shells. With the exception of Kling, Nebout, and Dr C. E. H. Flandin (brother of the politician) few of the scientists on the IEEC were in touch with the staff and with commanding officers; GQG was less open-minded in this respect than GHQ.[53] At the highest level, the friction between Albert Thomas and Joffre over more important issues reacted unfavourably on relations with the IEEC and the chemists were kept well away from the users.

There was very little change in the composition of the IEEC between 1915 and 1918, and its organization once fixed, never varied. Yet French research and development was conventional, undistinguished, and slow to respond to outside stimuli. The respirator designs were a disgrace until the German model was adopted and some gas shell fillings were retained long after their uselessness in the field had been demonstrated. The fault lay not with the organization of the scientific effort, but with the absence of a powerful personality among the scientists—someone with sufficient determination to stop lesser colleagues from pursuing hobby-horses and generally to inject some realism into the research work.

The Germans refined the French approach to its ultimate simplicity. As Haber had taken the lead from the outset, so his institute of physical chemistry at Dahlem became the centre of chemical warfare research. Throughout 1915 Haber recruited assistants largely on the old-boy net-work. Defence was first priority and he was able to draw on the support of some eminent people, notably Willstätter, Carl Neuberg, and Adam Bickel, the latter two from the neighbouring institute of biochemistry, which was later taken over and used as an annexe of Haber's. During 1916 the work load rose further, the site (in those days still largely rural) became dotted with hutments and animal houses, and presently was surrounded by a fence and guarded by troops.

Table 6.3 shows how changes in the priorities determined the evolution of the structure which became increasingly complex as the war intensified.[54] After

Table 6.3. *Development of Research Organization at KWI, 1915–1918*

Approximate Date	Section	Chief Functions and Name of Section Head
Sept. 1915	A	Respirator face pieces (Herzog)
Sept. 1915	C	Respirator drums (Pick; Willstätter, part-time)
Nov. 1915	B	Enemy chemical warfare; offensive research; technical and engineering design*, gas testing (Kerschbaum)
Spring 1916	D	New gases (Steinkopf, from late 1916 Wieland)
Spring 1916	E	Pharmacology and pathological work (Flury; Neuberg part-time)
Feb./Mar. 1916	F	Inspection and issue of respirators (Freundlich)
Winter/Spring 1917	G	Shell cases, fuses, components (Tappen)
Winter/Spring 1917	J	Proofing and issue of gas (Friedländer)
Date not available	H	Trench mortars (Poppenberg)
Sept. 1917	K	Particulate clouds (Regener)

* Gas shell design was added in February 1916, Livens type projectors in 1917. This section was responsible for offensive and defensive work on particulate clouds from late 1916 to September 1917.

the initial creative phase, the section heads became immersed in administration and the investigations and tests became routine. Haber relied on younger men from whom he demanded an unprejudiced approach, discipline, devotion to the job, enormous stamina, and compliance with his directives. Hartley was critical 'A great deal of careful methodical work was accomplished, but Haber seems to have become rather an autocrat, and consequently much of the research was carried out as prescribed tasks, little freedom being left to individual workers.' He compared unfavourably the German organization with the 'much greater freedom . . . given to our younger chemists and junior officers.' But Pick, a physical chemist seconded by the Auergesellschaft, looked at it differently: he found nothing wrong with the approach which was in accordance with German academic practice, and he admired Haber's inspiring leadership.[55] Both over-simplified. Neither considered the magnitude of the administrative tasks facing Haber. His organization resembled that of the big industrial laboratories with dozens of qualified men, supported by technicians, working on closely related subjects. During 1916 the section heads were allowed some more initiative. Kerschbaum, in particular, distinguished himself as an outstanding administrator and Freundlich managed the important, though dull, inspection department with great success. Tappen, the gunner whom we encountered at the beginning of the story, could be depended upon to keep the artillery staffs contented; he represented the OHL and was also the security officer. Von Poppenberg was an elderly regular officer from the Artillerie Prüfungsanstalt, and had a quasi-sinecure. A point worth noting is that Haber, then in his late forties, was less at ease with his contemporaries and seniors than with his younger collaborators—and his closest associates such as Kerschbaum, Pick, Freundlich, and Epstein (his personal assistant) were about ten years younger.[56]

The German organization in no way resembled the British committee procedures. The Germans had simple lines of command and held weekly meetings, but secrecy and strict compartmentalization sapped initiative despite the high standards of the routine work and the occasional brilliant initiatives to meet shortages. These defects, not incompetence, nor ignorance (as was the case with Jackson's group in 1915–17) explain the original neglect of mustard gas, the continuing reliance placed on diphosgene, the superficial testing of Blue Cross shell, and the delay over the Livens projector copy. Nor can the errors of judgement be ascribed to a failure of communications with the users. Haber's institute was under the control of the chemical section of the Kriegsministerium of which he was also in charge. (Until the end of 1916 he was responsible to the army medical services in all anti-gas matters.) He was, indeed, wearing a third hat as adviser to OHL. So far as I know, there were no such close personal links between research, development, supply, and use in France, Britain, and Russia. Since Haber played such a unique role, he must bear the chief responsibility for the weaknesses that characterized the organization in the latter part of the war.

The situation in the United States has been fully described by D. P. Jones[57] and need not long detain us, the more so as the impact of the organization on chemical warfare in Europe was minimal. Even before the USA entered the war, V. H. Manning, the Director of the US Bureau of Mines, told the National Research Council that the Bureau was familiar with noxious gases and with the protection against them. That was in February 1917 and may be taken as an indication of American unfamiliarity with war gases. A few weeks later Manning was asked to organize anti-gas research and in April work on the design of an American respirator began. It followed closely the SBR, but failed under thorough testing and the Americans later relied on the SBR. Manning's staff grew fast and soon about fifty people were working on anti-gas research in some twenty different university laboratories. He also assumed control over offensive research, and he subdivided these two branches into departments as necessary. There was a separate section for pilot plant production (something that the people in Berlin never had to bother about, and which Thuillier failed to set up). In order to simplify research management and to achieve quick results, he decided to concentrate production development on just four substances— phosgene, chloropicrin, hydrogen cyanide, and the tear gas xylyl bromide; mustard gas was not mentioned. He informed the Chief of Ordnance accordingly by letter dated 27 July, 1917.[58] The precise date is given to show, once again, the unrealistic attitude to fringe products (except phosgene) that were being abandoned in Europe, and also to draw attention to the absence of liaison between Washington and the British and French research groups.

Manning's organization soon became unwieldy and the quality of the work was unremarkable until the scope was broadened and the staff had been brought together. From November onwards the American University was fully operational and the situation improved. The Bureau of Mines now became involved in a dispute with the Army over control of research and the matter was not resolved until President Wilson created the autonomous US Chemical Warfare Service (CWS) at the end of June 1918. G. A. Burrell, a chemist of the Bureau of Mines, became head of the Research Division of the CWS. It ballooned swiftly into a major research enterprise, with fourteen sections corresponding to functions which resembled those of Haber's institute. Development and Proving, though closely related to Research, were made into separate Divisions of the CWS. This arrangement differed from that adopted by the British and the Germans and caused duplication of work and delay, which were aggravated by the remoteness from the gas troops in France.

Although the governance of research shows considerable variety some general conclusions may nevertheless be drawn. In every country the changing nature of chemical warfare and the leap-frogging contest between offence and defence created particular difficulties for research and development. Lack of time added to them. Good organization was therefore necessary, but itself insufficient unless it straddled defence and offence. Assuming these criteria were met (and they were not in Britain until late 1917), how would they work in practice? The answer would be by modern management methods, that is, setting objectives and securing the co-operation of people at different levels to achieve the desired results. But this was 1915 or 1918, and such concepts were unknown or at any rate unpractised. Instead two extreme positions may be noted. One was typified by German research management which failed because Haber over-extended

Fig. 13. Haber somewhere behind the Western Front. Date not known, but likely to be some time in 1917. The man to whom he is talking is carrying the standard-issue German respirator. (Author's collection)

himself and did not delegate sufficiently, and the work of his institute was only intermittently successful. The failure was not due to lack of willing collaborators: there is no evidence that German scientists boycotted chemical warfare, and those that went to the KWI were sufficiently good to occupy high industrial or academic posts after 1918. But Hartley's enquiries showed that Haber was not good as a communicator (though in seminars he was inspiring) and that as the war progressed he became increasingly reluctant to take criticism. Hartley visited him in 1921 and noted that during the war he had dispersed his energies and so accomplished less than he set out to do. But Coates who knew him better and enquired more thoroughly reached different conclusions. He thought of Haber not as an 'initiator', but as a 'propagator', driven by intense ambition, and a brilliant organizer.[59] No clear picture emerges. It seems to me that he was better at planning and establishing principles than at managing what he had created. In the last eighteen months of the war he was visibly tiring, and his attitude and letters reflect a growing pessimism: exhaustion and despair affected his judgement and decisiveness when they were most needed.[60]

The other extreme is exemplified by the British. They faced an entirely different situation, and the CWC was their characteristic response to it—collective responsibility for research and development through committee procedures. Theirs was not a one-man show with short lines of communication, but a system of groups—some of whom were quarrelling vigorously. Yet the roots of their difficulties lay elsewhere. Their research laboratories were dispersed so that good communications and frequent exchanges of view were essential and became an integral part of the Allied research organization. The details are important and warrant a digression.

At the level of scientific intelligence, the British and Germans put some faith into periodic, confidential bulletins: *Gas Warfare*, a monthly, was one of Hartley's earliest literary efforts and remains a source of much useful information. *Mitteilungen der Chemischen Abteilung des Kriegsministerium* was rather more scholarly, and was probably edited by Epstein. Both circulated more widely than anticipated and fell into enemy hands, thus providing a neat example of involuntary cross-fertilization.[61] This was an academic approach to communication—reading is good, but personal contacts are better. Haber's answer was to look for himself and he exhausted himself by incessant travels, which he ought to have delegated to younger men. Among the Allies, however, the difficulties took another form. For example the IEEC members (except Kling) were kept away from GQG and Jackson's group were not allowed even 'unofficial' contacts with Foulkes and the Special Brigade until well into 1917. Crossley was frustrated, and barely was the war over than he wrote that Porton had never been 'in direct touch' (his underlining) with the experimental work of the Allies and with the Special Brigade and 'never had any pretence of a liaison [*sic*] with the Artillery in France though nearly one half of the total work carried out affected artillery problems.'[62] He was a difficult man, and he exaggerated, but there was substance in his complaint: no one in chemical warfare could compel the artillery staff to do something if it was not so minded. Good communications would have helped (or might have overcome the obstacles), but the system then in force was the ultimate barrier to change.

These problems were not solved in Germany, and not for several years by the other side, but in the case of the Allies distance and language created further difficulties. The obstacle that needed to be overcome was how to get the right people to trust each other sufficiently so as to talk freely to each other at least at the technical level. The Chemical Advisory Committee met the IEEC members on a single occasion, in October 1916, but the French never returned the visit. Crossley, before he went to Porton, made occasional forays to Paris. There were rare meetings in 1915–16 with the Russians who puzzled the British. As to the Italians, the sole scientific contact before Caporetto (October 1917) was a visit by Starling. Only the Americans were always eager to exchange information.[63] By contrast the Anti-Gas Department had at all times the most cordial relations with the BEF.

Some improvements came from an unexpected and unlikely quarter. A junior officer in the Special Brigade, Victor Lefebure, happened to be a fluent French speaker. As he was unpopular with his superiors, but charmed the French, he was made unofficial liaison officer to them in the opening months of 1917.

Where others had failed, he succeeded. He got some useful information on French phosgene manufacture and then helped to organize the first Anglo-French conference on gas warfare (28–9 May 1917) and a larger Inter-Allied gas conference in September 1917. These meetings were very successful, and Terroine offered to put the IEEC staff at the disposal of a permanent secretariat which later organized two further meetings in March and October 1918.[64] The purpose of these gatherings was to review the progress in offence and defence and enable scientists to meet and exchange ideas. The quality of the papers varied and on offensive materials the contributions were marked by some reticence— they tended to be long on molecular structure and short on the results of field trials.[65] The personal contacts, however, were valuable in at least two respects: the treatment of gas casualties and the production of mustard gas. The difficulties posed by each would in any case have been surmounted, but better communications speeded the process and raised the intensity of the Allied effort whilst mitigating the consequences of similar German action. Limited collaboration continued after the war: Allied chemists visited the German factories in 1919 and worked together in the technical section of the Disarmament Commission.

Research policy and organization were important aspects of chemical warfare. Each country had its own particular approach, copying from others or improvising as circumstances dictated. Time was of the essence, and both sides wasted it. Ideally the management of research should have been characterized by flexible responses to military and technological changes, and also by quick decisions. The belligerents did not achieve either, except in a few instances, mainly in gas defence, throughout the three and a half years of chemical warfare. Perhaps neither side found the optimal solution (or an approximation to it) because the particular problems of military chemical research and development had not been encountered before and grew more complex as the war progressed. Relations with the users had no precedent, except in the supply of high explosives, and until a routine channel of communications had been established, the two parties, scientists and soldiers, failed to understand each other. As far as the former were concerned this is hardly surprisingly: their new jobs were so unusual by comparison with pre-war academic life, that a mental blockage was to be expected and would take time to remove. As for the latter, the situation as it unfolded never ceased to bewilder the regular soldiers. Their role as users and as victims of gas warfare has next to be considered.

It was believed in some quarters that chemists were seen to be on military service when gas troops were being raised, trained, and sent on operations. The facts were different. What was seen in reality was the reluctant acceptance by professional officers of a technological innovation.

In the British Army the formal link between offensive and defensive in chemical warfare dates from March 1916 when the first Director of Gas Services (DGS) was appointed. He was a senior officer of the Royal Engineers, Brig.-

Gen. Thuillier, who had commanded the support brigade of the 1st Division at Loos. He now took over the Special Companies, commanded by Col. (later Major-Gen.) C. H. Foulkes, RE, and the anti-gas organization under Col. S. L. Cummins, RAMC, who, with a small staff, had been doing this work since April 1915. Thuillier was stationed at GHQ. He had considerable delegated powers on defence. But on offensive matters, his men, though henceforth grouped for administrative purposes as the Special Brigade RE, continued to be employed, in company strength as GHQ, Army, or Corps commanders thought fit. Foulkes, though not Thuillier, was upset by such tactics, there were frequent clashes, and he became thoroughly unpopular among senior officers. Foulkes was not a chemist, so he was dependent on the advice of his gas officers—keen amateur soldiers, but not professional sappers and on T. H. Adams, the optimistic Brigade intelligence officer, who overrated the effectiveness of cloud gas.

Thuillier avoided arguments, and after the Somme became disenchanted with cloud-gas discharges. Instead he gave his support to Livens's projector and to gas bombs fired from trench mortars; in both respects he saw further than his deputy. In June 1917 he was promoted to the command of the 15th Division, which, by a curious irony, was to suffer heavy casualties a few weeks later when the Germans first used mustard-gas shell in the Salient. Foulkes succeeded Thuillier as DGS with the result that cylinder operations were again in the ascendant. At about the same time, Hartley took over Cummins's job, and Eddis, another regular RE, became Foulkes deputy on the offensive side.[66]

The numbers and duties of the Special Brigade varied a good deal. During the winter of 1915–16, about 1,000 RA drivers were winkled out from base depots and strengthened Foulkes's companies, until the Offensive Branch had about 5,000 men by early summer 1916. There were some reductions the following winter because of transfers to Helfaut, the Calais factory, and to the Anti-Gas side. But in 1917–18 the numbers increased again to about 6,000, of whom roughly 1,000 were not available for cylinder operations. The other 5,000 or so carried out normal RE duties, when not engaged in gas warfare operations.[67]

The German approach was different and simpler. Major (later Col.) Max Bauer, a gunner and staff officer of many years' standing, headed the technical section at OHL. He had operational control of chemical warfare and as far back as August 1915 had laid down the guide-lines for cylinder operations: cloud gas was to be employed for diversionary purposes or when it was desired to harass the enemy, without however, attacking him. Reports from observers at the front determined the location and provided the background against which H. Geyer, a staff officer in Bauer's department, would draw up the detailed plans with the technical assistance of Haber. Army or Corps commanders had to give their final approval and the special gas troops would then be sent to the particular sector. Bauer considered this the best way of using gas clouds, and his approach never varied in 1915–17; battalion and regimental COs who were at the sharp end, with little control over the operation, were naturally of a contrary opinion.[68]

The commander of the Gaspioniere, was a regular engineer officer, Otto Peterson, who became a major-general in 1917. He had little say in the employment of his men and was treated as the head of a technical group, rather than as a senior field commander. The German gas troops were formed into Pionier Regiments 35 and 36, each with a self-contained HQ section comprising cylinder- or projector-filling teams, signals and meteorological sections, and transport columns. The companies usually moved in small groups, called Gas Kommandos, and their principal duties were to ensure that the supplies were available when needed and to supervise the carrying parties provided by the infantry. They were not expected to have any particular chemical expertise, and specialist advice was obtained from men sent by Haber at Geyer's request.[69] When they were not on gas duties, the men worked as engineers.

The Gaspioniere gradually faded out of the picture in the last year of the war. But the organization was retained, in that Geyer remained in charge of plans, though he now dealt principally with Corps artillery commanders and prepared major gas shoots in association with them. Specialist advisers were sent from the OHL or Berlin to settle the technical details.

At first the French staff, and even Joffre himself, were enthusiastic about cloud-gas discharges. The Compagnies Z of the French Génie Corps were formed in December 1915. GQG had ambitious plans for them and the number of companies was quickly raised from three to six and then to nine. Soulié, who had been in command of the unsuccessful action in Champagne, was promoted to Lt.-Colonel, but the higher rank was of little help to him when it came to recruiting his men. Those he did find took longer to train than expected. He worked from an office at the War Ministry in Paris and executed such orders as he received from GQG at Chantilly. He made sallies to Le Bourget where the cylinders were filled and stored, and the Z companies had their depot. It was a prudent way of waging chemical warfare and it also reflected the growing lack of interest shown by GQG in gas operations. Nevertheless, the strength of the force gradually rose, and by mid 1916, the first two fully equipped battalions mustered 1,800 officers and other ranks, and a third was being formed. But GQG could not prevail on Army Commanders to put these specialists to work. Thus they were idle or served as pioneers. The better officers and NCOs were drawn into gas defence groups and the numbers employed in gas warfare fell. At the end of the war, the paper strength of the Z companies was 3,400, but the numbers trained and available for cylinder or projector operations was a fraction of that figure.[70]

The offensive actions of the other European belligerents can be quickly dismissed: the Russians claimed they discharged gas clouds against German and Austrian troops on 24 occasions in the twelve months to mid 1917. The Germans failed to notice them. The Italian gas troops, all 500 of them, went into action just once against the Austrians, and caused them casualties. The claim is not confirmed. [71]

But the Americans took gas very seriously indeed. Unlike the other belligerents they considered it a major new weapon. At a time when the Allies were cutting down on gas troops or used them for other duties, the American Expeditionary Force (AEF) was building them up. Men from the 30th Regiment of Engineers were seconded for training in August–September, 1917. A few months later the force was renamed 1st Gas Regiment, shipped to France, and continued to train there. To begin with, the American troops supported companies of the Special Brigade in operations during spring and early summer of 1918. The regiment was gradually reinforced so that the effective strength rose slowly to 3,400 men by autumn. The gas troops worked in the Meuse–Argonne sector in the last weeks of the war and carried out several projectile attacks on German strong-points.[72]

The 1st Gas Regiment was the first complete fighting unit of a new branch of the American armed forces—the Chemical Warfare Service (CWS). Created at the end of June 1918 it was entirely self-contained, complete with research and manufacturing facilities. The Americans signified to the world by this theatrical gesture that gas warfare would play an important role in the 1919 campaign. That was for the future. For the present, the service had as its head a General of the Engineers, W. L. Sibert, who had had an interesting but checkered career. The structure of his command was unconventional, but never had time enough to prove itself, though the approach was imaginative. Sibert's equivalent to Foulkes, the OC, 1st Gas Regiment, was another engineer, Amos A. Fries, renowned for building roads and bridges in the Yellowstone National Park. He was to play a big part in post-war military politics. In the latter half of 1918, he and his chief were busy empire-building and arranging maximum publicity for the exploits of their men.[73]

At the peak—around the middle of 1916—the European belligerents had between 15,000 and 16,000 men in offensive chemical warfare. Two years later the muster roll was well down, since the Russians were out of the war and the French and Germans gas troops were mostly on other duties. The British strength was roughly at the 1916 level, but the American forces were growing towards a planned year end-target of 13,500.

The numbers are hardly impressive and it is significant that among the hundreds of regimental histories and personal reminiscences, there are fewer than half a dozen accounts of the work of the gas troops. Why this reticence? First, and surely the main reason, there was not much of a story to tell. Secondly, whatever the scientists' excitement over gas in the early days, there was a certain futility about it—made by man, yet uncontrollable—which was difficult to explain away. By contrast the aircraft and the tank remained mechanical novelties, continued to develop fast throughout the war, were surrounded by romantic glamour and created a military tradition which cloud gas never achieved at the time, nor later in history books. Thirdly, the contribution made by cloud gas in 1915–16 was at best spasmodic and in the later stages of the war irrelevant to the collapse of Germany. Fourthly there was some embarrassment or perhaps guilty conscience about the evocation of poison-gas operations. This is no more than a feeling, but the users of gas remain an elusive and shadowy group of men.

Those who dealt with defence against gas began with a large measure of goodwill which they retained and indeed increased. They were articulate, knew they were doing an important job, and left behind much useful information. They were an energetic group, competent, and willing to put their hand to anything that needed attention. The job was, as Auld—one of them—said later, 'no sinecure' and they carried it out to the full. Their selection was peculiar: they were generally youngish dons or research assistants invited by Cummins, Haldane, or Haber to help out during the emergency. Among the British who later became FRS were A. J. Allmand, C. G. Douglas, and Harold Hartley. Arthur Smithells was already one, while L. J. Barley and S. J. Auld made names for themselves in the chemical industry and in agricultural science. Haber's role on the other side has already been noted, and his section heads in charge of protective equipment became important figures in post-war German science. The later careers of French or Italian gas officers are not known to me.

As there was no precedent for the work of gas officers, they tackled defence against gas as academics, not as regular soldiers. Here, at last, one could see scientists at war. Their purpose was to overcome ignorance through education, to help soldiers master their fear of the unknown by learning about gas, to have confidence in the respirator and, about all, to teach from experience. Initially the duties of the Chemical Advisers were not defined. At army or corps level, these advisers, usually lieutenants or captains, began by organizing crash courses in gas defence; then they established and supervised anti-gas instruction for NCOs; next they tried out every new pad, hood, or mask and endeavoured to improve them; later they began to collect chemical intelligence. At division, battery, or battalion level, specially trained junior officers or NCOs attended to the weekly inspection of masks, checked stores and gas-proof shelters, and gave lectures when the men were out of the line.[74]

The Germans were slower than the British in developing an equivalent service and recognizing its military importance. Up to the autumn of 1916, the Medical service was responsible for instruction and the issue of respirators, and the Army Gas Officer (Stabs-Offizier Gas, hence Stogas) reported to the head of the Army Medical Services, which burdened them with all the paper-work generated by supplies and stores; in the BEF the Ordnance Corps handled these chores. All this changed after mid 1916, not least because the events at Hulluch had shown grave defects in the German defences against gas (see Chapter 5). An energetic Stogas by name of Fuchs in the 6th Army made a big fuss and Haber's report on mask inspection and instruction generally alerted OHL and the Army Commanders to the potentially dangerous situation that might arise if nothing was done and the Allies increased the intensity of their gas attacks. Accordingly the position of the Stogas at army HQ was raised and full-time gas officers were appointed to each division. All had some knowledge of chemistry. In August and again in December 1916 (by which time Haber's section in the Kriegsministerium had taken over from the medical services) circulars spelled out the duties of the officers, and added two new ones to those of the Stogas:

he was to advice on planned gas-attacks and to collect chemical intelligence. The manning tables, especially at divisional level, were lower than in the BEF, mainly because there were no Gas Schools. Consequently there were probably no more than 200 or 250 people in the German anti-gas service.[75]

The other European belligerents followed British or German precedent, or rather copied what seemed most suitable, the difference being one of degree and of timing. There were, in addition, some other distinctions which, for the sake of completeness, call for brief mention. The British had a Central Laboratory at St Omer which reported to the DGS and was directed first by W. Watson FRS and later by B. Mouat Jones. It operated from Spring 1915 to the end of 1918 and, at its peak, employed about thirty people—chemists, physiologists, and other qualified scientists, assistants, technicians, and clerks. It served a useful purpose since it was fully equipped for every kind of analytical work and saved much time by making reference to UK laboratories superfluous. The Americans copied it, at first in temporary quarters outside Paris and later in elaborately fitted-out laboratories, built and crated in the USA, shipped to France and reassembled there. Around 65 scientists together with supporting staff, engaged in all manner of activity, some unconnected with the needs of the front; no less than a third carried out purely administrative duties.[76]

The French had the Centres Médicaux-Légaux which Kling had set up in mid 1915 and which he supervised for the duration. One of these mobile forensic laboratories was attached to each of the three Army Groups. With his police background, Kling approached defence against gas in the same way as he would have tackled a criminal investigation: determine the facts, then take appropriate action. His staff therefore began by studying the causes of death. When chemical warfare intensified, they were given additional duties. In particular they had to oversee the work of the newly created *Officiers ZP* who were posted to every army, corps, and division in the winter of 1916–17 to take charge of the issue and maintenance of respirators, technical intelligence, and scientific advice to senior commanders.[77] They resembled in many ways the German Stogas and *Gas Offiziere* of lower rank.

The Gas Schools, not the Special Companies nor the Gaspioniere or the Compagnies Z were the enduring monuments to the chemists. The first in the BEF opened in January 1916. Eventually every army and every corps had one. Here NCOs were trained intensively for a fortnight and then ran the instruction courses at divisional level. There were also shorter courses for regimental officers designed to impress upon them the necessity for high efficiency in defence against gas. At the base depots drafts fresh from England or the Empire were cursorily drilled and instructed. In this way millions of men learnt something about gas and many hundreds of thousands were subjected to more thorough anti-gas training which included lectures, films, and practical demonstrations in chlorine-filled trenches or gas-chambers. After Caporetto the Italians were prevailed upon by Gen. Plumer and others to take gas defence as seriously as their British allies. Despite their hurt pride they took their lessons. The Americans needed no urging and set up an elaborate instruction system.[78]

The Germans and the French had their gas schools in Berlin and Paris respectively. The scope was much more restricted, but a few days of lectures and the off-duty evenings had their pleasurable side and were almost like leave, so they helped boost morale. The German courses were given by Haber's staff. Those for infantry officers were superficial, while those for gas officers and gas NCOs were thorough, though unimaginative—cloud-gas operations still occupied an entire morning, as late as September 1918! In Paris, Col. Tassilly held lectures from August 1916 onwards at the École de Pharmacie. Up to 300 men attended each session held in the big auditorium, as was the French academic custom. There were no practical demonstrations, no question-and-answer period, but it was estimated that altogether 14,000 officers and NCOs attended in the last two years of the war.[79] Thus some useful advice and some sensible precautions were spread widely, if thinly.

Years later, Barley talked to me about the gas schools, his fellow Chemical Advisers, and their frequent meetings. 'We were,' he said, 'with one or two exceptions, a band of brothers.'[80] The passage of time has had its usual mellowing effect, for other sources show that there was a marked lack of cordiality among the scientists. Still, these chemists on active service in the anti-gas sections of the armies represented the only group in the entire chemical warfare effort that was in regular close touch with the practicalities of the new weapon. Their primary role was to monitor defence and to ensure that it was never far behind (and preferably ahead of) offence. By the end of 1916 this had been achieved, and though the balance tilted towards the other side in 1917, defence recovered and in the last year of war was well in the lead.

7

THE ORGANIZATION OF CHEMICAL
WARFARE

A NEW supply route had to be organized to link manufacturers with the troops. Chemical warfare was a weapon whose complexity had not yet been tamed by tradition and procedures; exceptional organizational skills were therefore needed. Men were required who could bring together chemistry with industry, and both with offence and defence. One might have expected, since the same experience was shared by all the belligerents, that sooner or later all would adopt the same, or at least a similar, approach. But that did not happen. In the first place the state and structure of the chemical industries of the various countries continued to evolve along different lines. Secondly, the management of chemical warfare was determined largely by the personalities of the leading men and they could, were they so minded, run the show as they thought best, at any rate up to the end of 1917. And thirdly, the established military supply procedures, which could not be bypassed, were not designed and staffed to adapt smoothly to a rapidly changing technology. Thus there were structural, personal, and institutional aspects to organization which more often diverged than converged and served to create different patterns which determined the value of the gas weapon.

We may conveniently begin with the Germans for they had a head start over their enemies. Contrary to received opinion their supply channels were informal and free from bureaucracy. Haber, wearing his manager's hat, at first operated behind the scenes. The military decisions were taken at OHL by Bauer and Geyer; shells and bombs were the responsibility of Gen. Tappen, and the Army Medical Services dealt with respirator production, inspection, and distribution. Haber advised all of them, but outside Research and Development had, at first, no executive authority. He formally joined von Wrisberg's Allgemeines Departement at the Kriegsministerium some time in 1916—I have been unable to discover the exact date. He was put in charge of Section A10, chemical warfare supplies, which, at the peak of activity, numbered less than ten officers and civilian staff and had the support of altogether 14 clerks, typists, and messengers.[1] Such manpower economy was unusual in the Kriegsministerium, but Haber wanted it that way and told Hartley that a small organization ensured greater speed and security. That was a *post hoc* rationalization: throughout 1915 and for most of 1916 there was no clear policy and various functional responsibilities were handed over to A10 as circumstances arose. For example gas shells were added in the first half of 1916, and respirator production as well as all anti-gas services were taken over from the medical services in the latter part of the year.

Haber's energy and his excellent contacts with the leaders of the chemical industry and the technical people at OHL ensured that A10 ran smoothly (see Diagram 7.1) the creation of the Kriegsamt under General Groener added complications and enlarged the bureaucracy, but hardly touched A10: chemical warfare was not sufficiently important to become involved in the intrigues, and Haber's unofficial channels of communication proved invaluable. With Groener's dismissal in 1917, the Kriegsamt lost a great deal of its influence.[2] Nevertheless there were problems. All observers are agreed that Haber and his closest colleagues were under great stress.[3] The administrative machinery, though simple on paper and uncluttered in practice, could not cope satisfactorily with the details of production and project management in the last eighteen months of gas warfare. For instance, quality control and examination of respirators entailed responsibility for the stores, the inspectorate, and the women

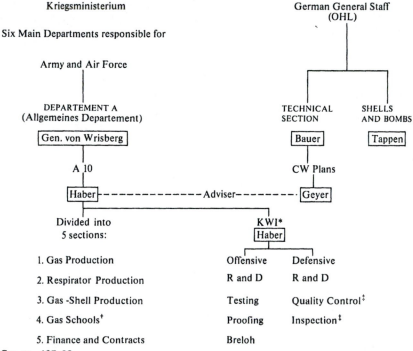

* See pp. 127–28.

† The organization of courses, selection of participants, etc. was handled by the administrative staff of the KWI.

‡ The management of the staff came administratively under the Respirator Section of A10.

Based on Hartley Report, pp. 14, 16, 18–19.

Diagram 7.1. German Chemical Warfare Organization from the end of 1916 to the Armistice who did the actual testing and packing. About four to five thousand civilians were employed on these tasks. The work was done in temporary accommodation in Dahlem at the KWI, but functionally came under A10. As the Dahlem site became increasingly congested, it was decided to build a large inspection centre at Adlershof in Berlin. The decision was right, but its implementation called for an immense effort which turned out to be wasted because the huge building was opened after the Armistice! Similar delays and frustrations surrounded the construction of the field research station at Breloh.[4] These were the collective failures of administrators, rather than of particular individuals. But it is interesting to note that while supplies moved smoothly from the factories, the timing of their use at the front was often faulty. This suggests that too much accumulated at the centre without considering the effect at the periphery: Haber could not be everywhere at once, nor was he good at delegating. So corners were cut and the pressure raised to save time and produce results. The outcome was to weaken the effectiveness of German chemical warfare as a whole.

The French were quickly off the mark. About the middle of June 1915, Weiss—whom we have already encountered in the preceding chapter in connection with research—was chairman of an inter-departmental committee dealing with gas and in that capacity he prepared for the Minister of War a scheme of organization. Its chief feature was that an additional Director-General would be appointed in the War Ministry with direct access to the Minister himself. The proposal came at an inopportune moment. A power struggle was developing in the Ministère de la Guerre, and Alexander Millerand, its political head, was forced to appoint four under-secretaries to appease the French Parliament. Among them was an energetic socialist politician, Albert Thomas, who took charge of guns and ammunition. Thomas had every intention of controlling chemical warfare supplies himself and therefore found the Weiss plan unacceptable. GQG also opposed it because it would leave the training of the Compagnies Z—which only existed on paper—in the hands of a civilian Director-General. So nothing was decided beyond establishing the Direction du Matériel Chimique de Guerre (DMCG) and restricting its activities to research and development. Thomas spent the next two months tightening his grip on the supply of munitions and when, in August, a group of Députés demanded the establishment of another Direction Générale, the thirteenth, specifically for gas warfare, he was ready for them. He merged all the various activities, offensive as well as defensive, loosely attached to the engineering and medical departments of the war ministry into the DMCG.[5] Then he got rid of Weiss, appointed Gen. Ozil, a regular officer from the Corps de Génie, and installed him and his staff at the École Supérieure de Pharmacie.

In the autumn of 1916 the supply of weapons was hived off from the Ministère de la Guerre and became a ministry of its own, the Ministère de l'Armement, under Thomas who was succeeded by Loucheur the following September. But the DMCG was not affected by the reorganization at the top: from September

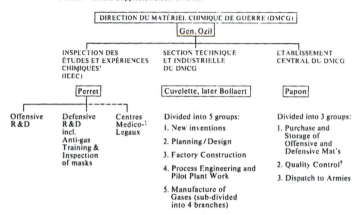

Ministère de la Guerre 1915–16
replaced by
Ministère de l'Armement 1916–18

Numerous *Directions Générales* (Departments) for Weapons, Munitions, Trench Warfare Supplies, Poison Gas, etc.

DIRECTION DU MATÉRIEL CHIMIQUE DE GUERRE (DMCG)

Gen. Ozil

INSPECTION DES ÉTUDES ET EXPÉRIENCES CHIMIQUES' (IEEC)	SECTION TECHNIQUE ET INDUSTRIELLE DU DMCG	ÉTABLISSEMENT CENTRAL DU DMCG
Perret	Cuvelette, later Bollaert	Papon

Offensive R&D	Defensive R&D incl. Anti-gas Training & Inspection of masks	Centres Medico-Legaux	Divided into 5 groups:	Divided into 3 groups:
			1. New inventions	1. Purchase and Storage of Offensive and Defensive Mat's
			2. Planning/Design	2. Quality Control'
			3. Factory Construction	3. Dispatch to Armies
			4. Process Engineering and Pilot Plant Work	
			5. Manufacture of Gases (sub-divided into 4 branches)	

* The Shell Filling Department was responsible for gas shells and the works at Vincennes and Aubervilliers which handled gas shells.

† See p. 126 for details.

‡ See p. 110 for details. Kling was the link between GQC and the IEEC.

§ Local offices at Lyon, Grenoble, Marseille.

Based on material in PRO/WO/142/176; PRO/MUN 5/386/1650/15; FMA 16N826 (d'Aubigny Report).

Diagram 7.2. French Chemical Warfare Organization 1915–1918

1915 to November 1918 there were no significant changes in the structure which remained simple. There were three sections or departments for research and development (the IEEC), for construction and production (Section Technique et Industrielle), and for purchase, quality control, and dispatch (Établissement Central du DMCG); the main outlines are shown in Diagram 7.2. Particulars of the numbers involved are not available, but the production section was certainly large since it had its own design and process engineering staff and eventually operated some chemical plants.[6]

The DMCG had all the advantages which continuity of management confers. It was also good on internal co-ordination. But Ozil was no Haber: he did not solve the chlorine shortage and, more seriously, made no impact on the scientists. He and his staff cannot have been unaware of the unsatisfactory condition of the French anti-gas measures and the importance of good respirators. In this, as in other ways, he was out of touch with GQG, though in fairness to the DMCG it must be remembered that the staff at Chantilly did not after 1916 take any particular interest in chemical warfare.

Before turning to Britain, the cursory treatment of the other belligerents calls for explanation. Next to nothing appears in the records, accessible to me, on Austria and Italy. But the gap is not serious since the only occasion on which gas played a significant role was at Caporetto in October 1917. The exclusion of Russia has other reasons. I have already mentioned that the British had chemical liaison officers in Petrograd and although their lengthy reports have survived, they were not interested in administrative details, nor were they asked about them. There is scarcely a reference to V. N. Ipatieff, a physical chemist who had contributed importantly to the Russian high explosives programme of 1915–16. In April 1916 he was appointed head of the Chemical Committee of the Chief Artillery Administration. Years later he described his activities, the account is one-sided, but there is no reason to doubt that he held far-reaching powers. Ipatieff was responsible for the supply of explosives, the chemicals used for them, gases, respirators, and pyrotechnic devices. Thus he was of all the professional scientists the one with the widest duties. He ran his large organization through five 'branches' or departments whose heads held weekly co-ordinating sessions. Regional offices handled supply matters and there were elaborate liaison arrangements with the Artillery Inspectorate which handled the dispatch and issue of all chemical warfare stores. It would be interesting to know how a backward bureaucracy dealt with the problems posed by the novel demands made on chemical manufacturers separated by vast distances; unfortunately such information is not available in the West.[7]

In contrast to Russia there is a wealth of material on the United States. But it can be briefly dismissed because the creation and organization of the CWS though a matter of official concern for many months, did not take place until the end of June 1918, and the effects were not perceived until the closing weeks of the war. Before then, several branches of the War Department had been involved and had proceeded independently so that there had been much conflict, many delays, and few links with Research and Development which came under the Bureau of Mines of the Department of the Interior (see Chapter 6). The CWS, when it was finally established, went much further than the measures adopted by Germany and France, and showed that something had been learnt from the British muddles with which people in Washington were familiar. It was an integrated and autonomous branch of the US armed forces with its own research and development facilities, manufacture, and issue to the troops.[8] It therefore secured a position which other belligerents never conceded to chemical warfare in their military–industrial planning. Gen. Sibert, the GOC, ran the CWS like a business: 'Divisions', that is departments with specific functional duties, were set up to deal with every aspect of chemical warfare, and indeed extended to the Gas Regiments in France which were to spearhead the final offensive in Spring 1919. These arrangements—some working, a few no more than ambitious paper plans—were in line with the American technological approach to the European war. The CWS was seen by its protagonists as a turning-point in the history of warfare. In practice it was nothing of the kind. The new branch made no significant contribution to the American military potential. The infantry were equipped with British respirators, the artillery used French shell cases, and the toxic ingredients were predominantly supplied by both allies. Only at the very end of the war, in September, and more particularly in October–November 1918 did American-made chemical supplies begin to reach the front. Thus the interest of the CWS lies not in its wartime role, but in its post-war influence and will be considered in its proper place.

The British went their own way. Their arrangements were unusual and remained inappropriate for over two years. We have seen in Chapter 6 (pp. 121–5) that offensive and defensive research were separate until October 1917, here we need to follow the tortuous arrangements for production. At the outset one may ask why an unsatisfactory state of affairs was tolerated far longer in Britain than in Germany or in France. The answers are to be found in the structure of the Ministry of Munitions (MoM) and particularly in the Trench Warfare Department (TWD) and in the War Office, specifically its Anti-Gas Department, and the reluctance of the latter to have anything to do with the TWD.

The Anti-Gas Department, initially known as the Anti-Gas Supply Committee, was from the outset in daily touch with the contractors who supplied mouthpads and gas helmets. Despite the manufacturing complexities of the SBR and the rapid increase in the scale of production, the organization, under Horrocks, remained simple and effective, and performed its job, as we shall see, satisfactorily. Meanwhile at the MoM, Lloyd-George had accorded the top officials, the Directors-General, wide powers. Delegation was all very well, but in the early months confusion and the lack of shells dominated everything. The TWD was also involved in the munitions crisis, but Jackson was not the man to cope with technical details, manage his scientific advisers, organize civil servants, and give orders to manufacturers. By mid October 1915 his staff numbered 182, among them 28 Section Heads, scores of clerks and messengers, and about 80 manual workers who filled grenades at Watford or handled trench stores. Diagram 7.3 displays the elaborate organization and shows the variety of activities for which Jackson was responsible. At the end of the year, his Financial Adviser, Alexander Roger, emerged victorious from a departmental reshuffle and became Head of Supply, while Jackson had to be content with Research and Design, but excluding the design of gas shells. The official explanation for the split in the TWD was that too much time was spent on research and not enough on production: judging by performance, both accurately described the situation, but the outcome of the new arrangement was not to strengthen either. Gas supplies, cylinders with their odds and ends, and grenades came under Henry Moreland, an accountant without chemical knowledge, like Roger.[9] There was no improvement in 1916, except for Roger who became a Director-General and was able to squeeze out Jackson altogether. Thus, by the autumn of that year the organization of British chemical warfare was divided into four: the Special Brigade in France, the Anti-Gas Department at the War Office, Jackson's small band in the Design Department of the MoM, and Roger's empire at the TWD (see Diagram 7.4). Roger was now in charge of ten sections, one of them being Moreland's with eight chief assistants, thirty-

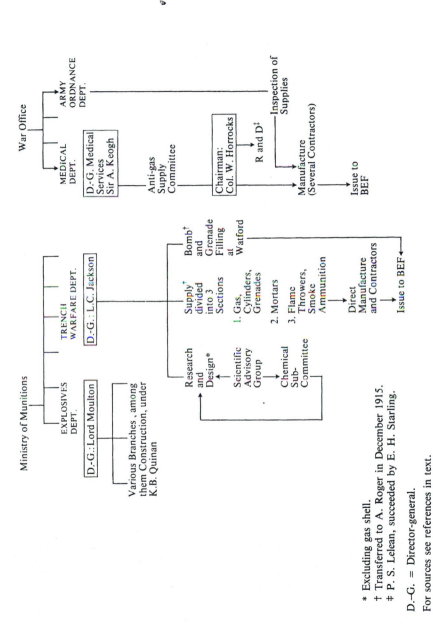

* Excluding gas shell.
† Transferred to A. Roger in December 1915.
‡ P. S. Lelean, succeeded by E. H. Starling.

D.-G. = Director-general.

For sources see references in text.

Diagram 7.3. British Chemical Warfare Organization, September 1915

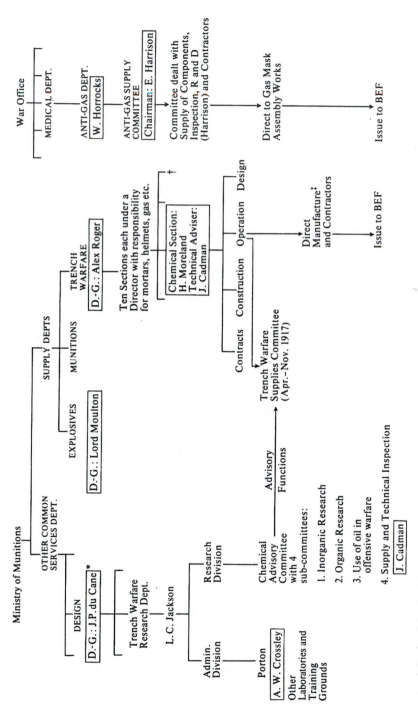

Diagram 7.4. British Chemical Warfare Organization, Autumn 1916

* Replaced by Gen. F. R. Bingham in August 1917.
† Filling trench mortar bombs and shells with chemical warfare materials did not form part of Moreland's section.
‡ Excludes phosgene plant and projectile filling unit at Calais which were run by RE men of the Special Brigade.

D.-G. = Director-general.

For sources see references in text.

four other employees, and hundreds of workers at Watford and Greenford filling chemical bombs and later also chemical shells. Moreland's lack of scientific knowledge was not considered a handicap, but for some months he had a technical adviser, John Cadman, who not only had a foot in Jackson's camp, but could not stand the incompetence of the bureaucrats, and was removed. Not everyone in the TWD was self-seeking or ignorant, but in general the department was not doing its job. E. S. Montague and Dr C. Addison, who followed Lloyd George as Ministers of Munitions, thought that chemical warfare was irrelevant compared with the supply of shell cases and HE, and therefore tolerated the failures of poison-gas supplies. But during 1917 the structure of the MoM came under increasingly effective attack: change was overdue and Churchill took charge in July. He was fascinated by military technology, interested in chemical weapons, and impatient of delay. He began to reorganize in August, went to France to discuss gas supplies and on return initiated moves which transformed the situation.[10]

Roger resigned in October and went to the Ministry of Reconstruction. Moreland (and others at Director level) lost their right of access to the Minister and became accountable to Controllers who, in turn, reported to Members of the Munitions Council which operated like a board of directors. With Roger as well as Jackson gone, the way was now open to end the absurdities of British chemical warfare organization. The Chemical Warfare Department (CWD) was established as one of the departments of the Design Group of the Munitions Council. Thuillier was recalled from France to become Controller of CWD. He had plenty of experience as a 'user' of gas, was accustomed to command, and turned out to be a good and conciliatory chairman. In Cols. Winsloe and Harrison he had some first-rate assistants who were excellent administrators. The CWC (see p. 125) turned out to be too large, so Thuillier divided it into three groups for offensive, defensive, and supply business. It should be noted that even at this late stage of the war the Controller was not directly responsible for supply. That function was entrusted to E. V. Haigh, in the newly created post of Controller, Trench Warfare Supply; he reported to Sir Keith Price, who headed the Explosives Group, but Thuillier was specifically authorized by Churchill to monitor and report on the progress of supplies. One branch, Gas Supply, depended on the indestructible Moreland (see Diagram 7.5).

Moving people about and creating a new organization can produce quick results. In this case it did not. In 1918 gas warfare was largely a matter for the artillery, but there were no formal links between the CWD and the Director of Artillery at the War Office. Equally troublesome was the continuing shortage of phosgene and the lack of mustard gas: both were to be used during 1918 and on a much larger scale in 1919. Another reorganization was needed to energize the production side. At the end of April 1918, the CWD was moved from the Design to the Explosives Group, and the Trench Warfare Supplies Department was broken up. Henceforth all production questions were settled at intra-departmental conferences chaired by Price and attended among others

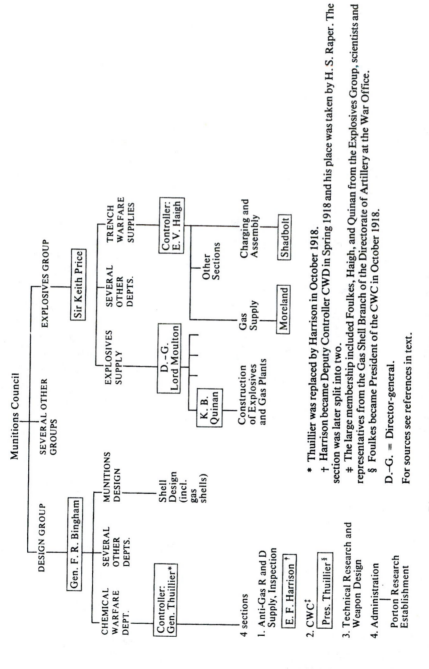

* Thuillier was replaced by Harrison in October 1918.

† Harrison became Deputy Controller CWD in Spring 1918 and his place was taken by H. S. Raper. The section was later split into two.

‡ The large membership included Foulkes, Haigh, and Quinan from the Explosives Group, scientists and representatives from the Gas Shell Branch of the Directorate of Artillery at the War Office.

§ Foulkes became President of the CWC in October 1918.

D.–G. = Director-general.

For sources see references in text.

Diagram 7.5. British Chemical Warfare Organization, end of 1917 by Lord Moulton and K. B. Quinan, of whom more will be heard later. At last every activity connected with chemical warfare came under a single head, Price: lines of command were now short and duplication ended. (There was yet another change to a new Group, W, of the Munitions Council in July 1918, but it does not affect the story.)[11] The April reforms strengthened the hands of the new men and created an organization which resembled that adopted by the French in September 1915 and by the Germans about fifteen months later.

The time wasted by mismanagement and the toleration of incompetence could not be made up. The effects would have been even more serious if inter-allied co-operation had been less effective. The chlorine for phosgene exchange between the British and the French enabled both to wage chemical warfare in 1916 and 1917. But as there were still severe production problems a year later, the British proposed and the French agreed to an inter-allied conference on chemical supplies. Ozil chaired the first meeting of the Comité des Fabrications Chimiques on 6 March 1918. It was such a success that a second meeting was held in mid May. The 'exchange-and-mart' approach was generally beneficial: the French needed bleaching powder and chlorine, had a surplus of phosgene, and might even have some mustard gas to spare later in the year. The British fielded Haigh, Pope, and Moreland who offered chlorine and bleach powder, and Fries on behalf of the Americans promised carbon tetrachloride, then used as a solvent for mustard gas. The meetings and deals continued during the summer and were based on production statistics which the DMCG. collated and circulated every month.[12] Thus, in the final phases of the war the organization of production was becoming increasingly business-like and assuming a multinational dimension.

Chemical warfare made unprecedented demands on the chemical industry, yet the scale of output by comparison with explosives, shell cases, or transport equipment was small. It also posed unusual problems because the manufacturers—excepting only the Germans—were working at the frontiers of applied science. Another curious aspect of this history, is that despite the intensive activities of all concerned, poison gases and respirators, made no lasting industrial impact. We shall be noting the acceleration of technical change in the production of liquid chlorine, phosgene, and ethylene which spread widely beyond Germany after 1915, but otherwise the numerous products and components vanished with the Armistice. After 1918, manufacture, where it continued at all, was transferred to Government establishments, so that poison gas and the defence against it cannot be said to have affected the structure of industry in the way that other 'war babies' such as dyestuffs intermediates, aero engines, or radio components did.

The following account is restricted to Britain, France, and Germany, and the United States are only mentioned to draw contrasts. Details on Russian activities were not available to me, but the documents at the PRO show that they produced liquid chlorine, chloropicrin, and even phosgene during

1916—though I was not able to reconcile the available statistics. Whatever the accuracy of the numbers, it is certain that the increasing volume came too late to have a bearing on the military effort.[13] In Italy production 'took off' even later than in Russia, but there appeared to be shortages and supply failures even in 1918. On Austria the reports are fragmentary, but it is known that the Germans supplied the bulk of what was used.[14]

In Spring 1915, the British and the French, eager to retaliate, had no idea whence to obtain the various chemical warfare agents. Military officialdom did not, at first, know where to look for liquid chlorine, nor were there any trade associations to which they could turn for help. The first formal enquiries were made by the Ministère de la Guerre towards the end of May, and the War Office finally got in touch with Castner-Kellner about liquid chlorine a fortnight later— eight weeks after the German surprise.[15] An early difficulty was how to distinguish between the rogues and the genuine contractors—for the majority of the chemical advisers as well as the TWD lacked commercial experience. Then there was the problem of prices and contracts. Gases and gas masks were new stores with no established costs. All purchases in Britain were therefore provisional until some months later formal supply contracts were signed. These ad hoc measures and the unconventional procedures for paying bothered conventionally minded Civil Servants and auditors. It's a wonder that anything got done. From May 1916 onwards the MoM supplied the raw materials (in particular bleaching powder and liquid chlorine) free of charge and paid the manufacturer 10 per cent on his invoiced price. There was no incentive under this system for economizing materials and much scope for padding out labour costs and overheads. Chloropicrin and tear gas were prepared under this arrangement, which was widely criticized at the time, for the next two years until the Department of Explosives Supply took over and introduced strict checks on costs. The Ministry usually paid for repairs and replacements and, where toxic materials were involved, covered the manufacturer against all risks. Capital expenditure was a charge on the Treasury. The orders for anti-gas equipment followed a different procedure and during 1915 were placed with a large number of contractors entirely 'by word of mouth', and formalized in writing much later.

The French dispensed with all pretence of costing and, initially, bought whatever was available regardless of price. The Germans had a great advantage over their enemies for many of the chemicals were on the manufacturers' lists and there were no particular shortages. The Kriegsministerium was therefore in a strong bargaining position, but did not exercise it. The supplies were ordered according to specification and the Ministry announced how much it was prepared to pay. The chemical concerns were left to work out the details among themselves. They usually chose a single producer, either because the company had spare capacity or the lowest costs (or both), and so the highest profit margin. In this way, everyone was satisfied. Capital expenditure on extra plant was generally small and not a contentious item.[16]

Thus production for chemical warfare got under way. One difficulty overlooked at the outset reflected the characteristic inter-dependence of chemical products. The Germans were occasionally bothered by it, the Allies frequently. The most persistent was acetic acid, while bleaching powder and ethyl alcohol, required in large volumes, created major bottlenecks. These supply links were not only technical, they were also at every stage a matter of priorities. All the belligerents discovered that as gas warfare intensified, so the price mechanism ceased to function and it became necessary to have 'friendly' negotiations between customer and contractors. Thus arose the other difficulty, how to make sure of the principal raw materials, and in this area the problems were never completely solved, except by some recourse to the black market. When negotiations failed, they were replaced by agreements within the industry and policed by it—the jargon term was 'informal general control'. This was widely used in Germany and Britain in about 1916–17, but when it too failed, formal allocations and rationing became unavoidable in 1917–18. In Britain bleaching powder, chlorine, and acetic acid were handled in this way, the first having been on allocation as early as October 1916.[17] In Germany the shortage of chemicals was not serious, but natural rubber and cotton were scarce even before the end of 1915 and disappeared altogether in the next eighteen months.

When we turn from raw material supplies to production, the story quickly becomes complex. To avoid repetition and to simplify matters we shall look at it from different viewpoints: first, the nature of the materials and of the components; next, manufacturing operations, their characteristics and efficiency; third, the principal firms involved in the preparation of gases and respirators; fourth, the trend in output. Finally, all these strands are combined in terms of the structure and state of the chemical and other industries.

Metal goods were essential to chemical warfare. Canisters, wire gauze, or expanded metal and other respirator components secured high priority and steel-strip or tin-plate were made available to contractors. But gas projectiles—as distinct from shell cases which were in short supply for most of the war—had a low ranking. Livens and his father showed ingenuity and persistence in locating stocks of 50 mm sheet at Stewarts and Lloyds which, somehow, had been overlooked. By contrast seamless drawn tube of about the same thickness, ideal for pressure gas cylinders, was hard to come by and the Special Brigade had to make elaborate arrangements to return empty cylinders to Britain for washing out, thence to the suppliers for refilling, and so back to the Front.[18]

Chemicals, above all chlorine and the products dependent on it—phosgene, chloropicrin, and later mustard gas, caused the Allies constant concern. They were required on the scale of up to several thousand tonnes a year and the necessary equipment had to be provided. There were many obstacles. Know-how was one, lack of plant designers and builders another, delays in obtaining the electrical components, copper conductors, compressors, and other machinery a third. In these respects the Germans and also the Americans were better provided. The situation with regard to organic chemicals was even worse. The Allied purchasing missions strove to cope with the shortage of acetate of lime, methanol, and ethyl alcohol, needed respectively for acetic acid, formaldehyde, and dichlorodiethyl sulphide. They were only partly successful.[19] Once again the Germans were unaffected. But they had their troubles too, and a few were insoluble. Lack of rubber and cotton forced them to adopt a small filter element with all the drawbacks this entailed. Recovered rubber, which they used for some months, disappeared in 1917 and they developed leather masks, cut from sheep- or goat-skins that had been dressed with a mixture of naphthalene and waste oil. The Germans asserted, and experience bore them out, that these leather masks performed as well as those made from recovered rubber.[20]

At first labour presented few problems, though skilled men such as bricklayers, plumbers, braziers, welders, and electricians were always scarce and commanded high wages. Later, when even reserved occupations were 'combed out' it became difficult to retain healthy, strong men who were essential for gas-shell filling: the work, though not physically very heavy, was exceptionally demanding because there were frequent gas leaks and dangerous spillages were unavoidable with mustard gas. Stamina, care, and quick wits were called for. The British were unable to find enough men for their mustard-gas programme, while the French employed a high proportion of men unfit for military service, prisoners, and foreigners in the chlorine and phosgene factories with the result that productivity per head was low. Respirators were regarded as women's work. The need to attract and retain sewing-machine operators and dextrous assemblers led to the establishment of special gas-mask factories in the most populous districts of London, Paris, Berlin, and ultimately, New York. Filling canisters with charcoal and permanganate granules was another kind of work, similar to that of bottling pills or packaging fine chemicals. Only a few firms had the necessary equipment and the trained women workers, so Boots at Nottingham, Bayer at Leverkusen, and Kahlbaum in Berlin, handled these operations.[21]

The nature and intensity of the demands made upon the contractors changed frequently. Most of the manufacturing problems were solved. But the solutions, often second best, and their timing, usually later than anticipated, were governed by the state of technology and the structure of the business which varied not only from product to product, but also from country to country.

On one side were the large firms which dominated the German dyestuffs industry. They appear to have had few production difficulties, except over ethylene where they could be attributed to construction delays. Even the copper shortage was circumvented by making wide use of aluminium for conductors and pipe-work, and the Allied teams inspecting the factories in 1919 were impressed by the quality of the workmanship and of the machinery. On the other side were the British and the French companies whose directors had first to catch up with the process technology and learn within months what the Germans had acquired by long experience. Secondly, they had to convert from the laboratory or pilot-plant scale to commercial production and obtain consistently good results. This called for machinery and plant which was often not quickly available. So it was necessary to improvise and hope that yields would improve.

With poison gas the problem was not the products, for these were known from the scientific literature, but how to make them quickly to strict specifications and in large quantities. With respirators the situation was entirely different. For example the SBR consisted of 195 parts—some of metal, others of fabric, rubber, or glass; chemicals were also needed. The masks were made at the rate of millions a month an output that required several hundred tonnes of charcoal in the same period. Some of the bits and pieces were sub-assembled like the canister or the face mask, and then dispatched for final assembly. The German respirator was simpler and had only twenty components, but the filter was much smaller than that of the SBR, so more had to be provided and that affected initial as well as final assembly. In anti-gas work, chemical know-how (except for charcoal) was irrelevant. The need was for production engineering, skill in applying mass production techniques, and the installation of machinery for pressing, die-stamping, fabric cutting, and stitching. The primitive pads and helmets of 1915 required only the most elementary mechanical aids, but the manufacture of masks on a huge scale in 1916–18 called for large buildings and labour-saving devices. E. W. Lucas and his colleagues installed conveyor belts and other mechanical handling equipment, as well as special soldering irons, compressed air-pipe systems, push-taps, and various testing devices in the London workshops, and we may be sure the Germans did the same. The French saved themselves all this trouble, because until the last year of the war they retained pads or snouts which were run up by the clothing firms in Paris and the South.[22]

All the belligerents had to accommodate their production schedules to the many small refinements introduced long after the basic design had been agreed and the parts therefore standardized. For example, the adaptability of rubber compounds was recognized and they were widely used. Phenolic resins were employed for some small components. The materials for eye-pieces changed from time to time: initially celluloid was preferred, later non-splinter glass, that is laminated glass with a gelatine layer, found favour and cellulose acetate was also used. A great deal of research and development went into the improvement of charcoal; it turned out to be of lasting value and one of the few positive results of chemical warfare. The type of wood used and the calcination method determined the characteristics of the charcoal which had to be hard, so as not to break into smaller pieces while being carried in the container, and also retain its absorptive power for months. The Germans relied on beechwood chips impregnated with zinc chloride. The British experimented with birchwood, logwood, nut shells, and fruit stones. None were entirely satisfactory or available in sufficient quantities (shipping constraints prevented the use of coconut shells, which the Americans used) and finally a specially briquetted mixture of charcoal and coal dust, activated with steam, gave the required dense material and increasingly displaced other forms of charcoal towards the end of the war.[23]

The quality of the products dispatched to the armies was supposed to be up to specification. That seems unlikely, if only because it was easier to establish standards on paper than check them at the point of destination. Only the British

Table 7.1. *Average British Plant Performance as percentage of Theoretical*

Input Material	End Use	%	Note
Bleaching Powder	Chloropicrin	81	average of 2 works
Chlorine	Phosgene	63	average of 2 works
Alcohol (92% C$_2$H$_5$OH)	Ethylene	48	
Sulphur and chlorine	Sulphur Chloride	95	average of 2 works

archives contain enough material to compare promise with performance. As regards toxic materials, a high standard of purity was regularly attained from mid 1917 onwards, but this was due in the main to stricter tests at the factories which condemned entire batches and so entailed a great waste of materials. The official figures given in Table 7.1 show the extent to which actual results differed, on average, from what was theoretically attainable. The latter would not be achieved in the laboratory except under ideal conditions, but, allowing for that, the British performance is unimpressive. The figure for bleaching powder reflects the great improvement in chloropicrin manufacture achieved in the last year of the war.[24] Up to then the performance of the suppliers had been only 60 per cent of theoretical.[25] Phosgene was throughout the war the great failure of the British chemical industry. As late as June 1918, 'firm' production represented about one-fifth of requirements—15 tons against 72 tons a week. The rest was bought from the French whose plants were more efficient. In 1916–17 they achieved 87 per cent of theoretical, whereas the British temporarily achieved 72 per cent (even that may have been too high because United Alkali's gas measurements were sometimes faulty) and Electro-Bleach and By-Products attained only 58 per cent.[26] The performance of the ethylene works was abysmal, but it is probable that the French (and possibly also the Germans) obtained similar low yields because the large-scale dehydration of alcohol was then a novel technique. There are other indicators of efficiency, notably output per head, but the only figures for this measure of productivity that I have been able to find are for French phosgene manufacture in July 1916.[27] It would be misleading to draw any conclusions from that information.

Quality control was the outstanding feature in respirator manufacture and productive efficiency took second place. Hence the extreme importance attached to testing procedures and the adoption of the principle, first by the British, later by the Germans, that examination formed an integral part of production. The Anti-Gas Department began by recruiting twenty inspectors, all of them men, and set them to work at the Camden Laundry, north London, in June 1915. Thereafter the numbers increased week by week, women replaced men, and in 1917 there were 2,800 of them in three stores depots and four inspection centres. Several hundred more tested finished masks as they came off the assembly lines in London and Nottingham. Altogether, about one-fifth of all direct employees on gas defence work were checking quality. Was this overdoing things? The answer is that it was unavoidable because of the adoption of a policy of sub-and sub-sub-contracting. The Anti-Gas Department was under great pressure to get the SBR into immediate quantity production from June 1916 onwards. If the orders were to be fulfilled, then the Department could not be choosy about the suppliers and must perforce make its own arrangements to ensure that the product was of a uniformly high standard. With over 160 contractors—some very small and most of them unable to control the quality of their materials and the finish of their product, it made sense to tolerate a high rejection rate, provided all worked flat out. Accordingly, the Department had teams of inspectors to examine every component on its arrival at the stores, that is at the 'input stage'. Each team was assigned a single part and worked in a separate room thereby ensuring uniformity. Ten per cent of all approved parts were checked a second time, and similarly the rejects were re-checked. In this way only components conforming to specification were accepted for sub- or final assembly. At the same time it did nothing to prevent waste, notably of parts made of rubber spoiled by poor workmanship. Nor did it penalize the careless contractors who presumably had to be tolerated since there were not enough of the good ones. Table 7.2 shows for a few components the average throughput, rejections, and other particulars between February 1917 and November 1918. The results from the Nottingham factory, which was somewhat smaller, also showed great variations in the proportion of rejects, and its is curious that the reject rates, where they can be compared, differ from the London results: expiratory valves averaged 13.3 per cent (nearly three times the top end of the London range), rubber mouth-pieces 6 per cent, angle tubes 12.7 per cent. On the other hand Nottingham got more reliable supplies of the metal containers (1.6 per cent rejected) and of the rubber connection tubes (5.8 per cent). Quality control was suited to statistical investigation, but beyond the 10 per cent sampling nothing was done, though it is apparent from the figures that have survived, that the contractors as a group did their work unevenly. There was also some waste at the 'output stage'. Every assembled mask was checked for air-tightness and for resistance to breathing through the filter. Before final packing, a 10 per cent sample test was made—if the mask failed in one particular, the entire batch was condemned.[29]

The German design was much simpler and there were fewer, but larger contractors, which—from the outset—were ordered to examine the quality of their goods. Because of the very large number of replacement filters the inspection staff for this sub-assembly was larger than the British. The German procedures were tightened up when the quality of the mask was criticized after the disaster at Hulluch in April 1916 (see p. 89). Moreover, the Germans could not afford to waste rubber. Accordingly the number of inspectors at contractors' factories was increased, and about 2,000 people were working in Berlin to check the final product, pack, and dispatch.[30]

Table 7.2. *Inspections and Rejections of Selected Gas Mask Components at London Depots*[28]

Description	Total inspected (mln.)	Daily average (in '000s)	No. of suppliers	Rejection range (per cent)	Remarks
Expiratory valves	15·4	35	17	3–5	Made of hard rubber by firms in rubber trade; a key part of SBR
Metal containers for filter mass	10·7	40	16	Best 0.5, generally 5–10	Some very large firms, e.g. Reads, Reckitt and Sons
Rubber connection tube	9·0	25	10	1–10	Very precise specification. Made by Dunlop, Leyland, and other firms in rubber trade
Rubber mouth-pieces	10·5	40	13	>2	Contains at least 50% rubber. Made by large firms
Inspiratory valves	n.a.	40	18	up to 70–80	Contains 80% pure rubber. High rejection rate due to bad cutting or shaping
Nose clips	16·9	40	6	1	Five suppliers from Birmingham
Angle Tubes	11·1	33	27	0.5–5.0	Made of brass. No large firms involved
Splinterless glass	7·4	75	1	10	Made by Roberts Capsule Stopper from purchased glass

There was no uniform pattern among the contractors, though collectively they mirrored the structure of industry among the belligerents. Relatively small firms might occupy important positions, whilst large companies—in the same sector—contributed very little. The initiative of the management, and sometimes good connections with Government departments, as well as spare capacity and technical competence, were important factors in the allocation of orders. It was rare for a company to supply the weapons for chemical warfare as well as the defences against it—Boots at Nottingham and Bayer at Leverkusen were the chief exceptions to this rule. At first there was no Government manufacture, but later 'national' factories were established because of the weaknesses, if not incompetence, in the private sector.

As far back as the autumn of 1914 Bayer had supplied lachrymatory substances to OHL and in the following year the Kriegsministerium first turned to them for gases. This may seem odd, for there were other large chemical firms which were not called upon to tender. The explanation is simple. Duisberg, the chief executive

Table 7.3. *Bayer's Production of War Gases 1915–1918*

Gas	Total (t)	Maximum Production Month	t/month
Chlorine	14,047	Oct. 1918	641
Diphosgene*	7,952	Apr. 1918	395
Mustard gas†	6,709	Mar. 1918	642
Chloropicrin	2,671	June 1917	277
Phosgene	938	June 1918	38

* Production started June 1915.
† Production started May 1917.
For sources see reference in text.

of Bayer maintained excellent relations with Bauer at OHL and so had access to the fulcrum of military−technical operations. Thus Bayer quickly became the most widely diversified chemical-warfare production unit and its activities ranged from gases to canister filling. Self-interest and the welfare of the enterprise were important, but then (as at other times) Duisberg was aiming at a 'rational' —that is non-competitive—organization of production. In 1916 this was formally recognized by the association of Bayer with other dyestuffs firms, in a combine known as the Interessengemeinschaft der deutschen Teerfarbenfabriken, for short IG. Meanwhile Duisberg and his colleagues so arranged matters that orders were accepted in a manner that enabled Bayer, BASF, Farbwerke Hoechst, and the rest to develop individually one or more specialities. Bayer's was the manufacture of war gases from materials purchased from other suppliers. The company had some spare capacity, particularly lead-lined reactors equipped with cooling coils, suitable for the hydrochlorination of thiodiglycol. This was the final stage in the production of mustard gas, but there was an unexpected hitch because Bayer could not find enough craftsmen. So the first batch of dichlorodiethyl sulphide was delayed until March 1917.[31] There were no such problems with diphosgene, which was prepared from phosgene supplied by BASF. Bayer also made, though on a small scale, arsenical compounds for sale to Hoechst. Moving chemicals or intermediates in bulk was nothing new in Germany—it made for better plant utilization. For Bayer it had the additional advantage that the finished toxic agents prepared at Leverkusen were close to Dormagen, on the left bank of the Rhine, where the company owned a large site which it developed into one of the principal shell filling plants. At an early date part of Bayer's pharmaceutical works was adapted for filling gas-mask drums with charcoal made at Leverkusen. At its peak, 75,000 drums a day were filled, and Bayer was the second largest supplier of filled canisters. It is worth noting that all this chemical warfare activity involved very little extra investment, apart from Dormagen which was paid for the Reich. The only

Table 7.4. *BASF's Production of War Gases and Intermediates 1915–1918*

	Total (t)	Maximum Month	Production t/Month	Start of Production
Chlorine	23,600*	not known	1,261	Before war
Phosgene	10,682	not known	621	Before war
Thiodiglycol	7,026	Oct. 1918	552	March(?) 1917†
Phenyl arsinic acid	1,600	Aug. 1918	178	July 1917
Ethyl arsenious oxide	840	not known	90	April 1917

* Includes chlorine for other than chemical warfare purposes.
† Small quantities available for sale before the war.

For sources see reference in text.

significant expansion took place in electrolytic chlorine capacity which was raised from 1,000 t a year in 1914 to 4,000 t two years later.[32]

BASF's chemical warfare 'specialities' were intermediates and phosgene. It was the cheapest producer of phosgene because a large volume of carbon monoxide was available as by-product from the gas separation plant of the adjacent Oppau ammonia works. The pre-war capacity of 1,800 t a year (probably not fully utilized) was raised to 7,200 t a year, and any surplus to requirements was sold to Hoechst. The chlorine capacity was raised from 13,000 to 16,000 t a year between 1914 and 1915, and additional supplies were bought when required. The company was also the sole supplier of the intermediates for mustard gas because it had been making them for several years. Ethylene chlorohydrin, required for the first stage of manufacture, had been employed in peace-time as the starting point for the preparation of indigo by the ethylene route. Thiodiglycol, derived from ethylene chlorohydrin, was sold in small quantities as a dispersing agent for certain dyes. As the demand for indigo was low, there was plenty of capacity for ethylene and derivatives and the company accepted orders for mustard-gas intermediates and undertook to enlarge its plants to meet all requirements. But BASF had not allowed for delivery and construction delays so that the additional alcohol dehydration units were not ready until June 1917; thus ethylene shortages held back the entire mustard-gas programme in the spring of 1917. But the chlorohydrin extensions caused no problems, and the thiodiglycol enlargement, which entailed an increase from three to eighteen units, was well in hand in the early months of the year. The uneven progress of the various sections was not due solely to shortages of materials: the company's engineering and design staff were stretched to the limit because work connected with the Leuna synthetic ammonia plant was even more urgent. BASF therefore informed the Kriegsministerium that it was unable to install equipment for the final or hydrochlorination stage of mustard-gas production. This was the most dangerous part of the process and the management feared the effect of air raids on the site at Ludwigshafen. In short, the company deliberately limited its commitment to chemical warfare. The preparation of intermediates for substituted

Table 7.5. *German Manufacturers of the Chief Arsenical Compounds 1917–1918*

Code Name	Company	Production started	Total Output (t)	% of total	Highest Month	Output t
DA	Hoechst	May 1917	645	8	Sept. 1918	300 (?)
DL	Hoechst	Aug. 1917	1,092	14	July 1918	150
DA	Agfa (at Wolfen)	May 1917	1,725	22	Aug. 1918	165
DA	Cassela (at Mainkur)	Aug. 1917	994	12	Aug. 1918	108
DC	Agfa (at Wolfen)	Feb. 1918	1,045	13	Aug. 1918	144
DC	Hoechst	May 1918	2,526	31	Sept. 1918	300
Total			8,027	100		

Note: DA = Diphenylchloroarsine; DC = Diphenylcyanoarsine; DL = Ethyldichloroarsine. These substances, used as filling for chemical shells, were collectively referred to as Blue Cross agents. For source see references in text.

arsines, though begun in 1917, was reined in until the pressure on the other sections had eased. As a result bulk production, for sale to Hoechst, did not get under way until the last year of the war.[33]

Farbwerke Hoechst became involved in the later stages of chemical warfare because it also had some idle capacity and considerable experience in handling arsenical compounds. The company was selected as one of several producers of intermediates and as the chief contractor for the supply first of Clark 1 (DA) and then of Dick (DL). It began manufacturing the former in May 1917 and the latter in August. Initially the quantities were small, but towards the end of the year they increased, and the firm of Cassella, a close associate of Hoechst, became involved. In spring 1918 Hoechst began the large-scale preparation of Clark 2 (DC). The pattern of production is illustrated in Table 7.5: the combined total of all three materials is substantial, though if we think of each of the finished compounds as a dye, the output would be well within Hoechst's or Cassella's azo- or aniline dye sections which were under-employed on account of the loss of export trade due to the war. Hoechst also made diphosgene and its wartime production of 3,600 t placed it next to Bayer.[34]

The remaining colour works played less important roles. Chemische Fabrik Griesheim-Elektron at Bitterfeld was designated as the leading producer of liquid chlorine of which it supplied altogether 34,500 t between 1915 and 1918; most of it was transferred to Bayer and to Agfa's nearby works at Wolfen. Agfa's main function was to fill Blue Cross shells at works it owned in Berlin, and to use equipment at Wolfen to manufacture Clark 1 and 2 from purchased intermediate products. All these firms were members of the IG and co-ordinated their manufacturing programmes. The arrangements worked very smoothly. Outsiders, such as Chemische Fabrik von Heyden, which had produced phosgene before the war, enlarged its capacity and augmented the supplies available to Bayer and to Hoechst.[35]

For their respirators the Germans relied on about twenty firms, of which seven were metal fabricators. Among them were several large companies in the rubber industry, and some big tanneries became involved after leather face-pieces were adopted. Charcoal was obtained at first from the Aussiger Verein (a large chemical enterprise in what was then Austrian Bohemia) and later also from Bayer and BASF. Siemens & Halske, one of the leading firms in electrical engineering, and Auergesellschaft were particularly important as they possessed the special machines for making electric-lamp bases which could be easily modified for shaping the container with its screw connection to the face-piece. Auergesellschaft was also the principal final assembler—buying parts from sub-contractors and the filled filter units from Bayer, Agfa, and C. A. F. Kahlbaum Chemische Fabrik; the last two converted their factories in Berlin to canister filling. The Auer company was also in Berlin; its pre-war specialities had been gas mantles and electric light-bulbs, but its export trade was languishing and there was not enough work for its women employees. Its involvement in anti-gas work from August or September 1915 onwards was due to Haber who was on excellent terms with Leonard Koppel, the chairman and principal shareholder.[36] An important feature of German respirator production was the extent to which the contractors and assemblers were concentrated in Berlin: it greatly simplified quality control and final examination as well as the overall management by Haber's staff.

When we turn to France the contrast with the size and the swift adaptability of the German enterprises is striking. Some of the large companies owned factories in the German occupied north or in the battle zone. The replacement of the customary sources of inorganic chemicals generated frantic building activity in other parts of the country and repeatedly dislocated the plans for poison-gas manufacture. These plans called, in the first place, for liquid chlorine. There wasn't any. Two factories had electrolysed brine before 1914, but their combined capacity was less than 5 t a day and neither had equipment for liquefaction. The larger of the two, once German-owned, was closed. The Government reopened it, but its former owners shelled it so that the equipment had to be dismantled and removed. Thus when, in the summer of 1915 GQG demanded cylinder gas, the DMCG had to ask for help from the British. Chlorine plants were hastily ordered and the first programme, adopted in August, envisaged the construction, with Government assistance, of about half a dozen works in the south-west. Their combined liquid chlorine capacity was 30 t a day (say 11,000 t a year). The second programme of spring 1916, envisaged a small increase and the third, in the following year, provided for a further enlargement to a total of 50 t a day (18,000 a year) from nine or ten works. Four of these were owned or controlled by the DMCG. The largest works were those of Chlore Liquide at Pont-de-Claix (near Grenoble), Electro-Chimie at Plombières in Savoy and Produits Chimiques d'Alais et Camargue at St Auban in the southern Alps. All three were to become important chemical undertakings between the wars, but meanwhile they were small indeed compared with the installations at Ludwigshafen or Bitterfeld. However, there was not enough time to develop hydro-electric resources for large installations and the plants had to rely of run-of-the-river driven turbines, and so on consequential seasonal fluctuations in power-generation. Despite Government help and the purchase of US equipment, the electrolysers started up months behind schedule. That put fresh pressure on British supplies which were essential to the French chemical warfare plans as well as to Britain's own phosgene requirements, of which the bulk was met by G. de Laire from Calais. On a good day he could produce 8 t, all of it for the BEF. In 1916 he opened a second phosgene factory at Pont-de-Claix and several other manufacturers also took up the production of the gas. By the end of 1917, the firms operated seven or eight phosgene plants with a total capacity of 22 t a day, which again contrasts with the German scale of operations. Extensions, notably at Pont-de-Claix, raised the daily potential to 39 t in August 1918.[37]

Chlorine and phosgene represented a big industrial effort for the French and strained the managerial and finanical resources of their businessmen. The Service des Poudres was called in, organized priorities, and eventually took over some of the factories which it transferred to the DMCG in the last year of war. Alongside these government-controlled enterprises there were about twenty contractors, most of them very small. While the Germans so arranged matters that economies of scale were achieved by the exchange of intermediate products, the French deliberately it seems, continued to rely on small operations even when there were no constraints on the site or on electricity supplies. For example, hydrogen cyanide and cyanogen compounds—both greatly favoured by their experts—were prepared in factories whose production, after extensions had been made, was at the rate of one or two tonnes a day! The conclusion must be that this was their traditional procedure.

The French were taken by surprise when the Germans introduced mustard gas and, like their Allies, they were eager to produce 'this masterpiece of gas warfare'.[38] The problem was how, given that there were no facilities for making ethylene, the intermediates used by the Germans were unknown outside the laboratory and there was, unlike Germany, no surplus dyestuffs-making equipment which could be readily adapted. The DMCG at first supported attempts to copy the process employed by the Germans and the construction of small works was begun in late summer by the Usines du Rhône at Péage du Roussillon (near Lyon) and the DMCG itself at Nanterre.[39] By November neither had made much progress and the following month this approach was abandoned because it was beyond the capabilities of the chemists and the engineers. Instead the DMCG instructed Usines du Rhône to adopt Guthrie's process and got the excise to waive all restrictions on alcohol. (The two routes are briefly explained in Chapter 6, note 18.) Job and Bertrand started, like Guthrie, from sulphur dichloride (SCl_2) and quickly realized that thorough mixing of ethylene and SCl_2 was essential. If the exothermic reaction was to yield dichlorodiethyl sulphide (instead of causing the decomposition of the material) the reaction temperature had to be carefully controlled: the best results were obtained between 30° and 38° C. If the ethylene was pumped under pressure into the vessel it would not only thoroughly react with the SCl_2, but also serve as a coolant. However, the lower the temperature, the longer the contact time and the greater the risk of the SCl_2 decomposing into sulphur and chlorine. Usines du Rhône was not successful at first and choked pipes testified to frequent breakdowns. Operating the process under partial vacuum also failed, and the engineers decided to dissolve SCl_2 in carbon tetrachloride (CCl_4) before introducing ethylene in the reaction vessel. This empirical approach, though adding greatly to the expense, prevented clogged pipes, and manufacture could now begin: Usines du Rhône obtained a mixture of dichlorodiethyl sulphide and CCl_4, and the latter had to be distilled off until the substance contained 85 per cent mustard gas and 15 per cent solvent as required by the shell-filling plants. This final stage was particularly difficult to design and control and also entailed the costly installation of recovery equipment for the CCl_4.[40] The staff at Usines du Rhône were driven on by J. de Kap Herr of the DMCG and by J. Frossard, a chemical engineer employed in the private office of Loucheur, the new Minister of Armaments. They spent the winter of 1917–18 on trials and by March 1918 had a pilot plant working at Péage du Roussillon. The company at once began to enlarge the installation and despite difficulties were in full production in May. Two other companies, Chlore Liquide at Pont-de- Claix and Stéarineries et Savonneries de Lyon were also involved in the mustard-gas programme and prepared test batches from sulphur monochloride (S_2Cl_2) during April. They too were in full production by the end of May. Three other small works, including one owned by the Service des Poudres, were built and operated before the end of the war. The six plants made a combined total of 1,937 t of mustard gas, of which Usines du Rhône accounted for 1,509 t.[41]

In the Spring of 1915 the British heavy chemical industry, though large, was unprepared for the demands of chemical warfare. Only two companies, Castner–Kellner Alkali of Runcorn and the Cassel Cyanide Company of Glasgow were in a position to make immediate deliveries and the former was the mainstay of British gas production for the remainder of the war. Other and less competent enterprises became involved until about 70 chemical works supplied toxic, lachrymatory, and smoke materials. At first all were private enterprise, but the MoM became so dissatisfied with their performance, that in 1917–18 it took over some of the worst, and converted surplus Royal Ordnance Factories to poison gas production.

Chlorine was the key chemical. Castner–Kellner made it electrolytically on a large scale and used it for bleaching powder; demand for liquid chlorine being small, its capacity was only 5 tons a week. In June 1915, the company, at the urgent demand of the War Office, agreed to raise liquid chlorine capacity to 150 tons a week (roughly 8,000 tons a year) and the Treasury paid £7,000 towards a new compressor installation. The actual capacity available in the second half of the year was nowhere near the target figure—it averaged about 30 tons a week—but it was enough for the battle of Loos and for the French. The implementation of the plans for 1916, which envisaged an intensification of chemical warfare soon ran into trouble. Castner–Kellner could not meet their targets because of insufficient generating capacity and as makers of bleaching powder they had forward commitments to other industrial users. Even after the latter problem had been settled, it emerged that other manufacturers would have to be approached. The obvious choice was Brunner, Mond and Company, then the leading soda maker, but they were too occupied with Government contracts. Nobel's Explosives, whose technical staff had a good reputation, could not spare anyone. So the UAC and Electro-Bleach and By-Products became suppliers. The first, though financially shaky, was trying to make a come-back and had opened just before the war a small electrolytic works at Gateshead. They did not initially supply liquid chlorine, but later enlarged the factory and installed liquefaction plant in 1916–17. They could, in theory, supply 70 tons a week of chlorine, of which 50 was available as liquid. Later UAC completed smaller units at Widnes and St Helens. Electro-Bleach of Middlewich, which had had an undistinguished record before 1914, was also approached by the TWD and undertook to supply 30 tons a week of liquid chlorine. Neither UAC nor Electro-Bleach ever fulfilled their promises. What made it worse was that the TWD, on behalf of MoM, and the Board of Trade, the sponsoring department for the textile trades, could not agree on priorities. Consequently there was much confusion in 1916 and 1917 and the Treasury, which was contributing £0.8–0.9 million towards the two companies' construction costs, became increasingly vexed.[42]

Though the gap between promise and achievement was large, the expansion was, on paper, impressive. By early spring 1918 capacity for making 10,000–11,000 tons a year of liquid chlorine was available, a further 28,000 tons a year had been authorized and was under construction, and another 28,000 tons was envisaged for 1919. This exceeded the German potential, but when Quinan investigated the position in mid June 1918 he discovered that of the available capacity of 10,000–11,000 tons, only 75 per cent were utilized in April and output was even lower in May; Castner–Kellner supplied three-quarters of the diminished total. Power shortages, especially at Gateshead, lack of electrical spares, poor maintenance, and not enough fitters served as excuses. The difficulties got worse and it became necessary to import chlorine from the USA so as not to jeopardize the chemical warfare plans.[43]

The failure to supply phosgene has been noted before. On paper, UAC, Electro-Bleach, and Ardol Ltd., had, by March 1917, a combined annual capacity of 1,800 tons a year; a year later it was 2,300 tons a year. That was a small fraction of the German potential, and in any case, the three firms were unable to reach more than a third of capacity. Thus it came about that the British firms supplied 1,362 tons during the war, while 6,148 tons were obtained from France. One must make allowances for start-up problems in 1916, but the difficulties persisted into 1917 and criticism mounted. Cadman as good as accused UAC of incompetence. That was one of the causes of his enforced departure, but it may be observed that the company ultimately adopted his advice and, as the French had done for many months, used liquid oxygen for the preparation of carbon monoxide. At Middlewich, Mr Hutchins, the manager, was said to be energetic and resourceful, but had little idea of phosgene technology. At the Ardol plant (where they had hydrogenated vegetable oil in better days) nothing worked, so the TWD took over in Autumn 1917 and later dismantled the plant. Electro-Bleach and Mr Hutchins struggled on, but never operated at planned output, not even after the MoM had taken over in August 1918. It was a sorry tale of general incompetence. Had the war continued, Castner – Kellner would have become involved. A similar story could be told of the chloropicrin programme. Two chemical tyros, but enterprising businessmen, undertook to produce this very simple compound from bleaching powder and picric acid supplied by the TWD. The companies, Sneyd Bycars of Burslem and the West Riding Chemical Company of Wakefield, were not impressive enterprises and when they could not meet specifications and contract dates, they blamed their suppliers for the low quality of their materials and the slow delivery. Whitehall put up with these excuses in 1916 and 1917, but in 1918 threatened to intervene forcefully with the result that quality and deliveries improved.[44]

The story, so far, is one of mismanagement and bureaucratic incompetence. The attempts to make mustard gas were an equally sorry tale of muddle and delays. The MoM's first programme, August 1917, envisaged a supply of 15 tons a week which became 200 tons a week by September. UAC was approached and told the MoM that it anticipated no process engineering problems. On 10 October, Threlfall was appointed to oversee the entire mustard-gas project which by then had grown to Teutonic proportions: 200 tons of mustard gas were to be produced by a variant of the German process in a 'National Factory' which would be equipped with its own sections for making sulphur trioxide, chlorine, and ethylene, and would operate its own power plant, workshops, laboratory, etc. It would cost £2 million and start in March 1918.[45] Some experts thought the project was wildly unrealistic and proposed that Britain should go in for the simpler technology of the Guthrie process. The two sides could not agree and Churchill settled the argument on 5 November by approving the plan. But the Treasury would not wear it, and three weeks later the Minister had to tell CWD that sanction, and so priorities, would only be given for a plant of about 75 tons a week. In December Nobel's Explosives were instructed to build a works for making thiodiglycol at Chittening near Avonmouth where the Ministry had a site. Chance and Hunt, a small alkali manufacturer at Oldbury, which had just been taken over by Brunner, Mond and Co., was awarded a contract for the supply of ethylene chlorohydrin and was also to prepare thiodiglycol on a pilot-plant basis. At that stage, no one had any practical experience of working the German process, but its supporters were acrimoniously disputing with the scientists who put their faith in the Guthrie process. Weeks passed and in February 1918 the CWD decided that Chance and Hunt should put up another pilot plant, this time for mustard gas starting from sulphur monochloride. It is to be noted that the company's progress with the German route to mustard gas was negligible. Meanwhile, at Chittening they had only got as far as site-clearing and preparation when a strike stopped work for most of March.[46] The French offered advice and details of their 'cold' working methods, but they were ignored, except by the dyestuffs firm of Levinstein Ltd. and their scientific adviser, Prof. A. G. Green. Some British chemists, and in particular Pope and C.

S. Gibson, insisted that by starting from sulphur monochloride and working the 'hot' process at 50°–70° C high yields of good quality dichlorodiethyl sulphide were obtainable and had repeatedly been obtained in the laboratory. They had Thuillier's support and Churchill endorsed their plans. We may recall that at this point in time, April 1918, the Germans were using unprecedented amounts of mustard gas on the Western Front and the French had virtually solved the engineering problems associated with the 'cold' process. But the gathering momentum of British mustard-gas development was devoted to making the unworkable work!

In April site work was resumed at Chittening, but made slow progress. In Manchester, Levinstein Ltd., using simple equipment and primitive working methods, were laboriously producing small batches of good quality mustard gas by the 'cold' process; the company was in touch with the Americans and licensed the know-how to them. The French continued to be co-operative and a full description of the work done at Usines du Rhône reached Whitehall towards the middle of May. Thus, when Green turned up at the offices of the CWD on 7 June to see Harrison and show him some specimens of Levinstein's material, there was surprise, envy, and also irritation when he declared that his employers were making mustard gas 'from patriotic motives and not for money'.[47]

The Trench Warfare Supply Department had, at last, been axed in April because its failures over the supply of gas could no longer to be tolerated. Quinan was henceforth in charge of construction and manufacture. He got rid of Threlfall, took over his group of scientists and engineers and decided that everything connected with mustard gas would henceforth be done in 'National Factories'. Nobel's, Castner–Kellner, and others would be relegated to the status of sub-contractors to these factories with precisely defined and limited responsibilities. So, at this late stage of the war, yet another programme was launched: Chittening was closed down and a new works on a green field site at Avonmouth was started. Throughout May and early June hundreds of builders and fitters worked round the clock to put together pipes and vessels originally intended for Chittening. The first batch of dichlorodiethyl sulphide by the 'hot' route was prepared on 15 June. Not surprisingly the reaction was incomplete and the product a mess. The next few trial runs were no better. By the end of June altogether 3.5 tons of mustard gas had been produced at the cost of immense effort, many injuries, and great frustration.[48] The disappointing results were due to a variety of causes, the principal ones being the continued adherence to the 'hot' process and the failure of the alcohol dehydration unit to provide ethylene of sufficiently high purity. At the beginning of July the superintendent Whitelaw and his staff were frantic, and he wrote later that everyone was 'more or less grasping at straws'. The French came to the rescue, Frossard, an unlikely *deus ex machina*, was asked to look over Avonmouth and his suggestion to adopt the 'cold' route was, according to Whitelaw, 'immediately seized upon'.[49] Yet the MoM had been told of the process by the DMCG, Lefebure and Levinstein's people for over two months! Why Quinan and his staff failed to act promptly in April or May has never been explained. At any rate the chemists at Avonmouth reduced the reaction temperature to 40° C and during the first half of July obtained, at long last, some good yields. But in the second half of the month the works had to be closed because the ethylene unit had to be completely overhauled. When that had been done, other problems emerged, notably sickness caused by mustard-gas poisoning and frequent shut-downs because there were not enough pipe-fitters in good health to repair blocked pipe-circuits. Nevertheless, the first batch of mustard gas to pass the acceptance test was triumphantly produced on 15 August. Although there were frequent interruptions in August and also in September, the improvement in the quality of the mustard gas was maintained and during the latter half of October production became regular, the peak being reached with 135 tons in the last week of the month. Avonmouth closed at 2000 on Armistice Day, having manufactured altogether 560 tons of mustard gas, of which 416 tons were acceptable for shell filling.[50]

The British quickly identified the contents of unexploded German shells with Blue Cross markings and the MoM deployed an intensive effort to retaliate in kind. But again there were difficulties. In the autumn of 1917, Nobel's Explosives, May and Baker, and Burroughs and Wellcome were asked to supply trial lots of DA. They were unable to do so. Lefebure was told to make enquiries from his French contacts, but all he discovered was that Poulenc Frères were investigating the manufacture of arsenical compounds. (When I went through the archives many years later I was unable to find any papers on the industrial development of substituted arsines.) Another crisis threatened, and as with mustard gas, Pope took a hand. He recommended triphenyl arsenic dichloride, code named TD, but it took several months before a manufacturer could be found to supply samples. When they became available at last in Spring 1918 they were tested and found useless. Unlike mustard gas, the MoM reacted at once. On 6 May, Quinan cancelled all development contracts, dropped TD, adopted DA, and ordered that a plant at Sutton Oak, near St Helens, which was no longer required for making synthetic phenol should be re-equipped to prepare DA. The intermediate materials were bought from chemical companies. The first batch was produced on 22 June. A few days later the CWD ordered the preparation of a related compound, diphenylaminechloroarsine, called 'Adamsite' or DM, after Roger Adams who had developed it at the American University. DM was made in another converted phenol plant and again the intermediate was bought from a sub-contractor. Altogether 61 tons of DA and 31 tons of DM were made in the remaining months of the war.[51]

By contrast the production of respirators in Britain was tackled most successfully. Within a few days of the first German gas cloud, E. W. Lucas, the manager of Bell, Hills and Lucas had organized the manufacture of simple pads which were soon to be followed by hoods. James Spicer and Co., the paper firm, were also involved and Boots of Nottingham became a contractor during 1916. When these three were unable to recruit more women and the rejection rate at final assembly became unacceptable owing to the pressure of orders, the Anti-Gas

Department stepped in and took the work to the women. The Department bought or rented warehouse space in east and north London, and requisitioned the Tottenham Hotspurs' football stadium: the stands were built up and roofed over, electricity installed, and sewing-machines fixed up. Thus private enterprise and six 'National Factories' between them were able to turn out up to 50,000 SBR's a day, repair damaged masks, and examine every single one of them. Bell's alone employed over 4,000 women, Boots about 1,000, the Tottenham National Factories over 1,100. Spicers and their satellite assemblers, formed the largest group and probably accounted for another 5,000 or thereabouts. In addition there were 2,000 inspectors, stores, and administrative staff. This complex and diverse activity, drawing on fifty main contractors and a further hundred or so sub-contractors and checking scores of millions of components and masks was run like a military organization by the Anti-Gas Department. The documents in the PRO show that there was never the remotest suggestion of incompetence.[52]

The Americans, late in the field, drew useful lessons from British and French experience. Haynes's comprehensive history of the American chemical industry contains few references to its contribution to chemical warfare. The larger firms, and in particular Du Pont, did not tender because they were fully committed to the explosives programme. Du Pont, though eager to invest its enormous profits in various diversification schemes, considered poison gases as too specialized a business with no post-war commercial potential. The Ordnance Department thereupon contracted with companies of the second or even third rank to supply phosgene and mustard gas. The projects were, by European standards, extremely large. For example, Zinsser and Company at Hastings-on-Hudson and the National Aniline and Chemical Company of Buffalo were each commissioned to build mustard-gas plants with a daily make of 22 tons (equivalent to a total of about 16,000 tons a year). But there were delays and neither seems to have been working by the end of the war.[53]

The manufacturers' lack of enthusiasm can be safely attributed to the fact that in the autumn of 1917 less troublesome and equally lucrative contracts could be had for the asking. At any rate, the Ordnance Department had to rely almost entirely on the works at the Aberdeen Proving Ground along the Chesapeake River not far from Baltimore. The site was named Edgewood, and the remarkable thing about this Federal arsenal was its conception, its size, and the speed of construction. In December 1917 the decision was taken to build a poison-gas factory there and combine it with the country's principal gas shell-filling plant. The site plans were ready in a few weeks, and a start was made on roads, railways sidings, water supply, and the power station. By spring 1918 the common services were sufficiently far advanced to allow the construction of the various sections to begin. Work on the electrolysers began on 11 May and the first units of what became the largest American chlor-alkali plant started up exactly three months later. What is even more noteworthy is that they worked without a hitch until the end of the war. The first plants for phosgene and chloropicrin became operational during August 1918. Conant, who was in charge of the technical development of

Table 7.6. *Production of War Gases at Edgewood, 1918*

	Initial capacity (tons/day)	Production in 1918	
		tons	Daily average (tons)*
Liquid chlorine†	89	2,433	27.0
Chloropicrin	n.a.	2,478	27.5
Phosgene	36	1,442	16.0
Mustard gas‡	27	897	10.0

* Based on 90 days' operation.
† The figure for liquefaction capacity was 36 tons a day. The rest was converted to bleaching powder.
‡ Pilot plant started up in July 1918 at 1.3 tons a day.
All figures have been converted from short tons to long tons. For sources see references in text.

mustard gas, was a supporter of the Guthrie process, accepted Levinstein's assistance and designed Edgewood to work the 'cold' method. The first experimental batches of dichlorodiethyl sulphide were made at Edgewood towards the end of May or the beginning of June and the works was in regular production from August onwards.[54] The figures given in Table 7.6 represent a mere three months' activity, including a brief cut-back in October owing to lack of shell cases. It was an extraordinary performance, made possible by the lavish use of manpower which the Europeans no longer possessed. On average 6,200 enlisted men worked at Edgewood and at the peak of activity—in the early autumn—there were over 7,000; in addition another 3,000, all of them civilians, were employed on the site in various capacities.[55] The Americans were also fortunate in having sufficient managerial talent for the arsenal. It was directed by Col. W. H. Walker, lately professor of chemical engineering at MIT and previously a consultant. Then in his prime he led or rather managed a group of uniformed civilians with experience in chemical engineering and seconded for the duration by their companies or colleges.

A similar approach was adopted for respirator manufacture and in this instance, British precedent was very important. The first contractor, the Hero Mfg. Company, chosen in 1917, was incompetent, and was quickly got rid of. It took somewhat longer to persuade the Americans to scrap their respirator design and use the SBR as their model. But Gen. Pershing insisted on the change with the result that the Federal Government established a factory at Long Island City to make the SBR American-style. No expense was spared, and between the latter part of November 1917 and March 1918, sheds, workshops, and warehouses were erected where all the components—except charcoal, soda-lime granules, rubberized fabric and rubber tubing—were made, cut or shaped and assembled, examined, and packed for dispatch. By July 12,000 people—two-thirds of them women—were employed. At the peak, in October 1918, the daily production rate was 44,000 which was only a little less than the half dozen or so British assemblers turned out at their peak rate.[56]

Table 7.7. *British and French Production of Chlorine and Phosgene*

	1915	1916	1917	1918	Total
Chlorine, liquid					
Britain (tons)	878	4,856	7,451	7,637	20,822
France (t)	nil	2,600*	5,800*	4,100*	12,500 †
Phosgene					
Britain (own make) (tons)	nil	131	561	670	1,362
France‡, (t)	80	1,718	·6,785	7,200§	15,703*

* Estimated.

† Excluding supplies from UK.

‡ Including supplies sold to Allies (sales to BEF amounted to 1,662 t in 1916, 2,877 t in 1917, and 1,598 t in 1918; the CWS bought 361 t in 1918 and the Italians 158 t).

§ Output figures for Jan.–Aug. and estimates based on available capacity in Sept.–Nov. For sources see reference in text.

Having described these activities it is necessary to give some indication of the results. The underlying statistics range from the adequate (collated by the MoM) to the incomplete or impressionistic (available in the French archives). The German documents have been destroyed and those given to the Allies in 1919–21 while offering some indication of the scale of operations do not lend themselves to comparisons and are sometimes inconsistent. It would be desirable to have monthly or quarterly data—but if such still exist, I have not located them. Table 7.7 summarizes the progress made by Britain and France in two areas of chemical warfare production. The improvisation phase of 1915 was followed by a large tonnage in the following year, most of it in the second half, as newly built capacity made its first contribution. There was a slowing-down of construction in 1917 and a resumption in late winter and spring – early summer of 1918, which extended from chlorine and phosgene to arsenicals and mustard gas. The European belligerents attained peak production in the summer of 1918; in the USA output rose sharply in the final months of the war (except briefly in October).[57] The international scale of the effort is illustrated in Table 7.8. One needs to bear in mind that neither Britain nor France were producing liquid chlorine in any quantity before the war. The very large German tonnage is due to the phosgene and even more so to the diphosgene programmes.[58]

Tables 7.7 and 7.8, despite their weaknesses, serve to show the order of magnitude and draw attention to national peculiarities. Purely in volume terms, chemical warfare was small business when set against the tonnage of essential inorganics such as sulphuric and nitric acids, and also ammonia. The German performance stands out, though they wasted much chlorine on diphosgene. The large tonnage of phosgene made by the French will be observed. The British put their trust in chloropicrin: that was the right decision, since they never had enough phosgene, but it was a second best. The French devotion to hydrogen cyanide, or

Table 7.8. *Production of the Principal War Gases by the Main Belligerents 1915–1918*

	Chlorine (liquid)	Phosgene	Diphosgene	Mustard Gas	Chloro-picrin	Cyanides
Germany (000 t)	58.1*	18.1	11.6	7.6	4.1	—
Britain (000 tons)	20.8	1.4	—	0.5	8.0	0.4
France (000 t)	12.5	15.7	—	2.0	0.5	7.7 †
USA (000 tons)	2.4	1.4	—	0.9	2.5	—
Total	93.8	36.6	11.6	11.0	15.1	8.1

* The figure excludes the production by Griesheim-Elektron at Bitterfeld, given as 34,500 t (see p. 159). Bayer and BASF used some chlorine in diverse manufactures not related directly to war gases.
† The figure includes Vincennite.

rather its mixture with arsenious chloride and other materials to form Vincennite, was less justified and their retention of it misguided. The French took second place to the Germans in mustard gas; the USA was in the first stages of a vast manufacturing programme.

The statistics do more than record numbers. They remind us that the structure of the supplying industry varied from country to country and they reflect the size and technical power of the contractors. Three or four firms accounted for the bulk of German production. But in France there were at the end of the war 18 specializing in chlorine and phosgene. In Britain there were about ten of which Castner–Kellner, the 'National Factories' and UAC, in that order, supplied most of the materials. In the USA there was, for all practical purposes, one enterprise— the Edgewood Arsenal.

The manufacture of poisonous gases, as distinct from other aspects of chemical warfare, was not particularly labour-intensive. But skilled manpower in general for the chemical industry became increasingly scarce as the war progressed and except in Germany and the USA the management was poor. The British reported that labour shortages were a 'constant obstacle' despite priorities. The Germans were short of fitters and maintenance men particularly in 1917, but otherwise their workers were exempted from call-up and were accustomed to matching strict specifications under quasi-military discipline. The Americans did best of all because they had, compared to the others, an abundance of everything and learnt from European mistakes.

It is not possible to segregate those making poison gas from others working on non-toxic chemicals in the same factories. There are not even complete records for those employed in the government-owned establishments. There were 7,000 direct workers at Edgewood, and from the fragmentary returns for Britain, France, and

Germany, I estimate that a similar number was employed by all three taken together. Very little is known of the financial effort. HM Treasury advanced altogether £1½ m, which includes the 'National Factories' at Chittening and Avonmouth. The French may have spent roughly the same, the Germans less, and the Americans a good deal more.

The manufacture of respirators depended on the smooth interaction of suppliers and contractors. The structure of industry and the state of its development were of less significance than the efficient organization of mass production processes at every stage of the assembly operations. Organizationally, defence against gas resembled a pyramid in structure. At the base, scores of firms—some of them highly specialized—were involved and the contracts generally represented only a small proportion of their turnover. Above them were a smaller number of sub-assemblers which put together components or materials from different sources to make the filter unit or the face piece. And finally at the top there were a few—in the USA only one—which assembled, tested, and packed the complete mask. The quantities were immense: 13 million SBRs were issued and another 4½ million made for stock. The German figure for complete masks was about half that, plus millions of spare filter units. The French produced about 5 million of the ARS type, which was modelled on the German mask, in the last year of the war and the Americans about a tenth of the British output. We have only incomplete employment statistics, but the work, especially in the latter stages, was extremely labour-intensive. There were roughly 12,000–15,000 assemblers, sub-assemblers, examiners, and packers—overwhelmingly women—in Britain at the peak of production. The Germans employed fewer than 10,000, the Americans around 12,000.

The industrial effort behind chemical warfare was more than the enumeration of output or of the factors of production. Access to materials and a well-developed chemical industry was of great importance, and so were the unquantifiable elements such as experience in large-scale production methods, familiarity with chemical technology, and good liaison with the forces. All this would now form part of normal management functions, but then only a few people were aware of the value of an efficient organization and fewer still in a position of creating one and working through it. Pope, Quinan, Harrison, Starling, Haber, and Walker were of that kind and left their stamp on production or research.

The Germans had for a long time the advantages of a head start. But the field eventually caught up with them. As the British mission on its travels through the Rhineland after the Armistice observed, 'the general impression . . . was that the technical practice in the factories visited was not markedly superior to that obtaining in England at the end of the war and in some respects it was inferior. The main source of strength of the German chemical industry appeared to lie in its organisation and in the large scale of its production.'[59] There was another characteristic, already noted by the Chemical Sub-Committee of the TWD in 1916[60]: the Germans were particularly competent and quick at scaling up from experimental plant to commercial production; the British were particularly slow at this right up to 1918.

Chemical warfare left its mark on the structure and location of the chemical industry in several countries. In 1919 all the belligerents had a large chlor-alkali capacity. The old Leblanc process lost its *raison d'être*, but its elimination still left a surplus of chlorine. The Americans simply mothballed parts of Edgewood and so dispelled the threat to the chlorine market. The French found themselves with a brand new electrolytic industry which contributed more to the modernization of their chemical manufacture than the reconstruction of the northern works. In Britain, the MoM's contracts with UAC did not rescue that company, but only confirmed the generally held low opinions of the firm. Castner–Kellner, however, emerged with an enhanced capacity and reputation, and was shortly to be taken over completely by Brunner, Mond and Co. This was one of the steps in the restructuring of the entire British chemical industry which led in 1926 to the formation of ICI, a concern in which Brunner, Mond was one of the two dominant factors and to which UAC had been reluctantly admitted. Only the Germans did not have to learn the industrial lessons of chemical warfare the hard way. Having lost the war, a different set of rules applied to them, but it is curious to note that this was not detrimental to their chemical industries.

The search for answers to the questions posed at the beginning of the previous chapter has led us to consider in turn the scientific effort, the nature and form of military and civilian organizations, and industrial patterns. What has emerged? In particular can one ignore the exceptions and generalize the problems posed by the introduction of a new weapon, and is it possible to identify the obstacles to its successful use? In both cases the answers are a qualified 'Yes'.

Rothschild's concept of customers and contractors in government research and development though clear, oversimplifies. Applied to chemical warfare in 1915–18 it would have implied that the staffs knew what they wanted, ordered it, and left the contractors to develop and supply the goods. That approach was, in fact, used for naval or ordnance work where metallurgy and power engineering led to advances in design and construction. So why didn't it work for poison gas?

One answer is that there was a great deal of confusion. Given the condensed time-scale of war it meant that the results were usually obtained when it was too late. Another answer is that the civilians and officers were not always up to their jobs; a third was the failure to provide from the outset for good communication channels. None of this is very surprising. One would hardly expect staff officers, vintage 1914, to be receptive to some esoteric applications of chemistry. A few examples from British experience will help to make the point. Until May 1916, the General Staff called for particular gases, thereafter the contractors were told what effect was desired. The change in policy influenced research as well as manufacture for it tended to reduce variety and so concentrated development and production on the tactically most useful substances. But another year passed before the Directorate of Artillery established a new section (A9) for gas shell and established formal direct links with the TWD of the MoM. And it was not until April 1918, that the CWD and the Department of Explosives Supply began to work in harness on gas shell requirements for 1919.

Not only in London, but also in Paris, Berlin, and Washington, the ramifications of the ordering procedures within and between Departments of State were such as to make delays unavoidable. In Britain the problems arising therefrom were aggravated because research and supply were divided. J. D. Pratt, an eye-witness, wrote later of 'the rivalry and jealousy which, as a rule, exists between corresponding sections of different Departments' and of the 'mutual lack of appreciation and understanding . . . between them'.[61] Matters came to a head over mustard gas, but the urgency at the top was not, it seems, felt lower down. Pope, addressing Churchill in Spring 1918 on the matter, observed that Supply Departments liked routine so that 'every suggestion of novelty is resented as a disturbance of business method [s] in which no risks are taken'.[62]

Secrecy (and not only in Whitehall) made matters worse. Over mustard gas and arsines it was counter-productive and the Germans were, if anything, even worse in this respect. Things improved somewhat among and between the Allies in the last six to eight months of the war. But relations between chemical warfare experts and the artillery in France left much to be desired. Some of the problems were common to all belligerents, the differences being one of degree rather than of kind. Tradition and temperament emphasized national characteristics. The committee procedure so beloved by the British civil service was often a handicap. But it should not be blamed for every failure. I suspect that Thuillier, despite his great qualities as a moderator, lacked the toughness to force through unpleasant decisions. There is some evidence for this in the 'Diary of Decisions', that is the record of 'actions' or of 'note taken' at the meetings of the CWC. There are about fifty such references to mustard gas between October 1917 and August 1918 when production was at last becoming satisfactory.[63]

The British performance over mustard gas was particularly bad. The other belligerents were quicker at locating pressure-points and applying leverage. They thus saved time, but made errors of judgement which often had serious consequences. In France, Ozil was put in charge and told to get on with chemical warfare: he achieved results because he was a good administrator, but the DMCG's products (phosgene and mustard gas excepted) were of little use because the scientists were allowed to ride their hobbies and testing was perfunctory. Ozil's attitude to protection against gas lacked imagination with the result that thousands became casualties. In Germany, Haber—who fulfilled a similar role—knew what he wanted and how to get it out of the manufacturers with the minimum of delay. His difficulties were peculiarly German and involved status and rank: at the top Bauer and the technical staff at OHL were receptive to innovation. Lower down it was different and particularly later in the war military hierarchies, especially in the artillery, created obstacles.[64] The Americans were best at managing chemical warfare. They were quick learners and generous spenders. Before 1917 it had been customary for the Corps of Engineers to carry out civilian construction jobs, and the regulars knew how to deal with contractors. As we have seen in connection with

Edgewood the blending of practical experience with public service, unfettered by military traditions and bureaucratic procedures removed obstructions and yielded high returns. That did not save them from making mistakes or prevent delays, but they caught up with the Allies in technology in less than a year and attained production levels after three months which had taken the British and the French about thirty.

This said, there was much more to chemical warfare than the formal relations between scientists, manufacturers, and military 'customers'. There were many small improvements, ingenious devices for attack, and sensible precautions in defence. There was, particularly in 1918, a good deal of co-operation between the Allies. But somehow it was less painful to copy the enemy than to learn from one's partners. The most extreme obscurantism and incomprehensible jingoism obtained among the French and Italians, and briefly even among the Americans, in the matter of respirators. The obtuseness of senior officers was to blame, and in this regard the British and the Americans were more adaptable and at least had the welfare and morale of their men at heart.[65] The British chemists in uniform were among the many specialists to be found at divisional, corps or army HQ. They could, if they showed tact and humour, make a contribution, have it accepted and witness its prompt implementation. General Curzon's cockney Gas Officer, Milward, the BSc. from London University, was not pure fiction, Forester drew him from life. He was an 'irregular', but he was often right and not even the GOC could entirely ignore him.[66] Barley, the fictional Milward's contemporary, wrote to me years later: 'my advice was invariably taken and I was left to run the defensive side' at 2nd Army HQ and later in Italy.[67] There is less evidence of such collaboration in the German and French armies. The German gas troops were not popular and the technical advisers carried little weight.[68] French infantry officers would very rarely encounter chemical warfare specialists because GQG would not let them stray far from Chantilly.

Conflicts abounded and were unavoidable. They were fiercest and least soluble in all matters concerning gas attacks. Defence also had its critics, but in general there was less friction between the various parties and after 1916 the machine ran smoothly in Britain and Germany. We will return to this dual aspect of chemical warfare in later chapters. Here it is sufficient to note that defence was perceived as a major factor in morale, while gas offence was considered, at best, an adjunct to strategy.

Some other conclusions emerge from the story so far. The technical condition and structure of the chemical industry could slow the response, but would not necessarily ensure success in the field. The ultimate decision rested with the staffs. When they had a clear objective and trusted their advisers, some remarkable results could be and were achieved in a short time. The SBR and the German mask, and their rapid introduction bear testimony to effective decision-taking. So does the Livens projector and German gas-shell tactics. Such instances however were rare; failures were frequent and combined with delays, caused distrust. The multiplication of committees, their endless meetings and the arguments they engendered, widened rather than narrowed differences.[69] But that was not the only problem: 'the worst about you scientists', Foulkes once said to Hartley, 'is that you don't know when to cut your losses.'[70] Someone had to decide. Academic chemists may have found such restrictions on discussion irksome and even unscientific, but they were necessary. Haber accommodated himself to this difficulty *vis-à-vis* the soldiers: he accepted his role as their adviser—an opinion was expected of him, not a decision. That was the job of the General Staff. But in order to give an opinion, the adviser had to be sure of his facts: with something as new as gas, how could one be certain? Defence in this respect was easier than offence—the objective was clear and the outcome, that is the mask, could be tested rigorously. Only the path had to be determined, and the relevant factors here were time, resources, and training. Offence called for the correct answer to a multiple-choice question. Chemists interested in their particular weapon, found that very difficult. They were not so much out of their depth, but ignorant of the consequences of their actions. And the soldiers were unable to enlighten them, the more so as their reactions were instinctive and pragmatic—the very opposite of the chemists' traditional background.[71]

Nowadays we would look for a solution in interdisciplinary defence research. That would certainly not have been acceptable in 1915–18. Haber thought of it, found in Koppel a sponsor, and enlisted some support among chemists and industrialists. The plan was to endow a Stiftung für Kriegstechnische Wissenschaft to link science and warfare. The Army insisted on packing the governing council of the foundation with their nominees and the project petered out soon after its launch in 1917. It was premature.[72] The increasingly technological war continued to be waged in the old and more familiar ways.

8

NEW WEAPONS, NEW TACTICS

ON the short time-scale of the Great War, 1917 occupies a special place. The year, or more precisely the spring and early summer witnessed a marked acceleration and diversification of the chemical warfare effort. Whereas 1915 and 1916 were characterized by the amateurishness that accompanies the early stages of military–technical developments, the unfolding of events in 1917 suggests that the specialists were becoming more experienced in the versatility and potential of their chemical weapons whose increasing importance lies, first in the more intensive use of a wider range of toxic substances, and secondly in the effect this had on many activities ranging from manufacture at one extreme to the development of gas tactics on the other. The ground covered by this span forms the subject of the present chapter. But before turning to the details it is necessary to outline the main characteristics of the military–chemical scene.

The chief claim made by proponents of chemical warfare was that it could achieve particular objectives which could not be obtained by conventional weapons with the same economy of effort. The assertion was unsubstantiated. Now other attributes were found, which, under the changed circumstances of 1917, carried more weight. Gas, it was said, harassed the opponent and so helped to wear him down. Moreover, experience had shown that chemicals injured rather than killed. The former proposition could be proved and it was unarguable that the dead soldier was beyond care, while the wounded called for treatment. Neither approach was clearly articulated for most of 1917, but they were influential in that they fitted in with the growing concern about manpower shortages. As the year wore on, manpower increasingly governed the overall strategy of the belligerents. Here was the central issue calling for action, and the measures taken had the unexpected result of strengthening the hands of those who propounded the wider and more intensive use of gas. For example in many quiet sectors—the Vosges, around the Aisne, along the Hindenburg Line—the opposing trenches were moving further apart. Elsewhere defence in depth was being adopted, notably at Ypres. But this sensible dispersal of soldiers, while it cut down casualties, also weakened, where it did not render useless, gas clouds blown from cylinders. For, to retain the same volume over a larger area entailed a quantitative increase in the ratio of the cube to the square. Such elementary considerations enhanced the value of alternative delivery methods: Livens's projectors were bound to hit some targets some of the time, and if more precision was called for, there was, henceforth, a selection of gas shells with specific effects.

The response of gas specialists to the opportunities presented by the manpower problems was, in practice, less smooth than the above summary would suggest. They played down the difficulties they encountered throughout 1917, which gave their operations, though large, a spasmodic and uncoordinated appearance. In particular, the rapid expansion of Allied chemical production turned out to be extremely labour-intensive and filling gas shells was especially slow. Gas might be labour-saving at the front, but required more hands at home. And it was dangerous, so that production schedules fell behind owing to sickness and absenteeism. The development of chemical weapons was paralleled by that of defence measures and medical facilities, and these too needed more people.

Despite all these qualifications and reservations, 1917 was a turning-point. The state of the art remained unchanged for the next quarter century. The Germans, having been in the lead, ceased to advance so that the British and later the Americans caught up and then overtook them as regards technology and means of delivery. The Allies also began to master the production problems. The following year they built up their capacity and in 1919 their output would have far exceeded that of the Germans. Finally, the polarization of the chemical conflict first became noticeable in 1917 and was to have important consequences as the war drew to a close and long after the Armistice. The Russian collapse put an end to chemical warfare on the Eastern Front, and it remained infrequent along the French front. That made poison gas a peculiarly Anglo-German mode of warfare to which the Americans made a contribution in the last months of the war. Such apparent limitation to a few of the belligerents, instead of proliferation, is contrary to the pattern followed by the introduction of a new weapon. The explanation would appear to be that chemical warfare entailed the development of so many specialities that some countries, having reached the limit of their professional and technically qualified manpower, could go no further. Thus the new forms of gas warfare imposed unexpected constraints which will be examined in due course.

Hartley, basing himself on interviews with Haber, wrote that as soon as the British Forces were equipped with the SBR, the Germans ended their cloud-gas attacks against them because 'it was not thought worthwhile to continue them against us'.[1] The chronology of events confirms the claim. The Germans discharged a mixture of chlorine and phosgene against the British at Wieltje, north-east of Ypres on 8 August 1916, and caused about nine hundred casualties. They planned more cloud attacks, but the intensity of the Somme fighting prevented all preparations and they knew that the SBR was being distributed along the Loos–Armentières sector. Wieltje (near Pilkem, where it had all begun eighteen months earlier) was not quite the last occasion: that incident took place under particularly horrifying circumstances 350 m down a pit east of Béthune in September 1917, killing soldiers and miners.[2]

The issue of the SBR coincided with a more critical attitude towards cylinder gas at German headquarters. The events of 1916 demonstrated that in Northern

France the prevailing winds jeopardized cylinder operations. Besides the troops were becoming increasingly critical of the activities of the Gaspioniere: they feared blow-back and the inevitable British artillery retaliation. As cylinder operations had the best chance of success in quiet sectors—which the Germans needed as much as the British—the staff at OHL came to realize that the occasional cloud-gas discharges were counter-productive.[3]

Against a weaker and less disciplined enemy who had no proper protection, cylinder discharges might still have some effect and accordingly the Germans mounted a few big operations against the French. The first took place on 31 January 1917 between Marquises and Aubérive just east of Reims. It was a cold winter afternoon and the wind, blowing gently at 2–3 m/sec, slowly pushed the gas obliquely down the shallow valley of the Vesle and the Suippe. The Germans had assembled 18,600 cylinders on a front of 11.5 km and so achieved a concentration of 40 t/km, high, but not exceptionally so. It was getting dark, the mouthpads were difficult to adjust with fingers numbed by the cold, and they were useless against dense gas. The French casualties were therefore high: 531 men were killed, half of them in the front line about 500–600 m from the cylinder emplacements. Another 1,500 were more or less seriously injured, a few of them at a distance of 22 km from the discharge. The German purpose was to give cover to several raiding parties and, perhaps more importantly, to cause anxiety and casualties in what was at the time a quiet sector. Both sides gave some publicity to the attack. The Germans used it as a warning to battalion commanders not to commit the same errors as the French and to be on the alert at all times. The French were more concerned: there was much evidence of neglected gas training, and though the German preparations had been heard, no preventive measure had been taken. Finally, inexperienced troops—territorials and a Russian Brigade—had suffered most. These matters were raised in the French Parliament.[4] The fuss probably saved some lives in later operations of which four are on record. Two, in April and June, were directed against French troops at Nieuport on the Channel coast. The front width was only 4 km, and the clouds killed and injured 470 in April and 367 three months later. The events in Lorraine on 7 April and 1 July were different in that the terrain favoured the Germans. The country, a plateau between the upper Meuse and the Moselle, had been bitterly contested in the opening weeks of the war and early spring of 1915. Since then it had witnessed little action, and the flat, marshy uplands, without hillocks and few hollows was ideal for gas clouds. Yet, so far as I know, the Gaspioniere had not operated there before. They opened their cylinders at night and at first the east wind carried the gas to the French lines between Limay and Remenauville. Then it turned. The outcome was 450–500 French casualties, a quarter of them killed; the Germans also suffered some losses. In July the Germans tried again nearby at Seicheprey. The width of the front was 5 km, 11,700 cylinders were used, and the concentration achieved was almost the same as that in Champagne at the end of January. But the French were more alert and perhaps also better trained. Their casualties, 500–600, of whom about 20–30 per cent were killed, were lower than at Marquises-Aubérive.[5]

Seicheprey was the last occasion the Germans used cloud gas on the Western Front. Why did they stop? The French respirators were no better than in 1916 and their anti-gas training remained unsatisfactory. The more likely explanation is that the Germans were cutting down on this particular employment of the gas troops. Only on the Eastern Front were they still in action with their cylinders. They were trying to harass the enemy and make him give up ground at no cost to themselves. While the available reports of the nine or perhaps ten gas clouds up to November 1917 are incomplete, they do confirm that they occurred in the central sector and east of Vilna. Their effect was small for as the Russian armies disintegrated, the lines moved so far apart and were so lightly held, that few troops were sufficiently close to encounter the full strength of the gas.[6]

Among the British, support of gas-cloud operations was increasing. This was almost entirely due to Foulkes. He was totally dedicated to chemical warfare, indifferent to the hostility of infantry commanders and skilled at making small successes look impressive. An analysis of his statistics shows that the most intensive use of cylinder gas was from 16 June 1916 to 4 April 1917, from the preliminaries to the Somme to the start of the artillery preparations for the battle of Arras. In these nine months 42,600 cylinders were discharged, equivalent to 1,163 t of gas, mostly White Star (half chlorine, half phosgene) and some Yellow Star (70 per cent phosgene: 30 per cent chloropicrin). The former was more effective.[7]

Foulkes's men were particularly busy with their cylinders in the area to the south and south-east of Arras. There the ground is open and slightly higher than the town and the boggy Scarpe, and the half-ruined villages of Ablainzeville, Ayette, Achiet-le-Grand, Gomiécourt, Mercatel, and Neuville-Vitasse offered some shelter to the Special Companies. The views are long towards the east where the Germans were entrenched on low ridges, their field artillery and stores invisible on the reverse slopes. The British trenches were somewhat exposed and emplacing cylinders, though done at night, was dangerous. A strong easterly was needed to push the gas cloud towards the enemy. In this sector the British operations were usually small, only 10–20 t of gas were released at a time, but the frontage was narow and so the concentration was higher. Further south, towards the valley of the Ancre the intensity of the Somme battles prevented cylinder operations from July onwards and later, at the beginning of 1917, the Germans withdrew eastward. To the north of Arras, especially between Loos and La Bassée, the terrain was also suitable and the corps commanders were well disposed towards Foulkes. The Germans had drenched this flat and featureless land with chlorine and phosgene in 1915 and 1916, but now it was quiet and the turn of the British had come. Foulkes carried out some substantial attacks here: on 1 September 1917, 1,334 cylinders (say 39 t) were opened, on

4–5 October, 1,250 (36 t), and on 5–6 November, 700 (20 t). That was the last cloud attack of the year: some gas drifted back and eleven men were severely injured. Altogether, the Special Brigade released gas on nine occasions between April and the end of November, in total 12,000 cylinders equivalent to 333 t of gas. It was not an impressive record and it was rare that the effect could be observed, let alone measured.[8] To Foulkes's chagrin the French could not be prevailed upon to combine their Compagnies Z with the Special Brigade, though they allowed him to empty 1,000 cylinders at Dixmuide, a channel port, on 26 October. For once the Germans were caught unawares and suffered heavily.

The DGS had to put up with many problems and sometimes they dented his optimism. The worst was the manpower shortage, and next to it the obstruction of regimental COs. Carrying parties became increasingly difficult to organize, even in sectors where senior officers were on good terms with Foulkes. So operations had to be cut down and at the beginning of 1917 the Special Brigade tried out small cylinders weighing 23 kg (50 lb.) filled. The idea was that one man could carry such a cylinder in a sling. It did not work in the narrow communication trenches and the manpower saving proved minimal. So a new tactic was developed—gas discharges from 'retired' positions. The men of the Special Brigade dug in the cylinders under the firestep in the accustomed manner. A short time before zero hour, the infantry retired to the support lines and the special troops took over the front line to open the cylinders. The job done, they withdrew and the soldiers returned. It is hard to see the justification of manpower savings, and Foulkes did not explain them. The enemy soon discovered the purpose of these comings and goings along saps and communication trenches. The German artillery was alerted, found the range, and soon struck the troops who were densely packed without proper protection. Soldiers were lost to no purpose.

Less committed men would have given up cylinder operations altogether. Foulkes thought otherwise. He recalled his troops from the front, sent them to Helfaut into winter quarters and made them practise new ways of generating even bigger clouds. Although cylinder operations had gained no ground and directly or indirectly had caused many British casualties, the year had gone well for the Special Brigade. The Livens projector and its gas-filled projectile or drum had emerged as a remarkably effective device which was first used on a large scale at the beginning of April 1917. For once, even Liddell Hart was impressed by the thoroughness of the preparations. Foulkes, who had consistently backed Livens could, and did, justifiably claim some of the credit for the initial success at Arras. Encouraged by the outcome, about 97,000 drums were thrown at the Germans between that date and the end of the following November.[9] A terrifying weapon had joined the chemical armoury.

Livens was a mechanical engineer who 'combined great energy and enterprise with a flair for seeing simple solutions and inventive genius'[10] and he was only in his late twenties when he made this signal contribution to the British war effort. We have encountered him in an earlier chapter and mentioned that he persuaded divisional commanders to try out his device in the closing stages of the Somme battle. The effect of oil- or gas-filled projectiles on enemy strongholds was noted with approval, and the idea was accepted subject to some changes. His father, then chief engineer at Ruston and Hornsby, had the right contacts so that when the first orders were placed, production began promptly. The final projector design of January–February 1917 was, even by the undemanding standards of the day, pretty rough. But it was an eminently practical weapon, and it was unusual in that the inventor himself developed every part of it and was also going to be the principal user. Livens's purpose was to provide something that could be carried by a soldier proceeding along a narrow trench in bad weather—hence limits on length and weight. The projector consisted of two pieces: a base plate and a tube. The first was shaped like a saucer and was rolled to 8 mm thickness in tin-plate mills. It weighed 18 kg. The tube came in 3 different lengths, but the most common type was 91 cm (36 ins) long with a diameter of 20 cm which weighed 45 kg. (The short version, 83 cm, had insufficient range, the long, 129 cm version, was too heavy.) The Livens, father and son, initially used the waste ends of the big hydrogen cylinders employed for filling observer balloons, but the weight was excessive. Then they found some stocks of 10 mm gauge Mannesmann seamless rolled steel-tube—light and strong. When supplies could no longer be obtained they turned to welded tube and finally to lap-welded tube, less strong, but adequate. Manufacture was simplicity itself: the tube was pressed close at one end and rough finished; no boring or turning was necessary. The machine and manpower inputs were negligible and the projector could be reused! The drum or projectile was made of light steel sheet, which was pressed to the shape of a wide bottle with a short neck. Two screw threads were cut into it, one in the neck for the gaine, the other in the bottom for the tapered filling-plug. Empty, it weighed 13 kg.[11] The projector called for less labour and fewer materials than gas cylinders and their paraphernalia of valves, gauges, manifolds, and pipework. The economies were even greater in terms of woman hours by comparison with filling and assembling gas shells.

Livens's device was not, and could not be, accurate and indeed from the outset he intended it to be a saturation weapon—a small area was to be drenched in gas. Livens's objective was to achieve a high-carrying capacity relative to weight and the ratio was almost 1:1, for the drum held 11 litres of phosgene, roughly 13 kg, and a little more if filled with the heavier chloropicrin. He accepted inaccuracy and turned it to advantage. For example, the wooden charge box at the bottom of the projector was filled with black powder, but did not fit closely. No matter if the propellant burnt evenly or not! But as the width of No Man's Land increased, the range had to be raised: cordite could do it, and extend the maximum distance from 1.4 to 2 km. But the effectiveness of cordite depends on regular combustion and pressure build-up, so the cylinder had to be provided with a steel ring or gas check, and the longer range was bought at the cost of extra stamping and some machining. But no attempt was made to improve accuracy. The results of a trial shoot of 7 projectiles speak for themselves. They were fired in rapid succession from the same point: their trajectory length was 870 to 1,215 m, and a brisk wind of 7–8 m/sec at 55–65° to the angle of fire deflected the drums by anything from 20 m to 150 m.[12] Again no matter! However the time fuse being found unsatisfactory, a percussion fuse was substituted.

Inaccuracy heightened the effect of the gas projectile. The discharge of several hundred simultaneously was like a spectacular fireworks display—a huge flash, clouds of smoke, and the rumble of an explosion. This was followed by the rustling sound of the projectiles as they tumbled and swayed in their slow descent. They took perhaps twenty-five seconds to hit the other side and could be seen easily in the light of flares. The target could not be plotted or even guessed, for they fell at random with devastating effect on dug-out entrances, trenches, and command posts; a gust of wind might deflect them at the last moment or a faulty fuse delay the detonation and prolong the terror.

The British seized the initiative: 15,000 projectors and 50,000 projectiles were ordered in December 1916. Some reached France the following month. The phosgene-filling plant at Calais was quickly adapted, and in March 1917 mass production began. The initial delivery of drums was 3,000 a week, raised to 4,000 a week in April, and raised again, in March 1918, to 6,000 a week. Altogether, 140,000 projectors and 0.4 mln projectiles were supplied between January 1917 and the Armistice.[13]

The enemy was taken by surprise. Livens's experiments in the closing months of 1916 had gone unnoticed, for no German eye-witnesses returned to tell the tale. The discharge and detonation of the projectiles near Arras on 4 April 1917, therefore, came as a terrible shock. The corps and army reports were not available to me, but it is easy to imagine the critical questions at OHL and in Berlin. Why had gas bombs been neglected? Why had Nernst's mortar operations been closed down eighteen months previously? Why had Haber and his boffins failed to anticipate the British? And so on. There could be no doubt that the British gas projectiles came at a most inconvenient time for the Germans because those who concerned themselves with chemical warfare were bending their energies to the production of new gases and gas shell-filling techniques which formed part of their plans to replace gas cylinder operations by gas shoots. So there were some excuses for doubts and delays, but the slow German reaction remains puzzling.

The Germans found an unexploded projectile in April or May, took it to pieces, and correctly deduced from it the size of the cylinder and the shape of the base plate. The next step was retaliation, but bureaucratic entanglements over seamless steel tube stopped progress. So OHL ordered the gas troops to use the obsolete smooth-bore trench mortar. It was a solid device, weighing 22.6 kg without accessories and base, clumsy to handle, and its inaccuracy had led to its relegation. Eventually some Mannesmann tubing was found and from

Table 8.1. *Comparison of the British and German Projectors and their Projectiles*

	Livens	Rifled German
Base plate, weight	18 kg	n.a.
Projector tube, diameter	20 cm	13.5 cm*
Projector tube, length	91 cm	125 cm
Weight of tube	45 kg	72.3 kg
Weight of gas projectile, filled	29.5 kg	36 kg†
Weight of phosgene content	13.6 kg	6.6 kg‡
Length of projectile	56 cm	64 cm
Range (min.)	1,300 m	1,600 m
Range (max.)	2,000 m§	4,500 m

* The smooth-bore trench-mortar tube had a diameter of 18 cm.
† The projectile of the trench mortar weighed 30 kg.
‡ Excluding pumice granules weighing 2–3 kg.
§ Reached by projectiles from tubes fitted with gas check.
For source see references in text.

midsummer onwards the German rifled projector went into production. It differed from the Livens type in being longer, much heavier, and carefully machined and turned. The accuracy and range were far superior to Livens's weapon, but to what purpose? The drum was also more elaborately fashioned and its smaller gas-carrying capacity was further diminished by the addition of pumice stone. The Germans claimed later that pumice improved the ballistics and prevented the rapid dissemination of gas.[14] These were unnecessary refinements, took up manpower, and missed the essential features of Livens's design: simple manufacture, ease of handling, high concentration at point of impact, and random dispersion over a narrow, shallow sector of the front. Furthermore, the use of two distinct types of projectors (for the old trench mortar was not withdrawn) for the same purpose called for more training and complicated operational plans. Finally the bulk and the weight of the rifled projector created major difficulties for the Gaspioniere who could no longer depend on infantry-carrying parties. Hence the absurd situation that at a time of growing manpower shortages, a new weapon was being issued that was even more labour-intensive than the cylinders.[15]

   The belligerents now had to rethink their gas tactics. Foulkes laid his plans on the assumption that infantry officers would not authorize carrying fatigues for *their* men. So *his* men had to do it. The practice was to dig in the projectors at night in groups of 25. They were emplaced at an angle of 45° towards the German lines and wired in series to a remotely controlled electrical firing-system. Digging-in and camouflaging took several nights and was dangerous because it had to be done 'on top', usually between the support and the reserve lines, perhaps 100–200 m behind the front. The working parties were threatened by enemy machine-guns and there were frequent casualties. On the other hand, the job was less back-breaking than humping cylinders to the very front and the 'carry in' took fewer men. The risk of premature or accidental release, ever-present with cylinders, was negligible. The British fired or 'pooped' several hundred tubes at a time, and if the exact location remained undetected and the site undamaged from artillery fire, another salvo was sent over a few nights later. In this way, the Special Companies could make life miserable for several hundred German troops and dislocate their ration parties. Eventually these procedures, from repetition, became routine, but the Germans thinned out their front positions and so there was less scope for the British to inflict casualties. The Germans, when at last they were ready, treated their projectors as if they were precision weapons and took much trouble emplacing them firmly and getting the inclination just right. Their thoroughness caused them to spend too much time on preparations and the work was liable to be detected from the air. Their instructions, as might have been expected, were detailed, paid great attention to wind speeds (which must not exceed 1.5 m/sec), and had as their objective the creation of miniature gas clouds on a few pre-selected targets. Foulkes and Livens saw it differently. They merely wanted to inflict casualties, any German would do, and did not worry unduly about the weather or any targets in particular, provided some were hit. German perfectionism created unnecessary delays and restricted the scope of the weapon whose effectiveness lay in its surprise, its unpredictability, and the fear it caused.[16]

The Allies having decided on one more frontal assault in Spring 1917, the British 3rd Army was ordered to break through the German defences between Croisilles, at the northern extremity of the Somme battles and Vimy Ridge which was to be taken by the Canadian Corps. Allenby was in command and was known to have an open mind on gas. Foulkes supported by Hartley, then Chemical Adviser to the 3rd Army, persuaded him to use gas not merely to kill and injure the enemy in the front trenches but also and just as importantly to neutralize the German field artillery. The chosen area was between Tilloy, just south of the river Scarpe, and Thélus under Vimy Ridge to the north, a straight line distance of about 8 km. To the north of the river the land between the N.25 (Arras–Lens) and D.919 (Arras–Henin) roads rises gently from about 60 m to 110–13 near Thélus, and then falls away steeply east of Vimy Ridge. Vimy village and Gavrelle, 8km north-east of Arras, where the British advance halted, are on the 60 m contour-line. A gas cloud was out of the question and Livens was to use his projectors.

The men began digging in their tubes on 31 March. They used underground passages and the shelter of ruined houses at St Nicolas and St Laurent to transport the projectiles and sited them in the dead angles of folds in the open ground. The German front observers did not spot them, had no inkling of what was afoot and the artillery had no target to aim at. At 0615 on 4 April, 2,300 projectiles were launched simultaneously; that corresponded to say 32 t of a

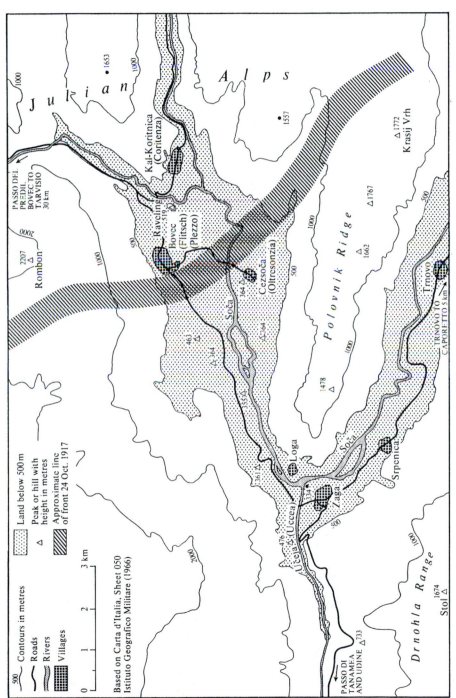

Map 5. The Valley of the Upper Soča

Contours in metres
Roads
Rivers
Villages

Land below 500 m
Peak or hill with height in metres
Approximate line of front 24 Oct. 1917

3 km

Based on Carta d'Italia, Sheet 050
Istituto Geografico Militare (1966)

0   1   2   3

J u l i a n   *A l p s*

• 1653

• 1557

△ 1772
Krasij Vrh

Kal-Koritnica (Coritenza)

PASSO DEI PREDIL
BOVEC TO TARVISIO
30 km

Raveline

Bovec (Flitsch) (Plezzo)

2207 △
Rombon

△ 1767

△ 1662

Cezsoča (Oltresonzia)

Soča

△ 364

P o l o v n i k   R i d g e

463 △

△ 364

△ 364

△ 364

355 △

1478 △

△ 1772

Trnovo

TRNOVO TO
CAPORETTO 5 km

Soča

361 △

Loga

Uccela (Uccea)

Srpenica

364 •

Zaga

476 •

D r n o h l a   R a n g e

Stol △ 1674

PASSO DI
TANAMEA
AND UDINE △ 733

mixture of chlorine and phosgene. The wind was blowing from the south south-west at about 4 m/sec, and the clusters struck trenches, gun emplacements, and command posts, the gas spreading out towards Vimy village in the north and Oppy in the east. Where the drums fell the Germans were overwhelmed, the noise and the density of the gas beyond their experience. Foulkes had foretold that Livens would disorganize the German defences and so facilitate the British advance on 9 April. He was right.[17]

The successful debut of the new British weapon failed to change the outcome of the battle of Arras which ended as yet another stalemate. But six months later, in the extreme north-west of present-day Yugoslavia, the German version, used at a critical hinge of the front, precipitated the collapse of the Italians at Caporetto.[18] The terrain, mountainous and difficult of access, gave the operation a unique character. Previous Italian attacks had taken them into the valley of the Soča (Isonzo) which, in the north, flows east to west before making a 90° turn to the south between Zaga and Loga. This northern sector of the Soča front was generally quiet and lightly held by the Italians. The Austrians occupied the high ridges of the Julian Alps and faced the Italians diagonally across the river on Mt Stol (the peak of the Drnohla range) and along the Polovnik ridge (see Map 5). The river has cut a deep valley through the limestone and the flood-plain is often wide, except at Loga and above Caporetto. The plan was to advance from Bovec (It. *Plezzo*, Ger. *Flitsch*) and in the centre from Tolmin, disrupt the Italian defences and seize the valleys on the west bank of the Soča, in particular that of the Učeja (Uccea) and the Nadiza (west of Caporetto). Progress along the former would endanger the entire front from the Alps to the Mediterranean, and along the latter would cut off the supply-lines to the middle and lower Soča.

The problem was how to do the job quickly, for if the attacks faltered, the Italians could regroup on higher ground and bar the passage to the Austrians. Haber was consulted. He recommended the use of the rifled projector. OHL was interested. Otto Hahn, Wilhelm König, and Blum, Peterson's chief of staff, were put into Austrian uniforms and told to find suitable launching-sites on the upper Soča. That was in September. They located a site, north of the river near Bovec. The Germans wasted no time and the next month Pionier Btn. 36 was sent to Tarvisio and thence to Kal-Koritnica (Coritenza) where the equipment could be safely stored. They emplaced 894 projectors by 23 October on the spot picked by Hahn and his party. The next morning the projectors were fired, but only 818 drums reached the target area across the river. The German weapon held less than the Livens projectiles, so that in total 5 or at the most 6 t of a phosgene−chlorine mixture struck the Italians between the river and the steep slopes of the Polovnik ridge. Not much by the standards of the day, but devastating all the same, because the Italians were not forewarned, were unprotected, and the mountain behind them prevented the gas from dissipating. The Germans then attempted to reload the projectors but failed, perhaps because some gas was flowing back. At 0900 the Austrians began their advance along the road from Bovec to Zaga. As they approached the defile and drew level with Loga there was no enfilading fire from the Italians across the river, for they were dead, struggling for breath, or clambering up the ridge to safety and eventual capture. By the afternoon the Austrians had seized Zaga and were following the road up the Učeja valley and the vital Col di Tanamea; they encountered little or no resistance.[19]

The aftermath of the Italian defeat at Zaga and of the capture of Caporetto further south is outside the scope of the book and in any case will be remembered by those who read Hemingway's *A Farewell to Arms*. On the purely technical level the impact was far-reaching. Chemical warfare was boosted and unlike first Ypres, the infantry was ready to follow up the initial breakthrough. As on the earlier occasion, the casualty figures enhanced the dramatic event. The Italians were so disorganized that they could not muster and soon reports spread that thousands had been gassed. The Germans counted 500–600 dead immediately after the projector attack east of the gorge. There were more casualties further south near Caporetto, where the Germans had used gas shells on October 23 just before the assult. When Barley arrived in Italy four or five weeks later he was told that 12,000 had been killed or injured by gas in that area, but the statistic had been inflated by repetition and was pure guess-work.[20] But it suited the Allies' propaganda to inflate the numbers and impress on their forces the need for more training and greater vigilance. The Germans incorporated the lesson in their plans for 1918.

The British projector operations of early April had no sequel worth detailing. Foulkes mentions twenty-five from the 4th of that month to the end of the year.[21] Many took place from the middle to the end of July around Ypres to distract the Germans and later to disorganize their counter-attacks elsewhere. The largest was at Bourlon Wood on the night of 19 to 20 November when 4,200 projectiles (about 57 t of gas) were fired to support the left flank of the British tank attack. It weakened the German defences for the next two to three days and so contributed to the initial success of the battle of Cambrai. In general however the Special Companies were employed at various points in small operations rarely exceeding 1,000 projectiles (13–14 t) to support raids or harass enemy troop-movements. It was an engineer's way of inflicting casualties at little cost in materials and manpower.

By the end of 1917 the war had become a routine business in which Livens projectors played a small role killing and injuring haphazardly, undermining morale, and keeping up the nervous apprehension. The Germans took the punishment, but their retaliation in kind was slow in coming. German prisoners, wishing to please their captors, inflated British gas superiority, and complained that their own experts were letting the side down.[22] One must allow for exaggeration, but the enemy, for once, was slow to react. Why? In the first place the manpower shortage was imposing delays. The gas troops having been sent to the Eastern Front with their cylinders, there were not enough in the west to begin practising. Secondly it took longer than anticipated to locate the old trench mortars, assemble them at the training depot, check them, and begin training. At OHL they were writing new manuals and the first instructions or *Dienstanweisung* issued in mid August covered every contingency except the absence of projectors![23] The preparations for the Soča operation were given overriding priority, and it was not until mid December that the Germans were ready. Then they struck six times in one month which suggests that they were waiting for several companies to be availabe for concentrated attacks. The French bore the brunt, first in Lorraine (5 December), twice in the Forest of Coucy between Chauny and St Gobain (13 and 22 December) and again in Lorraine at the end of the month. The British troops had their first experience of German gas projectiles on 11 December between Cambrin and Givenchy and on 30 December, north-west of Lens. The British collected every scrap of information on these two incidents and concluded that the German operational handling of the projectiles closely followed British practice. The Allies also suffered heavy casualties. The first salvoes on the French and the British caused respectively 113 and 78 casualties; 25 (= 22 per cent) of the former and 22 (= 28 per cent) of the latter died. In the later attacks there were fewer dead and injured.[24]

The offensive value of the projectiles was recognized before the year's end. Besides injury, they had a large psychological effect which increased its appeal to supporters of chemical warfare. They also gave the gas troops a new *raison d'être*, and this was appreciated in some quarters. But in the majority of operations on both sides, with the exception of Arras, the Soča defile, and near Bourlon Wood, the projectors had been used on their own without a strategic purpose. More was called for if the projectors were to become one of the instruments of victory. Foulkes was thinking in these terms, but to him it was simply a matter of more of the same recipe. The Germans, however, looked further. They envisaged the integration of gas shoots—artillery and projectors— with infantry attacks in a complex scheme. Their reasoning extended beyond volume to diversity of toxic materials and to specific effects. In this respect they differed from the British experts who, at the end of 1917, staked everything on the greater production of phosgene and chloropicrin. That might have been good in 1917, but was not good enough for 1918.

The title of the chapter and its position in the book would suggest that 1917 was an exceptional year in terms of discovery, manufacture, and application. This was not so as regards the first, but applied in part to the second, and completely fitted the third. I dealt with the first two in previous chapters; here we need to examine the implications of the decision to put mustard gas and arsenical compounds into shells and turn the artillery into the chief weapon of chemical warfare. Although development work remained incomplete and manufacture, except in Germany, was beset by problems, the artillery staffs went ahead with their plans. The intensive use of chemical shells required the assistance of chemical and ordnance experts for several distinct, but interconnected aspects: the design of shells; shell-filling techniques for mustard gas and arsenical compounds; use under varying conditions and interaction of artillery gas tactics with the infantry. As a consequence of and in step with changes on the offensive side of chemical warfare, defensive measures had to be adapted and, whenever possible, improved.

Mustard gas is a thick-flowing liquid and a few tests showed that the burster charge which opened the shell did not disperse it sufficiently. The belligerents therefore added a diluent, monochlorobenzene or carbon tetrachloride. The ratio of material to solvent, in the British nomenclature, of 'H' to 'S' was usually 4:1; so the specific gravity and the ballistics of the shell were altered. The Germans (and the Allies followed suit in 1918) altered their range tables, but they did not touch the shell design. The first Yellow Cross shells contained no HE beyond the burster charge and experienced troops soon learnt to associate the small flash and the 'plop' sound as the shell opened with mustard gas and were able to locate the point of impact. So the Germans looked for a shell case that would carry mustard gas and HE, and adopted a design introduced by the British earlier in 1917, but discarded because it leaked. It incorporated a partition to separate chloropicrin from the explosive. The Germans altered the shape of the diaphragm and hot-pressed it into a groove cut into an ordinary steel shell. Upon cooling the case shrank, making a gas-tight and leakproof fit between the two compartments. HE was poured in first, then the chemical filling was added. The noise made by the detonation was indistinguishable from an ordinary HE shell. The Diaphragm or *Zwischenbodengeschoss* went into large-scale production at the rate of 200,000 a month towards the end of 1917. It was also employed for ethylidichloroarsine (German code Dick, Anglo-American DL) which, being liquid, presented unusual shell-filling problems.

The solid arsenical compounds used as shell-filling had a complex evolution and the Germans never mastered all the technical problems. Their first product, Clark 1 (diphenylchloroarsine, DA) was supplied by Hoechst to the army's gas shell-filling plants in Warsaw and Mancieulles in eastern France. There it was dissolved in phosgene or diphosgene and filled into shells provided with a powerful burster. It was expected that the explosion would disperse liquid Clark 1 suspended in a toxic gas. Not only was the filling operation more than usually dangerous, but the Germans soon discovered that the liquid is corrosive. So a more cumbersome method was perforce adopted. Clark 1 and later Clark 2 were melted, filled into a small glass container which was inserted into the shell case, and TNT was poured around it. The idea was that the HE would break up and disperse the materials and the broken glass would further grind the mass. It did not work out in that way. The explosion compressed the solid and the detonation produced small, uneven pieces instead of a uniform particulate dust. Field trials would have demonstrated the error, but the Germans skimped them and the artillery were satisfied they had a new and effective weapon. It was largely wasted.[25] But that was not yet the end of the story. The army's filling stations did not have the equipment to carry out the whole complicated operation. Agfa and Schering were approached, and as they had assembly lines for filling bottles they were able to modify their installations in Berlin. Clark 1 and 2 called for equipment, glass, and, above all, womanpower on a scale which was out of proportion to the value at the front. The 'efficiency' of the shell, that is the proportion of arsenical compounds to gross weight was exceptionally low. In the field guns, 7.7 and 10.5 cm, it amounted to 1.6 and 2.6 per cent respectively and in the 15 cm howitzer it was 2.2 per cent. This was using a lot of metal to transport a very small mass of an ineffective material. The wonder is that this absurd arrangement was used for filling 15 million bottles which were inserted at the rate of one million a month in July 1918. Altogether about ten million of these shells were fired in 1917–18.[26] The figures represent a formidable waste of effort: filling with TNT only would have been more cost-effective.

By 1917 shell-filling everywhere had become a large industry. Gas shells, from the outset, were handled separately on green field sites at some distance from densely populated areas. But the introduction of mustard-gas shells forced the belligerents to rethink their approach. The Germans had no consistent policy. Bayer, as we have seen, made the bulk German mustard gas, but refused to fill it into shells, although they operated a large HE filling plant at Dormagen. The company claimed it was too dangerous to handle both materials on the same site. The army had a filling station behind the Western Front at Mancieulles, later moved to Saulnes near Longwy, but neither site was considered suitable for mustard-gas shell, possibly on account of the threat from air raids. The Kriegsministerium proposed to develop Breloh as a vast gas-shell complex, but the project had only been partly completed when the war ended. An interim solution was urgent, and Haber, who was in charge, negotiated with C. A. F. Kahlbaum, makers of fine chemicals, to build filling sheds, on a site it owned at Adlershof, then an outer suburb of what is now East Berlin. Transport was good and it was in a low-risk area. The works was completed in May 1917, but burnt shortly afterwards in a spectacular fire attributed to sabotage. The Germans were in a great hurry and rebuilt the sheds within four weeks: they identified handling as the key problem and devised mechanical turntables and dollies which saved labour. The shells were filled according to the constant volume method by a device which resembled that used in public houses to dispense spirits. The appliances were totally enclosed and provided with forced draught ventilation leading to tall chimneys. The site had storage tanks and railway sidings, and safety measures abounded. There were few reports of burns and other injuries and initially work was round the clock. Soon it was found that four short shifts and one four-hour break for maintenance and cleaning gave better results. At peak rates, 24,000 7.7 cm shells could be filled a day. Adlershof was the main gas shell-filling plant during 1918 and employed about 2,800 men and women. In the latter half of 1918 Breloh was able to deal with several thousand gas shells a day.[27]

The Allies had to make do with simpler installations. The Ministère de l'Armement added a mustard-gas filling line to an ammunition plant at Aubervilliers, just north of Paris. It worked for a few weeks in April 1918 and then closed because it was within range of Big Bertha. New purpose-designed plants with mechanical lifting devices were built at Salaise near Lyons and Pont-de-Claix, but neither worked at capacity until supplies from the mustard-gas factories became regular. The French would have liked to rely solely on constant volume filling, but their shells were not sufficiently uniform and a very small variation in volume could have a major effect on the ballistics of the 75 mm shell. So they were forced to depend on constant level filling, which caused more spillage, and had to design vacuum charging machines which retained the excess in the filling pipe. This method and the speed of operation were similar in principle to modern petrol-filling systems, but they were also extremely dangerous. Hence the wide fluctuations in the daily shell-filling rates attributed to the closure of one or more lines due to accidents. When the threat to Paris receded, Aubervilliers was reopened and enlarged, and was reported to be capable of filling 10,000 gas shells a day. French filling statistics for 1918 have not survived so the trend cannot be shown.[28] In Britain, the Chittening site, abandoned as a mustard-gas factory, became available for shell-filling and was hurriedly equipped with the necessary machinery. It opened for business on 8 July 1918, but as supplies from Avonmouth were irregular and minuscule for several weeks, the plant remained underemployed until September. A second factory, at Banbury, was converted for gas-shell filling during the summer of that year. By 11 November, almost 400,000 mustard-gas shells had been filled, half of them 18 pounders. The works at Edgewood was rather larger and handled only 75 mm shell cases. The Americans, of all the belligerents, had the best gas shell-filling facilities. The plant immediately adjoined the chemical works, and comprised a large refrigerating section for phosgene and a design based on bottle-filling machinery for mustard-gas shells. They were the first to employ compressed air-driven motors, set to give a uniform closing torque, to drive in the screw-plug. The system was simple, safe, quicker, and more dependable than the French or German manual devices to close the shell and render it leakproof. Here, as in other ways, the Americans quickly adapted engineering technology to the production of chemical weapons.[29]

In reviewing the progress of chemical shell we have run ahead in the chronology and must return to mid 1917 and describe the introduction of the new materials by the Germans and how they affected the course of artillery warfare. Shells filled with DA and marked with a blue cross were first used on a small scale on 10 July at Nieuport, but apparently went unnoticed. There were further shoots near Ypres on 20–1 July and a couple of nights later. Again nothing much happened. Then, on 28 July some unexploded shells with their distinctive blue markings were found by the British in the area of Wijtschate, south of Ypres. They were opened and the contents caused some sneezing. The chemists were busy on mustard gas and considered that the substance presented little danger, so that DA was not identified until some time in August. The

Germans were trying out the material, and in retrospect their efforts appear half-hearted. If they were counting on creating a noticeable effect and hoping to glean information from their front observers, they were disappointed. By contrast the début of mustard gas was dramatic and the first effects sensational. The British were making the final preparations for Third Ypres and were particularly sensitive to any interference with their preliminary artillery barrage. Their chemical advisers, like everyone else, were keyed up. The Germans benefited from a change in the weather. After some rain in the first week of July, it became hot and dry with wind-speeds below average for the time of year. Throughout the warm night of 12–13 July the Germans fired 50,000 mustard-gas shells into the area between St Jean and Potijze just east of Ypres.[30] The sector was held by the 55th and 15th Divisions, the latter, under Thuillier, who had just assumed his new command, was taking up positions. The Germans did not know that the former DGS was facing them, but Thuillier's presence sharpened the reaction. At the same time the Germans shelled some ammunition dumps and gun positions in the rear as well as French troops further north. Some shells were found marked with a yellow cross and fitted with the new instantaneous impact fuse EKZ 17. At the front and in the rear there were many casualties, but most were not severely injured. The alarming feature was the partial blindness of the casualties who also suffered from progressive conjunctivitis. It says a great deal for the morale and the discipline of the men that there was no panic, and somehow they were quickly guided to the CCS where doctors and nurses treated the unusual and indeed, alarming symptoms as well as they could. C. G. Douglas, Foulkes's physiological adviser, noted on his rounds that the men were rapidly developing blisters on buttocks, genitals, and armpits. In his report of 14 July he surmised that the Germans had fired some skin-irritating substance. But two days later many of the casualties were suffering from bronchitis and a few had died from inflammation of the lungs. The course of the infection and the aetiology of the disease were worrying because they followed no pattern and the delayed action of the poison was unheard of. By 18 July the eyes were generally improving, but the pulmonary symptoms remained severe. Six days later the sick still had bronchitis and noticeable skin rashes instead of blisters, but the conjunctivitis had disappeared.[31]

Identification and remedial action were given the highest priority. Hartley told me many years later how he was woken early on that 13 July and informed that the Germans had fired a new type of shell which made a plop-like sound when it burst. Hartley, newly in charge of the BEF's gas defence, and the Corps Chemical Adviser sallied forth and the next day had located some unexploded shells with yellow cross markings. They were defused, taken to GHQ, opened, the contents analysed by Mouat Jones and the findings compared with the entry in *Beilstein*, a copy of which was providentially on long-term loan from Balliol College! By 16 July, they knew what the stuff was and later analyses added little to this knowledge.[32] In retrospect it sounds like a jolly little scientific investigation with field work by dons in uniform. But the chemists had cause to be pleased with themselves. Their rapid and complete identification disposed of the fear of a new German wonder-weapon against which no precautions could be taken, nor treatment help.

In the following two to three weeks the Germans methodically shelled the area to the north and the south of Ypres, and occasionally targeted rear positions or quiet sectors such as Armentières, where at that late date civilians, inadequately protected by the French authorities, were still living. Thus on the night of 20–1 July and again a week later the town was shelled with mustard gas. In the built-up area the liquid clung to walls, gutters, and cellar floors, causing about 6,400 casualties, among them 675 civilians.[33] Thereafter the intensity of mustard-gas shelling diminished and for the rest of the year the Germans used it sparingly; they also continued to fire Blue Cross shells spasmodically. The Germans had some supply difficulties and they were taken aback by the prisoners' statements of the persistence of mustard gas and its blistering effect. The one called for more production and better distribution, the latter forced them to rethink their gas tactics. By December the Germans had plenty of mustard-gas shells and two different Blue Cross shells.[34] But the planning of artillery barrages using a variety of gases to achieve particular tactical results had to be tried out in battle, without, however, alerting British and French specialists. The closing stages of hostilities in Russia provided the Germans with just the experience they needed, and it may be doubted whether the details seeped through to the West. The Germans spent the winter months considering the lessons they had learnt in the late summer campaign in western Russia.

Among the problems which had to be tackled before detailed planning for 1918 could begin was what to do about the ammunition supply given the wide choice of shell fillings: one could carry the permutations too far. For example, at the end of 1917 the Central Laboratory of the BEF investigated the varieties of German gas shells and bombs and found that gas shells were available for nine different calibres of guns and mortars, and the gunners could select among twenty-two combinations of fillings and calibres. The 15 cm howitzer had an availability of five chemicals, the 7.7 and 10.5 cm field guns four each. Inevitably shell-filling programmes became extremely elaborate and the storage problems at rear dumps and forward stores excessively complicated. The work involved in scheduling supplies for a large gas-shell bombardment was of a different order of magnitude from that of an HE barrage. The British repeated the mistake, but at least they avoided the subtleties of the exact location of the diaphragm in the *Zwischenbodengeschoss* designed to keep the ballistics unchanged whatever the specific gravity of the filling. The really important thing was how to prevent gas shells from embedding themselves in the ground before detonation. For mustard gas and Blue Cross, an explosion just above ground was essential if the maximum dispersal was to be attained.[35] But this objective was not reached, for a reliable proximity fuse was not available during the war and a time fuse (as for shrapnel) could not be depended upon unless the fillings were absolutely uniform in volume or weight. The purpose of all these elaborate preparations and improvements was to optimize the use of gas shells, but how effective were they when Blue Cross was useless? The French (though not the British) avoided diversity, and from 1916 onwards concentrated on filling gas into 75, 120, and 155 mm cases. They claimed that the important element in gas-shell tactics was the rate of fire, and to make their point claimed that in October 1917 an entire German division had to be pulled out of the line owing to exhaustion due to wearing their respirators for seven and a half hours continuously in a gas bombardment which changed the rate of fire twenty-two times. The Germans confirmed the story, and the French tactic, which led to a small victory, was vindicated.[36]

Each side asserted that their chemical weapons and methods were superior to the enemy's. This was rarely true in 1917 and 1918, and as a rule one's own side was misled by expectations which remained unfulfilled. The claims could not be readily quantified, let alone verified, and so contributed to surround chemical warfare with an atmosphere of threatening but immeasurable implications. Thus the potential benefits for the innovator were weakened by ignorance of the precise effects at the front. It is interesting that the allegations of successful offence survived into the 1920s and 1930s thereby perpetuating the myth of a deadly weapon, without at the same time, drawing attention to its random nature, nor the parallel improvement in defence.

As the tempo of chemical warfare accelerated, so the defence against gas became yet more important, and by the end of the war, as we have seen, made appreciable demands on materials and scientific manpower, and employed many thousands of women. The Germans had been leading in the defence against gas in 1915 and for most of 1916, but the issue of the SBR gradually tilted the balance in favour of the British. At Arras the large scale use of Livens projectiles and of various chemical shells first showed the limitations of the German respirator. Circulars were issued to counteract any lack of confidence: they stressed the efficacy of the German anti-gas defences and belittled the casualties. The Gas Officer of the 4th German Army stated that the respirator protected *completely* and was *reliable* (his italics), but added that there had been 'considerable casualties' which were 'not always avoidable because a few breaths of the highly concentrated gas were enough to injure severely the unprotected [*sic!*] soldier'. It was not, the Stogas' circular concluded, that the Livens bomb contained a new gas against which the mask offered no defence: the trouble was that the men, hurriedly putting on the respirator accidentally trapped a little gas in its folds and breathed it in.[37] But what else were the troops supposed to do? It had been noted before that many soldiers became acutely uncomfortable after wearing the mask for more than an hour, especially at night, and, when anxious or tired they sweated, their veins swelled, and the fit ceased to be gas-tight.[38]

German confidence in their mask was shaken, but the Allies also had their problems. In this respect the night of 12–13 July 1917 was the testing time of the British anti-gas organization. The outward signs of mustard-gas poisoning—pain, fear, skin inflammations, embarrassment—and its potentially dangerous nature, had never been previously described and particulars of its aetiology and treatment were of the greatest urgency. Douglas rendered the BEF a great service when he issued instructions within forty-eight hours on treatment which 'needed only a trifling modification in the light of more experience.'[39] Douglas's improvisations and strict secrecy concerning the effect on the troops prevented a serious situation from getting out of control: the Germans had no idea of the brief and limited success they had achieved, while the detrimental effect on British morale was contained. The next job was detection and precautions. Mustard gas smells slightly of garlic or English mustard and in dispersions of as little as 0.2 ppm can still be detected by sensitive noses. The liquid is brown, easy to identify in a factory, but at the front it merged into the predominant day-time colours. Fortunately for the Allies, the plop sound of the burster was sufficient to alert the troops to the incipient danger. But when the Germans introduced the *Zwischenbodengeschoss* and new artillery tactics, this early warning system disappeared. Detection by chemical methods attracted much attention, but was useless in practice. When the Germans replaced the carbon tetrachloride diluent by monochlorobenzene, they added to the difficulties of the defence, for the new material lowered the viscosity of mustard gas and so contributed to a wider dispersion, while its higher boiling point (131° C against 76° C) slowed down evaporation.[40] The foolproof detection of this gas was never satisfactorily solved, so that even with good masks the precautions were inevitably incomplete. Those who minimized the danger from exposure to mustard gas and neglected to emphasize its varied character, caused much harm.[41] The heavy American casualties in Autumn 1918 bore witness to misleading instructions and lax precautions.

Although all gases had a debilitating effect, mustard gas and even more so Blue Cross introduced a psychological element into injury—depression and war weariness. Douglas and many RAMC doctors were not sympathetic and ascribed these symptoms to the 'neurasthenia which is so liable to appear in any case of gas poisoning'.[42] Yet there was a great deal more to it: the borderline between gas poisoning, battle fatigue and malingering was blurred in 1918 and it was fortunate for the Allies that the enemy rarely succeeded in producing effective particulate dispersions, for otherwise he could have done great damage to morale. The Germans were well aware of their own weakness in this respect, and in 1917 the KWI began the intensive study of protection against particulates.

All anti-gas measures had to be revised. Once mustard gas, Blue Cross shells, and Livens projectiles became a frequent hazard of life at the front, every aspect of the complex interlocking of alert, identification, individual and collective protection, treatment and morale was involved. Once again it is convenient to start with the Germans and their problems. The face-piece of their respirator was made of rubberized cotton fabric. When it became scarce chrome-tanned sheepskin, readily available from Bulgaria, was substituted. The first step was to dip it into sealing oil to render it waterproof. Next, a single piece was cut from the hide and rolled into the shape of a cone, cut in three places, the seams stitched and lacquered. The seams were designed to allow the eye-pieces to stand clear of the face, like goggles. The eye-pieces were double layered (celluloid and cellulose acetate respectively) and coated on the face side with gelatine to prevent misting up. The coating replaced the wiping folds of the fabric mask and so reduced the volume of dead space where stale air or gas might accumulate. The face line was made air-tight by fabric-covered twisted piano wire which, it was said, was as good as elastic tape. On paper the ingenuity of the design was undeniable, the Germans—making a virtue out of necessity—claimed that the leather mask was a considerable advance ('wesentlicher Fortschritt') over the rubberized fabric. It was nothing of the sort! The leather was smelly and rough, it was also stiffer and a good fit was therefore more difficult to achieve. The mask did not dry quickly, could not be patched with rubber solution, and had to be carefully stowed in its tin box to avoid chafing the seams. As if this were not enough, the eye-pieces were angled differently from those of the mask to which the soldiers had become accustomed. One got used to that, but aiming was very difficult.[43] Needless to say, the new mask required elaborate instructions. It was issued over a period of many months: there had been prisoner reports, in Spring 1917, of a leather mask, but a Bavarian document in September refers to their 'recent' introduction and the meticulous *Dienstvorschrift* describing its use was not printed until February 1918. The supply statistics of the 6th (Bavarian) Army, stationed between the Lys and Lens, confirm that the shift from fabric to leather began in the last quarter of 1917 and accelerated in the first quarter of 1918.[44] The final offensives of the war therefore found the German soldiers equipped with two respirators—one made of fabric, the other of leather—the latter gradually predominated, but was an inferior substitute and not suitable against particulates and mustard gas.

The design of the screw-on filter remained the same but the contents were changed in June–July 1917 in response to British gas projectiles. The potassium carbonate filter was reduced, because chloropicrin, being chemically neutral, does not require an alkali, while the activated charcoal content was raised. The 11-C-11 drum, though better than its predecessor, was still not good enough and a new drum was introduced in May 1918, code-named S-E and often referred to as *Sonntags-Einsatz*. It contained twice the weight of charcoal and there was a corresponding cut in the amount of impregnated pumice or kieselguhr granules. A small clip-on extension, filled with special rag paper had been devised by Drs Weigert and Pick at the KWI, and was issued in Spring 1918 to assault troops to protect them against the Blue Cross mists through which they had to advance.[45] The troops do not appear to have paid much attention to the changes in the filter contents, but the British who monitored them with great care, considered the thick paper discs of little use against DA in concentrations of 10 ppm or higher. The German scientists knew that the new filter offered much greater resistance to breathing, and they were aware that the respirator

Fig. 14. Soldier wearing German leather mask. Photograph taken by US Signal Corps in 1918. Note large eye-pieces, tight-fitting face line, and lacquered metal box for carrying respirator. The filter appears to have the clip-on extension to protect against Blue Cross materials. (Imperial War Museum)

had reached its limit. They feared, above all, that the British would introduce an efficient thermogenerator during 1918, against which the mask would be useless. As the danger receded they took comfort in the thought that at least the S-E filter would hold for twenty-nine minutes against a concentration of one part of phosgene in 200 of air, and up to eighteen minutes against 1:100, a concentration rarely encountered in the open.[46]

The Germans had no filter supply problems and the contents continued to be made chiefly by Bayer, Schering, and Riedel de Haen. The first two and also Kahlbaum handled the greater part of the filling work; the operation remained manual, though small electrically driven mixers were used to settle the mass. The KWI staff devoted much effort to the improvement of activated charcoal. From the end of 1916 onwards, Bayer at Leverkusen, and to a lesser extent Schering, accounted for most of it. They used fine wood chips, cheap and plentiful, and increased reactivity by treating the wood with a solution of zinc chloride and hydrochloric acid.[47]

During 1917 some changes were made to the SBR, notably the replacement of bone charcoal by wood charcoal and a new formulation for the soda-lime-permanaganate granules which slowed down their rate of decomposition. The contents of the filter unit were modified in August and October 1917 and again the following January. These improvements could be readily accommodated within the existing design, did not affect the breathing resistance, and called for only minor alterations in assembly.[48] The response to Blue Cross shell, which caused few casualties, was different because the filter of the SBR had not been designed with particulates in mind. The Anti-Gas Department put H. S. Raper in charge of the investigation, but he made little progress for several months because not enough material was available for tests, and unexploded German shells with their Blue Cross contents were difficult to extract from the morass of Third Ypres. Eventually some DA was found and Bertrand Lambert, working with Raper, devised a kind of jacket of cellulose wadding to surround the filter box, which may have been inspired by the French layered pads. At any rate on 8 February 1918 they reported to the Defence Committee of the CWD that 72 layers of such wadding gave 'satisfactory protection' against DA in a concentration of 10 ppm, but increased breathing resistance by 76 mm mercury. This was not a very impressive result, but the greater resistance was bearable in a system such as the SBR where breathing in was through the mouth. The Committee thought otherwise and asked them to find something better. Within a month they had brought the resistance down to 25 mm without loss of filter strength. The next problem was how to fit the wadding to the respirator and accommodate both in the haversack. A practical solution would take time, but the German attack was believed to be imminent and the War Office was extremely worried about Blue Cross shells. The Anti-Gas Department was told to order a 'slip-on jacket' which fitted over the bottom of the filter container. It gave adequate protection at the cost of increasing breathing resistance by about a quarter. Production started at once and the jacketed containers were issued in France from April onwards. Adhesive paper was also distributed, and the men were told to tape the jacket and its cellulose wadding tightly round the metal container. It was about as futile as the German attempt to generate particulate clouds, and the soldiers had no patience with the fiddly job. Nevertheless one million were issued until in May someone high up had the sense to cancel the order and the CWD were instructed to find something better. This took several months, because the best arrangement for placing the mechanical filter inside the redesigned container had to be devised and tested, the haversack had to be made from waterproof materials and the assembly lines reorganized to carry out the modification. Altogether it constituted a considerable research and development effort and the new SBR called the 'Green Band' at last went into production in September 1918, roughly a year after the start of work on protection against DA. Manufacture was increased very rapidly in response to

War Office demands. At the end of October the staff called for one million Green Band respirators in France by 1 January 1919 and sufficient for the entire BEF six weeks later.[49] The order was never completed, but the new gas mask was issued to the troops sent to Northern Russia.

Vinet wrote after the war that Lebeau took two years to design the Appareil Respiratoire Spécial, ARS, which implies that he began research before the German chlorine cloud of April 1915 made protection necessary! The facts are simpler. In the latter half of 1916 Lebeau and Dr Saulnier designed a good copy of the German mask, but the French version weighed less and the screw-on filter was a little smaller. The breathing system was very ingenious. It consisted of a mica, non-return, inlet valve, and an arrangement of rubber rings for the outlet valve. Breathing in was through the filter and the suction simultaneously opened the mica disc and pushed open the rubber flap. The French design was superior to the German in that the exhausted breath was expelled into the atmosphere instead of being pushed through the filter or the face line. The concept was very good, but depended in practice on the quality of the materials and the care taken in assembly and use. In particular the mica must not crack and operate smoothly and the rubber rings must be elastic and must remain air-tight. Failure of any of these weak spots would quickly lead to choking and gassing. The ARS, like the German model, was 'open', that is the wearer breathed in through the nose. A good, tight fit of the face-piece was therefore essential. The French made theirs of two layers—the outer of rubberized cloth, the inner of oiled cloth. It was more comfortable than the German leather mask, it was impermeable, washable, and did not smell, or at least not so much as the German. Unfortunately, French assertions notwithstanding, it did not protect very well. The reason was the smaller filter. So-called official tests made by the British, diplomatically placed it ahead of the German mask. In fact it should have been well behind.[50] During 1918 the French changed the composition of the filter granules (a mixture of sodium carbonate, charcoal, zinc oxide, and, incomprehensibly, caustic soda) and the new type was reported to give improved protection against acid gases. Claims that this ARS protected against phosgene concentrations of 1:500 for 3–3¼ hours and of 1:100 for 20–30 minutes need not be believed, though Lebeau had the nerve to quote these figures to an audience of Allied experts. Vinet merely noted that the ARS was not designed to deal with dense concentrations! Lebeau had also somehow contrived to insert a layer of cotton fabric into the filter to protect against Blue Cross, but it may be doubted whether it was of any use; obviously it added to the breathing resistance.[51] The French design served as model for later improvements, among them, though remotely, the British civilian respirator of 1938–45.

The Ministère de l'Armement accepted the ARS in February 1917, but deliveries did not begin until November. The delay is not surprising when one bears in mind the tooling-up and assembly problems the French had to face. They probably did not have the right kind of machinery, they had no experience of assembly-type operations, and it is likely that they had difficulties with the

Fig. 15. Soldiers wearing ARS mask. Note similarity to German respirator. The photograph is undated, but was taken some time in 1918. (Imperial War Museum)

mica and rubber shutters. Production was at the rate of 15,000–20,000 a day in the first quarter of 1918. Indeed up to 10 February, 1918, only half a million ARS had been issued, principally to the artillery, and distribution among the infantry was gradual 'pour ne pas jeter le discrédit sur le masque M2, d'ailleurs très efficace'.[52] The subtlety of the logic compels admiration, but it is only fair to add that the ARS proved helpful during the French retreats of March–April. Distribution was increased, and by May all the men at the front had one ARS. It was typical of the French approach to gas defence that the metal container was so small that the mask had to be shoved in and the fabric became abraded. More serious was the failure to provide a spare filter. Instead, the men carried the M2 device. By the end of the war, 3.7 million ARS had been issued, no mean feat of production, but the potential threat posed by Blue Cross shells could not be mastered by the small filter. A supposedly improved model, the 'Étoile Noire', was compared in September 1918 with the Green Band version of the SBR. The French experts had invited Lefebure, but they had no cause to be pleased by the unsatisfactory outcome of the trial. Indeed they were so chastened that they even considered a Gallic version of the SBR and Lefebure wrote of 'a common . . . allied mask as a not very remote ideal'. That was no more than wishful thinking and the French went back to their own design. They held another competition on 20 November; this time the wind changed direction, the observers had to withdraw, and the verdict was 'not proven'.[53] However, all were pleased to note that the German mask had failed, but by then, of course, the enemy was *hors de combat*.

The respirators of the other belligerents need not detain us long. The Americans developed two types. One was designed by a specialist in anaesthetic masks: it took several months to develop a working model consisting of a metal face-piece lined with sponge rubber and connected by rubber tubing to the filter unit at the back of the head. The contraption reached London in 1918 and was ridiculed there, whereupon Washington ordered it to be scrapped. The other was the USA version of the SBR and had a longer gestation period than the original. Tests demonstrated that it was no good, and for the duration the AEF in France was equipped with the British article. The Russians continued working on their own designs, of which the least impracticable was Avalov's, a fine piece of rubber moulding, with a very small filter directly attached to the face-piece. They badly needed good masks, for they were defence-less against some very intensive gas shelling in the autumn of 1917, the fore-runner of what the Allies were to experience six to seven months later. As to the Italians, they had nothing. Even in January 1918 they were still thinking in terms of an impregnated towel hanging over the chest to protect the wearer from mustard-gas splashes. But what was useful in a hairdressing salon was useless for the crouching soldier. Generally speaking there was much anxiety over the unprotected condition of the Italian army after Caporetto. It even reached the rarefied atmosphere of the Supreme War Council, which prevailed upon Gen. Cardorna, the CinC of the Italian forces, formally to ask for 1.6 million SBRs. He did, and before he could change his mind, half were dispatched from Calais. The rest got to Italy before Spring 1918;[54] later that year the local manufacture of a slightly modified version of the SBR was to begin.

Respirator improvements gave, or were supposed to give, better protection to the individual. But the introduction of mustard gas had much wider implications. Decontamination and collective defence at the front, at dumps and factories suddenly became very urgent. The protection of the guns was as important as that of the gunners and those who brought up the ammunition. Gas shells were to be stacked downwind from HE, preferably over trenches into which mustard gas could be dumped. Camouflage was the norm by 1917, but added to the troublesomeness of washing down and cleaning. Bleaching powder was the universal antidote—it breaks down dichlorodiethyl sulphide into sulphur chlorides and ethylene dichloride. The recommended practice after a bombardment was to rearrange the camouflage netting, or find fresh branches, and wipe the guns with a squee-gee dipped in chloride of lime. Next the ground was dusted with bleaching powder, and in order to hide the white patches from observation planes, earth was sprinkled over them. No wonder these jobs were rarely done by the rule book, and in July 1917 the gunners must have prayed for rain. It came the following month and the men then found that mustard gas remains dangerous for days in sheltered places. The infantry were just as sorely tried, because it clings to textiles and leather. The men had vaseline creams which did no harm, but did not stop itching or burns and blisters. Even if bleaching powder was in stock at trench stores, how was it to be taken up the line in the necessary quantities and how were the exhausted men to spread it over the churned up positions?[55] Barley, returning from leave, was sent for by Plumer, then in command south of Ypres, who was worried by high mustard-gas casualties. Barley recommended that troops should note the impact point of Yellow Cross shells, stake out the ground, and treat with bleaching powder. Beyond that he advised more drill in taking precautions, but how was it to be implemented in the mud of Flanders? The Germans were not bothered by mustard gas in 1917, but in spring 1918 they warned their assault troops to beware of ruins, and to dust walls and floors with bleaching powder, burn mattresses and straw, to air sheets and curtains and generally not to touch anything exposed to a barrage of Yellow Cross shells.[56]

Perversely, the further away from the front, the more elaborate anti-gas defences and decontamination became. For example the French and the Germans cut deep, artificially ventilated shelters into the limestone of the Chemin des Dames, and even thought of keeping them under slight pressure to prevent the entry of gas. That was not possible in Picardy, let alone in Flanders. There the British experimented with hand-powered lightweight fans sucking air through filters.[57] There were also decontamination squads, and various kinds of capes, overalls, and gloves were designed to enable men (and, at home, women) to clean up. The Germans used paper fabrics and impregnated leather gloves, both useless, but they had nothing else. The Allies had plenty of cotton and canvas, and finally adopted oiled linen suits, and leather gloves sheathed in disposable cotton gloves. Tambuté, who had made his reputation with the anti-gas snout, gained more fame in 1918 by designing a special outfit for decontamination troops. In Britain Whiteleys of Bayswater produced 58,000 oiled suits, but they were too heavy and uncomfortable for use with the BEF and were not suitable for wear in mustard-gas factories. The problem was insoluble: the tempo of the gas shell-filling lines called for easy movement and breathing. Where the specialists of 1917–18 failed, their successors twenty years or so later fared no better. The decontamination squads standing by for Hitler's war also needed to be shielded and it was found that rubber fabric was too hot, oiled cloth too heavy, and much trial-and-error work was required until suitable clothing for the ARP gas teams became available in 1940.[58]

A remarkable feature of the last eighteen months of the war was the extent to which civilians became involved in chemical warfare. The people of Armentières were the first non-combatant victims in 1917 and the next year they were joined by workers making dichlorodiethyl sulphide and organic arsenical compounds, both dangerous and debilitating occupations. The British were willing to take 'low medical category men', provided they had no heart or lung diseases, and women, provided they were not pregnant or nursing mothers. At Avonmouth they were employed for 44 hours spread over five-and-a-half days a week. The French took only 'Grade 1 whites', North Africans, or Indo-Chinese, and worked them on a 'six days on–two days off' rota. In both countries there were many injuries and at Avonmouth as at Aubervilliers, more than a thousand men and women were on sick leave at one time or another in the last four months of the war. At Morecambe the girls filling the thermo-generators were only two days in the danger section before being rotated to less unhealthy jobs. Yet the sickness rate was very high. Personal hygiene was not always good enough, but the chief difficulties were caused by the wooden floors, which soaked up the poison, by the absence of self-flushing toilets, insufficient eye-baths and showers, poor lighting, and inadequate ventilation. Collective protection and prevention had taken second place to production with the result that parts of works of Usines du Rhône and Avonmouth were closed from time to time owing to sickness and exhaustion.[59]

There were frequently moments of acute crisis over mustard gas. But what were the reactions of those directly exposed or injured? Nowadays an attitude survey would give us a clue, but in 1917–18 one had to guess. The matter was of more than passing academic interest, for the importance of civilian and military morale was recognized, and poison gas was among the causative agents which attracted increasing official attention. Attitudes reflect the individual's or group's temperament. When I talked to Chelsea pensioners and others who had known poison gas, the overwhelming impression I gained was the chanciness of gas, and the diversity of the men's reactions to it. Jack Berridge, James McLellan, and Lance Beales, whom I questioned in 1973, had been exposed to mustard gas. The first had been with the Sixth KRR and was not affected by Yellow Cross shells, though some of his comrades were burnt. McLellan, a lifelong non-smoker, was with the KOSB in March 1918, working a Lewis gun. He remembered that he breathed in some gas before putting on the mask: he was not burnt at the time but henceforth suffered from catarrh and bronchitis. His colleagues suffered no hurt whatever. Beales served with a siege battery behind Ypres in July 1917. An unusual smell one night alerted him and he, along with his comrades, put on their respirators. No one suffered except the CO who had not donned his mask; the next morning he was evacuated, blinded, and never returned. The post-war literature contains many descriptions of similar incidents. Two will suffice. Guy Chapman was at Ypres towards the end of 1917. The klaxon sounded, Chapman realized he had left his mask in the dug-out and was therefore greatly relieved when it turned out to be a false alarm. Yet he had heard some gas shells explode, there was some gas about, and his oversight cost him two days of conjunctivitis and tears which ten days' leave put right, though the slight injury was never forgotten. And another who remembered was Adolf Hitler. He had been through the war in Flanders unharmed, but on the night of 13–14 October 1918 the British fired mustard gas into the Wervik area near Menen, where Hitler served as runner in the 16th Bavarian Reserve Regiment. It is not stated whether he wore his respirator, but the dose was large and he was practically blind when he got back to regimental HQ. His eyes had become, he wrote later, 'glowing coals'. Hitler was invalided home and the war was over for him. He too remembered, and his experience was to have important consequences a quarter of a century later.[60]

The introduction of mustard gas and of arsenical compounds by the Germans and the repeated use of Livens projectiles by the British marked an escalation of the chemical war. On the technical level it drew attention to defects in the protective systems, notably to the effectiveness of respirators. In this respect the Germans laboured under a greater handicap than the Allies: they were short of rubber and cotton fabrics and the design of their mask could not be altered so as to incorporate additional filters for particulates.[61] Livens's projectile disrupted trench-warfare routines as no other weapon had done before. Like a raid, it was unpredictable and caused some casualties. Unlike a raid, one could see it coming without being able to judge where it would land. Uncertainty and fear magnified its effects, but against this was the infrequency of such attacks during 1917. For example, the war diary of the 10th BIR then at Auchy (south-west of Arras) records eight gas 'incidents' between 20 August and 24 December 1917. Six were definitely attributed to gas bombs. According to the incomplete records available they caused thirty fatal injuries. The papers of the 2nd Bavarian Corps which covered the area from the Lys river to the south east of Armentières, a frontage of around 10 km in a straight line, mention nine gas projectile attacks between 29 May and 28 October. There were twenty-two killed, but once again the returns are incomplete.[62] I mention these incidents because they introduced a new element into the gas war: occasional attacks, usually on a very narrow front, causing a few casualties of which a significant proportion were fatal. Such a form of harassment, unlike cloud gas or bombardments with gas shell which caused many casualties, relatively few of them fatal, was new. It increased uncertainty, struck at many different units, and had an effect on morale quite out of proportion to the expenditure of materials and manpower. The anxiety was enormous. Sergeant Hörnler's story was surely not exceptional: on the night in question he was near Ablainzeville when he heard the projectiles come over. He was warned in time and put on his respirator without swallowing any gas. Suddenly he noticed it coming through—'it took me all my will power not to pull off my mask', he told the regimental historian later. The only practical defence was to wear the respirator in the 'alert' position at all times, even when asleep in the dug-out, and that would not save the soldier at the point of impact when death was certain.[63] The Livens projectile ultimately became the chief British gas weapon. It had no tactical purpose other than to cause casualties and sap the enemy's fighting strength; as such it had considerable psychological impact. The Germans invariably retaliated with HE or gas shells against which the SBR gave good protection. The advantage thus rested with the British, though they did not exploit it fully for most of 1917. The Germans delayed the introduction of their projector, and did not make extensive use of it until the last weeks of the war when they caused heavy losses to the Americans.

The Allies also had technical problems over defence against novel chemical warfare materials, but they had the resources to improve or replace their respirators. They also had the manpower and the Anglo-Americans the organization to get better masks to the troops without delay and generally to tighten up on training. During the winter of 1917–18 the French finally decided to improve their anti-gas measures and, as noted, the Italians accepted the SBR and were being taught its use.[64] A repetition of the events on the upper Soča was therefore unlikely.

But on the level of perceptions, where scientific or design solutions did not apply, the events of 1917 ushered in a new phase. All the belligerents were aware of it and concerned about the effects of gas on morale, military no less than civilian. Apprehension grew and spread as additional substances and novel delivery methods were introduced. It was not merely the increasing strain on the medical services and the greater need for rest and recuperation for those injured by gas. The necessary arrangements could be anticipated and facilities provided behind the front or adjacent to the shell-filling plants. The problem was that the chemical substances, toxic or merely irritating, could weaken the soldier's effectiveness and, when employed against civilians, might have incalculable consequences for the home front. That is why the extension of chemical warfare to the air, though a non-starter on technical grounds was considered such an alarming threat.

Brock's experiments with hydrogen cyanide had come to an end in 1916 for there were no planes with sufficient carrying capacity. Besides the MoM had no confidence in the bombs nor their Jellite contents. The Germans initially considered that Zeppelins would be suitable for carrying gas bombs. Kerschbaum was put in charge of the project and Haber thought it might have a great future. Count Zeppelin supported the plan, and proposed to drop bombs on the French during the battle of Verdun. Falkenhayn vetoed the project and the matter was dropped. It was revived in 1917 when the Germans raided London and demonstrated the greater range and load-carrying capacity of their aircraft. This time Ludendorff stopped the proposal on the ground that it would lead to immediate reprisal raids on the towns of the Saar and the Palatinate.[65] The French were also involved. They investigated and concluded that many planes would be needed and that on a weight-for-weight basis gas was less efficient than high explosive. Later they changed their minds and in Spring 1918 tried out aerial bombs filled with phosgene in central France in the area of Clermont-Ferrand. Lefebure came to hear of the tests and reported that they were being terminated and that no further action was contemplated.[66] He explained that the French were reluctant to use gas against civilians, but a more likely reason is that they did not want to waste mustard gas, then scarce, by dispersing it very thinly in the rear of the German army. Pershing was approached by Fries with a similar proposal and turned it down: he did not want to initiate this form of warfare.[67]

So the introduction of aerial gas warfare against civilians was rejected. It is unnecessary at this stage to assess the relative importance of the technical constraints, moral scruples, and fear of retaliation, of which the last played an important role between the wars. What we may note, however, is that, as in the case of the Livens projectiles, the psychological and morale effects were taken very seriously. At a meeting in London chaired by Horrocks, the chemists from the TWD, as well as Home Office and Local Government Board representatives considered the effect of a 50 kg gas bomb (well within the carrying capacity of a Zeppelin) dropped on a town. They agreed that it would cause many casualties in a small area. The problem was, what could or should be done? Anti-gas instructions might alarm Londoners, already upset by air raids, even more. The issue of a simple civilian respirator might increase rather than reduce anxiety. Besides, millions would be needed and millions of Londoners taught how to use the mask. The matter came before the Smuts Committee on the Defence of London which rejected civilian respirators. It resurfaced in the War Cabinet where Lord Derby, then Secretary of State for War, declared that 'it would be almost impossible to train the London population to put on their masks even if they had them.'[68]

Here we come to a convenient end to the chapter: science and technology had given the military new weapons in 1917. Yet shortages of materials, technical backwardness, and military scruples or incompetence combined to prevent or delay the implementation of novel devices. Defence was therefore given time to catch up. Nevertheless, there were many new factors in chemical warfare. So the military and the politicians had a wider dimension to consider which went beyond manufacture and beyond use to such intangibles as how to deal with an unlimited potential threat. The chief consequence of Livens projectiles, mustard gas, and Blue Cross shells was to heighten the fear of the unknown and conversely increase the frustration caused by the inability to respond immediately to threats. These and the resulting attitudes rekindled the discussions on poison gas long after the war was over, and kept the subject of gas before the public as a whole. To this extent, late 1917 was *the* turning-point of chemical warfare.

9

1918: REALITY AND IMAGINATION

THE course of chemical warfare in 1918 was one thing, its interpretation afterwards quite another. What is beyond dispute is that the German staff made unprecedented use of gas shells. On their side the Allies hoped to retaliate more effectively with phosgene, and to surprise and demoralize the Germans with mustard gas. The summary omits the novel German gas-shell tactics which played an important role, and also sheds no light on the changing relationship of the artillery and the chemical experts. We may conveniently begin this chapter with an analysis of each.

After the war, some German writers declared that he new tactics had made gas shells into an instrument of victory, but that its potential had not been realized. Geyer, who should have known better, thought that through the development of gas tactics a 'new impetus was brought into warfare. But the full results were not achieved during the war'.[1] The man generally credited with the innovation was Major (later Colonel) G. Bruchmüller, recalled from retirement in 1916 to command the artillery of a territorial division on the Eastern Front.[2] He made a careful study of the methods first used by Germans and the French during the Battle of Verdun where they used a mixture of gas shells on a very narrow sector of the front. But the lack of gas shells prevented them from saturating the target area, and the rate of fire was slow. Bruchmüller, aware that conditions in the East were entirely different, adapted his tactics accordingly. He tried out brief, but intensive, gas-shell bombardments first at the Toboly bridgehead on the Stochod in April 1917 and, three months later, on the lower Seret in Galicia. The first of these bombardments lasted a mere five-and-a-half hours, the second five. Both were effective against a demoralized and ill-protected enemy. Bruchmüller employed various kinds of gas shells in combination with HE shell, and as the Germans colour-coded their shells, the practice grew up of referring to these shoots as *Buntschiessen* or *Buntkreuzschiessen*. He had a small staff, among them Major Marx, recommended by Haber, to represent, as it were, the gas interests. In the winter of 1917–18, this small group with their newly promoted chief, travelled west and, at OHL, joined the chemical warfare experts in Geyer's office. Yet another sign of the growing importance attached to gas shells was the transfer of Captain Meffert from the KWI in Berlin to OHL with the remit of reporting directly to Ludendorff on all trial shoots with gas shells.[3]

The successful implementation of the Bruchmüller tactics depended on the effective integration of gas specialists with artillerists who were every bit at hidebound as the infantry commanders at Ypres and Verdun. Depending on one's point of view one may look at the process in terms of experts permeating every branch of the forces or, alternatively, as the crumbling resistance of the gunners to chemical innovation. That was no small matter, for in Germany as in Britain, the artillery had its own technical service which had a scientific tradition of mathematics and physics, but not of chemistry, and a perception of its tactical role in support of troops that went far back into the nineteenth century. Neither country completely solved this problem. The French artillery staffs shouldered aside the IEEC specialists at GQG. The British approach of compromise by committee procedures failed to improve communications between Porton, Foulkes and his men in France, and the Artillery School in Salisbury Plain. At the end of June 1918, Churchill chaired a meeting of all parties, but was unable to reconcile the factions: Major Rendel of the Royal Artillery was differently minded from the chemists, and those with practical gas experience in France could not understand the theoretical work at Porton. The criticism voiced by Foulkes on 27 June may be contrasted with Crossley's observation after the war about the 'almost complete want of direct liaison with the various branches of the Army concerned.'[4] Similarly among the Germans. Bruchmüller's ideas were well received, but the testing of *Buntschiessen* with novel substances such as arsenical compounds and mustard gas was skimped because the facilities at Breloh were not ready. In this case, Haber's growing pessimism and the futility of much of the KWI's work in the last year of war may have been a contributory factor to its isolation and the bypassing of the scientists.

It we look at the situation from another angle, the above should not unduly surprise us. The gunners had to learn the contents of new range tables and cope with the complications of variable firing-rates and of unfamiliar *Buntschiessen* patterns. That was manageable, but there were further complications. Calibre and firing-rates were connected, the larger the shell the lower the rate, but persistent and non-persistent gases called for entirely different rates of fire to generate a desired concentration on the target, and so in turn influenced the consumption of shells, transport, and manpower. It was the combination of the various factors that gave the gas barrage of 1918 a new dimension. For example, the British 18 pdr. (88 mm calibre) could fire eight rounds a minute, a good rate, but the shell tended to embed itself before exploding. The German 77 mm field gun could fire up to ten rounds a minute, but the gas to total weight ratio, i.e. its effectiveness, was too low; the 10.5 cm howitzer shell had a superior effectiveness and a rather lower muzzle velocity, but could fire only four rounds a minute. In short, guns had been designed for HE and shrapnel and did not readily adapt to gases with varying properties. This particular constraint had been noted in 1915, but Bruchmüller's tactics in 1918 aggravated the problem. Thus there was some justification for the reserved attitude displayed by divisional and corps artillery commanders towards *Buntschiessen*.

The complications multiplied when big operations were planned in minute detail. Demand and supply, including reserves, had to dovetail. The logistical problems were unprecedented. The Germans had sufficient gas shells throughout 1918, and in the autumn rather more than they needed to cover their retreats. The Allies were also approaching sufficiency. The British programme for gas shells shows that the filling rates for the 4.5 inch gun and the 6.0 inch howitzer (both widely used) were working up to a peak of 45,000 a week in March and 50,000 a week in June, the latter corresponding to 163 t of phosgene. For once it was not the hardware, nor even the filling capacity that caused shortfalls, but simply the lack of phosgene and of mustard gas. During the summer of 1918, nearly one-third of the shells fired by the RA contained non-explosive chemical substances, not all of them toxic. If more gas had been manufactured, more shells could have been filled. But that position was not attained until the last week of the war, though many months previously the War Office had proposed to double the quantity for the 1919 campaign.[5] If we turn from production to the tactical employment of gas shells, yet another picture emerges. There was general agreement, even before Bruchmüller arrived on the scene, that gas could play a useful role in counter-battery fire: the enemy's guns could be 'neutralized' while one's own infantry moved forward. By 1918 aerial observation and the triangulation of gun flashes had progressed sufficiently to identify small targets at a distance of up to 8 km. The choice of gas presented some difficulties. It had to be persistent, unaffected by weather, and disperse evenly so that a direct hit was unnecessary. Mustard gas best met these criteria, and after mid 1917 the Germans (when they had sufficient supplies) were able to render Allied batteries *hors de combat* for several hours. The Allies, not having any, could not retaliate effectively. Thus they were at a disadvantage for the first half of 1918: the French obtained their first Yperite shells towards the middle and end of June, and found that salvoes, at intervals, gave the best results by maintaining the concentration on and around the target for a day or two. The British were delayed and were not able to follow the French until September.[6]

The belligerents had evolved some simple rules for the employment of gas shells against the infantry in the early months of 1916. The object was to create small gas clouds or drifts, but the results were disappointing. A large number of gas shells had to be expended to create cloud-like effects on the infantry positions; moreover the micro-meteorological conditions, particularly wind speed and direction at ground level, 3–6 km from the guns were unknown. Static tests in France were inconclusive, except for some evidence that after one minute and beyond a radius of 5–6 m from the shell burst, non-persistent gases were ineffective. That was not a startling discovery. So if the trench systems and lorry pick-up points were to be covered by a lethal concentration of phosgene or diphosgene, a great many shells had to be fired at very high rates. The French had investigated this problem, especially after deserters had told them that an intensive gas bombardment in October 1916 had been fruitless. An example will serve as illustration. To equate the discharge of 20 t of gas from cylinders over 1 km^2, by no means unusual in 1915–16, would require for the same area

1,300 guns firing at maximum rates 40,000 75 mm gas shells an hour. Such a paper exercise would have been impracticable in the field, which led the French specialists to recommend 'pas d'arrosages sur d'énormes surfaces et, au contraire, des tirs précis sur objectifs précis' (underlined in text). That was the position reached in the latter half of 1917 and shows to what extent the Allied situation differed from that of the Germans who had a persistent gas.[7] However, if one could not kill one's enemy with gas, one could always injure or harass him, so forcing him to wear his mask for hours on end. For that purpose low concentrations would suffice. Some people even suggested the combination of poison gas with a noisome gas—sulphuretted hydrogen or butyl mercaptans—so that the opponent would put on this mask as soon as *any* smell was perceived.[8] But that was to overrate one's cleverness and underrate the enemy's nerve. In any case we need not waste time on such elaborations; I have not come across any report of their being used, possibly on account of increasing confusion and of further complicating the instructions to the artillery.

The evolution of gas-shell tactics can be followed in the artillery manuals which the belligerents revised from time to time. The first German instructions of which I am aware were issued in August 1915. Two-and-a-half years later they had been elaborated to such an extent that I doubt whether they were ever followed to the letter. In 1917–18 the distinctions between types of bombardment were made with unnecessary precision. Consider the use of gas shell solely to harass the enemy (*Beunruhigungsschiessen*): diphosgene was to be used, at a steady rate, only during the hours of darkness at a wind speed below 1.5 m/sec. Alternatively, gas shells might be fired to prepare for an infantry advance. In that event the minimum prescribed area was 1 km², a maximum duration of eight hours using a mixture of two gases (one of them being mustard). The bombardment would be carried out at night by light and medium artillery which would put down altogether 42 t of gas. And so on. The result would be several gas drifts (hence the expression *Schwadenschiessen*), whose concentrations would be lower than those achieved by cylinder operations and therefore would not have a tendency to flow downhill. The instructions prescribed a high ratio of gas to HE. A third variant was the 'surprise shoot', a very intensive bombardment lasting a minute or so over a 'block' defined as an area of one hectare (10,000 m²). This was the method which Bruchmüller adapted to his purposes. Finally there was the 'interdiction shoot', designed to incapacitate batteries or deny the enemy a particular position: the area was always small, and the recommended material mustard gas.[9] Some of the implications of all that detail were important. A surprise shoot imposed tremendous strain on men and guns, and was known to overheat gun barrels. *Schwadenschiessen* provided for fifteen different gas combinations, two types of fuses, and various minimum safety-zones. The instructions assumed that organization and communications would be of a sufficiently high standard to take care of all the details and every hitch, and that the observers would at all times monitor the enemy's reactions. The French, not having the Germans superfluity of gas shells, gave up

Schwadenschiessen and turned instead to precision shooting. Their experts carried out trials from which they derived, by extrapolation, the minimum number of shells for a given concentration of gas per hectare. They assumed that the French artillery would have Yperite shells and also that the French mask was superior to the German respirator. This mixture of wishful thinking and results derived from static tests yielded some remarkable statistics for the recommendations to GQG, which ignored them. The British instructions also went through various stages of refinement, though it is not possible to discern what effect, if any, the work at Porton had on them. Even as late as March 1918, there was no mention of the use of mustard-gas shells.[10] When, at last, they became available six months later, the war had become one of movement. Nevertheless, the March instructions, unlike the German orders, were clear, simple, and distinguished between surprise bursts and harassing fire. They were also unrealistic: they assumed very high rates of fire, and for harassing fire recommended tear gas, though it was known that the German respirator protected against it; there was however much useful technical advice, and a supplement dated July 1918—provided a table of probability factors which showed how many shells had to be fired for a given proportion to hit the target. The Germans did not give that statistic, though it may be doubted whether their gunners could dispense with it. The technical advisers copied from each other and so their instructions converged. We should remember, however, that the Germans had a clear lead in gas supplies, and the British had by far the best respirator. What happened in practice?

The preliminaries to the battle of Arras in April 1917 were carfully monitored. The British alternated intense bursts with a slow and steady fire against enemy batteries and trenches. They used shells filled with a mixture of arsenious chloride and phosgene, code-named CBR, in combination with shells filled with a mixture of arsenious chloride, chloroform, and hydrogen cyanide jellified with cellulose triacetate, code-named JBR in the final gas bombardment on the 9th, which lasted from 0230 to 0630. Neither CBR nor JBR were of much use against experienced men wearing German respirators. Still, the programme unfolded according to plan and as the British infantry advanced at 0530, the guns raised their range to give the enemy batteries a final drenching. Alas, the wind speed at 6 m/sec (13.4 mph) at 0300 and 7.4 m/sec at 0600 was well above the recommended level of less than 1.3 m/sec.[11] In short, the expectations were not fulfilled, and if HE had been used in place of the toxic materials, the enemy would have suffered greater casualties.

The introduction of mustard gas in July 1917 transformed gas tactics and caused heavy casualties. One group considers that the Germans intended to spoil or delay the British preparations for Ypres, and that they aimed, in particular, at gun sites. Another view, less plausible, is that the first and second mustard-gas bombardments were in the nature of field trials which the Germans had neglected (or been prevented by supply difficulties) to carry out in the Reich. The results astonished the Germans, as they were not immediately aware of the blistering effect. I do not know to what extent Bruchmüller, then in Poland, was influenced by the information from Flanders, and in any event, he did not have mustard gas at the time. It seems more plausible to assume that he integrated Yellow Cross into his tactics later in the year.[12] He did not employ Yellow Cross shells in the Seret battle (19 July) nor did he provide for it when in August, he prepared for the crossing of the Dvina at Uexküll, 20km upstream from Riga. But his technique was maturing: there was to be no prior registration so as not to alert the enemy, and saturation bombardment targets were grouped into 'squares', later changed into rectangles of one hectare surface, with the long side facing the enemy. The use of the one hectare module was to allow for flexibility in target selection within the limits imposed by variable terrain and, perhaps more importantly, to make last-minute changes in the firing instructions to take account of the latest weather bulletins. The bombardment of the Uexküll crossing on 1 September lasted five hours. Phosgene and Blue Cross shells were mixed and, between them, represented four-fifths of the shell expenditure on Russian artillery positions, and one-half of that on the infantry. The operational area covered 10.5 km², only 38 per cent of which was shelled. The same tactic was employed later that month against the Russian bridgehead at Jakobstadt. Bruchmüller's operations differed profoundly from the typical area gas shoots of 1916 or 1917. His innovation consisted of short bombardments, varying in intensity, on pre-selected areas; the pattern of the gases was designed to have the maximum effect on particular objectives. Bruchmüller's instructions may be compared with Arras and Ypres which the British bombarded for five and sixteen days respectively in 1917.

What was so significant about the new German method? In the first place, the selection of targets was more careful and thorough than ever before: within each one hectare rectangle, there would be 100 m² 'blocks' in which there was something worth hitting. In short Bruchmüller put shells to better use than previous artillery advisers. In the second place the reconnaissance of potential targets and their position within a rectangle or block was done with typical Teutonic thoroughness and, one might say, scientifically. It was essential not to alert the enemy by long registration on the selected targets. Hence random shoots with smoke shells and, on the Western Front, targetting by map grid-reference which entailed a previously unheard of precision in aerial cartograghy. Thirdly, the firing pattern was so designed as to maintain the prescribed proportions against artillery targets and infantry positions throughout the bombardment. Fourthly, the ratio of gases to HE varied, depending on circumstances, and could be as high as 1:1. Finally, Bruchmüller first used the *Feuerwalze* (literally fire-roller, but usually translated as drum fire) at the Jokobstadt bridgehead (21 September 1917): the intensive creeping barrage lasted forty-five minutes and its object was to force the Russians to seek shelter and to keep their heads down. But the tempo overheated the barrels and the steel cartridge cases jammed. The lesson was learnt and in spring 1918, the *Feuerwalze* lasted only a few minutes. The German assault troops followed it closely, to within 300 m, and were on top of the enemy before he had recovered and trained his machine guns on them.[13] These, in essence, represented Bruchmüller's methods of 1917–18. They worked extremely well against the Russians, but one must remember that their armies were dissolving and they had no respirators. Geyer, writing after these events, ascribed to the tactics a role they did not have, asserting that they transformed Allied infantry dispositions, to which the Germans responded by changing theirs. He was referring to defence in depth and implying it was due to Bruchmüller's innovations. But the two were not related in any way. Hartley noted in Spring 1918 that the use of mustard gas on the artillery and flanks combined with a mixture of phosgene and Blue Cross shells on the first objectives, had caused higher gas casualties per shell. But the agent of change, the material which transformed the tactical use of gas, was mustard gas which caused casualties to gunners, and to infantry in the semi-open fighting of March-April; Blue Cross shells (to which the Germans attached so much importance in *Buntschiessen*) though expended at the rate of hundreds of thousands, were an inconvenience, but not a great danger.[14]

Bruchmüller's system and the German advances of March – June 1918 gave the proponents of chemical warfare the successes they needed: gas shells, so they argued, had brought them within reach of victory. The facts were different. Geyer wrote that more than a quarter of all the German shells fired in 1918 contained gas, but it was not enough. The average hides a wide dispersion. On paper, and on some occasions in March – April four-fifths of the shells against enemy batteries were gas shells, and two-fifths in the brief *Feuerwalze*. In many instances the local artillery conformed to Bruchmüller's prescriptions, but there were frequent occasions when his ground rules could not be followed. Besides, the majority of German gas shells in the last year of the war also contained HE—up to 30 per cent of the total content. The *Zwischenbodengeschoss* was an unnecessary complication: the sound of its explosion was not like that of the usual gas shell, but it achieved this advantage at the cost of the greater dispersion and smaller toxic content. Geyer's proportion of gas shells, if adjusted for the HE content, is rather less than a quarter, somewhere between a fifth and a sixth.[15] It seems difficult to believe that such a small proportion could have had such weighty consequences.

All the other belligerents, taken together, used as many gas shells as the Germans; it follows therefore that each made only negligible use of this weapon. According to the available statistics, whose reliability is doubtful, 6.4 per cent of the total German shell consumption, consisted of gas shells. For France the corresponding figure was 4.6 per cent and for Britain 2.2 per cent. On rare occasions the Allies fired a high proportion of gas, for example the French on the Ailette in October 1917 and the British in August in 1918.[16] Both sides augmented the use of gas by the frequent employment of gas troops to discharge cylinders or launch gas projectiles. The clumsy equipment and the troublesome installation precluded their use in battle areas, but in Picardy and on the Aisne, local operations harassed and worried the opponent.

The German spring offensive was heralded by a campaign of rumours. In the event these stories, in which gas and germ warfare featured prominently, were counter-productive, but in January and February 1918 their frequency caused alarm. Many of the reports picked up by French intelligence mentioned hydrogen cyanide and it is remarkable that this weapon should be trotted out again when the belligerents (France excepted) had abandoned it. Nevertheless there was concern at the highest level. Thuillier was called before the War Cabinet on 27 February 1918 to reassure ministers. 'If,' he said, 'as most of the evidence indicated, the Germans intended to use a gas of the hydrocyanic type', the SBR and the French masks were proof against it. Comforting, but only applicable to the SBR. He went on to talk about arsenical compounds for which the Germans had not yet found effective means of dispersion, so that they had not caused any British casualties. But to make doubly sure, the SBR was being strengthened, 'within 2–3 months' by a temporary extra filter.[17] The German tests with a sublimating device, the *Gas Büchse*, had been unsuccessful on several occasions, but the secret of the failures was well kept and the British, unaware of the facts, continued to worry.

Other, wilder, stories circulated, among them a rumour of a heavy, inflammable gas which 'floats harmlessly near the ground', but upon ignition destroys everything. And there was glanders, a contagious disease spread by infected horses behind the French lines. On one occasion the Red Cross passed on a German message that they would not introduce a new gas if the Allies stopped chemical warfare altogether. Since the Germans were stronger in gas and the Allies then had, beside chlorine, only phosgene and chloropicrin to retaliate with, the former were likely to gain more. The French and the Italians being weak in gas defence, were ready to accept, so was Pershing for he was against chemical warfare on principle. The Supreme War Council was undecided, except for Lloyd George who demanded watertight assurances from the Germans. Thuillier was called for: he suggested that the Germans be asked to surrender Alsace-Lorraine as a pledge of good faith. The Council accepted the proposal, though all knew the Germans would never swallow the bait. So the incident was closed.[18] True or false the stories are not without their significance, for the fact that they circulated enhanced the psychological effect of chemical warfare, extended the weaponry into the realm of science-fiction and spread anxieties from soldiers to civilians, particularly politicians. The alarms of 1917–18 passed, but were not forgotten: they resurfaced and were embellished in the 1920s. Meanwhile at OHL the technical experts and artillery staffs, advised by Bruchmüller, were putting the finishing touches to chemical warfare in the spring campaign.

The plans for the use of gas shells in 'Michael', the first German offensive, provided for a mixture of 50:50 of HE and gas (principally Blue Cross and phosgene) on the infantry and an 80:20 ratio of mustard gas to HE on gun positions. Yet another firing-pattern was adopted for areas which the Germans were not proposing to attack. For example they fired mustard-gas shells at a steady rate into the Flesquières salient, a bulge into the German lines, south-west of Cambrai. The two British divisions holding this uselesss salient suffered severely between 10 and 16 March. The German tactic put the British into a quandary: the Germans would not seize the salient, nor could the British break out to help the 5th Army when 'Michael' began on 21 March. So, still suffering unnecessary casualties, they gradually thinned out the troops—Bruchmüller's plan had worked at negligible cost to the Germans. Further south, the British defences were dispersed over a broad but lightly held strip of land—the front or 'Blue' line being 2–3 km across, then a gap and next the 'Red' line, or battle zone, which was under construction when the battle began. If the Germans were to win, they had to capture both lines, and confuse, seize, and injure the defenders. They planned a brief, intensive bombardment without prior registration on pre-selected 'blocks'. The duration was fixed at five hours and the last five minutes would be a hurricane of exploding HE shells. As the *Feuerwalze* crept forward, the British would have to seek shelter, and with their machine-gunners overwhelmed, the Germans would be on top of them before they had time to recover.[19]

Weather conditions remained of paramount importance. The belligerents scanned the rainfall records one side hoping that it would be dry and cold, the other praying for high winds and heavy spring showers to wash away mustard gas. For the general area of the Ancre–Somme the twenty-year March average was 49 mm, and in 1918 it turned out to be 52 mm. Further south the corresponding figures were 48 and 44 mm respectively. A dependable 24-hour forecast was vital and noon 20 March was the moment of decision for the start or the postponement of 'Michael', 16 hours hence. It was a squally day, the wind blowing from the west. Schmauss, still in charge of the meteorological services, reported to Ludendorff. He forecast calm and dry conditions for the 21st. OHL gave the order to go ahead. Ludendorff was, to say the least, relieved. Haber was told and later that day went to the south-west of Cambrai to watch the final preparations and then the bombardment.[20]

Most things went according to plan. The Germans worked frantically after nightfall to emplace the guns and aim them. The targets were given, registration was forbidden and punctually at 0440 the bombardment began along a front of 80 km. Bruchmüller's tactics and *Buntschiessen* proved to be effective on the 21st. Many of the objectives were hit repeatedly and the variations in the HE – gas-shell pattern were a great strain for the British who suffered severe casualties and were dismayed by the silence of their artillery. The Germans had indeed been thorough and their 'block' targets 'boxed in' the British guns with mustard gas, silencing them, and preventing relief from getting through to the crews. Bruchmüller was near the front: he was pleased with the reports from the 18th German Army (La Fère to the north of St Quentin) but less satisfied with the 17th Army (Cambrai northwards) where Captain Pulkowski, the artillery adviser to the commander, had issued imprecise and conflicting instructions. The ground mist, not forecast by Schmauss, was turning to fog through which some gas drifted back into the German positions. But in the centre, 2nd Army, all went well, despite the mist.[21]

At dawn both sides had their respirators at the alert. The British had the better protection, whereas many of the Germans had to make do with the clumsy leather mask which dangled round their necks. At 0940 the bombardment changed to a crescendo, the *Feuerwalze* rolled and behind it the storm troopers, now masked, advanced. They could hardly see through the thick mist and the gas drifts. They could not aim, nor were the British in a much better position—they had lost their bearings and what machine guns were still working, fired aimlessly. Only the drum fire went on for its full five minutes: it had, as we would now say, been programmed. The mist increased the effect of the gas shells and added to the confusion. It cleared after 1000, by which time the Germans had reached some of their first objectives. Hartley wrote later that 'some millions of rounds of gas shells were reportedly used', but it is difficult to estimate how much the enemy gained from *Buntschiessen*. The contemporary view of the Chemical Advisers was that 'the general impression, especially in the 3rd Army [south of Arras] seems to be that [the] enemy did not gain greatly by the use of gas shell.'[22] Despite all the qualifications, that verdict seems reasonable even now. Nevertheless the RA suffered severely, decontamination measures broke down, and the value of mustard gas as an agent causing extensive damage to men and equipment was demonstrated beyond all doubt. Until the Allies had their own supplies they would be severely handicapped.

Michael was followed by four other battles. The advance on the Channel Ports, 'Georgette', which began on 9 April and ended with the capture of Mt. Kemmel, west of Ypres, on the 25th; the attacks on the Aisne, the Chemin des Dames, and the march to the Marne, 'Blücher−Yorck', 27 May to 5 June; the short and unsuccessful break-out from Noyon-Montdidier, 'Gneisenau', 9 to 11 June; and the second battle of the Marne (west of Reims), 'Marneschütz', 15 to 17 July. According to Volkart, the use of gas shells on these occasions differed only in detail from the Michael tactics.[23] In that spring and early summer, Yellow Cross shells represented about one-third of the entire gas shell consumption, except for 'Georgette' when the proportion was two-fifths. Another small change was the cut in gas shells per km[2] for 'Blücher' and 'Marneschütz' and a shortening of the duration of the initial bombardment. The Germans repeated and intensified at Armentières what they had first practised at Flesquières: the gutters of the town were reported to be running with dichlorodiethyl sulphide and it was isolated from the battle. The procedure was repeated at Mt. Kemmel some ten days later. The hill was then held by French troops and the Germans soaked its north slopes with the stuff before scaling it from the south. In that manner they prevented the reinforcement of the French defenders, but also indicated that, for the time being at least, they were not advancing further. Finally, they introduced a new time-fuse, designed to detonate the gas shell a few metres above the target and so disperse droplets of gas more widely. However, the mechanism performed unsatisfactorily and when the

Germans went over to the defence they abandoned the fuse.[24] In June–July the gas-shell tactics were less effective than on earlier occasions, which may have been due in part to fatigue and loss of stamina among the assault troops who were wearing the leather mask; the weather had favoured the Germans on 9 April, 27 May, and 9 June, but on 15 July the wind turned and the gas drifted back.[25]

In August the tide turned and the Germans retreated in the centre and from Mt. Kemmel. The British who monitored chemical warfare with great care began to note that mustard gas was being used more frequently than before. British gas casualties which had been light in June–July, rose steeply in the last ten days of August and ranged from 3,000 to 4,000 a week in September–October. The troops were shelled daily and it was observed that Yellow Cross shells accounted for a larger proportion of gas shells. As the British advanced in the north, enemy artillery fire became disorganized—the bombardments were frequently heavy but scattered, and there were signs that targetting had become indifferent. The end was near, Bruchmüller's tactics had been abandoned, but gas-shell instructions still came off the presses. The circulars of the IVth Corps have survived: in mid and late October they drew attention to large stocks of gas shells and advised battery commanders to use them at all times, in any ratio they considered advisable (though one-third was generally recommended), to stem the Allied advance.[26]

From the above summary several generalizations emerge. In their advances, the Germans were assisted by gas shells. But the various accounts suggest that 'Michael', 'Georgette', and 'Blücher–Yorck' would have been initially successful even if no gas had been employed, because of the intensity of the bombardment and the favourable weather conditions. The British and the French were overwhelmed by the shock. I doubt whether the Germans could have taken Mt. Kemmel in late April without isolating its defenders from reinforcements by a strip of mustard gas. But what good did it do them? In the initial stages of the second battle of the Marne, gas blown about by a contrary wind hampered the Germans and the French gunfire killed many Germans before the *Feuerwalze* began to roll. It has been said that the entire operation was misconceived and would have failed in any case. These are matters of opinion, but it is certain that in the last three months of the war the Germans found the combination of machine guns and mustard gas invaluable: it gained them time, enabled them to retreat in good order, and kept the Allies at a safe distance. The retreat did not turn into a rout. Looked at differently, chemical warfare originally conceived as a means to break out of the stalemate of trench warfare turned out to be a versatile weapon in defence. Versatile because it slowed down the opponent who had to waste time bypassing contaminated terrain or face up to a higher casualty rate in the closing stages of the war. And all that at negligible cost to the defence. This characteristic was overlooked between the Wars when the experts thought of gas purely in terms of offensive use. It was not until 1940 when the Germans prepared to invade England that the circumstances of Autumn 1918 and the effectiveness of mustard gas were recalled.

But to return to the spring and early summer of 1918. The German successes and the intensive use of gas shells emphasized the weaknesses of the Allied chemical effort. When would they have sufficient mustard gas to fill shells? We have seen how the convulsions in the Ministry of Munitions failed to produce dichlorodiethyl sulphide. The French, though further ahead, were unable to retaliate when the Germans broke through on the Aisne. The Senate was told by Ozil at the beginning of April that large-scale production was due to start in July, and a month later the Commission de l'Armée heard that big filling plants were under construction while temporary facilities at Vincennes were even then in operation.[27] So the Anglo-French artillery staffs had to make do with other kinds of gas for a little longer: the first confirmed use of mustard-gas shells by the French was on two successive nights 16–17 and 17–18 June in the area then held by the 2nd German Army. There were 265 casualties, about a tenth of them serious. The incident, coming on top of earlier, unconfirmed reports during the 'Gneisenau' battles that the French had poured dichlorodiethyl sulphide into trenches and dug-outs before abandoning them to the advancing Germans, had a significance out of all proportion to the quantities involved. The Germans were taken completely by surprise. They analysed the stuff, expecting it to be German Yellow Cross laboriously extracted from unexploded shells. But their chemists soon identified that the Yperite had been prepared by the sulphur monochloride route. It represented, in fact, the first supplies from Usines du Rhône to have passed the acceptance tests. The German general staff was concerned, for the shortage of textiles prevented the replacement of contaminated clothing. Morale at the front had to be maintained at all costs and immediate steps were taken to organize detection and decontamination procedures. In July, *Entgiftungstrupps* consisting of an NCO and six men per battalion were formed, a 2 per cent clothing reserve was created, and there was a proposal to make a 'limited issue' of specially treated uniforms to the artillery. By September or October some stretcher-bearers and medical staff were given long gloves and impermeable aprons, and much ingenuity was devoted to the manufacture of impregnated paper overalls for the decontamination squads. All that is known of them is that they were uncomfortable as well as fragile.[28] The measures reflect moments of panic, and they were not fully implemented because they came too late: the troops were not adequately protected against mustard gas. They had to make do, when they were available, with unsatisfactory *Ersatz* materials. The best solution was to retreat, and indeed that is what saved them from even heavier casualties after their initial withdrawal in August.

The French employed Yperite at the second battle of the Marne, and on frequent occasions subsequently. The British fired some captured mustard-gas (or HS) shells from August onwards, though their first major bombardment with material from Avonmouth did not take place until 30 September in connection with an attack on the Hindenburg line.[29] In the final six to eight weeks of the war, the Allies increased the pressure of their chemical warfare. Ozil told a party of British chemists that the French had fired 1,000 t of Yperite into the German positions by the last week of September. It sounds a lot, but their productive capacity was up to it. The American forces carried out their first major gas bombardment on 1 November when they fired 36,000 rounds of mustard gas (probably of French origin) on the Bois de Bourgogne, north of Verdun. The target was at no great distance from the spot where the French had first tried out gas shells of a less sophisticated kind some three-and-a-half years earlier.[30] All these incidents came too late to hasten the German defeat—that event had taken place essentially through attrition—but gas, specifically mustard gas, contributed to the running down of the machine. The Allies did, however, inflict increasing gas casualties by artillery and by other means on the German infantry and so indicated their potential for the expected 1919 campaign.

In the last year of the war, the fortunes of the special gas troops revived. Their activities, though trivial alongside the much greater happenings on the Western Front call for mention and justify a digression on two grounds. First the technical devices introduced by the British illustrate the extremes to which the specialists were prepared to go, and secondly the emergence of the CWS which was to have significant consequences after the war in the USA.

It may be useful to give an indication of the manpower involved. In March 1918, at a high-level meeting in France, Foulkes said he had about 4,500 men under his command and if he were given more, he could achieve more. The Special Brigade had indeed suffered losses, not only from the Germans but also from manpower-minded army commanders. At its peak in 1917, the Special Brigade establishment numbered around 7,000. But a couple of thousand or so had been reassigned to the regular engineers and been set to work on the 'Blue' and 'Red' lines in Picardy. Foulkes and his staff had naturally made their plans for 1918, but the events of March and April postponed their execution.[31] Although the Brigade had lost British troops, it had been reinforced by the arrival of the first two American Special Companies. These men, volunteers from the 31st Regiment of the US Corps of Engineers, were the forerunners of what was intended to be a large chemical presence. Eighteen companies had been authorized in March and later in the year the establishment was raised to fifty-four, that is nine regiments. But only six companies reached France, were equipped and trained, and saw service there. At full strength, each had three hundred men, so that Col. E. J. Atkinson, the commander of the 1st (US) Gas Regiment had a substantial force under Gen. Sibert, the first head of the CWS. The first four companies spent the early summer working with the French and the entire regiment did not see active service until the battle of St Mihiel in September.[32] Soulié's Compagnies Z, though unpopular at GQG, owing to 'several bad accidents', as Foulkes put it, had not been disbanded and were last reported by him to be active in the Aisne area in the first ten days of

August.[33] In round figures the Allies may have fielded 8,000–9,000 men for cylinder and projector operations in the late summer of 1918. The Germans began to reorganize their gas troops towards the end of 1917 to handle gas projectors and raised an additional battalion of Gaspioniere in February 1918 and three more in June. By the end of September there were altogether eight battalions—their paper strength being 8,000, but by then all formations were under strength and at the most there were around 5,000 in the last stages of the war.[34]

The reason for all this activity is not difficult to find. The British and the Germans, short of men, considered that cylinders and projectiles would, on the fringes of the war, have a more than proportionate effect in hurting or, at least, harassing the enemy. The Americans had an additional motive: it was essential for Sibert to demonstrate or at least to assert that he was in command of a new branch of the American military machine, that it was functioning, and could act on its own directly under the orders of Pershing. All the gas troops commanders supported attempts to improve the equipment, notably the projectors, but the main engineering effort was devoted to better mechanical handling equipment to simplify the transport of cylinders and projectiles. That was increasingly necessary for Foulkes's requirements were on a vast scale. He had asked for 200,000 cylinders by the end of March, and got them! When Churchill, who was in the chair at the 19 March meeting, asked him how many cylinders were needed to saturate 250 km^2 for 48 hours so as to eliminate all German resistance, he answered 500,000 (say 15,000 t of chlorine or phosgene). That was asking too much, even from Churchill.[35] But Foulkes had the bit firmly between the teeth. Aware that the movement of thousands of cylinders for a single operation called for unprecedented measures he described some devices already available and recommended their adoption.

He had, he said, experimented with the discharge of a gas cloud from an underground gas pipe. But the trench had to be at least 2.50 m deep to withstand shell fire. Someone asked whether mechanical trench-diggers were available for this work. One can visualize these devices clanking away in the night behind the support lines, destroying telephone lines, waking the Germans, and inviting retaliatory shell fire. Everyone present could imagine the outcome and the matter was not pursued. However, there were ropeways and they showed some promise. Foulkes reported that 80 km were to be delivered in April–May and another 21 km were on order. It sounded like an everyday civil engineering contract for a brickworks, but the meeting was assured that the equipment had been tested by soldiers pulling or pushing cylinders carried in slings fixed to pulleys travelling on a single rail or a rope. I leave it to the reader to picture the installation and operation of such equipment in a quiet, flat sector somewhere between La Bassée and Loos. It was pointed out by someone hostile to the Special Brigade that on test, one line had been broken thirteen times by shell fire. Foulkes, unabashed, replied that he was willing to put up with that provided that GHQ did not prevent cloud-gas discharges on the sole ground of unreliability.[36] In fact the Special Brigade had used light railways whenever possible to reduce the length of the final carry-in. For another innovation, the so-called 'beam operations', narrow-gauge flat wagons were required. A light engine pushed the train into position, after which troops, specialists, and the locomotive withdrew smartly. Two or three train loads carried up to 1,200 cylinders, which were open but connected by short pipes to sealed nozzles. Once in position, a remotely controlled explosive device was wired up, and at the command was electrically detonated, blasting off the nozzle seals. The result was a flash, and the release of a narrow beam of dense chlorine or other gas. The successful outcome depended on the weather forecast being right twelve hours ahead, on the nozzles not freezing up, on the Germans not getting the range, on the small detonators working perfectly, and on other unpredictable factors. The first of these unusual operations was planned for March, but had to be postponed to 12 July, when altogether 1,250 cylinders (about 33 t) were 'beamed' in the general direction of Hulluch. Altogether nine of these operations were carried out in 1918.[37]

The object of these and related exercises with Livens's projectiles was to surprise, shock, and worry the opponent. They took place at irregular intervals but frequently, so that in the quiet sectors of the Western Front the men who had been sent to recuperate from the big battles, were kept on the alert and tense at night whenever the weather conditions were favourable. The Special Brigade carried out seventy to a hundred operations (precise figures are unobtainable) in the valley of the Lys, between Loos and La Bassée, and south-west of Arras in March, and again from May to late July. Some were substantial. For example during March, about 3,000 Livens projectors were dug in opposite St Quentin and another 2,900 in the area near Quéant. The Special Companies discharged the projectiles just before 'Michael' began. Within hours, the Germans had overrun the launching-sites which were recovered intact the following October during the British advance. In June, 4,000 cylinders were opened in one operation and as late as the second half of August, 60 t of cloud gas were released in Artois.[38] The American effort, though widely publicized for home consumption, was not of the same order of magnitude. Between March and July, the Americans working first with the British and then with the French, released about 60 t of chemicals using cylinders, Livens projectors, or Stokes mortars. From August onwards the 1st Gas Regiment carried out scores of operations, usually very small, amounting—in all—to 30 t of chemicals, explosives, and incendiary materials. The targets were German rifle and machine-gun positions.[39] The Germans were also extremely active and carried out almost 60 projector operations, two-thirds of them between April and August. The details have not survived, but from what other evidence is still available it appears that the scale was appreciably smaller than the British attacks.[40]

Each side justified its activities by claiming to inflict substantial casualties on the other. By 1918 such assertions, supported by phoney statistics, began to carry less weight, but it is a fact that the British had few casualties from

German projectiles. Foulkes attributed that to the delayed introduction of the German projectors and to the limited number of operations carried out against British formations. The French suffered more. They recorded 36 separate incidents in which 586 men were killed and 1,718 injured by gas. These figures suggest that the projectiles were less dangerous than the gas clouds of 1916 or 1917. It is probable, however, that gas defence training and respirator practice had improved by 1918 and that the M2 and the ARS., though only offering limited protection, were better than the pads.[41] What of the Germans? We need to bear in mind that the British effort was more intensive in every respect, frequently with 1,000 or more projectors, and that the Livens drum held more gas then the German projectiles. One might expect therefore that the British operations would yield better results than the German and this was indeed what Foulkes and Sibert proclaimed in order to bolster their case. But the evidence is conflicting. The CIGS told the Cabinet that 'there was no means of ascertaining the effect' of the very big cylinder and projectile operation on 13 May, and a few weeks later the Director of Military Intelligence informed the Cabinet that 'there was no evidence of the success or failure of our recent use of projector gas.' However McCombie, who spoke from first-hand experience as Chemical Adviser to the 1st Army, claimed that on 23 May, near Lens, a favourable wind drove gas clouds far into the German lines and that up to 4 km behind the front the bleaching effect of chlorine was noticeable.[42] Some of the German records can be matched with their British counterparts, and inconsistencies appear which are inexplicable unless we assume that one side was misinformed or lying. The incident mentioned by McCombie involved 1,175 Livens projectiles the Germans reported 'over 900', not a bad guess since it was night-time. There was a dense cloud which was quickly dispersed by a strong wind: according to the Germans it blew at 5.8 m/sec (13 mph) in a westerly direction, whereas in the British version it blew eastwards at 4.5 m/sec (10 mph). There were 148 German casualties, among them 28 killed. But if the Germans were right, why were there no British casualties from blow-back? On another occasion, 18–19 June, the British fired 975 drums into Ablainzeville, a ruined hamlet south-west of Arras. There were 118 casualties, including 53 dead. The large number of fatalities was due to a relief taking place at the time, an event of which the British were unaware. On both occasions, at negligible cost to the British, some injury had been done to the Germans.[43] But consider the 'beam' discharges of cylinders. Hartley asked Haber about them after the war. Haber said he was unaware of them. It is most unlikely that he should have been so ill-informed and out of character to lie. So what happened? A possible explanation is that the Special Brigade had learnt how to co-ordinate their operations with intensive bursts of shell-fire. The German observers, about a couple of kilometres away, kept their heads down and could not tell whether the cylinders were dug in, or loaded on flat wagons. Alternatively they may have reasoned that the bombardment presaged hundreds of Livens drums aimed in their general direction. It is also possible that a physical cause weakened the effect. Initially the cloud 'beam' would, owing to the density of the cold gas, roll along the ground, cooling it further. But soon it would begin to rise—still at some distance from the German front-line. And the dispersal accelerated with distance, for the fall in the density was greater through vertical than horizontal motion. By the time the gas cloud reached the German lines—now further away than in Spring 1915—what was left of the 'beam' was sufficiently thin to be neutralized by the German mask.[44] The phenomenon might explain Haber's ignorance and also Foulkes's satisfaction—each knew only part of the story.

What conclusions may be drawn from the chemical warfare tactics employed in 1918? First, as regards offensive materials the Allies were still not the match of their enemy. The Germans had a broader range of gases and integrated them ingeniously with their artillery tactics. The Allies had nothing to compare, chiefly because their production facilities did not equal those of Germany until August or September, by which time it did not matter any longer. Secondly, the Allies were, at last, producing enough shells and therefore, in respect of hardware (as distinct from chemical content) they were approaching and often surpassing German capabilities. The shortage was over, there were more guns to deliver more shells, and the British, presently joined by the Americans, were repeatedly using Livens projectors. In short, chemical warfare intensified. Finally, defence against gas improved, not so much in technical terms, but because more soldiers—the Americans, the Italians, and to a lesser extent the French—were provided with better respirators. Conversely, the quality of the German mask had peaked—the lack of rubber and of cotton fabric prevented any further development.

In March 1918 the Germans changed the rules of the game and put an end to traditional trench warfare. For the first time since the autumn of 1914 the war again become mobile and movement transformed gas warfare. What had failed in April 1915 now succeeded, not only because a wider choice of toxic materials was available, but also because such materials were specially suited for purposes not envisaged three years earlier such as neutralizing enemy artillery, incapacitating machine gunners and infantry before an attack, isolating areas from reinforcement by contaminating large tracts of ground, harassing and demoralizing the opponent by worrying or injuring him when he least expected it. For such particular end-uses differences in the degree of chemical sophistication mattered less than having several toxic materials so that somewhere, sometime one could frighten or hurt the opponent. The supporters of chemical warfare amongst staffs, chemists, and politicians changed their approach. They dropped all ideas of a breakthrough in the wake of a gas cloud and even showed less interest in the use of a gas cloud purely for purposes of retaliation. Contrariwise much was said about gas as an agent to incapacitate, to lower fighting efficiency, cause panic, depress morale, and, by attrition, to wear down the opponent's manpower. The revised claims and objectives reflected the novelty of mustard gas in particular, and also took into account the war weariness and physical exhaustion of the belligerents.[45] The American attitude was the exception: their troops were fresh, their gas companies had to prove themselves; they took a different line exemplified by Sibert who proclaimed: 'Gas warfare is not a fad, nor an experiment. It is a proven, powerful instrument of war, both in offense and defense . . . Contrary to the belief among many troops, the cloud gas is not obsolete and when more mobile methods of making cloud gas . . . are developed, its use may become more frequent.'[46]

In 1918 everything was on a huge scale, and as gas was being applied no less profligately than other weapons it was bound to have widespread effects. The Germans set the pace in March and April when they used gas shells by the hundred thousands for 'Michael' and 'Georgette'; even as late as 31 July—if Hanslian is to be believed—they saturated an area west of Verdun with 340,000 Yellow Cross shells to forestall a Franco-American attack. But they could not keep it up. In September, the supplies at dumps were somewhat less abundant, and they fired off what gas they had, to slow down the Americans at St Mihiel. Towards October, systematic *Buntschiessen* in a carefully planned pattern ceased.[47] That naturally defeated the whole object of the exercise, but the German organization was dissolving, and they were taking punishment from Allied gas shells. In mid-1918 almost one-third of the British shells were filled with gas and though their toxicity was not as high as the enemy's, such was the quantity that the Germans suffered more gas injuries than ever before. Towards the end of the war the Americans fixed the proportion of gas at 20 per cent of total shell consumption with effect from 1 November and at 25 per cent from 1 January 1919. Instead of the Germans worrying the Allies with threats of the unknown, it was now the other way round: the Anglo-American gas potential was no longer a public relations exercise, but a certainty. By the end of June 1918, the British had sufficient weekly capacity for filling phosgene into 21,000 shells and 4,000–5,000 Livens drums. That corresponded to 90–100 t a week of the gas. Separate figures for other gases, or mixtures of gases, are not available, but the production capacity for these was sufficient to raise the total by up to a half. For the 1919 campaign the British output of mustard gas was set at 200 t a week and at Edgewood the Americans had sufficient equipment in place by November 1918 to fill about 1,600 t of gas a month, sufficient for 2.7 million 75 mm shells.[48]

Apart from the artillery and directly under the control of the gas troops, there were the unconventional devices for delivering poison gas, in particular the gas projectors. Equally alarming was the possibility that planes might drop gas bombs on targets close behind the front. Churchill floated the idea at a meeting in March 1918 and justified it by claiming it would demoralize the Germans and cause them to put on their respirators every time they heard a plane. The objections to the proposal were not on grounds of retaliation, which would have been immediate, but because the RFC (soon to become the RAF) could not guarantee to deliver a bomb within 200 m of a given target. Hence there would be wasteful dispersion of the gas and the likelihood of injuring or killing non-combatants in such raids. Plausible, but not convincing. No one except Churchill and Thuillier was very interested in carrying out demonstration flights and nothing was done.[49] The idea was not new—Churchill was resuscitating a proposal he had made almost three years earlier—but the concept of spreading fear and uncertainty in the rear was new and re-emerged between the wars.

The nature of gas injury in the last year of war differed in several important respects from that of 1916–17. The arsenical compounds did not kill, they incapacitated: they caused such pain in the sinuses that the wearer would tear off his mask and seek more air, perhaps to be killed by breathing in phosgene. That, at any rate, was the intention, but as I mentioned before, the German shells did not usually disperse Blue Cross materials as particulates in which form alone they were effective. Sometimes however, by chance, the explosive charge had the desired result and the particulates caused the characteristic symptons of that arsenical form of poisoning: pain and 'a feeling of moral depression and weakness of the limbs.' For example on 27 May when yet another of Bruchmüller's bombardments heralded the German advance on the Aisne and the Marne, the 21st British Division suffered casualties from the intensive Blue Cross shelling. The soldiers had taken part in the March retreat, had been sent to the 'quiet' Chemin des Dames to reinforce the French, and were now exposed again to intensive *Buntschiessen*. Some of the men who got more than a small dose 'felt a general decrease in their stamina and power of resistance.' Recovery in fresh air was quick, but on defeated or demoralized troops the arsenicals had a pronounced effect for it rendered them 'distinctly unfit for . . . marching or hand to hand fighting.'[50] Even the Americans, well-fed, well-equipped, and untouched by war, became apprehensive. Brown who looked at the records of the 3rd and 42nd US Divisions which saw much fighting in Champagne during July and in the Argonne in September, reported that battle fatigue quickly followed intensive gas shelling.[51] Allied gas shells and Livens projectiles enhanced the increasing war-weariness of the Germans, whose spirits had been lowered first by heavy casualties, then by the evidence of vast Allied food and clothing stocks captured in spring, and later by the debilitating influenza epidemic.[52] We can therefore readily imagine the effect of mustard gas on the Germans, few of whom had heard of it, let alone seen the blisters or the inflamed eyes. From June 1918 onwards, French Yperite and three months later, British HS shells struck the enemy. At first there was surprise and concern and then, during the summer, a feeling that the situation was getting out of control. The first OHL circular acknowledging French mustard gas was dated 21 June 1918: it provided instruction on protection and decontamination, gave guidance on diagnosis and treatment, and specifically referred to malingerers who might take advantage of the delayed action of the substance by seeking, without justification, evacuation to the rear. (In the last months of the war the Germans adopted the practice of sending lightly gassed cases for a few days' observation and recuperation behind the front.) Rumours circulated about permanent injuries from gas. A circular, dated 27 September and signed by Haber, warned of unnecessarily alarmist stories, mentioned that arms and legs did not fall off, and that blindness was only temporary. But that did not suffice for, in October, MOs were given instructions on how to deal with such tales, among them impotence and damage to the genitals.[53]

What is remarkable about the mixture of common-sense precautions and morale-boosting is the stress on mustard gas. In the last months of the war this chemical warfare agent had an effect on the Germans out of proportion to the quantities used against them. Gas projectiles, fired randomly, also contributed to the weakening of morale. There is plenty of evidence to show what effect they had. For example a divisional order of 18 June 1918 reiterated the need for strict gas discipline and stressed that recruits and troops from the Russian front who had never encountered these projectiles were especially at risk. The Bavarian archives have particulars of many projector operations, some of them large: at Oisy-le-Verger (in the Quéant area) on 12 March the identification of the drums was too late, because British shell-fire masked the noise of the discharge; only two were killed and forty-four injured. (In that same week and in the same battalion, two men died and seven reported sick from carbon monoxide poisoning caused by a faulty stove.) In mid-May, at Carvin, north of Lens, about a hundred British projectiles slightly injured one man. But in the night of 23–4 May, at Merris, south-west of Bailleul, the British fired 1,178 drums on men of the 12th Bavarian Division, killing 27 and injuring 105. On 18–19 June, 975 Livens drums fell among the men of BRIR 12, who were being relieved in the Ablainzeville area, south-west of Arras. Once again, heavy shelling was co-ordinated with the operation, so that the sentries did not spot the discharge. The trenches were crowded, the gas dense, the wind light, and, in some cases, the respirator filters could not cope. As a result 53 men were killed and 66 injured.[54] And so it went on. By the standards of the day the incidents were merely the routine wear-and-tear of trench warfare, but they entailed loss of confidence in the mask and generally upset troops who were recovering from battle in these supposedly quiet sectors. Bauer, who had access to casualty statistics, attributed the 'overwhelming proportion of German gas fatalities' to the Livens projectiles.[55]

As gas warfare intensified, so did the German efforts to improve respirators. They did not know the facts, but anxiously anticipated the introduction of Allied arsenical compounds. The Germans feared that they had reached the physical and chemical limits to their mask, and though they issued special paper filters, they considered there was no further technical solution to the problems facing defence. Hence the increasingly gloomy attitude of the chemical warfare experts, and at the KWI development seems to have stopped in late summer, perhaps because it was thought no longer worthwhile. Haber and his friends had known for many months that the rising volume of Allied production would overwhelm the German defences in the spring offensive of 1919. The only answer, as they saw it, to the growing threat was to emphasize the need for discipline and safety drill whenever and wherever gas was likely to be encountered. A revision of the German gas manual, the February 1918 edition, served not only to introduce the leather mask, but also to prescribe safeguards against surprise attacks by Livens projectiles. There were recommendations on how to improve the protection of dug-outs against gas by more elaborate ventilation systems. But even that was not enough: there were, throughout that year, appeals for greater vigilance, instructions to post sentries at dug-out entrances, to check gas blankets, and sound the alarm, to order working parties to have the respirator at the alert at all times when within 1 km of the front, and so on.[56] We have seen that this did not prevent surprises and casualties. All the belligerents had learnt the need for anti-gas training and the drill was tediously repeated. But as the Allies increased their chemical operations, the Germans were pressed harder until, in the autumn, they obtained relief by putting a greater distance between the themselves and their opponents. The Americans were the exception again. Many learnt field craft and anti-gas precautions in the rear or in the quiet sectors. But as they were drawn into the June, July, and August battles their gas casualties mounted and were proportionately much higher than the British. The explanations were inexperience, bravado, and carelessness. But even seasoned British and French troops were caught unawares when in August, they began to advance. The elaborate precautions of trench warfare, the spare clothing, and the chloride of lime sacks had to be left behind. In August 1918 the British became concerned at the rising trend in their gas casualties and neither then nor later could they successfully counter the German practice of firing gas shells at random along the line of the advance.[57]

Tactically speaking the gas war of 1918 was no more decisive than the introduction of the chlorine cloud had been three-and-a-half years earlier. Then the Allies had no gas and could not retaliate in kind. In 1918, action and reaction were reversed: the British took the initiative in small gas operations and the Germans replied with whatever was at hand, chiefly artillery. Thus the activity of the Special Companies at Ablainzeville on 18–19 June, one out of many, had its predictable sequel twenty-four hours later, when the Germans shelled the presumed projector sites with mustard gas. The British had expected some form of retaliation, and when it came there were, for once, no deaths, but 126 men had to be evacuated for treatment. The night before almost the same number of Bavarians opposite had been injured by the gas projectiles![58]

In terms of manpower and cost-effectiveness it was a futile way of waging technological warfare. In this respect gas was no different from the other aspects of the local and wasteful character of trench warfare. The question may be asked: are we dealing here with some minor chemical–military gimmick adopted in 1915 to end that form of warfare, and after failing to produce the desired result, retained because no one could think how to abandon it? And could the Germans have won the war with poison gas, in the first half of 1918? High explosive, in an intensive and complicated firing pattern, enabled them to break out of trench warfare. If there had been no gas, they would still have been successful, for it was the combination of new artillery tactics with the specially trained

Fig. 16. American soldiers wearing the SBR. The photograph was probably taken in the second half of 1918; the location is not known. (Imperial War Museum)

infantry groups which overwhelmed the British, the Portuguese, and the French. Gas added to the confusion in the first stages and, in a few places, saved the Germans manpower. For example at Flesquières-Quéant, mustard gas signalled the enemy's intentions whilst inflicting avoidable losses on the British at negligible cost to the Germans. Similarly Armentières had to be evacuated after the Germans drenched it with mustard gas, and they were able to occupy it without trouble after the initial breakthrough of 'Georgette'. Gas undoubtedly contributed to occasional local successes, notably the capture of Mt Kemmel, of the Chemin des Dames, and the advance beyond the Aisne. But the German practice of sticking too long to a good idea had its disadvantages. The excessive use of mustard gas in a particular locality alerted their enemies to its particular significance and enabled them to make their dispositions accordingly, knowing that there would be no change in the next 48−72 hours. So the verdict is that gas was occasionally of some value to the Germans in their offensives. That raises the question whether gas served them better in defence. Here, the answer is that as long as the retreat was organized and co-ordinated, say from early August to early October, mustard gas made a useful contribution in keeping the Allied forces at a safe distance and also caused injury to the pursuers. When the transport system began to fail and ammunition trains were delayed, in the last three to four weeks, chemical warfare became irrelevant to the final outcome.

But for the Allies, the conclusion is entirely different. If the war had continued into the winter and spring of 1919, their chemical weapon production would have been very large, sufficient to give them local superiority, and enough to cause the Germans insoluble replacement problems. One way to deal with mustard gas was to kit out all soldiers in contact with it with new shoes, underwear, and uniforms. But the Germans were no longer in a position to do so. They had reached that condition months before the Armistice. Those who knew the supply position also knew that in 1919 the use of gas would bring the war to an end: the respirator could not be improved further given the available materials, and the other shortages—especially clothing and rubberized fabrics—could no longer be kept secret, for the Allies began to take thousands of prisoners on the Marne and at Amiens. That being so, could the war have been shortened if the British and the French had been in a position to use mustard gas and arsenical compounds intensively and repeatedly in June or July, instead of several weeks later? The answer, in the light of what is now known, is unquestionably, 'Yes'. From the end of June onwards, the Germans were profoundly apprehensive of gas and its effect on morale and equipment. If the Franco-British mustard-gas programme had gone according to plan, they would have had enough shells to stop 'Gneisenau' and the second battle of the Marne. But the plans went wrong, the supplies programmed for June were not available until August or September, and the Allies did not have a sufficiency of mustard-gas shells until October–November.

Allied gas could have shortened the war by up to two months, if—and it was a big if—their production capacity had developed more quickly. Two months seem little, but any saving would have been worth while. The greater potential benefit of gas to the Allies rested on supply considerations. If this is accepted, it helps to explain the great importance attached to the development and post-war maintenance of an organic chemical industry in Britain, France, the USA, and Italy, so that in another world war there would be no delays in the manufacture of toxic and other materials which might hold up their use at the front. Controversial as the value of gas in warfare must remain, there can be no doubt about its wider effects. Only the unimaginative remained unconcerned. The majority of the troops had encountered gas, if only through regular gas-mask drill. Scores of thousands were injured by it and many thousands killed. A few dozen artists and writers were so profoundly affected by poison gas that they transformed this relatively feeble weapon into something far greater than it ever was in practice. Imagination enhanced chemical weapons in subtle and unexpected ways and if one asks how effective poison gas was in the long run, one answer must be that seen through the eyes and the minds of the artists it became a powerful weapon and an enduring threat.

The title of the chapter refers to imagination and places it after reality. This was done purposely and by introducing the concept at this stage I am anticipating some of the conclusions. My reasons are as follows: one of the difficulties in writing about chemical warfare is that it was a peripheral activity of the war: it enhanced its awfulness, but made no great contribution to it. That particular aspect will be dealt with at greater length in a later chapter. Here, as an intermediate step, it may be useful to turn from technology and tactics, to writers and artists. How did chemical warfare appear to those who had experienced it at first hand, or at one remove through relatives and close friends, and how did these people interpret its significance? An exhaustive survey of the arts, literature, and personal reminiscences would answer the question, but there is a complication, important in the context of this book, which needs to be borne in mind: the passage of time alters perceptions. The contemporaries, unless they wrote in the heat of the moment, could have forgotten something or changed their minds. And historians, who have hindsight and are supposed to be detached, may yet reach the wrong conclusions.

So far in this chapter I have played down the importance of chemical warfare, and have relied on the evidence provided by the course of events. Further material bearing on the statistical and medical aspects will be found in the next chapter. But for the present I ask the reader to change his focus, to think in terms of sensations, and to tolerate generalizations drawn from particular incidents: in short to ignore facts and consider impressions.

No one who experienced gas forgot it: it may not have harmed their bodies, but it left an indelible stain on their minds. However—and this is a significant point—to some, chemical warfare was just a bothersome incident of war, to others it was the focal point of their fears then and later. Fear does not attack everyone in the same way, but when it strikes root and cannot be mastered, it works on the imagination and enhances the emotion. Look at Sargent's *Gassed* at the Imperial War Museum in London. It is not the best of canvasses, it is contrived and too orderly. He was not present when the Germans first fired Yellow Cross shells. But that does not matter because, when it was painted in 1918, it struck a chord. It still does—the helplessness of the blind, the pain of the burns. It does not matter that the blindness disappeared and the blisters only lasted ten days or a fortnight. Sargent may not have wanted to shock, he sanitized, as it were, the after-effects of a Yellow Cross bombardment, yet something remains, and the picture will not go away.[59] It is different with Owen's '*Dulce et Decorum Est*', one of the great war poems in the English language. He was in the line at the time, and wrote the short, burning verses in August 1917, just after a bombardment with gas shells. The poem is about exhaustion, fear, and choking to death. The scene is horrifying and the verses bring no relief. The detail of the reality was different, but that no longer matters. Owen intended the reader to be involved and achieved it by enhancing the effect of poison gas.[60]

The enlargement of incidents through the eye or the pen of the artist has had a powerful impact since 1918. There was also another stream, once important, but less significant since 1939. That was the clash between two forms of warfare, of the old weapons versus the new. I find it difficult to understand the difference between killing by phosgene and by HE—the end-result is the same. But romanticism versus technology had a powerful intellectual attraction to many famous authors, and it led directly to the campaigns for the control of what the French called '*armes déloyales*', for which the nearest translation is 'unfair weapons'. The argument even had its technical side: many infantry and artillery officers were baffled by poison gas, and some, no doubt, never 'communicated' with their chemical experts. From that situation it is but a short step to the role of the specialist in the Great War and his influence on the traditional element in warfare. Finally, we need to bear in mind that until 1918 the British and the French were more affected by gas than the Germans. My story so far shows why this was so, but in the course of 1918 the situation altered. Novelists are not chronologists, but in the last year of the war, German writers—particularly those whose novels were autobiographical—changed their perceptions. Remarque's *All Quiet on the Western Front* had a success—at a popular level— which Sargent, Owen, and British and French novelists never achieved. Remarque reached a vast audience and with him the box office and media-rating effects of the First World War on the minds of the masses began and has since continued. Plays, films, radio, and nowadays television have recreated for a generation who never experienced the 1914–18 horrors, the incidents on which imagination feeds, among them, poison gas.

Let us begin with 1915. The chlorine cloud at Second Ypres was a major journalistic event. Accuracy was less important than the message: the beastly Germans have tried out a new, i.e. an unfair weapon on the Allies who need to defend themselves and must retaliate at once. Sir Arthur Conan Doyle wrote of 22 April 1915 that the Germans 'took possession of . . . trenches tenanted only by the dead garrisons whose blackened faces, contorted figures and lips fringed with blood and foam showed the agonies in which they had died.' And of 1 May at Hill 60 he observed that the position was 'typical' for a German gas discharge, and that the British losses were 'nearly all from poison.'[61] That kind of exaggeration can be easily dismissed some seventy years later, but more skilful interpreters looked at gas warfare more perceptively. There was, for instance that unknown cameraman whose untitled film clips show scenes behind the front in 1917 or 1918, among them a scene near a CCS: a file of soldiers, each having his hand on the shoulder of the man in front, move slowly, are tired and dejected; they have been blinded by mustard gas and have gauze taped over their eyes. Contrast them—in the same scene—with the walking wounded cheerfully drawing on their cigarettes.[62] The silent film makes the point better, I think, than Episode 7 of *The Great War* BBC-TV series which dealt with Second Ypres and the effects of the chlorine cloud. The commentary was spoken by people who had not been personally involved in April 1915, abounded in clichés, and repeated, more than half a century later, Conan Doyle's observations including the blackened faces. More recently Vera Brittain's *Testament of Youth* showed us the young VAD on duty in the Salient in the winter of 1917–18. The yellow cream (vaseline?) smeared over the mustard-gas casualties made good colour television, but why it should be gas, instead of HE casualties, was not made clear.[63] Joan Littlewood's *Oh, What a Lovely War*, the film of the 1960s musical had several references to poison gas, made more poignant by the clever juxtaposition of events and characterizations: French appears at one point and declares that 'gas can be a winning weapon', while off-stage the troops sing 'Gas to-night . . . ' with its refrain of 'one mask for the four of us'. But that was Loos in September 1915 and by November 1918 only a masked soldier is left walking between the tapes marking the decontaminated path through the mustard-gas field.[64]

It has been said that universal literacy and the romance of technology gave science fiction and stories of future wars an appeal and an audience that they never had before. I have referred to H. G. Wells and others in my second chapter. But that was in the context of pre-war novels, and writers as well as painters did not perceive chemical warfare as science fiction come true. For example William Roberts, then a young artist, painted an incident of 22 April 1915: the work is entitled *The First German Gas Attack at Ypres*. Its bold colours, vertical strokes, and foreshortened scale show the Zouaves, shocked and contorted, stumbling into the Canadian battery whose gunners, cursing and sweating, are serving their weapons. The picture conveys chemical warfare better than anything else I have seen, except a work of Otto Dix, one of whose First World War etchings show five dead soldiers—gassed, black, bloated, no longer human—just dumped behind the First-Aid post. He had been in France and the etching was done at the end and not the beginning of chemical warfare.[65]

World war fiction, much of it semi-autobiographical, provides more insights even than the paintings. There is a great deal of it, and we may start with Erich Maria Remarque, not the best, but the most popular. Remark (his real name) served from 1915 to the end, and his novel recreates the story of a small group which gradually shrinks and ultimately disappears. The book is packed with incidents, some of them indeed banal, and the enormous and immediate success of *All Quiet on the Western Front* and the films made from the book enhanced the imagery of war. Remarque has several gas scenes which create the impression that it was not the numbers killed or injured that troubled him, but the fear of being cut off from fresh air and from contact with one's friends because the mask, though a safeguard, also increases one's sense of isolation. In this respect he was right, for speech was impeded by the German respirator as well as by the SBR. Remarque was obsessed by the symptoms of cyanosis—his injured always have blue faces—and by the mental shock of gas injury. When Paul Baumer, the hero, is gassed in 1918, there are no serious injuries, only distress. He is sent home on convalescent leave, recovers, and has moments of peace before he returns to the front when he is fatally injured.[66] The fate of a group of men is a recurring theme in war novels because author and reader can identify with it, compare impressions, and observe reactions. Raymond Dorgelès follows a section of French infantry from 1914 to the Armistice. He has no single hero, but like Barbusse's *Le Feu*, the description of trench life illuminates the miserable condition of the other ranks in the army. I have previously described the futility of the French anti-gas measures and these novels confirm that no one cared about protection—what was the point of it? Henri Barbusse wrote in the heat of the moment after the violent battles in Artois during the early autumn of 1915. He mentions occasional gas alerts but his little group is demoralized and in any case does not know how to make the best use of the muslin pads against the 'green cotton-wool' of German chlorine. No one bothered to train the men and they were too close to death to worry how they were going to die.[67] Jules Romains in his long and rambling novel about Verdun also stressed the neglect of the men by their officers. His chief theme is fear, always present, sometimes intensive, occasionally not very acute, from which there emerges a kind of fatalism which makes life endurable.[68]

We would not expect that everyone looked at the situation through the painters' and writers' eyes: what the one saw and the other sensed might well appear different to the man on the spot. Here, for example, is an extract from C. G. Douglas's report on his visit to No. 47 CCS on 14 July 1917 approximately 48 hours after the first mustard-gas shelling. He was most struck by the prevalence of conjunctivitis: 'There were very few who could keep their eyes open, so much so that when some of the milder cases were evacuated each man had to be led like a blind man by an orderly to the ambulance car.'[69] That is the fact behind Sargent's emotion, though I don't know whether the two ever met. Hartley, who knew Douglas, referred at the Bournemouth meeting of the British Association two years later to 'the pathetic appeal of Sargent's picture' and added that 75 per cent of the men would be fit for duty within three months, whereas those injured by HE suffered a far worse fate. One cannot compare the two types of injury—they were different—and it was the failure to emphasize the differences, to argue that gas was somehow less awful than shell, that led to so many fruitless discussions between the wars. Even as late as 1935 Thuiller, in a lecture to the Royal United Service Institution, referred to Gassed as that 'maudlin sentiment'.[70]

The intellectuals had the imagination, but as L. F. Céline wrote in his autobiography, 'if you have no imagination, dying is a small matter, but if you have, it's too much.'[71] The writers had the imagination, their work enhanced it, but what if they used their talents to give the story a particular twist or an 'angle' which it never had in real life? This takes us beyond chemical warfare as such and to the question of 'new' weapons against the old, specialists against regulars, gas clouds against rifles, and so on. Manning, like others, was aware of the conflict and in one vivid scene, which might have been tape-recorded, the hero—Bourne—and the CSM talk about how the artillery had changed things, how the old officers could not get on with the new, how the scale of operations had increased, and how the regular officers were amateurs by comparison with the specialists in Haig's New Army.[72] Siegfried Sassoon was also an eye-witness to the changes and he observed how, by the winter of 1916–17, 'the war had become undisguisedly mechanical and inhuman', and, in the context of a routine trench raid in 1918, of its 'business-like futility'.[73] There is, as I shall argue in the final chapter, no possible line of demarcation between different forms of inhumanity and from this it follows that those who wrote that gas was worse than shell because it was (in Sassoon's sense) 'mechanical' were not logical. But logic has nothing to do with feelings, which takes us to yet another aspect of the war-time literature. The widespread employment of specialists in the latter stages of the war was visible evidence of its technological character. Forester's general, Curzon (whom we first encountered at Loos) has been promoted to command a corps which entails unavoidable contact with the experts at HQ. Milward, the corps gas officer, is a chemistry graduate and, like other specialists, is treated as an 'irregular'. On the night of 20 March 1918 he has dinner with Curzon. Everyone around the table expects the Germans to attack and to use gas. Milward recalls that Curzon had discouraged him from experimenting with mustard gas because it was not lethal. Yet the next morning the Germans use it—Milward is proved right.[74] General Curzon represents the traditional military attitude to science which Forester and others blamed for unnecessary casualties and stalemate. From this one might conclude that if more attention had been paid to the gas specialists there might have been fewer wounded and—in Spring 1918—no need to retreat. That is unlikely, indeed wishful thinking, and assigns to the chemists a role they never occupied in the Great War. Curzon was badly wounded in the 'Michael' attack and that is the end of the story.

There were many other novels based on the stereotypes of regular officers and scientists at war. Malraux, who had romantic notions about individual courage, loyalty, and heroism uses a German cylinder gas discharge against the Russians as a background for his views on humanity and chivalry in war. The story is based on an actual event[75] and its purpose is to show that the professor of chemistry and his team contributed to the atrocious death of many Russians. The German soldiers, appalled by what they have seen in the Russian lines, retreat and a few are injured by their own gas. The chemist is satisfied with the outcome and defends the use of gas, but the intelligence officer, a regular of the old school, is shocked by the operation. Malraux makes him say that the new men who think in terms of numbers killed by different chemical formulae are destroying courage. Was this not also the attitude of many infantry officers in France to chemical warfare? They spoke of cylinder and projector operations as a waste of manpower and as provoking retaliation which would cause unnecessary casualties among their men.

Should all this be taken seriously? Are were not attaching excessive importance to those who enlarged commonplace incidents? I think we do, though I accept that those who have the imagination to dramatize an event, however small, also have the larger audience and operate on a different level from those who have no imagination. To enhance his story and make his point the narrator must ignore or at least neglect that side of chemical warfare which deals with the protection of the soldier, and so contributes to the support of morale. The descriptions invariably belittle the value of defence, or to put it the other way round, the development of anti-gas training, of better respirators, and improved medical services contributed to the containment of poison gas, but went unrecorded by novelists. This led me to the Chelsea Pensioners.[76] At the time they were in France they were aged between 19 and 24; five out of the ten had first-hand experience of gas, but none were injured; two were frightened by it. One of them, though not injured by gas, continued to worry about it and some sixty years after the event refused even to talk about the incident; this man was wounded in May 1915 and invalided out of the army. Another said that gas had left no particular impression on him, but he was frightened of mustard gas, apparently only at night: he explained that, in the dark, he might accidentally touch contaminated ground, a risk connected with his job as a telephone linesman. Questioned, he added that he had been deeply impressed by the tale of a soldier who got his buttocks and crutch badly burnt when relieving himself at night. It is one of the rare cases where I have been able to identify the causal mechanism of a man's fear.

A more common explanation of the fear of gas is equally plausible. Baynes, in his careful study of the battle of Neuve Chapelle,[77] has suggested that the mental age of the regular soldiers of those days was twelve to thirteen and that adults with a child's mentality behave like children: trustful of their leaders, resilient and optimistic, they like discipline, cope with drill, and in danger are sustained by the automaton-like carrying out of orders. Excellent qualities in trench warfare, but weakened by other characteristics, notably irresponsibility and fecklessness. We may contrast Baynes's description of responses to rifle- and machine-gun fire with an incident south west of Arras in 1917. The Germans shelled the particular position lightly and briefly. The British estimated that altogether 70–100 gas shells and 50–80 trench mortar gas bombs fell on their line at 1820 and again at 0320. Altogether 14 men were killed and 90 injured by gas. For some reason no warning was given and the impregnated anti-gas blankets had not been lowered at the entrances to the dug-outs. The adjoining sector was also shelled at the time and an estimated 250–300 gas shells were recorded; in this particular sector the warning was sounded and respirators put on. Result: no casualties.[78] Blunden had a similar experience. He was caught in the open by an intensive bombardment. Just as he scrambled into a dug-out two gas shells burst nearby. He warned the men to put on their masks, but two or three would not listen, they 'were gassed and fell exhausted'.[79] It may be that such stories are an indication of the fatalism mentioned earlier, an indifference to avoidable danger which in the latter stages of the war was observed in many armies. Those who were prudent and kept their nerve survived chemical warfare better, though, like Blunden, himself gassed, they were marked by it.

Apprehension and the fear of gas were extraordinary. At the beginning of 1915, when Sir Thomas Thorpe was experimenting with ethyl-iodoacetate (SK) at Chatham, they first came across the 'subjective effect' of gas. One officer who witnessed the test stood 50 m upwind from the burst of the SK bomb. He left the trench in some distress and told Thorpe that he felt very ill, yet the vapour could not possibly have reached him![80] The man had a very vivid imagination, and there must have been many who suffered agonies every time the gongs and klaxons sounded. Gladden reported that the anti-gas training at the base in Étaples was 'truly frightening' and one man fainted when told to walk through the gas chamber.[81] He also imagined too much. Bouffieux, the cook in Dorgelès's novel, went to pieces: he sniffed mustard gas everywhere and finally hid himself in the corner of a dug-out, never taking off his M2 respirator. No one, it may be noted, came to his help.[82] Bouffieux was one of those wretched people who would be destroyed by gas without ever being hurt by it.

So were imaginary and exaggerated fears an important element in chemical warfare? I have no doubt that this was indeed so, but gas spanned three-and-a-half years of war, time enough for character and perceptions to alter. Those of a nervous disposition might become indifferent to fear though constant exposure, while the unimaginative might be pushed beyond endurance and break down. Robert Graves is an interesting example. He served from August 1914 to December 1918. His descriptions of trench life remain a classic and his is the best eyewitness account we have of gas at Loos. The confusion near Auchy and Haisnes on 25 September 1915 was complete and two days later, another cylinder operation was called off after a wait of five hours. Neither disturbed his equanimity; the distress came a few weeks before the Somme when the new PHG helmets were issued. The device entailed breathing in through the nose and breathing out through a pipe-stem-like contraption held in the mouth. But Graves, as the result of a school accident, could only breathe in and out through the mouth. The helmet was therefore of no use to him and he needed to be operated upon to clear the passage. This circumstance probably saved his life, for he was convalescing when his comrades attacked on 1 July 1916. The combination of temporary defencelessness against gas and escape from death caused him, henceforth to be obsessed by the fear of gas: any unusual smell or even strongly scented flowers sent him trembling.[83] Though unharmed by gas, chemical warfare had scarred him. His friend, Siegfried Sassoon, had a similar reaction. At the beginning of his service in France, gas left no mark on his sensitive memory. But after his injury at Arras (April 1917) he was sent home and in the psychiatric hospital it began to weigh on his mind. A fellow-officer told him over a round of golf that half his company had been injured by a gas bombardment. This particular incident stuck in his memory where it became a growing problem, 'one might almost say more of a nightmare'.[84] Later he was sent to the Middle East and when he returned to France in February 1918 gas had receded for he no longer mentions it. Henry Williamson's leading character, Phillip Maddison, was also at Loos, within 2–3 km of Graves judging by the description. Yet there could not be a greater contrast. What is a horrible confusion to Graves is to Williamson a technical job. The two have not the same powers of description, but it is obvious that Williamson thinks of chlorine as a chemical not as a weapon that touches bodies and minds. And in this respect he reminds me of Otto Hahn who witnessed many gas operations, although his autobiography deals with them as if they were scientific phenomena, and the effect on the enemy only gets the briefest of mentions.[85]

Was the experience of gas warfare part of an individual's psychological condition? Always present, often suppressed, but apt to rise to the surface and disturb the emotional equilibrium when least expected? This possibility was ignored at first, but became increasingly important in the latter half of 1917 when the psychotropic effects of arsenical compounds were recognized, but could not be remedied except by breathing in uncontaminated fresh air. Since removing the mask would expose the wearer to chlorine or phosgene the protection of soldiers against particulates became an urgent problem. It was then discovered that individual reactions to Blue Cross shells varied. Scientists accustomed to handling poisonous substances managed better than laymen, yet their training and the nature of their work militated against self-analysis. If they could have conveyed their feelings when faced with the choice of toxic agents they might have turned into great novelists instead of, like Hahn, famous physicists.

Chapman, who joined the army towards the end of 1914, viewed his four years as a soldier with detachment and sympathy though never indifferently. He and Carl Zuckmayer in the German artillery served equal terms. Neither was more bothered by gas than by other ways of killing and injuring. Ludwig Renn who, between the wars, made his reputation as a socialist writer was another[86] and the list could be easily lengthened, the classification refined, further qualifications and explanations introduced (class, education, civilian background, rank, *et al.*) without materially altering the general conclusion: the artists and writers enlarged what they had observed. I have noted the reactions of some of them: their emotional response ranges from fear to indifference. The common thread is the neglect of the protection against chemical warfare. There was also another view, less articulate and imaginative, which characterized opposite attitudes. Gladden recalled that he thought at the time, 1916–18, 'that too much was being made of this horror' and he rated gas a lesser 'frightfulness' than high explosive.[87] The Chelsea Pensioners, to a man, praised anti-gas helmets and the SBR. But they also had less imagination than the intellectuals and more confidence in the drill and other routines of anti-gas measures.

Literature, painting, film, and radio have done more for gas since 1918 than the military use of chemical weapons up to then would justify. But gas injured and killed in unconventional ways to which contemporaries could not accustom themselves. It could be that the sensation of choking and slow suffocation releases fears which are stronger than the anticipation of pain from bullets or shell splinters. Who can say? The German doctor and novelist Peter Bamm, looking back on his life, considers that chemical warfare requires the courage of a fireman who must be brave but not foolhardy, and who must be sufficiently self-disciplined not to rush into action before calculating how long his breathing apparatus will last. You cannot be brave against gas, he wrote, and added 'we were in a position analogous to the knights when gunpowder was invented.'[88] Perhaps here is the nub of the problem—how do we react to a new weapon? And in particular to the effects of a weapon to which no one has become conditioned, because, with very few exceptions it has not been used from the Armistice of 1918 to the present day.

10

GAS CASUALTIES

THE casualty statistics of the Great War were a constant reminder of its horror; then and later they mesmerized public opinion and the numbers involved generated so much emotion that few attempts were made to examine them critically. This generalization applies with particular force to chemical warfare statistics and one of the chief purposes of this chapter is to investigate the reliability of the different sources and proceed thence to the compilation of a total which has greater meaning than the information hitherto available. Having estimated the scale and relative importance, I propose to analyse the findings and draw attention to the medical problems created by poison gas.

Between the wars, American and German specialist writers published various estimates of the total number of casualties from gas. Gilchrist, Prentiss, and Hanslian are the most widely used sources.[1] The first-named identified a total of 1,009,038, the second almost as precise, recorded 1,297,000, while the third offered an estimate of 880,000 in the 1927 edition of his book. Hanslian omitted this figure in the 1937 edition of *Der chemische Krieg*, but if one adds up the numbers one obtains yet another total—560,000! My own studies lead me to the conclusion that there is no reliable total; the principal source of error is the Russian data, and that if the Russian casualties are excluded, about half a million people were injured by or died from poison gas. If the totals published by Gilchrist and Prentiss are correspondingly adjusted, their figures are reduced to around 530,000 and 820,000 respectively.

Greater precision would be helpful. The chemical warfare experts of 1915–18 grounded their case on numbers, and in the post-war debates over poison gas these numbers were used to lend substance to their arguments or were extrapolated to indicate the potential threat in another world war. Whether different expert opinions and forecasts would have led to different political and military decisions after 1918 is an interesting exercise in which morality and 'cost-effectiveness' play important roles. I shall have more to say about that in the final chapter. But at this stage the search for greater accuracy is justifiable on other grounds, for I wish to show that the total casualties were usually overstated. For these reasons I propose to consider the background to the casualty statistics before discussing the numbers themselves and drawing conclusions.

We are dealing in the first place with the problem of definition and classification. Unless the cause of injury was specified, the gas casualty would be recorded by the armies under the omnibus heading 'other causes', and without criteria of severity the recovery time or morbidity of gas cases would remain unknown. To postulate these criteria assumes that counting the dead or diagnosing the wounded or gassed was a precise job: but in battle conditions there was not time for such niceties. Thus at the very start there is an element of uncertainty; the British system of casualty statistics, a very good one on paper, will illustrate the problem. It was evolved in the latter part of 1914 and rested on the medical history cards; fit men not accounted for at roll-call were 'missing', that is killed or taken prisoner. Thus the quick and the dead were numbered, and the regimental records were adjusted when the 'missing' turned up later. So everything depended on carefully filling in medical cards for the unfit, and keeping the records up to date. If there was no separate entry for gas, there would be no separate returns for those wounded or killed by gas; they would be recorded without identifying the cause. Even after the classification 'gassed' was introduced in the late summer of 1915 (the German army followed in January 1916 and the French in January 1918), the results were still uncertain at the height of a battle.[2] Failure to include gas would lead to understating at the beginning of chemical warfare, but there is some evidence that senior medical and staff officers introduced their own definitions and collected statistics without always forwarding them to headquarters or war ministries. Joffre complained about the lack of gas casualty statistics in November 1915, without any effect, and even for 1918 the data is incomplete for the four armies which then comprised the Groupe d'Armées du Centre.[3] That weakens the reliability of the French figures, and analogous omissions in 1915 render the Russian statistics useless.[4] The German defeats create further difficulties. They had an elaborate system of records forwarded to the Medical Department of the Prussian War Ministry where they were checked against the monthly hospital returns. But from August 1918 onwards the regimental returns became irregular and in the following month the hospital records also began showing gaps. When the monthly statistics were collated about ten years later, the compilers ceased to give details from 1 August 1918 onwards. However, other sources show that the Germans suffered severely from Allied gas in the next three-and-a-half months.[5]

The above suggests that the official records are likely to understate the total injured by gas. A further cause of understatement is the failure of the belligerents to list the cause of death and injury of enemy troops on the battle-field or in POW camps. This particular omission aggravates the unreliability of the Russian figures in 1915–16 and of the Allied losses in March–April 1918. Of all the statistical returns, the American and British are the most dependable, but the former are limited to 1918 and the latter are unreliable for 1915 and part of 1916. Nevertheless, a lot of detail is available, sufficient, it would seem, for grossing up the data to give totals for the nearly four years of gas warfare and for every country. But such extrapolations are useless. For example the British collected particulars of German bombardments and of casualties therefrom. But the resulting gas shell-to-casualty ratios differ so widely as to show no correlation at all between the number of shells and the number injured. That is hardly surprising, for estimating the number of shells is pure guesswork.

Another example is the detailed investigation of German gas clouds in 1915–16 by Allied specialists. Although the reports yield an abundance of numbers they cannot be used for estimating the effect of the Anglo-French gas clouds on the Germans. The reason is that the Germans used different concentrations and combinations of gases, and directed them against badly protected troops. The British efforts with chlorine cylinders were more frequent, though less intensive and were directed against men who wore good respirators. Thus correlation and sampling techniques are not helpful, nor do probability calculations provide a way out, for the certainty of casualties being inflicted still leaves in doubt the numbers involved and the severity of the injuries. One has therefore, to assemble what information there is and use one's judgement as to its quality. I have followed this approach in the table below, but where the data is too unreliable, I have omitted it altogether and put a question mark. The presentation of the statistics in two groups—'accurate' and 'incomplete' differs from that employed by other authors, as does the separation into two time periods, 1915–17 and 1918. This approach focuses attention on the Western Front and highlights the casualty rate for 1918 when chemical warfare reached unprecedented intensity.

The British figures come from an official publication compiled with scholarly care. Even so, there is some element of uncertainty, for no complete records were kept of those injured or killed by gas at the second battle of Ypres. The number runs to several thousand, a significant proportion of them being Canadians injured in the cloud-gas discharge of 24 April 1915. And, just to add a further complication, it would appear that Dominion troops were counted as British, except when they were treated in their own CCS or General Hospitals in England; this is likely to make a difference of several thousand for which I have allowed at the bottom of the table.[6] Although the British forces were exposed to repeated gas clouds in 1915 and the first eight months of 1916, Mitchell and Smith show that 90 per cent of all gas casualties admitted to CCS occurred in 1917–18.

The table shows that there is a large difference between my estimate and Prentiss's statistics for France. He relied on Gilchrist who, writing in 1927–8, did not give his sources, but they may have been German. The French official history is uninformative, and the archives, though incomplete, were not accessible to the public at the time. But if one pieces together the available data,[7] it emerges undisputably that the bulk of the gas casualties occurred in 1918, and that in 1915 the French experienced fewer cylinder operations than the British.[8] My estimate for 1915–17 may be too low, in particular there are few facts on the casualties caused by German gas shells in 1916–17, but for 1918 this is unlikely. The French failed to keep satisfactory records, and they did not care sufficiently about detail to reorganize their casualty statistics; I do not believe there was any deliberate intent on their part to suppress data or to manipulate what information there was. Did the Germans behave in a similar manner? Their statistics are impressive in their detail and the third volume of the *Sanitätsbericht* represents an elaborate compilation. The doubts arise because their figures are so low. When Hartley visited Germany in 1921 he was told that 3 per cent of the total admissions to Field Ambulances were gas cases, but could obtain no details and no figures for those killed.[9] The Germans were generally unforthcoming, although they had some rough figures at the time; they began the analysis of their medical records in 1927 and published their findings in 1934. The detailed breakdown was not taken beyond 31 July 1918, but that did not stop Prentiss from guessing that the total German chemical warfare casualties were 200,000. He exaggerated and ignored the significance of the monthly returns which can be compared with the reports of British cylinder and projectile operations and the effects of French gas-shell bombardments at Verdun.[10] The monthly average was 968 in 1916 (minimum 100 in January, maximum 1,726 in July) and 2,036 in 1917 (range 216 in January, 4,170 in August); there is no evidence that the data were selectively manipulated. The statistics suggest that Germans suffered relatively little from Allied chemical warfare until the late spring of 1917 when their losses began to mount. They abated during the winter of 1917–18, but rose further in Spring and Summer 1918, and were heavy in July–September. Finally, as regards the US casualties: the Americans tried harder than the other belligerents to obtain accurate figures; I have relied on Prentiss's, which are mid-way between the numbers given elsewhere.[11]

The total for the four belligerents shown in Group 1 of table 10.1 comes to just under half a million: it is substantially lower than Prentiss's and although it is based on a wider survey than that of other authors, it is still an estimate. It includes the German casualties on the Eastern Front—about 2,000, but excludes the estimated 20,000 losses of the smaller Allies: if we bear them in mind, the total approximately represents the human cost of chemical warfare on the Western Front. It needs to be contrasted with the roughly 15 million killed, missing, wounded, or sick on that front in 1914–18.[12] Thus the proportion attributable to gas is 3 to 3½ per cent, a range we need to recall in later discussions. The addition of the casualties suffered by the belligerents on other fronts changes the numerator as well as the denominator and leads from statistics to mere guessing. Prentiss, copying from Gilchrist, has 475,340 (!) Russian gas casualties, but did not give the source of his extraordinarily precise information. Indeed, the Western Allies had nothing reliable to go upon and post-war writers were in the same quandary.[13] The numbers quoted imply that the German cloud-gas operations in 1915–16 and gas shell bombardments in 1917 had a greater effect in the east than in the west, which is probable, but overlooks their comparatively small scale and infrequency. Prentiss's figure for the soldiers of the Austrian Empire are his guess, and as their exposure to Russian and Italian chemical warfare was minimal, it is of minor importance. In regard to Italian losses from Austrian and German chemical warfare the events on the Upper Soča in 1917 have been mentioned in Chapter 8; there was a major cloud-gas operation against unprotected troops in 1916; and some gas shelling

Table 10.1. *Estimated Casualties* from Chemical Warfare, 1915–1918†*

Country	1915–17	1918	Total	1918 as % of total	Prentiss's estimate‡
Group 1: Accurate or reasonably dependable information:					
UK (BEF)	72	114	186	61	189§
France	20¶	110	130	85	190
Germany	37	70‖	107	65	200
USA	—	73	73	100	73
Total	129	367	496	74	652
Group 2: Incomplete or unreliable information:					
Russia	?	—	?	?	475
Austro-Hungarian Empire	< 5	v. small	5	?	100
Italy	≏ 10	v. small	>10	—	60
Other**	5	15	20	75	10
Total	≏ 20 inc.	≏ 15	≏ 35 inc.	?	645
Grand Total	≏ 149 inc.	≏ 382	≏ 531 inc.	?	1,297

* Injured and dead; non-combatants excluded.
† All figures are in '000s; v. small = up to 1,000; inc. = incomplete; ≏ = approximate.
‡ *Chemicals in War*, pp. 653–4.
§ Excluding Dominion troops gassed in 1915.
¶ Assuming 2,500 casualties on 22 April 1915.
‖ Assuming 12,000 casualties from 1 October to 11 November.
** Canada, Australia–New Zealand (1918 only), India, Belgium, Portugal, Russian troops in France.

For sources see references in text.

in the Piave battles of June 1918.[14] Prentiss's figure, unsupported by evidence, is much too high bearing in mind the mountainous nature of the terrain, except in 1918 when the Austrians had reached the plains, but by then the Italians were protected by the SBR.

We shall never know how many were killed by gas, for throughout the war there were no accurate records of those whose death in action was directly attributable to this weapon. Nevertheless, it would appear that the number of fatalities was inflated and that specialist writers on the subject, instead of re-examining the evidence after 1918 merely repeated the numbers. We may start with Prentiss's statistics.[15] According to him precisely 91,198 men were killed by gas, that is 7 per cent of his estimate of all chemical warfare casualties shown in Table 10.1. But three-fifths of his total are accounted for by Russian dead and, as with their injured, it is impossible to tell, on the information currently available, whether this is anywhere near the actual total killed. It is more meaningful to confine oneself to the four major belligerents on the Western Front. Prentiss shows that 26.6 thousand died, corresponding to 4.1 per cent of his total. The numbers, as well as the percentage, are overstated, and the estimates given in Table 10.2 are considered to be more reliable.

Table 10.2. *Estimated Deaths from Chemical Warfare, 1915–1918**

Country	1915–17	1918	Total	Deaths as % of all gas casualties †		Prentiss's estimates‡
	'000s	'000s	'000s	1915–17	1918	'000s
UK (BEF)	3.2§	2.7	5.9	4.3	2.4	8.1¶
France	3.5‖	2.8	6.3	17.5	2.5	8.0
Germany	1.9**	2.1	4.0	5.0	3.0	9.0
USA	—	1.5	1.5	—	2.1	1.5
Total	8.6	9.1	17.7	6.6	2.5	26.6

* Non-combatants are excluded. Figures for German deaths refer to the Western Front only.

† The proportions were derived from the numbers in Table 10.1.

‡ *Chemicals in War*, pp. 653–4.

§ Mitchell and Smith, *Casualties and Medical Statistics*, p. 111. The figure for April–May 1915 is incomplete.

¶ Including Dominion troops killed by gas in 1915.

‖ Assuming 1,000 killed by gas on 22 April 1915.

** Including a small number (particulars are not available) killed by blow-back and Russian chemical warfare on the Eastern Front.

For sources see references in text.

The statistics indicate that the earlier phase of chemical warfare was the more deadly, and that though the total casualty figure in 1918 was nearly three times that of 1915–17, the fatalities were relatively lower. Nor is this surprising, for mustard gas dominated and its killing-power was reduced by improving protection and more effective treatment of the casualties. The British investigated the causes of gas fatalities with great care and paid particular attention to the deaths caused by German cloud-gas operations. They studied nine of these events from April 1915 to August 1916 and found that 7,296 men were injured by gas of whom 1,266 (17.4 per cent) died. Of those who died, 485 (almost two-fifths of the fatalities) were killed in the trenches before help could reach them or they could be taken for treatment.[16] The Germans abandoned the use of chlorine-phosgene gas clouds against the BEF when the SBR was introduced and employed more gas shells in 1917. Casualties rose steeply but mustard-gas injuries had a comparatively low mortality rate which varied with the weather and the degree of exposure. Thus it averaged 3.2 per cent from July to December 1917, fell to 1.3 per cent in the three months to March 1918 and rose again to 3 per cent in June–July only to fall once more to 2 per cent in August–September. Thus, though very large numbers of men were gassed, all were evacuated, and the slow development of mustard-gas burns and their secondary effects, meant that everyone was treated at a CCS or a special hospital and that every death was recorded.[17] The French, being less well protected and having medical services inferior to the British suffered more fatalities. They were, however, exposed to fewer German cloud-gas operations and, up to the beginning of 1918, to less shelling from mustard gas. There is information of sorts for 1918 which I have used in the table; it takes account of the heavy French casualties of April–June of that year.[18] Prentiss cast doubt on the German army's losses from gas, but they suffered very few fatalities in 1915–16 since the Allied chemical warfare effort was small and the German masks provided good protection. In 1917 the situation deteriorated sharply and there was only a small improvement in 1918. Geyer reported that in the last year of the war 3 per cent of the German gas casualties died, and the proportion, though higher than in the BEF and the French army, seems plausible to me bearing in mind the increasing debility of the troops.[19] There is some dispute about the American deaths; the bulk of them were attributed to the secondary effects of mustard gas.[20]

Some attempts were made to identify the branches of the army most exposed to injury by poison gas. Not surprisingly, most of the victims were to be found in the infantry. But as long as gas cylinders were employed, the men in the Special Companies faced additional hazards which other troops were spared. At Loos in September 1915, the British gas troops lost 14 per cent of their pre-battle strength. The French Compagnies Z had initially even higher losses, and the first two battalions of 1st US Gas Regiment lost 575 men, 36 of them killed, from gas and from other causes.[21] Although Foulkes and other chemical warfare specialists belittled the attrition rate among their men, it was sufficiently high to set limits to their recruitment.

The discussion and analysis of the available casualty returns has a wider purpose than the identification of wrong numbers and their replacement by more reliable statistics. Set against the millions killed and wounded on the Western Front, the casualties of chemical warfare were insignificant. But if we must not belittle the effect of gas, neither should we exaggerate it. Yet, throughout the war, depending on the needs of the moment, numbers or in their absence, incidents, were inflated or suppressed to increase or decrease the impact of the story. The novelty of the weapon, the secretiveness of the chemists, and the inexperience of the troops provided ideal conditions for the growth of legends, for claims and counter-claims, and for assertions that went unchallenged.

The Germans having started it, were in a dilemma. They had gained some ground at negligible cost to themselves on 22 April 1915, but had forfeited a valuable propaganda advantage because the Allies immediately accused them of introducing a 'horror' weapon, whilst wasting no time in preparing for retaliation. Leaving aside moral issues, what claims could be made for the usefulness of gas and could such claims be substantiated by numbers? The Germans decided to play down the casualties. Haber was questioned on this very point and answered that he had been over the ground an hour after the cloud had passed on 22 April 1915 and 'saw there a limited number of men killed by gas, not many'.[22] Neither he nor other Germans were more specific during or after the war. On the British side ignorance of the facts was no obstacle to sweeping claims: 'thousands of those in the support trenches and reserve lines and in billets . . . were suffocated—many to die later' wrote Auld before the war was over and Thuillier, some twenty years later, asserted that the death rate on that April afternoon was 'about 35 per cent of all casualties including those from shell and rifle fire as well as gas'. Two medical opinions, both French, may also be noted. Dr Sieur wrote to GQG that most of the men at the front were killed and that thirty-six hours after the cloud the French counted 625 gas cases of whom three died, and another doctor later told Mordacq that he had been taken to a German POW compound on 22 April where he had found about 800 men who were coughing 'something awful' and some of whom were very ill.[23] While it was in the German interest to belittle the consequences of chemical warfare, it was to the Allied advantage to inflate them. The outcome was unexpected. The Germans minimized the effect, with the result that when their gas casualties mounted during 1917 and rose further after mid-1918, their demoralization became worse. On the Allied side exaggeration helped to promote retaliation which led to empire-building by the commanders of the gas troops. But exaggeration also imprinted the fear of poison gas on the public imagination to an extent which few had anticipated; after 1918, Foulkes and others were to face a growing anti-gas lobby.

It was common practice to buttress one's case with the reports of front-line observers. Their 'facts' were often no more than wishful thinking, so whenever possible, the reports were compared with statements made by prisoners. Here is a typical example from a sensitive sector at the extreme right of the British 3rd Army: on 13 March 1918 Livens drums were fired into the German lines south-west of Quéant, and the observer reported that 'streams of ambulances were seen all day long leaving this sector'. A German POW later stated that forty men had been killed and a hundred injured by gas. But the battle diary of the 14 BIR, which faced the projector emplacement, recorded two men dead and forty-five men injured by gas on that day.[24] The observer had inflated and the prisoner had embellished, perhaps to gain goodwill. Enemy soldiers, though on the spot, were no better placed for observation than Allied specialists with their binoculars, and when they told their captors of companies or battalions withdrawing as the result of a gas attack they were, as likely as not, guessing. But such statements were taken at face-value by chemical advisers and intelligence officers and I have never seen any allowance being made for under-manning which was widespread on the Western Front in 1918. Thus a report of a battalion being 'wiped out by gas' was interpreted as 1,000–1,100 men *hors de combat*, whereas the actual 'trench strength' was probably nearer 600.[25]

In the early months of chemical warfare, the intensity of the fighting confused friend and foe alike. But by 1917 intelligence and casualty statistics had become sufficiently routined to enable us to match the claims of one side with the records of the other. Hartley made every effort to estimate the effect of gas at the battle of Arras (April 1917) because this was the first large-scale use of Livens's projectors, but obtained no coherent picture from the disjointed reports.[26] Conversely the Germans had no reliable information on the damage done by their mustard-gas shells in July 1917, or for that matter of earlier gas operations.

Heber wrote a long report some twenty years later which shows that he invariably recorded high Russian losses, but ignored those of the German gas troops which were often considerable. Of a gas-cloud operation against the British at Ypres on 19 December 1915 he wrote that 'agents' reported the deaths of 5,000 men from that attack. But Douglas investigated its effects and on going through the medical cards of the CCSs found that 1,069 men had been gassed of whom 116 died; he estimated that altogether 25,000 troops were in the area touched by gas.[27] Matters were no better eighteen months later when the Germans introduced mustard-gas shells, but remained ignorant of their effect for several weeks.[28]

The obsession with cause and effect became ludicrous. Gas projectiles were used by both sides in 1917–18 and became the chief weapon of the specialist companies on the Western Front. Hence their assertions of success served to underpin their demands for reinforcements, additional supplies, and recognition of their contribution to the war effort. It is not possible to verify the German claims because the records of the Gaspioniere were lost or destroyed at the end of the Second World War. But the claims made by Foulkes on behalf of the Special Brigade can, to a small extent, be compared with the war diaries of Bavarian regiments. Where this is possible, that is reports and records can be matched, the former are invariably higher than the latter.[29] The chemical warfare experts also concerned themselves with the effectiveness of gas shells. The British, at the request of Hartley and other chemical advisers, began to estimate the number of enemy shells, their contents, and the casualties they caused. The object was to correlate the intensity and duration of bombardment with the number of killed and injured by gas. Much time was spent on this useless exercise for the shells came over at night, whilst the gassed had to be counted the next day when many were at some distance from the explosion on their way to treatment.

What emerges? Reams of statements and claims which do not stand up to examination. But, as far as the Germans are concerned, there is no doubt that they deliberately played down the effect of Allied gas warfare. Haber told Hartley that they had had 'serious' gas casualties from only four causes—the battle of Loos, phosgene shells at Verdun in 1916, Livens drums in 1917–18, and French mustard gas shells in the summer and autumn of 1918. Haber exaggerated the first two, and was right about the other two, though phosgene and chloropicrin shells were also used extensively in the final year of the war.[30] Haber did not have the detailed German statistics at the time. When they were published in the 1930s they minimized the casualties inflicted by Allied cloud gas which were recorded as 4,926, including 448 killed. The figure is hard to believe, for among them are the German victims of blow-back—about 1,700 of whom 425 died.[31] The result of this manipulation was to give the impression that the vast majority of German chemical warfare casualties—over 90 per cent—were due to Livens projectiles and to gas shells. That is possible, but the way the German data are presented creates doubts about their veracity and strengthens the case for raising the published total.

On the British side, things were no different; how could they be when the cylinders and Livens projectors used by the Special Brigade were so inaccurate that they might strike a target of which the reporting prisoner, agent, or own observer was ignorant? Foulkes admitted this in his report to the War Office: 'no information has yet been obtained regarding half of these attacks' he wrote, and the only complete account of a gas attack 'ever received' was from a deserter who had been at Nieuport during the gas cloud operation on 6 October 1916; he concluded 'at present nothing but a rough estimate can be formed from the many scraps of intelligence that have been collected as well as from a comparison of our own losses.'[32] Here too there was a credibility gap. But the Special Brigade was not dissolved, it was merely bypassed and diverted to engineering duties whilst the pursuit of chemical warfare became, as in Germany, largely a matter for the artillery. But unlike the German army, the BEF improved its defences against gas and paradoxically the effectiveness of the SBR and of anti-gas training weakened the appeal of gas as an offensive weapon. This was also the attitute of the French, but it was not shared by the AEF, where the relatively high casualty rate from German mustard gas appeared to strengthen the CWS claim to offer a viable alternative to high explosive. These matters will occupy our attention in later chapters.

Chemical warfare also killed and wounded civilians, but despite the large numbers involved, they have been ignored by later historians. French and British records, though incomplete, suggest that more than four thousand farmers, townspeople, and factory-workers were injured and more than eighty died. The figures in Table 10.3 understate the position because I have not listed those incidents in which fewer than twenty people were gassed, nor have I been able to find any information on German civilian casualties and on French and Belgian civilians injured by British chemical weapons. Expressed differently, the total is certain to be considerably higher than the 5,200 listed in Table 10.3; the figure includes over a hundred known deaths.[33]

The belligerents avoided deliberate gas attacks on civilians. The French planned all their gas-cloud operations so that populous sectors behind the German lines were not involved; the Special Brigade took no such precautions. The Germans claimed that they had urged civilians to leave exposed areas, but that the French had opposed voluntary, let alone forced, evacuation.[34] That did not stop them from discharging cylinders or firing gas shells even when they knew that non-combatants were still living or working in an area. In general the careless indifference shown to civilians in the first 2 to 2½ years of chemical warfare does little credit to the military and the local authorities in northern France and the Belgian border villages. When, for example, the Germans opened their cylinders at Wulverghem in April 1916, farmers were working the land some 4 km away, and though the British had issued them with 'PH' helmets about twenty were gassed on that occasion. Just to the south, several thousand were still living in the western outskirts of Armentières. Although they knew

Table 10.3. *Known Civilian Casualties from Poison Gas in Britain, Belgium, France, and USA, 1916–1918*

Location	Date	Number
1. Towns and villages near Front:		
Armentières	July 1917	675*
Avelgem (on the Scheldt, SE of Kortrijk)	27–8 October 1918	>350
Annequin	April 1918	230†
Less (Belgium)	November 1918	50‡
Wulverghem	April 1916	*c.* 20
2. Factories and filling plants§		
Avonmouth (nr. Bristol)	15 June–15 December 1918 §	1,400
Chittening (nr. Bristol)	21 June–7 December 1918	1,213
Edgewood (nr. Baltimore)	June–December 1918	925
Vincennes (nr. Paris)	April–May 1918	300
Pont-de-Claix (nr. Grenoble)	August, 1918	33

* Including 86 killed.
† Including 19 killed.
‡ Including 6 killed.
§ The figures may include service personnel, but particulars are not available.

For sources see references in text.

about German gas, they were not prepared for the heavy mustard-gas bombardment in the night of 20–1 July 1917 and again eight days later. They went to the shelters, but upon returning touched brickwork and household objects and so came into contact with the liquid: 675 were injured and 86 of them died. It is not known whether these particularly serious incidents caused the French to appoint Dr Mazel to take charge of all civilian anti-gas precautions in the BEF zone. At any rate the mayors and the managers of the numerous coal mines were made responsible for the issue of M2 masks, the provision of one gas-proof room in every house, and for ensuring that everyone within 8 km of the front carried a respirator at all times. The British accepted responsibility for gas warnings. Since the mines in the Béthune area were still being worked and the country to the north-west of Lens was densely populated, the precautions were sensible and overdue. As a result many thousands of people became involved in gas alerts and gas defence. In 1918, chemical warfare became even more intense, but the civilians were better prepared. When the Germans bombarded Annequin and the mining villages between Hulluch and Béthune during April 1918, the local population in the area exposed to mustard-gas shells was estimated at over 4,000. Fortunately only 230 were gassed of whom 19 died.[35] These incidents went unpublicized at the time, the more so as the question of French civilians in the battle area created many difficulties. Moreover, as the Germans had involved the people of northern France in chemical warfare, they might do the same in south-east England using gas-filled bombs instead of shells. The effect on civilian morale was unpredictable and the Home Office decided to ignore poison gas in the revised leaflet on Air Raid Precautions issued on 1 October 1917, though it warned the public not to breathe 'the fumes' given off by bombs or buy respirators unless they had a War Office guarantee.[36]

Safety and health became important and urgent concerns only when the manufacture of poison gas began to assume large dimensions and hence a significant role in the industrial war effort. Throughout 1915–16 gas production was small business in Britain as elsewhere. Chlorine, however, though dangerous to prepare and use, was covered by the Factory Acts in England and by corresponding regulations in Germany. Practice and precautions minimized the danger. But the manufacture of derivatives was not regulated, and until well into 1917 mustard gas was not made outside laboratories. Although accidents were frequent in the early days of chemical warfare supplies, the consequences were trivial. Then, and later, everything depended on the care exercised by workers and foremen and—even more importantly—on the extent to which the employer provided good ventilation equipment, washing facilities, and first-aid stores. The Castner–Kellner Alkali Co., the largest supplier of liquid chlorine to the Allies, reported little trouble. The UAC had a contract to make phosgene at Gateshead. There the position was different because the effects of phosgene poisoning were not then on the list of 'scheduled' industrial diseases, so claims for injury were not covered by insurance, but negotiated between the manufacturers and the MoM. Under the circumstances, UAC sensibly introduced some precautionary measures: it provided 'PH' helmets for the workmen (who were handicapped by the poor visibility), paid for a works doctor at Gateshead, and even kept oxygen cylinders. All would have been of some help in the event of phosgene poisoning, but the poor quality of the material and the small output were the more important factors in accident prevention. The same reasons, with the addition of a great deal of luck, explain why Ellison's chloropicrin works reported no serious illness until mid-1916; when the returns for 1917 and 1918 became available, they showed seven fatal accidents in each year. De Laire's works at Paris and Calais, probably the largest until the government plants started in 1917, presented another picture: their ventilation and refrigeration equipment was carelessly supervised with the result that five men died of phosgene poisoning in Paris in January 1916 and conditions at Calais were disgraceful before the British took over. Even so, there were problems—two British workers were killed in Spring 1916 and eight others had to be hospitalized. The Special Brigade then assumed control, the strictest discipline was imposed, and though the men complained of ill-health, there were no further serious accidents.[37]

Filling gas into cylinders and shells was even more dangerous than making it. There were many accidents at Gateshead until UAC began filling phosgene into cylinders in specially designed vacuum cabinets. After use in France the cylinders were returned empty, or almost so, to Stoke-on-Trent where they were cleaned, repaired, and sent to the filling plants and thence back to France. A simple routine, one would have thought, but in the twelve months to October 1917, 459 minor accidents were recorded.[38] The Germans, great though their skills were at manufacture, also had their troubles. At Hoechst, where diphosgene was produced, there were many accidents and nine deaths during the war. Hahn spent some time at Leverkusen, a model chemical works, and wrote later that there were minor accidents in the phosgene section.[39]

Mustard-gas production was complicated and on a large scale. The Germans never had any trouble with their process,[40] but the Allies recorded thousands of accidents—many of them equivalent in their effects to serious gas injury in the field. They used Guthrie's method, which was dangerous and if employed on a factory scale called for the tiled construction and plumbing fixtures of a municipal wash-house, the ventilation system of an up-to-date coal mine, and the nursing facilities of a CCS in a quiet sector of the front. The French, and a few months later the British at Avonmouth, ignored all warnings and pressed on regardless: reaction vessels and pipe work were housed in brick buildings or sheds, wood was used everywhere, and the washing and sanitary facilities were primitive. There were frequent accidents caused by spillage and leaking joints, and the open mixing vessels gave off fumes which the fans could not extract quickly enough. Pressure jets failed to remove all toxic residues, and among the specially dangerous jobs were cleaning blocked pipes, repairing leaking pumps, and charging drums for dispatch to the shell-filling plants. Whatever was touched inflamed, whatever was breathed irritated. If the manufacture of mustard gas was hazardous in Britain, France, and the USA, filling the stuff into shells was dangerous everywhere. The German chemical companies refused to handle this business. Their attitude delayed the entire programme and led to the construction of the government filling works at Adlershof and Breloh. They employed women and soldiers declared unfit for active service; there were many accidents and injuries, and some deaths. The military left the job to Haber and his staff, and closed their eyes to the sickness reports. The French, having roughly adapted some sheds at Vincennes, began filling shells with mustard gas in April 1918, and complained afterwards that 300 men had been injured in a few weeks. The situation was no better at Lyons or Pont-de-Claix though both filling plants had been purpose-built. In England a section of the Chittening works had initially filled chloropicrin, but in June 1918 it was converted to mustard-gas filling: it was a disaster. At first one man reported sick for every nine shells filled! So, some improvements were introduced and, in particular, the working hours cut; nevertheless, between 21 June and 7 December 1918, 1,213 casualties were recorded, the weekly rate occasionally reaching 100 per cent of the labour force. The Banbury filling plant, designed with greater care and equipped with better machinery, opened later and had fewer accidents. Avonmouth and Chittening between them (there are no figures for Banbury) reported altogether 2,600 gas cases. The Americans combined production and filling at Edgewood where they had 925 casualties, including three dead, in the seven months' operation of 1918. Of these, 73 were attributed to mustard gas.[41]

Only haste in getting mustard gas out of the laboratory and into shells can explain the disgraceful statistics. As far back as July 1916, the Trench Warfare Supply Department appointed Dr F. Shufflebotham, a specialist in industrial diseases, to be their adviser; he also became medical superintendent of all British gas factories and shell-filling plants, to which medical officers were appointed the following April. They kept records and treated people, but were unable to obtain higher priorities for electrical fans, leak-proof joints, and corrosion-resistant pumps. They discovered the condition known as chronic mustard-gas poisoning; French workers also suffered from it, but it was unknown at the front. The symptoms in the usual mild form of the disease were listlessness, 'nervous debility' (nowadays identified as depression), headaches, indigestion, spasms of the eyelids, breathlessness, and inability to do a full day's work. It was found, not surprisingly, that leave was a good tonic and that shorter hours improved productivity. At Pont-de-Claix they sent the men into the nearby mountains and at Chittening a week's holiday after twenty days' work cut down absenteeism. The best remedies turned out to be the simplest—improved washing facilities, decent lavatories, free overalls, and, above all, job rotation.[42]

These improvements came too late to make any difference to the production schedules for the autumn, but they would have raised output in winter and the

Fig. 17. French civilians with gas masks, Marlache (St Mihiel sector), September 1918. The little girl on the right holds an M2 mask, the children in front have some kind of pad (perhaps Tambuté's) and separate eye-pieces. The young woman at the back is holding what looks like a German respirator container and a German mask. (US Signal Corps photograph, Imperial War Museum)

following spring had manufacture continued into 1919. Nevertheless some lessons had been learnt and were applied to the British arsenicals programme which envisaged the production of diphenylchloroarsine (DA) and the corresponding amine compound (DM) in the form of a very fine powder. The dangers of arsenic build-up in the body were recognized from the outset and job rotation as well as two weeks off for six weeks on were adopted from the start. Even so, the women filling DM into canisters, although working behind glass screens and using long gloves, developed blisters on arms, chest, and neck: the Morecambe factory reported 29 slight cases between August and the end of November 1918, and a faulty batch at the end of the period incapacitated several people who were transferring it to the filling chambers. The Germans had been making arsenicals for over a year, but continued to have health and safety problems with ethyldichloroarsine and the intermediate arsenious oxide. British investigators were unable to obtain particulars after the war, but it is likely that faulty equipment and the elaborate shell-filling procedures (see above, p. 189) were to blame.[43]

The treatment of civilians was in no way different from that adopted in the military hospitals of the belligerents, but as the specialists in respiratory diseases were working in France, the medical aspects of gas poisoning were best studied there.[44] The characteristics of chemical warfare on the Western Front from July 1917 onwards were the intensive mustard-gas bombardments, the large number of casualties they caused, and the elaborate methods adopted to treat the sick. Up to that date, phosgene, diphosgene, or chloropicrin had been the usual chemical shell-fillings and the first two, if sufficiently concentrated, killed. But at Ypres on the night of 12–13 July 1917, the German mustard-gas shells injured 15,000 men of whom 2–3 per cent died during the next fortnight. The numbers involved were unprecedented, as was the relatively low proportion of deaths. It was a foretaste of what was to happen on a larger scale in spring 1918. The important questions were how to deal with the enormous number of injured and how to treat their peculiar injuries.

By that time the medical services on the Western Front were highly organized and the evacuation of the wounded was an important link in an elaborate chain. Stretcher-bearers or walking parties went first to the Regimental Aid Posts at the Front, thence to Dressing Stations or Field Ambulances (FA) a little to the rear, and then to the CCS further back which had surgical facilities as well as oxygen cylinders. The CCS was beyond the reach of field and medium artillery, but it was a busy, restless place, equipped for urgent operations, for recording, classification, and oxygen treatment, but not designed for a long stay or recuperation. Hospitals yet further back or at base were better suited for gas cases. An important consideration with mustard gas was the careful observation of the symptoms as they developed and a reliable diagnosis of the extent of the exposure: the liquid quickly affected the eyes, but the inflammation of the skin took several hours to become painful and the men could walk, if guided, unlike those affected by phosgene who were told to avoid all exertion and await the stretcher-bearers. If the liquid touched the eye, a droplet was enough to produce conjunctivitis; it usually cleared, if mild, in less than a week. But apart from conjunctivitis, how extensive were the burns, how great the risk of bronchitis or inflammation of the lungs? It was generally impossible to make a prognosis within twelve to twenty-four hours of exposure—enough time for the men to get from the FA on foot or lorry to the CCS. At that stage the extent of the injured was 'not yet diagnosed' (abbreviated to NYD Gas), nor classified. The British practice was to get all gas cases to the CCS as quickly as possible because from October 1917 onwards there were physicians in attendance, ample supplies of hot water, clean clothes, and oxygen. On arrival, the men were carefully washed, classified, and medicated. But if the mustard burns were extensive, the CCS staff would not be able to cope, especially during a battle when the operating theatres had overriding priority. The British therefore tried to get the men moved as soon as practicable to so-called gas or recuperation centres at base where they could be treated more conveniently. Transfer of the convalescents to the UK exacerbated manpower wastage and was unusual for gas cases in 1918.[45] The French, until March or April 1918, tended to underrate the danger from mustard-gas injury, but the battle of the Lys and the operations around Mt Kemmel, where they had many gas cases, caused a change of mind. They reorganized their medical services and by August each corps had (or was supposed to have) two or three 'disinfectant points', that is, large wash-rooms complete with showers as well as *Ambulances* Z, each with 200–500 beds, oxygen equipment, and hastily trained medical aides. These arrangements were intended for the majority of the mustard-gas cases who would be treated there and also get some rest, before returning to the front within ten days or a fortnight. The minority suffering from extensive blistering or, more likely, inflammation of the throat and lungs went by rail or motor transport to specially built or converted hospitals in or near Paris where specialists were available for consultation. Thence, when able to travel, the injured were sent to convalescence centres.[46] The Germans initially made no special arrangements for gas cases, indeed to have done so in 1916 or 1917 would have been to admit that their respirators were not good enough and that the Allies had caught up with them. The picture changed in 1918 and they too introduced special centres for gas cases and convalescent homes or granted leave in Germany. One of the greatest problems, which could not be solved in the final months of the war, was the shortage of spare clothing and of dressings—paper was an unsatisfactory ersatz for cotton. The Americans who suffered comparatively more gas casualties than the other belligerents hesitated for a time and in the end also opted for a system of separate gas hospitals for treatment as well as for convalescence. These elaborately planned facilities come too late to play a significant role and the mobile bathing–decontamination stations were not introduced until the closing weeks of the war.[47]

The provision of separate facilities for gas cases at a time of acute manpower and material scarcities underlines the importance of chemical warfare injury at this late stage of the conflict. Expert medical opinion held that segregating the wounded from the gassed avoided unnecessary distress, but it is more likely that the post-operative care of shell cases differed entirely from the sickness-type nursing required by gas cases. I have described in Chapters 4 and 5 the treatment adopted in 1915–16 to deal with those gassed by chlorine, phosgene, or chloropicrin. In 1917–18, however these lung irritants had become less significant and therapy, without differing fundamentally from the principles adopted in the first months of chemical warfare, had been refined: absolute rest, warmth, a light diet, and plenty of fluid were the invariable rule everywhere. Venesection, common in 1915, had gone out of fashion in 1918, but intravenous saline drips were used occasionally to good effect, and so were digitalin or camphor injections to stimulate heart action. Oxygen treatment for several hours a day and repeated for several days was always employed in serious cases. With differences of degree this was the state of the art among the belligerents: those who survived were out of danger after about two weeks and took another two to five weeks to recover.[48] But the typical gas case of 1918 was not injured by lung irritants: depending on the extent of exposure, he suffered from mustard-gas injuries corresponding to first- or second-degree burns in civilian life, frequently accompanied by severe inflammation of the throat and (less often) of the lungs.

Conjunctivitis, painful and briefly frightening, was, by far, the commonest injury caused by mustard gas—86 per cent of the USA gas casualties experienced it—but also the least dangerous. It yielded after three or four days to boracic washes or colloidal silver in aqueous solution and disappeared entirely in ten days to a fortnight. Conjunctivitis by itself rarely led to complications but was a good indicator of the severity of the other injuries. One might say that the worse the state of the eyes, the worse would be the blisters and the inflammation of the mucous membranes. Early and accurate diagnosis of the extent of exposure, careful handling at the blistering stage, and good nursing throughout determined the course of the illness. At first the patient would look as if he was suffering from scarlet fever, then the rash turned into blisters which took up to four weeks to break. If the blisters became infected, which was common, the patient might take another five to six weeks to recover. This stage of the treatment called for careful nursing and frequent changes of dressings. Skin creams based on animal fats, much favoured by the French, were to be avoided because dichlorodiethyl sulphide is soluble in them and so the irritation would spread. Zinc oxide cream, hydrogen peroxide compresses, talcum powder, vaseline—magnesium carbonate ointment and such-like remedies were of some use, but the best treatment consisted of keeping the blisters aseptic, covering them lightly, and avoiding friction. These were counsels of perfection for the most tender parts of the body such as buttocks, genitals, armpits, and ears were often inflamed by contact with mustard gas. As the patient usually could not renew dressings or compresses himself, mustard-gas burns called for simple but meticulous care and when it was lacking, recovery took that much longer.[49] The inflammation of the throat presented the greatest potential danger and was usually followed by bronchitis which, in those days, called for frequent balsam inhalations. If the weather was mild and dry and the staff competent, the burns and the throat would clear in anything from four to six weeks, a little longer in difficult cases. But if bronchitis developed into pneumonia or worse, the patient was at risk and death from mustard gas, which ranged from 1 to 3 per cent of the cases, was due invariably to pulmonary complications. Douglas, a careful observer of mustard-gas injury from July 1917 onwards, was of the opinion that a very large proportion of the cases could be 'fit for duty in four to six weeks', which included one week in a convalescent depot and two to three weeks' light drill and 'recuperation' in a rest camp. This timetable applied to those whose exposure had been mild—perhaps some blisters and slight throat inflammation. The German experience was similar, and their survey mentions ten to twenty days for the lightly gassed, but those with bronchial infections or pulmonary complications required at least four weeks and more often eight before they were fit for light duties. The death-rate in a sample of 3,000 German mustard-gas cases was 3 per cent: all of them had had extensive blisters and pneumonia or pleurisy. It should be added that the poor physical condition of the German soldiers, bad food, and non-absorbent dressings aggravated the consequences of mustard-gas injury.[50]

Prolonged hospitalization and nursing were characteristic features of this form of poisoning and were often accompanied by a period of physical and mental exhaustion leading to depression. All the belligerents were aware of the link between injury, treatment, recovery, and morale, and in 1918 the interconnected problems were at their most acute. Hence the particular anxiety caused by the German Blue Cross shells with their arsenical fillings. Whilst the German method of dispersing the active agent by high explosive fragmentation ensured that it would have little toxic effect, there were occasions when particulates capable of penetrating the SBR were produced. The most remarkable consequences were then observed. Excruciating pains in nose, sinuses, mouth, and throat, and nausea were accompanied by 'intense mental distress . . . utter dejection and hopeless misery [which have] no counterpart in any other type of gas poisoning.' On war-weary men the effect could be devastating and turn them into useless troops. The symptoms disappeared within a few hours in uncontaminated air; the most serious cases were taken to a Divisional Rest Station and allowed a good night's sleep.[51] Blue Cross shells were a potential danger, and the Allied experts were concerned that the Germans might introduce arsenical smoke generators: soldiers would thereby be rendered so debilitated that they couldn't fight any more. At the very outset of chemical warfare, tear gas and incapacitating agents had been ridiculed. Now, in a more sophisticated form, novel compounds threatened morale and the will to fight.

Mustard gas transformed the medical picture. The large number of affected troops and the character of their sickness made heavy demands on scarce resources at the front—water, clothing, clean gauze, and hundreds of helpers and so created unexpected difficulties. Everyone considered it the dominant element of chemical warfare and the Germans were well aware of the danger it posed for them in 1919. The Allies were better equipped to deal with the consequences of mustard gas, but in the closing weeks of the war they were more concerned with the threat of arsenical smoke to their spring offensive. When the war ended, the image of chemical warfare in the future appeared even more alarming than the reality of mustard gas during 1918.

After the Armistice the gas warfare effort was quickly run down, yet the injuries continued: the troops cleaning away debris were contaminated by mustard gas, German soldiers destroying stockpiles at Breloh were poisoned from time to time, and the girls filling DM canisters at Morecambe reported sick with skin rashes. But the chemical war was over, or almost so for it was resumed, albeit briefly, in northern Russia in 1919. There were later, one-sided episodes in China and Abyssinia during the 1930s. These events, though not insignificant, do not add to our knowledge of First World War experience and statistics, nor do they help in reaching a conclusion on the role of poison gas in that war. Yet, when it was over, thousands were still being treated for gas injuries and would require medical attention for years, while thousands more, though apparently cured, would be marked for life.

Men who had lost limbs or their faculties were easy enough to identify, to compensate, and to sympathize with, but those hurt by gas presented unusual problems, for even when their symptoms were precisely classified, to what extent were they due to poison gas or to other factors? It was found that following the Armistice the strain relaxed, and as the tension eased so sickness became pronounced: the influenza pandemic hospitalized scores of thousands and, quite independently, extreme fatigue emerged as a major, if short-lived post-war development, called by the British 'neurasthenic disablement'. These illnesses often displayed the same symptoms which characterized those who had been gassed, treated, and returned to duty, or—in more serious cases—discharged as unfit. They easily fell victim to bronchitis, tended to asthma, and were often off work with throat or lung infections. Their 'wind was gone' and their hearts were 'irritable' as Macpherson was to describe it later, and the diagnosis DAH for disordered action of the heart was widely used as a catch-all for an undefined and unsatisfactory condition. Douglas, who had examined hundreds of gassed, wrote to Hartley after the war that few of those who survived gas 'exhibit in the end serious, morbid lesions'; some, however, continued to suffer from 'indefinite symptoms' of which he remarked: 'I fancy there is a good deal of the neurasthenic element in many of these DAH cases.'[52] It was realized quite early that some of the sick had had a history of chest diseases and should not have been called up, or if called up, not exposed to gas. But by 1919 that was water under the bridge, and in any case the immediate difficulty was caused by the demobilized soldier's work or environment. A severe gas injury left a man less able to cope with a tiring job in a dusty or humid atmosphere: the damp, cheerless, smoky winters of industrial England, northern France, or the Ruhr soon render-ed the ex-soldiers, many of them cigarette-smokers, unfit. Bronchitis was then a common illness, often associated with pulmonary infections, and it strained the heart muscle. There was also the danger that, as with tuberculosis, heavy, deep coughing would reopen scar tissue and lead to bleeding. Mustard gas had sequelae which were not perceived at the time, for conjunctivitis in 1918 some-times caused loss of vision forty or fifty years later and blindness in old age.[53]

The numbers involved are not precisely known. In Britain the Ministry of Pensions took over the records in April 1919, and its staff controlled hospital beds, rehabilitation centres, and the immense task of adminstering benefits—initially to more than 1½ million ex-soldiers. Medical Boards assessed the condition, made awards, renewed or altered them, and heard appeals. The British system, with considerable modifications and rather less generosity, was used elsewhere: it provided for two classes of pensioners—the stabilized cases, whose condition was unlikely to change either way, and the unstabilized whose disability was periodically reviewed. By 31 March 1929 there were still about 737,000 men drawing disability pensions arising out of the 1914–18 war of whom 427,000 received compensation for diseases, as distinct from wounds or amputations, among them tuberculosis, heart, respiratory system, and various neuroses, as well as 7,700 gas cases, the number being roughly equivalent to those certified insane as a result of the war! Before we rejoice too much at the apparently innocuous after-effects of gas poisoning, it is as well to remember that the unstabilized gas cases received variable awards, which were never large and subject to cuts by economy-minded Review Boards. There had been 19,000 of these cases in 1920, but death, weeding out, and reclassifications shrank them to 9,250 in mid 1922 and to 700 seven years later, of whom fewer than 100 received awards of greater than 50 per cent disability.[54]

Little purpose would be served by further examination of the numbers or extending the analysis to the other combatants.[55] What needs to be borne in mind is that even in 1918 chemical warfare was relatively unimportant. Of those gassed in all armies, the majority recovered sufficiently to lead a normal life. That is what one would expect from healthy people in their twenties and thirties. But the medical and pension services had not been designed to deal with those who, as a result of war service, found themselves not ill, but frequently unwell and subject to throat and chest diseases. It is possible that these men, in their maturity, would attribute their condition to the consequences of a gas attack ten or fifteen years earlier. The cause-and-effect connection between exposure to phosgene or mustard gas at 20 and bronchitis at 30-plus might often be tenuous, but it existed. In practice the connection was insufficient to justify an award, and if one was made, the payment was derisory. But it was enough for people to believe that being gassed was the cause of illness years later, and thus the special anxiety created by chemical warfare continued into the peace and was kept alive in the public's consciousness.

11

WAS GAS A FAILURE?

THE answer to this central question is 'Yes'. Why then proceed? Because chemical warfare was such an unusual military, industrial, and administrative phenomenon that a full explanation of its failure is justified. Moreover there were exceptional occasions or particular developments when gas was *not* a failure. And, as the continuing debate testifies, gas was a development of considerable military significance.

I am dealing in this chapter not merely with the conclusions to be drawn from numbers, but with matters of opinion where time has not smoothed over controversies. Several approaches are possible. Mine will be to identify the advantages and disadvantages of chemical warfare without, however, following the 'cost-effective' type of appraisal. That technique was not used in the First World War though Hanslian, Prentiss, and others who wrote from first-hand experience thought in terms of a 'balance sheet' of gains and losses, in which gas was judged 'profitable' or at any rate worthwhile if the gains exceeded the losses. Leaving aside all moral aspects, the writers never spelled out what they meant by gains and what by losses. A moment's reflection is sufficient to show that problems of definition and classification impose obstacles which become insurmountable when the available numbers are closely examined. The figures, such as they are, will not support an elaborate statistical analysis, let alone a profit and loss account. A common unit of measure is essential, but is unavailable: how can one 'value' the expenditure of gas cylinders, projectiles, or shells and the injury or death they inflict on the enemy soldier? Furthermore, all the calculations ignored the significance of defence, although experience during the war showed that the use of gas was invariably followed by counter-measures, with the result that the better the protection against gas, the greater the failure of offensive warfare. Gas weapons as well as repirators changed profoundly between April 1915 and November 1918: the changes were not at a constant rate, but came in variable, though discrete, steps, and were not the same for every belligerent. Thus the sequence of action − reaction had an effect analogous to a game of leap-frog, with the result that at any given moment observers could not tell who gained or lost. These difficulties led some people to adopt another approach: separate incidents were listed, and the particulars were then generalized into comparative judgements of different forms of gas warfare and between chemical and other weapons. There are weighty objections to this way of arguing. In the first place, that which is true of a part is not necessarily true of the whole. Secondly, the reasoning encourages the fallacy that a marginal addition to the deployment of resources leads to a more than proportionate result. Finally, only one side is represented and the role of defence is ignored. Although the compilation of incidents is superficially easy, it is just as misleading as the balance sheet approach. Notwithstanding these objections (and they were made at the time) Sibert and Foulkes employed the method, and Foulkes devoted many pages to innumerable examples. But he was fitting numbers into his preconceived scheme of things, and as an appraisal of a novel military technolgy it was useless.[1] In short there is no point in wasting time on a so-called cost-effective approach or in attempting a comprehensive survey of operations. But I consider it helpful to recapituate the numbers quoted in previous chapters to show the scale of the effort, before turning to the non-quantitative analysis of the successes and failures of gas warfare.

In 1918 the production of the various materials, respirators, shell- and projectile-filling, research and development, and not least the service personnel in the various specialist formations, may have involved a total of the order of 75,000 men and women. In Britain, France, Germany, and Italy the effort reached its peak in the summer of that year, though it continued to rise in the USA until November.[2] The manpower by comparison with, say, ordnance or the numbers of those serving on the Western Front was minuscule. The financial burden was also insignificant: in Britain the MoM spent altogether £6.5 million on poison gases and bleaching powder and £4.0 million on the wages and management fees of the contractors to the Anti-Gas Department. In addition £4.5 million and £2.0 million respectively went on plant, building, and equipment to make gases and respirators. This is not the complete total for chemical warfare because the cost of materials for respirators is excluded. We may nevertheless compare these expenditures with the £9.2 million spent on the large explosives factory at Gretna. The cost of Edgewood, which was not finished at the time of the Armistice, was $35.5 million (say £7 million). German figures were not available to me, but they were lower because the major chemical manufacturers had spare capacity which could be readily adapted to the preparation of war gases.[3]

The salient statistics of production are reproduced in Table 11.1. The large German figures for phosgene and mustard gas will be noted, and the lower Anglo-French output reflects the technical handicaps of the Allies. Germany made nearly 8,000 t of Blue Cross materials, whereas British production had not got beyond the pilot-plant stage. The astronomical figures for pads and respirators are a measure of the comprehensiveness of protective devices and of the introduction of several new and improved designs between 1915 and 1918.[4]

Perhaps the best way of putting chemical warfare into perspective is to look at the last line in Table 11.1. Millions of shells were filled with chemical warfare materials and used extensively in 1917–18. Taking the war years as a whole the proportion of gas shells to total shell supply was only 4 per cent for Britain. But in the last eleven months of the war the figure was 8.4 per cent. In France, the relative importance of gas to total shell supply was somewhat higher, and higher still in Germany. Almost three-fifths of all the German chemical shells were

Table 11.1. Production of the Chief Gases, Respirators, and Gas Shells, 1915–1918

	UK	France	Germany
Toxic materials (t)			
Chlorine (directly and for other gases), liquid	21,156	12,500	87,000*
Phosgene	1,384†	15,700	23,655‡
Chloropicrin	8,093	493	4,065
Mustard gas (including solvent)	522	1,968§	7,659
Tear gas and other irritants	1,819¶	481	3,710
Arsenical compounds (including Blue Cross agents)	98	n.a.	8,027
Hydrogen cyanide	small	4,160‖	—
Gas masks, etc. (millions)			
Helmets and pads	24.8**	40.6	n.a.††
Respirators (SBR, ARS, Germany)	17.5	5.3	12.0
Shells filled with chemical warfare agents (millions)	8.3	17.1	38.6‡‡

* Estimated. The figure includes supplies for purposes other than chemical warfare. 3,500 t of liquid chlorine were used for cylinder operations.

† The figure excludes 6,235 t obtained from France in exchange for chlorine. This amount is included with the French total.

‡‡ Includes 6,000 t of phosgene for diphosgene (of which altogether 12,190 t were made, but not shown in the table to avoid double counting). 4,000 t of phosgene were used for cylinder operations.

§ Includes 1,508 t produced by Usines du Rhône.

¶ Includes ethyl iodacetate (SK), not made in France or Germany.

‖ If the other ingredients of Vincennite, arsenic trichloride, stannic chloride, and chloroform, are included, the volume rises to 7,700 t.

** The figure is the total of 'P', 'PH', and 'PHG' helmets and of official pads.

†† Likely to be small (5 mln) and to consist principally of pads.

‡‡ Excluding about 1 mln shells filled with tear gas and other irritants between December 1914 and April 1915.

For sources see references in text and tables in Chapter 7.

supplied in 1918, and numerically the shells with Blue Cross markings were the most important. In that last year of the war, 28 per cent of all German shells contained chemical warfare agents—a proportion unsurpassed by any other belligerent.[5] Unquestionably 1918 was the chief year for gas warfare, and shells were the chief weapon employed, though the British were still carrying out cloud-gas operations and made frequent surprise attacks with Livens projectiles. The Germans abandoned gas cylinders in 1918 and made only spasmodic use of projectors.

The numbers show that in its requirements for labour and materials gas was not a demanding weapon, much less so than aircraft or tanks. This was a significant advantage, especially as manpower, fuels, and most metals were in short supply in the final year of the war. But the power to cause injury was also limited; at comparatively little cost in resources, the belligerents on the Western Front inflicted on each other about half a million gas casualties of whom under 20,000 died. Nearly three-quarters of those injured and half of those killed were recorded in 1918. That was the year of the most intensive use of gas. But it does not follow that more gas shells were a 'cheap' way, in terms of resources, of hurting the enemy. A statistical analysis of German bombardments and of British casualties in August–October 1918, of which details are given in the Appendix to this chapter, is inconclusive on the principal point at issue: the number of injured and killed was not directly related to the number of gas shells expended.[6] Other variables, which cannot be quantified because there is no numerical information or such information as is available is purely qualitative, also determined the outcome. The principal factors involved were the types of gas used, the proportion of each if the Germans had decided on a *Buntschiessen* pattern, the disposition of the British troops, the duration and intensity of the German bombardment, weather conditions and, not least, the accuracy of the count.

The statistical approach leads to a dead end. One answer to the question 'Was Gas a Failure?' is that, expressed numerically, the advantages and disadvantages of chemical warfare cannot be summed and compared, so that this line of enquiry leads to the conclusion that the case for and against gas is 'not proven'. That, however, still leaves open other approaches. Three are particularly relevant and in examining them we will come closer to the explanation as to why gas was a failure in 1915–18. The first is the belief that the military lacked commitment to this mode of warfare and pursued it haphazardly. The second is that the organization of gas warfare—research, development, manufacture, and application—was amateurish throughout the war. And thirdly that defence against gas was on the whole sufficient to contain the threat posed by this new weapon.

As the controversy over the use and effectiveness of gas began in April 1915 we must, perforce, go back to the beginning. Liddell Hart and Hanslian wrote that OHL had mishandled the introduction of gas: it should not have been wasted on a local operation north of Ypres. Hanslian explained that 22 April had been by way of an experiment, but regretted that the dress rehearsal for chemical warfare should have launched the second battle of Ypres. People on the Allied side asserted that the Germans had missed their chance. If they had released a really large cloud and followed it up 'resolutely', they could have ended the war there and then. OHL 'failed to realise what a powerful weapon they had and so did not apply it effectively.' The quotation is from Sir William Pope; others were of the same mind. But the issue was not so simple, and the implied incompetence of the General Staff has been challenged most recently by Trumpener who consulted the original documents.[7] Falkenhayn wanted a limited operation; the seizure of Pilkem ridge was a bonus on top of the experience which was essential. Large cylinder discharges had two major drawbacks—the need for suitable weather and extremely long pre-parations. Both bedevilled all planning, upset the troops, and also alerted the Allies who usually ignored the warnings. Falkenhayn, influenced by Haber's optimism, took a risk in backing chemical warfare, but had no conception of the likely con-sequences. On 22 April the Germans had beginner's luck against the French, but two days later and again in May the results were mixed, if not disappointing. The operations demonstrated that gas could not be controlled. If all went well, it was a novel and interesting form of attack, but one could not count on that with confi-dence. Bauer and Geyer became more cautious and argued that poison gas in cloud form did not lend itself as a spearhead for a major infantry advance and it followed that cylinder operations would not put an end to trench warfare. Hartley reported that by the fall of the year the Germans 'had lost practically all interest in chemical warfare'.[8] It had become for them an occasional weapon, with which to worry the opponents (especially the ill-protected Russians), to support a raid or to spoil or force the postponement of an enemy attack. Thus, on the German side, interest waned. The Germans also realized quickly that defence played the key role in defeating gas, but were slow to exploit the opponent's weakness in protective equip-ment. The French in particular were careless of the safety of their men, but OHL failed to turn this to advantage, and Geyer neglected the opportunities provided by the terrain to harass the French by repeated exposure to gas clouds. Hartley noted this failure and observed that the Germans did not consider gas 'an important weapon of attrition'; they abandoned the use of cylinder operations against the British after the introduction of the SBR.[9] In this important respect the tolerant and supportive attitude shown by GHQ towards the Special Brigade presents a striking contrast to German lack of imagination: various peculiar powders, liquids, or gases were filled into bombs or hand grenades and flung at the Germans to show that until the BEF could retaliate with poison gas, any 'annoyer' that came to hand would be a foretaste of more dangerous things to come, and come frequently![10] The British approach to poison gas was that of the injured party seeking quick re-dress at all costs. To this, there was a major obstacle. In 1915 and 1916, trench war-fare was interrupted by occasional major battles which called for large troop move-ments and various construction jobs. Accordingly, the manpower requirements built up rapidly several weeks before the attack. If, on top of them, there were added requests for carrying parties to emplace cylinders, something had to give . Cloud gas had been a fiasco at Loos, and GHQ, though sympathetic towards gas before the battle, became a little more restrained in its enthusiasm after it. While continuing to support chlorine, GHQ (like OHL) abandoned it as a breakthrough weapon. However (unlike OHL) the use of intermittent, relatively small, gas dis-charges in quiet sectors, continued to be sanctioned and even approved. The purpose was to inflict casualties, to upset the enemy, to keep his troops, sent there to recuperate from major battles, on the alert and to worry them. This led to many operations with a few hundred cylinders, say 7 to 15 t of gas. It cannot be claimed that they had any effect on the war (or even on the sector held by a particular unit), but they vexed the Germans and caused them some losses.

Both sides clung to their positions the evidence to the contrary notwithstanding: the Germans underrated and the British overrated cloud-gas operations. Such rigidly held views also impeded the most effective employment of a genuinely novel weapon. Livens's projectors which made their first large-scale appearance in April 1917 were a variant of the gas cloud. The latter ceased to be effective against well-protected troops, but the former could be deadly and took less time to set up than cylinder operations. They fulfilled the rule that resources must be concentrated at one point to achieve superiority and were used repeatedly by the British in 1917–18. The projectiles became the instrument of chemical warfare which the German experts considered 'the most dangerous gas weapon in existence and the most severe test of gas discipline', and according to Geyer, forced them to change their dispositions.[11] It is therefore inexplicable that he and Haber were so supine towards the introduction of similar projectors in the German army even after they had contributed to the victory at Caporetto. The German inflexibility is remarkable: could they only consider one chemical weapon at a time? First the cylinder, then the gas shell; projectors with their drums did not fit into either group and so were relegated. Thus OHL neglected the psychological effect which intermittent harassment by gas bombs produces.

The gas cloud and projector operations were not thought through. That was not to be expected at first. Here was a novel weapon, there was no precedent to go upon, so time was needed to make an impression on busy staff officers familiar with traditional arms and reluctant to accept the new and unproven. So gas had to be tried. It was, repeatedly, and the experiments did not fulfil expectations. Gas was too complicated and too dependent on wind and weather. The specialists were also surprised by the role of defence—it progressed more quickly than offence. Thus offence would be blunted unless new and more toxic chemicals could be manufactured or new and better delivery methods introduced. The engineers and their superiors at Headquarters were not quick enough to master these problems, with the result that chemical warfare as practised until 1917 made less of an impact than it might. With hindsight, the potential did not lie in its incorporation in the infantry tactics of the Great War. These tactics were, in any case, being modernized by the introduction of improved versions of customary weapons. In the two to two-and-a-half years after Second Ypres the role of gas was to act as a special psychological weapon to wear down the enemy. Too unreliable to win an action (except in the defiles of the Soča), let alone a battle, it yet had a place which the specialists failed to exploit and the generalists, that is the infantry officers, were not minded to promote. In this restricted field of harassment on a micro-scale, offence, very briefly, was stronger than defence. It could produce temporary and local demoralization, useful enough in trench war, but insufficiently important and too infrequent to engage the sustained attention of those who were in charge of larger schemes.

The introduction of gas shells in combination with HE produced some remarkable results in the last year and a half of the war. The shortage of shell cases having eased during 1917, the artillerists, prodded by innovative staff officers took the lead in looking for new ways of employing gas. The Germans on the Eastern Front and the French on the Chemin des Dames first used a large proportion of gas shells in their bombardments. Initially, the new artillery tactics created no great surprise, except, of course, for the shock caused by the introduction of mustard-gas shells in July 1917. The extension of chemical warfare to the artillery, gradual, but growing in volume, was accepted without the indignation that accompanied the chlorine clouds two years previously. The artillery gradually learnt new techniques, and the Germans had mastered them in time for their spring offensives of 1918. The artillery plans were thorough and the weather favoured them. But, unwisely, they fired millions of arsenical shells without previously testing their efficacy. They had convinced themselves that Blue Cross was a powerful chemical weapon. This mistaken conclusion, once reached, remained unaltered and it helped at this critical juncture to reduce appreciably the threat caused by gas, and so benefited the Allies.[12] Here was another instance of rigidity, not to say obtuseness by OHL and its technical experts. Nevertheless the German bombardments of March–June showed that *Buntschiessen* in association with HE had considerable synergistic action and was decisive on several occasions. German commanders also learnt quickly that gas shells, above all mustard gas, were valuable in defence, and after July employed them to slow their opponents' advance.

The Allies copied the German precedent and the revival of interest in all-out chemical warfare, including a vivified Special Brigade with its equipment supplementing a huge artillery effort, reflects the impact of the German offensives on British thinking. Chemical science might, after all, help destroy the enemy. The chosen instruments this time would be mustard gas and the Allied versions of arsenicals which, as particulate clouds 'developed suddenly and in overpowering volume' would break the German front more quickly than the tank. That was Barley's vision of 1919. Thuillier, writing later, claimed that DM (Adamsite) would 'almost inevitably' have led to a 'complete breakthrough'.[13] This takes us back to April 1915 and the confident faith in a chemical answer to the enemy's resistance. The war, however, had moved on. The Germans had not been beaten by their own invention as the Allied experts had predicted. Had the Germans managed to struggle on into 1919, chemical warfare, along with the tank, would have decided the issue, for their masks would not have been able to cope with particulate clouds, and they would have had to go over to an SBR-type respirator for which they lacked the rubber and fabric. More importantly, their field grey uniforms, contaminated by mustard gas, would have been irreplaceable, for the shortage of cloth was beyond remedy. That, however, was not to happen. Too many mistakes and muddles, by both sides, ensured that gas warfare ended in failure despite ingenious weapons such as mustard gas and Livens projectors. Thus we find that a weapon introduced in an *ad hoc* manner did not fulfil every expectation. Hartley gave that aspect much thought and concluded that chemical warfare had yielded some

tactical successes. His colleague Thorpe reflected that future governments would
have to decide whether they wanted to kill or to injure their opponent and make
their plans accordingly. Haber became disenchanted because it seemed to him
that the artillery was taking over without knowing what it wanted to achieve.
I think he was wrong in this assessment and that the artillery ultimately made
the best use of the novel weapon.[14]

The story of chemical warfare is largely one of imitation: the Germans usually
led and the Allies followed. Miscalculations, technical failures, and inertia on
both sides handicapped or delayed the most effective deployment of gas
weapons. Another, often underrated factor, was the unfamiliarity of
commanders and their staff officers with the whole concept of chemical warfare.
They had been trained to proceed along traditional lines, to remember the lessons
of past campaigns and to rely on conventional methods. But gas was an
unconventional weapon without precedent. There was no theory, no body of
knowledge, nothing apart from science fiction, about what could be achieved
by gas. To the German chemists the matter appeared to be straightforward:
once chlorine or a chlorine–phosgene mixture, had been released in sufficient
volume, the cloud would move with the wind and would overwhelm the enemy
and force him to retreat, pursued by the German infantry. The scenario
anticipated technical problems, but the military outcome would be to end the
trench stalemate. That appreciation was as original as it was optimistic, but
it was not grounded on experience and tradition and ignored or neglected such
difficulties as the width of the gap in the enemy line, the existence of undamaged
barbed wire, the role of the artillery, and how closely the infantry should follow
the cloud. These important military problems were submerged by the numerous
technical aspects which dominated cloud-gas operations to the detriment of the
operational aspects.[15] In retrospect it appears that the arrival of a totally new
weapon did more than upset well-established tactical doctrines. Its many
technical problems were unheard of and enabled laymen to intervene in the
running of the war. Why should chemists succeed where professional soldiers
had failed?

It was an awkward question, and goodwill and tact were unlikely to provide
the answers. Chemical warfare was outside the regular officer's frame of
reference. How then could it be turned into an effective infantry weapon? If
it were to be accepted and put to frequent use it had to be grafted on to something
familiar in the textbooks of *Kriegswissenschaft*. There were two ways of
achieving this. One was to adopt it purely as a psychological weapon which
would exploit the fear of gas and could be handled like propaganda.
Alternatively, gas could be integrated with the artillery, and that was the solution
ultimately favoured by the German staff. Initially, experience was all, the tactics
would follow. When one reads the analyses of cloud-gas attacks or the
monographs of the chemical warfare specialists one is struck by the pedantry
of the technical details and by the absence of all theory, or rather the inability

to fit the operations into existing military thinking. During the war nobody had the time and detachment to review the experience and consider how gas could serve to achieve particular objectives. After 1918 the general attitude was *post hoc ergo propter hoc* and the measures taken in 1915–18 were uncritically accepted. Publications and circulars issued from 1915 onwards were no more than 'instructions, for the use of . . .' and could not be called thought-provoking or original contributions to the science of war.

The German staff, disappointed by the gas shells of 1915 and baffled by the complicated nature of gas clouds, ran out of ideas. On the Allied side Foulkes and his colleagues developed something approaching tactics, but the job was not completed. Various books published between the wars did not fill the gap. Prentiss's *Chemicals in War*, published in 1937, was an important survey of the subject, and the rank of the author (he was a Brigadier-General in the CWS) lent it extra weight; its appearance just as rearmament in Europe was getting under way was significant.[16] The methods of chemical warfare were set out in six chapters, some 260 pages out of 700, which deal mainly with technical details. The principles are summarized as follows: the object of gas is to inflict casualties, to harass and reduce the enemy's combat efficiency, and to contaminate terrain so as to deny it to the opponent. To achieve these objectives, the gas troops were expected to work closely with the infantry but they had to remain mobile and Prentiss recommended that they form part of the GHQ reserves. There are long descriptions of the special equipment and ways in which it could be arranged so as to yield the best results. Precision mattered less than the appropriate mixture of persistent and non-persistent gases, the rate of fire and the concentration of gas shells on a particular target—the very problems that had puzzled French and German gunners twenty years earlier. Prentiss's detail and the care he took over the descriptions are impressive, and as a guide to the use of gas his book cannot be bettered, but he did not face up to the question: how can the tactical purpose of chemical warfare, if there is one, be achieved? Perhaps gas, unlike the other weapons of the Great War, did not have a tactical purpose, and failed because, for lack of one, it could not be properly employed. Prentiss overlooked the fact that the better the defence, the greater the likely failure of chemical warfare. All weapons are checked by defence, but the dependence of gas on wind and weather was unique: it strengthened the defence whereas bullets and shells were unaffected.

Foulkes thought at first, like the Germans, that gas could herald an infantry breakthrough. He changed his mind after Loos and henceforth considered it as a weapon to injure and to harass.[17] He pursued these objectives with remarkable single-mindedness, and unlike the Germans thought it worth while to dispatch his men on scores of small chemical sallies with up to a thousand cylinders of a few hundred projectors at a time, to irritate, to wear down, to demoralize, and to inflict losses on the enemy.[18] In these respects Foulkes was the better judge of what to do with gas the OHL: the Germans missed this opportunity. Foulkes seized and exploited it to the full. But he became preoccupied with technical details—improved handling methods, concentrated discharges from railway flat-cars—and ignored the different settings in which they took place.

The French artillery staffs perceived a solution sooner than anyone else. There is a circular in the French archives dated 11 August 1915 recommending that gas shells be used 'en masse' and 'en surprise', that is in large quantities and without preliminary ranging-shots. The author of the circular distinguished between the harassing effect of tear gas and the lethal effect of a toxic gas. He also recommended dug-outs and trenches as being more rewarding targets than open ground, and envisaged the use of gas shells just before the launch of an infantry attack.[19] At the time this was being wildly optimistic and not likely to be implemented because there were no gas shells except for experimental purposes. But the circular was a significant pointer to the future. The French first issued instructions for the use of gas shells on 12 March 1916, and in the following weeks carried them out. By then they possessed enough shells, sufficient 75 mm guns with a high rate of fire, and an enterprising artillery command. The first targets were the German infantry at Verdun and next their artillery on the Somme.[20] The French claimed later that they had invented 'neutralization' shoots—the technique first tested at Verdun in July or August 1916—whereby gas shells were fired steadily at the enemy, not necessarily to kill him, but to force him to wear his mask for hours on end and thus to weaken his resolution. In 1917 new instructions reflected more systematic thinking: 'boxes', that is pre-selected rectangles of terrain were to be shelled briefly but intensively so as to generate a dense cloud and force the enemy to evacuate the position.[21] Bruchmüller's innovations elaborated on earlier French concepts. He realized that the choice of gases, persistent, non-persistent, and harassing (respectively mustard, phosgene or diphosgene, arsenicals) provided greater variety for the artillery, enhanced its flexibility and so made it possible to design novel forms of bombardments. One new tactic was to silence the enemy guns, not as previously with a direct hit by HE, but by spattering the gun site and the shell dumps with mustard gas. The infantry would be subjected to another innovation, a very intensive, though brief, creeping barrage with gas, and HE. Bruchmüller's objectives were to prevent enemy gunners from serving their weapons until they had been decontaminated, and to force the infantry to don masks and seek cover instead of manning the trenches and repelling the Germans. These methods worked effectively against the Russians in the summer and early autumn of 1917.

The elaborate artillery tactics evolved by the French and the Germans incorporated the principles of massive use, harassment, counter-battery fire, denial of terrain, and support for attacking infantry. In turn the new gas-shell techniques called for fresh thinking by infantry officers. Thus, the men had to be trained to put up with intensive gas-shell bombardments or how to cross impassable zones created by drenching the ground with mustard gas.[22] There is no doubt that the incorporation of chemical warfare into the work and routines of the artillery made sense and did not create the animosities and tensions that were so characterstic of cylinder operations. For that reason gas shells developed naturally as it were within the artillery environment and became part of the artillery history of the Great War with which I am not concerned.

Those who sought to establish a framework for gas tactics during and after the war were unable to accommodate three variables: weather, nature of the chemicals employed, and the human factor. The weather, though a familiar enough problem, determined the success or failure of gas. The only thing to be done was to provide some elementary guide-lines on wind speeds and precipitation and leave the decision to the man on the spot. As to toxicity, some gases were more effective than others. Unfortunately for the staffs, the chemical experts spoke with different voices which explains why substances such as hydrogen cyanide and Blue Cross shell-fillings were retained though they did little damage. But bombardments, however carefully designed to meet certain criteria, would naturally not fulfil expectations if they incorporated faulty scientific information. The human element, particularly the attitude of infantry commanders, was the most difficult to fit into the scheme of things. We have seen that many officers disliked having to provide carrying parties for cylinders and projectors. The gas troops did their job and departed, but the enemy invariably retaliated and the infantry took the punishment. Brig.-Gen. Wigram, staff officer Personnel, at GHQ, spoke for many when he declared at the 19 March 1918 conference 'the armies do not like gas cloud work and there has been objection and obstruction to it all along.'[23]

The transport and handling of gas shells was, by comparison with the carry-in of cylinders, routine work. But the diversity of the contents created problems at the dumps and because these shells were of slightly different weights, the ballistics were affected and unless corrected the accuracy would be diminished. Nevertheless the limitations of chemical warfare were not so acute or obvious in the artillery, and the distance between gun and target was great enough to soften, if not to obliterate, the picture of men injured by gas shells. The other problems were part and parcel of the artillery in the Great War: gas neither added to nor diminished from them. They need not concern us here.

During the war, and even more so after it, the attitude towards poison gas of professional soldiers and those serving for the duration was not uniform. It was not condemned outright (except by individualists like Deimling), nor was support for it unstinted except among the cranks, the converts to chemical warfare, and the specialist troops. Cloud-gas operations were widely criticized for their inaccuracy and uselessness. Neither Brigadier Edmonds, who wrote the official history of the war, nor General Pershing, were enthusiastic. The latter commented that the CWS 'developed rapidly into one of our most efficient auxiliary services',[24] by which he meant, since gas was chiefly used in shells during 1918, that the CWS had the duty of looking after the anti-gas training of the AEF whose large casualties from gas were widely publicized. There was no need for Pershing to say more. At a less exalted level Foulkes and Fries were unreservedly for vigorous chemical warfare. The former wrote: 'GHQ was never in any doubt, during the whole war, about the value of our gas attacks.' Fries endorsed everything his British colleague, whom he described as a 'firm believer' in cylinder operations, had said and added for good measure that gas clouds were more efficient than shells 'for at least the first mile of the enemy's territory'. Thuillier, at one time Foulkes's CO, was more cautious: cylinders used purely for purposes of attrition had 'a very real effect' on the Germans.[25] Still lower down, opinions were divided. Livens considered that cylinders discharging gas were not worthwhile, but then he had an axe to grind. Pollitt was of the same mind. He had served first with the Special Brigade, then with the infantry. He thought that the gas troops asked for too much help from the overworked infantry, which 'combined with the absence of demonstrable results made the Special Brigade deservedly unpopular with formations in the line.'[26] Both agreed that the Special Brigade devoted too much time to cylinder operations and not enough to projectors, yet it was the latter which had the greatest effect owing to the combination of surprise and high concentration in a very small area. The weakening and undermining of the enemy's morale was what mattered most. Let Hartley have the last word; writing at a time when the casualty figures had not yet been collated, he suggested that as the effect of German cloud gas on the British had been so limited, it was unlikely that the British would be more successful in their operations against the Germans.[27]

All that is speculation. We are on more solid ground by returning to tactics. The likelihood of failure with chemical warfare was increased because of incomplete analysis. There were no gas tactics. The experience had to be learned on the job and there was not enough time. But other equally novel weapons seemed to be better managed in this respect. The tank, the aircraft, and the light machine-gun changed the face of war in 1918. It may be that poison gas was too unpredictable to fit into the military thinking of the time. It would indeed be expecting a lot of staff officers to be well disposed towards a weapon that was so troublesome and unreliable. Muddles and errors of judgement compounded the inherent weaknesses. Chemical warfare, hailed as a solution to trench warfare, turned out to be another false trail.

Suppose that the organization had been better, the amateurs less conspicuous, and that there had been less fighting between and within government departments. In such an ideal organization there would have been fewer delays, less confusion, and the supplies of poison gas would have been available sooner and in larger quantities. In the real world, however, things were very different indeed and the rest of the chapter will be largely concerned with the failures. The most conspicuous aspects were, in the first place, the scale and persistence of the muddles. Secondly, the Germans were also wrong, and their mistakes, though of a different kind, were just as far-reaching in their effects as those of the Allies. Thirdly, there were many delays before an error was corrected, and there were occasions when it was not put right at all.

At first all was confusion. Administratively speaking, the war was fought for several months by drawing on stocks, by scraping together, by luck, and by improvisation. In Spring 1915 they no longer sufficed and order had to be introduced. How was this to be done when there was little managerial talent, co-ordination and co-operation were unknown, and the war offices of the belligerents tended to requisition whenever they found civilian procedures too slow? On top of these difficulties were personal rivalries, delays over contracts, arguments about profiteering, and disputes over shoddy goods. These were the commonplace problems of a world war, and the waste of time and manpower was phenomenal. Superimposed on this chaotic state of affairs were the distinct requirements of poison gas which could only be dealt with by chemists and chemical manufacturers. The learned societies and individual academics had been occasionally consulted after August or September 1914, but had not been integrated into the war effort. But from April–May 1915 onwards all branches of chemistry became increasingly involved. It was soon discovered, however, that many of the advisers and administrators were better teachers than organizers, that taking decisions was not one of their strong points, and that all too often, time was not of the essence to them. That was bad enough; what made it worse was the mutual incomprehension of officers and scientists. And if the bureaucrats had been less concerned with red tape, accounting for candle-ends and, not least, with their dignity and their rank, less time would have been lost. It is also possible, though I have no evidence one way or the other, that too many civil servants, middle-ranking officers, and scientists were second- or third-raters. It would appear that in those hectic early months of chemical warfare some people got themselves into important positions whence it was difficult to dislodge them. There were, however, important exceptions: in Britain and in Germany (and rather later in France), extremely able as well as practical men emerged very soon to provide the defence against gas with the purposeful direction that was needed.

There were not enough chemical engineers in Britain. Some of the principal men in the TWD, Sir Louis Jackson and Henry Moreland, knew nothing of applied chemistry and appeared to be unaware of the role of research and development. They also lacked the drive and the skill for in-fighting which were essential in the early power struggles and manoeuvres at the MoM. For over two years there was no proper system of reporting, the available statistics were insufficient for comparisons and for planning, and there were too few meetings between sections to discuss matters of common interest. Those who should have been consulted were overlooked, those with deadlines to meet should have been warned of delays.[28] It was the familiar British muddle, this time with a special chemical flavour to it. The situation was, if anything, worse in France. The chemical industry there was fragmented and there were few competent managers, the best having been drafted into the Government explosives factories. During the summer of 1915 four distinct groups competed with each other to organize the supply of gas, cylinders, and protective pads. GQG was irritated by so much misplaced zeal and incompetence, and was instrumental in setting up a chemical warfare section in late summer. Interestingly, and in contrast to Britain, research and development were closely connected with the supply of gases and later also with that of shells, and offensive and defensive warfare formed part of the same organization.[29] The Germans, at first, had more luck. Their chemical industry was capable of meeting all demands, and there was no lack of qualified scientific staff and experienced foremen and charge hands. Haber, owing to his excellent industrial and academic contacts, had emerged at the beginning of 1915 as the principal consultant on chemical warfare, and he quickly impressed everyone with his organizational talents. Thus, his institute became the centre for research and development into weapons and respirators, and he was also given an office at the Prussian War Ministry where he co-ordinated the requirements of the army with the supply facilities of the manufacturers. Thus supplies, technical advice, research and anti-gas measures were under a single direction from 1915 to 1918.[30] The unified organization meshed with the manufacturing companies whose structure and experience contributed significantly to the successful working of the supply side of chemical warfare. But the advantages of single direction were weakened by marked lack of co-operation between those who designed weapons and those who used them. Development and testing were two functions which were less thorough than in Britain and relations with the artillery specialists were not sufficiently close in 1917–18. Hartley investigated the matter and concluded that the Germans had misjudged the importance of continuous field trials, and so they 'failed to reap all the advantages which their development of chemical warfare should have given them'.[31] The two chief instances of misjudgements were, as I have pointed out previously, the Blue Cross materials for shells—promising in the laboratory, but practically useless in the field, and the repeated malfunctioning of the arsenical smoke-generators.[32]

What is remarkable in the general context of organization and relations between administrators and scientists, is the delay in correcting mistakes and the ineffectiveness of the measures taken to avoid repetition. It seemed obvious to many people at the time that the new gas weapon called for the integration of all scientific and technical resources. The Germans adopted this concept, though the execution of it was far from perfect. The French, after some hesitation, followed suit. But the British kept offence and defence separated until November 1917, and it was not until April 1918 that the TWD, which handled supplies was reorganized. The verdict must be 'too little, too late', and it is not surprising that Pratt wrote soon after the war that the British organization 'might with perfect justice be very severely criticised'.[33] Why was this arrangement tolerated for so long? The answer is that until the second half of 1917 there was no one at the MoM sufficiently powerful *and* interested in chemical warfare to bring about reform. Foulkes, who possessed both characteristics, was busy in France and in any case had no patience with scientific experts. The TWD was not directed by men willing and sufficiently persistent to push, prod, and bully the contractors. At the very top, successive Ministers of Munitions were too preoccupied with the shortage of explosives and shell cases and the task of running a huge department of state to pay much attention to poison gas. For the first two years, chemical warfare was on a very small industrial scale and was neglected. Under Churchill's overall direction drastic changes were introduced and the situation improved. But a more business-like organization in the last year of the war was not enough to bridge the gap between makers and users. Relations between the RA and the Special Brigade HQ in France and the staff at Porton were often fraught: the serving officers accused the scientists of being too theoretical, and the 'boffins' were convinced that the soldiers were too impatient.[34]

The trouble was that, generally speaking, chemists and soldiers did not get on. There were exceptions, of course, but as a rule there was mutual incomprehension, different traditions and cultures, and the questioning attitude of the scientists contrasted with the unquestioning obedience to higher orders by officers. There were, in short, two differing and sometimes opposing ways of looking at things and doing a job. That had detrimental effects on every aspect of offensive gas warfare. Yet in everything connected with defence against gas—protective devices, training, and treatment—the co-operation between experts and officers was positive and fruitful, not least because civilian physiologists and army medical officers had a common educational background and were pursuing the same objectives. I shall return to the matter later in this chapter. Meanwhile, we may note that the artillery had their own specialists with a background of mathematics, gun design, and explosives expertise; chemical warfare was an intrusion, and the gunners were not prepared to put up with the chemists, unless the latter respected the primacy of the former. In fact the artillery integrated gas shells in its operations and its planning more successfully and quickly than the infantry commanders who found it difficult to accommodate themselves to cylinders and projectiles. Bruchmüller and his colleagues tolerated Haber and the chemists, but shunted them into sidings if they interfered. 'In Germany', Haber told an audience of officers after the war, 'generals, scientists and technologists lived under the same roof. They greeted each other on the staircase, but before the war, there was no fruitful exchange of views between them.'[35] He might have added that the situation changed very little after August 1914. Although Wrisberg praised the head of his chemical section and emphasized that the German officer corps was interested in and welcomed new technologies, the fact remained that with the exception of Bauer and Geyer at OHL chemists were held in little esteem by professional soldiers. Haber's personal standing was high for most of the war, but that did not mean that his advice was followed.[36] The role of chemists was no greater elsewhere. Pope, who spoke with great authority on British chemical warfare, wrote that 'the military mind always resents anything new' and his comments on civil servants were even less complimentary. That was in 1921; two years earlier he had had high praise for the MoM's management of gas warfare. The change of attitude may reflect a change of mood, but another chemist, Smithells, whose outspoken views had caused him to be sent back to England, declared at a meeting of the Committee on Chemical Warfare Organization, that he 'had found the General Staff bordering on illiteracy on scientific matters despite the fact that the conduct of the war depended more and more on the application of scientific principles and methods.' It was minuted that Pope agreed with Smithells.[37]

It is questionable whether in the short time available academic heavyweights could bring themselves to collaborate with Captains, Majors, or Colonels. Rank and seniority mattered in the army as well as in the enlarged civil service. Haber (who was promoted Captain from Sergeant-Major!) at one time thought that an Institute of Military Science and Technology would help to break down the traditional and institutional barriers, but the scheme never got off the ground. An imaginative and determined politician like Churchill would listen to advice and complaints (including Pope's), make up his mind, and force through overdue changes—among them the strengthening of the British gas programme in 1918. But he was the exception that proved the rule: the scientists were on tap, but carried little weight, except in matters connected with the defence against gas. Thus the likelihood of perpetuating errors was increased, and the delays and waste resulting from a wrong decision went unremedied. Examples from both sides abound, and they could be found in every branch of offensive chemical warfare. The most important in their effect was the excessive diversity in the range of toxic or lachrymatory agents, especially those employed in shell-fillings, as a result of which there was an insufficient supply of the effective substances and a surfeit of the useless. Development and manufacturing failures, notably phosgene and mustard gas in Britain, gas projectors and arsenical smoke-generators in Germany, represent other instances of conspicuous failure of the military – scientific organization.

The Great War was the first to involve science and technology on a large scale. The intervention of civilian specialists, temporarily in uniform, was bound to create friction, and they would inevitably be blamed for mistakes and technical errors of judgement. Some of the blunders connected with chemical warfare were serious and the effects far-reaching. Those who believe in conspiracy theory will see this as deliberate sabotage of the new chemical weapons by scientists or by soldiers. That is most unlikely. A more plausible explanation is that incompetence and bloody-mindedness were sufficient to frustrate the best use being made of gas. One may doubt, however, whether the choice of some of the leading people was wise: generally speaking the moderators and the compromisers achieved more than the bullies, but they also put up with the incompetent and the dilatory longer. General Thuillier and the mismanagement of mustard gas are a case in point. But the trouble was more deep seated: who selected suitable men—good scientists able to work as a team with civil servants and professional soldiers? The choice of chemical advisers was everywhere on the old-boy network and it was expected of those chosen that they would put up with the idiosyncrasies encountered on both sides of the line in France. On the other hand generals commanding armies, corps, and divisions, and their staffs, also share in the responsibility for failure. I doubt whether they gave much thought to their contribution to chemical warfare, and if they reflected on the role of the chemical experts—their juniors in rank and in military tradition— they would arrive at a simple answer: they would tolerate the advisers as long as they kept to their narrow terms of reference, but would exclude them if they ventured into matters of policy and strategy.

The half-hearted commitment to the new weapon as well as manufacturing and organizational weaknesses summarized in the preceding pages go far to explain the failure of chemical warfare. They need to be contrasted with defence against gas, which—on the whole—was handled competently and successfully. To a large degree this was the result of the clear objectives and the pressure from every quarter 'to do something' and to be seen doing it. The need was great and the response remarkable. It is possible too that the men involved in anti-gas work were more supple and adaptable in the way they tackled the job than their colleagues on the offensive side. And it is likely that their message and its implementation were acceptable to, and not questioned by, infantry officers. In Britain the success of defence against gas may have reflected the higher standing of physiology in British universities by comparison with chemistry or chemical engineering.

The better the defence against gas, the greater the failure of chemical warfare. The paradox held from April 1915 onwards, though it was not immediately accepted by every belligerent. Nevertheless, even the French, whose indifference to their conscript army was notorious, ultimately conformed. The proposition encouraged the leap-frogging of offence and defence. Initially offence held every advantage, then the first pads appeared, only to be rendered useless by phosgene. That event led to better pads, to gas helmets, and to respirators. There the defence stood until mustard gas, in mid 1917, shifted the advantage again to offence. Later more training, greater watchfulness, and better respirator drill, enabled defence once more to catch up. Arsenical compounds would have tilted the advantage again to the offensive, but they never worked as intended. Thus overall, except briefly, protection had the edge and throughout the tendency was to improve the quality and quantity of defence. In Britain and Germany from the start, in France and Italy not until much later, this was due entirely to substantial research and development and also to a manufacturing effort which in intensity was rarely matched, let alone surpassed, by the production of toxic gases.

The success of defence against gas sprang from the need to maintain morale. Good morale, endurance, and efficient soldiering go together; discipline and *esprit de corps* strengthen these characteristics, and in turn are reinforced by them. In this respect the threat posed by gas was taken as seriously as the outcome of the carnage wrought by conventional weapons on the Somme or at Verdun. A year later, British observers pointed out that the weakening of discipline during 1917 led to heavy casualties from gas among Russian troops in the Kerensky offensives. Contrariwise, the improvement of French anti-gas training and the issue of better masks is said to have reduced French casualties from mustard gas in March-April 1918, by comparison with the previous summer.[38] Gas was only one among a multitude of dangers in trench warfare, but my interviews with Chelsea Pensioners and others suggest that confidence in respirators, once established, greatly helped the soldier to emerge unscathed from a gas attack. The SBR, though complicated and calling for great discipline in breathing, was trusted because it provided very good protection.[39] By contrast the French with their nose pads, their M2s, and even their ARS were inadequately protected. Moreover, negligent training caused many unnecessary casualties not only in the French but also in the Russian and Italian armies. Good equipment was a necessary, but not a sufficient condition.

Training, experience, and endurance were equally important. Such principles may appear self-evident now, but were not universally applied then. Therefore the threat posed by gas had to be overcome not only by constant improvements to gas masks, but by constant practice in their use and by systematic checking of the soldier's equipment. Conscientious gas officers and their NCOs used to complain that the allotted time was not enough.[40] Training and refresher courses were relaxed in quiet sectors or were turned into meaningless routines, with the result that surprise projectile attacks exacted their toll. During 1918 this particular weapon caused so many alarms that some German formations took extreme measures: the men, masks at the ready, were kept on alert throughout the night, forbidden to rest in dug-outs, and ordered to carry their blankets at all times. When the projectiles came, the men slid on their masks, covered their heads with blankets and cowered against the trench walls. Thereafter, the casualties were negligible as was the fighting value of the units.[41] Without experience, instruction, some common sense and self-reliance, soldiers could be rendered helpless by unusual incidents like that described by Remarque when a fresh draft sheltering in a deep crater looked up to see men without respirators marching along its rim. So they took off their masks and were gassed because no one had told them that phosgene is heavier than air and lingers in shell holes, trenches, and dug-outs. The story finds an echo in the British suggestion that soldiers be taught the rudiments of science so as to be more aware of the dangers they would encounter.[42]

The introduction of mustard gas altered once again the nature of chemical warfare: in a sense it made it less dangerous, but the casualties were more widely dispersed and more frequent because of 'failure to appreciate the danger of a gas which does not cause immediate irritation'.[43] Poor anti-gas training and inexperience resulted in heavy losses. On New Year's Eve 1917, the wretched Portuguese north of La Bassée neglected all precautions in order to keep warm and so suffered badly when the Germans shelled them lightly, but enough to spatter Yellow Cross over their miserable shelters. The Americans, though well equipped and eager, had heavy casualties from mustard gas. Their gas training was inadequate, their gas discipline worse, nor did they learn readily from their Allies in adjoining formations. During the September–October 1918 battles the wastage from this one cause became so alarming that severe measures had to be taken to enforce discipline.[44]

Mustard gas and even more so arsenicals (provided they were in particulate dispersion) also operated in a subtler way because the conventional defences were useless against 'voluntary disablement'. For most of the war the type of gas employed prevented self-injury, but the heavy American losses and the demoralization of the German infantry exposed to French mustard gas, unexpectedly threw light on a new type of gas casualty. Whatever the individual's motives, these novel materials enabled him, were he minded to take the risk, to plead injury and avoid active service. While the symptoms of arsenical poisoning were easy to fake, the remedy was just as simple and effective, and there was little point in using Blue Cross as a pretext. It was different with mustard gas: the soldier could contaminate himself or, by sheer carelessness, extend the contact from the superficial to the serious, a difference in treatment from 7–10 days to 5–6 weeks. It sounds easy and was doubtlessly practised by a few, but was painful and also dangerous because bronchitis and its sequelae were then grave illnesses. I therefore disagree with those who adopted an extreme line, for instance Soldan, who wrote that gas encouraged skiving. Another example is provided by the author of a US War Department publication who, under the title 'Malingering' observed that the 'excessively high casualty list' combined with low mortality did not represent genuine gas injury, but signified that the men were suffering from other, unspecified and undiagnosed ailments. To suggest, as he does,[45] that only a third of those classified as 'gassed' were in fact involuntarily gassed, flies in the face of similar British experience in July 1917 when the men, like those of the AEF a year later, were fresh, but totally unprepared for mustard gas.

People familiar with chemical warfare were aware of the psychological element in defence against gas. Haber, who knew as much about it as anyone, considered that however well trained and practised, a soldier would always by apprehensive in an attack: 'Every change in sensation transmitted by smell and taste troubles the mind with fresh anxieties of unknown effects and further strains the soldier's power of endurance at the very moment when his entire mental energy is required for battle'.[46] Hanslian was less emphatic, but he too recognized the psychological significance of confidence in the respirator and of the link between training, good masks, and the prevention of panic. He noted, as did other German observers, that while the defeated British troops abandoned their equipment in March 1918, they invariably held on to the SBR. For Hartley the confidence factor was even greater. He told me that once the SBR had been issued and the men instructed in its use, the fear created by gas disappeared. I don't believe this to be true except perhaps for those bereft of all imagination, just as I don't believe Auld's remark that casualties were 'preventable' if the men were vigilant and 'well drilled' in the use and care of the respirator.[47] Gas bombardments were occasions when the well-protected man who kept his nerve stood a much better chance than the worrier, but to take the statement any further is absurd—everyone was at risk. Naturally good protection meant not only a reliable mask, but also an experienced response to poison gas. To this extent some gas injuries were avoidable. Good defence, in a broad sense, contributed most importantly to the failure of gas warfare because it stengthened the physiological and psychological barriers: the former blunted the power to injure, the latter reinforced the morale of the resolute. Whether this would also hold in 1919 when the Allies intended to smother the war-weary Germans with gas was never put to the test.

It is time to seek and answer to the question which forms the chapter heading. I anticipated the answer at the very outset: gas was a failure. It was more than a wartime scientific curiosity, but not a significant addition to the weaponry of armed conflict. Chemical warfare made few demands on resources such as labour; its raw material needs were unimportant and, with the exception of rubber and cotton in Germany, not critical for the belligerents. Poison gas had certain characteristics such as wide diffusion and variable persistency which HE with its instantaneous effect and limited range of dispersion, did not possess. However it was novel, complicated to handle, and lacked, except when part of a shell, a body of tactical experience. Gas in shells became part of the artillery, was found useful and readily accepted. But gas shells failed, as cloud gas and Livens projectiles and failed, to break the stalemate of trench warfare. Alternatively gas could be employed for harassing purposes and as a psychological weapon, but there were difficulties in adapting it to these purposes and in simplifying its use. The senior commanders were not wholly committed to chemical warfare and the muddles and mistakes that accompanied it from the outset diminished its appeal to the unconverted and hindered its development. Conventional weapons hurt the enemy just as much and were simpler as well as being less dependent on weather. The long production and administrative delays rendered gas a poor second best to staff officers. Finally, and most importantly, as the defence against gas strengthened, so its failure as a weapon became more pronounced: the genii out of the bottle remained at large, but its power to hurt was checked. And as its capacity to injure was weakened, so its effectiveness was diminished.

These drawbacks were recognized by many people. But the gas war, like the rest of the war machinery, built up momentum and became unstoppable. As defensive measures improved, so that elaborate set-piece cloud operations became irrelevant and futile. Yet these activities were publicized by the gas lobby who were equally concerned with empire-building as with justifying their existence. The clumsy and undependable gas cloud overshadowed the less remarkable but potentially more dangerous gas projectile which tended to be neglected. So, in 1915–17 the picture of gas warfare became unreal, its management routined and unimaginative, but its imprint fixed solidly on soldiers' minds. On its own it was a failure. In combination with artillery it caused casualties and denied access to terrain which HE would uselessly have churned over.[48]

Hartley was sure that propaganda and legends had distorted the facts and endowed chemical warfare with powers that it did not or ever could have possessed. But he also believed that training, experience, and resolution were within everyone's reach and so, armed with the SBR, it was possible to overcome successfully whatever the enemy might do. While German efficiency and technical skills were undisputed strengths there were also many personal weaknesses and in the end the disadvantages outweighted the gains: 'looking back [gas] wasn't such a godsend to the Germans'.[49] Haber's opinions went unreported and his two lectures, 'Zur Geschichte des Gaskrieges' and 'Die Chemie im Kriege', are disappointing. Nothing emerges beyond the brief descriptions. There are a few cautiously worded insights, much self-justification, but no critical analysis and no apologies. If there was more, he kept it to himself. His brainchild, in other hands, had failed and if this was hard to bear, it was harder still to watch the weakening of the German war effort which he had endeavoured to strengthen. By the Autumn of 1917 Haber was convinced that Germany would be beaten and during 1918 he grew more despondent as he envisaged the 1919 campaign when the army would be overwhelmed by gas against which there would be no defence.[50] This apocalyptic scenario was indeed what the Allies were planning.

The majority of the writers or participants in chemical warfare differed from Hartley and Haber. Hanslian, among the majority, stuck to the facts, specifically German technical superiority, and considered, however uncritically, that this was a sufficient conclusion. Foulkes and Barley, like Pope and Haldane, had no doubt as to the value of gas, but the first was fixated on cylinder operations, whilst the others took in every aspect of chemical warfare. Foulkes, though he had few facts to rely on, had convinced himself that the work of the Special Brigade had made a valuable contribution to the efforts of the BEF, and he certainly did not subscribe to German and other opinions as to the uselessness of gas clouds. Barley, an experienced Chemical Adviser, told me that in his opinion the Germans could have won the war on two occasions in 1915, on 22 April and in December, but they botched the job because their staffs were unprepared and their gas troops insufficiently trained. They missed yet another opportunity, this time with gas shells, in July 1917.[51] Such criticism expresses what Haber may have felt but left unsaid, and implies that in more competent hands, chemical warfare might have succeeded in winning the war. I don't agree. Such conclusions make no allowance for the inherent weaknesses of chemical warfare and exaggerate the impact of German clouds at a time when the Franco-British forces were not yet enfeebled by losses and would have stemmed the German advance whatever the temporary advantage obtained by the surprise of chlorine and of phosgene at Ypres. Foulkes and Barley, and more recently Brown[52] overrated the role of cylinder operations and neglected the contribution of gas to the artillery during 1918. Poison gas complicated warfare. This factor, on its own, was a serious drawback, for the battles, though repetitive in mode, were growing in complexity of preparation. The disadvantage was only partly compensated by the elements of surprise and harassment. Even here there were complications. The power of attrition was two-edged, and in no way ensured victory: the intensive use of gas by one side in an attack recoiled on that side because the advancing soldier wearing his respirator cannot aim properly and, more importantly, is more quickly exhausted, physically and mentally.

There were bouquets galore for the returning soldiers, and even in Germany criticism of the Army was muted. The gas specialists were welcomed back with less acclaim, as if the subject were embarrassing and now that the war was over the operators of unconventional devices could be shunted into sidings. The final verdict—when the official histories appeared decades after the events—was to say as little as possible.[53] Perhaps the military analysts found the matter too difficult to handle or wished to avoid rekindling old arguments. Yet, as we shall see, chemical warfare has not been forgotten and the subject refuses to be pushed into a historical limbo.

Technically, poison gas was an ingenious attempt to overcome trench warfare:

it was cheap, to produce and capable of further development. But in practice it was, until 1918, largely a waste of effort. In that year it helped the Germans rather more than the Allies, but it did not win them a battle, let alone give them victory. There were, however, some unusual features to gas. The entry of chemists into the business of war created more problems than it solved. They were not making a bid for power, but they wanted to be heard: they rarely were, except when some of them combined with physiologists and physicians to find ways of reducing the effectiveness of the weapon their colleagues had introduce and were striving to improve!

The sporadic employment of gas heightened its psychological effect, but did not add greatly to its usefulness. Yet, though very little was gained (and little had been risked), chemical warfare created, from the outset, arguments which ranged beyond technical or tactical controversies to touch upon moral issues and questions of principle. In this respect gas, like the submarine, was considered by some as wicked or wrong, though the criteria of right and wrong defied definition. Unlike the submarine, chemical warfare was counter-productive for those who used it. These matters may, more appropriately, be discussed in the final chapter. But let us pause for a moment's speculation. Suppose the Germans had not set the machinery in motion that led to 22 April 1915 and beyond. But if they hadn't, would someone else have started chemical warfare? The answer, I have no doubt, is 'Yes'. Such was the obsession with trench warfare and the pressure to find a technical solution that poison gas would sooner, rather than later, have made its appearance. Perhaps not dispersed from cylinders, for they were the response to the particular scarcity of shells in 1915. One should not take guesses too far, but there were many on both sides who sought solutions in novel ways. If Haber had not hit on chlorine clouds, someone else would have proposed chlorine bombs or phosgene projectiles. They appeared as the chemists' solution to the problem of the impregnable trench system. In this respect they failed, but failure has never stopped innovation in peace or in war.

Another question remains: if gas was a failure, why does it continue to attract so much attention? It is indeed extraordinary that this unreliable and ineffective weapon, magnified by propaganda and rumour; should survive into the 1920s and 1930s to trouble politicians and soldiers. One answer is that the myths surrounding gas give rise to endless discussion and speculation. Another answer derives from public attitudes during 1915–18 and specifically from the general impression created by chemists as military innovators.

Despite occasional expressions of horror by writers and artists, there were plenty of people in both camps who spoke up for and participated actively in the development of chemicals for warlike purposes. In so far as public opinion played a role, it tacitly condoned the use of poison gas. The Hague Convention, though relegated, had not been abandoned and its continued existence on the one hand stiffened the resolve of those few opposed to poison gas, and, on the other, was a godsend to Allied propaganda. So far as is known, there were only two public appeals to stop chemical warfare. The first was launched by President Wilson in May 1915, after the gas clouds at Ypres and the sinking of the Lusitania: he proposed that Germany end poison gas and attacks on merchant ships, in return for which Britain would lift the blockade of neutral ports. Neither side accepted. In February 1918 the International Red Cross appealed to all belligerents to abandon gas. Nothing happened.

The role of the scientists and of propaganda is more complicated to analyse and supplies an extra dimension to chemical warfare which the Germans had not anticipated when they began it. The subject is sensitive on personal grounds since a good deal of the opprobrium fell on my father and he carried a burden which others should have shared. His activities in the Great War need to be seen against the background of German science generally: in 1914 its prestige was at a peak and the reputation of the country's scientific establishment stood high. Should scientific or specifically chemical excellence be accompanied by equally elevated ethical standards? That question would excite Germans more than others not only on account of their predilection for discussing behaviour in philosophical and abstract terms, but also because the introduction of a wholly novel weapon inevitably led to a charge of 'unfairly' or 'treacherously' waging war from those who hadn't done it first. The fact that the British and the French were also testing chemical weapons was irrelevant, since the Germans took the lead on 22 April 1915. Thus the responsibility for the innovation rested on the Germans, and on Haber, their chief chemical figure-head. It would have been out of character for him to feel embarrassed. But the noisy self-righteousness of German scientists, including Haber, after the outbreak of war, though demonstrating their loyalty to Kaiser and army, left others to doubt their capacity for rational judgement and common sense on many subjects, not least that of chemical warfare. There were, of course, a few who disapproved of poison gas on principle, while others were animated by a vigorous dislike of Haber and his startling transformation from brilliant professor and innovator, to principal chemical adviser to the OHL and the War Ministry. Willstätter told Hartley that the German professorate had taken very little part in the war and many thought that chemical warfare might recoil on Germany. Hartley noted, but did not comment on the diverse opinions. It is likely that some German scientists were embarrassed by the introduction of gas and it is also likely that they exaggerated their feelings, perhaps to project them on to a wider audience. It seems to me just as plausible to suppose that, as patriotic Germans, they would subordinate their feelings to their duty. After 1918 it was sensible to change course and admit to some contrition, if German *Wissenschaftler* were to be readmitted to the international scientific community from which they had been excluded on account of gas and other sins.[54] Just as a good deal of the pre-1914 admiration had been uncritical, so much of the post-1914 criticism was unjustified. Haber, if he had any doubts about the moral aspects of his work, kept them to himself, whilst those who worked on gas defence suffered no opprobrium.

Amongst the Allies there were no exculpations and as they had won the war there was no need for recriminations as to the justness of the chosen weapons. Their chemists worked with a will. Pope was outstanding in this respect: he criticized his fellow-chemists and was scathing about those officers who regarded chemical warfare 'as a dirty weapon; the man who uses it would shoot foxes and net salmon'. The sentence neatly summarizes the views held by many in France—indeed the military establishment in France was more hostile to gas than the chemists in England. The most notable exception, apart from Foulkes and Thuillier, was Allenby, the GOC 3rd Army until he was sent to Palestine in 1917.[55] There was, apart from Pershing and a few senior commanders, little opposition to the development and use of chemical warfare in the higher American echelons. The French were noticeably uninterested in the human cost of the war and since they neglected the care of their own men it is unlikely that they would be squeamish about the effect of poison gas on the enemy.

The public at large was almost totally ignorant. Secrecy blanketed all research and development as well as preparations for gas clouds or Livens projectors. The women on the respirator assembly-lines knew a little and, of course, there were the occasional reports, misinformed and distorted in the press. The events of April-May 1915 gave the Allies a considerable propaganda advantage because the nature of the weapon and the spectacular flouting of the Hague Convention provided excellent copy. The results, in terms of attitudes to poison gas, were negligible. Later that year press comment became muted and ceased with the first cylinder operations by the British at Loos. There was a resurgence in 1918, by which time the Allies were in the ascendant, in order to enhance the propaganda campaign preceding the Spring offensive of 1919.[56] The widespread and overwhelming use of gas shells by both sides replaced the more dramatic image of the poisonous cloud. The remotely directed mustard-gas bombardment seemed, somehow, less awful, but it was forgotten that the shells caused more injuries than the clouds of 1915–16. At the front, there was a belief, however illogical, that bullets and shells were easier to avoid than gas clouds. That fantasy receded when high explosives dominated the trenches, but was replaced by the conviction of all the gas experts, many staff officers, and politicians that gas would be used in the next war, not only against soldiers but also civilians. Their predictions are difficult to reconcile with the equally widely held opinion that chemical warfare caused more trouble than it was worth. But the inconsistency of the opinion-formers and advisers is irrelevant when set against the possibility of more effective chemical technology in another war. The assertions of the experts gave rise to anti-gas attitudes which, feeble or suppressed in 1915–18, coalesced, gained strength, and attracted considerable attention in the inter-war period.

APPENDIX: A STATISTICAL NOTE ON GAS SHELLS AND CASUALTIES IN THE BEF

It is not known who first began to take an interest in the relationship of chemical shells to casualties. Perhaps it was Hartley. When he was put in charge of defence against gas (ADGS [D]) in the BEF in 1917 he began to list many of the German gas bombardments and in 1918 this became a regular monthly survey for the BEF, and was circulated under the title of 'Hostile Gas Activity'. The Hartley papers contained the tabulations for August–October 1918; there were earlier ones for March, and May to July, but they appeared to be incomplete which is hardly surprising when one considers what went on during the German offensives.

The monthly tabulations show the number of shells and of casualties, the location, the rate of fire ('heavy', 'intermittent', etc.), and what kind of gas (or gases) were used. Hence it is easy to establish a numerical relationship of casualties to shells and to express the result as a ratio of 1 casualty : n shells. It is to be noted that the ratios fluctuated enormously. In one instance 1,400 shells caused one casualty, i.e. 1 : 1400, in another, 500 shells injured 500 men, i.e. 1 : 1. There were also instances of no casualties at all (i.e. a nil ratio) and of direct hits in which there would be more than 1 casualty per shell.

The accuracy of the shell data is not satisfactory. Counting was done in daylight by sampling new shell craters and then grossing up by the estimated total areas covered by the bombardment. Sometimes gun flashes or bursts would be counted at night. The casualties would be obtained from the nearest Regimental Aid Posts, and would be

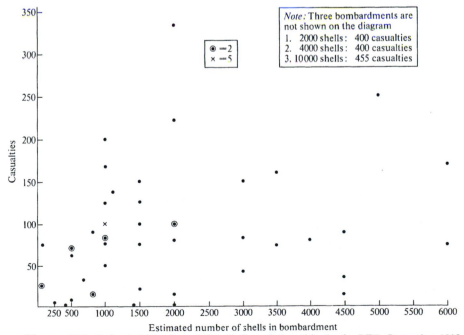

Diagram 11.1. Estimated Number of Gas Shells and Casualties in the BEF, September 1918

Table 11.2   *Statistical Analysis of Gs Shell Bombardments and Casualties,*
August–October 1918

	August 1918	September 1918	October 1918
1. Number of recorded bombardments used for regression equation*	37	55	54
2. Number of recorded bombardments which have numerical ratios of casualties per *n* shells+	35	52	50
3. Average of the monthly ratios of casualties per *n* shells (*x* as in line 2)	1 : 19	1 : 54	1 : 91
4. Highest (H) Lowest (L) ratios recorded in that month	H 1 : 80 L 1 : 1	H 1 : 1400 L 1 : 5	H 1 : 1000 L 1 : 1.4
5. Modal ratio (*n* as in line 2)	1 : 20	1 : 10 and 1 : 20	1 : 10
6. Correlation coefficient:	0.365	0.533	0.528
(a) Value at 1% level of significance	0.3810	0.3218	0.3218
(b) Value at 5% level of significance	0.3246	0.2732	0.2732
(c) Comment	Barely significant	Significant	Significant

Regression Equations (casualties regressed on shells)‡

	Casualties	Shells	R^2
August	53.51 (1.34)	0.06727 (2.32)	10.8%
September	49.9 (2.99)	0.02919 (4.58)	27%
October	4.81 (3.27)	0.03625 (5.44)	26.5%

* Every bombardment including those in which there were no casualties (nil ratio) and those in which there was more than 1 casualty per shell (direct hits).

+ Every bombardment excluding those with no casualties and direct hits.

‡ T-values in parentheses.

more accurate than the number of shells. Finally records were supposed to be kept of all the more important bombardments, but I have seen no definition of the term, the cut-off point seems usually to have been 100 shells.

Table 11.2 shows the results of the analysis of the ratios for August, September, and October 1918. The scatter diagram (Diagram 11.1) illustrates the dispersion of casualties and shells in September 1918.

The ratios are widely scattered and this is reflected in the usual measures of dispersion. Nevertheless, the correlation coefficient is in every case above the 5 per cent level of significance and in September and October also above the 1 per cent level. A regression analysis confirms this, but the August result is meaningless. For September and October, the explanatory value of the number of shells as a cause of casualties is relatively low. To improve it one would need to have a great deal more information— what did the shells contain, at what rate were they fired, what was the duration of the bombardment and the area covered, how many troops were in the target area, and so on? Other statistical approaches were tried but did not yield more meaningful results.

12

THE AFTERMATH

THE end of the First World War ended large-scale chemical warfare: since then gas has not been used, although there have been occasional incidents and many unconfirmed reports. This is one of the many unusual aspects of poison gas, and will be considered in due course. When one writes technological history a recurring problem is when to stop and which strands in the development to omit. Arbitrary decisions have to be made, and I have chosen to close the chapter in 1939: Hitler's war began with military thinking based on the materials employed in the earlier conflict, it ended with the large-scale production of nerve gases which, since the 1940s, have transformed offensive and defensive tactics.

Nerve gases require a book of their own, but the difficulty is that the archival material on poison gas—conventional or new—becomes scarce after 1939 and it is not yet possible to piece together the full story from the documents that have been released. Some general indications can be given, and where appropriate I have done so, but the purpose of the chapter is different. It is to draw attention to some issues that were left unresolved at the Armistice, and in particular, the place of poison gas in the peacetime armies, the future role of chemists and physiologists in chemical warfare research and development, and, generally the position of scientists as military advisers. This last issue is at the heart of a much wider debate which has generated its own literature, and which can only be summarized here. The inter-war years witnessed a sustained effort to restrict the scale and the scope of weapons. If that aspect of disarmament was to succeed, then poison gas had to be included. Its inclusion inevitably raised many technical questions of which manufacturing control and verification were the critical ones. At the political and intellectual levels there were the problems of first use, retaliation, and deterrence. Throughout the inter-war years the practical and the idealistic aspects of disarmament were intertwined. We therefore need to consider them as one, albeit the erstwhile Allies and the Germans looked at them from different points of view.

The debates on international relations often raised the spectre of another chemical war at a time when the events of 1915–18 were still influencing reactions to gas. It is indeed remarkable to what extent between the wars a weapon of such small effectiveness cast a threatening shadow over all questions of European dis- and rearmament. Gas had been a failure in the late war, but it continued to trouble people, and remained in the forefront of public concern for many years after its end. This chapter aims to provide some explanations for such an extraordinary phenomenon. But before coming to these unresolved and controversial problems, it is essential to sketch in the background, and draw attention to some strongly held lay and expert opinions on gas.

In Britain poison-gas manufacture stopped on, or very few days after, the Armistice, the only exceptions being DM and, for a few weeks longer, DA. At Morecambe, they continued to fill smoke-generators with both at the rate of 3,000–4,000 a day, equivalent to 30–40 per cent of capacity and by the end of January 1919, 150,000–170,000 were in stock awaiting shipment to northern Russia. The Anti-Gas Department was also being run down though the assembly of an improved respirator designed to withstand arsenicals, the Green Band type SBR, was maintained at a high level until one million were in reserve by the end of April. The Department employed about 12,500 people when the war ended; by mid January there were fewer than 5,000, early in March the numbers were down to 4,300, and six months later all had gone. Hartley, who was in charge of the CWD, must have felt that at times the baby was being thrown out with the bath water. Even Porton, to which he paid special attention, was marked down for closure. While its fate was being decided, the skilled men left and from February onwards experimental work became insignificant owing to lack of staff. The relegation to limbo ended, administratively speaking, on 1 July 1919 when the War Office took over from the MoM, and remained ultimately responsible for all chemical warfare activities until the creation of the Ministry of Supply twenty years later.[1] At dumps in England and in northern France, sappers, civilians, and prisoners of war were employed emptying gas shells and cylinders, tidying up sites, and decontaminating buildings and vehicles. The work, which was heavy as well as dangerous, took months and caused casualties. It was completed by early summer and with it any remaining danger from gas warfare ceased. The story was not greatly different elsewhere: the French dumped shells and cylinders at sea and where this was not possible, they decomposed mustard gas with bleaching powder, a process accompanied by a good deal of what is nowadays called environmental pollution.

More drastic measures were proposed in the USA: the Secretary of War intended to dissolve the entire CWS, a measure which the Chief of Staff, Gen. Peyton March, applauded because he was opposed to gas warfare. But Gen. Fries, who commanded the CWS, was a skilled lobbyist and he hurried back from France to enlist the help of Congress. The politicians came to his rescue, and the CWS was reprieved while both Houses proceeded to look at the service as part of an inquiry into the reorganization of the army. The situation was, to say the least, unusual, because while the CWS was ordered to discharge the men, it temporarily retained the unspent appropriations for 1918–19. Thus Edgewood, though inactive and in part 'moth-balled', was well endowed. As in Britain, the manufacture of respirators continued until more than a million were in stock.[2]

The Germans had been making gas up to the very end, but transport was disorganized and by mid November large quantities were held at the works or in railway sidings. It was decided to clear the lines of these dangerous goods and to move everything to Breloh and then wait for Allied instructions as to what to do next. The gas masks, several millions of them, were collected and stored at a depot in Hanover. The available evidence is conflicting but it would appear that Breloh held 85 rail tank cars, over 150,000 gas shells, 40,000 cylinders, and 638,000 glass bottles filled with various Blue Cross materials. No one bothered to keep a tally, and few people observed safety precautions. In 1919 an explosion destroyed the filling plant for mustard-gas shell, and that put an end to official German zeal to clear up the mess. The Military Inter-Allied Control Commission (the MICC) endeavoured to take stock and then appointed a French company to salvage the cylinders, but their employees were careless: they emptied the cylinders of their phosgene content by using the up-draught of a chimney, a dangerous practice which caused several deaths and some illness. Their method for dealing with mustard-gas shells was to arrange them in circles, fire one burster, and so detonate the lot, then sprinkle the ground with nitro-glycerine, set fire to it, and so destroy the toxic material. The men were given double pay for the work. The MICC disapproved, got rid of the French, and in 1920 negotiated with Dr Hugo Stoltzenberg. He was a plausible rogue and in other circumstances might have been believed if he had claimed to grow mushrooms successfully in the desert. As it was, he persuaded the MICC chemists that he could salvage the cylinders, recover phosgene, and destroy mustard gas. He was put in charge. The operation took years, instead of months, and resulted in the destruction of 1,303 t of poison gas, 3,560 cylinders, and 128,000 bottles filled with arsenicals; 1,088 cylinders were sold. Some of the stuff ended up in his junk-yard in the Hamburg docklands. It is not known what happened to the rest.[3] The Allies were more successful and much quicker at liquidating the mainsprings of German chemical warfare. Bayer at Leverkusen and Badische at Ludwigshafen were in the occupied zone, where the writ of the Control Commission ran large. Besides, neither company knew what to do with the greatly enlarged phosgene installation and both complied with the MICC's order to cut the capacity by half. Badische also reduced its ethylene capacity. Thus the supplies for the principal war gases were restricted. On paper these measures were far-reaching, but many people were convinced that the Germans were dragging their feet over the implementation of articles 171–2 of the Versailles treaty which provided for the disclosure of poison gas know-how and an end to all manufacture (Articles 169–72 will be found in the Appendix to this chapter). Lefebure was among them and his proposals for the industrial emasculation of the Reich gained some support.[4] The take-over of the dyestuffs works as security for Reparations and to prevent a recurrence of chemical warfare appears like special pleading, the more so as Lefebure was then on the staff of the British Dyestuffs Corporation. It was simpler and also less controversial to enforce the cessation of all research and development. By the time the Allied representatives arrived at the KWI, Haber had gone on medical leave, possibly on account of overwork and nervous exhaustion. His chief section heads, Freundlich, Flury, Herzog, and Friedländer were unemployed, but were trying to keep the staff together and working on the peaceful uses of toxic materials. Not surprisingly all the ingenuity proved to be useless, the money ran out, and many scientists and technicians were discharged during 1919 and 1920.[5]

Within a year of the Armistice not one of the former belligerents was in a position to manufacture poison gas on a large scale. The wartime installations had been scrapped or put on a care-and-maintenance basis, and those that remained would take several months to reactivate. The surviving government factories to assemble respirators were in rather better condition to resume production and testing. This might be taken to indicate a deliberate policy of phasing out offensive warfare, but retaining defence on a standby basis. The interpretation must not, however, be taken too far because it is doubtful whether, by the autumn of 1919, Ministers knew what to do about gas. Nevertheless a distinction was beginning to emerge between offensive and defensive preparations. Though there was no formal policy as yet, an important lesson had been learnt by the Allies: in the first place it was recognized that an indigenous chemical industry, capable of supplying at very short notice, chlorine, phosgene, and ethylene needed to be protected. Secondly, the poison gases which were expected to be used in the next war—phosgene, mustard gas, and arsenicals—should be prepared on a small scale in government-owned plants, from purchased intermediates. An important feature of these works was that they could be put on a war footing within a matter of days or, at the most, weeks. For Britain, this meant that wartime improvisations such as the works at Ellesmere Port, Avonmouth, and Morecambe would be closed and the equipment (if in good condition) moved to the larger site at Sutton Oak, near St Helens, where the first DA plant had been opened in spring 1918. By the end of 1919 the run-down had been completed and the British government, in a manner analogous to the USA at Edgewood, had its own permanent factory. The production of gas masks was initially concentrated at Watford and later moved to Porton.[6]

The demobilization of chemical warfare proceeded quickly, but not smoothly, for there were frequent, often serious, accidents among the demolition gangs. While other weapons were being paraded on every conceivable occasion, poison gas disappeared. More than that: the inter-allied liaison reports and information exchanges ceased, to be replaced by secrecy and suspicion. Details on arsenicals and particulate clouds were censored out of the the official records and only the German documents, in so far as these could be retrieved, survived in western archives.[7] But out of sight did not mean out of mind. Poison gas, though there was hardly any after 1919, appeared more alarming than before, and the paradox of a non-existent weapon accompanied by growing public awareness of its potential threat calls for comment.

The psychological aspects of gas had been noted from time to time during the war. The fear of choking to death and how to restrain that fear were behind the care taken over anti-gas training and the need to maintain discipline and morale. The problem did not end with the war and a peacetime infantry manual had to take this fact into account: 'A fundamental difficulty in anti-gas instruction arises from the mystery associated with the material used . . . There is an intensity not only of ignorance, but of what is almost superstition, attached to the material of gas warfare, that is found with no other branch of military training.'[8] So the instinctive recoil from exposure to gas was accepted and methods devised to blunt it, but the instructions were addressed to men subject to military discipline and accustomed to obeying commands. The new element after 1918 was the extension of gas warfare to civilians, not by accident, but deliberately, not behind the front, but on cities in the rear, and not by shells, but by aerial bombs. The threat changed the dimensions of chemical warfare and implied an escalation of death and injury. There were, it is true, neither the materials nor the means of delivery, but the frequent references between the wars to civilian casualties testify to the widespread concern about the consequences of another war. Surgeon Commander Fairley wrote of the 'neurotic element' inspired by the terror of mustard-gas poisoning and stressed the need to give those injured confidence in ultimate recovery. Haber also thought in psychological terms: before the experience of gas itself, the anxious would tend to exaggerate its effects, later—after the exposure—as if to compensate for the fear, the incident would be magnified. In short, there was nothing rational about the individual's reactions and the novelty of gas on untrained and undisciplined civilians would have a devastating effect: there would be panic and orderly government would become impossible. Expert opinions added to apprehensions which were further increased by newspaper reports, novelists, and not least by alarmist forecasts based on scientific rubbish disseminated by people who knew better.[9] The mixture of bizarre fantasies and plausible scenarios, together with the common experience shared by thousands of ex-soldiers had an enhancing effect so that poison gas held public attention throughout the 1920s and 1930s. The particular issue which touched a sensitive area of local and national government was that of civilian protection against gas and the extent to which the civilian population (as distinct from the military or public servants) should be forewarned of new dangers in another war. Ministers took it for granted that if an enemy were to employ gas, he would also use aerial gas bombs on cities. Heavy casualties and panic were unavoidable and one report spoke of 'disastrous' consequences.[10] So the questions that inter-war governments had to answer were whether the threat should be acknowledged, counter-measures such as Civil Defence be put in hand and to what extent the public need to be told.

European Cabinets avoided taking decisions as long as possible. In France, Germany, Czechoslovakia, and the Soviet Union some official publicity was given to the danger of gas warfare. In Britain the Home Office said very little at first, but after 1932 or 1933 some precautionary moves were deemed advisable and civilians had to be told. In any event an ostrich-like policy was ridiculous, because anyone who took the trouble to inform himself of what was happening on the Continent knew what had to be done. The first official leaflet, 'Air Raid Precautions', appeared in July 1935.[11] Thus chemical warfare was always subsumed, but the extent of the menace was ignored, because it was unknown. Gas inspired fear, but was difficult to comprehend. Collectively these attitudes influenced throughout the twenties and the first half of the thirties the debates on controlling certain classes of weapons, as well as the recurring discussions on the 'legality' and 'morality' of chemical weapons.

After fifty or sixty years it is difficult to imagine the intensity and acrimony of the arguments over 'unfair' weapons and the observance of the Hague Conventions. The Germans were accused of breaking 'the laws of war' in April 1915, were supposed to feel guilty, and to show some remorse; some did endeavour to exculpate themselves. There was also the wider problem of the morality of using science to kill or injure people.[12] Many of the points were of academic or philosophical interest and of no practical significance, some were totally irrelevant, and a few were special pleas of the worst hypocrisy. I would not waste the reader's time on these matters if it were not for the fact that they led to the well-intentioned inquiries on chemical warfare launched under the aegis of the League of Nations. The case for and against poison gas needs to be reviewed in the following pages because the threatened extension of chemical warfare to civilians sharpened the issue. It also forms a link with our present anxieties over the use of nuclear weapons.

The two Hague Conventions to which I referred at the beginning of the book expressly prohibited 'asphyxiating or deleterious gases' and 'poison or poisoned weapons'. The agreements were negotiated and signed at a time when statesmen were supposed to have moral standards, and it was generally expected that such declarations of principles (agreed to without duress) would be respected by all belligerents in a future war. The events of August–September 1914 dented these illusions, the German us of chlorine the following spring shattered them, and set a precedent. In the Great War, conventions and traditions were thrust aside and the language of contemporaries still conveys the emotional shock. Conan Doyle wrote that the Germans had 'sold their souls as soldiers' and Kitchener wired French that gas is 'contrary to the rules and usages of war . . . these methods show to what depths of infamy our enemies will go.' And so on.[13] But contrary voices were soon raised: Asquith wrote to George V that gas from cylinders 'is not perhaps an infraction of the literal terms of the Hague Convention': that was precisely the point the Germans were making—cylinders were not mentioned in Hague I or II—but where did that leave the spirit of the Conventions? From there it was only a short step to legitimize the use of gas at all times and not solely in retaliation against the enemy's first use. For example during the Gallipoli fighting in 1915 the Cabinet had decided against the use of gas, but less than two years later (shortly before the Palestine campaign) Ministers changed their minds, although the Turks had not discharged cylinders or fired gas shells at the British. The reasons given for authorizing

gas were the Turkish atrocities and the ill-treatment of Allied prisoners.[14] I
shall not labour the point further because 1915–18 was the open season as far
as chemical warfare prohibitions were concerned. The question to which we
need to address ourselves is what conventions, if any, should apply to a war
after 1918?

The German post-war attitude was that the Hague Conventions still applied,
indeed they had not been breached in 1915–18. So the *status quo ante* was
retained, and in any case the Germans had not been guilty of a precedent for
it was the French who had first used bullets and shells with toxic materials.
That was also Haber's opinion as recorded by Hartley in 1921 and subsequently
elaborated before a sub-committee of the Reichstag which investigated breaches
of international law during the late war.[15] He argued that gas did not cause
undue suffering and therefore was not inhuman. His logic satisfied sensitive
politicians: the German MPs felt absolved of all guilt—had not the army merely
done its duty by following the Allied example?—and in their report managed
to blame it all on the French. That was whitewashing a policy decision taken
at the highest level and methodically implemented by OHL. In his report Hartley
did not comment on Haber's views (or their accuracy), but it needs to be said
that they were shared by protagonists of chemical warfare after 1918 in Britain
and the USA. The practical effect of these attitudes was profound: international
resolutions or agreements to abandon poison gas would be meaningless unless
accompanied by verification of the binding undertakings in peacetime, and
sanctions against the transgressor in war.

One purpose of this book is to shed light on a brief, but important episode
of Fritz Haber's life. Though Germany was defeated, he did not change his
opinions: other Germans might talk about 'errors' or write of self-inflicted
'moral damage',[16] but Haber never retracted: he was not aware of having
broken Conventions or rules. He had done what was in the best interests of
the country. The same explanation has been used on many occasions since, and
it always appears incomplete. So it was in Haber's case. Coates, in his Haber
Memorial lecture, had to deal with his subject's attitude to gas. By then, 1936–7,
rearmament was getting under way and the threat of chemical warfare in the
next conflict aroused much attention. Coates was troubled: Haber had broken
the rules of war and though 'not guilty' in any legal sense, had acted in a way
that many perceived as going against custom and morality. Thus, he could be
held 'responsible for gas warfare'. Hartley was asked for advice and he
recommended to Coates that Haber must not be entirely absolved. It was sensible
advice, but Coates did not take it, preferring to gloss over the question of
responsibility for breaching the Hague Conventions.[17] My view is different:
governments are unprincipled and excuse their actions on the ground that the
national interest calls for them. Individuals aid and abet governments and seek
to justify themselves after the event. Regrets or remorse will soften the criticism
of history, but Haber was too self-righteous to adopt that line.

What is a 'humane' war? The adjective defies definition in this context, and so the question appears rhetorical, requiring no answer. But between the wars people thought differently and considered it relevant. They reasoned that if one could prove gas to be more humane than shells that would justify the continued existence of the chemical warfare services, and indeed raise their status. Furthermore the scientists would be rid of their particular guilt, for if gas was humane they would not have added something special to the horrors of war, they might even be commended for making it less awful. Such fantasies survived in the circumstances of the 1920s and even later and were taken seriously. C. G. Douglas, who had treated many gas casualties wrote to Hartley that 'really severe cases . . . are very distressing', although, 'in present day warfare any method of extermination is considered legitimate'. At least it may be said that the mortality from gas had been low. Some twenty years later, his colleague, Dr T. A. Elliott, in a letter to Hartley was more sensitive: 'It is a hateful and terrible sensation to be <u>choked</u> and suffocated and unable to get breath: a casualty from gun fire may be dying from his wounds, but they don't give him the sensation that his life is being strangled out of him.'[18]

Comparisons had a wide appeal, and, buttressed with statistics, were thought to be proof against all rejoinders. It is useful, even at this distance in time to draw attention to the arguments presented by each side. Few people would have been as extreme and outspoken as Gen. Sibert who stated 'that . . . it is impossible to humanize the act of killing and maiming', and added that there was no logic in condemning one weapon in particular.[19] That line justified all chemical warfare preparations after 1918 and the use of gas in another war. It was followed by those who compiled the entry for gas warfare in the 1929 edition of the *Encyclopaedia Britannica* and for Gilchrist's book on the comparison of casualties in the First World War.[20] Some scientists found this way of reasoning less satisfactory and others were confused. Otto Hahn's guilt feelings about gas seem in retrospect jejune. He was young at the time and against gas, but 'Haber put my mind at rest . . . I let myself be converted', and once he had seen the light he made a very good gas officer and special projects investigator.[21] But to be fair, there was a dilemma, for many chemists then believed that science was a force for good and that it ought not to be diverted to what they saw as inhumane purposes. That is how Hermann Staudinger, Hahn's contemporary, looked at the problem. Chemists, he argued, were not only scientists but also communicators and among their duties was the education of people in the effects of modern scientific warfare. He urged the Red Cross to issue an appeal against the use of gas in another war. Staudinger sent a reprint together with a respectful message to Haber who overreacted and in his answer accused his younger colleague of conduct unbecoming to a German. Staudinger replied placatingly, and his dignified pacifism contrasts sharply with Haber's intemperate self-justification.[22] The correspondence ended inconclusively but it showed that the chemical warfare controversy cut across professional lines.

When one turns from morality, humanity, and casualties to the arguments advanced by the other side, there appears—at least on first sight—clarity and no false sentimentality. The case for chemical warfare was practical, technologically powerful, and obviously appealed to self-preservation. The report of the Committee on Chemical Warfare Organization (the Holland Committee) asserted 'That gas is a legitimate weapon in war, the Committee have no shadow of doubt' and the members took it as a 'foregone conclusion' that gas 'will be used in the future' because no successful weapon has 'ever been abandoned by Nations fighting for existence'.[23] A few months later Sibert declared that he would use gas again 'as an aggressive weapon . . . to kill and maim enough men of the enemy to enable us to impose our will upon him before we can make peace.' He would even have aerial gas bombs.[24] The Holland Committee and Sibert took it as read that gas had been an effective weapon, though that assumption, as I have argued in the previous chapter, was unwarranted or, at best, not proven. They also linked chemical warfare with a diversified and prosperous chemical industry, and observed that such an industry would be playing a key role in the nation's preparedness. But the details of that link were never spelled out by the gas lobby, and we are left to assume that industry would supply the key materials, and the chemical warfare services would convert them into weapons.

Sibert was asked about civilians and the use of gas on undefended cities. He answered that he considered this form of warfare to be 'inhuman . . . except in the war area where it should be expected'.[25] No one asked him what he meant by 'war area' and he did not volunteer a definition. Questions about restraints on the employment of gas were not pressed by the investigating Congressmen. The professional soldiers did not raise the subject; if questioned at all they tended to skate over the difficulties and avoided discussing the implications of restraint. Chemists who approved of gas warfare, usually those who had been involved in it, took the same line. Sir William Pope condemned all anti-chemical warfare talk as mischievous and called on those who disagreed with him to explain why they wanted to abolish 'a very humane, although new instrument of warfare'. The subject was also examined wittily, and without false sentimentality by his colleague J. B. S. Haldane in *Callinicus*.[26] Haldane claimed that gas was an efficient weapon, capable of being integrated with tanks in breaking through a line of trenches. In his opinion those who objected to gas were pacifists, ignorant politicians, and military dunderheads: fear of the unknown, of the new and the incomprehensible, was at the root of the opposition. What was needed, in his opinion, was the education of people, though he did not explain how that would protect civilians from gas shells and bombs. There is no suggestion in Pope's or Haldane's writings that civilians should be, as it were, exempted from chemical warfare—the case for restraint or limitation was not mentioned at all. Hartley and Haber were more circumspect in their language, but their attitudes were broadly similar.[27] We may summarize their approach as follows: a new weapon is not necessarily less humane than existing ones; therefore neither traditional practices nor the Hague

Conventions are relevant, and accordingly questions of legality and morality do not arise. That being so, gas is like any other weapon. These opinions, sincerely held and vigorously propounded, had to be demolished by the other side.

The opposite point of view was simple, easy to understand, and had a great following not only among scientists, but also politicians, professional people, artists, and intellectuals. It rested on the premiss that war is sufficiently horrible, why make it worse? That appeal was first presented to the public by the leaders of the British medical profession in a letter to *The Times* a fortnight after the Armistice.[28] They condemned gas because it was uncontrollable and could injure non-combatants, because it led to 'death by long drawn out torture' and because new gases might 'blot out towns and even nations'. Science, they concluded, should not be used for 'causing death by chemical agencies' and they hoped that the Comity [i.e. The League] of Nations would abolish this weapon. The doctors said everything that the other side left unsaid, and it is no wonder that they were criticized for years afterwards by the supporters of chemical warfare. But the theme of scientists against gas appealed not merely in England and the USA, but also in France where Le Wita's woolly and well-meaning pleas not to put chemistry to destructive uses and to rally the League members in support of a country attacked by gas, attracted much favourable attention.[29] Le Wita and others like-minded were labelled pacifists, but rendered a service by drawing attention to what might happen in another war. The Women's International League for Peace and Freedom, an important pressure group, became convinced of the dangers from chemical warfare after witnessing a demonstration at Edgewood in 1924. The effect was the opposite of what the CWS intended to achieve by the open day and the Women's Committee on Scientific Warfare grew into an active lobby, and called a conference at Frankfurt in 1929. Its General Council included such luminaries as Einstein, Langevin, Gilbert Murray, Philip Noel-Baker, and Lord Cecil. The gathering attracted considerable publicity as it turned out to be an unusual mixture of feminism, pop-science, appeals to working-class solidarity against warmongers, and reminiscences, not always accurate, of 1915–18.[30] What matters in this context was that the lay public was told, very vividly indeed, what chemical warfare against civilians entailed.

The appeal to peace, to control of arms, and to international arbitration had its cranky as well as idealistic sides, but in the 1920s and even later was sufficiently influential to command the attention of politicians. As the Versailles Treaty held the threat of German chemical warfare in check, it was considered timely to extend the ban to the former Allies. The issue was first joined at the Washington Naval Conference 1921–2. France, Italy, Japan, the UK, and the USA met to agree on limiting their naval power. Americans who objected to the public relations exercises in which the CWS was then indulging, were able to have chemical warfare put on the agenda of the Conference. They also prevailed on the experts advising the USA delegation to recommend the complete prohibition of gas. The prospects for an agreement on the contractual prohibition of gas appeared good, because all the participating delegations reiterated their adherence to the Hague Conventions on poison gas. But the return to the pre-1915 status was not formally accomplished, because the French refused to ratify a clause dealing with submarines, and the proposed treaty, which was based on reciprocity became inoperative.[31] That put the whole issue into the lap of the League of Nations, which was to be concerned with chemical warfare for a great many years. An immense amount of time and paperwork led to a very small measure of success. The failure was due not only to the lack of goodwill and to mutual suspicions among members, but also to ignorance and the inability to come to grips with the problems of monitoring any agreement and of imposing sanctions against offenders. The stumbling-block was not the chemical industry, nor future military tactics and technology, but how to bring about a fundamental change in the relations between States.

The League had begun its work in 1920 by asking for information. It sent out a questionnaire on the use of poison gas, circulated the answers, and then proceeded to discussions in committee or referred the details to sub-committees of experts. Then and later there was usually a reference back to Governments before the next round of Inquiries began. Thus years passed, but there were occasional spurts of activity when a fresh initiative was launched and for a few months there was renewed optimism. But at working-party level the faces and the conclusions hardly changed—which was not surprising, for the specialists had actually waged chemical war only a few years before.[32] Under the impetus of Lord Cecil, the Temporary Mixed Commission for the Reduction of Armaments set up a committee which, in 1924 issued 'The Report of the Committee appointed to consider the Question of Chemical and Biological Warfare'. The authors rejected as impractical stopping chemical warfare by prohibiting the manufacture of certain chemicals; there was also, for the first time, a reference to bacteriological weapons, but they were not considered to be a threat. The report[33] still makes interesting reading for it shows 'the state of the art' in the mid-1920s: contamination by bacillae, staphylo- or streptococci, was thought to be ineffective and infestation by airborne parasites (envisaged by science-fiction writers and some intelligence officers) was unlikely. More alarming, in the opinion of the authors, was the use of planes to drop gas bombs, and in particular mustard gas on civilians. No new gases were anticipated.

There matters would have rested, but at the 1925 Conference on the Supervision of the International Trade in Arms, the subject of poison gas was introduced. Some skilful lobbying by American delegates led, after a relatively short time (by League standards), to the adoption of the Geneva Protocol on 17 June 1925. This brief document prohibited the use of chemical and bacteriological weapons, urged the signatories to ratify as soon as possible, and bound each signatory as regards other signatories—that is, it was multilateral. The Protocol, to this day, attracts attention and is given attributes which exceed its real significance. It is a declaration of intent and as such may have moral influence, but as there are no provisions for verification, or for enforcement of the ban, or penalties for infringement, it is without teeth. Between 1925 and 1930 many countries ratified the Protocol though they frequently qualified their adherence by adding that 'the Protocol ceased to bind if *any* enemy fails to respect it'. That was the safeguard adopted by Britain, France, and some other States. Italy and Germany, however, ratified unconditionally in 1928 and 1929 respectively. Russia did not sign, the USA signed but did not ratify because Fries once more rallied his supporters in Congress. Japan did not ratify the Convention until 1970 and the USA at last followed suit in December 1974, when it also approved a separate treaty on the development, production, and stockpiling of biological weapons.[34] The eagerness of some or the reluctance of others to adhere to the Convention are of more than purely chronological interest, as will emerge later.

The Protocol said nothing of research, development, manufacture, and stockpiling. These matters were left in abeyance and, in due course, came within the scope of the Preparatory Commission for the Disarmament Conference which met several times between 1926 and 1930. The Commission had the benefit of German expertise,[35] but the mountains of talk produced a mouse of practical solutions, and the problems of verification and of sanctions baffled everyone. The Disarmament Conference, convened in February 1932, adjourned in July, reconvened the following March, and petered out a few years later. As far as chemical warfare was concerned, the end came in May 1933 with the unanimous agreement on a draft submitted by the British delegation: it was, in effect, a reaffirmation of the Geneva Protocol, but allowed for chemical (though not bacteriological) retaliation. In one other respect the British draft broke fresh ground because it extended the Protocol by banning the preparation and manufacture of these weapons. Supervision was left to the Permanent Disarmament Commission.[36] The document remained a draft.

The summary calls for no comment except this: the chemical disarmament and control negotiations were overtaken by the Second World War. They have been resumed since, so far without success. The absence of results in the 1920s and 1930s showed that the Geneva meetings were a waste of time, but they were a constant reminder of what needed to be done.

The threat of nuclear warfare cannot be compared with that from gas more than half a century ago. But the scale and distance effect need to be recalled: gas was an important issue in those days and various pressure groups strove at all times to draw attention to it. An important aspect of chemical warfare which differentiates it from nuclear weapons, is defence. Since 1915–16 personal protection had been practicable and was being improved. This fact was glossed over, and often ignored altogether, by both sides. Thus attitudes to gas, though firmly held, were based on incomplete reasoning in that they took no account of defence and the contribution it could make to blunting the weapon.

The anti-gas movement would not have had such a wide following but for a combination of romantic idealism, fashion in science fiction, and journalism. The effect of the first is impossible to assess, but it was skilfully propagated by authors, playwrights, film producers, and intellectuals generally. They appealed to emotions, but avoided the obstacles that stood in the way of international agreement.[37] Science fiction had a wide appeal. The war years had shown that Robida's vision of a future gas war was no longer silly, but indeed entirely plausible.[38] The novelists of the 1920s and 1930s sometimes lost themselves in the most fanciful speculation—such as Will Irwin in a pacifist story, *The Next War* (1921) in which 'Lewisite' bombs achieved the most unlikely results. Sometimes they endeavoured to put a serious subject across and used a future gas war as a proxy for evil-intentioned scientists. Charlotte Haldane, for example, was concerned with women and eugenics in a muddled tale of a scientific community established after the first chemical war. *Man's World* (1926) was strictly for the feminists and was drafted before Charlotte married J. B. S. In general, however, the aim was simply to describe a future chemical war: M. S. Southwold's *The Gas War of 1940* (1931) and M. Dalton's *The Black Death* (1934) made aerial gas attacks the theme, and Dalton linked gas with the Nazis. The message conveyed by the science-fiction writers of those days was that the wars of the future would engulf civilians, putting at risk not only those caught in the battle zone, but non-combatants everywhere.[39]

Journalism made its own contribution to attitudes. The press featured incidents, usually small, but out of the ordinary because of some scientific peculiarity. Nor is this surprising: reporters cannot be expected to look at an accident through the trained eyes of a chemist or of an officer of the RE, and given the prevailing ignorance and secrecy, some embellishment was inevitable. Thuillier criticized the press for being 'unfair' owing to its sensational treatment of gas, whereas 'no one exaggerates the effects of rifles, machine guns or artillery . . . gross exaggeration regarding them would be ridiculed'. Thirty years' later newspapers were still being reproached for failing to inform the public of the danger of poison gas, let alone in educating it in the implications of chemical warfare.[40] But are the criticisms justified? Events are news: suppress them and you are accused of fostering public ignorance, enlarge them and you are called alarmist, describe them in unbiased detail and you lose the readers! Nevertheless, the Press kept poison gas before the public, radio also made a contribution and more recently we have had TV with its dramatic visual impact.[41]

Thus, the opponents as well as the proponents of gas warfare have not allowed the subject to fade into oblivion. They have maintained the awareness of gas among opinion-formers who, in turn, influence government policies. But how significant, in political terms, was this awareness and to what extent did the inter-war governments respond? Brown considers that governments overestimated the strength of feeling against the use of gas among the general public. I am not so confident. In the first place, what is the evidence? There were no European public opinion polls on the question in the 1920s and 1930s. Secondly, the failures at Geneva reflect a lack of urgency (or too much self-interest) at government level on the question of implementing the ban on gas. Thirdly, not enough is known of the attitudes of European politicians and soldiers to gas, especially in the later 1930s when rearmament was in the ascendant. But Brown is surely correct in drawing attention to opinions at Washington. Peyton March, who was chief of staff from 1918 to 1921, opposed chemical warfare on humanitarian grounds and restricted the CWS to such an extent that Fries asserted that March was out to destroy it. Pershing, who followed March, was also hostile, but Fries's lobbying ensured its survival; Douglas Macarthur and Malin Craig in the 1930s were opposed, and Roosevelt, throughout his life, did not countenance the use of gas.[42] What Americans thought and did about gas was less important than European reactions. There was no threat to American civilians, whereas in Europe the danger facing non-combatants was the driving force behind the pressure groups and led in the 1930s to Civil Defence. But the possiblity that protection against high explosives, gas, and incendiaries might deter the enemy from using them first, lest he invite retaliation on his towns, was not considered while disarmament was still being taken seriously.

The International Red Cross was the first to draw public attention to these matters. At conferences on the Protection of the Civil Population held under its auspices at Brussels in 1928 and Rome the following year, shelter design and gas-proofing methods were described at length.[43] But what were the governments to do? Acknowledging the potential threat might alarm civilians, but inactivity might encourage an aggressor to strike without warning. In the 1920s, the latter seemed unlikely, the more so as the Germans were prohibited from making or employing gas, and there appeared to be no threat from any other quarter. The early 1930s shattered this complacent view: aggression without formal warning and reported uses of gas had widespread repercussions. Chemical warfare quickly became an important policy matter, except in Germany where Hitler, until late in his war, opposed the use of gas. Other European leaders showed less opposition to it. Churchill's views were known, but long before he became Prime Minister, successive Home Secretaries had organized civilian defence against gas and so redressed the balance against the element of surprise in offensive chemical warfare.

In summarizing the disarmament debate and the evolution of attitudes, the emphasis has been all along on international organizations, or on groups or even on individuals whose aim was to stop gas warfare. There were others who took the opposite line and whose main planks were national defence, and more narrowly, a reorganization of the services so that chemicals would be more effectively deployed in the next war than in 1915–18.

It was not enough to proclaim, like Sibert, 'there is no field in which the future possibilities are greater than in chemical warfare', or agree with Fries and West that 'gas wave attacks may be expected to . . . reach a place of very decided importance'.[44] What needed to be demonstrated by the chemical warfare lobby was that gas had a great tactical or strategic potential, that its use would be better organized than in 1915–18, and that the next war would not be fought with the chemical weapons of the last. Those aware of the technical and operational obstacles were more cautious than the out-and-out enthusiasts of the CWS. Hanslian, for example, thought that gas would be a 'principal' arm, but no more. He forecast that mustard gas and the arsenicals would be the chief materials. Other experts concurred, except that the Americans patriotically, but misguidedly, ascribed to 'Lewisite' attributes it did not possess. Prentiss, in his methodical way, added a section on post-war developments to his book: it is short and uninformative by comparison with the rest, but what he writes on the artillery reflects the thought given by the CWS and the Ordnance Department to careful shell design, quicker fuses, and precise targeting.[45] These specialist authors, acting as spokesmen for the technical side, accepted two important lessons of the war: the necessity for less variety in the choice of offensive materials, and for greater carrying capacity and dispersing power in regard to gas shells.

The difference between war- and post-war thinking is not so noticeable in the emergence of novel tactical theories, but in the integration of gas with mechanized transport and, experimentally, with bomber aircraft. Cylinders and Livens's projectors were retained, but they were motorized to reduce manhandling. It was not yet possible to combine chemical with tank warfare: the choice was either one or the other, on account of the difficult problems of engine air-supply and the protection of the crew. Aircraft, however, were expected to play a major role in chemical warfare. The Americans, with their passion for technical gimmickry, thought in terms of fitting sprayers or sprinklers to the wings. The ideas were ingenious, but entailed specially adapted airccraft flying slowly at heights of about 100 m and so presenting a perfect target for anyone armed with a machine-gun. The German experts kept their opinions on aircraft to themselves, and recycled those of their American or Russian colleagues. After 1933 they were asked for their advice, but were enjoined to remain extremely discreet, and nothing significant was disclosed.[46] Of all the professional authors Thuillier, by then in retirement, judged the next chemical war with the greatest detachment. He dismissed the various technical innovations one by one, except gas bombs against civilian targets. They would be the decisive feature of another war, on account of the large casualties, but the bombs would lead to immediate retaliation. He was, so far as I am aware, the only one to consider the possibility of a stalemate in chemical warfare—the point when the defence against gas was equal to the enemy's offensive materials.[47] It is curious that the concept of mutual deterrence—which had been observed in the latter stages of Anglo-German gas warfare—was not resurrected in the 1920s and 1930s and discussed at length. Perhaps the semi-official positions occupied by some of the best-informed commentators led them, after 1936 or 1937, to exercise extreme discretion so as not to give anything away. The opinions of scientists, who were exerting considerable influence, were even more reserved. Hartley spoke of a triad of new weapons—aircraft, tanks, and poison gas, but he saw the last as being used predominantly on urban and industrial targets. That led him to speculate on the role of defence as a limiting factor to the effectiveness of gas, a theory which had been confirmed by events on the Western Front in 1917–18. The question to be answered in the inter-war years was whether the theory, extended to non-combatants, would also apply in the next conflict. Haber, independently of Hartley, also stressed the role of defence against gas in the next war.[48]

Gradually a consensus emerged from the advice which the military and scientific experts were offering to their war departments. We may summarize it as follows: experience had shown in the First World War that too many different materials had been employed. It would be better to concentrate on two or three with proven characteristics. Mustard gas was the preferred chemical agent, with phosgene in second place, and one of the arsenicals (DM was favoured by the British) third. The artillery, firing longer and thin-walled shell cases, was considered the most reliable and accurate mode of delivery. Everyone agreed that aircraft would become an instrument of chemical warfare, but the technical obstacles were great and the experts, instead of committing themselves to a forecast, recommended more research and tests. There was also entire agreement on the need for anti-gas training by troops, whose equipment must always be kept up to date. The greatest danger to the infantry would be shells or bombs filled with mustard gas.[49] Air-raid precautions and civil defence had received expert attention in the 1920s, and after 1933 were swept into rearmament. However, it may be doubted whether, regardless of advice, governments—except in Britain and the Soviet Union—made serious preparations for civilian protection against chemical warfare.

The use of gas as a surprise weapon of the first resort does not, from the documents accessible to me, seem to have been proposed or accepted by any government. The British Government discussed the matter in 1925, and—in line with its attitude to the Geneva Protocol—authorized the use of gas only for retaliatory purposes.[50] But the ability to retaliate was everywhere strictly limited. Contrary to what was said or written for public consumption, Britain, the USA, France, or Germany (I have no information on Japan or Russia) did not have the means to wage chemical warfare. For example the facilities at Sutton Oak were on a pilot-plant scale and in the mid 1920s it employed altogether 61 people. At the most it could produce 5 tons a week of mustard gas from thiodiglycol by the German process, and a few years later it had 2 tons in storage. DM was not made at all, but the large demonstration plant, rated at 2½ tons a week, could be started up within ten days; 5 tons of DM and 6,000 smoke-generators were in stock. In practical terms these did not constitute either offensive or retaliatory weapons. For the rest of its chemical armoury, the War Office relied on ICI's chemical works at Widnes which could be raised to emergency levels (though not to those achieved in 1917–18) with a delay ranging from one to three months. On the defensive side, to round off the picture of peacetime Britain, the Ordnance Factories at Woolwich had equipment and rubber moulds for a small production of SBRs. We may compare these modest volumes—at the height of disarmament—with the Services' anticipated requirements for the first six months of the next war: 1,000 t of mustard gas, 2,900 t of phosgene, 780 t of DM, and 390 t of tear gas (CAP).[51] The Special Brigade had been stood down in 1919. All this does not indicate any aggressive intent, nor the existence of a chemical deterrent. In the USA the situation was scarcely different. The National Defense Act (June 1920) set the establishment of the CWS at 100 officers and 1,200 other ranks. They were to handle research and development, anti-gas training, the manufacture of toxic, smoke-generating and incendiary materials, and the organization, training, and operation of the special gas troops. For the benefit of his readers, Pope inflated the role of the CWS to show how feeble were the British preparations, but in truth the CWS was in no position to do more than launch a token demonstration of gas warfare.[52] There was nothing of the kind in Germany, notwithstanding occasional stories of secret preparations.

For much of the war, the organization of chemical warfare, and in particular the link between Research and Development and the use of gas in the field had been incomplete and unsatisfactory. In the UK it remained so almost till the end. Those who supported the future use of gas were, in this one respect, in entire agreement with the Military Establishment. Change was overdue and the Holland Committee was set up in May 1919. Its remit was to advise and to make recommendations on an appropriate organization for war and for peace, to investigate the needs of peacetime research, and consider the role of scientists. Foulkes, Thuillier, Pope, Barcroft and Hartley were among its members, there were also representatives from the Navy and the Dominions, and Sir William Napier spoke for the RA. However, there was no delegate from the RAF, which was odd considering the role assigned to it in the post-war literature. The Committee held thirteen meeings, called many witnesses (among them Crossley, Rendel, and Levinstein) and issued, two months later, a long report which created the framework for British chemical warfare for the next twenty years.[53] The members dealt quickly with the pretensions of the artillery, and rejected Napier's suggestion that the top advisory body, the CWC, report to the Master General of Ordnance. (Napier recorded his dissent in a minority report.) The Committee recommended that there should be no separate chemical branch, as in the USA, and that in peacetime gas should form part of the RE, the officers being trained, like other sappers, at Woolwich. (In wartime, a special corps would be formed under the command of an RE general.) Up to that point, the recommendations followed the practice of 1915–19. The novelty lay in the proposed supply organization, and in that for research and development. The Committee proposed that the War Office (which at the time was taking over from the MoM) appoint a Director of Chemical Warfare Research and Supply who would be responsible for offensive and defensive equipment, for the State-owned factories, for Porton, and for liaison with the chemical industry. He would also be, ex officio, on the CWC. That Committee would, in future, be headed by the President who should have the rank of a Brigadier-General of the General Staff; he would have a small secretariat (J. D. Pratt being put in charge of that.) The CWC should consist of civilian scientists, military officers, and manufacturers who could co-opt others—among them the Chief Technical Officer at Porton, who came from the RA.[54]

The Holland Committee's report was accepted and put an end to the separation of offensive and defensive preparations, and to the segregation of supply from research and development. It also ensured that expert advice on a wide range of subjects reached those dealing with general policy and strategy at the highest military level. Some fresh problems emerged later and were not readily dealt with. In the first place the CWC found it expedient to work through sub-committees, whose numbers grew and the mass of detail they generated clogged the machinery. Secondly, and unexpectedly, the wartime energy and enthusiasm of the Porton staff waned. Perhaps it was because so much of the work tended to be repetitive, perhaps there was not enough of it to keep them alert, and secrecy as well as the generally held low esteem for chemical warfare research discouraged some of the scientists.[55] The academic advisers were aware of the difficulties, but no remedies were found until rearmament and civil defence preparations restored the self-esteem and morale of the staff.

Neither the War Office nor the Holland Committee were minded to abandon chemical warfare, but that was undoubtedly the intention of the US Chief of Staff when the expiration of the Overman Act, which had set up the CWS in June 1918, gave him the opportunity in 1919. The creation of a new branch of the American armed forces had aroused the hostility of the older services (the Army, the Marines, the Navy) and they now hoped, together with Peyton March, that the CWS could be killed off. Publicity, Congress, and Fries's energetic propaganda saved the CWS, but the National Defense Act of 1920 only ensured its survival as the merest rump of its former self. We may compare the establishment of 1,500 enlisted men in February of that year, before the run down to 1,200 prescribed by Congress, with the 12,000 men in the Corps of Engineers, 16,000 in the Air Force, and 36,000 in the artillery. Sibert had at one time hoped to see a CWS of 1,700 officers and men, but he was thinking in terms of a total army strength of 250,000.[56] The distinction with Britain, though important in principle, was irrelevant in practice. The Americans retained a separate service with an independent command, but the functions of the CWS were almost identical with those recommended by the Holland Committee the year before. The War Department cut the funds available to the CWS and channelled them into areas of which the Chief of Staff approved. A British observer noted impressive-sounding research activity accompanied by clever publicity at which Fries excelled. In this manner the small annual appropriations ($2 million, say £400,000 in 1920–1 and less than half that amount about ten years later) were made to yield apparently significant results. The charade deceived some people, but by 1939 the US army was untrained and unprepared for chemical warfare and the stocks of offensive materials were derisory; no toxic shells had been filled since 1922.[57]

Although chemical disarmament had gone far, an important lesson of the war had been learnt by the Allies and was being applied from about 1920 onwards. The supply constraints in Britain and France were unlikely to recur owing to the development in both countries of a chemical industry as diversified, and nearly as strong as that of Germany. The connection between chemical manufacture and poison gas was (and remains) direct, but involved several intermediate stages of diminishing commercial significance. Anglo-American policy aimed at protecting those branches of the industry which, though economically weak, were deemed essential in the national interest. The chosen instruments were tariffs and import licensing, and in this way the indigenous production of the appropriate organic compounds was enabled to survive and even prosper.[58] But who should be entrusted with the manufacture of poison gas in peacetime, and on what scale? What should be the relationship between Government and private enterprise for products for which there was only a single customer? The Holland Committee and Fries had ideas on the subject. The former recommended that the Government (i.e. the War Office or the MoM) should own and operate model factories (we would now call them pilot-plants), that there should be liaison through the CWC, and that the bulk production of gas in wartime should be handled by private enterprises acting as the agents of the Government. Fries, without the means to build a factory, was perforce of the same mind: Edgewood should be capable 'with moderate upkeep' to go into large-scale production 'without notice', while chemical companies were expected to be able to go into production with a minimum delay.[59] These were the principles followed between the wars, although the growth of the chemical industry was not as smooth as had been expected when protection was introduced soon after the war. The large firms did not maintain stand-by plant for national emergencies, but there is some evidence that a watchful eye was kept on potential needs, and where an essential branch of the industry required special protection in order to survive, it usually got it. Some observers had identified two key factors in the industrial preparations for chemical warfare. The first was the availability of technically qualified manpower, the second was an assured supply of chlorine, arsenic, ethyl alcohol, and carbon monoxide.[60] During the 1920s there were no supply problems and the growth of the chemical industry after 1935 ensured that materials for chemical weapons would be quickly available on a large scale.[61] The German policy and timetable were not significantly different from the British, and the USA followed suit from 1941 onwards.

Between the wars the stocks of gas and the capability of making gas were so limited everywhere, that they cannot be considered a credible deterrent. That remained the situation even after rearmament with conventional weapons had begun in about 1935. The latter may have been considered a more reliable safeguard and so given priority treatment. But protection against gas was another form of deterrent, and from 1936 onwards civil defence began to play a growing role in containing the threat of aerial gas attacks. Many governments professed to be studying appropriate measures, a few took elementary precautions,[62] but only in the UK, where German air raids in 1916–18 had made a profound impression, was there an organization and adequate equipment by September 1939. In the 1920s the behaviour of civilians and the decontamination of buildings and streets had been studied; the Royal Navy appointed an anti-gas officer for the Portsmouth dock-yard and the CWC busied itself with the design of decontamination centres. In 1929, ventilation tests were carried out at the Down Street and Maida Vale stations of the London Underground, and it was found that air locks at the entrances were useless and that the powerful draught created by the tube trains was ideal for quickly dissipating the gas.[63] Of much greater significance were the studies of different designs for civilian gas masks, and of rubber compounds and rubber accelerators to cut moulding times. It became obvious that something much simpler than the SBR was required, but the most suitable alternative—the German respirator—had poor visibility and the screw-on filter unit was an unnecessary complication. Nevertheless, it served as model for the experimental masks, which were extensively modified before the first prototypes went into production.[64] British civil defence began in earnest in 1935 when the Home Office took over from Sir John Anderson's ARP Committee which had met infrequently. The ARP Act of 1937 came into effect on 1 January 1938 by which time large contracts for civilian respirators had been let. Local authorities were responsible for protecting civilians, but at the outbreak of war, despite great activity on paper, training of wardens, police, and the fire services was incomplete.[65] Gas masks, by the million, had been issued, but their uselessness against arsenicals remained a well-kept secret. The citizenry, with their little respirators, had no idea what arsenicals were and remained blissfully ignorant of the most elementary precautions to be taken in the event of an attack with mustard gas. The measures may have deceived the civilians, but not the German specialists, and yet the combination of the public gas-mask distributions, press and radio coverage, official exhortations, as well as ignorance or suppression of muddles and technical failures sufficed: they gave comfort and strengthened resolve at home and signalled a warning to the enemy abroad. For as long as the Germans were less well protected than the British, they would, other things being equal, suffer the greater casualties from retaliatory gas raids. The message from London was unmistakable: as signatories of the Geneva Protocol we will not use gas first, but we are protecting our civilians against attacks from you, and we will injure your people if you strike against ours. That was a plain enough warning, but how great was the danger from Germany?

The Versailles Treaty prohibited all manufacture and trade in poison gas and instruments of delivery, and, it would appear, respirators. The production of gas (or equipment) by Germans outside the Reich was not explicitly forbidden. The MICC, set up under Article 208, was charged with the implementation of the disarmament clauses. It had a chemical section in Berlin under Henri Muraour and H. E. Watts, both qualified chemists. They were in touch with

Stoltzenberg whose slow progress in dismantling Breloh was notorious and they knew that in 1923 he had rented a site in Hamburg's dockland whence he traded in second-hand gas as Chemische Fabrik Stoltzenberg. They may have had their suspicions about the Reichswehr, but for several years the Waffenamt, its supply organization, operated very discreetly. When the Reichswehr began its secret discussions with the Russians, the manufacture and testing of poison gas were put on the agenda. The big chemical companies were approached but were not interested and in any event were under the surveillance of the MICC. So the choice fell on Stoltzenberg and in the latter half of 1923 he accompanied a German mission to Moscow. Among the Russian negotiators was V. N. Ipatieff who, a few years before, had been responsible for the Tsarist chemical warfare programme. It did not take Ipatieff long to see through Stoltzenberg whom he dismissed later as 'untrustworthy . . . I never believed what he said.'[66] An important part of the deal was the reactivation of a chemical factory built, but never operated, during the war at Ivashchenkovo in the province of Samara. A joint company was formed: the Russians put into it the value of the site and of the installations, the Germans contributed know-how and special equipment, in particular plant for making mustard gas. But the Waffenamt had underestimated the cost, and Stoltzenberg who was the contractor for the poison gas section, was not paid on time and had to borrow. By 1925, he was in trouble with the Russians for non-fulfilment of the contract. He now insisted that the Waffenamt put up more money. But the officials were becoming suspicious and decided to take the dispute to arbitration. Haber was asked to mediate. He asked for particulars of Stoltzenberg's design, was not satisfied that it would work and ruled against him. That was the end for Stoltzenberg: the creditors moved in and in 1926 a scandal threatened. If Stoltzenberg was not bailed out he would be bankrupted and that would attract much unwelcome publicity. On the other hand, if the Russo-German project was abandoned, the Russians would be sure to demand a revision of the 1923 agreement, and again publicity was most undesirable. At this awkward stage the German Foreign Office and the Reich Chancellery became involved. Stresemann's policy of peace and reconciliation had just been launched and clearly something had to be done quickly. It was decided to pay Stoltzenberg's creditors one-third of what they demanded and to take over his chlorine works (or what there was of it) north of Leipzig, and sell it for what it would fetch. The settlement with the Russians took much longer. The Germans withdrew from Ivashchenkovo (which still had not been completed) in 1928, and renounced all claims for equipment delivered but not paid for by the Russians. In return they obtained permission to attend chemical warfare field-trials.[67]

I have summarized the story at some length to show how German officials circumvented the peace treaty and became involved in a shady deal which did not yield them much. It remains to tell the sequel. Stoltzenberg was officially dropped and became a trader in dangerous scrap. All attempts to hush up the Russian agreement failed. The *Manchester Guardian* of 3 and 6 December 1926, using German sources, revealed a great deal and in all essentials it reported accurately. What is more, the articles alerted people that the Reichswehr was developing chemical warfare by proxy and it was rightly suspected that this was condoned if not connived at by senior politicians and civil servants. Articles in left-wing papers (possibly planted by Soviet agents to put pressure on the Germans to pay up) were noted abroad. German participation in Russian field-trials with poison gas had been authorized by Stresemann in 1928 and added to suspicions outside Germany.[68] Accordingly, when a storage tank holding 10 t of phosgene blew up on a hot Sunday afternoon on Stoltzenberg's site on the Müggenburger Kanal in Hamburg it created a sensation. The phosgene cloud of 20 May 1928 killed eleven people and injured several hundred. The German Cabinet expressed concern, the British Ambassador made official enquiries in Berlin, and there was a question in the House of Commons. It had been mischance: a welding seam had burst owing to a rise in pressure which was caused by the hot weather. Stoltzenberg was accident-prone, but as he was bankrupt there was no point in fining him. The army and the fire brigade took over the site and found 3,000 gas cylinders and altogether 50 t of toxic materials which they loaded on a freighter and dumped in the North Sea.[69]

We shall hear again of Stoltzenberg. Meanwhile, what was the extent of secret German chemical rearmament? During the Weimar Republic the Reichswehr schemed and relied on amateurs, but was unable to develop further the knowledge gained in the war. Stories circulating abroad of German research and development activities, though fanciful, were widely believed.[70] Defence was another matter. In the late 1920s Haber, Jaenicke, and, separately from them at Würzburg, Flury, were working on devices to clear gas-filled rooms, and the Auergesellschaft was reported to be studying new filters against particulate substances.[71] This was interesting, but not significant. A new impetus was given to chemical warfare after Hitler became Chancellor. With Haber's departure from the KWI in mid 1933, more compliant men took over: under G. Jander, who was shortly to be followed by P. Thiessen (who remained head of the Institute until 1945), much work was done on particulate clouds and on respirators, while Flury resumed his pharmacological investigations which had been interrupted in 1918. However by far the most important discovery was made in the Bayer research laboratories at Leverkusen where Dr G. Schrader had, in 1935, begun to study organic fluorine compounds with a view to investigating their insecticidal properties. When that line led to no results, he turned to organic phosphorus compounds. One of them, a cyanogen phosphoric acid amide, discovered in December 1936, was extremely toxic. Though commericlally useless it was patented and brought to the attention of the experts in the army. Schrader and his colleagues moved to Elberfeld and the product—the first nerve gas—called 'Tabun' (GA in the USA), began to be developed intensively. It went into large-scale production at Dyrhernfurth (in Silesia, now Poland) in Spring 1942. It was never used.[72]

Looking back at it all, the 1915–18 experience remained a major influence on defence up to 1939. Its effect on offensive warfare was chiefly noticeable in organization and supply arrangements. In practice, poison gas presented no serious military threat to soldiers and civilians. Yet, so powerful were the recollections of 1915–18 and so enduring the legends surrounding the events of that period, that public awareness of gas remained high throughout the inter-war years. It was a case of the shadow cast being larger than the substance.

Poison gas has been employed on some occasions in the past sixty years, but not all the details have been released. In what follows I have generally relied on published sources since the relevant archives were not accessible to me. It is, however, beyond question that in every case after 1918 and up to Hitler's war, the use of gas was sporadic and quite unlike the experience of 1915–18. The nature of the wars of 1918–39 and the terrain over which they were fought were different from the earlier conflict, so that gas was not being used for the same purpose, and indeed it seems to have been employed as much for experimental as for tactical ends. Gas remains the only weapon to have been introduced in one major conflict and not used in the next one.

The first of these episodes began even before the Great War was over, and took place during the British campaign in Northern Russia, initially on the Murmansk front, later south of Archangel. The CWC was consulted about mustard-gas shells, but that plan was not pursued. The War Office was more interested in testing arsenical smoke-generators. Major J. H. Davies was appointed CO of the Special Companies with the BEF in Northern Russia and the equipment was sent out in Spring 1919. Livens projectors were to be used in support of the advance from Archangel; they arrived without their base-plates and so were useless. The DM-generators arrived complete and were ignited on several occasions, the last time on 2 September 1919. But the trials were a fiasco and London lost interest. However, some useful observations were made: many generators failed to ignite, or when ignited did not sublimate the DM; none the less a sufficient number did work and the arsenical smoke penetrated the 'Green Band' type SBR. Davies was an ingenious commander and was able to attach 200 of the devices to the wings of aircraft, to have them ignited, flown over the Russian lines, and dropped. Only four generators broke, the rest worked, and when the British 'walked across' the position 36 hours later, they reportedly captured 700–800 Red Army soldiers 'who could hardly stand'. It sounds unbelievable and I have found no corroboration. When the British began to evacuate the bridgeheads, Davies was ordered to dump his equipment in the Dvina or the White Sea, and 47,000 smoke-generators were later sunk off-shore Murmansk.[73] The censorship was severe and few details of this miserable episode have survived in the accessible parts of the PRO. But it is reasonable to surmise that as a result of the events in North Russia, DM and the use of aircraft in chemical warfare were re-examined at Porton.

There were allegations that the Spanish army used gas in Morocco during the mid-1920s to crush a rising of tribesmen.[74] A few years later there were frequent reports of Japanese chemical warfare against the Chinese. According to Brown, the Japanese were producing mustard gas from 1928 onwards and they employed it intermittently in shells and bombs in Manchuria and elsewhere in China.[75] The League of Nations was repeatedly asked to verify and to condemn the Japanese, but it was impossible to obtain sufficient evidence to convince all the members. The Japanese were in possession of the field and having left the League in 1933, refused to collaborate. It was an entirely different matter in Abyssinia. Hailé Selassié complained about the use of gas by the Italians in December 1935, and the League had no difficulty in ascertaining that Abyssinian soldiers and civilians had been treated for mustard-gas burns. The Italians did not deny the accusations and claimed that they were merely retaliating against Abyssinian atrocities. When they felt sufficiently confident of winning the war, they walked out of the League (May 1936), asserting that Abyssinia was an internal Italian matter, and the military operations were of no concern to other states.[76] The Emperor's men were not surprisingly untrained in gas defence and in no position to retaliate, and these incidents yielded no tactical lessons on what would happen if the opponents were equally matched in chemical warfare.

During and after the Second World War there were occasional mentions of gas, but no reliable documentation appears to exist. In the early stages of Hitler's war, the belligerents did not have the means of delivering gas on a substantial scale. And when they did—in 1943–5—the fear of retaliation and the lack of preparedness of the Home Front (excepting the UK) kept the principals in check. The Nazis took their cue from Hitler. When he changed his mind about gas in the second half of 1944, it was too late and the instinct of self-preservation too strong among the German generals directly concerned with the implementation of the new policy. Similarly the Japanese. They had gas troops and equipment in the Pacific theatre, but never used them in their advance. When the tide turned against them, they were careful to avoid any provocation which would, after Roosevelt's death, have led to retaliation from the better-equipped American forces.[77]

Chemical warfare brought many chemists to military prominence. Most of those mentioned in this book would have made their mark in any case, indeed some of the older ones had done so before the war. Their activities after 1914 did not go unrewarded. Many were decorated for bravery, others were honoured for their scientific or practical achievements. So far as I have been able to discover, only a handful made money out of their ingenuity. The Royal Commission on Awards to Inventors received applications on behalf of a few who were well known. Bertram Lambert, who had invented the soda-lime-permanganate granule for the filter of the SBR, got £12,500—one of the rare large awards. Livens received £4,500 for his projector. H. B. Baker and S. J. Auld applied, but were turned down, for their anti-gas appliances. Levinstein, Green, and the British Dyestuffs Corporation also expected to be rewarded for their mustard-gas process.[78] The Levinstein—Green claim caused controversy and embarrassment, for it was exacerbated by the hostility between Herbert Levinstein and his group on the one hand, and Pope, C. S. Gibson (his assistant), and Thuillier on the other. Pope's group had taken out a secret wartime patent which was a rehash of Guthrie's old process, while Levinstein's claim to originality consisted of working at low temperature. It, too, was without substance because Kap Herr and the team at Usines du Rhône had used the technique some weeks before the people at Blackley had adopted it. The Royal Commission heard both sides, but eventually rejected the Levinstein—Green claim. The episode soured Levinstein's relations with many leading figures in the British chemical industry.[79] There was also controversy in Germany, and it is pleasant to record a favourable outcome. The Kaiser had been generous with his decorations, but a certain Pochwadt felt he had gone unrewarded for suggesting to Haber the use of phosgene as an offensive weapon. He bided his time, and after the Nazis came to power, judging the moment opportune, he appealed to the new masters. But the old connection still worked: Geyer or someone else in high command, took Haber's side in the defamatory allegations, and the Reichswehrministerium rejected Pochwadt's claim for a reward.[80]

Most of the scientists who had been commissioned to work as chemical advisers in the field or in the laboratories of the KWI, Porton, or the American University went back to teaching and research. Those on the Allied side usually retained some connection with chemical warfare and sat on the chemical, medical, or technical advisory committees. In Britain, several were elected Fellows of the Royal Society, and Pope was knighted for services in connection with chemical warfare.[81] Haber's colleagues had equally distinguished careers. Hahn, Hertz, and Franck, his trouble-shooters, became Nobel laureates. Freundlich, who had been in charge of filter-testing, stayed on at the KWI and was appointed deputy director; in 1933 he went to London and thence to the USA. Kerschbaum, Epstein, and Just were rewarded with honorary professorates for their war work and found jobs in industry. Epstein emigrated to France after 1933, was caught by the Nazis, and perished in one of their camps. Herzog became director of the Kaiser Wilhelm Institut für Faserstoffe and left Germany in 1933. Richard Willstätter and Hans Pick, who had done the fundamental work on the German respirators, had very different later careers. The first withdrew from the KWI in the latter part of 1915, but the decision in no way impaired his lifelong close friendship with Haber; he too was a Nobel Prize winner. Pick, a specialist in charcoal, joined the Aussiger Verein company after the war and died in the Terezin camp.[82] The American chemists who had flocked in great numbers to the CWS went back to teaching in 1919. J. B. Conant ultimately became President of Harvard, G. N. Lewis (another foreign member of the Royal Society) was the senior professor of chemistry at the University of California, and W. Lee Lewis, the discoverer of Lewisite, was appointed director of research at the Institute of American Meat Packers. V. H. Manning, the Head of the US Bureau of Mines who had been in overall charge of chemical warfare research at the American University in 1917–18, left government service in 1920, when he was chosen to be the first director of the Research Division of the American Petroleum Institute. There he initiated some of the fundamental work into the composition of properties of oil. In that position he must have come across one of the most unusual personalities among the scientists turned military organizers. V. N. Ipatieff[83] survived the Revolution, played an active role in the rebirth of the Russian chemical industry, only to fall foul of the Communist leadership. He emigrated to the USA in 1930 where he became a senior consultant to Universal Oil Products, then the leading independent research and patent licensing company in the American petroleum industry.

Of those who went into industry, G. P. Pollitt had a meteoric career: he joined Brunner, Mond and Co. and played a leading part in the introduction of the Haber–Bosch nitrogen fixation process into England. He was one of the original directors of ICI at the time of its foundation in 1926. R. E. Slade met Pollitt in the Special Brigade and instead of returning to his lectureship in Liverpool after the war, he too joined Brunner–Mond and was later an important figure at the Billingham works. Barley stayed with Hartley until the winding-up of the CWD had been completed, had several jobs offered to him and finally joined Nobels Explosives; later he took charge of ICI's Development Department in London, an appointment he held for many years. Victor Lefebure, a difficult man in the Special Brigade, made an excellent liaison officer in France and in 1919 joined the newly formed British Dyestuffs Corporation. He attracted attention with a badly written book, *The Riddle of the Rhine* (1921), about the past threat and future danger from the German chemical industry. He appears to have had something of a sinecure at the Dyestuffs Corporation, but lost his job in an economy drive and became technical adviser to a London firm of builders.[84] Many of the members of the CWS were industrial chemists who after, serving briefly, went back to their businesses; several became directors in the late 1920s and 1930s. I have been unable to trace the careers of the more senior German businessmen employed on war work by Auergesellschaft, Schering, Bayer, and other firms closely connected with chemical warfare. However, two Frenchmen, Joseph Frossard and Jacques de Kap Herr who developed mustard-gas production in 1917–18 call for mention. The former had been Assistant to the director of the Matériel Chimique de Guerre and took charge of the entire programme. In 1919, he became head of the Cie. Nationale des Matières Colorantes, and when it merged with the Kuhlmann Company he was appointed managing director of the new concern's organic chemical division.[85] Frossard later became chief executive of the company and played an important role in French industrial politics during the 1930s. Kap Herr also became a senior manager at Kuhlmann.

Some of the regular officers who had been in chemical warfare between 1915 and 1918 were pensioned off, but a few continued to serve for many years. Among the Germans, Peterson retired, but Hermann Geyer remained in the army and eventually became a general. He commanded a Corps from 1935 to 1942 and died in 1946. Hanslian was a freelance writer, but the Reichswehr paid for his editorial job at *Gas- und Luftschutz*, for his lectures at the army's gas training school, and assisted him to compile his books on gas warfare. He retired on grounds of ill-health from all public activities before the Second World War. Foulkes, by contrast, was indestructible. He reverted from his wartime rank of General to Colonel and in 1919 turned down the offer of Commandant of Porton. Thereupon he was gazetted a Brigadier-General in the RE and served in England and India. He was promoted Major-General in 1930, but as he had differences of opinion with his superiors he retired into civilian life as a director of John Oakley and Sons. One might be excused for thinking that the job was entirely appropriate because the company was (and remains) a leading British manufacturer of abrasives. Foulkes held the post until 1960, and died nine years later.[86] His one-time chief, Henry Thuillier, retained a military connection throughout his long life. After the war he became Commandant of the School of Military Engineering (1919–23) and that was followed by Director of Fortifications and Works at the War Office (the job held by Jackson before he became involved with gas) from 1924 to 1927, and he was GOC 52nd (Lowland) Division TA until 1930 when he retired and was knighted. In the 1930s he was Col. Commandant of the RE, became known for his writings on chemical warfare, and during Hitler's War served as a major in the Ministry of Supply where he dealt, once again, with poison gas. He died, aged 85, in 1953. Gen. Fries, another engineer, remained in charge of Edgewood and the CWS until his retirement in 1929. Throughout his service he boosted the CWS, but on the whole had little influence on policy-makers in Washington.

I have left Hartley and Haber, who had so much to do with the writing of this book, to the last. There is no doubt that the events of 1918–19 accelerated Hartley's career. He had arrived on the scene at a favourable juncture. The war had shown the value of practical scientists in important positions. Sir Harold (he was knighted in 1928) was the right man at the right time, and he did much to apply sensible scientific thinking to critical pressure points. After serving as Controller CWD in 1918–19 he combined a senior fellowship at Balliol with the direction of research at the Gas Light and Coke Co. (now the North Thames Gas Board). This large enterprise knew little and cared less about modern gas technology, but Hartley helped to drag it into the twentieth century, and extended the reforms to its domestic appliance business. He left Oxford in 1930, joined the London, Midland and Scottish Railway as director of research, and thenceforth his public appointments were as diverse as they were important, among them the chairmanship of Imperial Airways. He was one of the few to bridge the two cultures, and until his very last years was busy and fulfilled. Hartley died, aged 94, in 1972.

Haber's life after 1918 took a different and less happy turn. He was overwhelmed by the outcome of the war and, for several months, nervously exhausted. The Swedish Academy of Science having passed him over for the Nobel Prize in chemistry in 1918, decided a year later to award that for 1918 to him.[87] Despite that great honour, Haber's leading role in chemical warfare isolated him from the foreign scientific community for several years and may have decided him to campaign for the readmission of Germany in international institutions. But some people continued to distrust him, the more so as he spoke and wrote on poison gas and was, correctly, thought to have retained contacts with the Reichswehr on matters relating to chemical warfare.[88] This is not the place to summarize Haber's last fifteen years, spent, except at the very end, entirely at the KWI which became under his direction a centre of intellectual brilliance in physical chemistry. When Hitler became Chancellor and Jewish academics were purged, Haber prepared for emigration. It is known that he would have preferred to go to Switzerland for language and health reasons, but he received no invitation. The former enemies now rallied: in the summer of 1933 Haber was in London, spoke to Donnan, who alerted Hartley, who contacted Pope, and so the old-boy network worked again in unexpected ways. Pope offered laboratory space and other facilities and in September wrote about arrangements for Haber, his sister, his secretary, and a studentship for Dr Weiss, his last assistant. And so Haber left Germany for good and was made welcome in Cambridge by the Vice-Chancellor. He did not stay long. Ill-health and the climate depressed him: *en route* to southern Switzerland he died in Basle on 30 January 1934. He was just over 65.[89]

The purpose of the foregoing mention of the great and the deserving is not merely biographical listing and occupational classification, but to draw attention to the importance of wartime chemistry. Up to 1918 the specialists rarely made the contribution they thought they were entitled to make. But in the peacetime armies facilities were provided to enable chemists, physiologists, and technologists to work towards well-defined objectives. It is likely that some of the work was wasted and some badly directed, but in general the scientists had enhanced their status. They retained it and could count on the support of the eminent people who made up the advisory committees.

After 1918 the concept of an inter-disciplinary approach to chemical warfare gained ground. But there were practical difficulties. The Armistice had left a great deal of research and development incomplete. What was to be done about it? Who would give orders to whom? Who would determine priorities, bearing in mind that anti-gas work was finding greater favour with politicians than the pursuit of offensive research? And what about the staff themselves—were they to be officers in white laboratory coats or quasi-academics in a government department, with tenure but without the right of publication and unable to exchange views with others? The British advisers, notably Pope and Hartley, were all for 'unfettered' research, but the 'regulars', among whom we must count Crossley, the wartime head of Porton and his successor Rendel, supported a military environment and more emphasis on empirical testing. Beyond the legitimate differences of opinion over methods, there was the unresolved dispute over secrecy. The War Office took an extreme line, only to discover that too much secrecy had a detrimental effect on the recruitment of qualified staff, and in the end had to relax the rules a little.[90] The CWC, as recommended by the Holland Committee, was formally constituted in 1920. One of its chief functions was to advise on and monitor research and development activities at Porton. In the late 1920s Col. H. A. Lewis was president of the committee, and in addition to twelve representatives from the armed forces, there were more than eighty members. The real work was performed by specialist sub-committees and a co-ordinating Chairmen's Conference. But the Commandant of Porton, its military head and chief administrator, was not happy with the scientific management. He complained that military requirements were neglected, that there were not enough men with 'expert C.W. technical experimental knowledge', and of continuing differences between the research and development staff, that is the scientists, and the Director of Experiments, a regular soldier who was in charge of field trials.[91]

Lack of money and of staff imposed severe restraints on Porton. The recurring expenditure—salaries, wages, materials—was budgeted at £170,000 for the financial year 1922–3, and though some additional funds became available for civilian respirator work in the early 1930s, money remained tight. In 1922 the total establishment was 428. Three years later there were 51 qualified staff, 57 technical assistants, and about 300 others—for the most part men of the 58 (Porton) Coy., RE.[92] They did much repetitive work and as far as particulate clouds were concerned, the inadequate equipment (in part due to the instruments available in those days) seriously handicapped research. One gains the impression that the practical tests were more successful in answering some of the questions left unresolved by the war. Nor is this surprising. People were convinced that new toxic substances were unlikely to be found, and that success in offensive warfare lay in improving the quality and delivery of products such as phosgene, mustard gas, and DM. At Porton, as well as at Edgewood, a good deal of attention was paid to the reliability of the smoke-generators and Porton also carried out the design studies for the process improvements at Sutton Oak. Mustard-gas spraying from aircraft was often discussed, but was extremely expensive because planes had to be modified and elaborate tests needed to be organized to monitor airborne contamination. The Americans tried to finance this work on the back of crop-spraying trials and the British experimented with glass bombs holding 20 kg of mustard gas. The results were disappointing.[93] A great deal of study was devoted to the optimal configuration of gas masks and to raising the quality of charcoal, filter-papers, and granules. About 1926 the British began to redesign the respirator and after several years the 'GS Respirator' evolved. It resembled the SBR and remained in use throughout the Second World War. In the early 1930s work began on the civilian respirators and about 1935 the prototypes were undergoing tests. After further refinements they went into large-scale production from 1937 onwards.[94]

In the USA, the CWS made much of the commercial value of the research at Edgewood. The respirator studies and the filters had potential civil uses, but the chief significance lay elsewhere. All this activity helped to create the impression that chemical warfare had important scientific aspects which research was enlarging. Britain and America were signalling to potential enemies that if gas was used against them, they would retaliate with better offensive and defensive devices. No doubt there was some bluff in the scale and scope of what the scientists were doing, but it helped to make the German staff question the value of chemical warfare on Britain and its allies in the Second World War.

A good deal of the technology developed and first applied in the war was exploited commercially afterwards. The research centres devoted to poison gas endeavoured to find peaceful uses for their materials and devices. They were, everywhere, unsuccessful, and such 'fall-out' as has been recorded was modest and would have taken place anyway. At the KWI and also at Edgewood the chemists hoped that some of the organic substances on which they had been working could serve as starting-points for the preparation of pharmaceuticals or of insecticides. Nothing came of it. A few enterprising businessmen were quick off the mark and adapted wartime inventions to products such as gas-flow meters, non-toxic insecticide sprays, and materials for large-scale fumigation.[95] In Britain, it had been observed that workers in plants making chlorine and arsenicals were little affected by the influenza pandemic of 1918; it had also been noted at a hospital in North Staffordshire that gas-poisoning cases responded favourably to oxygen inhalation in an air-conditioned atmosphere. Neither the one nor the other turned out to be of medical significance.[96]

But the use of tear gas in the early months of the war had not been forgotten. After the war several lachrymatory substances were thoroughly investigated, and some American police authorities were readily persuaded to try out tear gas on demonstrators. Chloroacetophenone (code names CN or CAP) had been rejected in 1916–18 owing to its low vapour pressure which rendered it useless for trench warfare. But when dispersed as a smoke by a small burster charge, it was startingly effective. Edgewood designed a grenade, manufactured CN, and sold both through Federal Laboratories Inc. Its reception in Europe was more guarded, but it was gradually adopted in many countries for controlling civil disorder and was the principal tear gas for many years. It has now been replaced by CS (o-chlorobenzalmalononitrile) which disperses more easily and is quicker-acting.[97]

The one area in which a contribution of major peacetime value was made was industrial respirators. Considerable progress had been made during the war to elucidate the characteristics of different charcoals, and simultaneously special paper filters against particulates were found to have excellent dust-resisting properties, and could therefore be employed in lightweight filter-pads. Porton designed an industrial respirator which complied with British safety regulations and was produced commercially for many years.[98]

This short list covers all the projects that had some measure of success. One can think of other areas where chemical warfare technology might have made a contribution, for example crop-spraying, locust control, or insecticides. Considerable progress was made in these fields during the 1920s and 1930s, but the chemical companies, which had greater resources, made all the running.

It will be recalled that Bayer's entomologists noted the striking results of a phosphorus compound which was later developed as 'Tabun'. That would confirm the link between chemical warfare and chemical industry, but in general the connection is rarely so direct. The First World War had demonstrated that without a diversified and advanced technological base the production of military stores could be subject to long delays or forced to use inferior substitutes. The problems encountered with mustard gas in France and Britain, pointed to chemical backwardness and necessitated remedial action in the inter-war years.[99] But we would be stretching cause-and-effect relationships too far if we claimed that chemical warfare in 1915–18 caused the emergence of petroleum-derived chemicals. Poison gas was only one of many factors, and a minor one at that, behind the growth of aliphatic chemicals during the 1920s and 1930s.

At the end of a long history, I have reached several firm conclusions and have, on certain subjects, changed my views since, at Harold Hartley's suggestion, I began to study the subject. In the first place I have a better understanding of my father and of his work in those few war-time years: my admiration for him as an organizer and military thinker have grown. Secondly, the consequences of chemical warfare have been greater than the tactical effects of the use of gas itself. Thirdly, science and technology as applied to gas did change military thinking: they were ignored up to 1915, tolerated by 1918, and had become indispensable by 1939. The members of the Holland Committee were aware of the trend when they recommended that in future officers should be given sufficient scientific education at Woolwich as well as at Sandhurst to understand the language of scientists and to talk to them about science applied to war 'on terms of an intelligent equality'.[100] A generation or two passed before their advice had been taken. This leads me to the fourth conclusion: collectively, scientists collaborating with the military during 1915–18 required an unusual sense of purpose. Haber possessed to a high degree the right blend of innovation and communication in an extremely conventional setting, so also did the Chemical Advisers and the officers in special gas formations. Up to 1918, and often beyond, military thinking was still so inflexible as to reject most of the experts' advice. But applied science is an irresistible force, and traditional attitudes had to give way. At first, the services had demanded more of technology than it could deliver, but within twenty years or so they had grown sufficiently confident of the specialists to put to use what the advisers were in a position to supply.[101] Fifthly, research for its own sake rarely turned up something of immediate use. The conclusion, though contradicted by a few exceptions in 1915–18 and by Schrader's work at Bayer in the 1930s, still held generally true, at any rate until the Second World War. The reason is that the pressure of time and the need to achieve quick results defeat the thorough-going academic approach. Adaptations and improvements on what has been tried and tested are of the essence. In the chemical war trial-and-error empiricism were all important, the fundamental approach had a nil short-term yield. Hence the important devices turned out to be not the uncontrollable clouds and the DM smoke-generators, but Livens's rough and ready projectors and the gas-filled shell. But as the German failure with Blue Cross materials shows, it was not the shell that was to blame, but insufficient field tests. Sixthly, the bizarre forms an important part of the poison gas story. No doubt other weapons also have their demonology (and an older one at that), but poison gas, though hardly used since 1918, still haunts the memory. There are occasions when the past returns under extraordinary circumstances, and sets one thinking of history's strange ways. Take, for example, Speer's plan to kill Hitler. The story may be untrue, yet sounds plausible when one recalls the background: Speer proposed to suck gas into the Führer bunker through the air intakes of the ventilation system. That was in February or March 1945. Hitler who had complained of stale air and feared plots against his life recalled his First World War experience of heavier than air gases. He ordered the intakes to be raised to 4 m. Speer was foiled and Hitler survived for another few weeks.[102] More recently there was another strange event, and it involved, once again, Stoltzenberg. He had got through the war, rebuilt the business in Hamburg where he produced smoke devices and experimental quantities of poison gas for testing the respirators of the Bundeswehr. Occasionally he also obliged the Hamburg municipality by storing or disposing of toxic or explosive materials. In the 1960s, Stoltzenberg moved the business to Eidelstedt, a northern suburb of the city. He sold it to his manager in 1969 and retired. The enterprise decayed, the site became derelict, and children used it as a playground. Predictably, there was an accident: in 1979 one child was killed, two seriously injured. When the specialists began to clear up the mess they found 500 t of assorted explosives and small quantities of nerve and other gases. Stoltzenberg, once again, escaped punishment, for he had died in 1974. His offence had been to dump the dangerous stuff into disused peat-cuttings, to cover with earth, and then forget all about it. The army was called in and moved everything to a site near Münster in the Lüneburg Heath where decades earlier that very same Stoltzenberg had so incompetently destroyed the poison gas of the First World War.[103] Such episodes are absurd, but they are out of the ordinary and they do much to keep the legends surrounding poison gas before the public.

From these half-dozen conclusions, I turn to the threat of gas in another war. The range of toxic materials and the means of delivery have been perfected since 1918. Only the deterrent of effective and powerful retaliation can diminish, but not eliminate, the likelihood of chemical and biological warfare in another conflict. The concept of deterrence through the ability to retaliate was recognized in 1917–18. It led at the time to competition of being first with the latest, but the then existing limitations of chemistry restricted the scope of the race, and—just as important—the quality of the available gas defences weakened the effectiveness of the offensive materials. Everything is more complex now, but it is worth recalling that well before 1933 civilians were considered targets for chemical warfare. It was recognized even then (or, at the latest, early in Hitler's war) that the potential threat to unprotected non-combatants could only be averted if the deterrent power of retaliation was credible.[104] Stocks of poison gas and civil defence equipment (respirators, shelters, decontamination services) were the prerequisites for protection. But the means to retaliate (and so give the deterrent credibility) did not exist at the outbreak of Hitler's war; they were developed after its outbreak, yet gas was not used between 1939 and 1945.

Something else is needed to explain the absence of any kind of chemical warfare. Brown has suggested that 'coalition warfare' and 'escalation' were novel and potent barriers to the introduction of gas. By the first he means that Germany refrained from using gas against the Russians, lest the British use gas on German civilians or that the Americans refrained from gas warfare in the Pacific, lest the Japanese employ it against the Chinese. The second means that the introduction of gas in the battle area would be followed by retaliation behind the lines and so spread this form of warfare even more widely with unpredictable results.[105] I accept this reasoning because it makes sense and provides an explanation, though until the documents are released the details of the decisions will not be known. But what of international agreements? Ever since the Hague Conventions and the Geneva Protocol there has been an air of unreality about the prohibition of chemical warfare. Agreements are meaningless unless there are penalties. But who will impose the penalties? And if the more modest aim of verification is sought, who will investigate and monitor? The MICC had access to Germany's chemical potential for seven or eight years after the Armistice, but was unable to control Stoltzenberg's ludicrous activities. It may be that these things would be better managed now, but the problem remains of making an agreement stick.

Thus fear and uncertainty continue. Do we have to live with them? I am sure we have to, but I also think that, as time passes, we will learn to live with our anxieties. Some latter-day Dr Strangelove may press the buttons that unleash another chemical war, kill millions, and end the debate. But even here, there is a comforting thought: the introduction of a new form of warfare in April 1915 created its own mythology. And one legend, in particular, is especially tenacious. It is that gas warfare is continuously being bettered and rendered ever more dangerous. That is indeed likely, but what is overlooked now, as it was in 1915, is that wind, rain, and heat are potent obstacles to the effective use of gas. It may be more dangerous than ever before, but it remains subject to the elements. Meanwhile, there are many other weapons besides chemical and biological devices, and they are being improved so that they are certainly better than their forerunners in two World Wars.[106] The final lesson that I have learnt from this book is that gas has no unique claim to novelty. Better ways of killing and injuring continue to be invented, are tested and appeal to those in command. That is regrettable, but it's the way of the world. Still, it is a fact that the improvements to conventional weapons have made the rifle and the gun a much greater danger to soldiers and civilians than the chemical weapons that were introduced from 1915 onwards. The image of future chemical warfare is worse than its present reality.

APPENDIX:
ARTICLES 169–172 OF THE TREATY OF VERSAILLES

Article 169

Within two months from the coming into force of the present Treaty German arms, munitions and war material, including anti-aircraft material, existing in Germany in excess of the quantities allowed, must be surrendered to the Governments of the Principal Allied and Associated Powers to be destroyed or rendered useless. This will also apply to any special plant intended for the manufacture of military material, except such as may be recognised as necessary for equipping the authorised strength of the German Army.

The surrender in question will be effected at such points in German Territory as may be selected by the said Governments.

Arms and munitions which on account of the successive reductions in the strength of the German army become in excess of the amounts authorized by Tables II and III annexed in this Section must be handed over in the manner laid down within such periods as may be decided by the Conferences referred to in Article 163 [which deals with the first reduction of German forces to 200,000 within three months of the coming into force of the Treaty].

Article 170

Importation into Germany of arms, munitions and war materials of every kind shall be strictly prohibited.

The same applies to the manufacture for, and export to, foreign countries of arms, munitions and war material of every kind.

Article 171

The use of asphyxiating, poisonous and other gases and all analogous liquids, materials or devices being prohibited, their manufacture and importation are strictly forbidden in Germany.

The same applies to materials specially intended for the manufacture, storage and use of the said products or devices.

The manufacture and the importation into Germany of armoured cars, tanks and all similar constructions suitable for use in war are also prohibited.

Article 172

Within a period of three months from the coming into force of the present Treaty, the German Government will disclose to the Governments of the principal Allied and Associated Powers the nature and mode of manufacture of all explosives, toxic substances and other like chemical preparations used by them in the war or prepared by them for the purpose of being so used.

Source: *The Treaty of Peace between the Allied and Associated Powers and Germany . . . signed . . . 28 June 1919,* HMSO, 1919.

NOTES

Chapter 1

1. Hartley, Sir Harold: 'Fritz Haber' (typescript, 1961), p. 1.
2. The material was collected in 1934–5. Apart from letters, Coates's manuscript notes run to about 100 pages and shed a most revealing light on Haber. The lecture was given in 1937. After Professor Coates's death in 1973, his son very kindly gave me the papers.
3. The letters, among the Hartley papers, are dated 26 March, 3 and 15 May respectively.
4. Letters to Sir Solly (now Lord) Zuckerman of 10 May and 22 June 1961 among the Hartley papers.
5. Cf. *Memorial lectures delivered before the Chemical Society 1933–42*, vol. IV (1951), pp. 127–57.
6. It is not known who coined this apposite verb. I have used the conjugation employed by the late Sir David Martin replying on behalf of the Royal Society Club at the dinner in Celebration of the 90th birthday of Sir Harold Hartley. *Notes and Records of the Royal Society of London*, 24, 1 (June 1969), p. 115.
7. Schwarte, M. (ed.): *Die Technik im Weltkriege* (1920). The chapter runs to only thirty pages in a book of 600.
8. Hanslian, R. (ed.): *Der chemische Krieg*, 3rd edn. (1937). References throughout this book are to the 3rd edition unless expressly stated otherwise.
9. The files, together with Hartley's other papers, were deposited at Churchill College in 1973.
10. Hartley papers, in particular files on German gas attacks.
11. The techniques and substances will be described in later chapters.
12. The reports are among the Hartley papers. Another report—'Les Gaz de Combat'—is dated 12 Oct. 1922. It is at the PRO, WO/188/176, French Questionnaire on German Factories. I do not know whether Hartley ever saw it.
13. Letter from J. Davidson Pratt, then Secretary of the CWC, to Hartley, 9 June 1921. Hartley papers.
14. It contains pencil notes, in telegraphese, of his meetings. The hand-writing is atrocious. Bruce Wilcock and others at the Oxford University Press were able to decipher many difficult passages, and Hartley himself was able to interpret some, but large gaps remain. These notes were essentially personal 'background' information.
15. Introduction to Hartley Report.
16. For example there should be ample documentation on Russia and Italy. There is very little of the former and the meagreness of the latter could fortunately

be supplemented by official reports and memoranda which Lt.-Col. Leslie Barley kindly put at my disposal.

17. *Notes of the Royal Soc.*, 24, p. 112.
18. Information from Dr. J. Jaenicke, who investigated the whereabouts of the KWI documents. He showed me his copy of the report on organic compounds, a highly technical report, analogous to those prepared at Porton in 1917–18 and now at the PRO.
19. Stahl, F. C.; 'Die Bestände des Bundesarchiv-Militärchiv', *Militärgesch. Mitt.*, 2 (1968), pp. 139–40.
20. Report No. 2547, A.10. It was translated by T. H. Adams on 9 Dec. 1918.
21. Interview with Dr Heyl, director of the archive, 6 Sept. 1971.
22. Box 16N827, GQG, État Major, 1er Bureau, file 342/3.
23. *History of the Ministry of Munitions*, vol. XI (n.d., ? 1921), pt. II, 'Chemical Warfare Supplies', p. 1. hereafter abbreviated to MoM History.
24. Bloch, J. von: *Der Krieg*, vol. I (1899), p. xix.
25. Prentiss, A. M.: *Chemicals in War* (1937). The author, it might be noted, was American, a Ph.D. in chemistry, and a Brigadier-General in the CWS.
26. Lanchester, F. W.: *Aircraft in Warfare* (1916). Lanchester was an outstanding engineer. His law is based on the relationship of the squares of the numbers opposing each other multiplied by the fighting-value of the individual units.
27. Pope, Sir W.: 'Presidential Address to the Chemical Society', *Tr. Chem. Soc.*, 115 (1919), pp. 397, 405.
28. It now hangs in the Imperial War Museum.
29. The classification and definition of poison gas creates endless difficulties. The materials may not be poisonous, that is destroying life or injuring health, below a minimum level, nor are chemical warfare agents invariably gaseous. Some are liquid at ordinary temperature and pressure, others are employed as a very fine dust of microscopic particles. Nevertheless poison gas is a suitable collective noun for the various materials. The characteristics of the principal poison gases employed during the First World War will be discussed in their proper place.
30. Brown, F. J.: *Chemical Warfare. A Study in Restraints* (1968), pp. 290 ff.
31. The British figures are based on a 1:23 random sample which excludes Commonwealth and Colonial troops and foreign contract labour. The German casualty statistics, though detailed, do not cover the entire war period. The French information is not systematically presented.

Chapter 2

1. *Dictionary of National Biography*, article on Thomas Cochrane, 10th Earl of Dundonald (1775–1860). Dundonald was no scientist, but a distinguished naval officer with a great interest in marine engineering. His father was an early, but unsuccessful industrial chemist, his nephew, Col. William Francis Cochrane (1847–1928) vainly attempted to interest the War Office in poison gas in 1914.
2. Carbon disulphide would have been the toxic ingredient obtained if one followed his advice of passing sulphur vapour over red hot coke. Carbon disulphide

became an important chemical once the viscose rayon process developed industrially just before the First World War. The liquid boils at 46° C and is inflammable.

3. For further information see in particular: Davis, Sir Robert H.: *Breathing in Irrespirable Atmospheres* (1948), pp. 16 ff; and Hanslian: *Chem. Krieg*, p. 6.

4. See the present author's *Chemical Industry during the 19th Century* (1958), pp. 8–9, 96–7.

5. Nagel, A. von: 'Fuchsin, Alizarin, Indigo', BASF (n.d.), *Schriftenreihe des Firmenarchivs*, pp. 35–7; Haynes, Williams: *American Chemical Industry, a History* (1954), vol. I, pp. 276–80.

6. Blücher's *Auskunftsbuch für die chemische Industrie* (1926), articles on Coal Tar Dyes and Phosgene; Kirk–Othmer: *Encyclopedia of Chemical Technology* (1969) 2nd, rev. edn., vol. XX, articles on triphenylmethane dyes.

7. There are seventy-five references to masks and respirators before the First World War in a typed bibliography of gas masks prepared by Dr W. P. Kennedy in 1951 at the Library of the Chemical Defence Research Establishment, Porton.

8. Davis: *Breathing in Irrespirable Atmospheres*, pp. 188 ff.

9. Robida, A.: *La Guerre au vingtième siècle* (1887), pp. 17, 27.

10. Pp. 137, 142–3, 144, 212 in the Heinemann edition (1963) refer to Black Smoke.

11. Colomb, P., Maurice, J. F., *et al.*: *The Great War of 189–: A Forecast* (1893), pp. 228–30. The authors, though professionals, were not scientists. Their bomb would have been highly unstable and the hoped-for additive effect unlikely to materialize. The point is only worth mentioning as an instance of the gap between applied science and conventional land warfare.

12. Driant (1855–1916) was Boulanger's son-in-law. Though well over military age, he volunteered in 1914 and soon attracted attention by his criticism of the neglect of the Verdun defences. He was killed fighting the Germans at the Bois des Caures.

13. Clarke, I. F.: *Voices Prophesying War 1763–1984* (1963), pp. 231–9.

14. *International Encyclopedia of the Social Sciences*, vol. IV (1968), p. 197: article on Disarmament by J. D. Singer.

15. Ibid., vol. X (1968), pp. 317–18: article on Military Law by J. W. Bishop jnr.

16. Prentiss,: *Chemicals in War*, p. 685.

17. Ibid., p. 686.

18. The tortuous reasoning can be seen at its best in the proceedings before a Committee of the German Reichstag (*Völkerrecht im Weltkrieg*), 3rd series, vol. IV: 'Gaskrieg, Luftkrieg . . .' (1927), pp. 1–42.

19. The story appears to have originated in an article by Major West in *Science* of 2 May 1919. It was repeated by Haber: *Fünf Vorträge* (1924), p. 83; Hanslian: *Chem. Krieg*, pp. 10–11; Prentiss: *Chemicals in War*, p. 132, and others.

20. *The Times*, *Le Temps*, and *Le Figaro* of 29 April 1912. The French papers devoted almost an entire page to the event.

21. Florentin, D.: 'Les Poudres, les explosifs et les gaz de combat', in *Dix ans d'efforts scientifiques et industriels 1914–24*, vol. I. (1926), pp. 682, 694.

22. PRO/MUN 5/197/1650/6: 3rd Liaison Report on Gas Warfare by Lt.-Col. Crossley; 2 Nov. 1916, pp. 13 ff.
23. Interview with Dr Jaenicke 23 Sept. 1972. He apparently got the information from the Company's archives.
24. BA, folios 95–139 Bauer papers. The report is undated, but from the context was written after 1918, possibly for the German delegation at Versailles.
25. BMA, File N 221/32, letter from Fritz Haber to Gen. Geyer, 1 Aug. 1933 describing the background to the German use of phosgene.
26. MoM History, p. 1.
27. Ibid. and PRO/MUN5/385/1650/4, first draft of a 'History of Chemical Supply', April 1915–July 1917 by Mrs L. J. Redstone of the Historical Section of the Ministry.
28. PRO/WO/143/53. Report by Professor Steele to the General Chemical Sub-committee of the Trench Warfare Department, 26th Meeting, 4 Aug. 1915.

Chapter 3

1. BMA, N221/223, Geyer papers. Memorandum by Geyer, dated 29 March 1922.
2. Hartley Report, p. 2.
3. The French chemist Moureu later discovered an acrolein stabilizer.
4. By a curious coincidence Bauer and Jackson, both closely connected with chemical warfare, had similar pre-war jobs. In 1914 the former was chief of the fortress and heavy artillery section at OHL, the latter was in charge of Fortifications and Works at the War Office.
5. MoM History pp. 1–2. PRO/MUN5/385/1650/7, 'History of SK' by J. F. Thorpe (typescript, 10 Feb. 1919).
6. PRO/CAB 21–83: Cabinet file on correspondence re gas, Jan. 1915 onwards.
7. Trumpener, H. U.: 'The Road to Ypres', Jnl. of Mod. Hist., 47, 3 (1975), p. 462.
8. Haber: Fünf Vorträge, p. 83.
9. FMA 16N832, folder 1080/0, item 1. The particulars of the telegram of 30 March 1915 are quoted in a letter of 17 April 1915 from 4ème Section Génie to Joffre. I have found no confirmation that the Germans employed tear gas against the French in that month.
10. FMA 16N832, folder 1080/0, item 21. Telegram from Foch's HQ to GQG, 26 April 1915, asking for Bertrand No. 1 (chloroacetone) grenades.
11. Trumpener: 'Road to Ypres', p. 463.
12. Haber: Fünf Vorträge, p. 83.
13. Nernst knew Bauer and on a visit to OHL at the end of September lunched with him and Geyer. Both officers were interested in what Nernst had to say about chemicals in war. See note 1 above for source.
14. Trumpener: 'Road to Ypres', p. 465. His figure of 17,000 shells filled cannot be reconciled with the amount ordered. Either the former is much too high or the latter much too low.
15. Schwarte: Technik im Weltkriege, p. 279.

16. Vinet, E. G.: 'Report on the German C.W. Organisation, translated from French by the War Office 1 Dec. 1920, p. 27, in PRO/WO/188/114.

17. Taken from Vinet op. cit., p. 26; Memorandum by H. E. Watts dated 15 Feb. 1922. When the two sources conflict I have relied on Watts who is more precise on dates.

18. Schwarte: *Technik im Weltkriege*, p. 280.

19. Trumpener: 'Road to Ypres', p. 469.

20. Col. Belaiew, of the Military Artillery Academy in St Petersburg, described the shelling when he visited Britain in July 1915. The date and location tally with German accounts, but his story that the Germans also discharged chlorine from cylinders is pure imagination. It would appear that the Russians did not report the use of tear gas at Bolimów to their Allies until Belaiew's visit. PRO/WO/142/134, file CWD 386.

21. BA, Bauer papers, folios 8–11; letter from Duisberg to Bauer 3 March 1915 and folios 50–61, letter to the chairman of the artillery proof commission Berlin, 6 April 1915.

22. Coates, J. E.: 'Haber Memorial Lecture', *Memorial lectures delivered before the Chemical Society*, vol. IV (1951), p. 143.

23. Vinet: 'Report on the German C.W. Organisation', pp. 6, 27.

24. German replies to Questionnaire of Allied Military Control Commision 1920–1, Hartley papers. This particular piece of information was supplied by Professor Fritz Epstein, Haber's personal assistant.

25. Hartley Report, pp. 2–3 and family information.

26. Haber: *Fünf Vorträge*, p. 76 (tr.).

27. Interview with Hartley, 9 Jan. 1972; Trumpener: 'Road to Ypres', pp. 470–3.

28. Deimling, B. von: *Aus der alten in die neue Zeit* (1930), p. 201.

29. BMA N 56/4, Tappen papers. Tappen's reply, dated 19 March 1927 to a questionnaire by the Reichsarchiv on Ypres. BA Bauer papers, folios 185–90, letter from Bauer to Haber, 20 March 1927.

30. Mordacq, J. J. H.: *Le Drame de l'Yser* (1933), p. 48.

31. FMA 16N826, GQG 1er Bureau, Cie Z: report of the head of the meteorological services to GQG, 12 Jan. 1916.

32. The four worst months were Jan. March, Dec., and Oct. in that order. PRO/WO/142/153, file CL/3/15. The report is dated 20 May 1915.

33. Interview with Dr Canepeel, Ypres, 7 April 1972.

34. Schroth, A.: *Bilder aus dem Leben der Gaspioniere im Feld* (n.d.), p. 6.

35. A second regiment, No. 36, was formed early in May. Meier-Welcher, H. and von Groote, W. (ed): *Handbuch zur deutschen Militärgeschichte*, 3rd series, V (1968), pp. 254–5. Hanslian (*Chem. Krieg*, p. 17) says that Peterson's men consisted of large numbers of chemists and chemistry students besides engineers, but there is no confirmation for that statement from other sources.

36. This statement and others later in the chapter are based on visual evidence. An enthusiastic and competent amateur photographer accompanied the observers. He used excellent film and well over a hundred photographs have survived for the period April–Oct. 1915. They are dated, have brief captions, and so provide precise detail often not elsewhere available. The collection was

in Haber's possession and was found at the bottom of an old chest in my mother's flat in March 1973. They are now in the IWM.

37. Hahn, O.: *My Life* (1970), pp. 118–19. The autobiography is always interesting, but the details are sometimes unreliable.

38. Photographs dated 10 Feb. (1915), captioned *Gaswolke in Wahn.*

39. Hanslian: *Chem. Krieg*, p. 87; Trumpener: 'Road to Ypres', pp. 473–4.

40. Schwarte: *Technik im Weltkriege*, p. 281; Hartley Report, p. 3.

41. Vinet, E.: 'Report on the Organisation and Working of the Four German Field Ammunition Depots' (June 1920), no page no.

42. Hanslian: *Chem. Krieg*, p. 87; Deimling: *Aus der alten*, pp. 202–3; Interview with Dr Canepeel.

43. Hartley Report, p. 3; 'Report of Chemical Dept. of (German) War Ministry', No. 2547, 11.17.A.10, 21 Dec. 1917, translated by T. H. Adams for DGS 9 Dec. 1918 (hereafter referred to as report No. 2547), Hartley papers.

44. Prentiss: *Chemicals in War*, p. 663.

45. Hartley Report, p. 3; Schwarte: *Technik im Weltkriege*. Haber's letter to the Draeger company appears as facsimile at the end of Hanslian's *Der deutsche Gasangriff bei Ypern am 22. April 1915* (1934).

46. BMA, N221/23 Geyer papers: *Denkschrift betreffend des Gaskampf und Gasschutz* (n.d.), covering letter of memorandum is dated 27 March 1919.

47. Trumpener: 'Road to Ypres' pp. 476–7; Hanslian: *Chem. Krieg*, p. 88. All times are GMT, one hour behind German time.

48. Liddell Hart, B. H.: *Foch*, vol. I (1937), p. 183. FMA 16N832, folder 1080/0, items 5–8. Isorni, J. and Cadars, L.: *Histoire véridique de la Grande Guerre*, vol. III (1970), pp. 208–15, state (p. 212) that the 11th Division which occupied the sector around Langemark had prepared mouthpads and told the Algerians who relieved them that the Germans might use chlorine against them.

49. PRO/MUN5/198/1650/17, historical surveys prepared by Captain Atkinson in Jackson's office in 1917 or 1918.

50. PRO/CAB/21/83. Cabinet file on gas. Hankey's note was written on 24 April; his visit to the BEF took place earlier.

51. Morddacq: *Drame de l'Yser*, pp. 55, 59; Nicholson, G. W. L.: *The Canadian Expeditionary Force 1914–19* (1962), p. 56.

52. Report no. 2547 and FMA 16N826, GQG; Report of Médecin Inspecteur Sieur of the DAB, dated 25 April 1915.

53. BMA, N 102/10, Heber, K: 'Aufzeichnungen', p. 4, (n.d., but *c*. 1937–8). Heber was a gas observer and his report compiled years later from notes is not always dependable. Interviw with Dr Canepeel. Liddell Hart, B. H.: *History of the First World War* (1970), pp. 243 ff. Nearly sixty years later, gunner Bloye, who was near Vlamertinge on that day, some 8 km from the gas discharge still remembered the foul smell. Interview with Mr Bloye 8 Oct. 1973.

54. Report No. 2547; Mordacq: *Drame de l'Yser*, pp. 105, 135; Trumpener: 'Road to Ypres', pp. 23–5.

55. Hartley's notes on interview with Nernst in Berlin 23 June 1921. Nernst nursed a further grievance: his trench mortars capable of firing tear-gas projectiles had not been used.

56. Hanslian: *Gasangriff*, pp. 82, 87–90. The opinions were of the *post hoc* kind; one would like to know what these eminent officers had thought of the operation before the event.
57. Dispatch No. 140, Hartley papers.
58. PRO/CAB/21/83.
59. Nicholson: *Canadian Expeditionary Force*, pp. 72–5; Heber: 'Aufzeichnungen', p. 6; Anon: 'German Gas Warfare' (typescript, n.d.), p. 2, Hartley papers. This well-informed report may have been written by C. G. Douglas. Neither Hartley nor Barley claimed authorship.
60. I have omitted reports of gas on 26 April and 2 May (mentioned by Nicholson, p. 85 and Hanslian, p. 91 respectively) because they were not confirmed by other German and British sources. The chief references used are 'German Gas Warfare'; Schroth: *Bilder . . . der Gaspioniere*, p. 8–9; PRO/WO/142/91, folder DGS 23; summary of Court of Enquiry on 24 May 1915; Hanslian: *Chem. Krieg*, p. 91.
61. Hartley Report, pp. 4–5.
62. Heber: 'Aufzeichnungen', p. 7; Trumpener: 'Road to Ypres', p. 479. The collection of phots (see n. 36 above) has provided some useful pictorial support for the statements in this and the following three paragraphs.
63. PRO/WO/142/98, folder DGS 90: Typed notes by Captain C. P. Schwabe, British Military Mission in Petrograd, undated. Letter and sketch map from W. L. Hicks, Petrograd, to Col. Cummins, 7 May 1917, Hartley papers.
64. Hoffmann, M.: *Der Krieg der versäumten Gelegenheiten* (1923), pp. 113 ff. The main German efforts were to be made from the north (where the 12th Army advancing from East Prussia was reinforced by divisions drawn from the 9th) and from the south.
65. Heber: 'Aufzeichnungen', p. 9, gives 5 per cent. Vinet's 'Report on the German C.W. Organisation', pp. 16–17, mentions 20 per cent.
66. Schwabe's notes; Heber: 'Aufzeichnungen', pp. 10, 11; Reichsarchiv: *Der Weltkrieg*, vol. VIII (1932), pp. 134–5.
67. Hahn: *My Life*, p. 120; *Der Weltkrieg*, VIII, pp. 135–6; Heber: 'Aufzeichnungen', pp. 11, 12.
68. Heber: 'Aufzeichnungen, p. 13. *Der Weltkrieg*, VIII, p. 334. The official history states that the cylinders were opened at 2145. This is surely a misprint. Heber claims there were no German losses; I have preferred to rely on the official version of the incident.
69. BA, Schwertfeger papers, folios 43–5, letter from Nernst to Valentini 12 Aug. 1915 enclosing report on the two actions, dated 5 Aug. 1915. The first trials took place on 17 and 18 June at Neuville on the western front. No visible evidence of casualty-inflicting power was discovered. I consider that the trench mortar episode reflected the antagonism between Haber and Nernst which dated back to the 1900s. The former was in the ascendant and ousted his rival.
70. Schroth: *Bilder . . . der Gaspioniere*, pp. 12, 13.
71. BA, Schwertfeger papers, folios 37–8: letter from Haber to Valentini, dated 2 Jan. 1916 in which he reviews chemical warfare in 1915.

72. Hanslian: *Chem. Krieg*, p. 91. Barley roughly estimated gas casualties on 24 April and during May at 2,000 and 6,000 respectively. PRO/WO/142/109, folder DGS M/95. Much later, Nicholson (*Canadian Expeditionary Force*, p. 83) went through the records and estimated the Canadian losses from all causes on 24, 25, and 26 April at 1,500.

Chapter 4

1. Sartori, M.: *The War Gases* (1940). This book contains detailed descriptions of all war gases used in 1915–18.
2. A memorandum in PRO/WO/142/115 by Professor B. Moore of the London Hospital Medical College dated 7 July 1915 is of considerable interest in this connection because he demonstrated that short bursts of gas were the best method of generating a dense cloud. Moore did not concern himself with diffusion. Among the Hartley papers there is only one description of an experimental gas discharge—590 kg, of chlorine on 17 Nov. 1916. The details given do not permit any rigorous analysis, and the only firm conclusion is the not very original one that concentration diminishes rapidly with distance. Years later, Prentiss (*Chemicals in War*, pp. 59–75) addressed himself to the subject, but his formulation of a theory of gas clouds is incomplete. It was examined very thoroughly by Dr Jonathan Shoham who came to the conclusion that Prentiss's aim was to draw up a mode of working and not a framework for a physical law on poison gas clouds. All that emerges is that if a certain average concentration up to a height of 2 m above ground is to be achieved at a known distance, then given wind speed, drag and distance, the volume to be released will vary directly with the cube root of the weight of the chemical discharged.
3. Interviews with Dr. E. Gold, FRS, 19 and 26 Feb. and 1 April 1972.
4. The following sources have been used (numbers in brackets refer to columns): (1) W. G. Macpherson *et al.*: *Medical Services*, vol. II (1923), pp. 254–5; (2) Haber: *Fünf Vorträge*, p. 92 and Hartley Report, pp. 52–3; (3) Prentiss: *Chemicals in War*, pp. 14–16; (4) Clark, D. K.: 'Effectiveness of Chemical Weapons in WWI', (1959), p. 16.
5. Monkeys were found to be more responsive to phosgene than dogs: $0.4 \mathrm{g/m^3}$ was lethal to them within three minutes, as compared to $1.5 \mathrm{\ g/m^3}$ for dogs. Rabbits were the least sensitive ($7.5 \mathrm{\ g/m^3}$). The results were challenged after the war. West, C. J.: 'Phosgene'. Monograph No. 4 of War Gas Investigations, American University Experiment Station, Washington (typescript, 24 May 1918), p. 88 in PRO/SUPP/10/129 (Quinan papers).
6. Boyland, E. and Goulding, R. (eds.): *Modern Trends in Toxicology* (1968), pp. 1–2.
7. German wartime data would be especially interesting. The first German to write on the subject was F. Flury who worked in Haber's institute. He gives some experimental data in 'Über Reizgase' in *Z. f.d.g. exp. Med.*, 18 (1921), pp. 1–15 but the article is of little scientific value and the statistical approach to the experiments is so incompetent that one cannot draw any conclusions from them.
8. Freundlich: 'The German Gas Mask Filter' (typescript, n.d.), among Hartley

papers; Heeres-Sanitätsinspektion . . .: *Sanitätsbericht . . . 1914–18*, vol. III (1934), p. 180.

9. Haldane's scathing comments were made on 24 May 1915 to the Adjutant General (PRO/WO/142/91, file DGS 23). Carey Morgan, M.: 'Report on the Work of Women in Connection with the Anti-Gas Department' (typescript in IWM Library, 1919), pp. 3 and 5; typed note by L. J. Barley, 2 Oct. 1918.

10. PRO/WO/142/153, file CL 3/15; PRO/WO/142/90, file DGS 3; PRO/MUN/5/198/1650/17. Interviews with Hartley, 10 Oct. 1971 and Barley, 8 March 1972. Notes among Hartley papers.

11. FMA 16N832, folders 1080/0 to 3 and 16N823.

12. Mouat Jones, B.: 'Development of German Gas Defence Appliances', 17 Dec. 1918 in PRO/WO/142/162, file CL/23/18–19 and a report by G. M. W. MacDonogh, DGMS 280/2/37 dated 12 Sept. 1915 among the Hartley papers. German sources hardly mention this respirator and I have seen no report of a general issue to troops.

13. Hartley, H.: 'Chemical Warfare', paper read to Section B of the British Association 1919. Raper, H. S.: 'History of the Anti-Gas Department' (n.d.), PRO/MUN 5/386/1650/13. Interview with Barley, 8 March 1972. Memorandum by P. S. Lelean, 20 June 1915 in PRO/WO/142/182, file AGD/4. Letter from E. F. Harrison to Barley dated 18 Feb. 1916, Barley papers.

14. Interview with Barley 8 March 1972. Barley's note 2 Oct 1918. Fox, M. S.: *Corporals All* (1965), pp. 2–3. 'The Work of the Royal Engineers . . . 1914–19', *RE Jnl.* (1921), pp. 105–20.

15. Circulars and Instructions among Hartley papers. The most detailed, though not the first, is dated GHQ 4 June 1915.

16. FMA 16N826, GQG, État Major 1er Bureau, Cie Z.

17. Circular (translated), dated 28 June 1915, HQ German 4th Army, Thielt, among Hartley papers. Hartley Report, p. 29.

18. 'Gas Defence; Men's Reactions 24.5.1915 in German Gas Warfare', unsigned, undated report (possibly written by C. G. Douglas) among Hartley papers.

19. Barbusse, H.: *Le Feu* (1917), p. 30.

20. MoM History, *passim*. Interview with J. E. Coates on 22 Nov. 1972. He was one of those who answered the appeal of the Institute of Chemistry. Letter from R. C. Gale to Harold Hartley, 5 Oct. 1970, in Hartley Papers.

21. The order was given on 19 June 1915. MoM History, pp. 2–4.

22. MoM: 'First Report of Chemical Sub-Committee of the Scientific Advisory Committee of the Trench Warfare Department, for period ending 16.8.1915', pp. 7–8, in Hartley papers (hereafter referred to as 1st, 2nd . . . Reports of the CS-C).

23. The meeting at Boulogne was attended be Gen. Ivor Philipps, MP (Parliamentary Secretary to the Ministry of Munitions), Foulkes, and Cummins of the RAMC, in PRO/MUN5/197/1650/8. Moreland, H.: 'Chemical Warfare Record of Chemical Supplies' (1919), pp. 44–5, in PRO/MUN5/386/1650/10. MoM History, XI, pt.I, 'Trench Warfare Supplies' (n.d.), p. 95 and MoM History, p. 3.

24. Fox: 'Corporals All', pp. 2–3, 12–13.

25. 6th Army HQ, 7 July 1915 (British translation of German circular) and German circulars issued in Aug.–Sept. 1915 among Hartley papers.
26. PRO/MUN5/198/1651, file 1.1 and FMA 16N827, letter from 4ème Direction Ministère de la Guerre to GQG, dated 17 Oct. 1915.
27. *Les Armées françaises*, III, p. 617, alleges that the number of Z companies was to be brought to six in mid-Nov. If so, this was wishful thinking. By the middle of Jan. 1916, there were three companies, say 1,300 men, of which one was operational, one resting, and the third training. FMA 16N826, letter from Joffre to Ministère de la Guerre 22 Nov. 1915, and report dated 17 Jan. 1916. Also various signals and letters in 16N827, July to Nov. 1915 and *Les Armées françaises*, Annexe iv to vol. III, item 3068, pp. 247–8.
28. FMA 16N832 file 1080/2.
29. MoM: 2nd Report of the CS-C from 1 Oct. 1915 to 10 Jan. 1916, pp. 10–11. Hartley papers.
30. Liddell Hart: *History of First World War*, pp. 256–68. Isorni and Cardas: *Histoire véridique*, vol. III, pp. 231–59. Foulkes, C. H.: '*Gas!*' (1934), describes the role of gas at Loos on pp. 55–84. His account may usefully be compared with that of Robert Graves who was at the front during the battle: see his *Goodbye to All That* (1957), pp. 145–63.
31. Interviews with Dr Gold, who kindly lent me the records of wind speed and direction.
32. PRO/WO/143/44, 105th Meeting of the General Chemical Sub-Committee of the Scientific Advisory Committee of the Trench Warfare Department, 6 Nov. 1915. Williamson, H.: *Fox under my Cloak* (1955), pp. 292 ff.
33. Anon: 'The first British Gas Attack', *Chem. and Ind.* (12 Nov. 1960), no page nos. Conan Doyle, Sir Arthur: *The British Campaign in France and Flanders*, vol. III (1917), p. 181; *Der Weltkrieg*, vol. IX, pp. 56–7 (tr.).
34. *RE Jnl.* (Feb. 1921), pp. 105–20 and Foulkes: '*Gas!*', p. 76.
35. BMA, HO2—107/5, Report of the Medical Services of the VII Corps from 25 Sept. to 15 Oct. 1915. BA, Schwertfeger papers, No. 209, folios 37–8, letter from Haber to Valentini, 2 Jan. 1916, in which he writes of a Division '*die dem seelischen Eindruck der heranrollenden Rauchmasse unterlag*' and retreated. Letter from Pollitt to Harold Hartley, 30 June 1960 in Hartley papers and letter from Hartley to author 25 Feb. 1972.
36. Graves: *Goodbye*, pp. 152 ff. Interview with Cpl. Duncan on 8 Oct. 1973 and with C. Kerpen on 25 Feb. 1974. Both men took part in the advance towards Hulluch.
37. PRO/WO/142/100, file DGS/M/12; C. G. Douglas collated the statistics after the Armistice.
38. Foulkes: '*Gas!*', pp. 88–90 and Fox: 'Corporals All', *passim*. The two authors often disagree on details. The German gas casualty figures appear in their official medical history for the first time in Jan. 1916.
39. The chosen site was in the Mt. Têtu–Maisons de Champagne area; there is now no public access to the uplands which form part of a training area. The details of the plans are in FMA 16N826 and 827, file 342/1. A brief description is in *Les Armées françaises*, III, p. 674 and Annexe iv, item 3170, pp. 459–61.

40. *Der Weltkrieg*, IX, p. 92. German replies to Allied Questionnaire, *c.* 1921, no page ref. in Hartley papers. Dated photographs in IWM.

41. Heber: 'Aufzeichnungen'. In Oct. 1915, Heber, was attached to Pionier Rgt. 36. His descriptions can be checked occasionally with the summary in *Les Armées françaises*, III, pp. 668–9 and with the report from the GOC 5ème Armée to GQG on 22 Oct. 1915 in FMA 16N826. Sometimes the three accounts tally. Hanslian: *Chem. Krieg*, pp. 92–3, differs from both.

42. *Les Armées françaises*, III, p. 669 and Annexe iv, item 3036, p. 147. R. Buisson, a young artillery observer, was at Pompelle on 19 October and his account, typed years later, may be consulted in the museum which now occupies the reconstructed casemates of the fort. Conditions were very bad, but the trenches down to the canal remained passable. Buisson, who was wounded records that the pad was 'assez efficace'. He was lucky.

43. There are three different casualty statistics for this operation. *Les Armées françaises* (III, p. 675) states 500, including 50 killed. I have used the numbers given by Gen. Herr to Foulkes on 23 Dec. 1918 (PRO/WO/142/109, file DGS/M/94). Slightly lower figures are quoted in PRO/WO/142/99, file DGS/M/9.

44. Interview with Barley, 8 March 1972. Heber's 'Aufzeichnungen', p. 20. Hartley papers: 'German Gas Attacks and German Gas Warfare' (n.d.). PRO/WO/142/99, file DGS/M/1A and 142/102, file DGS M/25. The documents at the PRO show that great care was taken by Douglas and others to obtain accurate casualty figures.

45. PRO/MUN5/197/1650/6: Lt.-Col. Crossley's first liaison Report on Chemical Warfare (in the form of a letter to Gen. Jackson, 13 Dec. 1915). FMA 16N 826, the drawing is dated 20 June 1915, but does not indicate whether S_2Cl_2 or SCl_2 was to be used.

46. Vinet, E.: 'La Guerre des gaz', *Chim. et Ind.*, 2, 11–12 (1919), pp. 1403–6. Letter from E. F. Harrison to L. J. Barley, 25 Feb. 1916 Barley papers.

47. Vinet: 'La Guerre des gaz'. Vincennite contained 50 per cent HCN, 30 per cent $AsCl_3$, and 20 per cent other compounds.

48. '3rd report of the CS-C', 1 Oct. 1915 to 10 Jan. 1916, p. 16, among Hartley papers. Admiralty Technical History Section: *The Technical History and Index*: vol. I, pt. II, 'Lethal Gases' (1919), pp. 6–7. MoM: 'Trench Warfare Supplies', pp. 46–7.

49. 'Notes on German Shells', 2nd edn., GHQ 1 May 1918. Prentiss: *Chemicals in War*, pp. 459–50. Notes among Hartley papers.

50. The 75 mm shell was of monoblock construction so that canisters could not be inserted through the base. The details of the French work on tear-gas shell, which led to the adoption of glass-lined shell-cases towards the end of 1915 are in Vinet: 'La Guerre des gaz', p. 1414 and in IEEC, *Cours spécial sur l'emploi militaire des gaz*, 'Les Projectiles spéciaux' (n.d., ? April 1918), p. 8 among Hartley papers. Schwarte: *Technik im Weltkriege*, p. 283, has a description of the German techniques written by Kerschbaum.

51. An example, kindly contributed by Dr J. Shoham, will ilustrate the difference: the target area is 200 x 100 m. Assume that the shell burst has the configuration

of a circle with a radius of 1 m. Find the number of shells required (*a*) with bursts not overlapping, but tangential to each and (*b*) with bursts not overlapping by more than one quarter of the radius (ignore bursts at the edge of the area). The answer to (*a*) is 100 x 50 = 5,000. The answer to (*b*) is that along the horizontal there will be $200/\sqrt{3}$ bursts (rounded to 116) and along the vertical $100/^3/_2 = 67$, therefore 116 x 67 = 7,772. The overlap, which is approximately hexagonal and is the practical minimum, entails in increase of 55 per cent in the consumption of shell. I am grateful to Mr M. G. Willis of the IWM for some of the other technical details in this paragraph.

52. Hanslian: *Chem. Krieg*, pp. 48–54. Hartley Report, pp. 45–6.
53. Hartley: 'A General Comparison of British and German Methods of Gas Warfare', *Jnl. of the Royal Artillery*, *46*, 11 (1920), p. 18.
54. 'Chemical Warfare Record of Chemical Supplies for Offensive Purposes' (typescript, 1919: PRO/MUN5/386/1650/10) has a detailed description, running to 50 pages, of the filling technique. The Trench Warfare Chemical Supply Committee agreed at its meeting of 15 June 1917, that it was impossible to achieve 'a universal dead weight for all fillings' and that 'a constant percentage volume' was the most satisfactory method (PRO/MUN5/197/1650/11). Lefebure, V.: 'Report on Chemical Warfare Liaison with France' (1920), p. 34, PRO/MUN5/386/1650/15. The French practice is described in IEEC: 'Les Projectiles spéciaux', pp. 12–13 and Crossley's '3rd Liaison Report on Chemical Warfare' (in the form of a letter to Jackson) 2 Nov. 1916 (PRO/MUN5/197/1650/6). The German method in Vinet: 'Report on . . . the Four German Field Ammunition Depots' (1920), no page nos.
55. German replies to Allied questionnaire, no page ref., Hartley papers. Crossley's Report of 2 Nov. 1916. Vinet: 'La Guerre des gaz', p. 1414 and also his 'Report on . . . the Four German Field Amunition Depots', pp. 5, 25–6, 33, 56 and MoM: 'Trench Warfare Supplies', pp. 27–8. '2nd Report of the CS-C', pp. 18–19 and '3rd Report of the CS-C', p. 44.
56. Hartley Report, p. 5.
57. Ministère de la Guerre, 'Note sur le chargement . . . des obus spéciaux', 4 Aug. 1916, no page number, among Hartley papers. *Les Armées françaises*, III, p. 617 and Annexe vol. IV (1926), item 2974, pp. 10–12; item 3248, pp. 596–8; item 3304, pp. 706–7; and item 3335, pp. 737–8.
58. The correspondence in PRO/WO/142/155, files CL 7/15 and 8/15 recounts the British anxieties. The Germans were occasionally worried about retaliation and their incomplete preparations against it. Their detailed Instructions Regarding Gas Warfare, were translated at GHQ, BEF in July 1916 (ref. SS 449, among Hartley papers), and were probably issued earlier that year.
59. Hartley Report, p. 34. Hartley: 'Fritz Haber' p. 7. Interview with Dr Jaenicke 23 Sept. 1972. Willstätter, R.: *Aus meinem Leben* (1949), pp. 237–8. BMA, Nachlass Bauer, folios 44–54, letter from Duisberg to Bauer, 24 July 1915, contains interesting technical details.
60. Interviews with Hartley 8 Aug. and 10 Oct. 1971. Letters from Harrison to Barley 18 and 25 Feb. 1916, Barley papers. Douglas, C. G.: 'John Scott Haldane', *Obiit FRS*, ii (n.d.). p. 131, wrote that he 'had nothing to do with

its [the respirator's] design for he was not appointed to the Committee . . . his profound knowledge would have rendered his services invaluable.'

61. Vinet: 'La Guerre des gaz', pp. 1379–80. FMA 16N826: 'Rapport sur l'Organisation du Matériel Chimique de Guerre', mimeographed 25 August 1915, *passim*.

62. Schwarte: *Technik im Weltkriege*, pp. 295–7. (The section on respirators was written by Pick.) Hartley, 'Chemical Warfare', p. 9. Anon: 'The SBR', no date, no pagination, in PRO/WO/124/122, file CWD/167.

63. Letter from Cummins to Horrocks dated 1 May 1916 in PRO/WO/142/169, file CL/40/17.

64. Pick, in *Technik in Weltkrieg*, p. 298. Clark: 'Effectiveness of Chemical Weapons', p. 31. Breathing out in the German mask was through the filter box which required some effort and unavoidably led to breathing in some stale air. The Germans provided the mask with a non-return valve after the war.

65. Memo by P. S. Lelean, RAMC, 20 June 1915 in PRO/WO/142/183, file AGD/14. Chronology of the British respirator in Hartley papers.

66. Hartley Report, pp. 39–40. Willstätter; *Aus meinem Leber*, Freundlich: 'The German Gas Mask Filter', typed reply (translated) to an Allied questionnaire (n.d.), no page nos. among Hartley papers. Léon Dehorter, a French pharmacist, first worked with hexamine on 18 Aug. He was in touch with Foulkes later that month about phosgene, but it is not known whether he told him also about hexamine. The first Central Laboratory report on a dipping solution containing hexamine is dated 15 Oct. 1915; PRO/WO/142/91, file DGS/23. Hexamine is the commonly used trade name for hexamethylene tetramine; the Germans and French frequently called it urotropine.

67. Letter to N. Garrod Thomas, 15 Nov. 1915 in PRO/WO/142/155, file CL 8/15.

68. Lelean memo (see n. 65).

69. Letter from Macready to Kitchener, 7 July 1915 in PRO/WO/142/91, file DGS 23.

70. Hartley: 'Chemical Warfare', p. 8. MoM History, pp. 65–6. PRO/WO/142/155, file CL/7/15 contains much correspondence on different aspects of the 'P' helmet programme, and file CL/8/16 on the PH-helmet. Large-scale dipping of the 'PH' helmet began on 20 Jan.

71. PRO/WO/142/155, file CL/10/15 and PRO/WO/142/156, file CL/10/15 contain correspondence on the prototypes and details of the 'Tower'. Sadd, J. A.: 'Evolution of Anti-Gas Appliances up to the Introduction of the SBR' (PRO/MUN5/386/13) has the best general account of the events in summer and autumn 1915.

72. Hartley Report, pp. 39–40. The earliest date-stamp found on the new drum filter was 23 Jan. 1916, cf. Mouat Jones: 'Development of British Gas Defence Appliances' in PRO/WO/142/162.

73. Vinet: 'La Guerre des gaz', p. 1390, 1395. Note by Professor Lebeau on the M2 mask dipping fluid, dated 16 May 1917 among the Hartley papers.

74. In 1973–4 I interviewed six men, five of them Regulars, who had been trained in the use of the various helmets and had worn them on occasion. Their opinions were not hostile, but unenthusiastic. By contrast all liked the SBR.

The French tests with hoods are mentioned in FMA 16N832, folder 1080/2.

75. Various reports in Hartley papers and West; 'Phosgene', p. 163.

76. Raper: 'History of Anti-Gas Department', p. 18. Gimingham, T. C.: 'The Evolution of the SBR', p. 6 in PRO/MUN 5/386/1650/13. The figures on the German respirator are taken from Mouat Jones, B.: 'Development of German Gas Mask Appliances', 17 Dec. 1918 in PRO/WO/142/162, file CL/23/18–19.

77. Among the Hartley papers, there is a note by Professor Lebeau, dated 16 May 1917 whch makes the most sweeping claims for the M2. An early French complaint about the tampons is in a letter from Gen. de Langle to Joffre, dated 31 Oct. 1915, in Annexe iv of *Les Armées françaises*, p. 147, item 3036. Other criticisms and reproaches will be found in FMA 10N57 and 16N827 (item 29), and there is a very critical report on the performance of the French masks during a cloud gas attack by Major A. de la Chapelle, dated 26 Feb. 1916, among the Hartley papers. The most thorough recent study on the subject is by Clark: 'Efectiveness of Chemical Weapons', pp. 30, 33.

78. On the German mask see Schwarte: *Technik im Weltkriege*, pp. 299–301 and Hanslian: *Chem. Krieg*, pp. 195, 199. On charcoal, interviews with Hartley 25 Dec. 1971 and Jaenicke 23 Sept. 1972. Gimingham: 'Evolution of SBR'. Freundlich: 'The German Gas Mask Filter' (tr.), among Hartley papers. On soda-lime granules, Raper: 'History of Anti-Gas Department', pp. 16–17. Sadd, J. A.: 'The Evolution of the Anti-Gas Appliances up to the Introduction of the SBR', p. 4 in PRO/MUN5/1650/13 and letter from Cummins to Horrocks 4 May 1916 in PRO/WO/142/162, file CL/40/17. Lloyd, S. J. and West, C. J. (eds.): 'Soda-lime Granules', pp. 1–14 in US Bureau of Mines, Monograph No. 9 of War Gas Investigations in PRO/WO/143/33.

79. Interview with Hartley 19 Sept. 1971. PRO/WO/124/122, file CWD/167. Hanslian: *Chem. Krieg*, pp. 207–8, 210.

80. According to Geyer (BMA N 221/23; 'Denkschrift', p. 18) the first masks were issued on 15 Sept. The face-piece was made from cotton fabric impregnated with natural rubber solution. On 30 Sept. the machine-gunners and telephonists of the 5th BIR got '*Zeppelin Masken*'—the face pieces of these respirators were made from the rubberized silk fabric of the captured French dirigible 'Alsace' (War Diary of 5 BIR at BHSA). BA, Schwertfeger Nachlass, No. 209, folios 37–8. Circular on Gas Masks, German War Ministry No. 1514/15, 17 Jan. 1916 at BHSA. Hartley Report, pp. 4–5: Hartley was told after the war that manufacturing difficulties imposed delays. But troops movement in Feb.–March 1916 were on such a scale that hold ups were unavoidable.

81. Graves: *Goodbye*, p. 146, mentions the helmets at the start of the battle. Raper: 'History of Anti-Gas Department', p. 6. Circular No. 8 dated 14 Nov. 1915 shows that the 3rd Army received its tube helmets during Nov. (Hartley papers).

82. FMA 16N832, folder 1080/1. PRO/WO/142/98, file DGS 84. Hartley Report, p. 38 and Coates's interview with Hartley 8 Jan. 1935 among Coates papers.

83. PRO/WO/142/98, file DGS/90; PRO/WO/142/99, file DGS/M/10C; PRO/WO/142/195, R-O-A 5, 6, 10 and 13; PRO/WO/143/134, files CWD/379 and 386. Hanslian: *Chem. Krieg*, pp. 218–19. The British Chemical Advisers in Petrograd sent comprehensive reports to London for most of 1917,

which provide many details, not elsewhere available, of Russian designs.

84. Letter from Barley to Harrison and Report by Barley to DGS; both dated 24 Dec. 1917 among Barley papers. PRO/WO/142/135, file CWN/403 and PRO/WO/142/138, file CWD/431.

85. The chief tear-gas shoots took place on 20 June, 30 June, 1–2 July, 13–14 July in the Argonne and on 13–14 Oct. against the British. On the first occasion, the bombardment was heavy, but the figure of 40,000 T shells fired in six hours is implausibly high given the number of 15 cm howitzers then available and their firing rate. On the last occasion the British were doubly unlucky, because a German shell hit some cylinder emplacements, so that they suffered from chlorine as well as from tear gas. Clark: 'Effectiveness of Chemical Weapons', pp. 83–4. PRO/WO/142/100, file DGS/M/12.

86. There are gaps in the German statistics, especially in the volume released on the Eastern Front and near Verdun in Nov. I have not found particulars of the small British clouds in Oct.–Nov., but the amount involved is unlikely to have a significant effect on the total British gas usage.

87. Interview with Barley, 8 March 1972.

88. BMA HO2-107/5 and BHSA, circular of 6th Army dated 29 Dec. 1915. It is likely that the appointment of Braun and of other officers was timed to coincide with the issue of the new respirators.

89. Interview with Claud Kerpen, 25 Feb. 1974; the sequel of the story is as follows: Kerpen was passed fit for the RFC, led a very active business life and died in his late seventies.

90. The title of the poem is '*Dulce et decorum est*', from Wilfred Owen: *The Collected Poems* (1969), pp. 55–6.

91. Macpherson *et al.*: *Medical Services*, pp. 389–99.

92. A. T. Sloggett, the Director-General of the BEF's Medical Services, issued his first memorandum on gas poisoning on 20 July 1916. Achard's and Flandin's 'Notice thérapeutique des intoxications par les gaz' is very similar and was also issued in July 1916.

93. Richards, O.: 'The Development of Casualty Clearing Stations', Guy's Hosp. R., *70* (1922), pt. III, pp. 115 ff. Schroth: *Bilder . . . der Gaspioniere*, p. 6. Mignon, A.: *Le Service de santé pendant la guerre 1914–18*, vol. IV (1926), pp. 771–2.

94. Macpherson *et al.*: *Medical Services*, pp. 411–14. BMA HO2-107/5; Report by the Medical Service of VII Corps for 25 Sept. to 15 Oct. 1915. Hartley Report, pp. 53–4. Letter from C. G. Douglas to Cummins 21 Dec. 1915 in German Gas Attacks among the Hartley papers. Thiess, A. M. and Tress, E.: 'Phosgene Intoxication in the Chemical Industry', *Therapie-Woche*, *41* (1975), p. 5900. Dr W. J. Grant has very kindly guided me through the intricacies of the modern pharmacopœia; codeine has taken the place of atropine, meperidine hydrochloride that of morphia, strophantin that of the old cardiac tonics.

95. BMA HO2-107/5, papers of the VII Army Corps; the circular is dated GHQ 13 Jan. 1916 (N-21896). Hartley, undated memo (*c.*1960) and Fritz Haber (n.d., *c.*1960–1), pp. 15–16, both among Hartley papers.

96. In winter, according to Churchill, there were frequent south-westerly gales

'which would afford a perfect opportunity for the employment of gas by us . . . I trust that the unreasonable prejudice against the use of gas upon the Turks will now cease.' Note to Dardanelles Committee 20 Oct. 1915, PRO/CAB/42/4 item 14.

97. Foulkes '*Gas!*', pp. 90–1. Fox: *Corporals All*, pp. 28, 30, 36. Barley, L. J.: 'Notes of provisional organisation for protection against gas', 2 Oct. 1918 among Barley papers.

98. *Les Armées françaises*, III, pp. 634–5; Foch's question is in Annexe vol. IV, p. 427, item 3149.

99. 'It is doubtful whether chlorine alone can maintain its military value much longer' wrote the secretary of the Chemical Sub-Committee in or about March 1916. '3rd Report of the CS-C', p. 40, among Hartley papers.

Chapter 5

1. I am grateful to Dr. L. Burstall and Dr M. Burstall for checking the references in *Beilstein* and the *Chem. Zentrablatt*. They found altogether twenty-five references to chloropicrin between 1848 and 1914.

2. American experiments showed that eleven out of a group of twenty-one men could detect phosgene at concentrations of 1 ppm, the maximum safe concentration. But another group could not detect the gas at the much higher concentration of 5.6 ppm (0.25 mg/1). West: 'Phosgene', p. 89 ff. in PRO/SUP/10/129.

3. MoM History, pp. 41 ff., 98. Letter from W. Watson to P. B. Lelean 29 June 1915 in PRO/WO/142/153, file CL 3/15. West: 'Phosgene', pp. 17 ff. De Mouilpied, A. T.: 'Review of C. G. Position', typescript, 6 June 1918 and notes by Quinan, dated 12 July 1918 in PRO/SUP/10/128. Rough Design Voucher [for a phosgene plant for 1919 Programme] dated 12 July 1918 in PRO/SUP/10/164.

4. The table is based on information in PRO/MUN5/198/1650/14; PRO/WO/143/56; PRO/WO/142/114, file CWD 87 and FMA 16N832, files 1080/1 and 1080/2. The rate of exchange used is £1 = 25 fr. The first two agreements with de Laire provided for a considerable reduction in price after 400 t of phosgene had been supplied. Since particulars of weekly or monthly deliveries are not available, I have based the calculations on the total delivered during the year (1389 t). The third agreement, like the purchases by the French Government, was a flat rate per kg $COCl_2$.

5. Moreland: 'Chemical Warfare Record', p. 191 ff. MoM History, p. 44.

6. Sartori; *The War Gases*, pp. 99–115. West, C. J., and Harned, H. S.: 'Superpalite', Monograph No. 11 of War Gas Investigations, American University Experiment Station, Washington, typescript (18 Aug. 1918), pp. 25–6, 38–9 in PRO/WO/142/35. ('Superpalite' was the French code name for diphosgene.)

7. Interview with Hartley, 16 May 1971 and Hartley Report, p. 6.

8. Watts, H. E.: 'Production of Gas . . . in Germany during War'(typescript, 15 Feb. 1922), p. 10, Hartley papers. Vinet, E.: 'Report on . . . the Installations

... for ... Gases in the German Chemical Factories', typescript (22 March 1921), pp. 6–7, Hartley papers. Letter from Hartley to J. E. Coates, 26 April 1937.

9. Crossley, A. W.: 1st Liaison Report, 13 Dec. 1915, and 3rd Liaison Report 2 Nov. 1916 both in PRO/MUN5/197/1650/6. MoM History, p. 6.

10. Moreland: 'Chemical Warfare Record', pp. 51–2, 220, 224. 3rd Report of the CS-C. (n.d. c.March 1916), pp. 19–21, 32–3, 43. Allmand, A. J.: 'Report on War Work for German Gas Services ... at ... Leverkusen ...' (typescript, 31 Jan. 1919), Hartley papers.

11. Hartley Report, pp. 4, 14. Geyer: 'Denkschrift', p. 9, in BMA N 221/23. GHQ, BEF, translation of rough notes taken at a German Gas Course and found on a prisoner, 3 July 1917, Hartley papers. Letter from Cummins to Horrocks, 1 May 1916 in PRO/WO/142/169, file CL/40/17.

12. FMA 16N827, file 342/2. Letter from Thomas to the President of the Senate Army Commission dated 3 March 1916 in FMA 10N57 and Reports among Hartley papers of German cylinder attack on French on 21 Feb. 1916 by A. de la Chapelle and B. Mouat Jones dated 26 Feb. 1916.

13. Hanslian: *Chem. Krieg, passim.* Heber: 'Aufzeichnungen', pp. 25–7, BMA N 102/10. Typed enclosure to Sir George Buchanan's dispatch No. 193 of 17 August 1916 in PRO/WO/142/99, file DGS M/10C and PRO/WO/142/38, file CWD 431. The Austrians probably also used gas. Mr V. G. Raitz told me that his father, then serving as a doctor with the Russians near Czernowic, was gassed, but although he had no mask, recovered completely.

14. Attack of 8 August 1916 and 'German Gas Warfare', typescript; both reports without date among Hartley papers. Auld, S. J. M.: *Gas and Flame* (1918), p. 114. A total of 370 men were killed and 434 injured by gas. There were several explanations for the exceptionally large proportion of fatalities. The German gas mixture contained more phosgene than previously and a relief was taking place at the time. The trenches were therefore crowded and swift movement prevented. It was also noted that the fresh troops lacked anti-gas training.

15. The principal British documents are the reports prepared by Mouat Jones on 30 April 1916 and by Hamilton McCombie (the Chemical Adviser of the 1st Army) on 4 May 1916, both among the Hartley papers as well as Elliott, T. R., and Douglas, C. G.: 'A Report on the Casualties due to Gas ...' (n.d.), in PRO/WO/142/102, file DGS/M/25; PRO/WO/142/97, file DGS/69; PRO/WO/142/99, file DGS/M/1A; and 'Lessons to be learnt from recent gas attacks', GHQ, BEF (May 1916), SS III, Hartley papers. The German documents are in BHSA: 6th Army papers, Bavarian 2nd Corps papers, the war diaries of the 5, 9, 17, 18, and 23 BIR; the 9th suffered most. Haber's scientific report on the disaster at Hulluch is dated 9 July 1916 (ref. 151/5.16 Z. Chem.) and Heber, who was present on both occasions, described the event in his 'Aufzeichnungen', pp. 21–3. Except for Heber (whose numbers are wrong) the various accounts agree with each other. One further point may be noted. Haber's report, though secret, reached the Allies in 1917 or 1918 for Auld (*Gas and Flame*, pp. 101–2) quotes figures from it.

16. The incident took place at Aubérive either on 21 May or a couple of days earlier.

The Pioniere opened some cylinders, the French spotted the gas at once, set up an intense artillery barrage, and scored direct hits on a group of cylinders. The gas escaped, drifted along the trench, and into a dug-out. A total of 25 Pioniere were asphyxiated and 42 injured by gas. In addition the infantry suffered casualties. Schroth: *Bilder aus . . . Gaspioniere*, pp. 17–19. (Schroth was the MO of the gas battalion involved in the story.)

17. It will be recalled that Nernst had taken an active interest in this weapon during 1915 and found a supporter in Major Lothes. When Lothes was killed at Verdun, the special section was disbanded. Hartley Report, p. 13.

18. MoM: 'Trench Warfare Supplies', p. 95. Minutes of Meeting of General Chemical Sub-Committee of Scientific Advisory Committee on 24 Feb. 1916 in PRO/WO/143/57. Moreland: 'Chemical Warfare Record', pp. 49–50.

19. Edmonds, J. E.: *Military Operations in France and Belgium, 1916*, vol. I (1932), p. 78

20. Interviews with Hartley, who disliked Foulkes. The MoM papers show the extent of the dispute over phosgene: in fairness to Foulkes it must be said that he was right to castigate the incompetence of British manufactures and civil servants.

21. Miles, W.: *Military Operations in France and Belgium, 1916*, vol. II (1938), pp. 543–4. Foulkes: '*Gas!*', pp. 123–4. Foulkes claims that on the left flank of the 4th Army, gas was wasted by the carelessness of Divisional Staffs. Although he gives no evidence, he is likely to have been correct.

22. Crossley's 3rd Liaison Report, *passim*. 'Gas Attacks', Hartley papers. Fox: *Corporals All*, p. 49 ff. 'The Work of the Royal Engineers in the European War', *RE Jnl.* (Feb. 1921), pp. 105 ff. 'Report of British Cylinder Gas Attack in French Sector wear Nieuport', GHQ 4 April 1917, SS/549, Hartley papers. Foulkes: *Gas!*, pp. 121–2.

23. Foulkes: 'Report on the Activity of the Special Brigade', dated 19 Dec. 1918 in PRO/SUP/10/292. Foulkes's information is in the form of a bar diagram, which I have converted into numbers. The figures agree with those quoted in MoM: 'Trench Warfare Supplies', p. 95.

24. Sassoon, S.: *Memoirs of an Infantry Officer* (1930), p. 64. Manning, F.: *Her Privates We* (1930), p. 57.

25. Foulkes: '*Gas!*', p. 157. At Laventie, on 19 June 1916 the Germans suddenly shelled the British lines hit a cylinder, and the wind blew the gas along the trench: 80 were gassed of whom 11 died. PRO/WO/142/87, file AGD, 36 A–E.

26. Livens, W. H.: 'The Livens Gas Projector' (n.d.), PRO/WO/188/143, file R8/A/1. Earlier in the year Harrison, in a letter to Barley (among Barley papers), dated 25 Feb., had suggested glass vessels filled with phosgene fired from a Stokes Mortar. Liddell Hart: *History of First World War*, p. 329.

27. In 1917 Poincaré intervened to stop a gas-cloud attack near Thann in Alsace. I have not come across a similar example of restraint in northern France. There were considerable civilian gas casualties in 1917 and 1918 in the densely populated industrial districts.

28. Crossley's 2nd Liaison Report, dated 11 March 1916, in PRO/MUN 5/197/1650/6: he was told in mid-February that six large chlorine plants had started up and that by mid June France would produce 50 t/day. This was

wishful thinking. Joffre's letter is in FMA 16N827, file 342/1, item 73.
29. The French official history for 1916 is uninformative on gas cylinders. There are some details in FMA 16N827, files 342/2 and 342/3, in BMA N 233/23 (diary of O. von Trotta, xiv, pp. 107–12), and among the papers of the 1st Bavarian Corps in BHSA. The German reports rarely confirm the French, and where they are specific, mention extremely low casualties: 35 (none fatal) at La Pompelle on 26 March and 19 around Nampcel between the Oise and Aisne on 13 April. The number of cylinders employed is not a reliable indicator of volume, because the French used large and small cylinders indiscriminately. The carrying capacities ranging from about 20 to 30 kg.
30. FMA 10N57 (written answers by Ozil dated 10 Nov. 1916, 9 Dec. 1916, and 23 Feb. 1917). Vinet: 'La Guerre des gaz', p. 1408, mentions 20 gas clouds, but does not list them. According to him, phosgene was first used at the beginning of 1917.
31. Hanslian: *Chem. Krieg*, p. 101. The British did not have a permanent chemical mission in Petrograd during 1916. The visiting British specialists recorded what information they were given. PRO/WO/142/98, file DGS 90 and 142/134, file CWD 386, contain some brief reports. PRO/WO/142/138, file CWD 431 has a report on the Italian gas organization and the general background.
32. Hanslian: *Chem. Krieg*, p. 20. Hartley Report, pp. 5–6 and interview with Hartley on 31 Oct. 1971. Vinet: 'Report on the German C. W. Organisation', p. 28 and 'Report on . . . the four German Field Ammunition Depots', *passim*; both reports among Hartley papers.
33. IEEC: 'Le Tir des projectiles spéciaux', *passim*, Hartley Papers. Altogether 400 75 mm shell were detonated at the February shoots.
34. IEEC: 'Cours spécial sur l'emploi militaire des gaz', pp. 57–8, Hartley papers. The volume of the 75 mm shell is 525 cc ± 30 cc. This corresponds to about 735 gr ± 42 gr of phosgene. Some room for expansion was always allowed for so that the net weight ranged from 600 to 650 gr. The first instructions on the use of gas shell were issued by GQG on 12 March, 1916. Cf. *Les Armées françaises*, IV, pt. I, p. 530.
35. Hartley Report, pp. 5–6. IEEC: 'Cours spécial', pp. 24–6.
36. BA Bauer Nachlass, folios 217–25.
37. Hanslian: *Chem. Krieg*, pp. 21–2. Mignon, A.: *Le Service de santé*, II, pp. 543–4. Mignon gives 9 March for the first use of gas, but this is not confirmed by other sources. Horne, A.: *The Price of Glory* (1962), has the best account of the battle in English: see in particular pp. 285–7 and 291.
38. 'Renseignements sur l'emploi des obus spéciaux à la VIème Armée' (n.d.), Hartley papers. Minutes of 295th meeting of Chemical Supply Sub-Committee, 18 July 1916, PRO/WO/142/58.
39. Miles: *Military Operations*, frequently refers to gas bombardments during July; Hartley was wrong when he reported only two; see his Report to C. G. Douglas dated 25 Jan. 1919 entitled 'British Gas Casualties in German Gas Cylinder Attacks', Hartley papers.
40. Hartley 'A General Comparison of British and German Methods of Gas Warfare', *Jnl. of the Royal Artillery*, *46*, 11, (1920), p. 3. Auld: *Gas and Flame*,

p. 143. Schwarte: *Technik im Weltkriege*, p. 276. Memorandum Regarding the Employment of Gas Shell, OHL 6 August 1915, translated at GHQ BEF in Hartley papers: this instruction recommends firing twelve shells (calibre not specified) per rectangle of 150 m x 25 m and moving the rectangles in bands 25 m wide from the rear to the front across 400 m. I have converted these measurements into the equivalent of 1 km^2 for purposes of comparison with the gas cloud and with the document of 18 Feb. 1917, 'Anwendung für die Verwendung von Grünkreuzgeschossen' (among Hartley papers) which prescribed the number of shell per km^2.

41. IEEC: 'Le Tir des projectiles spéciaux', pp. 29–30, 76, and Hartley's undated notes, probably made at the second conference on gas shells.

42. Miles: *Military Operations*, p. 298. The story of the British gas shell and its introduction is exceptionally confusing because the people involved made every effort to put the blame on someone else. The main sources are MoM History, p. 6, Memorandum on Steps taken by MoM to provide Chemical Shell, dated 4 May 1916 in PRO/MUN5/187/1360/1; and Redstone, J. L.: 'History of Chemical Supply April 1915–July 1917', first draft dated 25 April 1918, PRO/MUN5/385/1650/4.

43. Crossley's 3rd Liaison Report, p. 35.

44. Horne: *Price of Glory*, p. 300.

45. Miles: *Military Operations*, p. 298 and previously cited French and German sources.

46. Heeres-Sanitätsinspektion . . .; *Sanitätsbericht* . . ., III, p. 180. BHSA, 6th Army folder with Allgemeines Kriegs Departement papers, and 1st Bav. Corps papers. Schwarte: *Technik in Weltkriege*, p. 297, 301. C. G. Douglas translation of German memorandum on the Recognition and Treatment of Gas Poisoning dated 3 Oct. 1916, GHQ BEF 11 Jan. 1917, Hartley papers. Memo, by Hartley (?), dated 13 April 1916 among his papers. GHQ BEF, 'Lessons to be learnt from recent Gas Attacks'.

47. Gladden, N.: *The Somme* (1974), p. 141.

48. Undated note on the German Gas Warfare among Hartley papers and letter from Horrocks to Cummins dated 20 April 1916 in PRO/WO/142/169, file CL 40/17.

49. Fox: 'Corporals All', p. 46. Carr, F. H.: 'Harrison Memorial Lecture', *Pharmaceutical J.* (26 July 1919), p. 96. Hartley papers (in particular an undated memo (1916?) by him, ref. HH/S/35 B). Exhibit of respirators at Imperial War Museum.

50. Diary of Development of British Respirator (n.d., *c.* 1919?) among Hartley papers. Carr: Harrison Memorial Lecture, pp. 96–7. Raper: 'History of the Anti-Gas Department', pp. 7–8, PRO/MUN5/386/1650/13, and interview with L. J. Barley 8 August 72 at which he told me that Harrison knew Jesse Boot and the directors of Spicer's, the paper manufacturers.

51. Diary of Development of British Respirators.

52. Correspondence between the Ministère de l'Armement and various Députés in 1916 in FMA 10N57. GQG, circular dated 1 April 1916 in FMA 16N826, Report by Dr Flandin on the German Gas Attack in Champagne on 31 Jan. 1917 in

PRO/WO/142/154, file CL/5/18. Various reports between April and June 1916 in FMA 16N827, files 342/2 and 342/3. Letter from Cummins to Horrocks 1 May 1916 in PRO/WO/142/169, file CL 40/17, and interview with Harold Hartley 23 April 1972.

53. Hanslian: *Chem. Krieg*, pp. 222–3. Enclosure to Sir George Buchanan's dispatch referred to in note 13 and Report by W. L. Hicks and C. P. Schwabe, Petrograd, 28 June 1916 in PRO/WO/142/195 (R.O-A/10).

54. Auld: *Gas and Flame*, p. 43.

55. Baynes, J.: *Morale. A Study of Men and Courage*, (1967), pp. 195–6. This is a case study of men's behaviour at the battle of Neuve Chapelle in March 1915. Heber ('Aufzeichnungen', p. 23) writing about the Bavarians at Hulluch more than a year later also remarks on the connection between morale and behaviour during a cloud-gas attack.

56. A circular in Hartley papers by Gen. Kiggell (Haig's Chief of Staff) dated 22 Jan. 1916 is explicit on this point and obviously draws on the experience gained at Ypres four weeks earlier.

57. BMA N 233/23, diaries of O. von Trotta, xiv and xx. Various German circulars dated 1915 and 1916 in BHSA and, among the Hartley papers, 'Report on German Gas Attack . . .' on 19 Dec. 1915, ref. HH/S/45 (n.d., ? Jan. 1916).

58. Interviews with Chelsea Pensioners in October 1973. All except one recalled having some instruction, but its thoroughness varied.

59. Elliott and Douglas: 'Report on Casualties'.

60. Report on German Cylinder Attack on French 21 Feb. 1916, dated 26 Feb. 1916, Hartley papers. FMA 16N827, file 342/2. Letter from Ozil (?) to Député Laval dated 23 Feb. 1917 in FMA 10N57. Report No. F/D/C35 by Dr Flandin entitled 'Vague Allemande du 7 Avril [1917] a Limey-Remenauville', in PRO/WO/142/173. Geyer: 'Denkschrift', p. 18.

61. The following statistics from Elliott and Douglas: 'Report on Casualties' speak for themselves.

Date and Location	Gas Casualties Admitted to CCS	Died at CCS as % of Admissions
19 Dec. 1915, Ypres	1,017	3.5
27 April 1916, Hulluch	377	4.2
29 April 1916, Wulverghem	610	7.9
30 April 1916, Hulluch	474	10.5
17 June 1916, Wulverghem	530	12.1
8 Aug. 1916, Wieltje (Ypres)	540	19.6

At Wieltje the fatal casualties at the front or in the communication trenches were exceptionally heavy, see note 14, above.

62. Sloggett, A. T.: 'Memorandum on Gas Poisoning . . . its Pathology and Treatment', 20 July, 1916, pp. 12, 14, 17–19. German memo, dated 3 Oct. 1916, tr. by C. G. Douglas, Hartley papers.

63. Gas Shell Bombardment of Arras 27–8 December 1916, 3rd Army G10/33, dated 5 Jan. 1917, Hartley papers. Circular of 5th German Army dated 15 March 1916 on pyridine solutions for spraying, tr. from French in Hartley papers. 'German Instructions Regarding Gas Warfare' tr. at GHQ BEF July 1916, SS 449, pp. 12–13. BHSA, First Bavarian Corps, Report No. 23/190/6650 on Eneny Gas Attack on 26 March 1916.

Chapter 6

1. There are plenty of numbers, but few stand up to close scrutiny. For Germany, the best source is the Hartley Report (p.45) and an undated note (probably 1935) from Professor Epstein to Professor Coates among the Coates papers. Some American data have been collated by D. P. Jones for his dissertation, 'The Role of Chemists in Research on War Gases in the US'(University of Wisconsin, Ph.D. (1970), (pp. 97, 122–3) but I have relied on A. A. Fries: 'Chemical Warfare in *Journal of Ind. and Eng. Chem.*, 12, 5, (1920) p. 427, where he gives the numbers of 'technical' men (some probably only partly qualified by European standards) and their 'assistants' in the Research Division of the American University, Washington. For Britain, I have used Raper's 'History of the Anti-Gas Department', pp. 1–2 and various references in PRO/WO/142/133, file CWD 375; WO/142/187, file AGD 25/26; and a note dated 2 Dec. 1918 (ref. WO, AGDJ) in the Hartley papers and A. W. Crossley, 'The R.E. Experimental Station, Porton, 1919',PRO/MUN 5/386/1650/4, p. 15. The French statistics are incomplete, and the only comprehensive survey is to be found in Vinet's 'La Guerre des gaz', p. 1408.
2. Hartley Report, *passim*. Jones: 'The Role of Chemists', pp. 111, 113–14 and Brown: *Chemical Warfare*, p. 22.
3. Davidson Pratt, J.: 'Memorandum on the Organisation for Chemical Warfare Reseach', 3 April 1919, pp. 122–3 (PRO/MUN 5/385/1650/8) and papers in PRO/WO/142/133, file CWD/375. Towards the end of the war, the number engaged on offensive research (excepting Porton) was slightly higher than that of scientists and their assistants working on gas defence in London, 110 as against about 100.
4. Vinet: 'La Guerre des gaz', pp. 1381, 1389, also FMA 16N832, file 1080/1 (item 1) and file 1080/3 (item 45).
5. The facilities in Italy were primitive and the research amateurish. Fewer than a dozen chemists were working in the chemical warfare centres at Rome and Bologna universities. Barley Papers: Note on a Conversation with Col. Penna, 19 Feb. 1918 and Report on a visit to Rome 12–16 Feb. 1918.
6. I have relied on British sources (Davidson Pratt: Memorandum, pp. 196–7 and the minutes of the CWC (PRO/WO/142/71 and 72), but there are some German reports mentioning similar problems.
7. Hartley Report, pp. 50–1 and notes on his visit in 1921.
8. They are stored at the PRO under reference WO/142/172–82.
9. On Mayer, cf. Vinet: 'La Guerre des gaz', pp. 1407 and 1409. The British

statistics are based on a survey of the material at the PRO. The eight volumes of product entries and abstracts will be found at the PRO in boxes under WO/142/82 to 84 and 86. Other details from Moreland: 'Chemical Warfare Record', pp. 281–2 (PRO/MUN 5/386/1650/10).

10. There are scores of these reports, each running to many typed pages. They are now at the PRO under WO/142/1–5.

11. Davidson Pratt: Memorandum, pp. 107–8.

12. A few examples must suffice. In 1916 Bragg and Donnan were invited to design silencers to stop the characteristic hiss of discharging gas cylinders. Their work and failure are recorded in PRO/WO/143/55 and 56. Even that late, others, less eminent, were still porposing to kill the enemy with carbon monoxide (cf. PRO/WO/142/144, file 82). The Hartley papers contain a circular issued by the 3rd Army, dated 10 April 1917, on how to take air samples with a vacuum flask and what to do with the plasticine stopper. Finally the arrival of the Americans led to two discussions on the use of poison ivy. Someone had the sense to get in touch with the Royal Botanical Gardens at Kew and was told to let the folk in Washington deal with the weapon. (Cf. minutes of the Chemical Advisory Committee for 14 Sept. and 19 Oct. 1917, PRO/WO/142/60.)

13. Letter from Kling to Mouat Jones dated 8 March 1916 in PRO/WO/142/165, file CL/32/16.

14. Mignon: *Le Service de santé*, iv, p. 768. FMA 16N832, file 1080/1, item 23.

15. The British and the Americans used different materials than the Germans. The Americans eventually relied entirely on coconut shell. The absorptive capacity, governed by the moisture content of the charcoal, was the critical factor. This varied greatly according to the particular calcination and drying techniques used.

16. Terroine's paper to the Gas Conference on 27 Oct. 1918 (among the Hartley papers) is a good example of the muddled approach to what was supposed to be a 'scientific' test of the French ARS mask. The French used small groups of volunteers to perform various tasks who were rewarded for their endurance. But the French neglected to have any controls to evaluate the performance of unmasked men under the same conditions. British investigations are mentioned in a Report of Central Laboratory and a letter from Cummins to Horrocks, both in August 1918 in PRO/WO/142/155, file CL 7/15.

17. PRO/WO/142/83 deals with the mustard-gas detector and WO/142/93, file DGS 43/44 gives the background to Foulkes's comments on Lt. Hemens's gas detector in a report dated 5 Oct. 1916. Tests at Porton showed it to be useless and it had to be redesigned. All work was suspended in April 1917.

18. The chemical name of mustard gas is dichlorodiethyl sulphide. Guthrie first described it comprehensively in two contributions to *Qly. J. Chem. Soc.*, 12 (1860), pp. 109–20 and 13 (1860–1), pp. 129–35 entitled, 'On Some Derivatives from the Olefines'. He noted the smell, which resembled 'oil of mustard', and that it tasted of horseradish. Guthrie observed skin blisters and symptoms of conjunctivitis. He prepared it initially from sulphur dichloride (SCl_2) and ethylene, and later used sulphur monochloride (S_2Cl_2). The distinction is important and troublesome. The dichloride is obtained by the chlorination of the monochloride. The two have similar specific gravities, but can be

distinguished by their boiling-points and colour. Pure S_2Cl_2 decomposes above 100° C and boils at 138° C. The dichloride decomposes above 40° C and boils at 60° C. The dichloride is reactive, but is less satisfactory than S_2Cl_2 for the preparation of dichlorodiethyl sulphide, because the sulphur tends to settle out and it behaves like an unstable mixture of S_2Cl_2 and chlorine. Guthrie was unaware of these characteristics because he operated at 100° C for many hours: under such conditions the yields were negligible—which was just as well, because he would have badly burnt his mouth if the end product had been purer. Meyer described his work in 'Ueber Thiodiglykolverbindungen' (*Ber.*, 19 (1886), pp. 3259–66). His starting-point was ethylene chlorohydrin which he dissolved in potassium sulphide (later replaced by sodium sulphide). This yielded the thiocompound, and upon chlorinating it with phosphorus trichloride, dichlorodiethyl sulphide separated out. Meyer noted its blistering power and pointed out that it was very toxic ('äusserst giftig'). Years later, H. T. Clarke—a pupil of Meyer—wrote a paper ('On 4-Alkyl-1,4 Thiazans', *J. Chem. Soc.*, 101 (1912), pp. 1583–90) in which he demonstrated that the chlorination stage of the thiodiglycol could be simplified by using hydrogen chloride. This was the method afterwards employed by the Germans at Leverkusen to make mustard gas.

19. The memo will be found in PRO/WO/142/196, file DES 1/36–80. The provisional application for Pope's process was dated 4 Feb. 1918. It was given a number, 142,875, and was secret. Pope's co-patentees were C. S. Gibson, his principal assistant, and Thuillier, at that time Controller CWD. The complete specification was lodged on 2 Oct. and accepted on 5 Nov. The patent remained secret until 22 April 1920. These dates are given in PRO/WO/142/129, file CWD 289. The file also contains a memorandum by W. J. Gidden on the subject of mustard gas work.

20. The various sources are agreed on dates and details. The minutes of the Chemical Advisory Committee and of the CWC (PRO/WO/142/60 and 84) show the progress made. Moreland: 'Chemical Warfare Record', pp. 330–6 fills in the details as do files 257 and 295 in PRO/WO/142/127. After the war Levinstein and Green challenged Pope's claims to the prior development of a satisfactory route and the Hartley papers contain Davidson Pratt's letters of 5 March 1920 and 31 Jan. 1921 to Hartley and to Thuillier respectively which give details of the litigation.

21. Jones: 'The Role of Chemists', p. 136 ff.; PRO/SUP/10/125 and 126 (Quinan papers H 135–6 and H 366) and West, C. J.: 'The History of Mustard Gas', *Chem and Met. Eng.*, 22 (1920), p. 542. For their large-scale manufacture the Americans used what became known as the Levinstein process, which differed slightly from Pope's method.

22. I have not been able to discover the precise date when the French found that a reaction temperature of 30°–40° C gave the best results, but it appears to have been early in March. PRO/WO/142/127, file CWD 272 (note on meeting with Moureu on 14 Dec. 1917) and PRO/WO/142/136, files CWD 417 and 423.

23. Badische introduced a new indigo synthesis in 1909 for which the starting materials were ethylene chlorohydrin and aniline. The process was simpler than

the other two syntheses then being worked by the company but the ethyl alcohol cost too much and the preparation of chlorohydrin was complicated. At its peak in 1913, 400 t of alcohol were processed and 1,100 t of 'ethylene indigo' supplied. After the war the company adopted Gomberg's process for making chlorohydrin, but this route to indigo remained uneconomic and was stopped in 1924. It is piquant to recall that Gomberg developed his process in the USA during 1918 to obtain supplies of ethylene chlorohydrin for the mustard gas programme. Nagel: 'Fuchsin, Alizarin, Indigo', p. 48 and by the same author 'Athylen', BASF No. 7 (1971), pp. 7–8; Jones: 'The Role of Chemists', pp. 137–8.

24. The main authority on arsines was the German chemist Michaelis who became interested in them in 1880. There are numerous literature references before 1914 to phenyldichloroarsine, several to diphenylchloroarsine and a few to the ethyl- and vinyl- compounds. Dr and Miss Burstall kindly compiled the citations.

25. Hartley's notebook jottings and his Report, pp. 11–12. German replies to Allied questionnaire in Hartley papers. The prototype of a *Gas Büchse* was tested at Wahn in August 1917: the device was supposed to generate intense heat for a short time, sufficient to sublimate a mixture of the arsenical compound, initially DA, and pumice. But the high temperature produced a convection current which caused the particulate to rise and disperse too quickly. The device was modified, tried out in Russia, but failed again. Another field trial against the French was organized before the end of 1917. It was another failure. OHL lost interest and the entire programme was wound down.

26. Hartley Report, pp. 12, 44. Hartley was invariably scathing about German research on substituted arsines. Otto Hahn (*My Life*, p. 128) mentions that in October 1918 he was sent to the Hela peninsula (near Gdansk) to try out yet another smoke generator.

27. PRO/WO/142/122, file CWD 163; PRO/WO/142/98, files DGS 84 and 85: Work on the structure of particulate clouds. The minutes of the CWC (PRO/WO/142/60, 70–2, 122) contain many references to Wilson. Two American groups in the Organic Unit at the American University were also studying these compounds. 'Adamsite' after Roger Adams and 2-chlorovinyldichloroarsine or 'Lewisite' after W. L. Lewis were prepared in March 1918, but a reliable means of dispersion could not be found, nor had the Americans tested both materials in the field. But they decided to manufacture Lewisite and the British were also going to make it at Stratford; by the end of the war neither plant had been completed. It was found much later that Lewisite was unsuitable for chemical warfare. There are frequent references to the American research in the minutes of the CWC (PRO/WO/142/72) and also in PRO/WO/142/83 ('Lewisite and Analogous Substances', pp. 68–70). Jones: 'The Role of Chemists', p. 148 ff.

28. Dimethyl sulphate was turned down at the highest level at Millbank; Leonard Hill termed it 'fairly harmless stuff' (PRO/WO/142/169, file CL/40/17). P. S. Lelean, an important person at Millbank, proposed calcium arsenide (PRO/WO/142/183, file AGD/4). At its meeting on 13 April 1917 the Chemical Advisory Committee turned down arsine because of its 'delayed toxic effects' (PRO/WO/142/59).

29. Schwarte: *Technik im Weltkriege*, p. 286. Hartley Report, p. 7; interview with Hartley, 10 Oct. 1971; and Hartley: 'Fritz Haber', p. 10. The suggestion to

introduce mustard gas was made, apparently independently, by Prof. Steinkopf at Dahlem and Dr Lommel at the Bayer research laboratories. Mustard gas was often called 'Lost' by the Germans after the names of the two chemists.

30. Interview with Hartley 10 Oct. 1971 and *Notes of the Royal Soc.*, 24, p. 149. Starling would not be aware that the detonation of the shell would disperse droplets of mustard gas over a considerable area. Dr Dudley, then at Millbank, knew of Starling's 'discovery', He may even have prompted it, because he had been witness to an accident in Fischer's laboratory in Berlin were an assistant had been burnt so badly by mustard gas that he spent six weeks in hospital . The story appears in an extract of the minutes of a meeting of the Anti-Gas Committee on 20 July 1917 among the Hartley papers.

31. Vinet: 'La Guerre des gaz', p. 1406. Moureu, C.: *La Chimie et la guerre* (1920), p. 67. Moureu told Moreland, Lefebure, and others this story at a meeting in Dec. 1917 (PRO/WO/142/127, file CWD 272) and Gen. Pedoya's report to the Commission de l'Armée, 14 May 1918 also refers to it (FMA 10N57).

32. Hartley Report, p. 49; interview with Barley 8 March 1972. Vinet: 'The Dismantling of the Gas Plants in German Factories', English version of a French report (1921), p. 19, among Hartley papers.

33. Hartley Report, p. 6; IEEC: 'Les Projectiles spéciaux', *passim*, in Hartley papers. The British and the French had plenty of experience of diphosgene and thought very little of it.

34. Chemists and officers of the Special Brigade were working on and with Green Star from August 1915 to the autumn of 1916. MoM History, pp. 7, 40–1. Fox: *Corporals All*, p. 78.

35. Barley to Harrison 18 Feb. 1918, Barley papers. Similar observations were made by Thuillier writing to the War Office on 30 Jan. 1918, PRO/WO/142/135, file CWD/403.

36. Lord Rothschild much later wrote pithily, 'applied research must be done on a customer-contractor basis. The customer says what he wants; the contractor does it (if he can); and the customer pays.' 'A Framework for Government Research and Development', Cmnd. 4814 (1971), p. 3, para. 6.

37. MoM History, pp. 8–9. The 3rd Report of Chemical Sub-Committee, 1 Dec. 1915 to 10 Jan. 1916, pp. 26 ff., gives other examples where tests eliminated useless materials.

38. The volumes of the French 155 and 75 were approximately in the ratio of 7 : 1, but repeated shoots gave results which corresponded to a volume ratio of 5 : 2. This was based not on 'raisonnement', but 'un résultat constaté'. It is worth noting that the French were aware of the role played by rate of fire, calibre, wind speed, and gas used, but did not have the statistical techniques to evaluate the significance of each of the four variables. IEEC: 'Les Projectiles spéciaux', pp. 94 f., Hartley papers.

39. Wrisberg, E. V.: *Wehr und Waffen* (1922), p. 116. Hartley Report, pp. 8, 11, 46–7. The German proof commission was staffed almost exclusively by mathematicians and engineers and there was little liaison with the infantry.

40. Crossley: 'R.E. Experimental Station'; Davidson Pratt: Memorandum, *passim*.

41. Bacon, R. F.: 'The Work of the Technical Division CWS AEF', *Jnl. Ind. and*

Eng. Chem., 11, 1 (1919), pp. 13, 14. Prentiss: *Chemicals in War*, p. 84. Mignon: *Le Service de santé*, p. 769.

42. Hartley Report, pp. 46 ff. Letter from Haber to Geyer, 15 May 1933, BMA N 221/32.

43. It may be recalled that the first demonstration was held at Porton in Dec. 1916, weeks after Livens had fired his weapon on the Somme. PRO/WO/142/82 ('The Livens Gas Projector', pp. 82–4). MoM History, 'Trench Warfare Supplies', pp. 99–100.

44. MoM History, pp. 1, 14. Davidson Pratt: Memorandum, *passim*. Papers in PRO/WO/142/104, and the Reports of the Medical Research Committee. For completeness' sake, we may note that the Admiralty, prodded by Churchill, carried out research on cyanides between May 1915 and Spring 1917.

45. Raper, 'History of Anti-Gas Department', *passim*. MoM History, pp. 19–20. Carr: 'Harrison Memorial Lecture', pp. 95–8.

46. MoM History, *passim*. Minutes of Scientific Advisory Committee in PRO/WO/142/52.

47. 1st, 2nd, and 3rd Reports of the CS-C in the Hartley Papers; PRO/WO/143/53–6 (minutes of meetings); interview with Davidson Pratt on 7 May 1973 for views on Crossley and other members.

48. Davidson Pratt: Memorandum, p. 36'. PRO/WO/142/59 and 69–70 for minutes of the joint meetings.

49. Letter from Pope to Hartley 20 August 1917, Hartley papers. William Jackson Pope (1870–1939) became professor of chemistry at Cambridge in 1908. He undertook a good deal of research for Government departments after August 1914, but his active involvement in chemical warfare research, especially over mustard gas, dates from Sept. or Oct. 1917. For this work he was knighted in 1919. He was fluent in German and French, well informed, and possessed great drive—attributes that were to vivify the entire British chemical research and development effort in the last year of the war. Cf. Gibson, C. S.: 'Sir William Jackson Pope', *Obiit FRS*, 3 (n.d.), pp. 321, 323.

50. MoM History, p. 95 has the full list. Baker, Beilby, Thorpe were on the main committee, but represented a minority of scientists. Several of the names mentioned by Pope in his letter to Hartley were Associates.

51. PRO/WO/142/71 and 72 contain the minutes of the Committee and 86 has the index to the products. In a dispute between A. V. Hill and Barcroft about the toxicity of chlorarsines, Pope was appointed 're-examiner' (cf. PRO/WO/142/71, minutes of meeting on 25 Jan. 1918). The mustard-gas conference took place on 11 July 1918 and the report of it takes up 18 foolscap pages of single-space typing in PRO/SUPP/10/126, Quinan papers (1918), H 387.

52. FMA 16N832, files 1080/0 and 1. 'Rapport sur l'Organisation du Matériel Chimique de Guerre' dated 25 August 1915, 16N826. Vinet: 'La Guerre des gaz', p. 1380. PRO/WO/142/176 (lefebure papers). Interview with Hartley, 31 Oct. 1971. F. A. V. Grignard (1871–1935) left his chair at Nancy in 1914 and spent the war years in Government service, though he was not particularly involved with chemical warfare.

53. Vinet: 'La Guerre des gaz', p. 1386. Nebout published a booklet on gas shells

which was elementary as well as obscure, but at least could be taken as an attempt to link theory with practice.

54. Hartley Report, pp. 34–5, 44–5. Epstein's report among Hartley papers. Interview with Dr Jaenicke, 23 Sept. 1972.

55. Hartley Report, p. 58 and letter from Pick to J. E. Coates, 4 Jan. 1935 in the Coates papers.

56. Hartley Report, *passim* and interview with Jaenicke, 23 Sept. 1972.

57. The following section draws heavily on Jones: 'The Role of Chemists'.

58. Ibid., p. 130.

59. Transcript of Hartley's notes on meetings with Haber, Willstätter, and others in June 1921. Interview with Professor J. E. Coates 22 Nov. 1972. *Notes of the Royal Soc.*, 24, 1, p. 152 and Hartley: 'Fritz Haber', p. 14.

60. H. H. Wille in his biographical novel *Der Januskopf* (1969), pp. 212–16, implies that Haber may have delayed the introduction of mustard gas and the copy of Livens Projector because he thought it was too late to change the course of the war with chemical weapons. The novelist's perception may see further here than the historian. The hypothesis is plausible, although no written evidence is available to confirm it.

61. *Gas Warfare* was published in France. The issues for September to November 1917 were summarized in the *Mitteilungen* for June 1918 which will be found among the papers of the 16th Bavarian Division in the BHSA.

62. Crossley: 'R.E. Experimental Station', pp. 78–9.

63. Crossley's liaison reports to Jackson in PRO/MUN 5/197/1650/6 and the minutes of the CS-C in PRO/WO/143/54, 56, and 71 contain useful information on the absence of links. French officers were invited to attend tests with chlorine gas in Cannock Chase in the latter part of 1915 (FMA 16N832, file 1080/0 item 53 and 1080/2 items 21 and 22); I have not found particulars of later contacts. The meetings with British specialists from Petrograd are recorded in PRO/WO/142/74 and with the Italians in 142/138. US technical experts were frequently in attendance at British scientific meetings, and on June 6 1918, Fries, Kendall, and others reviewed their work on mustard gas at a conference attended by senior members of the Chemical Warfare Department (PRO/SUP/10/125, Quinan papers (1918), H 135–6).

64. Lefebure: 'Report on Chemical Warfare Liaison with France'. The report runs to 41 foolscap pages of single-space typing and is dated 25 May 1920: the key facts tally with information from other sources. Lefebure emerges as a self-satisfied busybody, an impression confirmed by talks with Hartley (22 August 1971) and Pratt (29 June 1972 and 7 May 1973). But even busybodies can play a useful role. Lefebure became official resident liaison officer to the French in November 1917.

65. The Hartley papers contain membership lists and the texts of some of the papers. Good linguists were in great demand on these occasions. See also Vinet: 'La Guerre des gaz', pp. 1386–7.

66. I had several talks with Hartley about Foulkes. Hartley was prejudiced against him, chiefly on the ground of his inflexibility in 1917–18. Those less closely involved to whom I spoke, namely Barley and Gold, were also less critical. All

were agreed that Foulkes was exceptionally brave and a good commanding officer.

67. Foulkes: '*Gas!*', pp. 182–3, 258. Also Fox: *Corporals All, passim* and *RE Jnl.* (February 1919), pp. 105–20 (Foulkes's report on the Special Brigade). There are no satisfactory manpower statistics for the Special Brigade.

68. BA Bauer Nachlass, Draft (?) memo on Chemical Warfare, (n.d., probably August 1915), folios 87–8. Captain Hermann Geyer (1882–1946) was a staff officer and at OHL throughout the war.

69. Peterson was about 55 in 1915, and his previous job had been commander of the fortress engineers at Königsberg. His staff consisted of Otto Hahn (1879–1968), another physicist by name of Lummitzsch, a meteorologist, and a medical officer. They travelled extensively throughout 1915–17. Hahn: *My Life*, p. 125; Hartley Report, pp. 29–31; Petter, D.: *Pioniere* (1963), pp. 189–91.

70. FMA 16N826, Cie. Z and 16N827, files 342/1–3. The files are incomplete and such numerical information as they contain is contradictory and misleading. Letter from H. E. Reynard to Foulkes, 12 Dec. 1918 in PRO/WO/142/176, Lefebure papers.

71. PRO/WO/142/134, file CWD 386 and 142/195, R-O-A2 and A9. On Italy see PRO/WO/142/138, file 431 and Barley's report on Anti-Gas Organization with the Italian Army, 11 Feb. 1918.

72. Fries and West: 'Chemical Warfare', pp. 34–5. Schulz, J. S. N.: *Textbook on the Chemical Service* (1923), pp. 56–7.

73. Sibert (1860–1935) had managed several of the big projects in the construction of the Panama Canal. He was appointed GOC 1st US Division and, a signal honour, took it to France in June 1917. But he was brusquely relieved of his command six months later and put in charge of American railway transport in France. In May 1918 he was promoted again to head the CWS which was then being formed. Schulz: Textbook . . ., pp. 56–7; Brown: *Chemical Warfare*, pp. 24, 31; *J. Ind. and Eng. Chem.* (12 May 1920), p. 423; *Dicty. of American Biography* (Supplement 1).

74. Hartley: 'Chemical Warfare', p. 9; various circulars and memos among the Hartley papers, interview with Hartley 23 Jan. 1972. Auld: *Gas and Flame*, p. 122. Foulkes: '*Gas!*' p. 258.

75. The earliest German circulars on defence against gas are dated 4 Dec. 1915 and 28 Feb. 1916. They show that Haber was aware of the need for an efficient organization, but as none existed on the Western Front, he was prepared to send instructors from Berlin as and when needed. This was locking the stable-door after the horse had bolted, because Fuchs's and Haber's reports on Hulluch (dated 9 July 1916) showed that senior commanders usually took the advice of their Stogas *after* something unpleasant had happened to their troops. There are many papers on the subject in the AOK6 files of the BHSA. The first German brochure on defence against gas that I have seen was issued by the Stogas of the 3rd Army (Champagne Front) and is dated 1 Oct. 1916. The English translation, dated 19 June 1917, is among the Hartley papers.

76. Interviews with Hartley on 14 and 28 Feb. 1971; Various memos in the Hartley papers and 'Chemical Warfare' p. 10. Bacon: 'Work of Technical Div.', p. 14

and 'Special Summary Report of Work of the C. W. S. Laboratory, A. E. F.' (Nov.–Dec. 1918), vol. I—Introduction in PRO/WO/142/7.

77. Report by Député E. Vincent to the Public Health Committee of the Chambre des Députés on 13 June 1917 in FMA 10N57 and also PRO/WO/142/176, Lefebure papers.

78. The IWM has an interesting film clip on cloud gas and gas drill (112–01 PA); see also Gladden: *The Somme*, p. 66. The training of the Italian instructors by British personnel under Barley's direction was accompanied by unexpected difficulties, but as the chemists often spoke some German, the specialists of the two Allies could communicate at the technical level. I am indebted to Col. Barley for this information on Italy (interview 8 March 1972 and letter to me dated 20 Oct. 1972) and for the use of his typescript, dated 2 Oct. 1918, 'Notes of [*sic*] Provisional Organisation for Protection against Gas'. For Hanlon Field see Bacon: 'Work of Technical Div.', p. 65.

79. Hartley Report, p. 28. BHSA, AOK 6 documents. BMA HO2—234/2, pp. 92–3 and HO2—52/1. Vinet: La Guerre des gaz', pp. 1414–15. FMA 16N832, file 1080/0, 1080/2 and FMA 10N57, written answer to Député Laval on 23 Feb. 1917.

80. Conversation 8 March 72. Raper: 'History of the Anti-Gas Department', p. 3. The minutes of the Chemical Advisers' meetings are in PRO/WO/142/95, files 65A and 65B. The list of topics is in PRO/WO/142/68.

Chapter 7

1. Hartley Report, *passim*. Reply, undated, from H. E. Watts to Hartley's letter of 21 Sept. 1921 in Hartley papers.

2. Hartley: 'Fritz Haber', p. 25. Memorandum from Hartley to Coates (n.d., (*c*. 1934) among Coates papers. A full account of the German economic warfare organization will be found in Feldman, G. D.: *Army, Industry and Labor in Germany 1914–18* (1966), and (from a different political viewpoint) in Klein, F. (ed.): *Deutschland im ersten Weltkrieg*, vol. II (1971). See also Wrisberg: *Wehr und Waffen, passim*.

3. Personal information from Charlotte Haber. Letters from Haber to his wife 1917–18 and conversations with Dr Jaenicke and Mrs D. Freund.

4. Sources as note 1 above. Vinet's Report on German Chemical Warfare Organization, p. 9 in Hartley papers.

5. PRO/WO/142/176 (Lefebure papers). FMA 16N832, files 1080/1 and 2. 'Rapport sur l'Organisation du Matériel Chimique de Guerre by député d'Aubigny', 25 August 1915 in FMA 16N826 (hereafter referred to as d'Aubigny Report). Vinet: 'La Guerre des gaz', p. 1383.

6. Memorandum by Albert Thomas, 18 August 1915 in FMA 16N832, file 1080/2, item 46. Lefebure: 'Chemical Warfare Liaison'. *The Times*, 31 August 1920.

7. Ipatieff, V. N.: *The Life of a Chemist* (1946), *passim*. Meeting of Jackson, Baker, and others with C. P. Schwabe on 8 Jan. 1917 in PRO/WO/142/74 and typescript by Schwabe (undated, but likely to be 1918) in PRO/WO/142/98, file DGS 90; and Schwabe's reports in PRO/WO/142/198, file R-O-A 13.

8. Fries and West: *Chemical Warfare*, p. 35. 'C. H. H': 'Gas Offense in the U. S. a Record Achievement', *Jnl. Ind. and Eng. Chem.*, 11, 1 (1919), p. 7. Sibert took up his new command on 11 May 1918 but the CWS was not formally constituted until 28 June 1918 when President Wilson signed the Overman Act.

9. While these intrigues went on at the MoM, the Navy (encouraged by Churchill) was making hydrogen cyanide at Stratford. Its purchasing officers requisitioned sodium cyanide without regard to the TWD, so creating more confusion. The details of this sub-plot which would unnecessarily complicate the main story will by found in PRO/MUN 5/198/1650/13 and in the minutes of 29 June, 7 and 20 July 1916 of the Chemical Supply Committee of the TWD in PRO/MUN 5/196/1650/11.

10. The entire complicated story is well documented and though the interesting bits have been omitted from the official history, the drafts contain the important details. MoM History, pp. 11, 13, 14, 69, 74–5 and also History of the Ministry of Munitions, vol. II, part 1—'Adminstrative Policy and Organisation' (1921), *passim*, and 'Trench Warfare Supplies' pp. 8–11. Interview with Davidson Pratt, 7 May 1973 and his 'Memorandum', pp. 15–16, 40–5, 48, 60–2, 68–70, 72, and 74–5. Moreland: 'Chemical Warfare Record', *passim*. Minutes of the Chemical Advisory Committee, various dates in PRO/WO/143/157. A recent and valuable source on the MoM in 1917–18 is Gilbert, M.: *Winston S. Churchill*, vol. IV (1975), pp. 28, 42, 47.

11. Moreland: 'Chemical Warfare Record' pp. 34, 340–1; Davidson Pratt: Memorandum, pp. 91, 98–100, 115–19; MoM, p. 11; 'Administrative Policy', pp. 77–8. Raper: 'History of the Anti-Gas Department', pp. 23–4. Gilbert: *Churchill*, IV, pp. 73–4 mentions in connection with the plans for 1919 that the Cabinet at its meeting on 11 March 1918 learnt that the War Office did not favour Churchill's proposal to make massive use of gas: they argued it would prevent the infantry from advancing. Within less than a fortnight, the Germans demonstrated the exact opposite.

12. Vinet: 'La Guerre des gaz', pp. 1387, 1415. Minutes of the Inter Allied Commission Meeting, 11 May 1918, PRO/SUP/10/127, Quinan Papers M 14–16.

13. The only production figure which inspires some confidence is that for liquid chlorine of which 3,000 tons were made in the year to end April 1917. This was roughly of the same order as French output, and well below that of Britain and Germany. See PRO/WO/142/195 (R-O-A9), report by W. L. Hicks, 30 July 1917. Other interesting information on Russia is contained in C. P. Schwabe's typed notes (n.d., probably late 1918) in PRO/WO/143/57, PRO/WO/142/98 (D.H.S.90), and in PRO/WO/142/134 (CWD 386). 'The Russian Shell Shortage 1914–17', contributed by N. Stone to Best, G. and Wheatcroft, A. (eds.): *War Economy and the Military Mind* (1976), pp. 112–17, which provides valuable background information.

14. On Italy, see report by Starling on Italian Gas Organization in PRO/WO/143/138, file CWD 431 (n.d., probably late summer 1917). On Austria, Wrisberg: *Wehr und Waffen*, pp. 217–18.

15. D'Aubigny Report, p. 2; Moreland: 'Chemical Warfare Record', pp. 150–3.
16. D'Aubigny Report, *passim*; MoM History, pp. 27–8, 69–70 and Hartley Report, pp. 19–20.
17. Acetic acid was the starting point for cellulose acetate employed as aircraft dope. It was chlorinated to chloracetic acid used for tear gas (ethyl iodo-acetate) and dyestuffs intermediates. Bleaching powder was needed by the textile industries, for export and as an indispensable disinfectant behind the lines.
18. Moreland; 'Chemical Warfare Record', p. 142. Livens: 'The Livens Gas Projector', no page nos.
19. Moreland; 'Chemical Warfare Record', pp. 267–8, 297. Correspondence in PRO/WO/142/155, file CL 8/15 and, more generally, in MoM History.
20. Hartley Report, p. 39.
21. Moreland; 'Chemical Warfare Record', p. 142; Hartley Report, p. 27.
22. Among the French contractors was the young Marcel Boussac whose textile interests, small in 1914, benefited from these military orders, and grew fast between the wars and became a large concern in the 1950s and 1960s. FMA 16N832, file 1080, Ministère de la Guerre to GQG 17 July 1915 and written answer from Thomas to Député R. Pevet, 3 June 1916 in FMA 10N57.
23. Report by Anti-Gas Department dated 20 Jan. 1919 in Hartley papers. Hartley Report, pp. 25, 41–2. Schwarte: *Technik im Weltkriege*, p. 585. The special charcoal briquettes were developed by Sutcliffe, Speakman and Co. of Leigh which, to the present day, specializes in filtrating materials.
24. MoM History, p. 98.
25. PRO/SUP/10/122, Quinan Papers, Book 41, pp. C2 and C24.
26. Review of C. G. Position by A. T. de Mouilpied, report dated 6 June 1918, p. 38 in PRO/SUP/10/128, Quinan papers.
27. FMA 10N57: written answer by Albert Thomas to Senator H. Berenger, 2 Sept. 1916.
28. Compiled from particulars in Anti-Gas Department, Historical Notes, typescript in PRO/MUN 5/386/1650/12.
29. Pinsert, A.: 'Report on the Nottingham Gas Factory', pp. 30–1, PRO/MUN 5/586/1650/11. Carey Morgan, 'Report on the Work of Women in . . . the Anti-Gas Department', *passim*. MoM History, pp. 72, 77–81.
30. Letter from Hartley to Watts 21 Sept. 1921 and Watts's undated reply in Hartley Papers. Schwarte: *Technik im Weltkriege*, p. 304.
31. The hydrochlorination stage called for precise temperature control, forced ventilation, thorough safety precautions, and, generally, good chemical engineering practice. It is interesting to observe that the Bayer people could have made the last stage continuous, but preferred to operate a batch system because the equipment was in place and worked well with manual controls. Interview with Jaenicke, 3 April 1971. Hartley Report, pp. 7, 48. 'Report of the British Mission . . . to . . . Enemy Chemical Factories', Department of Explosives Supply (Feb. 1919), p. 7 (for details see Bibliography, Ministry of Munitions). Note by Prof. J. Thorpe on conversation with Haber, 28 Nov. 1924 in Hartley papers. German Replies to Allied Questionnaire in Hartley papers and documents in PRO/WO/88/288 and 289.

32. 'Report of the British Mission, pp. 11, 14, 15, 19, 23–7. H. E. Watts's letter to Sir F. E. Bingham, 8 March 1921 in Hartley papers. Muraour, H.: 'Les Gaz de combat', typescript dated 12 Oct. 1922, pp. 1–4 in PRO/WO/188/176. Vinet: 'Report on the Present Condition of the Installations . . . for the Manufacture of Asphyxiating Gases', typescript dated 22 March 1921 in Hartley papers.

33. 'Report of the British Mission', *passim*; Vinet as in note 32, p. 3.

34. Muraour as in note 32, *passim*; Vinet as in note 32, pp. 3, 11, 12, 14. Watts's letters to Bingham, 8 March 1921 and to Hartley, 15 Feb. 1921, both in Hartley papers. The various sources agree with each other.

35. 'Report of the British Mission', pp. 54, 56 ff. Vinet's Report as in note 32, pp. 6–7, 9. Muraour as in note 32, pp. 5–7. Watts's letter to Hartley 15 Feb. 1921 in Hartley papers. I have deliberately simplified the account, but for the sake of completeness it is worth adding that a small mustard gas plant, identical with Bayer's, was operated by Griesheim-Elektron at its Griesheim works between March and Nov. 1918; it produced altogether 850 t of mustard gas.

36. Letter from Hartley to H. Watts, 21 Sept. 1921, and Watts's undated reply in Hartley papers. Coates's preliminary notes for lecture (n.d., ? February 1936) among Coates papers. Letter from Duisberg to Bauer, 24 July 1915 in BA Bauer Nachlass, folio 48. Hartley Report, p. 27. The relationship between Haber and Koppel, a much older man, went back to the early years of the century when Haber was consultant to the Auergesellschaft. Koppel was a great admirer of Haber, endowed the KWI, and it was his express wish that Haber should become its first director. The contract for the gas masks may have been a quid pro quo. It is an example of Haber's preference for the 'old-boy network', and turned out to be an excellent choice.

37. Various documents dated 1916 in FMA 10N57. PRO/WO/142/182, 'F' series of reports: French output of CW Material. Vinet: 'La Guerre des gaz', p. 1412. Tissier, L.: 'Les Poudres et explosifs'; in Chimie et Industrie: *10 ans d'efforts . . . industriels* (1926), p. 1343. Lefebure, V.: 'Report on Chemical Warfare Liaison with France', pp. 31–2, hereafter referred to as Lefebure's Report.

38. Vinet: 'Report on the German C.W. Organisation', p. 18.

39. FMA 10N57, report by Gen. Pedoya to Commission de l'Armée of the Chamber of Deputies on 14 May 1918. Lefebure's Report, pp. 22–5.

40. Memorandum by J. D. Pratt dated 15 Feb. 1919 in PRO/WO/142/128, file CWD 272. Report by Lefebure dated 25 Jan. 1918 in PRO/WO/142/200, file DES 10/1–6. Crossley's Liaison Reports PRO/MUN 5/197/1659/6. Usines du Rhône was a manufacturer of dystuffs, but at the time of which I am writing it specialized in a wide range of organic chemicals and also cellulose acetate dope and plastics. Smaller than the German dye works, it was the only French firm to approach them in technical performance. Later it merged with Poulenc Frères and ultimately became the largest business in the industry. Two of the other firms mentioned are still trading today. G. de Laire's successors continue making speciality chemicals (though not, so far as I am aware, phosgene) and Gillet & Fils are now called Progil SA.

41. Florentin, D.: 'Les Poudres . . . et les gaz de combat'; in *10 ans d'efforts . . . industriels*, p. 698. Vinet.: 'La Guerre des gaz'. p. 1413.

42. MoM History, p. 96. Moreland: 'Chemical Warfare Record', pp. 46–7, 150–1. Quinan papers, Book 41, C2 in PRO/SUP/10/122. Four chlorine programmes can be distinguished. They covered military and civilian supplies and were invariably expressed in terms of weekly bleaching powder (36–7 per cent Cl_2) output. First programme: supplies available by end 1916: 3,500 tons (including 2,100 tons civilian deliveries); second programme: by mid 1917: 4,100 tons; third programme by January 1918: 4,800 tons; final programme, availability by January–April 1919: 9,600 tons.

43. MoM History, pp. 34–5, 38. Moreland: 'Chemical Warfare Record', pp. 163–4. Quinan Papers in PRO/SUP/10/121, p. C11.

44. The phosgene scandal is well documented and the different sources confirm each other. Cf. in particular the Reports and Minutes of Chemical Sub-Committee of the TWD in PRO/WO/143/56 and 57. Moreland: 'Chemical Warfare Record', pp. 196–8, 201, 204, 224. Mouilpied, A. T. de; 'C.G. Production', report dated 15 August 1918 in PRO/WO/142/138, DES 8/1–60. Redstone, L. J: 'History of Chemical Supply' (first draft dated 25 April 1918) pp. 12–13 in PRO/MUN 5/385/1650/4. MoM History, pp. 47–8. Cadman's reports on his visits are in PRO/MUN 5/197/1650/12 and PRO/WO/142/114, file CWD 86.

45. An example will indicate the difficulties which were likely to arise with the German (or Meyer's) process to make dichlorodiethyl sulphide. In August or Sept. 1917 Thomas Kerfoot and Co. of Ashton-under-Lyne, then the only firm making thiodiglycol in Britain, were asked if they could supply it in large quantities. They replied that they had been preparing it for the past eighteen months, using thionyl chloride bought from UAC, at the rate of about 25 kg a week. They sold it for pharmaceutical end-use. The Ministry's requirements called for 25 tons a day! MoM History, pp. 49–50. Moreland; 'Chemical Warfare Record', pp. 270–1 and 275–6.

46. MoM History, pp. 50–2. PRO/WO/142/71, PRO/WO/142/196, and PRO/DES/1/36/80 for minutes of the CWC meetings on the subject of mustard gas.

47. Green's samples were immediately analysed and tested 72, 75, and 76 per cent dichlorodiethyl sulphide. That was approaching German standards. The various claims and the conflicting assertions are fully documented, e.g. Pope, Sir William: 'Mustard Gas', *Journal of the Soc. of Chem. Industry* (30 Sept. 1919), *R* p. 344. See also PRO/SUP/10/126, Quinan papers, pp. H 303–6, 344, 'The Levinstein Plant', report dated 20 August 1918 and PRO/WO/142/129, file CWD 289, Levinstein–Green Claim. Draft Instructions to Adviser Letters Patent 142,875, 2 July 1920 in Hartley papers. For Prof. Green's activities and visit to London see PRO/SUP/10/124, Quinan papers, H 127, Report from Levinstein Ltd, 3 June 1918 and SUP/10/125, Quinan papers, H 210–11, Prof. Green's Visit, 7 June 1918. Copy of letter from J. D. Pratt to Thuillier, 31 Jan. 1921 in Hartley papers.

48. Moreland: 'Chemical Warfare Record', pp. 335 ff. Whitelaw, R. P.; 'Report on the Manufacture of Mustard Gas at HM Factory Avonmouth' (typescript, n.d., probably 1919 or 1920), pp. 1–2, in Hartley papers. I have been unable

to find a single dependable figure for the rated capacity of dichlorodiethyl sulphide at Avonmouth. It varied greatly, depending on the number of reactors in operation at any one time.

49. Copy of letter from Whitelaw to J. D. Pratt, 2 Feb. 1921 in Hartley papers and Whitelaw: 'Report on . . . Mustard Gas', p. 14.

50. Draft Instructions to Adviser . . . (see n. 47). Whitelaw: 'Report on . . . Mustard Gas', pp. 21–8. PRO/WO/142/71, minutes of the CWC meetings.

51. PRO/WO/142/200, file DES 12/1/60, notes by Prof. Steele on DA, dated 1 Oct. 1918. Job, 'Progrès accomplis dans la fabrication des Arsines', typescript of paper read to Interallied Gas Conference, 29 Oct. 1918 in Hartley papers. MoM History, pp. 52–4. Sartori: *War Gases*, pp. 320 ff. PRO/WO/142/117, file CWD/115 A, note on DM Manufacture (n.d.), PRO/SUP/10/128, Quinan papers, pp. 19–20. It was planned to disperse DA and DM as particulate clouds and for this purpose 200,000 'thermo-generators' were ordered in July 1918. But the final design for these sublimators was only approved in October and the first assembly line at Morecambe, with a capacity of 50,000 a week, was not ready until just before the Armistice. Finely ground DA or DM, packed in drums, was received from Sutton Oak. The material was mixed with kieselguhr, poured into tin boxes, and equipped with an ignitor and friction tape. The women who did this work wore special protective clothing and elaborate safety precautions were taken. Nevertheless there were some cases or arsenic poisoning during Nov. and Dec. PRO/WO/142/116 and 117, files CWD 114, 115, and 117, Visit by J. D. Pratt to Morecambe, 5 Dec. 1918. Moreland: 'Chemical Warfare Record', pp. 355–6. PRO/WO/142/98, file DGS 84.

52. Sinclair, M.: *Lest we forget* (n.d.), no page nos; this is the story of the wartime activities of John Bell, Hills and Lucas. The firm, under the name of John Bell and Croyden, continues to trade to the present day and many will know it best as the large chemist's in Wigmore Street, London. Anti-Gas Department, Historical Notes in PRO/MUN 5/386/1650/12. Raper: 'History of the Anti-Gas Department', *passim*. Carey Morgan: Report, *passim*. Carr: '*Harrison Memorial Lecture*, *passim*.

53. Haynes, W.: *American Chemical Industry*, vols. II and III (1945), deal with the war years. Zinsser specialized in fine and photographic chemicals, National Aniline and Chemical was a new company formed to make dyestuffs. A document in PRO/WO/142/19, 'Report on Present Position . . . at Edgewood Arsenal and Branches' (n.d., *c*. Summer 1918) mentions that these and several other firms were 'under construction' or 'in course of completion' and as they had lower priority than Edgewood, they were overtaken by it.

54. Whittemore, G. F. jr.: 'World War 1 Poison Gas Research and the Ideals of American Chemists', *Soc. Studies of Science*, 5, 2 (1975), p. 151. 'C.H.H.': 'Gas Offense in the US', p. 6. PRO/SUP/10/125, Quinan papers, H 135–6: Meeting with Americans at Storey's Gate on 5 June 1918. The American team was high-powered and described their plans for Edgewood. According to them the pilot plant had made two tons in May and was scheduled to produce ninety in June. It is likely that the Americans visited Levinstein Ltd in Manchester at about the same time.

55. Fries and West: *Chemical Warfare*, pp. 33, 56. C.H.H.: 'Gas Offense in the US', pp. 6–12. The mustard gas plant was constructed from drawings sent by Levinstein Ltd, free of charge. A French company offered its design for $250,000, but was rejected—PRO/WO/188/185, file R/15/4.2.

56. Fries and West: *Chemical Warfare* pp. 50–1. Charcoal was made at a nearby factory operated by the National Carbon Co. Sodium permanganate granules were supplied by the Kalbfleisch Corp.

57. The figures in Tables 7.7 and 7.8 have been compiled from several sources, cross-checked, and where all else failed estimated on such fragmentary daily or weekly returns as were available. For the UK I have relied on MoM History, p. 97, for France on Tissier, reference 37 and Florentin, reference 41. Lefebure's 'F' reports, complete except for August, Sept., and Nov. 1918, in PRO/WO/142/182. Production reports (incomplete for 1917 and 1918) and Ozil's notes in FMA 10N57 and graphs in Thomas' and Loucheur's notebooks in FMA 10N58. For Germany, 'Report of the British Mission', *passim*. Watts: 'Production of Gas . . .', 15 Feb. 1922 in Hartley papers and his letter to Bingham of 8 March 1921 in Hartley papers.

58. Sources as in previous reference. For the USA the information is based on Col. R. F. Bacon's memo to Quinan of 12 August 1918 in PRO/SUP/10/127, p. M 36–8 and 'C.H.H.': 'Gas Offense in the US', *passim*.

59. 'Introduction to the Report of the British Mission', Cmd. 1137 (1921), p. 10.

60. 3rd Report of the CS-C (n.d., March? 1916), p. 7, in Hartley papers.

61. Davidson Pratt: 'Memorandum', pp. 32, 34. See also MoM History, pp. 9–10, 22–3 and Moreland: 'Chemical Warfare Record', *passim*. Moreland had much to say about red tape. He attributed delays to frequent personnel changes which were due to the game of musical chairs much in vogue at the MoM.

62. The memorandum is dated 12 April 1918, PRO/WO/142/128, file CWD 270. See also 'Mustard Gas', p. 343.

63. Before the Committee was constituted at the beginning of Nov. 1917, there are only three references to mustard gas in the relevant War Office files PRO/WO/142/84. Two of them noted reports by Professor Irvine on Guthrie's process, the one eventually chosen. The item appeared ten times on the agenda in Nov.–Dec. 1917, six times in Jan.–March, thirteen times in the April–June quarter and nineteen (!) times in the following five weeks. From 7 August to the Armistice, the Committee dealt seven times with mustard gas.

64. Hartley Report, p. 20. Haber's letter to Valentini of 2 Jan. 1916 in BA, Schwertfeger Papers 209 (folios 37–8) shows how important the captaincy was for him. It was indeed unusual in that he had been promoted to it directly from his reserve status of NCO and it gave him a certain standing in the Kriegsministerium. On Bauer's role, see Feldman: *Army, Industry and Labor in Germany*, pp. 37, 150 and 172 and Klein: *Deutschland im ersten Weltkrieg*, vol. II, pp. 462, 593, 769–71.

65. The adoption of the SBR by the Americans, once their own mask had turned out to be 'a fiasco' was quick. The Italians took longer to persuade, but eventually they too accepted it. PRO/WO/142/188, file AGD 28 for letter from Harrison to Barley of 10 Jan. 1918 on this subject and letter from B. B. Cubitt

(Army Council) to GOC., British Forces in Italy, 8 Feb. 1918 in Hartley papers.
66. Forester, C. S.: *The General* (1936), pp. 185, 224.
67. Letter dated 7 Apr. 1975. Hartley's conversations with me a few years earlier were along the same lines and support the view that 'irregulars' could work happily with field officers.
68. Arnold Zweig in *Erziehung vor Verdun* (1935) used Eberhard Kroysing, a very brave pioneer lieutenant, to contrast the arrogance and narrow-mindedness of regular infantry officers with the competence and devotion to his job of the specialist.
69. In Britain, eleven committees—some functioning at the same time—dealt with, or rather advised on, chemical warfare. They are listed in MoM History pp. 94–5. The minutes are often not a record of decisions, but spell out the positions taken by individuals on particular issues. A good example of such irreconcilable differences is the meeting on toxic substances for shells. It took place on 31 May 1917, was chaired by Bingham and attended by Thuillier, Foulkes, Crossley, Moreland, Cadman, Thorpe, and other less important individuals. It ended inconclusively and thus entailed further delays in the gas shell programme.
70. Foulkes, T.H.F.: 'Memoirs' (reprint ?1969, from *RE Jnl.*), pp. 238–9.
71. My talks with Hartley after reading his report (particularly pp. 29 and 49) and his notes on the visit to Germany in 1921 have helped me reach these conclusions. See also Haber: 'Die Chemie im Kriege' in *Fünf Vorträge*, pp. 25 ff.
72. Letter from Haber to Valentini, 24 Dec. 1916, BA Schwertfeger papers, 209. This episode in Haber's wartime activities is badly documented.

Chapter 8

1. Hartley Report, pp. 4, 55. The interviews with Haber took place in July 1921.
2. The second battalion of Pionier Rgt. No. 38 discharged 8 t of a chlorine-chloropicrin mixture down a shaft near Hulluch. The upcast ventilation shafts, in the British sector at the Béthune end of the coal mine, sucked the gas through the pit. The alert came too late and all those on the bottom level were killed. Particulars are given in Hanslian: *Chem. Krieg*, p. 100; in the translation of a captured report from the Kriegsministerium, No 2547, Nov. 1917 A 10 (21 Dec. 1917, in the Hartley papers); and in Macpherson *et al.*: *Medical Services*, vol. II, pp. 548–9.
3. Geyer: 'Denkschrift', pp. 10–11.
4. The French and the German sources complement each other and agree on everything except casualties, which the French revised downwards, while the Germans retained their inflated guesstimates. Hanslian: *Chem. Krieg*, pp. 97–9; Kriegsministerium Report, as in note 2 above. PRO/WO/142/154, file CL/5/18, Mimeographed report by Dr Flandin. Diary of O. von Trotta, vol. xxvi, 4–6 March 1917, in BMA N233/30–5. Written answer by Ministère de l'Armement to Député Laval, 23 Feb. 1917, FMA 10N57.
5. List of German gas attacks prepared by C. G. Douglas, dated 6 Apr. 1918, and his report of gas casualties dated 30 Nov. 1918 both in PRO/WO/142/99, file DGS/M/16D. PRO/WO/142/109, file DGS/M/94, letter from Gen. Herr

to Foulkes, dated 23 Dec. 1918. PRO/WO/142/173, file F/D/C 35, 'Vague Allemande du 7 Avril à Limey-Remenauville'. (The two villages are 10 and 17 km respectively west of Pont-à-Mousson on the Moselle.)

6. PRO/WO/142/98 and 195, file DGS 90 (C. P. Schwabe's reports from Petrograd and various 'Gas Service Reports from Russian Front'). The British observers, hundreds of miles from the front, had no means of checking the information. Dr K. Heber, on the other hand, accompanied the Gaspioniere on some of the occasions and twenty years later wrote down what he could remember. His impressions rarely coincide with the British reports. Heber ('Aufzeichnungen', p. 27) mentions that the last gas cylinder discharge took place on 12 Nov. 1917, east of Baranovitchi and south-west of Minsk in White Russia.

7. Foulkes: '*Gas!*', *passim*. Fox: Corporals All, *passim*. 'M. S. F.' [Fox]: 'With the Special Brigade' (n.d., 1957), p. 22.

8. Foulkes: '*Gas!*', *passim*, Fox: 'Special Brigade', p. 22.

9. Liddell Hart: *History of First World War*, p. 413. Foulkes, C. H.: 'The Work of the Royal Engineers in the European War', *RE Jnl.* (Feb. 1921), *passim*.

10. Harold Hartley in his Tribute to Captain William Howard Livens, DSO, MC, 1889–1964, *The Times*, 6 Feb. 1964. Livens: 'Gas Projector', *passim*.

11. MoM History, p. 7. MoM: 'Trench Warfare Supplies', pp. 99–100. Foulkes: '*Gas!*', pp. 171–3.

12. Experimental Data and Notes in Hartley papers. The test was made in France on 3 April 1917. A fortnight earlier the Chemical Advisory Committee noted (PRO/WO/142/59, 338th meeting on 16 March 1917) that a test shoot at Porton had gassed three people at a range of 2 km. That put an end to further experiments for the time.

13. MoM: 'Trench Warfare Supplies', pp. 99–100.

14. Heber: 'Aufzeichnungen', p. 29. Hartley Report, pp. 12, 13. Central Laboratory Report 3395, 22 Sept. 1918 in Hartley papers.

15. Schroth: *Bilder aus . . . Gaspioniere*, pp. 28–9.

16. Foulkes: '*Gas!*', *passim*. Fox: *Corporals All*, pp. 96–7, 98; BHSA, 1st Bavarian Reserve Infantry Div., Circular of OHL, II, IV 62282, dated 16 Aug. 1917; the circular contained the instructions for the newly formed Minenwerfer Kompagnie 500.

17. See Liddell Hart: *History of First World War*, pp. 407 ff, for the battle as a whole. Livens's 'The Livens Gas Projector' is the best account of the preparations and the firing of the cylinders. Foulkes ('*Gas!*', pp. 211–12) was present on 4 April.

18. There were several separate attacks. All took place in a political and linguistic frontier area. Until 1918 it formed part of the Austrian Empire. It was then disputed by Italy and Yugoslavia and handed over to the latter by the Treaty of St Germain (1919). German, Italian, and Croatian was spoken. I have kept to the present-day place-names and given their Italian or German equivalents in brackets, except Caporetto: it was one of the great events of the First World War; changing it to Kobarid would, in the present context, be historical pedantry.

19. Seth, R.: *Caporetto* (1965), pp. 147, 157, does not mention the gas drums near Bovec. Hahn: *My Life*, pp. 126–7, describes the preliminaries, but he was back on the Western Front when the battle began. Hanslian: *Chemische Krieg*, pp. 181–2, has the most detailed account of the operation.

20. BMA F5026, PG MP IV/II, typed memo from OHL, II No. 71673 dated 29 Nov. 1917. Interview with L. J. Barley 8 March 1972.

21. Foulkes lists the operations, though not in any particular order between pp. 192 and 230 of his book. The largest involved 4,800 projectors (65 t) dug in between Messines and Ploegstreet. They were to be fired in June at the same time as the famous underground mines, but the operation was cancelled.

22. British gas officers interrogated many German prisoners during the battle of Arras. The stories were collated by Hartley ('Effects of British Gas Shell Bombardment April 8–9, 1917', Report dated 13 April 1917) and Adams ('4th Report for period July–Dec. 1917', dated 27 Feb. 1918), both in the Hartley papers. The prisoners' evidence of the damage caused by gas is conflicting, and the answers are occasionally totally implausible. A man is captured during a battle and questioned: what weight should be given to his claim that his battalion, and in one case, his Division, suffered heavy casualties? Yet Foulkes was convinced and used these reports to strengthen his case. Hartley was much more cautious in his conclusions.

23. BHSA, papers in AOK 6 files and OHL Circular No. 62282, dated 15 Aug. 1917 among papers of 1st Bavarian Reserve Infantry Div.

24. Memo No. 412, ref. DGS 'B', dated 13 Dec., Memo No. OB 492, dated GHQ 1 Feb. 1918 and signed B. Wigram, both in Hartley papers. PRO/WO/142/109, file DGS/M/94, letter from Gen. Herr to Foulkes dated 23 Dec. 1918 and Hanslian: *Chem. Krieg*, p. 25.

25. Douglas, C. G.: 'Effects of Blue Cross Shells on the Troops in the Field', typescript dated 16 Nov. 1939 in Hartley papers.

26. Notes on German Shells, 2nd. edn., GHQ (Intelligence), 1 May 1918. I am grateful to Mr Willis of the IWM for explaining some of the technicalities to me. Schwarte; *Technik im Weltkriege*, pp. 288–91 has a section on gas shells contributed by Kerschbaum: it is interesting, but not entirely correct. Prentiss: *Chemicals in War*, pp. 458, 473. It may be noted that Agfa filled 4.8 million bottles and Schering presumably most of the rest, letter from Watts to Sir F. B. Bingham of 8 March 1921 in Hartley papers.

27. Vinet: 'Report on the German C.W. Organisation' pp. 31–2 and his 'Report on the Organization and Working of the four German Field Ammunition Depots', *passim*, both in Hartley papers. German Replies to Allied Questionnaire, *passim*. Schwarte: *Technik im Weltkriege*, p. 286; *Schering Blätter*, No. 5 (1971), p. 12, has a picture of Adlershof in the 1920s and some of the filling sheds can easily be discerned.

28. PRO/WO/142/129, file CWD 289, notes by T. M. Lowry (n.d.), and also 136, files CWD 417 and 423, memos by Lefebure dated 29 April and 6 June 1918. PRO/SUP/10/126, Quinan papers 1918, H 307–8, (notes by Lefebure on Aubervilliers 10 August 1918) and H 332–7 (notes by R. T. F. Barnett on Pont-de-Claix and Salaise 12 August 1918).

29. MoM History, pp. 31, 48, 50, 52, 56–7. Moreland: 'Chemical Warfare Record', p. 91. PRO/WO/142/98 (Foulkes's Periodic Reports). Fries and West: *Chemical Warfare* pp. 56 ff. Edgewood did not have enough bursters for shells above 75 mm, and this explains why some gas was sent in bulk containers to France and Britain from August 1918 onwards.

30. Volkart, W.: 'Die Gasschlacht in Flandern im Herbst 1917', Beiheft 7, *Wehrwissenschaftliche Rundschau*. (1957), pp. 47, 51–2. Volkart's article is based on regimental histories which are dependable on dates, but unsatisfactory on casualties. PRO/WO/142/10, file M60/A1. Reports by C. G. Douglas dated 17 and 24 July 1917. Douglas: 'Effects of Blue Cross Shells'.

31. PRO/WO/142/106, folder DGS/M60/A; Hartley's Report to GHQ, 19 July in Hartley papers.

32. Interviews with Hartley on 14 Feb. and 9 May 1971. Some British chemists had been studying dichlorodiethyl sulphide the year before in London, and may have been consulted by Mouat Jones.

33. Volkart: 'Die Gasschlacht', pp. 51–2. The figures mentioned by Volkart are lower than those quoted by Macpherson *et al.*: *Medical Services*, pp. 294–5, which show that from 12 July to the end of the month there were over 14,000 gas shell casualties, overwhelmingly from mustard gas.

34. Hartley Report, p. 48 and German circular dated 11 March 1918, Ref. 169/18/A1 in Hartley papers.

35. Hartley: 'A general comparison of British and German methods of Gas Warfare', *passim*. Central Laboratory GHQ, Report No. 2626, dated 21 Dec 1917, in Hartley papers. Hanslian: *Chem. Krieg*, p. 55. Schwarte: *Technik im Weltkriege*, p. 288: Kerschbaum mentioned that gas mines were designed with fuses set to explode from 10 to 100 m above ground. I have not seen any confirmation of this statement in British reports.

36. Hanslian: *Chem. Krieg*, pp. 26–9; IEEC: 'Le Tir des projectiles spéciaux', p. 85.

37. BMA, Stogas 4th Army, circular (tr.) dated 26 Sept. 1917, ref. F 5026, PG Mk. IV/II. This circular replaced that of 4 June 1917 (ref. 1903/17) which is not in the BMA.

38. BHSA, 2nd Bavarian Corps, Report dated 23 May 1917 of a conversation with Dr Blumenreuther, adjutant to the Stogas of the 4th Army.

39. Cunningham, D. J. C.: 'C. G. Douglas', Obit FRS, NS 10 (1964), p. 59. The instructions predated the positive identification of mustard gas.

40. Note on mustard gas (n.d.), Hartley papers. Reports DGS B/412 dated 19 and 24 July 1917 in Hartley papers. Report by A. E. Boycott, Porton, dated 12 June 1918 in Hartley papers. Grignard, F. A. V.: 'Propriétés physiochimiques des solutions d'Yperite', Third Inter-Allied Conference on War Gases, 29 Oct. 1918 no page nos. in Hartley papers.

41. Auld: *Gas and Flame*, pp. 171, 178–9.

42. Douglas, C. G.: 'Effects produced in the field by shell containing chlorarsines', Report dated 22 Oct. 1918, ref. M 73/B/15 in Hartley papers. Also PRO/WO/142/122, file CWD/167, Report (n.d., ?1918) on protection against particulate clouds.

43. H. Pick in Schwarte: *Technik im Weltkriege*, p. 300 and Hanslian: *Chem. Krieg*, pp. 200–1. Both authors praise the leather mask.

44. BHSA, records of 16 Bavarian Infantry Div. and papers of AOK 6, records of the Stogas. Between 1 Oct. 1917 and 31 Dec. 1917 131,000 complete leather masks were issued, packed. From 1 Jan. 1918 to 31 March 1918 155,000 were issued, mostly loose, that is, ready for immediate use.

45. Freundlich: 'The German . . . Filter', no page nos., in Hartley papers. Hartley Report, pp. 42–3. PRO/WO/142/116, file CWD 113; memo by J. D. Pratt on use of M-Generator in North Russia, 2 June 1920. Hanslian: *Chem. Krieg*, p. 303 states that Blue Cross was 'in mässigem Grade abgefangen', i.e. stopped to a limited extent, by the S-E drum.

46. Hartley Report, pp. 37, 40, 42; Freundlich: 'The German . . . Filter', *passim*. PRO/WO/142/162, file CL/23/18–19, Mouat Jones, B., 'Development of German Gas Defence Appliances', 17 Dec. 1918. PRO/WO/142/72, Minutes of CWC. Schwarte: *Technik im Weltkriege*, pp. 301–2; Hanslian: *Chem. Krieg*, pp. 204–5. Carpenter, J. A.: 'Report on German Respirator Drums with New Fillings', ref. DGS B/275a, dated 18 August 1918 in Hartley papers. The measurement of breathing resistance was not systematic, let alone—judging by the available documents—scientific. The paper filter added 36 mm (1.5 in) mercury to the 11-C-11 filter which itself was 12–14 mm above the old filter. Testing for mask break-down was as follows: as one observer left the gas chamber he handed the mask to the next until phosgene or chloropicrin became noticeable. This was the 'breakdown' point and the time was recorded.

47. Freundlich: 'The German . . . Filter', *passim*. Hartley Report, *passim*. Report of British Mission', pp. 26–7. Interview with Dr Jaenicke, 23 Sept. 1972.

48. 'Diary of Development of British Respirator' (n.d.), in Hartley papers. MoM History, pp. 67–8. Hartley: British Association lecture, *passim*. PRO/MUN 5/386/1650/13, Raper: 'History of the Anti-Gas Department', pp. 16–17 (this file also contains drawings of the various filters).

49. Hartley: British Association lecture, *passim*; Raper: 'History of The Anti-Gas Department', p. 11. PRO/WO/142/71, Minutes of CWC. PRO/WO/142/98, file DGS 84, Development of Thermogenerator Type M.

50. The comparisons were elaborate, but the findings were not always circulated among the Allies. For example in one report the Italian respirator was said to give 'practically no protection' and that of the ARS 'was of a different order to that given by [the] S.B.R.' PRO/WO/142/71 Minutes of the 10th and 14th meetings of the CWC, 4 Jan. and 8 Feb. 1918.

51. Lebeau: 'Sur la valeur de protection actuellement conferée par l'appareil ARS', Third Inter-Allied Conference on War Gases 27 Oct. 1918, in Hartley papers. Bloch, D.-P.: *La Guerre chimique* (1929), pp. 70–1. Vinet: 'La Guerre des gaz', pp. 1393–4, 1395.

52. FMA 10N57, Report by Sen. Cazeneuve (1 Feb. 1918) and amendment by Commission de l'Armée (21 Feb. 1918). In March output fell to 15,000 a day (covering note by Ozil to the above report, dated 22 March 1918). PRO/WO/142/176, file F/M/C/5, 'L'Action des gaz pendant l'offensive Allemande de Mars/Avril', 1918 by Dr Flandin (n.d.), p. 5.

53. Lefebure's Report, pp. 19–21. Mignon: *Le Service de santé*, vol. III, pp. 780–1. PRO/WO/142/98 file DGS 84, Development of Thermo-Generator Type M.

54. Fries: 'Chemical Warfare', pp. 423–9. PRO/WO/142/195, file R-O-A 13, Captain Hicks's Report (n.d., from context Oct. or Nov. 1917). Letter from Barley to Harrison 17 Jan. 1918 in Barley papers.

55. Memorandum circulated by Hartley dated 9 Aug. 1918 (ref. DGS B/461) in Hartley papers. Shufflebottom, R.: 'Medical Aspects of the Production of Mustard Gas', Jan. 1919, Report No. 18 of the Medical Research Council, pp. 10–11.

56. Conversation with Barley, 8 March 1972. BHSA, 16 Bavarian Infantry Div. papers, Circular No. 1519/5.18 A 10 dated 18 May 1918, issued by Kriegsministerium.

57. Circular (n.d., 1917), on fans in Hartley papers. Vinet: 'La Guerre des gaz', p. 1399. Mignon: *Le Service de santé*, vol. III, p. 252.

58. Hartley Report, p. 42. MoM History, p. 68. Vinet: 'La Guerre des gaz', p. 1398. Achard and Flandin: 'Traitement des Brûlures par Yperite', Third Inter-Allied Conference on War Gases, 30 Oct. 1918, Summary, no page nos., in Hartley papers. Carey Morgan: 'Work of Women in . . . the Anti-Gas Department', p. 25. O'Brien, T. H.: *Civil Defence* (1955), pp. 142, 234. PRO/WO/142/196 for papers on impregnated materials. The disadvantages of oil impregnants were known, but no alternative was available.

59. PRO/SUP/10/126 Quinan papers, H 286–7, Lefebure's Notes on Hygiene in French HS Factories, 10 Aug. 1918. Shufflebotham: 'Medical Aspects . . . of Mustard Gas', pp. 8–9. Lowry, T. M.: 'Chemical Research and Munitions Work at Guy's Hospital Medical School', *Guy's Hosp. R.*, *70* (1922), pt. III, p. 18. Whitelaw: 'Report on . . . Mustard Gas', pp. 54, 76–7.

60. Interviews with Messrs Berridge and McLellan on 5 Nov. 1973 and with Dr Beales on 1 Dec. 1973. Chapman, G.: *A Passionate Prodigality* (1966), pp. 219–20. Fest, J. C.: *Hitler* (1973), pp. 113, 121. Note by B. L. Eddis on the Wervik shelling dated 5 Nov. 1918 in Hartley papers: over 1,000 'HS' shells were fired.

61. Hartley Report, pp. 8, 44.

62. BHSA, various Corps and Regimental records. Volkart: 'Die Gasschlacht', pp. 39, 56.

63. BHSA, papers of BRIR 10, 'History of 3rd Btn.', prepared by men of 2nd Btn.; Volkart: 'Die Gasschlacht . . .', pp. 37–8, 39 quotes from several other regimental battle diaries. For British views see Hartley's British Association lecture, pp. 4–5 and Report, p. 55. PRO/WO/188/143, file RA/A/1, has a collection of notes by Livens on casualties. They do not carry precise dates.

64. BMA, F 5026, Stogas 4th Army previously cited. Hartley Report, pp. 21–3, 35, 60–2. The Barley papers throw much light on the change in Italian attitudes from ignorance and neglect to the gradual acceptance of protection and training. In December 1917 they were prickly and stubborn, but by February 1918 they had accepted the SBR and within six or seven weeks hundreds of instructors were being taught its use. BBC TV, in Episode 25 (2 March 1975) of *The Great War* showed the Italians being led into captivity after Caporetto: none carried respirators. British POW's were never taken without them.

65. PRO/WO/143/57 for minutes of CS-C meetings of 11 March and 17 April

1916 which considered Brock's bombs. Admiralty Technical History Section: *The Technical History and Index*, vol. I, pt. II, pp. 7, 30. *Chemical Age* (10 July 1926), p. 30. Hartley Report, p. 49. BMA, file No. 221/23, Geyer: 'Denkschrift', pp. 7–8. BA, Bauer Papers, folios 93–139, Memorandum on Gas Warfare and Gas Defence (n.d., ? 1919), no page nos. BA, Schwertfeger Papers, folios 37–58, letter from Haber to Valentini, 2 Jan. 1916.

66. Lefebure's Report, p. 34. FMA 10N57, Senator Cazeneuve's Report.

67. Brown: *Chemical Warfare*, p. 45. Pershing had strong views on chemical warfare which were of some importance after the war.

68. PRO/CAB/23–4, War Cabinet 306, 26 Dec. 1917. PRO/WO/142/187, file AGD 25/26, meeting held at Adastral House on 18 July 1917.

Chapter 9

1. Schwarte: *Technik im Weltkriege* (Geyer's contribution), p. 277 (tr.).

2. Hoffmann, M.: *Der Krieg der versäumten Gelegenheiten* (1923), pp. 135–6. He described Brüchmuller as an 'artillery genius'; I will leave it to the reader to form his or her own judgement.

3. Bruchmüller, G.: *Die deutsche Artillerie in den Durchbruchschlachten des Weltkrieges* (1921). This slim book of 118 pages is a collection of eight case-studies. A few years later, the author revised and enlarged it, and under the title of *Die Artillerie beim Angriff im Stellungskrieg* it was published in 1926; see in particular pp. 41–2, 68. BHSA, Papers of AOK 6, Circular of German War Ministry, 11 Sept. 1917.

4. Crossley was thinking not only of the Directorate of Gas Services but also of the artillery at GHQ. Particulars of this acrimonious meeting are in PRO/MUN5/198/1650/28 and in Note of Meeting at MoM, 27 June 1918 in Hartley papers. For Crossley see Kent: 'History of Porton', p. 23.

5. MoM History, p. 11. PRO/MUN 5/187/1360/10, Report of a Conference on General Gas Policy held at the Ministry of Munitions on 27 Nov. 1917. The figures shown in that report are surpassed by those in MoM History, p. 93, for April 1918. Mr M. G. Willis of the Imperial War Museum was very helpful over guns and firing-rates and I take this opportunity of gratefully acknowledging his assistance.

6. Auld: *Gas and Flame*, pp. 157–61. Note by B. L. Eddis for DGS, 5 Nov. 1918, ref. DGS/A/96 in Hartley papers.

7. Notes by Hartley in his papers on a conference of Chemical Advisers, 15–21 May 1917 at which the static tests were made. Nebout, J.: 'Les Projectiles spéciaux: organisation, fonctionnement et conditions d'emploi', (n.d., ?April 1918), pp. 57–61, in Hartley papers. Given the lack of data, regression analysis to determine the effect of the numerous variables is impossible. It should also be noted that the surface area covered by a cylinder attack differed from that of a gas shoot, thus the common denominator, 1 km², represents variable terrain conditions.

8. Nicolet, N. H.: 'The Problem of Gas Camouflage from the Laboratory Viewpoint', Third Inter-Allied Conference on War Gases, 25 Oct. 1918 in

Hartley papers. Bacon: 'The Work of the Technical Division, CWS, AEF', p. 14

9. The Hartley papers contain a copy of the instructions dated 6 Aug. 1915 and 21 Feb. 1917. The instructions of 1 Dec. 1917 were prepared by the CO of the Artillery Training School of Valenciennes, see BMA H02–52/1 (Buntschiessen Anweisungen) and BHSA Ref. no. R 2874. Hartley was aware of the German instructions which he summarized in his article, 'A general comparison . . . ', pp. 7–8.

10. IEEC: 'Le Tir des projectiles spéciaux', pp. 44–5 in Hartley papers. 'Instructions on the Use of Lethal and Lachrimatory Shell', rev. edn. (March 1918), SS 134 in Hartley papers.

11. 'Effect of British Gas Shell Bombardment 8–9 April 1917', in Hartley papers.

12. Volkart; 'Die Gasschlacht', made a thorough study of the use of gas shell at Third Ypres and in Spring 1918. He relied principally on German sources which may explain why, on p. 39 of the article, he accepts—without questioning—the assertion that diphosgene (Green Cross) shells were very effective against gun positions. (I am assuming that he did not confuse Green with Yellow Cross.) He does not refer to the possibility of field trials for mustard gas. However Haber's frequent journeys to Belgium in the early summer of 1917 suggests that more than counter-battery work was involved.

13. Bruchmüller: *Die Artillerie . . .*, pp. 26, 41–2, 68, 170–3. It should be noted that his 'case studies' are incomplete, do not lend themselves readily to comparisons and are designed to show him, at all times, in the best possible light. The German War Ministry Circular No. 2547, 11.17A10, of 21 Dec. 1917, reports on the new methods on the Eastern Front. It was found among captured Bavarian records, was translated at GHQ, BEF and is now among the Hartley papers. See also Hartley Report, pp. 8–9 and Clark: 'Effectiveness of Chemical Weapons', pp. 66–7, 69 and 78 ff.

14. Schwarte: *Technik im Weltkriege*, p. 277. PRO/WO/142/71, Minutes of CWC (Defensive), 19 April 1918. Memo on Defence against Yperite, signed by Hartley (n.d., ?May 1918) in Hartley papers. Douglas, C. G.: 'Effects of Blue Cross Shells on the Troops in the Field', *passim*.

15. Geyer: 'Denkschrift', p. 5. Hartley Report, pp. 11, 48.

16. Clark: 'Effectiveness of Chemical Weapons', pp. 99–100. She relies on Prentiss who, like everyone else on the subject, is not dependable, but the proportions give the order of magnitude. IEEC: 'Le Tir des projectiles spéciaux', pp. 8–9.

17. PRO/CAB/23/5, War Cabinet 355, item 10, 27 Feb. 1918. Thuillier was called to attend, because at the meeting on 20 Feb. (item 6), the possibility of gas bombs on London and stories of new chemical weapons had been raised, but no one present had been able to give a technical opinion.

18. Hartley: 'Note on conversation with Sir Henry Thuillier', 14 Aug. 1945 in Hartley papers. PRO/CAB/23/5, War Cabinet 350, item 6, 20 Feb. 1918. PRO/WO/142/71 Minutes of CWC (Offensive) 21 Feb. 1918. Direction des Services Chimiques de Guerre: 'Rapport sur les Bouffées Periodiques de Renseignements . . . ', 23 Feb. 1918 in Hartley papers. Hartley's speech to Royal Society, pp. 150–1. On glanders, see PRO/WO/118/117, where the story was reported from Geneva, dated 2 Sept. 1927. This supposed wartime plot stretches

credulity, particularly when one reads that the name of the German agent was Schreck!

19. See Middlebrook, M.: *The Kaiser's Battle* (1978), which gives a very thorough account of the last 10 days of March 1918.

20. PRO/WO/142/153, file CL3/18, Central Laboratory, has the rainfall statistics. Hartley: 'Fritz Haber', *passim*. Middlebrook: *The Kaiser's Battle*, pp. 123–4. There is a story, told by Haber to Hartley which, though apocryphal, bears repeating. Haber heard Schmauss's forecast and at once reported to Ludendorff. The Quartermaster-General relaxed and became genial. The attack was imminent and 'if the wind were unfavourable, I am uncertain as to what we should do. Go tell the Field Marshal.' Haber went and said, 'the wind will be favourable tomorrow morning in obedience to your orders.' Hindenburg stood up, raised his right hand and announced 'Not in obedience to my orders, but by the will of God.' Haber told Hartley that the Field Marshal spoke from his heart and added 'there were some peculiar (*merkwürdige*) people about.'

21. 'Box' fire, that is, shelling small rectangular or square targets, depended on the close co-operation of several batteries, careful aiming, and on gun barrels being in good condition. An example will show how it worked: the Germans put down a 'box' of mustard gas on either side of the duckboards which took the place of a communications trench, but left the front line undisturbed. Shelling lasted forty to fifty minutes: the duckboards were smashed and the shell holes had a layer of mustard gas on the water. For a time there was no possible path to the front. The incident took place at Hoge near Ypres, in Spring 1918 and was described by G. Chapman, who witnessed it (*A Passionate Prodigality*, pp. 229–30), as 'weird and disturbing'.

22. Bruchmüller: *Die Artillerie . . .*, pp. 112, 188–9. BHSA, Reg. Diary of 14 BIR, then in the Quéant sector. Middlebrook: *The Kaiser's Battle*, pp. 328–9, 330–1, 340–1. Hartley: 'A general comparison . . . ', p. 8. DGS: 'Notes on German Gas Shell Bombardment', 21 March 1918, dated 9 April 1918, in Hartley papers.

23. Volkart: 'Die Gasschlacht', *passim* relied on Prentiss (*Chemicals in War*, pp. 665–6) and he, in turn, on various British and German sources. Neither had access to the actual consumption statistics. Instead they multiplied the maximum number of rounds fired by a combination of German field and medium artillery by the duration of the bombardment. Some of the estimates are plausible, others—such as the pattern of *Buntschiessen* for each operation—pure guesswork. Volkart also estimated the area of the initial bombardment but failed to make clear whether the numbers refer to total area or the 40 per cent or thereabouts represented by Bruchmüller's rectangles and blocks. It is therefore not possible to use his figures for any worthwhile comparative analysis.

24. Volkart: 'Die Gasschlacht', pp. 66–7, writes that the Germans took Kemmel wearing respirators. Judging by my experience they must have been supermen— the hill is steep! On some of these occasions, Armentières, Kemmel, etc. gas shells represented 80 per cent of total shell expenditure. See Hartley: 'A general comparison', and lecture given at London University on 25 Nov. 1926. PRO/WO/142/176, file F/M/C/5. For the sake of completeness I should point out that Germany's allies hardly ever used Yellow Cross shells.

25. Hartley Report, p. 10.

26. BHSA: papers of 16 Bavarian Infantry Div. The circulars are dated 19 and 26 Oct. 'Particulars of [German] Gas Shellings August–October 1918' in Hartley papers.

27. FMA 10N57. Letter dated 2 April 1918 to the President of the Senate Army Committee and General Pedoya's report on Yperite of 14 May 1918 to the Commission de l'Armée of the Chambre des Députés.

28. PRO/WO/142/177, German reports on French gas and WO/142/165, file C/L/31/18. Hartley Report, p. 49. Volkart, 'Die Gasschlacht', p. 69. Memo of Stogas of 4th Bavarian Army, dated 20 June 1918, on Anti-Gas Precautions in Hartley papers. *Sanitätsbericht*, III, p. 181.

29. Hartley: British Association lecture, p. 4 and 'A general comparison', p. 12. PRO/WO/142/129, file CWD 289. Hanslian: *Chemische Krieg*, pp. 30 f., states that the British captured a large stock of Yellow Cross shells during the battle of Cambrai and used them on 17 Nov. 1917. His source is an article by M. E. Backer in *Chemical Warfare*, 20 March 1934; I have found no corroboration elsewhere.

30. PRO/WO/142/198, file DES 5/391–440. Hartley: 'A general comparison', *passim*. Schulz: *Textbook*, pp. 79–80.

31. *History of the MoM*: II, pt. I, 'Administrative Policy and Organisation', p. 99. PRO/MUN5/198/1650/29. Minutes of Conference at GHQ to consider supply of Gas for 1919, 19 March 1918 (hereafter shortened to 19 March Conference), pp. 2–3.

32. Fries and West: *Chemical Warfare*, p. 94. Fries: 'Chemical Warfare', p. 427. Hanslian: *Chem. Krieg*, p. 30. US National Archives, CWS, RG 120, Entry 124 and Boxes 1249 and 1250.

33. PRO/WO/142/98, file DGS 84, Circular issued by Foulkes dated 25 July 1918. The story is not confirmed by Lefebure in his reports, nor is there any information about these accidents. I have not found any reference in the FMA to Soulié and his men in 1918. Clark: 'Effectiveness of Chemical Weapons', p. 21, states that according to Hanslian, the French carried out twenty cylinder operations in 1916–18. Since they were inactive in 1916, the majority of the attacks must have taken place in 1917 and 1918. The French archives contain no particulars (date, location, scale, etc.) so that I have no means of confirming or denying Hanslian's statement. Foulkes: '*Gas!*', p. 332. PRO/WO/142/109, file DGS/M/94, contains Foulkes's papers and notes, many of them undated, but from the context written after the Armistice.

34. Heber: 'Aufzeichnungen', pp. 30–8. On 26 Sept. 1918 the French (or perhaps the Americans) captured an entire Pionier Btn. and also some men from the HQ company of Pionier Rgt. 36, among them Heber. Meyer-Welcher, H. and Groote, W. von (eds.): *Handbuch zur deutschen Militärgeschichte*, vol. V, pp. 254–5.

35. PRO/MUN 5/386/1650/101. Moreland: 'Chemical Warfare Record', p. 53. 19 March Conference, p. 8. PRO/WO/142/71, Minutes of CWC, meeting 7 March 1918. PRO/WO/188/143, file R/8/A/1, papers written by Livens. The people who attended the 19 March Conference knew that there was not sufficient

phosgene to fill the order and that chlorine and chloropicrin would also have to be used. There was no mustard gas at the time.

36. 19 March Conference, pp. 5, 9. Foulkes, C. H.: 'Report on the Activity of the Special Brigade', 19 Dec. 1918, p. 2.

37. Fox: *Corporals All*, p. 101. 'M. S. F.': 'With the Special Brigade', p. 21. Foulkes, 'Report on the Activity', p. 2. Grantham, D. R.: 'The Great War: Gas—The Development of Weapons' (typescript, n.d.), *passim*, in IWM Library. Grantham served in the Special Brigade. He mentions that on one occasion he detonated more than a thousand cylinders simultaneously. This suggests that elaborate electrical devices were being used.

38. Note from C. G. Douglas to Hartley dated 15 June 1921, in the Hartley papers; 'M. S. F.': 'With the Special Brigade', p. 21. The dates given by the authors do not always coincide, but such precision does not matter too much in the present context. Middlebrook: *The Kaiser's Battle*, pp. 125–6.

39. Clark: 'Effectiveness of Chemical Weapons', p. 50 quoting Addison, J. T.: *The Story of the 1st Gas Rgt.* (1919). Schulz: *Textbook*, pp. 81–2. Fries and West: *Chemical Warfare*, pp. 96 ff.

40. PRO/WO/142/109, file DGS/M/94, letter from General Herr to Foulkes dated 23 Dec. 1918 and other memoranda written or received by Foulkes. Heber's 'Aufzeichnungen', though useful in many respects never give the number of projectiles fired in an operation. Each battalion of the Gaspioniere was normally issued with 1,000 projectors which, after an operation, were supposed to be dug out and re-used. Among the papers of 1st Bavarian Reserve Infantry Div. there is a report, dated 1 May 1918, of a German projector attack between Lens and Hulluch in which 800 projectors were used.

41. Foulkes: '*Gas!*', p. 332. Herr's letter of 23 Dec. 1918.

42. PRO/CAB/23/6, Cabinet No. 411, item 5, 14 May 1918 and No. 425, item 5, 4 June 1918. PRO/WO/142/72, Minutes of CWC, (Offensive) meeting; 31 May 1918.

43. GHQ, BEF, Circular dated 12 Sept. 1918 in Hartley papers. Demmler, E. *et al.*: *Das K.B. Reserve Infanterie Regiment 12* (1934), pp. 264–5. BHSA, papers of BRIR 2, 10 and 12.

44. Interviews with Hartley on 21 March 1971 and Dr Gold on 1 April 1972. Hartley Report, p. 5 and Hartley: 'Fritz Haber', p. 18.

45. Cf. Clark: 'Effectiveness of Chemical Weapons', p. 54. She used German, British, and US sources to draw attention to the change in attitude and aims of the chemical warfare lobby.

46. Circular from CWS, dated 11 July 1918 in Hartley papers.

47. Hanslian: *Chem. Krieg*, p. 37. 'Summary of Hostile Gas Activity for October 1918' in Hartley papers. The two sources complement and confirm each other.

48. *History of the MoM*: 'Administrative Policy', p. 99. Moreland: 'Chemical Warfare Record', pp. 388–9. Mouilpied: 'Review of the C.G. Position', 6 June 1918 in PRO/SUP/10, Quinan Papers, p. 38. Schulz: *Textbook*, p. 59. Fries and West: *Chemical Warfare*, p. 59.

49. 19 March Conference, p. 16. Thuillier talked about porcelain-filled vessels.

Bingham squashed that one by asking what would happen if the pilot could not jettison the bombs before he crash-landed!

50. Jessup, A. C.: 'Summary of Blue Cross Casualties suffered by V Corps, May–October 1918', memo dated 5 Dec. 1918 in Hartley papers. (Jessup was Gas Adviser to the Corps.)

51. Brown: *Chemical Warfare*, pp. 36–7. For a British view see Douglas's memo cited in ref. 14.

52. There are many references to outbreaks of influenza in June–July in the BHSA papers. I have used those of the BRIR 10 at Ablainzeville-Gomiecourt because it was also involved in British gas operations. Demmler *et al.: Das . . . BRIR 12*, p. 264.

53. Schwarte: *Technik im Weltkriege*, p. 278. *Sanitätsbericht*, III, pp. 179–81 which specifically mentions the undermining of morale by 'many false rumours' (tr.) about mustard gas. BHSA, papers of 16 Bavarian Infantry Div. Translation, by T. H. Adams of Ludendorff's Circular of 21 June 1918, dated G.H.Q., B.E.F., 30 July 1918 in Hartley papers.

54. The incidents are recorded in the papers of BRIR, 2, 10, 12, BIR, 14, and of 16th Bavarian Infantry Div., all at BHSA. Demmler *et al.: Das . . . BRIR 12*, pp. 264–5. Many of the German regimental battle-diary entries can be compared with British reports, e.g. GHQ, BEF circular, dated 12 Sept. 1918 in Hartley papers.

55. BA, Bauer Nachlass, folios 95–139, No. 1a.

56. Official Instructions on [German] Gas Defence, translated by T. H. Adams, 18 June 1918, SB/1.0/103 in Hartley papers. Hartley: British Association lecture, p. 5.

57. 'Summary of Hostile Gas Activity for August 1918', in Hartley papers.

58. Translation of German Document on the projector operation at Ablainzeville, made by Intelligence, GHQ, BEF, 12 Sept. 1918 together with Hartley's notes on the incident in Hartley papers.

59. J. Singer Sargent (1856–1925) painted several war pictures, generally undistinguished. *Gassed* is dated 1918 and was based on descriptions of the scene at a CCS on the Doullens–Arras road in August 1918. The foreground is filled with blinded soldiers, recumbent or being led, while in the middle distance some convalescent men are playing football.

60. Wilfred Owen (1893–1918) wrote many war poems in his short life. He was killed in the last week of the War. *Collected Poems*, pp. 55–6.

61. *The British Campaign in France and Flandres*, III, pp. 48–9 and 80.

62. IWM Film Library, ref. No. 184-PA, no caption, nor date is available for the clip. I am indebted to Mr Bridger for the showing of this film. I do not know whether Sargent ever saw the film.

63. BBC-TV, *The Great War*. The serial was first screened in the mid-1960s; Episode 7 was repeated on 29 July 1974. BBC-TV *Testament of Youth*, part 4, repeated on 24 August 1980.

64. The film was made in 1969. A World Record Club LP has the tunes of the film.

65. William Roberts (1895–1980) did other First World War paintings. He was, at the time, a Vorticist. The painting of the gas cloud was commissioned by the Canadian War Memorials Fund in 1918 and now hangs in the National

Gallery of Canada, Ottawa (No. 8729). Otto Dix (1891–1969) was a member of the Neue Sachlichkeit group.

66. *Im Westen nichts Neues* was first published in 1929 and at once translated into English. I may add that the face is not blue, but pallid in the final stages of gas cyanosis.

67. Roland Dorgelès's (pseudonym of Roland Lécavelé, 1886–1973) *Les Croix de bois* was first published in 1919, while Henri Barbusse's (1873–1935) *Le Feu* appeared in 1916 and was translated into English the following year.

68. Romains, J.: *Les Hommes de bonne volonté, XVI, Verdun* (1938).

69. 'Mustard Gas Casualties', report dated 17 July 1917 in PRO/WO/142/106, file DGS/M 60/A.

70. Hartley: British Association lecture, p. 6 and Notes on conversation with Sir Henry Thuillier 14 Aug. 1945, both in Hartley papers.

71. Céline, L.—F.: *Voyage au bout de la nuit* (1962), p. 23 (tr.). Céline was severely wounded by a shell splinter in the early months of the war. He was invalided out of the French army and it is likely that the effects of the injury led to the recurring depressions which he describes in this autobiographical novel.

72. Manning: *Her Privates We*, p. 78.

73. *Memoirs of an Infantry Officer* (1930), p. 147 and *Sherston's Progress* (Penguin edn., 1948), p. 135. Sassoon (1886–1967) was in France from Spring 1916 to April 1917 when he was wounded at Arras. He returned to the Western Front in 1918.

74. Forester: *The General*, pp. 185, 224, 226.

75. Malraux A.: *Les Noyers d'Altenburg* (1948), pt. III, pp. 157–234, especially p. 179. The entire passage is extraordinary. Bolgako is not known to me, but the attack took place in June 1915 (see Chapter 3) and some of the details of the professor, my father, are accurate. In the story, his son, a veterinary, accompanies him. But in real life, Hermann, Haber's son by his first marriage, would have been a teenager and he never visited the Eastern Front. Who was Malraux's informant?

76. My interviews with them took place in Oct. 1973.

77. Baynes: *Morale: A Study of Men and Courage*, pp. 157–9, 195–6. The battle was fought in March 1915 and was inconclusive. Baynes was a regular officer in the Cameronians and the son of the CO who had taken part in the battle.

78. Report HH 91/E, 18 Feb. 1917, Third Army, in Hartley papers.

79. Blunden, E.: *Undertones of War* (1929), p. 251. The incident took place not far from Zillebeke, near Ypres, towards the end of 1917.

80. Thorpe, Sir Thomas: 'History of SK', in PRO/MUN 5/385/1650/7, no pagination.

81. Gladden: *The Somme*, p. 66.

82. *Les Croix de bois*, pp. 331–2.

83. *Goodbye*, pp. 146–163. 198, 267–8.

84. *Sherston's Progress*, p. 34.

85. *Fox under my Cloak*, pp. 309–10. The hero, Maddison, is a chemist and his cylinders were emplaced between Loos and the Vermelles-Hulluch road. Hahn: *My Life*, pp. 130–2.

86. Chapman: *A Passionate Prodigality*. Carl Zuckmayer's autobiography, *Als wär's ein Stück von mir*, was published in 1966. His reminiscences of the First World War take up about seventy pages of a very long book and are less dramatic than his account of the theatre in Weimar Germany. Renn, L.: *Krieg* (1929), had not the same success as Remarque's *All Quiet . . .*

87. *The Somme*, p. 16. Gladden's notes were enlarged between the wars, but were not rewritten until the 1960s or early 1970s.

88. Bamm, P.: *Eines Menschen Zeit* (1972), p. 320, (tr.). Kurt Emmerich, (1897–1975), the pseudonym of Bamm, served in both World Wars.

Chapter 10

1. Gilchrist, H.L.: *A Comparative Study of World War Casualties from Gas and other Weapons* (1931), p. 6; Prentiss: *Chemicals in War*, pp. 653–4; Hanslian: *Chem. Krieg*, 2nd edn. p. 24; 3rd edn., pp. 35 f. It is worth adding that all three had served in the chemical warfare services during the war.

2. Middlebrook paid particular attention to this question in the March 1918 battle. He reached the conclusion that the statistics of the British dead for the 21st, the first day of the German offensive, were poor whilst the records of the injured at CCS in the 5th Army are 'virtually non-existent' and he could not even find an estimate for gas casualties. Very high mustard-gas casualties—3,000—were reported from the Flesquières salient where the 3rd and 5th Armies joined, but these could have been an accumulation of several days. Middlebrook: *The Kaiser's Battle*, pp. 312, 316–17, 321.

3. French casualty statistics are unsatisfactory. There is some information in FMA 16N521 and 524, but it is of no use in the context of this book. FMA 16N523 has graphs showing gas and other causes of injury in 1918 for each army. The scale is not uniform and the lines cannot be read with precision; the underlying numbers cannot be located.

4. Hanslian: *Chem. Krieg*, p. 36, quotes an article in *Wehr und Waffen* for Feb. 1935, p. 83 by K. Leppa which, in turn, is based on Russian sources.

5. Heeres-Sanitätsinspektion: *Sanitätsbericht . . .*, III, pp. 1,7,17.

6. Mitchell, T. J. and Smith, G. M.: *Casualties and Medical Statistics of the Great War* (1931), contains all the relevant information. The Canadian history (Nicholson: *Canadian Expeditionary Force 1914–19*, p. 548) gives a figure of 11,600 injured by gas out of a total of 227,400 dead, wounded, and injured. The Australian History (Bean, C. E. W.: *The Australian Imperial Force in France*, vol. V (1937) of *The Official History of Australia in the War of 1914–18*) and Stewart, H.: *The New Zealand Division 1916–19*, (1921)) have nothing to say on the subject. The number of men in the Dominion forces in France during 1918 was of the order of half a million.

7. There is no methodical survey of the French gas casualties. Apart from the graphs in FMA 16N523, the letter from Gen. Herr (GQG) to Foulkes dated 23 Dec. 1918 (PRO/WO/142/109, file DGS M.94) gives some useful details of the 11 cylinder operations and 39 projector attacks which the Germans carried out against the French in 1915–17. The compilations show an aggregate of about

2,600 killed and 10,500 injured, but exclude the casualties on 22 April 1915 for which I have allowed 2,500. Herr derived his information from the reports of the Centres Médico-Légaux; some of these have survived and, in general, are slightly lower than the dispatches from Army commanders. There are two other sources of information, the authors being senior medical officers with access to original hospital records. Toubert, J.: 'Étude statistique des pertes subies par les Français pendant la Guerre de 1914–18' (n.d., reprint of a lecture given at the Val-de-Grâce hospital in July 1920) and his *Le Service de santé militaire au GQG français 1918–19* (1934), pp. 34, 39, 45–6, 58, 67, 95–6, and Mignon: *Le Service de santé*, II, p. 664, 672–4; III, pp. 251–2, 467–8. Toubert relied in the main on the records of the Groupe d'Armées du Centre and on the returns furnished by the hospital train organization which was the chief mode of evacuation in 1918. His statistics exclude those killed by gas at the front (likely to be very small in 1918), those lightly gassed and not sent to the rear, and those transported by motor ambulance. Mignon gives much more detail and his statistics, unlike Toubert's, purport to show the number of gas cases, including those injured by gas shells in 1917. His figures, where they can be compared, are lower than Toubert's.

8. British and Canadian troops, 6 (24 April; 1, 6, 10, and 24 May; 19 Dec.); French, 4 (22 April; 19 and 27 Oct.; 26 Nov.).

9. Hartley Report, p. 53. The percentage was taken from Geyer's report (see next note), but the Germans chose not to divulge more to their visitor.

10. Geyer: 'Denkschrift' gives a figure of 58,000 German casualties, of whom 1,755 (3 per cent) died, from 1st Jan. to 30 Sep. 1918. Geyer was in a position to know the facts and his report was prepared for the German delegation to the peace talks. The *Sanitätsbericht*, III, pp. 130, 176, and 177 gives separate gas casualty figures for the Eastern and Western fronts annually for the twelve months ending 31 July until 1918 and also monthly figures from Jan. 1916 to July 1918 inclusive. The former are shown separately for field ambulances and for hospitals, the latter for hospitals in the field army (*Feldheer*) and the occupation army (*Besatzungsheer*). There is a risk of double counting, so I did not add the two sets of figures, but have relied on the higher of the two, that is respectively the returns from the field ambulances and the field army.

11. Gilchrist: *A Comparative Study*, pp. 17–18, has 70,500, excluding the Marine Corps. Gen. Sibert in his evidence to the House of Representatives Committee on Military Affairs in 1919 spoke of 75,767 (US National Archives, RG 287, Box Y5890, Ar5, Part 10, pp. 537, 543).

12. I have consulted the *Encyclopaedia Britannica*, the *Grand Larousse*, V (1962), p. 691, and its *Macropaedia* (XIX, 1973–4, p. 966), and the *Grosse Brockhaus*, without finding a consensus on the casualties of the First World War.

13. Hanslian: *Chem. Krieg*, p. 36, mentions that the Russians reported 38,600 men were killed by gas. He reproduced the monthly totals from an article in *Wehr und Waffen*, (see note 4 above) but considered the figures unreliable, not least because there were only 46 dead between 1 May and 1 August 1915 when the Germans carried out some of their largest cloud-gas operations in Poland, and almost 14,000 in Nov., when chemical warfare activity was minimal.

Independently of Hanslian, Capt. W. L. Hicks, the representative of the DGS in Petrograd, wrote to London that Russian statistics were untrustworthy. 'Report on Russian Gas Services' (n.d., [Oct.–Nov. 1917]) in PRO/WO/142/195, R-O-A13.

14. The gas cloud at San Michele del Carso (at the southern end of the Soča (Isonzo) front) on 29 June 1916 is mentioned by three writers, and it is indicative of Italian casualty statistics that they quote three different figures. Hanslian wrote (pp. 23, 105–6, 182) that 5,000 Italians were gassed and a further 1,000 taken prisoner. Col. Starling on a visit to Italy in August or Sept. 1917 was told there had been 7,000 gas casualties of whom 4,000 died (PRO/WO/142/138, file CWD 431). Finally, A. Lustig, the head of the Italian chemical warfare service, stated in 1919 that 8,000 were injured, but did not mention the number of dead (Lustig's report is reproduced in Valori, A.: *La guerra italo-austriaca*, 2nd edn. (1925), p. 242). It may be noted that there are few reports of gas clouds or gas shells by either Austrians or Italians along the Isonzo front. The Italian Official History for the year 1918 was not available to me.

15. *Chemicals in War*, pp. 653–4.

16. The treatment of casualties and the effectiveness of the different types of gas helmets and respirators required as much information as possible on the morbidity of gas injury. Elliott, T. R. and Douglas, C. G.: 'A report on the casualties due to gas', PRO/WO/142/102, file DGS/M/25 (n.d., probably late 1917 or 1918). PRO/WO/142/109, file DGS/M/95, letter from Douglas to Barley 25 Nov. 1918 on the events in Spring 1915. PRO/WO/142/97, file DGS 69, undated reports by Mouat Jones and Barley. WO/142/99, file DGS M/1/A and WO/142/102, file DGS/M/1/A. Anon. [probably C. G. Douglas]: 'German Gas Warfare', pp. 3, 4, 5, 8–10, 13 in Hartley papers. Macpherson, *et al.*: *Medical Services*, II, pp. 274, 280. Macpherson's contributors were experts: the long section on chemical warfare was by Drs C. G. Douglas, T. R. Elliott, and A. B. Soltau.

17. Douglas, C. G.: 'Casualties caused by Yperite', 22 Oct. 1918 in Hartley papers. Macpherson *et al.*: *Medical Services*, II, pp. 303, 309; Mitchell and Smith: *Casualties . . .* , p. 111. Douglas, Mitchell, and Smith and others sampled medical record-cards and thus obtained information on the injuries caused by different gases. For example A. C. Jessup reported that between 25 May and 9 Oct. 1918, 83 per cent of the gas casualties in V Corps were attributable to mustard gas, 10 per cent to Blue Cross and 7 per cent to Green Cross (diphosgene), report dated 5 Dec. 1918 in Hartley papers. According to Mitchell and Smith the 114,000 gas casualties represented 18.2 per cent of admissions to medical units in 1918.

18. Mignon: *Le Service de santé*, II, pp. 664, 672–4, III, pp. 450–1. Toubert: *Service de santé . . . au GQG*, pp. 34, 39 mentions that in the May 1918 battles almost all the French gas casualties were attributable to mustard gas. The French troops which participated in the defence and evacuation of Mt. Kemmel in April 1918 also suffered severely from that gas. But from late July 1918 onwards French forces were less actively engaged and suffered correspondingly less. PRO/WO/142/109, file DGS/M/94, letter from Gen. Herr to Foulkes, 23 Dec. 1918.

19. Hanslian: *Chem. Krieg*, p. 35, states that the Germans lost 2,300 men killed by gas. This is about one-half of the more likely figure of 4,000 shown in the table. The *Sanitätsbericht* (III, p. 177) gives an estimated mortality of 2.9–3.0 per cent in 1918 for all gas casualties, but as the latter are incomplete, the deaths are understated. The figure of 1,900 for 1915–17 is an assumption based on the German statistics of injured for those years and includes the fatalities caused by blow-back on the Eastern Front in 1915. For 1918 I have relied on Geyer's 'Denkschrift' and his mortality rate of 3 per cent for the nine months to 30 Sept. 1918, but applied the proportion to the estimated number of gas casualties to 11 Nov. 1918, shown in Table 10.1.

20. On average 27 per cent of all USA battle casualties in 1918 were attributed to gas, a proportion occasionally equalled by the other belligerents on the Western Front. Schulz: *Textbook* . . ., pp. 7–8. I have used Prentiss's estimate for death from gas; Gilchrist: *A Comparative Study*, p. 17 has a slightly lower figure—1,221—to that shown in Table 10.2.

21. Fox: 'Corporals All', p. 25. According to Foulkes's report to the French GQG dated 11 Oct. 1915, 161 men of the Special Companies were gassed, wounded, or killed at Loos: 15 were killed, 87 were gassed, the rest were wounded or missing, FMA 16N826, GQG État Major, Cie. Z. There are several reports on the accidents which dogged the men in the Cies. Z during 1916, FMA 16N827 files 342/2 and 3. Schulz: *Textbook*, p. 81.

22. Bell, J. (ed.): *Völkerrecht im Welkrieg 1914–18*, IV, p. 24 (tr.). The statement was made in the course of Haber's evidence to a committee of the Reichstag. The German is as follows: 'habe dort in beschränkter Zahl Gastote gesehen, nicht viele'. He went on to say that the majority of the French escaped death.

23. Auld: *Gas and Flame*, p. 14. Thuillier, Sir Henry: 'Can methods of warfare be restricted?', *RUSI Jnl.* (May 1936), p. 272. FMA Box 16N826 Report of Med. Inspecteur Sieur to Méd.Inspecteur Général dated 25 April 1915. Mordacq: *Le Drame de l'Yser*, p. 76.

24. The particulars will be found in *Gas Warfare* (edited by Hartley), No. 9 (March 1918), p. 3 and No. 10 (April 1918), p. 5; and the diary of 14 BIR at BHSA.

25. Middlebrook: *The Kaiser's Battle*, pp. 43–4, 84–5, and Field Notes on Belgian, French, and German Armies (n.d., ?1918). Only the AEF and Dominion formations remained at full strength throughout 1918.

26. 3rd Army HQ, memo dated 20 May 1917, ref. 142/5 in Hartley papers.

27. Heber: 'Aufzeichnungen', *passim*. Letter from C. G. Douglas to Col. Cummins 21 Dec. 1915 on the subject of German Gas Attacks, N. of Ypres 19 Dec. 1915, in Hartley papers. PRO/WO/142/97, file DGS 169, Report of German Gas Attack . . . on 19 Dec. 1915 (n.d.), ref HH/C/45.

28. In July and perhaps also for part of August 1917, the Germans had no idea of the incapacitating effect of mustard gas. But prisoners taken at Third Ypres told them of blisters, temporary blindness, and contaminated trenches (see file of the gas officer of the 2nd Bavarian Corps at BHSA).

29. Although there are many references to the use of Livens projectiles, few incidents can be matched according to three criteria: date and time; precise location; weapon (Livens projectiles or gas bombs). In preparing the following table I

have relied on Foulkes's book or *Gas Warfare* and the regimental or divisional records in BHSA.

British Claims compared with German casualty figures:

Date	Location	Weapon	Claim	Killed	Injured	Total
21 July '17	Hoge (Ypres)	Livens	more than 100 casualties	n.a.	n.a.	43
13 March '18	Quéant Salient	Livens	40 dead and 100 injured	2	44	46
6 Nov. '17	Auchy	Cylinders	considerable losses		not shown separately	8
12–13 May '18	Auchy-Hulluch	Livens and Cylinders	severe casualties	1	3	4

30. Hartley: 'Fritz Haber', *passim.*
31. *Sanitätsbericht*, III, pp. 176, 177. The internal inconsistencies of this official history are remarkable. Particulars of the blow-backs and the casualties they caused will be found in *Der Weltkrieg*, III, p. 334, for the incident at Sochazew in Poland on 6 July 1915 (see also Chapter 3) and in BHSA, papers of the 2nd Bavarian Corps for the accidents at Hulluch on 27 and 29 April 1916.
32. Foulkes: 'Report on the Activity of the Special Brigade', p. 4 in Hartley papers. The deserter was misinformed. He said nearly 1,500 Germans were killed at Nieuport. This is extremely unlikely because the *Sanitätsbericht* records 1,373 injured (including those who died in hospital) for the whole of Oct. The Oct. figure may be compared with 1,928 for Sept. and 1,492 in August.
33. Macpherson *et al.*: *Medical Services*, II, pp. 282, 294. PRO/WO/142/176, file F/M/C/5, Report (n.d.) by Dr Flandin: 'L'Action des gaz pendant l'offensive Allemande de Mars–Avril 1918', pp. 8, 22, 36. 'Summary of the More Important German Gas Bombardments', Oct. 1918, Hartley papers.
34. Letter from D. M. Wilson to Hartley 24 May 1917 in Hartley papers. Evidence of Lt.-Col. O. von Stülpnagel to German Parliamentary Commission in Bell: *Völkerrecht*, p. 25. Stülpnagel then GSO1 to Army Group I failed to persuade the mayors of Lorraine villages to evacuate when the Americans began gas and projectile bombardments. He and Haber agreed that there had been gas casualties among French civilians.
35. Dr Flandin's report (see n. 33).
36. PRO/WO/142/187, file AGD/25/26.
37. In Britain, the injuries caused by poison gas (except for chlorine which was scheduled under the Workmen's Compensation Act of 1906) went unrecorded until 1917. It may be noted that deaths from TNT poisoning were notified: they averaged one a week during 1916, all due to neglected safety precautions. MoM

History, pp. 28, 59. MoM History, V, pt. 3, 'Welfare and Control of Working Conditions' (1920), pp. 74–6. PRO/WO/142/104, file DGS M/41, letter from E. Haworth of Castner–Kellner to Crossley (n.d., probably first half of 1916). PRO/MUN 5/198/1650/14, French Phosgene Works. PRO/SUPP 10/129, West: 'Phosgene', pp. 34–5. It may also be noted that there was never a single serious accident at Stratford where they were using hydrogen cyanide to make 'Jellite' between 1915 and 1917: the works were run by chemists and naval ratings; J. E. Coates, letter to author, 6 Aug. 1973.

38. MoM History, pp. 61, 64.

39. 'Report of the British Mission', pp. 55, 56. Hahn: *My Life*, p. 124.

40. Meyer discovered the thiodiglycol route which presented no danger until the last stage. 'Über Thiodiglykolverbindungen', p. 3261. H. J. Allmand ('Report on War Work for German Gas Services . . . at Leverkusen . . . ') reported there was not a single casualty in the section where thiodiglycol was hydrochlorinated to dichlorodiethyl sulphide. This final stage was the only dangerous step in the German process, and if Allmand was correct, it shows a high standard of works and safety practice.

41. Hartley Report, pp. 21, 22. Whitelaw: 'Report on . . . mustard gas', pp. 23, 28, 77–8. PRO/WO/142/98, file DGS 84. PRO/WO/142/136, file CWD 417, letter from Lefebure to Dr Young 7 June 1918. PRO/WO/142/129, file CWD 289, notes by T. W. Lowry (n.d., [1918]) on French filling plants; at Pont-de-Claix, 120 men were employed on average during August 1918: of these 26 needed first aid and seven hospital treatment. Fries and West: *Chemical Warfare*, p. 59.

42. Shufflebotham: 'Medical Aspects of . . . Mustard Gas', pp. 5–6. Barcroft, J.: paper read at Third Inter-Allied Conference on War Gases, 25–30 Oct. 1918, in Hartley papers. PRO/WO/142/182, file F/P/C/2, letters from Lefebure to Dr Young 7 June and 10 Aug. 1918 and memorandum by Lefebure in PRO/SUPP/10/126, ref. H 286–7.

43. MoM History, p. 63. Hartley Report, p. 22. 'Report of the British Mission', pp. 55, 71. CWD, Demobilization, First Stage, memoranda dated 10 and 11 Jan. 1919 in Hartley papers. PRO/WO/142/116, files CWD 114 and 115.

44. There was no significant difference in the treatment of gas cases in the factory hospitals at Runcorn and Avonmouth and the RAMC hospitals in France. It is probable that the same remarks apply to the medical facilities at Leverkusen and Höchst and the German military hospitals. Cf. MoM History, pp. 63–4 and Whitelaw, 'Report on . . . mustard gas', pp. 74 ff.

45. Macpherson *et al*.: *Medical Services*, II, pp. 496 ff. Mitchell and Smith: *Casualties . . .*, pp. 24–5, 28.

46. The appointment of Dr Paul as head of the gas section in the office of the Under-Secretary of State for Health in July 1918 was an important step in the organization of French gas treatment. A month later a special mustard-gas centre was opened at the Hôpital Necker in Paris. It is interesting to note that the French were less bothered than the British about sending gas cases for convalescence to Paris or provincial towns. Mignon: *Le Service de santé*, III,

pp. 162–3, 202–3, 449, 778. Toubert: *Service de santé . . . au GQG.*, pp. 20, 40, 125. PRO/WO/142/176, report F/M/C/5.

47. Macpherson *et al.*: *Medical Services*, II, pp. 503–4.

48. The pathology of the diseases caused by chlorine, phosgene, and chloropicrin made great progress in the three years after April 1915. In particular the aetiology of the throat and lung inflammation and of pulmonary oedema leading to heart failure became well known. Rather less progress had been made on treatment with the important exception of oxygen inhalation which became by 1918 the single most effective weapon available to doctors in saving the patient's life. The design of the inhaler had been improved and simple rubber face-pieces were in use everywhere. There is some evidence that the death-rate from lung irritants fell in the last year of the war, but this may be due as much to faster evacuation to the CCS as to oxygen therapy. The best information on medical practise is to be found in the memoranda on gas poisoning issued by the office of the DGMS France in July 1916 and April 1918, and in the English translation of the official German booklet on gas injuries, 1916 edn., in the Hartley papers. See also Macpherson *et al.*: *Medical Services*, II, pp. 333, 364 ff., 390 ff.; the Reports of the Medical Research Committee (MRC), No. 4, April 1918 and Nos. 10 and 16, both Oct. 1918, and *Sanitätsbericht*, III, pp. 180 f.

49. Achard and Flandin: 'Traitement des Brûlures par l'Yperite', paper read at Third Inter-Allied Conference on War Gases, 25–30 Oct. 1918 in Hartley papers. Mignon: *Le Service de santé*, III, pp. 354, 454–6. Macpherson *et al.*: *Medical Services*, II, pp. 428 ff. Gilchrist: *A Comparative Study*, p. 29, based his analysis on a sample of 6,980 mustard-gas cases in the AEF. The British experience was similar (cf. Statistical Reports of the MRC dated 22 Jan. 1919 and 13 Jan. 1920).

50. Douglas, C. G.: 'Note on Gas Casualties caused by Yperite', 22 Oct. 1918, in PRO/WO/142/106, file M732 [16]. Douglas's medical reports dated 17 and 24 July 1917 (M/60/A/1 and 2) in Hartley papers. Macpherson *et al.*: *Medical Services*, II, p. 445. *Sanitätsbericht*, III, pp. 179–81.

51. Douglas: 'Effects of Blue Cross Shells'. Jessop, A. C.: 'Summary of Blue X casualties suffered by V Corps May to October 1918', memo dated 5 Dec. 1918 in Hartley papers. Davis, T. H.: 'Report on Smoke Generators, No. 1, MK1 in Nth Russia', 15 Sept. 1919, PRO/WO/142/116.

52. Letter from C. G. Douglas to Harold Hartley (n.d., probably early 1919) in Hartley papers. Macpherson *et al.*: *Medical Services*, II, pp. 402 ff. Macpherson (pp. 387–8) has an interesting summary of what happened to the Canadians injured by chlorine clouds in April and May 1915: 332 of these men were sent back to England for rest and recuperation. Of these, 80 (24 per cent) were eventually declared fit and returned to duty, 48 (15 per cent) remained in the UK for 'home duty' and 204 (61 per cent) were returned as invalids to Canada. Of these invalids, 188 reported for examination in 1919 and were found to suffer from the following conditions: 'irritable heart', 78; bronchitis and asthma, 26; neuroses, 18; no significant ailments or no sickness at all, 66. H. L. Gilchrist and P. B. Matz, in *The Residual Effects of Warfare Gases* (1933), concluded

(pp. 49–51) that in general lung irritants led to a tendency towards bronchitis, emphysema, and tachycardia in civilian life. They also quoted from the medical records of 89 men injured by mustard gas to show (pp. 92 f.) that about ten years after the injury the men still suffered from chronic bronchitis and asthma.

53. Gilchrist and Matz: *Residual Effects*, pp. 54 f., 76–8. Jones, R.: 'Chemical Warfare, the Peacetime Legacy', *New Scientist*, 24 April 1975, p. 202. On blindness in old age see *Sunday Times*, 19 March 1972, p. 5 and letter from Miss Rose Coombs (IWM) to author, 17 Dec. 1971.

54. Mitchell and Smith: *Medical Services*, II, pp. 320, 321, 340.

55. Gilchrist: *A Comparative Study*, pp. 37–8. In 1924 a sample survey showed that the US Veteran's Administration was still paying some compensation to one-fifth of those who had been gassed during 1918. There are no figures for French soldiers drawing disability pensions as a result of gas poisoning. They were included with the 236,000 who, on 1 Jan. 1927, were drawing pensions for various chest ailments and who, at that time, represented one-third of all those receiving payments for wounds and sickness caused by the war. Toubert: *Service de santé . . . au GQG*, pp. 130–1.

Chapter 11

1. Hanslian: *Chem. Krieg* (in particular 2nd edn. (1927), p. 24; the calculations were omitted from the 3rd edn.); Prentiss: *Chemicals in War* (Chapter 24: 'The Effectiveness of Chemical Warfare') and Foulkes: '*Gas!*' (*passim*). The comparisons are invariably descriptive and qualitative because it is not possible to assign numbers to each of the separate constituents of overall effectiveness (such as manpower requirements, dependence on weather, toxicity of material employed, psychological effect, etc.). Thus the different chemical weapons cannot be put into a ranking order and attempts to do this are merely playing with numbers, and the efficiency ratings reflect the observer's personal assessment, retroactively, of a gas operation.

2. The British data on manpower are extensive and will be found in PRO/MUN 5/386/1650/11 and 12. Box 13 in this group contains Carey Morgan's 'Report on the Work of Women'. Note prepared by Lt. Cheesewright of the War Office (n.d., ?August 1919) in Hartley papers. PRO/WO/142/138, file CWD 429E, memo by Barley dated 24 June 1919.

3. French and German information is incomplete, but I have used the list of factories and the numbers they employed on 1 August 1916 in the records of the Ministère de l'Armement in FMA 10N57; Hanslian: *Chem. Krieg*, pp. 211–13; Vinet: Report on the German C.W. Organization', pp. 8–9; Prentiss: *Chemicals in War*, pp. 85–6; MoM History, pp. 43–4; Moreland: 'Chemical Warfare Record', p. 363; and PRO/WO/142/197, file DES 3 and 188/377, file R 960/7, report by the PSOC Sub-Committee, No. 1, 24 Sept. 1927.

4. The principal British sources are the MoM History (pp. 31, 81, 97) and Moreland: 'Chemical Warfare Record', p. 204. Carey Morgan: 'Report on the Work of Women', pp. 14, 17–18, has slightly higher totals than the MoM History. Moreland mentions that 224,000 cylinders were sent to France between

Sept. 1915 and Nov. 1918. They contained altogether 6,700 t of gas (chlorine, phosgene, chloropicrin, or mixtures of these). The number is very much higher than that given by Foulkes; the difference is largely due to the shipments to the French government under the chlorine–phosgene swap deal. For Germany, H. E. Watts's papers in PRO/WO/118/114, file R7/G4, contain the statistics which he obtained from German sources. They were used by Hartley for his report and are plausible except for the number of tear gas shells in 1914–15 which seem to me to be much too high. For France, Vinet: 'La Guerre des gaz', pp. 1412–13 gives the most detailed information. It tallies in general, with what is available elsewhere. PRO/WO/188/176 contains a comparison of the French and the German outputs based on Vinet's article and Muraour's questionnaire to the Germans which agrees with Watts's enquiries. For pads and respirators, FMA 10N 57 has some numbers. Also Hanslian: *Chem. Krieg*, pp. 211–13 and Prentiss: *Chemicals in War*, p. 85.

5. Letter from Secretary of CWC to Hartley, 3 Dec. 1921 in Hartley papers. Vinet: 'La Guerre des gaz', p. 1414; of the 17 mln French gas shells, 13.2 mln were 75 mm, and one-sixth of these were filled with mustard gas. PRO/WO/118/114, file R7/G4 for German statistics and also Vinet: 'Report on the Organization . . . of the four German Field Ammunition Depots', *passim*. Hartley Report, pp. 11, 24.

6. I take this opportunity of thanking Mr Frank Fitzpatrick, then a statistician in the Department of Industry, and Dr Chris Rowlands, lately Research Fellow in the Department of Economics of Surrey University, for discussing the variability in the measures of dispersion and the regression analyses with me. Foulkes was, I think, the first, to believe, mistakenly as it turned out, that the ratio of shells or cylinders expended to enemy casualties was a valid indicator of the 'efficiency' of chemical warfare. More recently, V. C. Marshall has investigated the relationship in 'How Lethal are Explosions and Toxic Escapes?' (*Chem. Eng.*, Aug. 1977, pp. 576–7). While sceptical of First World War data, his 'Mortality Index'—the fatalities per t of gas released—has the serious purpose of measuring the hazards caused by dangerous goods in peace-time owing to accidental discharge or fire.

7. Liddell Hart: *History of First World War*, pp. 247 f. Hanslian: *Der deutsche Gasangriff bei Ypern . . .* , passim. Pope, Sir William: The 'Case for Chemical Warfare', reprint from *Chemical Age*, 7 May 1921, p. 3. Trumpener: 'The Road to Ypres', p. 479.

8. Hartley Report, p. 57.

9. Ibid., p. 13. The Germans paid much attention to the question of maintaining a high level of concentration in order to penetrate and so break down the protection afforded by gas helmets and later by respirators. But on the Western Front it was difficult to generate and maintain a dense cloud. Hartley: 'Chemical Warfare', lecture given on 25 Nov. 1926.

10. They included finely ground hot pepper! GHQ had a low opinion of these materials. PRO/MUN 5/177/1650/6, Crossley's letter to Gen. Jackson, pp. 17–18. Third Report of the CS-C (n.d., March ? 1916), p. 44 in Hartley papers.

11. Hartley Report, p. 13.

12. Douglas later observed that arsenicals were *not* of minor importance. If the Germans had been able to master the dispersal of the material, they would have caused temporary incapacity among a large body of British troops which would have been of great help to the attacking enemy. Douglas: 'Effects of Blue Cross Shells'.
13. Barley, L. J.: 'Suggestions for the tactical use of DM', memo dated 26 Aug. 1918 in Barley papers. Thuillier, H.: *Gas in the next War* (1939), p. 66.
14. Interview with Hartley, 2 Jan. 1972. Thorpe: 'History of SK', p. 5. The evidence for Haber's disenchantment is circumstantial and rests mainly on information provided by J. F. Thorpe, for I have found no written record of Haber's opinion. Thorpe met Haber at a conference in 1924 and asked him about mustard gas. Haber confirmed what he had told Hartley during the interviews in 1921 and added that in late spring 1917 he had been consulted on the question of introducing mustard-gas shells. Haber, as reported by Thorpe, said that the substance should only be used if Germany was certain of winning the war quickly because the Allies would be able to produce it within six months and would proceed to smother the German infantry with the stuff. Note by Thorpe: 'Conversation with Haber in Washington on 29 Sept. 1924', forwarded by J. D. Pratt of the CWC to Hartley on 28 Nov. 1924 in Hartley papers.
15. The critical technical question was how to achieve the desired concentration over the enemy trenches and how to maintain it. From it flowed a mass of detailed instructions and measures. At first the Germans aimed at 1½ cylinders per metre of trench. Later they wished to penetrate the protection offered by the 'PH' helmet. This called for a dense cloud to be maintained for 15–20 minutes which, in turn, required 2–2½ cylinders per metre and a windspeed of 1–2 m/sec (2.2–4.4 mph). Only in some Valhalla of the Gaspioniere could such objectives be achieved, let alone repeated. Anon. [C. G. Douglas]: 'Gas Warfare', p. 14. Heber: 'Aufzeichnungen', *passim*.
16. The book's subtitle is *A Treatise on Chemical Warfare*. Chapter XVI, 'The Technique and Tactics of Chemical Troops', takes up about 90 pages (pp. 343–431) and XVII, which deals with the Artillery, about 140 pages (pp. 432–574). Both are principally concerned with techniques. There are shorter chapters on General Tactics, The Infantry, the Cavalry, and the Air Corps.
17. Foulkes told Gold before Loos that cylinder gas was to be used 'strategically' in combination with the infantry and the artillery. But in his report in 1919, he emphasized that the surprise tactics had been introduced by the Special Brigade and had later been taken over by the artillery and finally by the Germans. Foulkes, like Prentiss after him, underrated the role of defence. When he finally wrote his memoirs he enlarged the scope of gas: 'The reduction of enemy manpower was our main preoccupation' he wrote, but the Special Brigade also tried 'on every possible occasion to combine this object with the endeavour to assist our own infantry in the accomplishment of their immediate tasks'—as at Loos or the incendiary bombs on 8 Nov. 1918, the Brigade's first and last actions respectively. Foulkes: *'Gas!'*, p. 302 and 'Report on the Activity of the Special Brigade during the War'. Interview with Mr E. Gold, 26 Feb. 1972.

18. Fox: Corporals All, pp. 105, 112–14 lists several of these mini-operations in Aug. and Sept. 1918. Occasionally Livens drums were filled with smoke-generating materials or with oil.

19. FMA 16N832, folder 1080/2, item 160, circular, author unknown, signed by Joffre at GQG, 11 August 1915.

20. IEEC: 'Cours spécial . . . les projectiles spéciaux', pp. 22, 39. 'Renseignements sur l'emploi des obus spéciaux à la VIème Armée' (Autumn ? 1916), in Hartley papers.

21. IEEC: 'Le Tir des projectiles spéciaux', pp. 73, 76, 77, 98, 107, in Hartley papers.

22. Foulkes, C. H.: 'Enemy Use of Gas Shells during 1918', memorandum dated 19 Nov. 1918. Summary of Hostile Gas Activity, Sept. 1918, 18 Oct. 1918, both in Hartley papers.

23. PRO/MUN 15/198/1650/29, 19 March Conference, p. 3.

24. Pershing, J. J.: *Final Report* (1920), pp. 76–7. Pershing was of the anti-gas school of thought.

25. Foulkes: '*Gas!*', pp. 139, 175. Fries and West: *Chemical Warfare*, pp. 17–18. Thuillier; *Gas in the Next War*, p. 71.

26. PRO/WO/188/143, file R8/A/1, Livens: 'The Livens Gas Projector', *passim*. Letter from G. P. Pollitt to Harold Hartley, 11 August 1919 in Hartley papers. Douglas, in a letter to Hartley dated 11 March 1958, was in no doubt that the Livens projectile was the most deadly gas weapon.

27. Hartley: 'A General Comparison', p. 4.

28. Moreland: 'Chemical Warfare Record', pp. 15–16 and interview with J. D. Pratt, 7 May 1973. Pratt was severely injured in 1915, invalided out of the army and joined the TWD. He and the documents at the PRO shed interesting light on the situation in London. In Sept. 1916, Alexander Roger, at the time head of Supplies attempted unsuccessfully, to reorganize the common services (transport, contracts, etc.). The following spring the TWD introduced a Central Statistical Section, but it did not work, and concern over security leaks led to its closure. In March 1918, K. B. Quinan, head of the Factories Branch of the Department of Explosives Supply, became responsible for poison-gas production—specifically mustard gas at Avonmouth and arsenicals at Morecambe. He introduced the organizational procedures which had worked in the HE plants. (Cf. Robinson, C. S.: 'Kenneth Bingham Quinan', *Institution of Chem. Eng.* (n.d., ?1970), pp. 4–5.) An early example of poor communications is furnished by the following quotation from the Minutes of the 12th Meeting on 24 May 1916 of the Scientific Advisory Committee of the Trench Warfare Department in PRO/WO/142/52: 'The Committee desired unanimously to record their opinion that, had the demands for chemicals now made known, been put forward in the latter part of last year, those demands could have been, by this date, adequately met'.

29. FMA 16N826, 'Rapport sur l'Organisation du Service du Matériel Chimique de Guerre', by Deputé d'Aubigny, 25 Aug. 1915 and *The Times*, 31 August 1920, 'Development of Chemical Warfare Organisation', probably contributed by Lefebure.

30. Wrisberg: *Wehr und Waffen*, pp. 122–3. Feldman: *Army, Industry and Labor in Germany 1914–18*, p. 179. Hartley Report, p. 57.

31. Hartley Report, p. 47.

32. Ibid., p. 12.

33. Pratt, J. D.: 'Memorandum on the Organisation for C. W. Research, December 1914–November 1918', dated 30 April 1919 in PRO/MUN 5/385/1650/8.

34. Minutes of the Committee on Chemical Warfare Organization, 10th meeting, 2 June 1919, Hartley papers. Interview with Hartley, 13 Feb. 1972. Hartley and Foulkes often disagreed, but they were united in condemning Rendel, Porton's artillery specialist, on the grounds that his advice on gas shells was unpracticable. Rendel was a gunner on detachment from the RA.

35. Haber: *Fünf Vorträge*, p. 29 (tr.).

36. Hartley Report, pp. 19–20. Wrisberg: *Wehr und Waffen*, pp. 115, 169. It is worth mentioning that at a late stage in the war, an OHL circular dated 19 April 1918 (in the BHSA papers of the 6th Army) criticized army staffs for not consulting their gas officers often enough, and Hanslian in *Der deutsche Gasangriff bei Ypern*, p. 117, wrote that Haber was not sufficiently forceful in his dealings with senior officers and this weakness was 'one of the tragic happenings of the war' (tr.). Hanslian showed insight, but who would dare argue with the officer corps?

37. MoM History, p. 22. Pope, Sir William: 'The Case for Chemical Warfare', *Chem. Age* (7 May 1921) and 'Chemistry in the National Service', p. 399. Minutes of 2nd meeting of the Committee on Chemical Warfare Organization, 21 May 1919 in Hartley papers.

38. Baynes: *Morale: A Study of Men and Courage*, pp. 94–102. Sassoon: *Memoirs of an Infantry Officer*, p. 218, has a scene involving a frightened and undisciplined battalion near Arras in April 1917. Renn: *Krieg*, frequently comments on the decline in the morale of German troops, during the spring battles of 1918. Dr Flandin: 'L'Action des Gaz . . . Mars–Avril 1918' (n.d.), in PRO/WO/142/176, file F/MK/5 and Hicks's reports from Petrograd in WO/142/195, files R-O-A9 and 13.

39. Interviews with Messrs Avery, Lawrence, and McLellan at Chelsea Hospital, Oct. 1973 and with Hartley on 30 May 1971. The SBR, it will be recalled, required breathing in and out through the mouth; the nose was blocked by a clip.

40. Brown: *Chemical Warfare*, p. 27. The AEF, following BEF practice, allotted two days out of three months combat-training for anti-gas instruction. That was later cut to six hours.

41. Papers of BIR 12 and 14, 2nd Bavarian Corps and 22 (German) Reserve Infantry Div. at BHSA. The regimental records list as 'gassed' those who were killed by carbon monoxide poisoning from smouldering stoves in dug-outs. On the question of neglected precautions among the French, see Report by L. J. Barley dated 9 Feb. 1917 in the Hartley papers, concerning the outcome of a German cylinder operation in Champagne.

42. *Im Westen nichts Neues*, p. 134. BHSA, papers of 1 Bavarian Reserve Infantry Div. and draft of training manual for gas defence, July 1919, Hartley papers.

43. 'Yellow Cross Gas Shells and the Measures to be taken to counter-act their Effects' (April 1918), SS 212 (GHQ) in Hartley papers. The leaflet describes the dangers and points out that more could be done to keep gas casualties down.

44. Clark ('Effectiveness of Chemical Weapons', pp. 46–8, 131) reports that those men who were gassed because they had taken off their respirators without orders were classed 'wounded not in the line of duty', and all it entailed. Those who lost or damaged their SBRs were fined $4.44.

45. Soldan, G.: *Der Mensch und die Schlacht der Zukunft*, quoted in Hanslian: *Chem. Krieg*, pp. 251–2. The German text, as given by Hanslian, is as follows: 'Kein Mittel hat es im Krieg gegeben das derartig die Druckerei förderte wie das Gas.' Dr Matthew Meselson drew my attention to the American Reference, USA War Department: *The Medical Department of the U.S. Army in the World War*, XIV, 'Medical Aspects of Gas Warfare' (1926), p. 65.

46. Haber: *Fünf Vorträge*, p. 37 (tr.).

47. Hanslian: *Chem. Krieg*, pp. 249 f. Auld: *Gas and Flame*, p. 46. Interviews with Hartley, 2 and 9 Jan. 1972. In fairness to Hartley I should add that he considered the mustard-gas phase of the war as an exceptionally testing time. He remarked that in March 1918 the Guard's Division did not suffer as badly from gas, as other, less disciplined formations.

48. Letter from Hartley to author dated 25 Feb. 1972. Hartley: 'A General Comparison', p. 20. Hartley wrote in that article that gas 'is a very valuable weapon', but fifty years later he had become much more cautious, even about gas shells, because their efficacy greatly depended on the weather.

49. Interview with Hartley, 12 March 1972. Hartley Report, pp. 58–9.

50. Interview with Dr J. Jaenicke, 3 April 1971. Fritz Haber's letters to his second wife in the autumn of 1917 have survived and reflect his growing despondency.

51. Hanslian: *Chem. Krieg*, p. 37. Interview with Barley, 8 March 1972, Barley's notes for author dated 8 March 1972 and letter to author of 12 July 1976.

52. *Chemical Warfare*, pp. 4–5, 10.

53. Edmonds: *Military Operations in France and Belgium*, II, pp. 137–8, refers briefly to the use of mustard-gas shells at Ypres in July 1917. He singles out the 15th (Scottish) Division of which Thuillier had just taken command: it suffered heavy casualties from gas, but took part in the capture of Pilkem ridge on 31 July 1917—a poignant moment for Thuillier, for the Germans had seized it with the help of chlorine gas in April 1915. There is no mention that German mustard gas delayed the launching of third Ypres.

54. Hartley Report, p. 2. Interview with J. E. Coates, 22 Nov. 1972. Letter from Max Born to J. E. Coates, 1 March 1937 in Coates papers. Haber had no difficulty finding willing helpers among the younger scientists, among them Hahn, Franck, and Kerschbaum. It may be added that the Chemical Society of London expelled Haber because of his connection with chemical warfare, but later readmitted him and after his death invited Coates to give the Haber Memorial Lecture in 1937.

55. Pope: 'The Case for Chemical Warfare', *passim*. Thuillier, Sir Henry F.; 'Can methods of warfare be restricted?', p. 272. Interview with Hartley, 30 Jan.

1972. Thuillier's approval of cylinder operations was qualified, but whole-hearted in respect of mustard gas.

56. Brown: *Chemical Warfare*, p. 79.

Chapter 12

1. MoM History, p. 70. PRO/WO/142/138, file CWD 429/E, Hartley's report dated 22 July 1919 and memo by Barley, 24 June 1919. PRO/WO/142/98, file DGS 84, Development of Thermo-Generators. Letters from Hartley to Foulkes, 16 Nov. and 6 Dec. 1918 and notes by Wingate and Foulkes, 27 and 28 Jan. 1919 respectivley. Hartley papers, memos by Hartley 10 and 11 Jan. 1919 and by Col. Bythell, 13 June 1919. PRO/WO/142/190, file AGD 30. PRO/WO/142/72, Minutes of CWC, (Offensive), 28 Feb. 1919.

2. Brown: *Chemical Warfare*, pp. 75 ff. Hearings before the Committee on Military Affairs (House of Representatives) on HR 8287, pt. X, 1919 Army Reorganization (hereafter abbreviated to Army Reorganization): Sibert's evidence in NA, RG 287, Box Y 5890, pp. 551–2; the figures quotes are not consistent; at one point Sibert said he had $23 mln. for new projects, but he did not say that he was authorized to spend that money at once. NA, Gen. Fries's Files, RG 175, Entry 7, Box 17, letter from Fries to Doherty, 12 July 1919, about gas masks and their possible sale.

3. Hartley Report, p. 26. Vinet, E.: 'Report on the Present Condition of the Installations set up for the Manufacture of Asphyxiating Gases', pp. 15 f., 33, 37 in Hartley papers. Letter from Hartley to H. E. Watts (then a British member of the chemical industry section of the MICC), 21 Sept. 1921 in Hartley papers. PRO/WO/188/212, MICC (in French) 'Rapport Final' (1927), pp. 241–2, 266–8. Muraour: 'Les Gaz de Combat', *passim*. (Muraour was Watts's colleague on the MICC) *The Times*, 26 May and 2 June 1928.

4. Various notes (undated, probably 1919 or 1920) about Lefebure in the Hartley papers. Lefebure's views, in a somewhat toned-down version, were published in his *Riddle of the Rhine* (1921), Chapter 12 ('Chemical Warfare and Disarmament') and his Conclusion (pp. 260 ff). The arguments over the respirators stored at Hanover are a good example of German obstruction. The leather face-pieces were rotting by 1921, nevertheless the Reichswehr wanted to equip its men with them. The Allies objected. In 1925 however they agreed that each soldier should have one respirator and that half that number again should be in reserve—altogether 150,000. German records showed precisely that number, but British intelligence claimed that in 1924, 250,000 were in good condition and the next year a MICC team found (*sic!*) half a million filter units at Hanover. The MICC claimed later to have destroyed altogether 5.3 million gas-masks. The story sheds interesting light on veracity and verification. Hartley Report, p. 39; MICC, 'Rapport Final', pp. 290, 299, 338 and PRO/WO/190/20, memo from DMI, 10 Jan. 1924.

5. Coates's interview with Freundlich, 22 May 1934 in Coates papers.

6. Memo from H. E. Watts to Hartley, 8 August 1919 in Hartley papers. 'Report of the Committee on Chemical Warfare Organization', hereafter the Holland Committee (1919), pp. 10–11 in Hartley papers. PRO/WO/142/117, file CWD

117, report by J. D. Pratt on a visit to Sutton Oak on 6 Dec. 1919. Sutton Oak remained the only Government factory concerned with gas manufacture (as distinct from Agency Factories in the Second World War) until the 1950s when it was closed and operations transferred to Nancecuke in Cornwall.

7. An example will suffice: a comparison between the typed draft and the printed version of the MoM History shows what was omitted. The gaps in the story of British arsenicals are obvious. See also PRO/MUN 5/386/650/16, letter from J. D. Pratt to Miss Redstone, dated 4 Nov. 1920, warning her of careless disclosures.

8. 'Training in Anti-Gas Measures', WO ref. 40/WO/7338, July 1919, p. 3 in Hartley papers.

9. PRO/WO/188/265, Report by Surgeon Commander A. Fairley, dated 16 June 1927: at the time Porton was studying the effect of a gas-bomb attack on HM Dockyards. Haber's views are in Bell (ed.): *Völkerrecht im Weltkrieg*, IV, p. 25. A lecture by Haber along similar lines was summarized by *The Times* on 3 July 1926. Foulkes told the Holland Committee (minutes of meeting on 2 June 1919) of chemical super-weapons which were colourless and invisible and killed by blood poisoning. Lefebure (*Riddle of the Rhine*, pp. 214-16) wrote of chemicals which could disturb the balancing mechanism of the ear or anaesthetize the enemy and so immobilize him!

10. PRO/WO/144/44, file R8/C/22, Memorandum on the Protection of the Civil Population against Gas Attack (n.d., 1924? or 1925), pp. 7, 8, 12–13. It is worth recalling that in December 1917 the War Cabinet turned down the proposal to issue gas masks to civilians and that in May 1918, Thuillier told Ministers that it would be difficult to devise protection against gas bombs on cities (see PRO/CAB 23/4, War Cabinet 306, item 2 and CAB 23/6, War Cabinet 411, item 20).

11. The leaflet cost 2*d*. O'Brien: *Civil Defence*, pp. 19, 50, 56.

12. Best, G: *Humanity in Warfare* (1980), has recently looked at these problems with almost philosophical detachment, and the book has much to say that is relevant on the extension of war to non-combatants.

13. Conan Doyle, A.: *The British Campaign in France and Flanders*, III, p. 50. A copy of Kitchener's telegram is in the Hartley papers.

14. PRO/CAB 37/127, item 40, Asquith's letter of 27 April 1915 and CAB 23/1, War Cabinet 38, 19 Jan. 1917, item 5.

15. Hartley Report, pp. 1–2, where Haber is quoted as saying that the words 'poisons' and 'poisoned weapons' in Hague II were not intended to apply to war gases. He added that the German tear-gas shells of 1914–15 contained very little active material and that the bulk consisted of HE. Bell: *Völkerrecht im Weltkrieg* gives Haber's evidence on 4 Oct. 1923 verbatim. It takes up about thirteen pages and amounts to a skilful defence of an inexcusable action. 'I would have been deterred from collaborating', he said, 'if Falkenhayn's orders on chlorine had been in conflict with international law' (p. 13, tr.). Haber's last published statement on the legality of chemical warfare appeared in *Kriegskunst in Wort und Bild*, III, p. 12, Sept. 1927, p. 535: it is a piece of revanchist propaganda and it is surprising that he allowed his name to be used for such a jingoistic article.

16. The second expression was used by Hanslian: *Der deutsche Gasangriff bei Ypern* p. 81. See also Trumpener: 'The Road to Ypres', pp. 468–9 for a good discussion of the German case.

17. J. E. Coates's notes on interviews with Hartley (8 Jan. 1935) and Pope (2 Oct. 1938). Draft of a letter by Coates to Hartley (n.d., probably late 1936 or early 1937) and letter from Hartley to Coates, 20 April 1937. In a subsequent letter, dated 17 Oct. 1938, when Coates was preparing the lecture for the printers, Hartley wrote: 'If I were you I shouldn't appear quite so anxious to acquit Haber of all responsibility . . . that will attract notice'. The notes and letters are in the Coates papers. Coates delivered the lecture on 29 April 1937. It is reprinted in *Memorial Lectures, 1933–42*, esp. p. 145.

18. Letter from Douglas to Hartley (n.d., but probably early 1920s) and from Elliott to Hartley, 3 Sept. 1944, both in Hartley papers. Elliott underlined the word 'choked'. Some other opinions are relevant in this context. Duisberg and Quincke of the Bayer Co. were questioned immediately after the war, and compared gas with HE shell to the advantage of the former, Allmand: 'Report on War Work for German Gas Services', *passim* in Hartley papers. H. A. L. Fisher, in his contribution to the Report of the Temporary Mixed Commission for the Reduction of Armaments, wrote that chemical warfare could not 'necessarily inflict more pain than high explosives'. Reprinted in League of Nations Union: *Chemical Warfare*, (1924), p. 2.

19. Introduction, p. ix, to Fries and West: *Chemical Warfare*. Sibert, it may be noted, was merely following Admiral Mahan's opinion at the first Hague conference in 1899.

20. Jones: 'Chemical Warfare—The Peace Time Legacy', pp. 202, 203 mentions that Fries and Zanetti compiled the entry. Gilchrist: *A Comparative Study*. . . . Gilchrist was a medical officer in the CWS during and after the war. Lest it be thought that only the Americans relied on numbers, let me add that J. B. S. Haldane and Sir Henry Thuillier used the same approach, the former in *Callinicus* (1925), pp. 38, 52 ff.), the latter in 'Can methods of warfare be restricted?', pp. 271–2.

21. Hahn: *My Life*, pp. 130 f.

22. Hermann Staudinger (1881–1965) was a distinguished, south German chemist and a Nobel laureate (1953). He had been Haber's colleague at Karlsruhe and was professor at Zürich from 1912 to 1926. The correspondence with Haber in Oct.–Nov. 1919 is in the Staudinger papers at the Deutsche Museum in Munich. The article was entitled 'La Technique moderne et la guerre' and appeared in the *Rev. Int. de la Croix Rouge*, 1 (15 May 1919), pp. 514–15.

23. Holland Committee, p. 5.

24. Army Reorganization, pp. 546, 549.

25. Ibid., pp. 549–50.

26. Pope: 'The Case for Chemical Warfare', reprint, pp. 3, 5. The article was written before the Washington Naval Conference had come to an inconclusive end. Haldane was at the time Sir William Dunn Reader in Biochemistry at Cambridge and in every other respect the extreme opposite of Pope, the professor of chemistry in that university. *Callinicus, a Defence of Chemical*

Warfare, was originally given as a public lecture in August 1924 at, of all places, Mürren in Switzerland. Haldane was so encouraged by its reception that he had it printed (1925) and its appeal was boosted by the publicity surrounding the coincident signing of the Geneva Convention. The booklet, despite its irrelevancies and several gross mistakes, is well worth reading even now. Callinicus was said to have discovered the Greek Fire, which Haldane believed to have been the greatest advance in warfare before black powder.

27. Hartley in 'A General Comparison', reprint, p. 2, wrote: 'When a nation is fighting for its existence, there will be an overwhelming temptation to use whatever developments of science seem most likely to give it success'. He spoke in a similar vein in a lecture at the University of London, 25 Nov. 1926. For Haber, see 'Zur Geschichte des Gaskrieges' in *Fünf Vorträge*, pp. 79, 91.

28. *The Times*, 29 Nov. 1918. The letter was signed by the Presidents of the Royal College of Physicians and of the Royal College of Surgeons, by their colleagues in Scotland and Ireland, and by the Regius Professors of Medicine and Physics at Oxford and Cambridge respectively.

29. Le Wita, H.: *Autour de la guerre chimique* (1928), pp. 32, 186–7. Memories are short: what happened seven years later when the Italians droped gas bombs on the Abyssinians?

30. Women's International League . . . : 'Abridged Report of papers presented at the Conference', 1930. Victor Lefebure had also got on to the Council. A case of the poacher turned gamekeeper?

31. Brown: *Chemical Warfare*, pp. 64–72. Goldblat, J.: *CB Disarmament Negotiations 1920–1970*, SIPRI, IV (1971), pp. 19 ff. In this and the next two paragraphs I have followed the chronology given by Goldblat; the Stockholm International Peace Research Institute's (SIPRI) work extends beyond chemical and biological warfare, but is probably the most detailed source on the subject. Sir Edward Thorpe in 'Chemical Warfare and the Washington Conference' published in the *J. of the Soc. of Chem. Industry*, 41, 3 (15 Feb. 1922), pp. 43–4, considered that Washington marked a turning-point and given some goodwill, ultimate success in controlling gas was within reach. He wrote before the negotiations ended inconclusively.

32. SIPRI. IV *passim*. Paterno and Angeli from Italy, J. E. Zanetti (then at Columbia University), and J. D. Pratt, were regularly among the experts. There were usually also some neutrals, often Swiss, in that group.

33. League of Nations Union: *Chemical Warfare*, pp. 12, 17, 18–19. SIPRI, IV, pp. 49, 55.

34. Bacteriological warfare was an after-thought andd was added at the suggestion of the Polish delegation. SIPRI, IV, pp. 19–21, 341–2. *Nature*, 243 (10 Jan. 1975), p. 82.

35. These were the years of goodwill, engendered by the Locarno Treaty. But the Germans could not add anthing to what was already known. Haber, in a lecture on Disarmament and Gas Warfare to the German section of the Inter-Parliamentary Union (*The Times*, 3 July 1926, carried a summary), urged a total ban on chemical warfare. It would restore equality to Germany which had been prohibited by the Versailles Treaty from developing and testing chemical

weapons. He went on to say that Germany's chemical industry did not want to be involved in something that had earned the country so much opprobrium.

36. SIPRI, IV, pp. 89, 102–3, 133–73.

37. André Malraux who extolled the soldierly virtues of some bygone age was obsessed by gas—'la lutte contre les gaz m'habite' he wrote at the end of his life, and he equated gas with death (*Le Miroir des limbes: Lazare* (1974), p. 154). Hochhuth used chemcial warfare to enhance the drama of the situation. Thus Churchill in *The Soldiers* (German edn., 1970, p. 169), says to the Bishop of Chichester that if the Germans had invaded he would not have felt bound by the Geneva Protocol—they would have been eradicated (literally etched away or cauterized) with mustard gas. Sir Henry Thuillier anticipated some of Malraux' and Hochhuth's points. He was not a novelist but an RE general, perceptive and humane, who realized that the League of Nations as it existed in the 1930s, would never have the power to stop gas warfare agianst non-combatants ('Can methods of warfare be restricted?, p. 274).

38. Robida: *La Guerre au vingtième siècle*; all the inhabitants of a French town are asphyxiated by German gas bombs. Only the hero of the story survives. Robida observes—'Ce sont là des accidents de guerre auxquels depuis les dernières conquêtes de la science, tous les esprits sont habitués' (p. 13).

39. Clarke in his *Voices Prophesying War*, has a detailed analysis of changing styles in science fiction.

40. Thuillier: *Gas in the next War*, pp. 123–4. Cookson, J. and Nottingham, J: *A Survey of Chemical and Biological Warfare* (1969), p. 364.

41. O'Brien: *Civil Defence*, p. 50 mentions articles in *The Listener* in 1934 by a former member of the Porton staff and whilst this book was being written Jeremy Paxman devoted one evening of the BBC's *Panorama* programme (2 June 1980) to chemical warfare. Nothing much emerged from the various film clips, one dating back to the First World War, but it was better to show the material, than leave the subject unmentioned. The title of the programme was 'A Higher Form of Killing', an expression attributed to Fritz Haber, but which I have not traced to its source. *The Listener* (5 June 1980), *103*, No. 2664, p. 706 f.

42. Brown: *Chemical Warfare*, pp. 83–4, 92, 124–5, 145, 178–83, 291. NA Gen. Fries's Files, RG 175, Entry 7, Box 15 (letter to E. J. Atkisson, 5 Sept. 1919) and Box 19 (letter to Pershing 25 Sept. 1919—inviting him to Edgewood. Pershing, apparently, never went).

43. PRO/WO/188/257 and 258. The proceedings of the second conference ran to 140 foolscap pages of text. The Red Cross even offered a prize, 10,000 Swiss Fr., for a device to detect mustard gas in the atmosphere.

44. Fries and West: *Chemical Warfare*, pp. ix and 17–18. Fries was given to hyperbole and it is difficult to take him seriously when he declared (*Jnl. Ind. and Eng. Chem.* 12, 5 (May 1920), p. 423) that gas 'is making or will make in the future' the most profound changes since the introduction of gunpowder. In that same article he wrote of surrounding aircraft with a poisonous atmosphere instead of directing rapid fire at it.

45. Hanslian: 'Chemical Means of Warfare in the Future', translated at Porton from *Wissen und Wehr* (1926), 3, pp. 129–44, with comments by Porton staff,

in Hartley papers. Prentiss: *Chemicals in War*, pp. 490–514.

46. Hanslian (see n. 45) envisaged a considerable future role for aero-chemical warfare against civilian targets. By contrast, F. von Tempelhoff's *Gaswaffe und Gasabwehr* (1937), devoted only 12 out of 200 pages in his compilation to gas bombs and gas sprays. All his information was drawn from non-German sources, which suggests that some people wanted no publicity whatever for German thinking on gas.

47. Thuillier: *Gas in the Next War*, pp. 61, 79–82, 172.

48. Hartley: 'Chemical Warfare', p. 250. Haber, as quoted in *The Times*, 3 July 1926. Geyer; 'Denkschrift', p. 21.

49. The Tempelhoff papers (BMA N 102/5) contains a translation published in *Gasschutz und Luftschutz* (n.d.) of provisional Russian instructions, dated 15 Dec. 1935, for protection against mustard gas sprayed from planes. A similar War Office circular, 'Defence against Gas', dated 31 Oct. 1935 (in Hartley papers) also deals with protection against airborne mustard-gas droplets. The thoroughness of anti-gas training in the British forces is illustrated by 'Training in Anti-Gas Measures' (40/WO/7338, July 1919, in Hartley papers). The Committee of Imperial Defence, though unsure about a policy for offensive chemical warfare, agreed with the CWC that everyone in the Services should have adequate training in personal and collective protection against gas (PRO/WO/144/144). In the USA, Peyton March suspended anti-gas training in the forces after the war; Pershing reintroduced it when he replaced March. It is worth noting that governments, irrespective of their opinions on gas, authorized some expenditure on research and development. A Cabinet decision on the continuation of Porton's work was taken in 1920 (PRO/CAB 27/20, CP 1218, Conclusion 5, 12 May 1920), but money was always tight. Edgewood was not treated more generously though there was some money for field trials with aircraft sprays.

50. PRO/WO/188/377, file R 960/12.

51. PRO/WO/188/377, file R 960/2, 'Short Description of the Chemical Warfare Research Department', 1926, by J. D. Pratt; file R 960/5, undated memo (probably about 1929), 'Supply of CW Agents'; file R 960/6, undated memo (from context probably written in late 1920s) on the use of gas in war. PRO/WO/188/288 and 289: Progress Report on Sutton Oak, 31 July 1926.

52. Prentiss: *Chemicals in War*, pp. 99–100. Pope: 'The Case for Chemical Warfare', pp. 7–8.

53. The report runs to 25 single-spaced foolscap sheets; a copy is in the Hartley papers.

54. The minutes of the Holland Committee, and the papers submitted by Thuillier, Napier, and Foulkes show that some of the lessons of the First World War had been thoroughly digested. I am grateful to the late Mr J. Davidson Pratt who wrote to me on 11 April 1973 and gave me much interesting information about the Committee and some of its personalities.

55. PRO/WO/144/144, file R/8/C/26, memorandum (n.d., April? 1922), from Commandant of Porton.

56. Army Reorganization, pp. 538, 540, and House of Representatives Reports, 66th Congress, 2nd Session 1919–20; II, No. 680, 26 Feb. 1920, pp. 16–20 and III, No. 1049, 27 May 1920, p. 12.

57. The British Air Attaché in Washington, Group-Captain M. G. Christie, was taken on a visit to Edgewood and reported at some length (Report No. 653, 16 June 1924, in Hartley papers). He was particularly interested in vertical smoke curtains, obtained by spraying titanium tetrachloride at high pressure in the direction of the tanker aircraft's flight. Fries told Christie he hoped to develop mustard-gas dispersion from specially adapted aircraft and had plans for bombs bursting in the air. It turned out that these were still ideas and no tests had been made. Christie was impressed by the public relations content of Fries's Annual Report and he noted that Fries 'uses the fact that some of the Edgewood chemicals are valuable for certain medicinal purposes to cover up the military aspect of his work.' There was, assuredly, nothing like it at Porton in the 1920s. Lefebure, who had been shown the sights of Edgewood when there was more money about, came away with similar impressions. PRO/WO/88/123, file R7/US/B4, report by V. Lefebure, 29 July 1920. Annual Reports of the Chief CWS to the Secretary of War in PRO/WO/88/124, files R7/US/B/29 and 35. Brown: *Chemical Warfare*, pp. 89–90, 133–4, 139–40, 146–7.

58. 'Introduction to the Report of the British Mission', p. 9. Brown: *Chemical Warfare*, p. 57–9.

59. Holland Committee, minutes of meetings on 30 May and 5 June 1919 and Report, pp. 6–7. Fries: 'Chemical Warfare', pp. 427–8.

60. Muraour: 'Les Gaz de combat', p. 18. It is worth mentioning in this context that the British Board of Trade appointed a Committee in 1935 to examine the continuation of the so-called Key Industry Duties, first imposed under the Safeguarding of Industries Act, 1921. Hartley was a member and Davidson Pratt gave evidence on behalf of the chemical manufactures. The War Office, in its evidence, recorded that protection had been of great value and recommended continuation. It also recommended that activated carbon should be given special protection. About 20–5 tons a year were currently required for gas masks, but the quantity 'will be considerably increased in the near future'. The War Office was misinformed—a tariff of 20 per cent had been imposed in 1933. The details are in PRO/BT/55/42, files K13 and K16, the report, recommending continuation of the duties, was published in 1936 (Cmd. 5157, PP. 1935–6, *14*).

61. Altogether £19.2 m. was spent by the Ministry of Supply on the construction and equipment of poison-gas factories which were built and operated by ICI's General Chemicals Group under the Agency Factory Scheme. The first to be completed was Randle Works, opened in April 1938, to make gas; the second, Rocksavage, started the production of intermediates in Sept. 1939. Two other gas and two intermediates works were opened at various dates between April 1940 and Feb. 1942. The largest, Hillhouse, in Lancashire, made ethylene dichloride for thiodiglycol and after the war was bought by ICI for its vinyl chloride operations. ICI's Dyestuffs Division also made a small tonnage of mustard-gas intermediates, tear-gas, and phenylarsinic acid between 1938 and 1940. Reader, W. J.: *Imperial Chemical Industries*, II (1975), pp. 262, 275, 276.

62. PRO/WO/188/121 contains the translation of a manual, edited by J. M.

Fishman, 1928, for the use of Russian ARP staff. The civil defence preparations are thoroughly described and range from organization and camouflage of potential targets to gas-proof shelters and gas masks. Without access to the Russian archives it is not possible to say how much was being done in practice. German anti-gas measures of civilians were unimportant until 1941–2.

63. PRO/WO/188/boxes 67, 256, 257, 317 contain many reports on civil defence tests carried out by the ARP Sub-Committee of the Committee of Imperial Defence and by the staff at Porton. Down Street no longer exists, but those familiar with Maida Vale station and its unusual stairwell will be aware of its natural, forced draughtiness!

64. PRO/WO/188/378 and WO/142/78 and 79 have much material on the details of the respirator designs. Large supplies of reactive charcoal were identified at an early stage as essential. Sutcliffe, Speakman, and Co. had provided some of this material for the SBR in the First World War and became the chief manufacturer before and during the Second World War. They still make charcoal.

65. O'Brien: *Civil Defence*, pp. 5, 14, 107–8, 120, 144.

66. Ipatieff: *The Life of a Chemist*, p. 382. Ipatieff's memory misled him on many details, but some of his recollections can be independently checked against the German record of the events, in *Akten zur deutschen auswärtigen Politik 1918–1945* (hereafter *Auswärtige Politik*), Serie B, II/1 (1967), pp. 457–9 and II/2 (1967), pp. 262–71, 312–14.

67. *Auswärtige Politik*, document No 248,009 for Stoltzenberg's finances and production statistics. From this document it emerges that he did not make or sell dichlorodiethyl sulphide. He bought 'Glykol' (i.e. thiodiglycol) for resale to customers in Spain and possibly also the Soviet Union. (As noted earlier, upon treatment with hydrochloric acid, thiodiglycol yields, under suitable conditions, mustard gas). Stoltzenberg also sold small quantities of phosgene, chlorine, and some other products. The value of his company's sales in the three years ending 31 March 1926 was 2.5 mln. RM (say £126,000). A good account of the story, to which Evelyn Waugh or Graham Greene would have done justice, will be found in Gatzke, H. W.; 'Russo-German Military Collaboration during the Weimar Republic', *Am. Hist. Rev.*, (April 1958), pp. 575–88. According to a note by Dirksen of the German Foreign Office, dated 15 Dec. 1926, the Russians demanded 8 mln. RM for non-completion of the contract, but the Reichswehr thought that 5 mln. (RM £250,000) would satisfy them. One can almost hear the diplomatic sigh of relief. *Auswärtige Politik*, B, II/2, pp. 425–7. I have no information on the size of the Ivashchenkovo factory, but the Randle and Rocksavage plants built in England about 10 years later cost altogether £4.9 mln.

68. *Auswärtige Politik*, B, IV (1970), pp. 571–3, memorandum from Gen. Schleicher to German Foreign Office, 16 March 1927, and vol. VIII (1974), pp. 580–1, note by Dirksen 29 Dec. 1927. Gatzke; 'Russo-German . . . Collaboration', pp. 586–8.

69. *The Times* 22, 23, 25, 26 May and 2, 15, and 25 June 1928. *Frankfurter*

Allgemeine Zeitung, 19 Sept. 1979; *Der Spiegel, 33*, No. 39, 24 Sept. 1979. PRO/WO/118/115 contains translations of Stoltzenberg's publicity brochures; the last one, No.6 (1928) has a description of the accident. *Auswärtige Politik*, B, IX (1976), pp. 81–4 has a report of Gen. Ludwig's attendance at a Cabinet Meeting and his assurance to Ministers that the Reichswehr had nothing to do with Stoltzenberg. Hansard, 217 (1928), 23 May 1928, col. 1857 and 6 June 1928, cols. 168–9. On the former occasion the Foreign Secretary promised to make enquiries, on the latter the Home Secretary said that there were no specific regulations in the UK concerning phosgene and its storage, but that the Department of Scientific and Industrial Research was carrying out an inquiry into the handling and storage of dangerous gases.

70. Haber spoke before a Reichtstag sub-committee in October 1923 and poured scorn on allegations that Germany was surreptitiously continuing the development of poison gas. That would require testing and involve hundreds of people, and if discovered would have a detrimental effect on Germany. Bell (ed.): *Völkerrecht im Weltkrieg*, p. 15. I think (but I have no evidence one way or the other) that Haber did not know at the time that Stoltzenberg was *en route* to Moscow. There is no doubt that he knew two years later. PRO/WO/188/117 contains a note by the War Office dated 26 Oct. 1927, that the Germans were experimenting with glanders to infect horses. The story was about ten years old. Le Wita: *Autour de la guerre chimique*, p. 66, without giving the source, alleged that the Germans were working on some entirely novel weapons.

71. Interviews with Dr J. Jaenicke on 3 April 1971 and 23 Sept. 1972. 'Reports on German Chemical Warfare R&D', CDR5, 25 Aug. 1941 in Hartley papers.

72. Jacobi, F. (ed.): *Beiträge zur hundertjährigen Firmengeschichte: G. Schrader, Planzenschutz* (1964), pp. 115–16, Clarke, R.: *We all fall down* (1968), pp. 33–4. Brown: *Chemical Warfare*, p. 232 f.

73. Letter from Major G. F. R. Wingate of the WO Research and Designs Department to Hartley 14 Oct. 1919 in Hartley papers. Wingate had worked closely with Hartley in the summer of 1919 winding up the CWD, PRO/WO/142/116, file CWD 113, 'Use of DM in North Russia'. According to Davies, as related by Wingate, the reports on the smoke-generators were destroyed in Russia on WO instructions and never reached London. That may explain the paucity of the material at the PRO.

74. Stoltzenberg, in a long interview with Clodius of the German Foreign Office on 10 May 1926, claims to have organized a factory in Spain and to have supplied materials (possibly phosgene and thiodiglycol) for use in the Rif campaigns. Stoltzenberg invariably exaggerated, but I believe there is substance in what he told Clodius. *Auswärtige Politik*, B, II/2, p. 457.

75. Brown: *Chemical Warfare*, pp. 247–8, 257. Tempelhoff (BMA N 102/5) in his compilation mentions that in 1933 the Japanese had special decontamination vehicles for use against mustard gas in Manchuria.

76. SIPRI, IV, pp. 177, 178, 184. PRO/CAB 4/24 Committee of Imperial Defence, ref. 1226, April 1936: a sample of material collected after an air raid on Daghabur on 3 Dec. 1936 was identified at Porton as mustard gas.

77. Speer, A.: *Erinnerungen* (1970), p. 421. During the summer of 1944 German production of mustard gas and of 'Tabun' was very high. But the production of civilian respirators was insufficient. Letter from L. J. Barley to author 7 April 1975: Barley was a chemical observer in New Guinea where he saw Japanese DA smoke-generators; the same material had been used in German shells a quarter of a century earlier!

78. Second Report of the Royal Commission on Awards to Inventors, Cmd. 1782 (1922), PP. 1922, Session 2, 17, pp. 15, 17 and Third Report . . . Cmd.2275 (1925), PP. 1924–5, 9, 225, p. 11. Most of the awards were in respect of aircraft, communication equipment, and navigation instruments.

79. A full version of Pope's side of the business will be found in his article, 'Mustard Gas'. Thuillier, who had been Controller of the CWD in 1918, seems to have been aware of a possible conflict of interest as co-patentee and head of the Department. Most of the people involved, R. P. Whitelaw, Quinan, and Davidson Pratt among them, sided with Pope. Levinstein's case, as summed up in the brief for Counsel, is unconvincing, but Lefebure (then an employee of the British Dyestuffs Corp.) lobbied energetically on behalf of his managing director. PRO/WO/188/185, file R/15/H/2 and 142/129, file CWD/289 (Levinstein–Green Claim), and correspondence, various dates in 1920–1, in Hartley papers.

80. Letter from Beer, Kiesel & Krause (a firm of solicitors) to Rita Cracauer (Haber's secretary), 25 Oct. 1933, in Levy papers. Haber was living in Cambridge at the time.

81. Apart from Hartley, the following were elected FRS after the War: A. J. Allmand, C. G. Douglas, E. Gold. Barcroft, Baker, Crossley, Donnan, Pope, J. F. Thorpe, and Smithells had been elected before the war. Freundlich was a foreign member of the Royal Society.

82. Interview with Dr Jaenicke, 23 Sept. 1972. Jaenicke joined the KWI in the latter part of the War and later moved to the Metallgesellschaft where he attained a leading position in the research department. He died in 1984.

83. Whittemore: 'World War 1 Poison Gas Research and the Ideals of American Chemists', pp. 152, 157. I am indebted to Professor Y. M. Rabkin for information on Manning. Browne, C. A. and Weeks, M. E.: *A History of the American Chemical Society* (1952), pp. 118–19. Haynes, Williams: *American Chemical Industry*, IV (1948), p. 252. Ipatieff: caps. 49 and 50.

84. Interviews with J. D. Pratt, 29 June 1972 and 7 May 1973 and with L. J. Barley, 8 March 1972. Pratt was on the staff of the CWC until 1928 when he became Director of the Association of British Chemical Manufactures (now the Chemical Industries Association). He was seconded to the Ministry of Supply in 1940 to take charge of poison gas and returned to the Association after the war.

85. Établissements Kuhlmann: *Cent ans d'industrie chimique* (1925), pp. 45 ff.

86. For Geyer, see BMA, N 221/23, Geyer papers. He remained on friendly terms with Haber and was, it seems, helpful over the Pochwadt affair; there is a letter from Haber, dated 1 August 1933, which refers to the matter. Col. Max Bauer, Geyer's superior until the Armistice, became an extreme right-wing militant and earned his living as an industrial-military consultant on assignments in various parts of the world. His last employer was Chiang-Kai-Shek and he died in China

in 1929. BA, Bauer papers. For Foulkes, see Obituary in *RE Jnl.*, (1969), p. 239.

87. In 1918 the Chemistry Prize Committee was not unanimous. One member argued that the Haber–Bosch process was still secret, which was against the principles of the Nobel Foundation. Another member considered that the fixation of atmospheric nitrogen had prolonged the war and on those grounds Haber should be disqualified. No criticism of chemical warfare is recorded. There was also the question to what extent Haber had been assisted by Le Rossignol, Mittasch, and Bosch. The discussions are a curious mixture of ignorance and irrelevance. In November 1919, the same committee reversed its decision, and without dissent awarded the chemistry prize to Haber. (Karl Bosch shared the chemistry prize in 1931 with Bergius for their work on high-pressure synthesis.) I am grateful to Dr W. Odelberg of the Royal Swedish Academy of Sciences and to Professor A. Magneli of the Nobel Committee for Chemistry, for locating and making available to me the relevant documents. Dr G. Andermann of Surrey University kindly translated them.

88. Cf. his evidence to the Reichstag sub-committee in 1923 (in Bell (ed.): *Völkerrecht im Weltkrieg*); he spoke on disarmament and chemical warfare in 1926 (*Chem. Age*, 10 July 1926, p. 30) and his lectures on chemistry and war were published in *Fünf Vorträge*. Letters from him to Geyer are in the BMA (N 221/32) and show that he had thought about army reform (26 July 1919) and the use of the KWI for chemical warfare research (15 May 1933). Haber was a subject of great interest to Hartley, and a note by J. F. Thorpe—'Conversation with Haber in Washington on 29 Sept. 1924' (attached to a letter by J. D. Pratt dated 28 Nov. 1924) has survived in the Hartley papers. Thorpe and Haber had been shown over Edgewood, and Haber declared he was no longer interested in poison gas. Thorpe did not believe him: 'I think the man, throughout, was acting a part. His face was always a mask'.

89. Letters from Pope to Hermann Haber 29 July 1933 and to Fritz Haber, 25 Sept. 1933, and from the Vice-Chancellor, 20 Nov. 1933. Haber was invited to undertake research at the Cavendish and to supervise research students until he was 70. No remuneration was offered. Weiss went to the University of Newcastle-upon-Tyne where he taught for many years. It may be added that Pope also invited Willstätter who declined and remained in semi-retirement in Munich for several years and eventually settled in Switzerland. Several letters from Haber in the collection of Dr F. Levy shed light on these matters (to Weizmann, 26 July 1933 about contacts with Donnan and Hartley; to von Laue, 9 Dec. 1933 about official government permission to emigrate; to Karl Bosch, 28 Dec. 1933 about Switzerland being his first choice).

90. Crossley and Rendel gave evidence to the Holland Committee (minutes of 5th meeting, 27 May 1919 and Report, p. 7). Sibert's views on the matter are in Army Reorganization, pp. 544–5: he said that the universities must second good men to Edgewood for one or two years. The contribution of these academics was essential because a 'permanent Government establishment is liable to get into a rut and to get in deeper the older it gets', and they would provide a leavening of fresh minds. He was against publications by the staff and, to him, secrecy 'is all important'. Memorandum by Hartley, dated 16 August 1919, after the

completion of the Holland Committee's report, in Hartley papers. Hartley proposed a salary of £2,000 for the Director of Research. That was above the level then paid to a professor, but was necessary according to Hartley, because to Director would have no opportunities for outside earnings.

91. PRO/WO/144/144, file R/8/C/26, memorandum (n.d., April? 1922), from Commandant. WO/188/214 has particulars of the CWC organization in 1927. There were eleven sub-committees at the time: three dealt with respirators, one with chemical weapons, one with medical aspects. The Chairman's Conference brought together, in a small group, the heads of the sub-committees. Hartley was on every committee, except physiology, and chairman of four. Thorpe, Pope, and C. G. Douglas were also prominent.

92. PRO/WO/144/144, memorandum by the Chancellor of the Exchequer, 22 June 1922. Kent, A. E.; 'A History of Porton', *passim.*

93. PRO/WO/188/318. The contents of this box end in 1930, and the rest has either been destroyed or was closed to the public at the time I was working on the subject. PRO/WO/188, boxes 44 to 46 contain material on the work done between 1920 and 1926 to determine the concentration of DM in a cloud. Particle behaviour and counting were then a new subject. Boxes 66 and 68 have material on research connected with contamination caused by mustard gas. Interview with J. D. Pratt 7 May 1973.

94. PRO/WO/188/1 and 2 lists some of the patents issued as a result of research done at Porton. Not all the patents were secret. The work at Edgewood appears less impressive by comparison with what was being done at Porton. The reason is that the Americans were not concerned about civilian involvement in another chemical war and so did not study civil defence. British Air Attaché, Washington; Appendix 1 to Report No 653, 16 June 1924 and notes by Group-Captain Christie, in Hartley papers. Anon: *A Brief History of the Chemical Defence Experimental Establishment (CDEE)* (1961), pp. 16–17. O'Brien: *Civil Defence*, pp. 46, 47, 77.

95. Epstein, F. and Freundlich, H.: typescript of a history of the KWI (n.d., 1929?) in Coates papers. PRO/WO/88/123, file R7/US/B19. Ship fumigation with poisonous chemicals had been tried before the war. The most effective gases were also the most dangerous—hydrogen cyanide in particular carried very considerable risks in a confined space.

96. MoM History, pp. 63, 64. At Edgewood they went several steps further than in Britain and recommended the inhalation of chlorine as treatment for colds and bronchitis. initially a high success-rate was claimed, but no more was heard of this after a few years. PRO/WO/88/123, files R7/US/B29 and 35.

97. It is interesting that CAP was discussed on at least two occasions during the war, in March 1916 and August 1918, but there was no follow-up. (PRO/WO/143/57, 211th meeting of the General Chemical Sub-Committee, 14 March 1916 and WO/142/72, 40th meeting of the CWC (Offensive, 23 August 1918). In the first half of 1919 the Army Council enquired about tear gas, but apparently refused permission for tests when it was pointed out that the extent of damage to the eye was unknown. CAP was not specifically mentioned on this occasion, PRO/WO/142/131, file CWD 344, 'Chemicals

to deal with Civil Disturbances'. Edgewood vigorously promoted CAP and Group-Captain Christie reported that the CAP installation could produce 1,000 lb. (say half at) a day (Appendix 1 to note of 16 June 1924 in Hartley papers). CS was developed at Porton and patented in 1960, Rose, S. (ed.): *London Conference on CBW* (1968), p. 20.

98. Bertram Lambert wrote to Hartley on 13 June 1921 about the special treatment given to German charcoal and wanted more information. There is also a letter from Kerschbaum at the Aussiger Verein to Haber (20 Dec. 1922, in Levy papers) that a highly absorbent charcoal, suitable for oil refining was then under development. O'Brien: *Civil Defence*, pp. 78, 332. *A Brief History of the . . . CDEE*, p. 19.

99. Interview with Hartley 22 Aug. 1971. Ethylene was the critical material in the supply of mustard gas. It was then obtained by the dehydration of fermentation alcohol, and the Germans had no difficulty in manufacturing it. The Allies devoted much effort to finding other sources: in America, J. B. Conant worked on cracking crude oil to obtain mixed olefines whence ethylene was extracted. In Britain, Soddy studied its extraction from coke oven gas and the Skinningrove Iron Co. proposed to use charcoal for the operation. The Hall Motor Co. reported work on the high-temperature cracking of kerosene to yield olefines, thus anticipating the UK petroleum chemical industry by about thirty years. The details are in PRO/SUP 10/123, Quinan papers, Book 41, Sept. 1918, pp. E81ff.: Report summarizing ethylene position, and SUP10/125 pp. H 135–6, Meeting at Storey's Gate with Americans on 5 June 1918.

100. Holland Committee, Report, p. 14.

101. R. V. Jones, in the concluding programme of *The Secret War* (BBC-TV, 9 Dec. 1977) used this argument. He was primarily concerned to contrast the state of military science in Britain and Germany during the Second World War.

102. Speer: *Erinnerungen*, pp. 437–9.

103. *Frankfurter Allgemeine Zeitung*, 15 and 18 Sept. 1979; *Essener Tagblatt*, 15 Sept. 1979.

104. 'Memorandum on the Protection of the Civil Population against Gas Attack', (n.d., about 1924 or 1925), p. 9, PRO/144/144, file R 8/C/22.

105. Brown: *Chemical Warfare*, pp. 295, 296–7.

106. Meselson, M. and Robinson, J. P.: 'Chemical Warfare and Chemical Disarmament', *Scientific American*, 242, 4 (April 1980), deal clearly and thoroughly with the lack of progress on chemical disarmament since 1925, and with the changing technology of 'conventional' and 'chemical' weapons.

BIBLIOGRAPHY

IN the following pages I have listed the printed publications (books, articles, etc.) which are available in the larger libraries. But, as explained in the Chapter 1, I have relied extensively on unpublished material from a variety of sources. It seemed to me unnecessary to repeat here in full all the references given in the notes, but the more important primary sources warrant listing and are described in as much detail as is necessary to identify them in archives or specialist libraries such as that of the IWM. As far as possible I have followed a strict alphabetic order, but where necessary have provided cross-references or explained authorship more fully.

Admiralty Technical History Section: *The Technical History and Index*, vol. I, pt. II, 'Lethal Gases', London (1919).

Allmand, A. J.: 'Report on War Work for German Gas Services carried out at the Leverkusen Works of the Farbenfabriken vorm. Fr. Bayer', typescript, dated 31 Jan. 1919, in Hartley papers.

Auld, S. J. M.: *Gas and Flame*, New York (1918).

Auswärtige Politik (Akten zur Deutschen Auswärtigen Politik 1918–1945), see under Germany.

Bacon, R. F.: 'The Work of the Technical Division, CWS AEF', *Jnl. Ind. and Eng. Chem.*, 11, 2 (1919).

Bamm, P. (Kurt Emmerich): *Eines Menschen Zeit*, Zurich (1972).

Barbusse, H.: *Le Feu*, Paris (1917).

Barnett, C.: *The Swordbearers*, London (1963).

Baynes, J.: *Morale, a Study of Men and Courage*, London (1967).

Bean, C. E. W.: *The Australian Imperial Force in France*, vol. V, Sydney (1937).

Bell, J. (ed.): *Völkerrecht im Weltkrieg*, 3rd series, vol. IV, 'Gaskrieg, Luftkrieg . . .', Berlin (1927).

Best, G.: *Humanity in Warfare*, London (1980).

——and Wheatcroft, A. (eds.): *War, Economy and the Military Mind*, London (1976).

Bloch, D.-P.: *La Guerre chimique*, Paris (1929).

Bloch, J. von: *Der Krieg*, vol. I, Berlin (1899).

Blunden, E.: *Undertones of War*, London (1928).

Boyland, E. and Goulding, R. (eds.): *Modern Trends in Toxicology*, London (1968).

Brown, F. J.: *Chemical Warfare, a Study in Restraints*, Princeton (1968).

Browne, C. A. and Weeks, M. E.: *A History of the American Chemical Society*, Washington (1952).

Bruchmüller, G.: *Die deutsche Artillerie in den Durchbruchschlachten des Weltkrieges*, Berlin (1921).

——: *Die Artillerie beim Angriff im Stellungskrieg*, Berlin (1926).

Carey Morgan, M.: 'Report on the Work of Women in Connection with the Anti-Gas Department', typescript (1919) in IWM. (The draft is in PRO/MUN 5/386/1650/13.)

Céline, L.-F.: *Voyage au bout de la nuit*, Paris (1962).

Chapman, G.: *A Passionate Prodigality*, New York (1966).

Chimie et Industrie: *10 ans d'efforts scientifiques et industriels*, Paris (1926), *see* Florentin, D., and Tissier, L.

Clark, Dorothy K.: 'Effectiveness of Chemical Weapons in WWI', (Operations Research Office, The Johns Hopkins University), Bethesda (1959).

Clarke, I. F. 'The Othello Syndrome', *History Today*, Aug. 1965, pp. 559–66.

——: *Voices Prophesying War, 1763–1984*, London (1970).

Clarke, R.: *We all fall down*, Harmondsworth (1969).

Coates, J. E.: 'Haber Memorial Lecture', *Memorial lectures delivered before the Chemical Society 1933–42*, vol. IV, London (1951), pp. 127–57.

Colomb, P., Maurice, J. F. *et al.*: *The Great War of 189–. A Forecast*, London (1893).

Conan Doyle, Sir Arthur: *The British Campaign in France and Flanders*, vol. III, London (1917).

Cookson, J. and Nottingham, J.: *A Survey of Chemical and Biological Warfare*, London (1969).

Dalton, M.: *The Black Death*, London (1934).

Davis, Sir Robert Henry: *Breathing in Irrespirable Atmospheres*, London (1948).

Deimling, B. von: *Aus der alten in die neue Zeit*, Berlin (1930).

Demmler, E. *et al.*: *Das K.B. Reserve Infanterie Regiment 12*, Munich (1934).

Dorgelès, R.: *Les Croix de bois*, Paris (1919).

Douglas, C. G.: 'Effects of Blue Cross Shells on the Troops in the Field', typescript dated 16th Nov. 1939 in Hartley papers.

Edmonds, J. E.: *Military Operations in France and Belgium, 1916*, London (1932).

Ellis, J.: *Eye Deep in Hell*, London (1977).

Feldman, G. D.: *Army, Industry and Labor in Germany 1914–1918*, Princeton (1966).

Fest, J. C.: *Hitler*, Frankfurt (1973).

Florentin, D.: 'Les Poudres, les explosifs et les gaz de combat', Chimie et Industrie, *10 ans d'efforts scientifiques et industriels*, vol. I, Paris (1926), pp. 680–700.

Forester; C. S.: *The General*, Harmondsworth (1968).

Foulkes, C. H.: *'Gas!' The Story of the Special Brigade*, Edinburgh (1934).

——: 'Report on the Activity of the Special Brigade', typescript 19 Dec. 1918 in PRO/DUP10/292.

Fox, M. S.: 'Corporals All, with the Special Brigade RE 1915–1919', typescript (1965) IWM library.

French Official History: *Les Armées françaises dans la Grande Guerre*.

Fries, A. A.: 'Chemical Warfare', *Jnl. of Ind. and Eng. Chem.*, 12, 5, May 1920, pp. 423–9.

——and West, C. J.: *Chemical Warfare*, New York (1921).

Gatzke, H. W.: 'Russo-German Military Collaboration during the Weimar Republic', *Am. Hist. Rev.*, LXIII (Apr. 1958), pp. 575–88.

Germany: *Akten zur deutschen auswärtigen Politik*, Bonn/Koblenz, 'Serie B', II (1967), IV (1970), VIII (1974), IX (1976).

Geyer, H.: 'Denkschrift betreffend des Gaskampf und Gasschutz', n.d. (?March 1919) in BMA N221/23 (Geyer Nachlass).

Gilbert, M.: *Winston S. Churchill*, vol. IV, London (1975).

Gilchrist, H. L.: *A Comparative Study of World War Casualties from Gas and other Weapons*, Washington (1931).

——and Matz, P. B.: *The Residual Effects of Warfare Gases*, Washington (1933).

Gladden, N.: *The Somme*, London (1974).

Goldblat, J.: *CB Disarmament Negotiations*, being vol. IV of SIPRI: 'The Problem of Chemical and Biological Warfare', London (1971).

Graves, R.: *Goodbye to All That*, New York (1957).

Guinn, P.: *British Strategy and Politics 1914 to 1918*, Oxford (1965).

Guthrie, F.: 'On Some Derivatives from the Olefines', *Qly. J. Chem. Soc.*, 12 (1860), pp. 109–20 and 13 (1860–1), pp. 129–35.

Haber, F.: *Fünf Vorträge*, Berlin (1924).

Haber, L. F.: *The Chemical Industry 1900–1930*, Oxford (1971).

——: 'Gas Warfare 1915–45', Stevenson Lecture 1975, London (1976).

Hahn, O.: *My Life*, London (1970).

Haldane, Charlotte: *Man's World*, London (1926).

Haldane, J. B. S.: *Callinicus. A Defence of Chemical Warfare*, London (1925).

Hanslian, R. (ed.): *Der chemische Krieg*, 3rd edn., Berlin (1937). (1st edn., Berlin 1925, 2nd edn., Berlin 1927.)

——: *Der deutsche Gasangriff bei Ypern am 22. April 1915*, Berlin (1934).

Hartley, H.: 'Chemical Warfare', paper read to Section B of the British Association, 1919.

——: 'A General Comparison of British and German Methods of Gas Warfare', *Jnl. of the Royal Artillery*, 46, 11 (1920).

——: 'Report on the German Chemical Warfare Organisation and Policy, 1915–1918', n.d. (?1921–2, revised ?1925), PRO/WO/33/1072.

——: 'Chemical Warfare', reprint of a lecture given in the University of London, 25 Nov. 1926.

——: Sir Harold: 'Fritz Haber', typescript, 1961.

——: Speech on the occasion of the Royal Society Club Dinner on 14 Nov. 1968, *Notes and Records of the Royal Society of London*, 24 (1 June 1969), pp. 146–55.

Haynes, Williams: American Chemical Industry, *A History*, vol. I, New York (1954), and vol. IV, New York (1948).

Heber, K.: 'Aufzeichnungen', typescript, n.d. (*c*.1938), in BMA N 102/10.

Heeres-Sanitätsinspektion des Reichskriegsministerium: *Sanitätsbericht über das deutsche Heer im Weltkriege 1914/18*, Berlin (vol. I, 1935; vol. II, 1938; vol. III, 1934).

Heinrici, P. (ed.): *Das Ehrenbuch des deutschen Pioniers*, Berlin (1918).

Hoffman, M.: *Der Krieg der versäumten Gelegenheiten*, Munich (1923).

Holland Committee (Committee on Chemical Warfare Organization): 'Report' (1919) in Hartley Papers.

Holley, I. B. Jr.: *Ideas and Weapons*, Hamden, Conn. (1971).

Horne, A.: *The Price of Glory*, London (1962).

IEEC, *see* Ministère de L'Armement, IEEC.

Inventors, Reports of the Royal Commission on Awards to: Second (Cmd. 1782, 1922), Third (Cmd. 2275, 1925).

Ipatieff, V. N.: *The Life of a Chemist*, Stanford (1946).

Isorni, J. and Cadars, L.: *Histoire véridique de la Grande Guerre*, vol. III, Paris (1970).

Jackson, R.: *At War with the Bolsheviks*, London (1972).

Jacobi, F. (ed.): *Beiträge zur hundertjährigen Firmengeschichte: 'G. Schrader, Planzenschutz'*, Leverkusen (1964).

Jones, D. P.: 'The Role of Chemists in Research on War Gases in the United States during World War I', Ph.D. Thesis, University of Wisconsin (1969).

Jones, R.: 'Chemical Warfare, the Peacetime Legacy', *New Scientist*, 24 Apr. 1975.

Kent, A. E.: 'History of Porton', typescript (1960).

Klein, F. (ed.): *Deutschland im Ersten Weltkrieg*, Berlin (1971).

Lanchester, F. W.: *Aircraft in Warfare*, London (1916).

League of Nations Union: *Chemical Warfare*, London (1924).

Les Armées françaises dans la Grande Guerre. Text, vol. VIII, Paris (1923); Annexe, vol. IV, Paris (1926).

Lefebure, V.: 'Report on Chemical Warfare Liaison with France', typescript dated 25 May 1920 in PRO/MUN 5/386/1650/15.

——: *The Riddle of the Rhine*, London (1921).

Le Wita, H.: *Autour de la guerre chimique*, Paris (1928).

Liddell Hart, B. H.: *Foch: Man of Orleans*, London (1937).

——: *History of the First World War*, London (1970).

Livens, W. H.: 'The Livens Gas Projector', typescript (n.d.) PRO/WO/188/143, file RA/A1.

McCarthy, R. M.: *The Ultimate Folly*, London (1970).

Macdonald, L.: *They called it Passenchendaele*, London (1978).

——: *The Roses of No Man's Land*, London (1980).

Macpherson, W. G. et al.: *Medical Services, Diseases of the War*, vol. II, London (1923).

Malraux, A.: *Les Noyers d'Altenburg*, Paris (1948).

——: *Le Miroir des limbes: Lazare*, Paris (1974).

Manning, F.: *Her Privates We*, London (1930).

Marshall, V. C.: 'How Lethal are Explosions and Toxic Escapes?', *Chem. Eng.*, Aug. 1977, pp. 576–7.

Meier-Welcher, H. and von Groote, W. (eds.): *Handbuch zur deutschen Militärgeschichte*, 3rd series, vol. V, Frankfurt (1968).

Meselson, M. and Robinson, J. P.: 'Chemical Warfare and Chemical Disamament', *Scientific American*, 242, 4 (1980), pp. 34–43.

Meyer, J.: *Der Gaskampf und die chemischen Kampfstoffe*, Leipzig (1925).

Meyer, V.: 'Ueber Thiodiglykolverbindungen', *Ber.*, 19 (1886), pp. 3259–66.

Middlebrook, M.: *The Kaiser's Battle*, London (1978).

Mignon, A.: *Le Service de santé pendant la guerre*, Paris (1926).

Miles, W.: *Military Operations in France and Belgium, 1916*, London (1938).

Ministère de l'Armement, IEEC: 'Cours spécial sur l'emploi militaire des gaz, les projectiles spéciaux' (n.d., ?April 1918), in Hartley Papers.

Ministère de l'Armement, IEEC: 'Le Tir des projectiles spéciaux', (n.d., ?Oct. 1918), in Hartley Papers.

Ministry of Munitions, Department of Explosives Supply: 'Report of the British mission appointed to visit enemy chemical factories in the Occupied Zone engaged in the production of munitions of war', February 1919. Confidential, No. 5889. [All references in the book are to this report, unless the shortened, published version is expressly mentioned. This is entitled 'Introduction to the Report of the British Mission . . .' and was published as Cmd. 1137 in 1921 (PP 1921, 20, 583).]

MoM (Ministry of Munitions): *History of the Ministry of Munitions*, II, pt. 1, 'Administrative Policy and Organisation' (1921); v, pt. III, 'Welfare and control of Working Conditions' (1920); XI, pt. I, 'Trench Warfare Supplies', n.d., XI, pt. II, 'Chemical Warfare Supplies', n.d. (?1921).

Mitchell, T. J. and Smith, G. M.: *Casualties and Medical Statistics of the Great War*, London (1931).

Moore, W.: *See how they ran*, London (1975).

Mordacq, J. J. H.: *Le Drame de l'Yser*, Paris (1933).

Moreland, H.: 'Chemical Warfare Record of Chemical Supplies', typescript (1919) in PRO/MUN 5/197/1650/8.

Moureu, C.: *La Chimie et la guerre*, Paris (1920).

'M. S. F.' (M. S. Fox): 'With the Special Brigade: A brief story of 186 Coy. RE and "C" Special Coy. RE 1915–1919', typescript (n.d., ?1957), IWM library.

Muraour, H.: 'Les Gaz de combat', typed report for the Comité Militaire Interallié Chimique (CMIC), Berlin, dated 12 Oct. 1922 in PRO/WO/188/176.

Nagel, A. von: 'Fuchsin, Alizarin, Indigo', BASF, 1 (n.d.); 'Äthylen', BASF, 7 (1971).

Nicholson, G. W. L.: *The Canadian Expeditionary Force 1914–1919*, Ottawa (1962).

O'Brien, T. H.: *Civil Defence*, London (1955).

Owen, Wilfred: *The Collected Poems*, London (1969).

Pershing, J. J.: *Final Report*, Washington (1920).
Petter, D.: *Pioniere*, Darmstadt (1963).
Pope, Sir William: 'Presidential Address to the Chemical Society', *Tr. Chem. Soc.*, 115 (1919).
——: 'Mustard Gas', *Journal of the Soc. of Chem. Industry* (30 Sept. 1919), **R**, pp. 343–4.
——: 'The Case for Chemical Warfare', reprint from *Chemical Age*, 7 May 1921.
Prentiss, A. M.: *Chemicals in War*, New York and London (1937).

Raper, H. S.: 'History of the Anti-Gas Department' (n.d.), in PRO/MUN 5/386/1650/13.
Reader, W. J.: *Imperial Chemical Industries*, vol. II, Oxford (1975).
Reichsarchiv: *Der Weltkrieg*, vol. VIII, Berlin (1932), vol. IX, Berlin (1933).
Remarque, E. M.: *Im Westen nichts Neues*, Berlin (1929).
Renn, L.: *Krieg*, Frankfurt (1929).
Richards, O.: 'The Development of Casualty Clearing Stations', *Guy's Hosp. R.*, 70 (1922), pt. III.
Riebicke, O.: *Unsere Pioniere im Weltkrieg*, 2nd edn., Berlin (1925).
Robida, A.: *La Guerre au vingtième siècle*, Paris (1887).
Robinson, J. P.: *The Rise of CB Weapons*, being vol. I of SIPRI, 'The Problem of Chemical and Biological Warfare', London (1971).
Romains, Jules: *Les Hommes de bonne volonté*, vols. XV and XVI, Paris (1938).
Rose, S. (ed.): *London Conference on CBW*, London (1968).

Sanitätsbericht, *see* Heeres-Sanitätsinspektion.
Sartori, M.: *The War Gases*, London (1940).
Sassoon, S.: *Sherston's Progress*, Harmondsworth (1948).
——: *Memoirs of an Infantry Officer*, London (1930).
Schroth, A.: *Bilder aus dem Leben der Gaspioniere im Feld*, Stuttgart (n.d.).
Schulz, J. W. N.: *Textbook on the Chemical Service*, Ft. Leavenworth (1923).
Schwarte, M. (ed.): *Die Technik im Weltkriege*, Berlin 1920.
Seesselberg. F.: *Der Stellungskrieg*, Berlin (1926).
Seth, R.: *Caporetto*, London (1965).
SIPRI, *see* Goldblat, J. and Robinson, J. P.
Southwold, M. S.: *The Gas War of 1940*, London (1931).
Speer, A.: *Erinnerungen*, Berlin (1970).
Stahl, F. C.: 'Die Bestände des Bundesarchiv-Militärchiv', *Militärgesch. Mitt.*, 2 (1968), pp. 139–44.
Staudinger, H.: 'La Technique moderne et la guerre', *Rev. Int. de la Croix Rouge*, 1 (1919), pp. 508–15.
Stewart, H.: *The New Zealand Division 1916–19*, Auckland (1921).

Tempelhoff, F. von: *Gaswaffe und Gasabwehr*, Berlin (1937).
Terraine, J.: *Impacts of War*, London (1970).
Thorpe, Sir Edward: 'Chemical Warfare and the Washington Conference', *J. of the Soc. Chem. Industry*, 41, 3 (1922).

Thuillier, Sir Henry: Can Methods of Warfare be Restricted?', *RUSI Jnl.*, May 1936.
——: *Gas in the Next War*, London (1939).
Tissier, L.: 'Les Poudres et explosifs', Chimie et Industrie, *10 ans d'efforts scientifiques et industriels*, vol. I, Paris (1926), pp. 1320–45.
Toland, J.: *No Man's Land*, London (1982).
Toubert, J.: 'Étude statistique des pertes subies par les Français 1914–1918' (n.d.), reprint of a lecture given in July 1920, IWM library.
——: *Le Service de santé militaire au GQG français: 1918–19*, Paris (1934).
Trumpener, H. U.: 'The Road to Ypres', *Jnl. of Mod. Hist.*, 47, 3 (1975).

USA War Department: *The Medical Department of the U.S. Army in the World War*, vol. XIV, 'Medical Aspects of Gas Warfare', Washington (1926).

Valori, A.: *La guerra italo-austriaca*, 2nd edn., Bologna (1925).
Vinet, E.: 'La Guerre des gaz et les travaux des services chimiques français', *Chim. et Ind.*, 2, 11–12 (1919), pp. 1377–1415.
——: 'Les Gaz de combat', typescript, 12 Oct. 1922, PRO/WO/188/176 (file French Questionnaire on German Factories).
——: 'Report on the German C.W. Organisation', typescript, translated from the French, 1 Dec. 1920, Berlin, PRO/WO/188/114, file R/7/G/4.
——: 'The Dismantling of the Gas Plants in German Factories', typescript (1920), translated from the French, in Hartley papers.
——: 'Report on the Present Condition of the Installations set up for the Manufacture of Asphyxiating Gases in the German Chemical Factories', typescript, 22 Mar. 1921, Berlin, in Hartley papers.
——: 'Report on the Organisation and Working of the four German Field Ammunition Depots', typescript, June 1920, Berlin, in Hartley papers.
Volkart, W.: 'Die Gasschlacht in Flandern im Herbst 1917', Beiheft 7 of *Wehrwissenschaftliche Rundschau*, Berlin (1957).

Wells, H. G.: *The War of the Worlds*, London (1898).
West, C. J.: 'Phosgene', typescript, 1918 in PRO/SUPP10/129 (Quinan Papers).
——: 'The History of Mustard Gas', *Chem. and Met. Eng.*, 22, (1920), p. 542.
Whittemore, G. F.: 'World War I Poison Gas Research and the Ideals of American Chemists', *Social Studies of Science*, 5, 2 (1975) pp. 135–63.
Wille, H. H.: *Der Januskopf*, Berlin (1969).
Williamson, H.: *A Fox under my Cloak*, London (1955).
Willstätter, R.: *Aus meinem Leben*, Weinheim (1949).
Women's International League for Peace and Freedom: *Chemical Warfare*, London (1930).
Wrisberg, E. von: *Wehr und Waffen*, Berlin (1922).

Zuckmayer, C.: *Als wär's ein Stück von mir*, Berlin (1966).
Zweig, A.: *Erziehung vor Verdun*, Amsterdam (1935).

INDEX

Printed in the United States
1237000001B/117